THE VISIONS OF
Anne Catherine Emmerich

BOOK III

THE VISIONS
OF
Anne Catherine Emmerich

BOOK III

The Final Teachings, Passion, & What Follows
With a Day-by-Day Chronicle
February AD 33 to May AD 33
(Hour-by-Hour during the Passion)

The Life of Mary After the Ascension
June AD 33 to August AD 44

From the Notes of
CLEMENS BRENTANO

Revised and Supplemented
by James Richard Wetmore
General Editor

Daily Summaries, Chronology, & Appendices
by Robert Powell, Ph.D.

 Angelico Press

First published in the USA
by Angelico Press 2015
Revised Text, New Text, Supplements,
Translations, and Layout
© James Richard Wetmore, 2015
Daily Summaries, Chronology, Appendices
© Robert Powell, 2015

For information, address:
Angelico Press
4709 Briar Knoll Dr.
Kettering, OH 45429
www.angelicopress.com

Book I: ISBN 978-1-59731-146-5 (pbk)
Book II: ISBN 978-1-59731-147-2 (pbk)
Book III: ISBN 978-1-59731-148-9 (pbk)

⊕

Cover Images:
J. James Tissot (French, 1836–1902)
Front: *The Magnificat* (detail)
Back: *Feed My Lambs* (detail)
Brooklyn Museum, purchased by
public subscription: 00.159.337, 00.159.347
Reproduced by permission
of the Brooklyn Museum
Cover Design: Michael Schrauzer

CONTENTS

Day-by-Day, then Hour-by-Hour, Chronicle of the Passion and Death of Jesus Christ

February 19–April 1, AD 33: *Final Weeks Leading Up to the Passion*

The Last Weeks before the Passion • Jesus's Discourse in the Temple 1 — Jesus's Solemn Entrance into Jerusalem 5 — [*Magdalene Repeats her Anointing of Jesus 10 — Instruction at Lazarus's • Peter Receives a Severe Reprimand 12 — The Widow's Mite 13 — Jesus Speaks of the Destruction of the Temple 14 — Jesus in Bethany 16*] — Jesus's Last Discourse in the Temple 16 — Magdalene's Last Anointing 19

April 2–April 3, AD 33: *Holy Thursday to Earliest Hours of Good Friday • Jesus's Arrest*

The Last Passover Supper 71 — The Washing of the Feet 77 — The Institution of the Most Blessed Sacrament 78 — Private Instructions and Consecrations 80 — Jesus on the Mount of Olives 82 — Judas and his Band • The Wood of the Cross 94 — The Arrest of the Lord 96 — Means Taken by Jesus's Enemies for Carrying Out Their Designs 102 — Glance at Jerusalem at this Hour 103

April 3, AD 33: *Early Morning of Good Friday • Jesus Taken before Annas and Caiaphas, Imprisoned, then Taken to Pilate*

Jesus before Annas 106 — Jesus Led from Annas to Caiaphas 107 — Jesus before Caiaphas 109 — Jesus Mocked and Insulted 112 — Peter's Denial 113 — Mary in the Judgment Hall of Caiaphas 114 — Jesus Imprisoned 116 — Judas at the Judgment Hall 117 — The Morning Trial 117 — The Despair of Judas 118 — Jesus is Taken to Pilate 119 — The Palace of Pilate and its Surroundings 120

April 3, AD 33: *Morning till Noon of Good Friday • Jesus before Pilate and Herod • Seven Falls beneath the Cross • Raising of the Cross, and the Crucifixion*

Jesus before Pilate 192 — Origin of the Devotion of the "Holy Way of the Cross" 195 — Pilate and his Wife 196 — Jesus before Herod 197 — Jesus Taken from Herod to Pilate 199 — The Scourging of Jesus 201 — Mary during the Scourging of Jesus 203 — Personal Appearance of Mary and of Magdalene 204 — Jesus Crowned with Thorns and Mocked 204 — "Ecce Homo!" 205 — Jesus Condemned to the Death of the Cross 206 — Jesus Carries his Cross to Golgotha 209 — Jesus's First Fall under the Cross 211 — Jesus, Carrying his Cross, Meets His Most Holy and Afflicted Mother • His Second Fall under the Cross 212 — Simon of Cyrene • Jesus's Third Fall under the Cross 213 — Veronica and her Veil 213 — The Weeping Daughters of Jerusalem • Jesus's Fourth and Fifth Falls beneath the Cross 215 — Jesus on Golgotha • The Sixth and the Seventh Falls of Jesus • His Imprisonment 216 — Mary and the Holy Women Go to Golgotha 217 — Jesus Stripped for Crucifixion and Drenched with Vinegar 218 — Jesus Nailed to the Cross 219 — The Raising of the Cross 221 — The Crucifixion of the Thieves 222 — The Executioners Cast Lots for Jesus's Garments 222 — Jesus Crucified • The Two Thieves 222 — Jesus Mocked • His First Saying on the Cross 224

April 3–April 4, AD 33: *From Noon of Good Friday to Sunset of Holy Saturday • Sayings from the Cross • Death of Jesus • Descent from the Cross • Preparation of the Body • Burial • Descent into Hell*

The Sun Obscured • The Second and the Third Sayings of Jesus on the Cross 300 — Fear Felt by the Inhabitants of Jerusalem 301 — Jesus Abandoned • His Fourth Saying on the Cross 301 — The Death of Jesus • Fifth, Sixth, and Seventh Sayings on the Cross 303 — The Earthquake • Apparitions of the Dead in Jerusalem 305 — Joseph of Arimathea Requests the Body of Jesus from Pilate 309 — The Side of Jesus Opened • The Legs of the Thieves Broken 310 — Some Localities of Ancient Jerusalem 312 — Garden and Tomb Belonging to Joseph of Arimathea 313 — The Descent from the Cross 313 — The Body of Jesus Prepared for Burial 315 — The Sepulcher 318 — The Return from the Burial • The Sabbath 319 — The Imprisonment of Joseph of Arimathea • The Holy Sepulcher Guarded 320 — The Friends of Jesus on Holy Saturday 320 — Some Words on Christ's Descent into Hell 323

The Resurrection • The Ascension • and the Descent of the Holy Spirit

April 4–May 31, AD 33: *The Resurrection • Love Feasts* (Agapes) *and Appearances of the Risen One • The Ascension, Pentecost, and Some Early Events in the Community*

The Eve of the Holy Resurrection 386 — Joseph of Arimathea Miraculously Set at Large 386 — The Night of Resurrection 386 — The Resurrection of the Lord 388 — The Holy Women at the Sepulcher 389 — The Guards' Statements 391 — The First Love Feast (*Agape*) after the Resurrection 392 — Communion of the Holy Apostles 393 — The Disciples Going to Emmaus • Jesus Appears to the Apostles in the Hall of the Last Supper 393 — The Apostles Preaching the Resurrection 396 — The Second Love Feast (*Agape*) • Thomas Puts his Hand into the Marks of Jesus's Wounds 398 — Jesus Appears to the Holy Apostles at the Sea of Galilee 400 — Jesus Appears to the Five Hundred 404 — Love Feast (*Agape*) in Bethany and in the House of the Last Supper • The Destruction of the Holy Places by the Jews 405 — The Majesty and Dignity of the Blessed Virgin 406 — Increase of the Community 407 — The Days Immediately Preceding the Ascension 409 — Jesus's Ascension into Heaven 410 — The Holy Day of Pentecost 412 — The Church at the Pool of Bethesda 414 — Peter Celebrates the First Holy Mass in the Last Supper Room 416 — First General Communion of the New Converts • Choice of the Seven Deacons 418

The Life of Mary After Christ's Ascension

June 1, AD 33–August 15, AD 44: *The Life of Mary Following Christ's Ascension, Up Until Her Death and Assumption at Ephesus*

The Blessed Virgin Goes with John to the Neighborhood of Ephesus 419 — Mary's "Holy Way of the Cross" near Ephesus • She Visits Jerusalem 422 — The Apostles Arrive to be Present at the Blessed Virgin's Death 424 — Death, Burial, and Assumption of the Blessed Virgin 425

Appendices

Appendix I: *Chronology of the Life of Jesus Christ* 477

Historical Overview 477 — The Date of Birth 478 — The Date of the Baptism 482 — The Date of the Crucifixion 484 — The Duration of Jesus's Ministry 485 — The Gap in Anne Catherine Emmerich's Account of the Ministry 486 — The Dates of Some of the Major Events in the Ministry of Jesus 489 — The Probative Value of the Visions 490 — The Names of Places 492

Appendix II: *The Hebrew Calendar* 493

Appendix III: *Reconstruction of the Hebrew Calendar for the Time of Jesus's Ministry Based on Anne Catherine Emmerich's Calendar Indications* 495

Remarks Concerning the Reconstruction of the Table of Months of the Hebrew Calendar from June AD 29 to May AD 33 497 — Discussion of Anne Catherine Emmerich's Calendar Indications 498

Appendix IV: *A Summary of the Chronicle* 500

Preliminary Remarks 502

Appendix V: *Commemoration of Events in the Life of Jesus Christ* 508

Index of Persons 515
Index of Places and Subjects 523

ILLUSTRATIONS

Tomb in the Valley of Hinnom (Interior) · · · · · TOC
The Two Angels at the Sepulcher · · · · · · · · · Part div.
Olive Trees on the Mount of Olives · · · · · · · · · · · 8
Kidron Bridge on the Way to the Temple · · · · · · · 16
Gethsemane Road to Jerusalem · · · · · · · · · · · · · 17
Gethsemane Road among the Olives · · · · · · · · · · 22

TISSOT SECTION G—*The Passion and Death of Jesus Christ*: 23 Paintings · · · · · · · · · · · 23–69

Angelic Dial of the Hours of the Passion · · · · · · · 70
Narrow Village Street · 98
Valley of Kidron (*Mar Saba*) · · · · · · · · · · · · · · 101
The Temple & Its Environs at Time of Christ · · · 104

TISSOT SECTION H—*The Passion and Death of Jesus Christ*: 35 Paintings · · · · · · · · · · 122–191

Caravan Resting Place · · · · · · · · · · · · · · · · · · · 194

Pilate's House · 201

TISSOT SECTION J—*The Passion and Death of Jesus Christ*: 37 Paintings · · · · · · · · · · 225–299

Tombs in the Valley of Hinnom · · · · · · · · · · · · 304
Our Lord Jesus Christ · · · · · · · · · · · · · · · · · · · 326

TISSOT SECTION K—*The Passion and Death of Jesus Christ*: 29 Paintings · · · · · · · · · · 327–385

Tiberias · 399
Sea of Galilee from Heights of Safed · · · · · · · · · 402
Boat on the Shore near Joppa · · · · · · · · · · · · · · 420

TISSOT SECTION L—*The Passion and Death of Jesus Christ*: 22 Paintings · · · · · · · · · · 429–473

Ancient Stairwell in Jerusalem · · · · · Appendices div.
Station of Mary's Way of the Cross · Appendices div.

Tomb in the Valley of Himmon (Interior)

YEAR 4

Day-by-Day, then Hour-by-Hour

CHRONICLE

OF THE PASSION AND DEATH OF JESUS

Final Weeks Leading Up to the Passion
February 19–April 1, AD 33

Holy Thursday to the Earliest Hours
of Good Friday • Jesus's Arrest
April 2–April 3, AD 33

Early Morning of Good Friday • Jesus Taken before
Annas and Caiaphas, Imprisoned, then Taken to Pilate
April 3, AD 33

Morning till Noon of Good Friday • Jesus before
Pilate and Herod • Seven Falls beneath the Cross
Raising of the Cross, and the Crucifixion
April 3, AD 33

From Noon of Good Friday to Sunset of Holy Saturday
Sayings from the Cross • Death of Jesus • Descent from the Cross
Preparation of the Body • Burial • Descent into Hell
April 3–April 4, AD 33

The Resurrection • Love Feasts (*Agapes*) and Appearances of the
Risen One • Ascension, Pentecost, and Early Events in the Community
April 4–May 31, AD 33

The Life of Mary Following Christ's Ascension
Her Death and Assumption in Ephesus
June 1, AD 33–August 15, AD 44

The Two Angels at the Sepulcher

THE PASSION AND DEATH OF JESUS CHRIST

The Last Weeks before the
Passion • Jesus's Discourse in the Temple

Thursday, February 19, AD 33 (Shebat 30)

IN the morning, Jesus, accompanied by Lazarus, left Alexandrium and went to Bethany. He repaired to the temple to teach, and his most holy mother accompanied him a part of the way. He was preparing her for his approaching Passion, and he told her that the time for the fulfillment of Simeon's prophecy, that a sword would pierce her soul, was near at hand. They would, he said, cruelly betray him, take him prisoner, maltreat him, put him to death as a malefactor, and all would take place under her eyes. Jesus spoke long upon this subject, and Mary was grievously troubled.

Jesus put up at the house of Mary Mark, the mother of John Mark, about a quarter of an hour from the temple and, so to say, outside the city.

ADAR (29 days): February 19/20 to March 19/20, AD 33 Adar New Moon: February 18 at 6:45 AM Jerusalem time

Friday, February 20, AD 33 (Adar 1)

Next day, after the Jews had left the temple, Jesus began to teach in it openly and very earnestly. All the apostles were in Jerusalem, but they went to the temple separately and by different directions. Jesus taught in the circular hall [the portico of Solomon] in which he had spoken in his twelfth year. Chairs and steps had been brought for the audience, and a very great concourse of people was gathered.

Jesus's Passion, properly speaking, was now begun, for he was undergoing an interior martyrdom from his bitter sorrow over humanity's corruption.

Saturday, February 21, and Sunday, February 22, AD 33 (Adar 2–3)

Today, Jesus taught again in the temple, beginning his teaching after the Pharisees had ended theirs. The next day Jesus was again in the temple.

On this and the following day he lodged in the house outside the Bethlehem gate where Mary had put up when she brought him as a child to present in the temple. The lodgings consisted of several apartments adjoining one another, and a man acted as superintendent. When Jesus went to the temple, he was accompanied by Peter, James the Greater, and John; the others came singly. The apostles and disciples lodged with Lazarus in Bethany.

Monday, February 23, AD 33 (Adar 4)

From the morning on, Jesus taught in the temple. During the afternoon, he left to go to Bethany.

On the next day, after teaching in the temple from morn till noon, the Pharisees having been present at his instructions, Jesus returned to Bethany, where he again spoke with his mother of his approaching Passion. They talked standing in an open bower in the courtyard of the house.

Nicodemus, Joseph of Arimathea, Simeon's sons, and other secret disciples did not appear openly in the temple during Jesus's discourses. When the Pharisees were not present, these disciples listened to Jesus from distant corners.

Tuesday, February 24, AD 33 (Adar 5)

In the morning, Jesus made his way back to Jerusalem after visiting a little place, Bethphage, on the outskirts of the city.

Wednesday, February 25, and Thursday, February 26, AD 33 (Adar 6–7)

Jesus continued to teach in the temple. He spoke of the parable of the field overgrown with weeds that had to be carefully uprooted so that the good grain would ripen and not be uprooted together with the weeds—meaning the Pharisees.

In his instruction on this day, Jesus repeated the parable of the field overgrown with weeds. It was to be worked cautiously that with the weeds the good grain, which was to be allowed to ripen, might not be rooted up also. Jesus presented this truth to the Pharisees in words so striking that, though full of wrath, they could not stifle a feeling of secret satisfaction.

Friday, February 27, AD 33 (Adar 8)

Today Jesus was in Bethany and spoke at length with his mother, the holy Virgin, about his approaching suffering. This evening he went to the temple in Jerusalem for the onset of the sabbath. After the Pharisees had left, Jesus taught late into the night.

At a later instruction, their vexation led the Pharisees to close the entrance to the hall so that the listeners might not increase. Jesus taught on this day till late into the night.

Saturday, February 28, AD 33 (Adar 9)

Jesus taught this morning in the temple. Around three o'clock, he shared a meal with about twenty of his apostles and disciples at the house of Mary Mark.

Jesus made no violent gestures in preaching, but turned sometimes to this side, sometimes to that. He said that he had come for three sorts of people, and saying this, he turned to three different sides of the temple, indicating three different regions of the world, wherein were all the elect comprised. Before this, on his way to the temple, he had said to the apostles with him that when he should have departed from them, they should seek him *in the noonday*. Peter, always so bold, asked what that meant, "in the noonday." Then I heard Jesus saying: "At noon the sun is directly above us and there is no shadow. At morn and eve shadows follow the light, and at midnight darkness prevails. Seek me, therefore, in the full noonday light. And you shall find me in your own heart, provided no shadow obscures its light." These words bore some allusion also to different parts of the world, though I cannot now recall it.

Sunday, March 1, AD 33 (Adar 10)

Jesus taught again in the temple. He spoke of John the Baptist, and many pupils of John were present, but they did not display themselves openly. That evening he went to Bethany and spoke with the holy women. Afterward, he retired to sleep at Lazarus's house.

The Jews had become still more insolent. They closed the railing around the teacher's chair and even shut in the chair itself. But when Jesus, with the disciples, again entered the hall, he grasped the railing and it opened of itself, and the chair was freed by the touch of his hand. I recall that many of John the Baptist's disciples and some secret partisans of Jesus were present, and that he began by speaking of John and asking what they thought of him and what they thought of himself. He desired that they should declare themselves boldly, but they were afraid to speak out. He introduced into this discourse the parable of a father and two sons. The latter were directed by their parent to dig up and weed a certain field. One of them said "Yes," but obeyed not. The other replied "No," but repenting, went and executed the order. Jesus dwelt long upon this parable. Later on, after his solemn entrance into Jerusalem, he again taught upon it.

Tuesday, March 3, AD 33 (Adar 12)

Jesus taught in the temple. He returned to sleep that night in Bethany.

Wednesday, March 4, AD 33 (Adar 13)

Next day when Jesus was going from Bethany to the temple, whither his disciples had preceded him to make ready the lecture hall, a blind man cried after him on the road and implored him to cure him, but Jesus passed him by. The disciples were dissatisfied at this. In his discourse,

Jesus referred to the incident, and gave his reasons for acting as he did. The man, he said, was blinder in his soul than in the eyes of his body. His words were very earnest. He said that there were many present who did not believe in him and who ran after him only through curiosity. They would abandon him in the critical hour of trial. They were like those that followed him as long as he fed them with the bread of the body, but when that was over, they scattered in different directions. Those present, he added, should now decide. During this speech I saw many going away, and only some few over a hundred remaining around the Lord. I saw Jesus weeping over this defection on his return to Bethany.

Thursday, March 5, AD 33 (Adar 14)

It was toward evening on the following day when Jesus left Bethany to go to the temple. He was accompanied by six of his apostles, who walked behind him. He himself, on entering the hall, put the seats out of the way and arranged them in order, to the great astonishment of the disciples. In his instruction he touched upon his reason for so doing, and said that he was now soon to leave them.

Friday, March 6, AD 33 (Adar 15)

This afternoon Jesus came from Bethany to Jerusalem before the onset of the sabbath. He ate at the home of John Mark. The holy women and Lazarus were also present. But Lazarus did not go with Jesus to the temple when the sabbath began. Later, Jesus returned to Bethany.

Saturday, March 7, AD 33 (Adar 16)

Jesus taught in the temple again this morning and, after a short pause around midday, he continued teaching. He said that one should not hoard up perishable treasures (Matthew 6:19–21). He spoke, too, of prayer and fasting and of the danger of hypocrisy with regard to these practices (Matthew 6:5, 16). He referred to his approaching end, indicating that he would make a triumphant entry into Jerusalem beforehand. Addressing the apostles, he revealed to them something of their future tasks. Peter, John, and James the Less would remain in Jerusalem; the others were to spread out and teach in various lands, for example, Andrew in the region of Gilead, and Philip and Bartholomew around Gessur. Jesus told them that they would all meet again in Jerusalem three years after his death, and that John and the holy Virgin would then go to Ephesus. He taught many other things as well. The Pharisees were enraged by what they heard and wanted to stone Jesus as he made his way out of the temple. Jesus, however, managed to elude them and returned to Bethany. After this, he did not teach in the temple again for about three days.

On the next sabbath Jesus taught in the temple from morning till evening, part of the time in a retired apartment in presence of the apostles and disciples only, and another part in the lecture hall where the lurking Pharisees and other Jews could hear him. He foretold to the apostles and disciples, though in general terms, much of what was to happen to them in the future. Only at noon did he pause for awhile. He spoke of adulterated virtues: of a love wherein self-love and covetousness predominate; of a humility mixed up with vanity; and he showed how easily evil glides into all things. He said that many believed it was an earthly kingdom and some post of honor in it that they were to expect; and that they hoped by his means to become elevated without pain or trouble on their own part, just as even the pious mother of the sons of Zebedee had petitioned him for a distinguished place for her children. He forbade them to heap up perishable treasures, and he inveighed against avarice. I felt that this was aimed at Judas. He spoke also of mortification, of prayer, of fasting, and of hypocrisy which influences many in these holy practices; and here he made mention of the wrath of the Pharisees against the disciples when the latter, one year before, had stripped some ears of corn. He repeated many of his former instructions, and gave some general explanations upon his own manner of acting in the past. He spoke of his recent absence from them, praised the conduct of the disciples during it, made mention of those that had accompanied him, commending their discretion and docility and recalling in what peace the journey with them had been made. Jesus spoke with much emotion. Then he touched upon the near fulfillment of his mission, his Passion, and the speedy approach of his own end, before which, however, he would make a solemn entrance into Jerusalem. He alluded to the merciless treatment he would undergo, but added that he must suffer, and suffer exceedingly, in order to satisfy divine Justice. He spoke of his blessed Mother, recounting what she too was to suffer with him, and in what manner it would be effected. He exposed the deep corruption and guilt of humankind, and explained that without his Passion no man could be justified. The Jews stormed and jeered when Jesus spoke of his sufferings and their power to satisfy for sin, and some of them left the hall to report to the mob whom they had appointed to spy Jesus. But Jesus addressed his own followers, telling them not to be troubled, that his time was not yet come, and that this also was a part of his Passion.

In this instruction he made some allusion, though without naming it particularly, to the Cenacle, to the house in which the Last Supper was to be eaten and in which later on they were to receive the Holy Spirit. He spoke of their assembling in it and of their partaking of a strengthening and life-giving food in which he himself would remain with them forever. There was some mention made also of his secret disciples, the sons of Simeon, and others. He excused them before the open disciples and designated their caution as necessary, for, as he said, they had a different vocation. As some people from Nazareth had come to the temple out of curiosity to hear him, he said, in a way for them to understand, that they were not in earnest.

When the apostles and disciples alone were standing around Jesus, he touched upon many things that would take place after his return to the Father. To Peter he said that he would have much to suffer, but he should not fear, he should stand firm at the head of the community, which would increase wonderfully. For three years he should with John and James the Less remain with the faithful in Jerusalem. Then he spoke of the youth who was to be first to shed his blood for him, but without mentioning Stephen by name, and of the conversion of his persecutor, who would afterward do more in his service than many others. Here too, he forbore giving Paul's name. Jesus's hearers could not readily comprehend his last words.

He predicted the persecutions that would arise against Lazarus and the holy women, and told the apostles whither they should retire during the first six months after his death: Peter, John, and James the Less were to remain in Jerusalem; Zacchaeus was to go to the region of Gilead; Philip and Bartholomew, to Gessur on the confines of Syria. At these words, I saw in a vision the four apostles crossing the Jordan near Jericho, and then proceeding northward. I saw Philip healing a woman in Gessur where at first he was greatly beloved, though later on he was persecuted. Not far from Gessur was Bartholomew's birthplace. He was descended from a king of the city, a relative of David. His refined manners distinguished him among the other apostles. These four apostles did not remain together; they worked in different parts of the country. Gilead, whither Andrew and Zacchaeus went, was at no great distance from Pella, where Judas had passed his early years.

James the Greater and one of the disciples were sent to the pagan regions north of Capernaum. Thomas and Matthew were dispatched to Ephesus, in order to prepare the country where at a future day Jesus's mother and many of those that believed in him were to dwell. They wondered greatly at the fact of Mary's going to live there. Thaddeus and Simon were to go first to Samaria, though none cared to go there. All preferred cities entirely pagan.

Jesus told them that they would all meet twice in Jerusalem before going to preach the Gospel in distant pagan lands. He spoke of a man between Samaria and Jericho, who would, like himself, perform many miracles, though by the power of the devil. He would manifest a desire of conversion, and they must kindly receive him, for even the devil should contribute to his glory. Simon Magus was meant by these words of Jesus. During this instruction the apostles, as in a familiar conference, questioned Jesus upon whatever they could not understand, and he explained to them as far as was necessary. Everything was perfectly natural.

Three years after the crucifixion all the apostles met in Jerusalem, after which Peter and John left the city and Mary accompanied the latter to Ephesus. Then arose in Jerusalem the persecution against Lazarus, Martha, and Magdalene. The last-named had up to that time been doing penance in the desert, in the cave to which Elizabeth had escaped with John during the Massacre of the Innocents. The apostles, in that first reunion, brought together all that belonged to the body of the church. When half of the time of Mary's life after Christ's Ascension had flown, about the sixth year after that event, the apostles were again assembled in Jerusalem. It was then they drew up the Creed, made rules, relinquished all that they possessed, distributed it to the poor, and divided the church into dioceses, after which they separated and went into far-off pagan countries. At Mary's death they all met again for the last time. When they again separated for distant countries, it was until death.

When Jesus left the temple after this discourse, the enraged Pharisees lay in wait for him both at the gate and on the way, for they intended to stone him. But Jesus avoided them, proceeded to Bethany, and for three days went no more to the temple.

Sunday, March 8, AD 33 (Adar 17)

Jesus remained hidden for three days in the house of Lazarus in Bethany. The apostles came to him and asked him about what he had taught in the temple on the sabbath.

Jesus wanted to give the apostles and disciples time to think over what they had heard. Meantime they referred to him for further explanations upon many points. Jesus ordered them to commit to writing what he had said relative to the future. I saw that Nathaniel the bridegroom, who was very skillful with the pen, did it, and I wondered that it was not John, but a disciple who recorded the predictions. Nathaniel at that time had no other name. It was only at baptism that he received a second.

Monday, March 9, and Tuesday March 10, AD 33 (Adar 18–19)

Today Jesus stayed in Bethany. Three Chaldeans arrived to see him, having heard of his teaching in Chaldea.

Jesus spoke with them only briefly and referred them to the centurion Cornelius in Capernaum.

During these days, three young men came to Lazarus at Bethany from the Chaldean city of Sikdor, and he procured them quarters at the disciples' inn. These youths were very tall and slight, very handsome and active, and much nobler in figure than the Jews. Jesus spoke only a few words to them. He directed them to the centurion of Capernaum, who had been a pagan like themselves, and who would instruct them. Then I saw the youths with the centurion, who was relating to them the cure of his servant. He told them that through shame of the idols that were in his house, and because it was just the time at which the pagan carnival was celebrated, he had begged Jesus, the Son of God, not to enter into his idolatrous household. Five weeks before the Jewish Feast of Easter, the pagans celebrated their carnival, during which they gave themselves up to all kinds of infamous practices. The centurion Cornelius after his conversion gave all his metallic idols in alms to the poor, or to make sacred vessels for the temple. The three Chaldeans returned from Capernaum to Bethany and thence back to Sikdor, where they gathered together the other converts, and with them and their treasures went to join King Mensor.

Wednesday, March 11, AD 33 (Adar 20)

Early this morning, Jesus went to the temple with about thirty disciples. He taught concerning his approaching suffering. Later, he returned to Bethany.

Up to this time Jesus had gone to the temple with only three companions; but now he began to go thither escorted by his whole company of apostles and disciples. I saw the Pharisees retiring from Jesus's chair into the surrounding halls, and peering at him through the arches when he began to preach and to predict his Passion to the disciples.

In the wall of one of the forecourts just in front of the entrance of the temple, seven or eight vendors had taken up their quarters to sell eatables and some kind of red beverage in little flasks. They were like sutlers, and I know not whether they were very devout or not, but I often saw the Pharisees sneaking around to them.

Thursday, March 12, AD 33 (Adar 21)

Today, Jesus taught again in the temple and stayed in Jerusalem overnight.

Friday, March 13, AD 33 (Adar 22)

This morning, all the disciples accompanied Jesus as he went to the temple. There were several vendors selling their wares in one of the forecourts to the temple. Jesus commanded them to leave. As they hesitated, he himself began to gather their things together, and some people carried them away. Later, in the afternoon, Jesus went to the house of John Mark. As the sabbath began, he returned to the temple. He taught until late and stayed in Jerusalem that night.

When Jesus, who had passed the night in Jerusalem, went next morning to the temple and reached the hall in which these vendors were, he ordered them to be off instantly with all their goods. [G1] As they hesitated to obey, he put his own hand to the work, gathered their things together, and had them removed. When he afterwards entered the temple, he found the teacher's chair occupied by others, but they retired as hurriedly as if he had chased them away.

On the following sabbath, after the Jews had finished their sacred services, Jesus again taught in the temple and prolonged his instruction late into the night. In it he made frequent allusions to his journey among the pagans, so that it could be easily understood how good they were and how willing to receive his teachings. In support of his words, he appealed to the recent arrival of the three Chaldeans. They had not seen Jesus when he was in Sikdor, but they had heard of his doctrine, and were so impressed by it that they had journeyed to Bethany for more instruction.

Saturday, March 14, AD 33 (Adar 23)

On the following day Jesus caused three arches in the lecture hall to be closed, that he might instruct his apostles and disciples in private. He repeated on this occasion his early instructions upon his own fast in the desert. He alluded also to many events connected with his own past life, and said why and how he had chosen the apostles. During this last part of his discourse, he placed the apostles in pairs before him. With Judas, however, he spoke but few words. Treason was already in his heart. He was becoming furious, and had had an interview with the Pharisees. After finishing with the apostles, Jesus turned to the disciples, and spoke of their vocation also.

Sunday, March 15, AD 33 (Adar 24)

Jesus taught again in the temple concerning his approaching suffering (Matthew 20:17–19). The disciples were downcast.

I saw that all were very sad. Jesus's Passion was near.

Monday, March 16, AD 33 (Adar 25)

Today, Jesus taught for about four hours in the temple. Once again, he described what would happen to him and how many of the disciples would forsake him. He spoke of his forthcoming triumphant entry into Jerusalem and said that he would then remain with them for fifteen days. The disciples did not understand the "fifteen days" and believed that he meant a longer period. Jesus repeated "three times five days."

Jesus's last instruction in the temple before Palm Sunday lasted four long hours. The temple was full, and all who wanted to hear him could do so. Many women listened from a space separated by a grating. He again explained many things from his former instructions and his own actions. He spoke of the cure of the man at the pool of Bethesda, and said why he had healed him just at that time; of the raising of the son of the widow of Nain, also that of the daughter of Jairus, and said why the former had immediately followed him, but the latter not. Then he referred to what was soon about to happen, and said that he should be abandoned by his own. At first he would with splendor and openly, as in triumph, enter the temple, and the lips of the suckling that had never yet spoken would announce his entrance. Many would break off branches from the trees and strew them before him, while others would spread their mantles in his way. The first, he explained, namely those that strewed branches before him, would not renounce for him what they possessed, and would not remain faithful to him; but they that spread their garments on the way would detach themselves from what they had, would put on the new man, and would remain faithful to him. Jesus did not say that he was going to enter Jerusalem on an ass; consequently, many thought that he would celebrate his entrance with splendor and magnificence, with horses and camels in his train. His words gave rise to a great whispering in the crowd. They did not take his expression, "*fifteen days,*" literally. They understood it to mean a longer time; therefore, Jesus repeated significantly: "Three times five days!"

Tuesday, March 17, AD 33 (Adar 26)

This instruction occasioned great anxiety among the scribes and Pharisees. They held a meeting in Caiaphas's house, [G2] and issued a prohibition against anyone's harboring Jesus and his disciples. They also set spies at the gates to watch for him, but he remained concealed in Bethany with Lazarus.

Jesus's Solemn Entrance into Jerusalem

Wednesday, March 18, AD 33 (Adar 27)

Today, in a basement room in Lazarus's house, Jesus told Lazarus, Peter, James, and John that tomorrow would be the day of his triumphant entry into Jerusalem. The remaining apostles came and when all were gathered together, Jesus spoke with them at length. Then he went to a room where his mother, the holy Virgin, and six other holy women were gathered. He told them a parable. Afterward, they all ate.

JESUS along with Peter, John, James, and Lazarus, and the

blessed Virgin with six of the holy women, remained hidden at Lazarus's. They were in the same subterranean apartments in which Lazarus lay concealed during the persecution that had risen against him. These apartments were under the rear of the building, and were comfortably fitted up with carpets and seats. Jesus, along with the three apostles and Lazarus, was in a large hall supported by pillars and lighted by lamps, while the holy women were in a three-cornered apartment shut in by gratings. Some of the other apostles and disciples were at the disciples' near Bethany, and the rest in other places. Jesus told the apostles that next morning would usher in the day of his entrance into Jerusalem, and he directed all the absent apostles to be summoned. They came, and he had a long interview with them. They were very sad. Toward the traitor Judas, Jesus was gracious in manner, and it was to him that he entrusted the commission to summon the disciples. Judas was very fond of such commissions, for he was desirous to pass for a person of some consequence and importance.

After that, Jesus propounded to the holy women and Lazarus a great parable, which he explained. He began his instruction by speaking of Paradise, the fall of Adam and Eve, the Promise of a Redeemer, the progress of evil, and the small number of faithful laborers in the garden of God. From this, he went on to the parable of a king who owned a magnificent garden. A splendidly dressed lady came to him, and pointed out near his own a garden of aromatic shrubs, which belonged to a good, devout man. She said to the king: "Since this man has left the country, you should purchase his garden and plant it with aromatic shrubs." But the king wanted to plant garlic and similar strong-smelling herbs in the poor man's garden, although the owner looked upon it as a sacred spot in which he desired to see only the finest aromatics. The king caused the good man to be called, and proposed that he should remove from the place or sell his garden to him. Then I saw the good man in his garden. I saw that he cultivated it carefully and was desirous of keeping it. But he had to suffer great persecutions. His enemies went even so far as to attempt to stone him in his own garden, and he fell quite sick. But at last the king with all his glory came to naught, while the good man, his garden, and all belonging to him prospered and increased. I saw this blessing spreading out like the branches of a tree, and filling all parts of the world. I saw the whole parable while Jesus was relating it. It passed before me in tableaux and looked like a true history. The flourishing of the good man's garden was shown me under the figure of gain, of growth, of the development of all kinds of shrubs, also as a watering by means of far-flowing streams, as overflowing fountains of light, and

as floating clouds dissolving in rain and dew. The blessing arose from these sources and spread around and abroad even to the ends of the earth. Jesus explained this parable as having reference to Paradise, the Fall of Man, Redemption, the kingdom of this world, and the Lord's vineyard in it. This vineyard, Jesus said, would be attacked by the prince of the world, who would ill-treat in it the Son of God, to whom the Father had entrusted its care. The parable signified also that as sin and death had begun in a garden, so the Passion of him who had taken upon himself the sins of the world would begin in a garden, and that after satisfying for the same, the victory over death would be gained by his resurrection in a garden.

This instruction was followed by a short repast, after which Jesus continued to speak with the disciples, who as soon as it grew dark had gathered in the neighboring houses.

Thursday, March 19, AD 33 (Adar 28)

Early this morning Jesus instructed Silas and Eremenzear to go to Jerusalem, not by the main road, but along a secondary route via Bethphage. He told them to clear the way. He said that they would find a donkey and a foal in front of an inn at Bethphage and that they should tether the donkey to a fence. If asked what they were doing, they should reply that Jesus had need of these animals (Matthew 21:1–6). After the youths had been gone for a time, Jesus divided the disciples into two groups. Sending the older disciples on ahead, Jesus followed with the apostles and the younger disciples. His mother, the holy Virgin, accompanied by six other holy women, followed at a distance. When they arrived at Bethphage, the two youths brought the donkey and the foal to Jesus. He took his seat on one of them. The apostles and disciples bore branches from palm trees. They began to sing. Thus they made their way into Jerusalem. The news spread quickly of the procession of Jesus and the disciples into the city, and people came from everywhere to see it. There was great jubilation. Jesus wept, and the apostles also wept, when he said that many of those now rejoicing would soon mock him. He wept too in beholding Jerusalem, which would soon be destroyed (Luke 19:41–44). When he arrived at the city gate, the jubilation grew and grew (Matthew 21:10–11). Jesus rode up to the temple and dismounted there. (Anne Catherine saw that something took place in the temple, but she could not recall what. In all probability, Jesus taught there, surrounded by the apostles and disciples, in the presence of the priests and Pharisees and crowds of people.) The holy women returned to Bethany that evening, followed later by Jesus and the apostles (Matthew 21:17).

Early next morning Jesus sent Eremenzear and Silas to Jerusalem, not by the direct route, but by a road that ran through the enclosed gardens and fields near Bethphage. They were commissioned to make that road passable by opening the hedges and removing the barriers. He told them that in the meadow near the inn outside Bethphage (through which ran the road) they would find a she-ass with her foal; [G3] they should fasten the ass to the hedge, and, if questioned as to why they did that, they should answer that the Lord would have it so. Then they should remove every obstruction from the road leading to the temple, which done, they were to return to him.

I saw the two setting out on their journey, opening the hedges, and removing all obstructions from the way. The large public house, near which asses were grazing in a meadow, had a courtyard and fountain. The asses belonged to some strangers who, on going to the temple, had left their beasts here. The disciples bound the she-ass, as directed, and let the foal run at large. Then I saw them continuing their journey to the temple and on the way putting to one side whatever might prove an obstruction. The vendors of foodstuffs, whom Jesus had recently dispersed, had again taken up their stand at a corner near the entrance to the temple. The two disciples went to them and bade them retire, because the Lord was about to make his solemn entrance. After they had thus executed all points of their commission, they returned to Bethphage by the direct route, the other side of the Mount of Olives.

Meanwhile Jesus had sent a band of the eldest disciples to Jerusalem by the usual route with orders to go, some to the house of Mary Mark, others to that of Veronica, to Nicodemus, to the sons of Simeon, and to friends like them, and notify them of his approaching entrance. After that, he himself with all the apostles and the rest of the disciples set out for Bethphage. The holy women, headed by the blessed Virgin, followed at some distance. When the party reached a certain house on the road surrounded by gardens, courtyards, and porticos, they paused for a considerable time. Jesus sent two of the disciples to Bethphage with covers and mantles which they had brought with them from Bethany, in order to prepare the ass of which they had been directed to say that the Lord had need. Meantime he instructed the immense crowd of people that had gathered under the open portico. The latter was supported by polished pillars, between which the holy women took up a place to listen to him. Jesus stood on an elevated platform; the disciples and the crowd filled the courtyard. The portico was ornamented with foliage and garlands. The walls were entirely covered with them, and from the ceiling depended very fine and delicate festoons. Jesus spoke of foresight and of the necessity of using one's

own wits, for the disciples had questioned him upon his taking that by-route. He answered that it was in order to shun unnecessary dangers. One should protect himself, he said, and take care not to leave things to chance; therefore he had beforehand ordered the ass to be bound.

And now Jesus arranged his procession. The apostles he ordered to proceed, two by two, before him, saying that from this moment and after his death, they should everywhere head the community (*the Church*). Peter went first, followed by those that were to bear the Gospel to the most distant regions, while John and James the Less immediately preceded Jesus. All carried palm branches. [G4] As soon as the two disciples that were waiting near Bethphage spied the procession coming, they hurried forward to meet it, taking with them the two animals. The she-ass was covered with trappings that hung to its feet, the head and tail alone being visible.

Jesus now put on the beautiful festal robe of fine white wool which one of the disciples had brought with him for that purpose. It was long and flowing with a train. The broad girdle that confined it at the waist bore an inscription in letters. He then put around his neck a wide stole that reached to the knees, on the two ends of which something like shields was embroidered in brown. The two disciples assisted Jesus to mount the cross-seat on the ass. The animal had no bridle, but around its neck was a narrow strip of stuff that hung down loose. I know not whether Jesus rode on the she-ass or on its foal, for they were of the same size. The riderless animal ran by the other's side. Eliud and Silas walked on either side of the Lord, and Eremenzear behind him; then followed the disciples most recently received, some of whom he had brought back with him from his last great journey, and others that had been received still later. When the procession was ranged in order, the holy women, two by two, brought up the rear. The blessed Virgin, who up to this time had always stayed in the background, now went at their head. As the procession moved forward, all began to sing, and the people of Bethphage, who had gathered around the two disciples while they were awaiting Jesus's coming, followed after like a swarm. Jesus reminded the disciples of what he had previously told them to notice, namely, those that would spread their garments in his path, those that would break off branches from the trees, and those that would render him the double honor, for these last would devote themselves and their worldly goods to his service.

From Bethany to Jerusalem, the traveler in those days met Bethphage to the right and rather more in the direction of Bethlehem. The Mount of Olives separated the two roads. It lay on low, swampy ground, and was a poor little place consisting of only a row of houses on either side of the road. The house near which the asses were grazing stood some distance from the road in a beautiful meadow between Bethphage and Jerusalem. On this side the road ascended, but on the other it sank into the valley between the Mount of Olives and the hills of Jerusalem. Jesus had tarried awhile between Bethany and Bethphage, and it was on the road beyond the latter place that the two disciples were waiting for him with the ass.

In Jerusalem the vendors and people whom Eremen-zear and Silas had that morning told to clear the temple because the Lord was coming, began straightaway and most joyfully to adorn the road. They tore up the pavement and planted trees, the top branches of which they bound together to form an arch, and then hung them with all kinds of yellow fruit like very large apples. The disciples that Jesus had sent on to Jerusalem, innumerable friends who had gone up to the city for the approaching feast (the roads were swarming with travelers), and many of the Jews that had been present at Jesus's last discourse crowded to that side of the city by which he was expected to enter. There were also many strangers in Jerusalem. They had heard of the raising of Lazarus, and they wished to see Jesus. Then when the news spread that he was approaching, they too went out to meet him.

Olive Trees on the Mount of Olives

The road from Bethphage to Jerusalem ran through the lower part of the valley of the Mount of Olives, which was not so elevated as the plateau upon which the temple stood. Going up from Bethphage to the Mount of Olives, one could see, through the high hills that bordered the route on either side, the temple standing opposite. From this point to Jerusalem the road was delightful, full of little gardens and trees.

Crowds came pouring out of the city to meet the apostles and disciples, who were approaching with songs and canticles. At this juncture, several aged priests in the insignia of their office stepped out into the road and brought the procession to a standstill. The unexpected movement silenced the singing. The priests called upon Jesus to say what he meant by such proceedings on the part of his followers, and why he did not prohibit this noise and excitement. Jesus answered that if his followers were silent, the stones on the road would cry out. At these words, the priests retired.

Then the high priests took counsel together, and ordered to be called before them all the husbands and relatives of the women that had gone out of Jerusalem with the children to meet Jesus. When they made their appearance in answer to the summons, they were all shut up in the great court, and emissaries were sent out to spy what was going on.

Many among the crowd that followed Jesus to the temple not only broke off branches from the trees and strewed them in the way, but snatched off their mantles and spread them down, singing and shouting all the while. I saw many that had quite despoiled themselves of their upper garments for that purpose. The children had rushed from the schools, and now ran rejoicing with the crowd. Veronica, who had two children by her, threw her own veil in the way and, snatching another from one of the children, spread that down also. She and the other women joined the holy women, who were in the rear of the procession. There were about seventeen of them. The road was so thickly covered with branches, garments, and carpets that the procession moved on quite softly through the numerous triumphal arches that spanned the space between the walls on either side. [G5]

Jesus wept, as did the apostles also, when he told them that many who were now shouting acclamations of joy would soon deride him, and that a certain one would even betray him. He looked upon the city, and wept over its approaching destruction. [G6] When he entered the gate, the cries of joy became still greater. Many sick of all kinds had been led or carried thither, consequently Jesus frequently halted, dismounted, and cured all without distinction. Many of his enemies had mingled with the crowd, and they now uttered cries with a view to raise an insurrection.

The nearer to the temple, the more magnificent was the ornamentation of the road. On either side hedges had been put up to form enclosures, in which little animals with long necks, kids, and sheep, all adorned with garlands and wreaths around their neck, were skipping about as if in little gardens. The background of these enclosures was formed of bushes. In this part of the city there were always, and especially toward the Passover feast, chosen animals for sale, pure and spotless, destined for sacrifice. To move from the city gate to the temple, although a distance of about half an hour only, the procession took three hours.

By this time the Jews had ordered all the houses, as well as the city gate, to be closed, so that when Jesus dismounted before the temple, and the disciples wanted to take the ass back to where they had found it, they were obliged to wait inside the gate till evening. In the temple were the holy women and crowds of people. [G7] All had to remain the whole day without food, for this part of the city had been barricaded. Magdalene was especially troubled by the thought that Jesus had taken no nourishment.

When toward evening the gate was again opened, the holy women went back to Bethany, and Jesus followed later with the apostles. [G8] Magdalene, worried because Jesus and his followers had had no refreshment in Jerusalem, now prepared a meal for them herself. It was already dark when Jesus entered the courtyard of Lazarus's dwelling. Magdalene brought him a basin of water, washed his feet, and dried them with a towel that was hanging over her shoulder. The food that she had prepared did not amount to a regular meal, it was merely a luncheon. While the Lord was partaking of it, she approached and poured balm over his head. I saw Judas, who passed her at this moment, muttering his dissatisfaction, but she replied to his murmurs by saying that she could never thank the Lord sufficiently for what he had done for her and her brother. After that Jesus went to the public house of Simon the leper, where several of the disciples were gathered, and taught a little while. From there he went out to the disciples' inn, where he spoke for some time, and then returned to the house of Simon the leper.

Friday, March 20, AD 33 (Adar 29)

Today, as Jesus and the apostles made their way to Jerusalem, Jesus was hungry. This was a hunger to convert the people and to fulfill his mission. As he passed by a fig tree, he cursed it when he saw that it had no fruit (Matthew 21:18–19). The fig tree symbolized the old Law and the vine the new Law. Then Jesus went to the

temple. Many vendors were again selling their wares in the forecourt. Jesus drove them all out (Matthew 21:12–13). He taught in the temple. At this time, some travelers from Greece told the apostle Philip that they wished to see Jesus. Philip spoke with Andrew, who told Jesus. Jesus continued his teaching. With his hands folded, he gazed up to heaven. From a cloud of light, a ray descended upon him, and a voice like thunder resounded: "I have glorified him, and I will glorify him again" (John 12:20–36). Later, Jesus left the temple and disappeared into the crowd. He went to John Mark's house, where he met and spoke with the travelers from Greece. They were good and well-respected people. Hearing Jesus's words, they were converted. In fact, these Greeks were among the first to become baptized by the disciples after Pentecost. Jesus then went to Bethany for the beginning of the sabbath and ate a meal with the disciples at the inn of Simon the leper, whom Christ had earlier healed of his leprosy. At the end of the meal, Mary Magdalene came up to Jesus from behind and poured a vial of costly ointment upon his head and feet. She then dried his feet with her hair and left the room. Judas was incensed by this, but Jesus excused Mary Magdalene on account of her love. That very night, Judas ran to Jerusalem to Caiaphas's house. This was Judas's first step toward the betrayal of Jesus.

As Jesus next day was going to Jerusalem with the apostles, he was hungry, but it seemed to me that it was after the conversion of the Jews and the accomplishment of his own mission. He sighed for the hour when his Passion would be over, for he knew its immensity and dreaded it in advance. He went to a fig tree on the road and looked up at it. When he saw no fruit, but only leaves upon it, he cursed it that it should wither and never more bear fruit. [G9] And thus, did he say, would it happen to those that would not acknowledge him. I understood that the fig tree signified the Old Law; the vine, the New. On the way to the temple, I saw a heap of branches and garlands from yesterday's triumph. In the outer portico of the temple, many vendors had again established themselves. Some of them had on their backs cases, or boxes, which they could unfold and which they placed on a pedestal. The latter they carried along with them. When folded, it was like a walking stick. I saw lying on the tables heaps of pence, bound together in different ways by little chains, hooks, and cords, so as to form various figures. Some were yellow; others, white, brown, and variegated. I think they were pieces of money intended for ornamental pendants. I saw also numbers of cages with birds, standing one above another and, in one of the porticos, there were calves and other cattle. Jesus ordered the dealers to be off, and as they hesitated to obey, he doubled up a cincture like a whip and drove them from side to side and beyond the precincts of the temple. [G10]

While Jesus was teaching, some strangers of distinction from Greece dispatched their servants from the inn to ask Philip how they could converse with the Lord without mingling with the crowd. Philip passed the word to Andrew, who in turn transmitted it to the Lord. [G11] Jesus replied that he would meet them on the road between the city gate and the house of John Mark when he should have left the temple to return to Bethany. After this interruption, Jesus continued his discourse. He was very much troubled and when, with folded hands, he raised his eyes to heaven, I saw a flash of light descend upon him from a resplendent cloud, and heard a loud report. [G12] The people glanced up frightened, and began to whisper to one another, but Jesus went on speaking. This was repeated several times, after which I saw Jesus come down from the teacher's chair, mingle with the disciples in the crowd, and leave the temple.

When Jesus taught, the disciples threw around him a white mantle of ceremony which they always carried with them; and when he left the teacher's chair, they took it off so that, clothed like the others, he could more easily escape the notice of the crowd. Around the teacher's chair were three platforms, one above the other, each enclosed by a balustrade, which was ornamented with carving and, I think, molding. There were all sorts of brown heads and knobs on them. I saw no carved images in the temple, although there were various kinds of ornamentation: vines, grapes, animals for sacrifice, and figures like swathed infants, such as I used to see Mary embroidering.

It was still bright daylight when Jesus and his followers reached the neighborhood of John Mark's house. Here the Greeks stepped up, and Jesus spoke to them some minutes. The strangers had some women with them, but they remained standing back. These people were converted. They were among the first to join the disciples at Pentecost and to receive baptism.

MAGDALENE REPEATS HER ANOINTING OF JESUS

FULL of trouble, Jesus went back with the apostles to Bethany for the sabbath. While he was teaching in the temple, the Jews had been ordered to keep their houses closed, and it was forbidden to offer him or his disciples any refreshment. On reaching Bethany, they went to the public house of Simon, the healed leper, where a meal awaited them. Magdalene, filled with compassion for Jesus's fatiguing exertions, met the Lord at the door. She was clothed in a penitential robe and girdle, her flowing hair concealed by a black veil. She cast herself at his feet and with her hair wiped from them the dust, just as one would clean the shoes of another. She did it openly before all, and many were scandalized at her conduct.

After Jesus and the disciples had prepared themselves for the sabbath, that is, put on the garments prescribed and prayed under the lamp, they stretched themselves at table for the meal. Toward the end of it, Magdalene, urged by love, gratitude, contrition, and anxiety, again made her appearance. She went behind the Lord's couch, broke a little flask of precious balm over his head and poured some of it upon his feet, which she again wiped with her hair. [G13] That done, she left the dining hall. Several of those present were scandalized, especially Judas, who excited Matthew, Thomas, and John Mark to displeasure. But Jesus excused her, on account of the love she bore him. She often anointed him in this way. Many of the facts mentioned only once in the Gospels happened frequently.

The meal was followed by prayer, after which the apostles and disciples separated. Judas, full of chagrin, hurried back to Jerusalem that night. I saw him, torn by envy and avarice, running in the darkness over the Mount of Olives, and it seemed as if a sinister glare surrounded him, as if the devil were lighting his steps. He hurried to the house of Caiaphas, and spoke a few words at the door. He could not stay long in any one place. Thence he ran to the house of John Mark. The disciples were wont to lodge there, so Judas pretended that he had come from Bethany for that purpose. This was the first definite step in his treacherous course.

NISAN (30 days): March 20/21 to April 18/19, AD 33 Nisan New Moon: March 19 at 3:30 PM Jerusalem time

Saturday, March 21, AD 33 (Nisan 1)

When, on the following morning, Jesus was going from Bethany to Jerusalem with some of his disciples, they found the fig tree that Jesus had cursed entirely withered, and the disciples wondered at it. I saw John and Peter halting on the roadside near the tree. When Peter showed his astonishment, Jesus said to them: "If ye believe, ye shall do still more wonderful things. Yea, at your word mountains will cast themselves into the sea" (Mark 11:20–25). He continued his instruction on this object, and said something about the signification of the fig tree.

A great many strangers were gathered in Jerusalem, and both morning and evening, preaching and divine service went on in the temple. Jesus taught in the interim. He stood when preaching, but if anyone wanted to put a question to him, he sat down while the questioner rose.

During his discourse today, some priests and scribes stepped up to him and inquired by what right he acted as he did. [G14] Jesus answered: "I too shall ask you something; and when you answer me, I shall tell you by what authority I do these things" (Matthew 21:23–32). Then he asked them by what authority John had baptized, and when they would not answer him, he replied that neither would he tell them by what authority he acted.

In his afternoon instruction, Jesus introduced the similitude of the vine dresser, also that of the cornerstone rejected by the builders (Matthew 21:33–46). [G15] In the former, he explained that the murdered vine dresser typified himself, and the murderers, the Pharisees. Thereupon these last-named became so exasperated that they would willingly have arrested him then and there but they dared not, as they saw how all the people clung to him. They determined, however, to set five of their confidential followers, who were relatives of some of the disciples, to spy on him, and they gave them orders to try to catch him by captious questions. These five men were some of them followers of the Pharisees; others, servants of Herod.

As Jesus was returning toward evening to Bethany, some kindhearted people approached him on the road and offered him something to drink. He passed the night at the disciples' inn near Bethany.

Sunday, March 22, AD 33 (*Nisan 2*)

Next day Jesus taught for three hours in the temple upon the parable of the royal wedding feast (Matthew 22:1–14), the spies of the Pharisees being present. Jesus returned early to Bethany, where he again taught.

Monday, March 23, AD 33 (*Nisan 3*)

After teaching in Bethany, Jesus went to the temple to teach there. He was approached by five men who were in league with the Pharisees and Herodians. They asked him if they were allowed to pay tax to the emperor. Jesus replied as reported in Matthew 22:16–22. That afternoon, seven Sadducees came to him and asked him about the marriages of a woman after the death of her husband. Jesus answered as recorded in Matthew 22:23–33. He also said that love was the highest commandment (Matthew 22:34–40). Then he spoke of the Messiah (Christ) as being a "son of David" (Matthew 22:41–46). That evening, Jesus and the apostles dined with Lazarus, and he taught until late that night.

As he mounted the teacher's chair next day in the circular hall of the temple, the five men appointed by the Pharisees pressed up through the aisle that ran from the door to the chair, the space all around being filled by the audience, and asked him whether they ought to pay tribute to Caesar. Jesus replied by telling them to show him the coin of the tribute; whereupon one of them drew from his breast pocket a yellow coin about the size of a Prussian dollar [or a US quarter] and pointed to the image of the Emperor. Then Jesus told them that they should render to Caesar the things that are Caesar's. [G16]

After that Jesus spoke of the kingdom of God, which he likened to a man who cultivated a plant that never ceased to grow and spread its branches. To the Jews, it would come not again; but those Jews that would be converted would attain the kingdom of God. That kingdom would go to the pagans, and a time would come when in the East all would be darkness, but in the West, perfect day. He told them also that they should perform their good works in secret, as he himself had done, and that he would receive his reward at noonday. He spoke too of a murderer's being preferred to himself.

Later in the day, seven of the Sadducees went to Jesus and questioned him upon the resurrection of the dead. They brought forward something about a woman that had already had seven husbands. Jesus answered that after the resurrection there would be no longer any sex or any marrying, and that God is a God of the living and not of the dead. I saw that his hearers were astounded at his teaching. The Pharisees left their seats and conferred together. [G17] One of them, named Manasseh, who held an office in the temple, very modestly asked Jesus which of the commandments was the greatest. Jesus answered the question, whereupon Manasseh heartily praised him. Then Jesus responded that the kingdom of God was not far from him, and he closed his discourse by some words on Christ (the Messiah) and David.

All were dumbfounded; they had nothing to reply. When Jesus left the temple, a disciple asked him: "What mean the words that thou didst say to Manasseh, 'Thou art not far from the kingdom of God'?" The Lord answered that Manasseh would believe and follow him, but that they (the disciples) should be silent on that head. From that hour Manasseh took no part against Jesus. He lived in retirement till the Ascension, when he declared himself for him and joined the disciples. He was between forty and fifty years old.

That evening Jesus went to Bethany, ate with the apostles at Lazarus's, then visited the inn where the women were assembled, taught them until after nightfall, and lodged at the disciples' inn.

While Jesus was teaching in Jerusalem, I saw the holy women frequently praying together in the arbor in which Magdalene was sitting when Martha called her to welcome Jesus before the raising of Lazarus. They observed a certain order at prayer: sometimes they stood together, sometimes they knelt, or again they sat apart.

Tuesday, March 24, AD 33 (Nisan 4)

Jesus taught in Bethany and then went to the temple. This morning the Pharisees were not present and he was able to teach the apostles and disciples undisturbed. They asked him about the meaning of the words: "Thy kingdom come." Jesus spoke at length about this. He also said that he and the Father were one (John 10:30) and that he would be going to the Father (John 16:16). The disciples asked why, if he and the Father were one, did he need to go to the Father? Jesus spoke of his mission, saying that he would withdraw from humanity, from the flesh, and that whoever— with him, through him, and in him—separated himself from his own fallen nature, would at the same time commend himself to the Father. The apostles were deeply moved by these words and cried out joyfully and full of enthusiasm: "Lord! We will spread your kingdom to the end of the world!" Jesus answered that whoever spoke like this would not accomplish anything. They should never boast: "I have driven out devils in your name!" or "I have done this and that!" Also, they should not carry out their work publicly. That afternoon a great many scribes and Pharisees were present. Jesus spoke the words recorded in Matthew 23:2–39. He added: "You do not lay hands on me yet, as my hour has not yet come." At this, the Pharisees left the temple. It was already dark when Jesus made his way back to Bethany.

On the next day Jesus taught about six hours in the temple. The disciples, impressed by his instruction of the preceding day, asked what was meant by the words: "Thy kingdom come to us!" Jesus gave them a long explanation, and added that he and the Father were one, and that he was going to the Father. Then they asked, if he and the Father were one, why was it necessary for him to go to the Father. Thereupon he spoke to them of his mission, saying that he would withdraw from the humanity, from the flesh, and that whoever separated from his own fallen nature, to go *by him to him*, went at the same time to the Father. Jesus's words on this head were so touching that the apostles, ravished with joy and transported out of themselves, started up and exclaimed: "Lord, we will spread thy kingdom to the end of the world!" But Jesus responded: "Whoever talks in that way accomplishes nothing." At this the apostles became sad. Jesus said again: "You must not say, 'I have cast out devils in thy name, I have done this and that in thy name,' nor should ye do your good works in public." And then he told them that

the last time he had left them, he had done many things in secret, but that they had at the same time insisted that he should go to his own city (Nazareth) although the Jews, on account of the raising of Lazarus, wanted to kill him! But how then would all things have been accomplished? The apostles then asked how could his kingdom become known if they had to keep all things secret. But I do not remember what answer Jesus gave them. They again grew quite dejected. Toward noon the disciples left the temple, but Jesus and the apostles remained. Some of the former returned soon after with a refreshing drink for Jesus.

After midday, the scribes and Pharisees crowded in such numbers around Jesus that the disciples were pushed to some distance from him. He spoke very severely against the Pharisees, and I heard him say once during this stern lecture: "You shall not now arrest me, because my hour has not yet come." [G18]

INSTRUCTION AT LAZARUS'S • PETER RECEIVES A SEVERE REPRIMAND

Wednesday, March 25, AD 33 (Nisan 5)

Today, Jesus spent the whole day with Lazarus and the holy women and the twelve apostles. During the morning, he taught the holy women. Then, around three o'clock in the afternoon there was a meal, after which they prayed together. Jesus spoke of the nearness of the time of delivery of the Son of Man, saying, too, that he would be betrayed. Peter asked why he always spoke as if one of them would betray him, as he, Peter, could testify for the twelve that they would not betray him. Jesus answered that if they were not to receive his grace and prayer, they would all fall, and in his hour of reckoning they would all forsake him. They also asked him about his kingdom. He said that he had to go to the Father and that he would send them the Spirit which proceeds from him and the Father. He said that he had come in the flesh for their salvation and that there was something material in his influence upon them, that the body works in a corporeal manner, and for this reason they could not understand him. However, he would send them the Spirit who would open up their understanding. He also spoke of the coming of a time of tribulation, when all would be filled with fear, and he referred to a woman in the pangs of giving birth. He spoke of the beauty of the human soul, created in God's image, and how wonderful it is to save souls and lead them to their salvation. He taught until late into the night. That night, Nicodemus and one of Simeon's sons came secretly from Jerusalem in order to see him.

JESUS spent the whole of this day at Lazarus's with the holy women and the twelve apostles. In the morning he instructed the holy women in the disciples' inn. Toward three o'clock in the afternoon, a great repast was served in the subterranean dining hall. The women waited at table, and afterward withdrew to the grated, three-cornered apartment, to listen to the instruction. In the course of it, Jesus told them that they would not now be together long, they would not again eat at Lazarus's, though they would do so once more at Simon's, but on that last occasion they would not be so tranquil as they now were. He invited them all to be perfectly free with him, and to ask him whatever they wanted to know. On hearing this, they began to ask numerous questions, especially Thomas, who had a great many doubts. John, too, frequently put a question, but softly and gently.

After the meal, as Jesus was speaking of the approach of the time when the Son of Man would be treacherously betrayed, Peter stepped forward eagerly and asked why he always spoke as if they were going to betray him. Now, though he could believe that one of the others (the disciples) might be guilty of such a thing, yet he would answer for the twelve that they would not betray him! Peter spoke boldly, as if his honor had been attacked. Jesus replied with more warmth than I ever before saw in him, more even than had appeared when he said to Peter: "Get thee behind me, Satan!" He said that without his grace, without prayer, they would all fall away, that the hour would come in which they would all abandon him. There was only one among them, he continued, who wavered not, and yet he too would flee, though he would come back again. By these words Jesus meant John who, at the moment of Jesus's arrest, fled, leaving his mantle behind him. All became very much troubled, excepting Judas who, while Jesus was talking, put on a friendly, smiling, and insinuating air.

When they asked Jesus about the kingdom that was to come to them, his answer was inexpressibly kind. He told them that another Spirit would come upon them and then only would they understand all things. He had to go to the Father and send them the Spirit which proceeded from the Father and himself. I distinctly remember his saying this. He said something more, but I cannot repeat it clearly. It was to this effect, that he had come in the flesh in order to redeem man, that there was something material in his influence upon them, that the body works in a corporeal manner, and it was for that reason they could not understand him. But he would send the Spirit, who would open their understanding. Then he spoke of troublous times to come, when all would have to suffer like a woman in the pains of childbirth, of the beauty of the human soul created to the likeness of God, and he showed how glorious a thing it is to save a soul and lead it home to heaven. He recalled to them how many times they had misunderstood him, and his own forbearance with them; in like manner should they, he said, treat with sinners after his departure. When Peter reminded him that he had himself been sometimes full of fire and zeal, Jesus explained the difference between true and false zeal.

This instruction lasted until late into the night, when Nicodemus and one of Simeon's sons came to Jesus secretly. It was past midnight before they retired to rest. Jesus told them to sleep now in peace, for the time would soon come when, anxious and troubled, they would be without sleep; this would be followed by another time when, in the midst of persecution, a stone under their head, they would sleep as sweetly as Jacob at the foot of the ladder that reached to heaven. When Jesus concluded his discourse, all exclaimed: "Lord, how short was this meal! How short this evening!"

THE WIDOW'S MITE

Thursday, March 26, AD 33 (Nisan 6)

Early this morning, Jesus went to the temple. Today was a day of sacrifice for all who wanted to purify themselves for the feast of the Passover. Jesus and the apostles waited in the temple and watched the people coming with their contributions for the treasury. The last person was a poor widow. It was not possible to see what the people contributed, but Jesus knew what she had given. He said to the disciples that she had given more than anyone else, for she had given all that she had (Mark 12:41–44). That afternoon Jesus taught in the temple. Addressing some Pharisees, he said that they should not expect a peaceful Passover this year; they would not know where they should hide themselves; all the blood of the prophets whom they had murdered would be upon their heads. He also said that the prophets would arise from their graves and that the earth would quake. Later, Jesus went with the disciples to the Mount of Olives. On the way, a disciple showed Jesus the temple and spoke of its beauty. Jesus answered that not one stone would be left upon another (Matthew 24:1–2). On the Mount of Olives, Jesus sat down and some apostles asked him when the temple would be destroyed. Jesus spoke of his second coming, as recorded in Matthew 24:1–14. The last words he spoke here were: "Blessed is he who perseveres until the end."

VERY early the next morning, Jesus repaired to the temple—not, however, to the common lecture hall, but to another in which Mary had made her offering. In the center of the hall, or rather, nearer to the entrance, stood the money box, an angular pillar, about half the height of a man, in which were three funnel-shaped openings to receive the money offerings, and at its foot was a little door. The box was covered with a red cloth over which hung a white transparent one. To the left was the seat for the priest who maintained order, and a table upon which could be laid doves and other objects brought as offerings. To the right and left of the entrance stood the seats for the women and the men, respectively. The rear of the hall was cut off by a grating, behind which the altar had been put up when Mary presented the child Jesus in the temple.

Jesus today took the seat by the money box. It was an offering day for all that desired to purify themselves for the Passover feast. The Pharisees, on coming later, were greatly put out at finding Jesus there, but they declined his offer to yield to them his place. The apostles stood near him, two by two. The men came first to the money box, then the women, and after making their offering, they went out by another door to the left. The crowd stood without awaiting their turn, only five being allowed to enter at a time. Jesus sat there three hours. Toward midday, as a general thing, the offerings ended, but Jesus remained much longer, to the discontent of the Pharisees. This was the hall in which he had acquitted the woman taken in adultery. The temple was like three churches, one behind the other, each standing under an immense arch. In the first was the circular lecture hall. The place of offering in which Jesus was, lay to the right of this hall, a little toward the sanctuary. A long corridor led to it. The last offering was made by a poor, timid widow. No one could see how much the offering was, but Jesus knew what she had given and he told his disciples that she had given more than all the rest, for she had put into the money box all that she had left to buy herself food for that day.[G19] He sent her word to wait for him near the house of John Mark.

In the afternoon, Jesus taught again in the customary place, that is, in the portico of the temple. The circular lecture hall was just opposite the door, and right and left were steps leading to the sanctuary, from which again another flight conducted to the Holy of Holies. As the Pharisees approached Jesus, he alluded to their not daring to arrest him the day before as they had intended, although he had given them a chance to do so. But his hour had not yet come, and it was not in their power to advance it; still, it would come in its own time. The Pharisees, he went on to say, should not hope to celebrate as peaceful a Passover as in former years, for they would not know where to hide themselves; the blood of the prophets whom they had murdered should fall upon their heads. The prophets themselves would rise from their graves, and the earth would be moved. In spite of these signs, however, the Pharisees would remain obstinate. Then he mentioned the poor widow's offering. When toward evening he left the temple, he spoke to her on the way and told her that her son would follow him. His words greatly rejoiced the poor mother. Her son joined the disciples even before the crucifixion. The widow was very devout and strongly attached to the Jewish observances, though simpleminded and upright.

JESUS SPEAKS OF THE DESTRUCTION OF THE TEMPLE

AS Jesus was walking along with his disciples, one of them pointed to the temple and made some remark on its beauty. Jesus replied that one stone of it would not remain upon another.[G20] They were going to the Mount of Olives, upon one side of which was a kind of pleasure garden containing a chair for instruction and seats cut in the mossy banks. The priests were accustomed to come hither to rest at evening after a long day's work. Jesus seated himself in the chair, and some of the apostles asked when the destruction of the temple would take place. It was then that Jesus recounted the evils that were to fall upon the city, and ended with the words: "But he that shall persevere to the end, he shall be saved." He remained scarcely a quarter of an hour in this place.[G21]

From this point of view the temple looked indescribably beautiful. It glistened so brightly under the rays of the setting sun that one could scarcely fix his eyes upon it. The walls were tessellated and built of beautiful sparkling stones, dark red and yellow. Solomon's temple had more gold in it, but this one abounded in glittering stones.

The Pharisees were very greatly exasperated on Jesus's account. They held a council in the night[G22] and dispatched spies to watch him. They said, if Judas would only come to them again, otherwise they did not well know how to proceed in the affair. Judas had not been with them since that first evening.

Friday, March 27, AD 33 (*Nisan 7*)

Jesus and the apostles and disciples returned to the Mount of Olives early in the morning. Jesus spoke of the destruction of Jerusalem and of the end of the world (Matthew 24:15–31), referring, by way of analogy, to a fig tree standing there (Matthew 24:32–35). He also referred to his betrayal, saying that the Pharisees were longing to see the betrayer again. Judas listened with a smile. Jesus also warned the apostles not to be burdened with worldly cares. Later, he taught in the temple, employing the parables of the ten virgins (Matthew 25:1–13) and of the talents (Matthew 25:14–30). He also repeated his words to the Pharisees concerning the shedding of the blood of the prophets (Matthew 23:29–39). Jesus then spent the night at a place at the foot of the Mount of Olives.

Early on the following day Jesus returned to the resting place on the Mount of Olives, and again spoke of the destruction of Jerusalem, illustrating with the similitude of a fig tree that was there standing. He said that he had already been betrayed, though the traitor had not yet mentioned his name, and had merely made the offer to betray him. The Pharisees desired to see the traitor again, but he, Jesus, wanted him to be converted, to repent, and not to despair. Jesus said all this in vague, general terms, to which Judas listened with a smile.

Jesus exhorted the apostles not to give way to their natural fears upon what he had said to them, namely, that they would all be dispersed; they should not forget their neighbor and should not allow one sentiment to veil, to stifle another; and here he made use of the similitude of a mantle. In general terms he reproached some of them for murmuring at Magdalene's anointing. Jesus probably said this in reference to Judas's first definitive step toward his betrayal, which had been taken just after that action of hers—also, as a gentle warning to him for the future, since it would be after Magdalene's last anointing that he would carry out his treacherous design. That some others were scandalized at Magdalene's prodigal expression of love arose from their erroneous severity and parsimony. They regarded this anointing as a luxury so often abused at worldly feasts, while overlooking the fact that such an action performed on the Holy of Holies was worthy of the highest praise.

Jesus told them, moreover, that he would only twice again teach in public. Then speaking of the end of the world and the destruction of Jerusalem, he gave them the signs by which they should know that the hour of his departure was near. There would be, he said, a strife among them as to which should be the greatest, and that would be a sign that he was about to leave them. He signified to them also that one of them would deny him, and he told them that he said all these things to them that they might be humble and watch over themselves. He spoke with extraordinary love and patience.

About noon Jesus taught in the temple, his subject being the ten virgins, the talents entrusted, and he again inveighed severely against the Pharisees. He repeated the words of the murdered prophets, and several times upbraided the Pharisees for their wicked designs. He afterward told the apostles and disciples that even where there was no longer hope of improvement, words of warning must not be withheld.

When Jesus left the temple, a great number of pagans from distant parts approached him. They had not, indeed, heard his teaching in the temple, since they had not dared to set foot therein; but through the sight of his miracles, his triumphal entrance on Palm Sunday, and all the other wonders that they had heard of him, they wanted to be converted. Among them were some Greeks. Jesus directed them to the disciples, a few of whom he took with him to the Mount of Olives where, in a public inn formerly used by strangers only, they lodged for the night.

Saturday, March 28, AD 33 (*Nisan 8*)

Early this morning, Jesus taught the apostles and disciples at the place at the foot of the Mount of Olives where he had spent the night. Then he went to the temple. There he spoke of his departure, saying that he was going to the Father. He described how the fall into sin had begun in a garden and that it would end in a garden. His enemies would lay their hands on him in a garden. They had wanted to kill him, following the raising of Lazarus. He had gone away in order that everything could be fulfilled. He characterized the journey that he had made after the raising of Lazarus by dividing it into three parts, each several weeks long. (The journey had lasted five months.) He spoke also of Eve and said plainly that he was the Savior who would free human beings from the power of sin.

Next morning, when the rest of the apostles and disciples came thither, Jesus instructed them upon many points. He said that he would be with them at two meals more, that he was longing to celebrate with them the last Love Feast in which he would bestow upon them all that humanly he could give. After that he went with them to the temple, where he spoke of his return to his Father and said that he was the Father's will, but this last expression I did not understand. He called himself in plain terms the salvation of humankind, said that it was he who was to put an end to the power of sin over the human race, and explained why the fallen angels were not redeemed, as well as man. The Pharisees took turns, two at a time, to spy. Jesus said that he had come to put an end to the domination of sin over man. Sin began in a garden, and in a garden it should end, for it would be in a garden that his enemies would seize him. He reproached his hearers with the fact of their already wanting to kill him after the raising of Lazarus, and said that he had kept himself at a distance, that all things might be fulfilled. He divided his journey into three parts, but I no longer recollect whether it was into thrice four, or five, or six weeks. He told them also how they would treat him and put him to death with assassins, and yet they would not be satisfied, they would not be able to effect anything against him after his death. He once more made mention of the murdered just who would arise again; yes, he even pointed out the spot in which their resurrection would take place. But as for the Pharisees, he continued, in fear and anguish they would see their designs against him frustrated.

Jesus spoke likewise of Eve, through whom sin had come upon the earth; therefore it was that woman was condemned to suffer and that she dared not enter into the sanctuary. But it was also through a woman that the cure of sin had come into the world, consequently she was freed from slavery, though not from dependence.

Jesus again took up quarters in the inn at the foot of the Mount of Olives. A lamp was lighted, and the sabbath exercises were performed.

JESUS IN BETHANY

Sunday, March 29, AD 33 (Nisan 9)

Today Jesus went with the disciples across the brook Kidron to Gethsemane. He pointed out to the apostles the place where he would be seized and added that here they would forsake him. Jesus was very downcast as they went toward Bethany. That evening, they took a meal together at the house of Lazarus.

NEXT morning, Jesus went with his followers across the brook Kidron, and then northward by a row of houses between which were little grass plots on which sheep were grazing. Here was situated John Mark's house. Jesus then turned off to Gethsemane, a little village as large as Bethphage, built on either side of the brook Kidron. John Mark's house stood a quarter of an hour outside the gate through which the cattle were led to the cattle market on the north side of the temple. It was built upon a high hill which, at a later period, was covered with houses. It was from here to Gethsemane one-half hour; and from Gethsemane across the Mount of Olives to Bethany, something less than an hour. The last-named place lay almost in a straight line east of the temple and, by the direct route, it may have been only one hour from Jerusalem. From certain points of the temple and from the castles in the rear, one could descry Bethany. Bethphage, however, was not in sight, as it lay low; and the view was, besides, up to the point at which the temple could be seen through a defile of the mountain road, obstructed by the Mount of Olives. As Jesus was going over the brook Kidron to Gethsemane with the disciples, he said to the apostles as they were entering a hollow of the Mount of Olives: "Here will ye abandon me! Here shall I be taken prisoner!" He was very much troubled. He proceeded afterward to Lazarus's, in

Kidron Bridge on the Way to the Temple

Bethany, thence to the disciples' inn, after which he went with some of them around the environs of the city consoling the inhabitants, like one bidding farewell.

That evening there was a supper at Lazarus's, at which the holy women assisted in the grated apartment. At the close of the meal Jesus told them all that they could have one night more of peaceful sleep.

Jesus's Last Discourse in the Temple

Monday, March 30, AD 33 (Nisan 10)

Early this morning, Jesus went with the disciples to Jerusalem. In the temple, he spoke of union and separation. He used the analogy of fire and water, which are inimicable. When water does not overpower fire, the flames become greater and more powerful. He spoke of persecution and martyrdom. By the flames of fire, he was referring to those disciples who would remain true to him, and by water he meant those who would leave him and seek the abyss. He spoke also of the mingling of milk and water; this symbolizes an inner union which cannot be separated. With this he meant his union with them. He referred to the mild and nourishing power of milk. He also spoke of the union of human beings in marriage. He said that there are two kinds of marriage: that of the flesh, where the couple become separated at death; and that of the spirit, where they remain united beyond death. He spoke also of the bridegroom and of the church as his bride and went on to refer to the union with them through the Last Supper, which union could never be dissolved. He spoke also of the baptism of John, which would be replaced by the baptism of the Holy Spirit, whom he would send, and gave instructions to the disciples to baptize all who came to them to be baptized. That evening he returned to Bethany.

EARLY the next morning, Jesus went with the disciples to Jerusalem. Having crossed the Kidron in front of the temple, he continued his course outside the city toward the south, till he came to a little gate, by which he entered, and, crossing a stone bridge that spanned a deep abyss, he reached the foot of Mount Zion. There were caverns also under the temple. Here Jesus turned from the south side of the temple and proceeded through a long vaulted corridor, which was lighted only from above, into the women's portico.

Here, turning toward the east, he passed through the doorway allotted to women condemned on account of their sterility, crossed the hall in which offerings were made, and proceeded to the teacher's chair in the outer hall of the temple. This door always stood open, although at Jesus's instructions, all the other entrances to the temple were often closed by the Pharisees. They said: "Let the sin-door always remain open to the sinner!"

In words admirable and deeply significant, Jesus taught upon union and separation. He made use of the similitude of fire and water, which are opposed to each other, one of which extinguishes the other, though if the latter does not get the better of the former, the flames become wilder and more powerful. He next spoke of persecution and martyrdom. Under the figure of fire, Jesus alluded to those disciples that would remain true to him; and under that of water, to those that would separate from him and seek the abyss. He called water the martyr of fire. He spoke also of the mingling of water and milk, naming it an intimate commingling that no one could separate. Jesus wished under this figure to designate his own union with his followers, and he dwelt upon the mild and nutritive properties of milk. From this he passed to the subject of marriage and its union, as the disciples had questioned him upon the reunion after death of friends and married people. Jesus said that there was a twofold union in marriage: the union of flesh and blood, which death cuts asunder, and they that

were so bound would not find themselves together after death; and the union of soul, which would outlive death. They should not, he continued, be disquieted as to whether they would be alone or together in the other world. They that had been united in union of soul in this life, would form but one body in the next. He spoke also of the Bridegroom and named the church his affianced. Of the martyrdom of the body, he said that it was not to be feared, since that of the soul was the more frightful.

Gethsemane Road to Jerusalem

As the apostles and disciples did not comprehend all that he said, Jesus directed them to write down what they failed to understand. Then I saw John, James the Less, and another making signs from time to time on a little tablet that they held before them resting on a support. They wrote upon little rolls of parchment with a colored liquid, which they carried with them in a kind of horn. They drew the little rolls out of their breast pockets, and wrote only in the beginning of the instruction.

Jesus spoke likewise of his own union with them, which would be accomplished at the Last Supper and could by nothing be dissolved.

The obligation of perfect continence, Jesus exposed to the apostles by way of interrogation. He asked, for instance, "Could you do such and such a thing at the same time?" and he spoke of a sacrifice that had to be offered, all which led to perfect continence as a conclusion. He adduced as examples Abraham and the other patriarchs who, before offering sacrifice, always purified themselves and observed a long continence.

When he spoke of baptism and the other sacraments, he said that he would send to them the Holy Spirit who, by his baptism, would make them all children of Redemption. They should after his death baptize at the pool of Bethesda all that would come and ask for it. If a great number presented themselves, they should lay their hands upon their shoulders, two by two, and baptize them there under the stream of the pump, or jet. As formerly the angel, so now would the Holy Spirit come upon the baptized as soon as his blood should have been shed, and even before they themselves had received the Holy Spirit.

Peter, who had been appointed by Jesus chief over the others, asked as such whether they were always to act in this manner without first proving and instructing the people. Jesus answered that the people would be wearied out with waiting for feast days and pining meantime in aridity; therefore they, the apostles, should not delay to do as he had just told them. When they should have received the Holy Spirit, then they would always know what they should do. He addressed some words to Peter on the subject of penance and absolution, and afterward spoke to them all about the end of the world and of the signs that would precede it. A man enlightened by God would have visions on that subject. By these words, Jesus referred to John's revelations, and he himself made use of several similar illustrations. He spoke, for instance, of those that would be marked with the sign on their forehead, and said that the fountain of living water which flowed from Golgotha's mount would at the end of the world appear to be almost entirely poisoned, though all the good waters would finally be gathered into the valley of Jehosaphat. It seemed to me that he said also that all water was to become once more baptismal water. No Pharisees were present at any part of this instruction. That evening Jesus returned to Lazarus's, in Bethany.

Tuesday, March 31, AD 33 (Nisan 11)

Today, Jesus taught for the last time in the temple. He spoke of the truth and of the necessity of fulfilling what one teaches. He wished to bring his teaching to fulfillment. It was not enough to believe; one must also practice one's faith. Thus, he would bring his teaching to fulfillment by going to the Father. Before leaving his disciples, however, he wished to bestow on them all that he had; not money and property, which he did not have, but his power and his forces. These he wanted to give them, and also to found an intimate union with them to the end of the world, a more perfect union than the present one. He asked them to become united with one another as limbs of one body. By this, Jesus referred to that which was to be accomplished through the Last Supper, but without mentioning it. He also said that his mother, the holy Virgin, would remain with them for a number of years after his ascension to the Father. As he left the temple that evening, he took leave of it, saying that he would never enter it again in this body. This was so moving that the apostles and disciples cast themselves down on the ground and wept. Jesus also wept. It was dark as he made his way back to Bethany.

The whole of the next day Jesus taught undisturbed in the temple. He spoke of truth and the necessity of acting out what they, the apostles, taught. He himself, he said, was now about to fulfill it. It is not enough to believe, one must practice one's faith. No one, not even the Pharisees themselves, could reproach him with the least error in his teaching, and now by returning to his Father he would fulfill the truth he had taught. But before going he would give over to them, would leave to them, all that he possessed. Money and property he had not, but he would bequeath to them his strength and power. He would establish with them a union which should be still more intimate than that which now united them to him, and which should last till the end of time. He would also bind them to one another as the members of one body. Jesus spoke of so many things that he would still do with them that Peter, conceiving new hope that he would remain longer on earth, said to him that if he were to fulfill all those things, he would have to abide with them till the end of the world. Jesus then spoke of the essence and effects of the Last Supper, without, however, mentioning it by name. He said also that he was about to celebrate his last Passover. Peter asked where he intended to do so. Jesus answered that he would tell him in good time, and after that last Passover he would go to his Father. Peter again asked whether he would take with him his mother, whom they all loved and reverenced so much. Jesus answered that she should remain with them some years longer. He mentioned the number, and in it there was a five. I think he named fifteen years, and then said many things in connection with her.

In his instruction upon the power and effects of his Last Supper, Jesus made some allusion to Noah, who had once become intoxicated with wine; to the children of Israel, who had lost their taste for the manna sent them from heaven; and to the bitterness they tasted in it. As for himself, he was going to prepare the bread of life before his return home, but it was not yet ready, was not yet baked, not yet cooked.

He had, he continued, so long taught them the truth, so long communicated with them; and yet they had always doubted, indeed they doubted still! He felt that in his corporeal presence he could no longer be useful to them, therefore he would give them all that he had, he would retain only what was absolutely necessary to cover his naked body. These words of Jesus the apostles did not understand. They were under the impression that he would die, or perhaps vanish from their sight. As late as the preceding day, when he was speaking of the persecution of the Jews against him, Peter said that he might again withdraw from these parts and they would accompany him. He had gone away once before after the raising of Lazarus, he could now go again.

When toward evening Jesus left the temple, he spoke of taking leave of it, saying that he would never again enter it in the body. This scene was so touching that all the apostles and disciples cast themselves on the ground crying aloud and weeping. Jesus wept also. Judas shed no tear, though he was anxious and nervous, as he had been during the past days. Yesterday Jesus said no word in allusion to him.

In the court of the temple some pagans were waiting, many of whom wanted to give themselves to Jesus. They saw the tears of the apostles. On learning their desire, Jesus told them that there was no time now, but that they should later on have recourse to his apostles and disciples, to whom he gave power similar to his own. Then taking the way by which he had entered on Palm Sunday, and frequently turning with sad and earnest words to gaze upon the temple, he left the city, went to the public inn at the foot of the Mount of Olives, and after nightfall back to Bethany.

Here Jesus taught at Lazarus's, continuing his instructions during the evening meal, at which the women, who now kept themselves less aloof, served. Jesus gave orders for a plentiful meal to be prepared at Simon's public house on the following day.

It was very quiet in Jerusalem all this day. The Pharisees did not go to the temple, but assembled in council. They were very anxious on account of Judas's non-appearance. Many good people of the city were in great distress at Jesus's predictions, which they had heard from the disciples. I saw Nicodemus, Joseph of Arimathea, Simeon's sons, and others looking very troubled and anxious, though they had not yet withdrawn from the rest of the Jews. They were still mixing with them in the affairs of everyday life. I saw Veronica also, going about her house sad and wringing her hands. Her husband inquired the cause of her affliction. Her house was situated in Jerusalem between the temple and Mount Calvary. Seventy-six of the disciples lodged in the halls surrounding the Cenacle.

Magdalene's Last Anointing

Wednesday, April 1, AD 33 (Nisan 12)

Early this morning many disciples assembled at the home of Lazarus in Bethany to hear Jesus teach. In all, about sixty people were gathered together. Toward three o'clock that afternoon, tables were prepared for a meal at the house of Simon the leper. At the meal, Jesus and the apostles served, Jesus going from one table to the other, exchanging words with the disciples as he went. Mary was indescribably sad, as Jesus had told her that morning of the nearness of his approaching death. Jesus also spoke with the disciples of this, saying that one of them would betray him to the Pharisees for a sum of money. The disciples wept bitterly and were so downcast that they could no longer eat. But Jesus bid them to partake of the food. He also gave instructions as to what they should do and where they should go after his death. At the end of the meal, while Jesus was teaching, Mary Magdalene entered the room bearing a costly ointment that she had bought in Jerusalem that morning. She cast herself down at Jesus's feet, weeping, and anointed his feet with the costly ointment. Then she dried his feet with her hair. Jesus broke off what he was saying, and some of the disciples were irritated by this interruption. Jesus said: "Do not take offense at this woman!" Then he spoke quietly with her. Mary Magdalene took the remaining ointment and poured it upon his head and the fragrance filled the room. Some of the apostles muttered at this. Magdalene, who was veiled, wept as she made her way from the room. As she was about to walk past Judas, he held out his arm and blocked the way. Judas scolded her on account of the waste of money, saying that it could have been given to the poor. However, Jesus said that she should be allowed to go, adding that she had anointed him in preparation for his death and burial, and that afterwards she would not be able to do so again. He said that wherever the Gospel would be taught, her deed and also the disciples' muttering would be remembered (Matthew 26:13). Judas was quite furious and thought to himself that he could no longer put up with this kind of thing. He withdrew quietly and then ran all the way to Jerusalem. It was dark, but he did not stumble. In Jerusalem the high priests and Pharisees were gathered together. Judas went to them and said that he wanted to give Jesus over into their hands. He asked how much they would give him and he was offered thirty pieces of silver. After concluding this agreement by shaking hands, Judas ran back to Bethany and rejoined the others. That night Nicodemus came from Jerusalem to speak with Jesus, and he returned to Jerusalem before the break of day.

NEXT morning, Jesus instructed a large number of the disciples, more than sixty, in the court before Lazarus's house. In the afternoon, about three o'clock, tables were laid for them in the court, and during their meal Jesus and the apostles served. I saw Jesus going from table to table handing something to this one, something to that, and teaching all the time. Judas was not present. He was away making purchases for the entertainment to be given at Simon's. Magdalene also had gone to Jerusalem, to buy precious ointment. The blessed Virgin, to whom Jesus had that morning announced his approaching death, was inexpressibly sad. Her niece, Mary Cleophas, was always around her, consoling her. Full of grief, they went together to the disciples' inn.

Meantime, Jesus conversed with the disciples upon his approaching death and the events that would follow it. One, he said, that had been on intimate terms with him, one that owed him a great debt of gratitude, was about to sell him to the Pharisees. He would not even set a price upon him, but would merely ask: "What will ye give me for him?" If the Pharisees were buying a slave, it would be at a fixed price, but he would be sold for whatever they chose to give. The traitor would sell him for less than the cost of a slave! The disciples wept bitterly, and became so afflicted that they had to cease eating, but Jesus pressed them graciously. I have often noticed that the disciples were much more affectionate toward Jesus than were the apostles. I think as they were not so much with him, they were on that account more humble.

This morning Jesus spoke of many things with his apostles. As they did not understand everything, he commanded them to write down what they could not comprehend, saying that when he would send his Spirit to them, they would recall those points and be able to seize their meaning. I saw John and some of the others taking notes. Jesus dwelt long upon their flight, when he himself would be delivered up to the Pharisees. They could not think that such a thing would ever happen to them, and yet they really did take to flight. He predicted many things that were to follow that event, and told them how they should conduct themselves.

At last he spoke of his holy mother. He said that through compassion, she would suffer with him all the cruel tor-

ture of his death, that with him she would die his bitter death, and still would have to survive him fifteen years.

Jesus indicated to the disciples whither they should betake themselves: some to Arimathea, some to Sichar, and others to Kedar. The three that had accompanied him on his last journey were not to return home. Since their ideas and sentiments had undergone so great a change, it would not be well for them to return to their country, otherwise they might give scandal or, on account of the opposition of friends, run the risk of falling back into their former way of acting. Eliud and Eremenzear went, I think, to Sichar, but Silas remained where he was. And thus Jesus went on instructing his followers with extraordinary love, counselling them on everything. I saw many of them dispersing toward evening.

It was during this instruction that Magdalene came back from Jerusalem with the ointment she had brought. She had gone to Veronica's and stayed there while Veronica saw to the purchase of the ointment, which was of three kinds, the most precious that could be procured. Magdalene had expended upon it all the money she had left. One was a flask of the oil of spikenard. She bought the flasks together with their contents. The former were of a clear, whitish, though not transparent material, almost like mother-of-pearl, though not mother-of-pearl. They were in shape like little urns, the swelling base ornamented with knobs, and they had screw-tops. Magdalene carried the vessels under her mantle in a pocket which hung on her breast suspended by a cord that passed over one shoulder and back across the back. John Mark's mother went back with her to Bethany, and Veronica accompanied them a part of the way. As they were going through Bethany, they met Judas who, concealing his indignation, spoke to Magdalene. Magdalene had heard from Veronica that the Pharisees had resolved to arrest Jesus and put him to death, but not yet, on account of the crowds of strangers and especially the numerous pagans that followed him. This news Magdalene imparted to the other women.

The women were at Simon's helping to prepare for the entertainment, for which Judas had purchased everything necessary. He had entirely emptied the purse today, secretly thinking that he would get all back again in the evening. From a man who kept a garden in Bethany, he bought vegetables, two lambs, fruit, fish, honey, etc. The dining hall used at Simon's today was different from that in which Jesus and his friends had dined once before, that is, on the day after the triumphal entrance into the temple. Today they dined in an open hall at the back of the house, and which looked out upon the courtyard. It had been ornamented for the occasion. In the ceiling was an opening which was covered with a transparent veil and which looked like a little cupola. On either side of this cupola hung verdant pyramids of a brownish-green, succulent plant with small round leaves. The pyramids were green likewise at the base, and it seemed to me that they always remained green and fresh. Under this ceiling ornamentation stood the seat for Jesus. One side of the table, that toward the open colonnade through which the servings of food were brought across the courtyard, was left free. Simon, who served, alone had his place on that side. There too on the floor, under the table, stood three water jugs, tall and flat.

The guests reclined during this repast on low cross-benches, which in the back had a support, and in front an arm upon which to lean. The benches stood in pairs, and they were sufficiently wide to admit of the guests' sitting two by two, facing each other. Jesus reclined at the middle of the table upon a seat to himself. On this occasion the women ate in an open hall to the left. Looking obliquely across the courtyard, they could see the men at table.

When all was prepared, Simon and his servant, in festal robes, went to conduct Jesus, the apostles, and Lazarus. Simon wore a long robe, a girdle embroidered in figures, and on his arm a long fur-lined maniple. The servant wore a sleeveless jacket. Simon escorted Jesus; the servant, the apostles. They did not traverse the street to Simon's, but went in their festal robes back through the garden into the hall. There were numbers of people in Bethany, and the crowds of strangers who had come through a desire to see Lazarus raised somewhat of a tumult. It was also a cause of surprise and dissatisfaction to the people that Simon, whose house formerly stood open, had purchased so large a supply of provisions and closed his establishment. They became in a short time angry and inquisitive, and almost scaled the walls during the meal. I do not remember having seen any foot-washing going on, but only some little purification before entering the hall.

Several large drinking glasses stood on the table, and beside each, two smaller ones. There were three kinds of beverages: one greenish, another red, and the third yellow. I think it was some kind of pear juice. The lamb was served first. It lay stretched out on an oval dish, the head resting on the forefeet. The dish was placed with the head toward Jesus. Jesus took a white knife, like bone or stone, inserted it into the back of the lamb, and cut, first to one side of the neck and then to the other. After that he drew the knife down, making a cut from the head along the whole back. The lines of this cut at once reminded me of the cross. He then laid the slices thus detached before John, Peter and himself, and directed Simon, the host, to carve the lamb down the sides, and lay the pieces right and left before the apostles and Lazarus as they sat in order.

The holy women were seated around their own table.

Magdalene, who was in tears all the time, sat opposite the blessed Virgin. There were seven or nine present. They too had a little lamb. It was smaller than that of the other table and lay stretched out flat in the dish, the head toward the Mother of God. She it was who carved it.

The lamb was followed by three large fish and several small ones. The large ones lay in the dish as if swimming in a stiff, white sauce. Then came pastry, little rolls in the shape of lambs, birds with outstretched wings, honeycombs, green herbs like lettuce, and a sauce in which the last-named were steeped. I think it was oil. This course was followed by another of fruit that looked like pears. In the center of the dish was something like a gourd upon which other fruit, like grapes, were stuck by their stems. The dishes used throughout the meal were partly white, the inside partly yellow; and they were deep or shallow according to their contents.

Jesus taught during the whole meal. It was nearing the close of his discourse; the apostles were stretched forward in breathless attention. Simon, whose services were no longer needed, sat motionless, listening to every word, when Magdalene rose quietly from her seat among the holy women. She had around her a thin, bluish-white mantle, something like the material worn by the three holy kings, and her flowing hair was covered with a veil. Laying the ointment in a fold of her mantle, she passed through the walk that was planted with shrubbery, entered the hall, went up behind Jesus, and cast herself down at his feet, weeping bitterly. She bent her face low over the foot that was resting on the couch, while Jesus himself raised to her the other that was hanging a little toward the floor. Magdalene loosened the sandals and anointed Jesus's feet on the soles and upon the upper part. Then with both hands drawing her flowing hair from beneath her veil, she wiped the Lord's anointed feet, and replaced the sandals. Magdalene's action caused some interruption in Jesus's discourse. He had observed her approach, but the others were taken by surprise. Jesus said: "Be not scandalized at this woman!" and then addressed some words softly to her. She now arose, stepped behind him and poured over his head some costly water, and that so plentifully that it ran down upon his garments. Then with her hand she spread some of the ointment from the crown down the hind part of his head. The hall was filled with the delicious fragrance. The apostles whispered together and muttered their displeasure—even Peter was vexed at the interruption. Magdalene, weeping and veiled, withdrew around behind the table. When she was about to pass before Judas, he stretched forth his hand to stay her while he indignantly addressed to her some words on her extravagance, saying that the purchase money might have been given to the poor. Magdalene made no reply. She was weeping bitterly. Then Jesus spoke, bidding them let her pass, and saying that she had anointed him for his death, for later she would not be able to do it, and that wherever this Gospel would be preached, her action and their murmuring would also be recounted.

Magdalene retired, her heart full of sorrow. The rest of the meal was disturbed by the displeasure of the apostles and the reproaches of Jesus. When it was over, all returned to Lazarus's. Judas, full of wrath and avarice, thought within himself that he could no longer put up with such things. But concealing his feelings, he laid aside his festal garment, and pretended that he had to go back to the public house to see that what remained of the meal was given to the poor. Instead of doing that, however, he ran full speed to Jerusalem. I saw the devil with him all the time, red, thin-bodied, and angular. He was before him and behind him, as if lighting the way for him. Judas saw through the darkness. He stumbled not, but ran along in perfect safety. I saw him in Jerusalem running into the house in which, later on, Jesus was exposed to scorn and derision. The Pharisees and high priests were still together, but Judas did not enter their assembly. Two of them went out and spoke with him below in the courtyard. When he

told them that he was ready to deliver Jesus and asked what they would give for him, they showed great joy, and returned to announce it to the rest of the council. After awhile, one came out again and made an offer of thirty pieces of silver. Judas wanted to receive them at once, but they would not give them to him. They said that he had once before been there, and then had absented himself for so long, that he should do his duty, and then they would pay him. I saw them offering hands as a pledge of the contract, and on both sides tearing something from their clothing. The Pharisees wanted Judas to stay awhile and tell them when and how the bargain would be completed. But he insisted upon going, that suspicion might not be excited. He said that he had yet to find things out more precisely, that next day he could act without attracting attention. I saw the devil the whole time between Judas and the Pharisees. On leaving Jerusalem, Judas ran back again to Bethany, where he changed his garments and joined the other apostles. [G23]

Jesus remained at Lazarus's, while his followers withdrew to their own inn. That night Nicodemus came from Jerusalem, and on his return Lazarus accompanied him a part of the way.

Gethsemane Road among the Olives

TISSOT ILLUSTRATIONS
[SECTION G]

The Passion and Death of Jesus Christ

⊕

Jesus Forbids Carrying Loads in Forecourt · · · · · · 24
The Chief Priests Take Counsel Together · · · · · · · 26
The Foal of Bethphage · · · · · · · · · · · · · · · · · · 28
The Procession on the Mount of Olives · · · · · · · · 30
The Procession in the Streets of Jerusalem · · · · · · 32
The Lord Wept · 34
The Procession in the Temple · · · · · · · · · · · · · · 36
Jesus Goes in the Evening to Bethany · · · · · · · · · 38
The Accursed Fig Tree · · · · · · · · · · · · · · · · · · 40
The Merchants Chased from the Temple · · · · · · · 42
The Greeks Ask to See Jesus · · · · · · · · · · · · · · 44
The Voice from on High · · · · · · · · · · · · · · · · · · 46

The Ointment of Magdalene · · · · · · · · · · · · · · 48
By What Right Does He Act in This Way? · · · · · · · 50
The Corner Stone · 52
The Tribute Money · 54
The Pharisees Question Jesus · · · · · · · · · · · · · · 56
Woe unto You, Scribes and Pharisees · · · · · · · · · · 58
The Widow's Mite · 60
The Disciples Admire the Temple Buildings · · · · · 62
Prophecy of the Destruction of the Temple · · · · · · 64
Conspiracy of the Jews · · · · · · · · · · · · · · · · · · 66
Judas Goes to Find the Jews · · · · · · · · · · · · · · · 68

Jesus Forbids the Carrying of Loads in the Forecourt of the Temple [G1]

⊕

WHEN Jesus, who had passed the night in Jerusalem, went next morning to the temple and reached the hall in which these vendors were, he ordered them to be off instantly with all their goods. [5]

[Mark 11:16] And he would not allow any one to carry anything through the temple.

JESUS, *having undertaken to restore order in the house of his Father, did not content himself with the first sweeping reform just described. Yet another abuse had crept in: namely, the crossing of the temple with various vessels in which to fetch water more conveniently than by going round. To understand more clearly how this custom came to be introduced, what has already been said about the system of the water supply of Jerusalem must be borne in mind. We know that all those portions of the temple open to the sky were paved with polished stones and, in some parts, with many-colored marbles intended to receive rain water and take it to the cisterns or reservoirs. These reservoirs were numerous, and were much frequented by the women of the town, who flocked to them to draw water for their domestic needs. Besides rain water these reservoirs received the water from the sealed fountain on the further side of Bethlehem and Etam, beyond the Wady Urtas. The water from Solomon's Pools was also diverted to them by means of the aqueducts already referred to. The reservoirs thus fed were celebrated, and their water was much sought after on account of its freshness and purity; the people, however, preferred to draw it from the cisterns adjoining the temple to going to fetch it from outside the town at Amygdalum, or in the reservoirs of the Valley of Gihon. This was the cause of the perpetual going and coming which destroyed the retirement of the temple. It was not, however, the only one, for all those who wished to go to any place beyond the temple preferred taking a short cut through it to going around the whole of the vast enceinte, which would have involved a very wide detour. But Jesus could not bear to look on at such an abuse; he therefore forbade everyone to cross the temple carrying loads, so as to restore to the consecrated spot the quiet and seclusion which rightly belonged to it.*

The Chief Priests Take Counsel Together [G2]

⊕

THIS instruction occasioned great anxiety among the scribes and Pharisees. They held a meeting in Caiaphas's house, and issued a prohibition against anyone's harboring Jesus and his disciples. They also set spies at the gates to watch for him, but he remained concealed in Bethany with Lazarus. Then the high priests took counsel together, and ordered to be called before them all the husbands and relatives of the women that had gone out of Jerusalem with the children to meet Jesus. When they made their appearance in answer to the summons, they were all shut up in the great court, and emissaries were sent out to spy what was going on. [5]

[MARK 11:18] 18 And the chief priests and the scribes heard it and sought a way to destroy him; for they feared him, because all the multitude was astonished at his teaching.

THE triumphal procession had passed by, quiet had been restored to the Royal Porch, for the crowd had gone after Jesus and none were left but a few groups of the usual frequenters of the colonnades, such as the doctors and their attendants of various sects, among whom Pharisees predominated. It was easy enough for them to convince themselves of the growing importance of the Nazarene, for tidings, and indeed fresh sounds of excitement, reached them from the town and its environs every moment, confirming the signification of the events of which they had all just been witnesses. There was no doubt that the resurrection of Lazarus had forcibly appealed to the imagination of all, kindling the hopes of everyone, so that the official authorities were beginning to find themselves at the mercy of every caprice of the new Prophet.

Now, from the first he had shown little favor to the Pharisees, and they might, therefore, well fear that he would not hesitate to make a dead set against their influence. There was, then, no time to be lost; they must have done with this man. The secret meeting in the house of Caiaphas was known, its probable results were commented on, and what would be the best measures to take to counteract this increase of popular favor were eagerly discussed. As for Jesus himself, all he did on that day was to pass through the temple, which he entered from the town and left by the Susa Gate. Then, traversing the Valley of Jehosaphat, he was able, by climbing obliquely the Mount of Olives, to make his way to Bethany, where, no doubt, he lived until the following Thursday. However that may be, we shall leave him no more, and the gospel will give us details as numerous as they are precious on this last period of his life on Earth. It will show him going to the temple sometimes before daybreak, spending long hours there, and only returning home at nightfall. It will explain to us every act of his, however apparently trivial, in every hour, nay, every minute; enable us to listen to his discourses; will invite us to receive his supreme admonitions, given in the addresses which became ever more and more frequent. In a word, the gospel will initiate us into all the mystery of those last days which were to end with the greatest event in the history of the human race.

The Foal of Bethphage [G3]

EARLY next morning Jesus sent Eremenzear and Silas to Jerusalem, not by the direct route, but by a road that ran through the enclosed gardens and fields near Bethphage. They were commissioned to make that road passable by opening the hedges and removing the barriers. He told them that in the meadow near the inn outside Bethphage (through which ran the road) they would find a she-ass with her foal; they should fasten the ass to the hedge, and, if questioned as to why they did that, they should answer that the Lord would have it so. Then they should remove every obstruction from the road leading to the temple, which done, they were to return to him. [7]

[LUKE 19:29–35] 29 When he drew near to Bethphage and Bethany, at the mount that is called Olivet, he sent two of the disciples, 30 saying, "Go into the village opposite, where on entering you will find a colt tied, on which no one has ever yet sat; untie it and bring it here. 31 If any one asks you, 'Why are you untying it?' you shall say this, 'The Lord has need of it.'" 32 So those who were sent away and found it as he had told them. 33 And as they were untying the colt, its owners said to them, "Why are you untying the colt?" 34 And they said, "The Lord has need of it." 35 And they brought it to Jesus, and throwing their garments on the colt they set Jesus upon it.

The Procession on the Mount of Olives [G4]

⊕

AND now Jesus arranged his procession. The apostles he ordered to proceed, two by two, before him, saying that from this moment and after his death, they should everywhere head the community. Peter went first, followed by those that were to bear the gospel to the most distant regions, while John and James the Less immediately preceded Jesus. All carried palm branches. As soon as the two disciples that were waiting near Bethphage spied the procession coming, they hurried forward to meet it, taking with them the two animals. The she-ass was covered with trappings that hung to its feet, the head and tail alone being visible.

Jesus now put on the beautiful festal robe of fine white wool which one of the disciples had brought with him for that purpose. It was long and flowing with a train. The broad girdle that confined it at the waist bore an inscription in letters. He then put around his neck a wide stole that reached to the knees, on the two ends of which something like shields was embroidered in brown. The two disciples assisted Jesus to mount the cross-seat on the ass. The animal had no bridle, but around its neck was a narrow strip of stuff that hung down loose. I know not whether Jesus rode on the she-ass or on its foal, for they were of the same size. The riderless animal ran by the other's side. Eliud and Silas walked on either side of the Lord, and Eremenzear behind him; then followed the disciples most recently received, some of whom he had brought back with him from his last great journey, and others that had been received still later. When the procession was ranged in order, the holy women, two by two, brought up the rear. The blessed Virgin, who up to this time had always stayed in the background, now went at their head. [7]

[LUKE 19:37–40] 37 As he was now drawing near, at the descent of the Mount of Olives, the whole multitude of the disciples began to rejoice and praise God with a loud voice for all the mighty works that they had seen, 38 saying, "Blessed is the King who comes in the name of the Lord! Peace in heaven and glory in the highest!" 39 And some of the Pharisees in the multitude said to him, "Teacher, rebuke your disciples." 40 He answered, "I tell you, if these were silent, the very stones would cry out."

The Procession in the Streets of Jerusalem [G5]

⊕

MANY among the crowd that followed Jesus to the temple not only broke off branches from the trees and strewed them in the way, but snatched off their mantles and spread them down, singing and shouting all the while. I saw many that had quite despoiled themselves of their upper garments for that purpose. The children had rushed from the schools, and now ran rejoicing with the crowd. Veronica, who had two children by her, threw her own veil in the way and, snatching another from one of the children, spread that down also. She and the other women joined the holy women, who were in the rear of the procession. There were about seventeen of them. The road was so thickly covered with branches, garments, and carpets that the procession moved on quite softly through the numerous triumphal arches that spanned the space between the walls on either side. [8]

[MATTHEW 21:10–11] 10 And when he entered Jerusalem, all the city was stirred, saying, "Who is this?" 11 And the crowds said, "This is the prophet Jesus from Nazareth of Galilee."

THE streets of Jerusalem are nearly all steep, being built along the flanks of the four hills on which the town is situated. These hills have been worked as quarries from the very earliest times, first for the construction of the temple and then for the walls surrounding the suburbs round about Mount Zion and Mount Moriah.

The Lord Wept [G6]

⊕

JESUS wept, as did the apostles also, when he told them that many who were now shouting acclamations of joy would soon deride him, and that a certain one would even betray him. He looked upon the city, and wept over its approaching destruction. [8]

[LUKE 19:41–44] 41 And when he drew near and saw the city he wept over it, 42 saying, "Would that even today you knew the things that make for peace! But now they are hid from your eyes. 43 For the days shall come upon you, when your enemies will cast up a bank about you and surround you, and hem you in on every side, 44 and dash you to the ground, you and your children within you, and they will not leave one stone upon another in you; because you did not know the time of your visitation."

The Procession in the Temple [G7]

⊕

IN the temple were the holy women and crowds of people. All had to remain the whole day without food, for this part of the city had been barricaded. [9]

[MATTHEW 21:15–16] 15 But when the chief priests and the scribes saw the wonderful things that he did, and the children crying out in the temple, "Hosanna to the Son of David!" they were indignant; 16 and they said to him, "Do you hear what these are saying?" And Jesus said to them, "Yes; have you never read, 'Out of the mouth of babes and sucklings thou hast brought perfect praise'?"

THE temple was entered from the right and worshippers went out again on the left. The orientation of the temple being from west to east, the right half of it was on the south and the left on the north. It was, therefore, possible to go in by the door at the northwest angle and leave again by that on the northeast corner, after having gone twice round the temple. To reach it from the town, therefore, Jesus must necessarily have passed over the so-called Xystus Bridge on to which opened the Royal Porch on the south of the temple. This porch or gallery which had recently been completed by Herod, consisted of five naves formed by four rows of Corinthian columns; there were one hundred and sixty of these columns, and in the center, to uphold the cupola, were four thicker columns which four men together were scarcely able to encircle with their arms. This part of the temple was shady throughout the day, and was, therefore, much resorted to by the people; the Pharisees preferred it as did the Sadducees and other sects each of which had its doctors and its preachers who drew around them a crowd of adepts. It was, moreover, a convenient spot for watching what was going on in the Court of the Gentiles, a considerable portion of which is situated between the Royal Porch and the balustrade of the Chel, or the little rampart, already described, surrounding, as we have explained, the buildings of the actual temple. Here might be seen this or that celebrity, this or that fashionable doctor or teacher surrounded by his disciples, the crowd of lookers-on gathering wherever the interest of the moment happened to be concentrated.

Jesus Goes in the Evening to Bethany [G8]

FULL of trouble, Jesus went back with the apostles to Bethany for the sabbath. [9]

[MARK 11:11] 11 And he entered Jerusalem, and went into the temple; and when he had looked round at everything, as it was already late, he went out to Bethany with the twelve.

THE day had been a very full one for Jesus and, as the evangelist tells us, "he had looked round about upon all things," he had taken care for everyone, he had put everything in order, making himself alike a providence for the poor and a terror to the sinful merchants. But now that the eventide had come and the crowd had quitted the temple, the Lord, accompanied by the twelve apostles, who followed him at a distance down the slopes of the Mount of Olives, set forth on his return to Bethany. After passing through one of the two gates of the temple on the northeast side, they left the town by the Sheep Gate, then, going down the Valley of Jehosaphat, they would reach at its lower extremity a spot full of tombs of some importance hewn in the rock. There, at the base of the Mount of Olives, were gardens with caves to which Jesus often resorted with his disciples. These gardens belonged to different owners, and in one of them was an oil-press called Gethsemane, belonging to one of the friends of our Lord. Crossing the bridge over the brook Kidron, generally dried up at that spot, a road was reached, overshadowed by great pine trees full of doves, and beneath the shade of which were shops, frequented by those who wished to buy suitable offerings for the temple. After skirting along the gardens the travelers crossed the slopes of the Mount of Olives by a path leading also to the summit of the neighboring Mount Scopus, where Titus established his camp when he besieged Jerusalem. This same Mount Scopus was reserved during the Feast of Pentecost as a resting-place for the people of Galilee, and it was on this account, no doubt, that Jesus chose this route, reaching Bethphage first, and going from thence to Bethany, which was on the right, about half an hour's walk farther on.

It was by this route, also, that the venerable David made his way to the desert weeping, with his head covered and his feet bare as he fled before his son Absalom, who had usurped his throne. Once arrived at the summit of the Mount of Olives, the traveler turning round had the whole of the Valley of Jehosaphat spread out beneath him, that valley already shrouded in the shadows of the eventide, with the grand walls of the temple beyond dominating the whole scene. From this point could be made out all the most important portions of the superb structure, with the enceinte of the temple itself, the walls encircling it, the massive supplementary buildings dedicated to various purposes, while on the right, rising above everything else, were the towers of the Antonia Citadel. It was in this citadel that the Roman troops were stationed, and now and then could be heard the shrill blasts of their trumpets, breaking for a moment into the silence of the evening only to render it all the more solemn when the sound died away again. The groups of buildings were succeeded by a vacant space known as the Tyropeon valley, beyond which again rose the rest of the town, extending to Herod's Palace situated on Mount Zion, which formed the culminating point of the city. Farther away were the western slopes behind which the sun was setting; Jerusalem, with her back turned toward the light, seeming to wrap herself in a shroud of darkness before sinking to sleep. All was calm, the west wind from the Mediterranean sweeping in its passage over the surface of the calcareous rocks baked through and through with the heat of the day's sunshine, brought to the eastern district where Jesus was walking an atmosphere still hot and laden with the scent of the incense which had recently been offered up in sacrifice. In fine weather, and with a favorable wind, the column of scented air which went up from the temple services would be dispersed all over the country; under certain conditions reaching even to the Jordan.

The Accursed Fig Tree [G9]

⊕

AS Jesus next day was going to Jerusalem with the apostles, he was hungry, but it seemed to me that it was after the conversion of the Jews and the accomplishment of his own mission. He sighed for the hour when his Passion would be over, for he knew its immensity and dreaded it in advance. He went to a fig tree on the road and looked up at it. When he saw no fruit, but only leaves upon it, he cursed it that it should wither and never more bear fruit. And thus, did he say, would it happen to those that would not acknowledge him. I understood that the fig tree signified the Old Law; the vine, the New. [9]

[MATTHEW 21:18–22] 18 In the morning, as he was returning to the city, he was hungry. 19 And seeing a fig tree by the wayside he went to it, and found nothing on it but leaves only. And he said to it, "May no fruit ever come from you again!" And the fig tree withered at once. 20 When the disciples saw it they marveled, saying, "How did the fig tree wither at once?" 21 And Jesus answered them, "Truly, I say to you, if you have faith and never doubt, you will not only do what has been done to the fig tree, but even if you say to this mountain, 'Be taken up and cast into the sea,' it will be done. 22 And whatever you ask in prayer, you will receive, if you have faith."

The Merchants Chased from the Temple [G10]

I SAW lying on the tables heaps of pence, bound together in different ways by little chains, hooks, and cords, so as to form various figures. Some were yellow; others, white, brown, and variegated. I think they were pieces of money intended for ornamental pendants. I saw also numbers of cages with birds, standing one above another and, in one of the porticos, there were calves and other cattle. Jesus ordered the dealers to be off, and as they hesitated to obey, he doubled up a cincture like a whip and drove them from side to side and beyond the precincts of the temple. [10]

[MATTHEW 21:12–13] 12 And Jesus entered the temple of God and drove out all who sold and bought in the temple, and he overturned the tables of the money-changers and the seats of those who sold pigeons. 13 He said to them, "It is written, 'My house shall be called a house of prayer'; but you make it a den of robbers."

WE have already said a few words on the circumstances which led to this action of Jesus, an action apparently violent, but in reality quite natural. Between Solomon's Porch and the outer wall of the temple on the eastern side, there was a certain space set apart for the animals to be offered up in sacrifice. It was from this space, after a first selection had been made, that they were taken to the priests whose duty it was to examine them carefully according to rigidly prescribed rules, when they were led to the sheep-pool to be purified. In the space above referred to, which was a kind of long narrow passage, there were beneath the portico a number of little vaulted rooms resembling the shops in a bazaar, where congregated the buyers, money-changers, and merchants. The premises, however, soon became too small, and the traders in animals gradually encroached on the other portions of the temple. To begin with, the money-changers, going up a few steps, took their stand on the right and left of Solomon's Porch, others imitated their example, and soon the entire colonnade was invaded, especially at the time of the great festivals. Nor did the abuse end there; even the Court of the Gentiles was in its turn invaded and defiled by the animals bought and sold in it.

Now, this court was paved with large polished stones with a slope managed, as already explained, so as to receive rain water and conduct it to the cisterns. The water in the cisterns of the temple, must, therefore, have been contaminated by impurities, while the silence of the sacred precincts was broken by all the confused noises of the market. Preaching, prayer, and quiet meditation were all alike impossible; the state of things was scandalous; no one could now retire to the cool shade of the temple in the morning, for it was then that the traffic was at its height. Everyone realized the abuses resulting from the deplorable invasion; but no one had the courage to take the initiative in trying to put a stop to it. Jesus alone, with the authority which radiated forth from his personality, could have hoped to bring such an attempt to a successful issue. He took off a kind of girdle, made of rope, which he wore round his robes, twisted it into a sort of scourge and used it as a whip to drive out them that sold. Behind him in procession followed his disciples who, amid great confusion, gradually cleared out the purchasers, till the portico was restored to its original tranquillity.

The Greeks Ask to See Jesus [G11]

⊕

WHILE Jesus was teaching, some strangers of distinction from Greece dispatched their servants from the inn to ask Philip how they could converse with the Lord without mingling with the crowd. Philip passed the word to Andrew, who in turn transmitted it to the Lord. [10]

[JOHN 12:20–24] 20 Now among those who went up to worship at the feast were some Greeks. 21 So these came to Philip, who was from Bethsaida in Galilee, and said to him, "Sir, we wish to see Jesus." 22 Philip went and told Andrew; Andrew went with Philip and they told Jesus. 23 And Jesus answered them, "The hour has come for the Son of man to be glorified. 24 Truly, truly, I say to you, unless a grain of wheat falls into the earth and dies, it remains alone; but if it dies, it bears much fruit."

OF *the three approaches to the temple open to those who came from the town, the most remarkable and at the same time the most modern was that which, spanning the Tyropeon valley on the southwest, led across a bridge of three arches abutting on the Mount Zion side on the remains of the ancient Millo bastions near the Xystus porticoes, and on the other side on the Royal Porch or Naos Basilica, built by Herod some thirty years previously. It was at this point that the Tyropeon valley, or the valley of cheeses, was deepest. There seems to be no doubt that it was by this, the grandest of all the approaches, that the Greeks arrived who came to the temple asking to see Jesus. From it, in the shade of the Naos Basilica and through the forest formed by the seventy-two columns, the outlines of all the buildings of the temple would rise up before them, glowing in the midday sunlight.*

The strangers who came to the temple to see Jesus were probably from Cyprus. Out of respect for the Master, they were not likely to address him directly, but probably preferred their request through Philip.

The Voice from on High [G12]

JESUS continued his discourse. He was very much troubled and when, with folded hands, he raised his eyes to heaven, I saw a flash of light descend upon him from a resplendent cloud, and heard a loud report. The people glanced up frightened, and began to whisper to one another, but Jesus went on speaking. This was repeated several times, after which I saw Jesus come down from the teacher's chair, mingle with the disciples in the crowd, and leave the temple. [10]

[JOHN 12:27–38] 27 "Now is my soul troubled. And what shall I say? 'Father, save me from this hour'? No, for this purpose I have come to this hour. 28 Father, glorify thy name." Then a voice came from heaven, "I have glorified it, and I will glorify it again." 29 The crowd standing by heard it and said that it had thundered. Others said, "An angel has spoken to him." 30 Jesus answered, "This voice has come for your sake, not for mine. 31 Now is the judgment of this world, now shall the ruler of this world be cast out; 32 and I, when I am lifted up from the earth, will draw all men to myself." 33 He said this to show by what death he was to die. 34 The crowd answered him, "We have heard from the law that the Christ remains for ever. How can you say that the Son of man must be lifted up? Who is this Son of man?" 35 Jesus said to them, "The light is with you for a little longer. Walk while you have the light, lest the darkness overtake you; he who walks in the darkness does not know where he goes. 36 While you have the light, believe in the light, that you may become sons of light." When Jesus had said this, he departed and hid himself from them. 37 Though he had done so many signs before them, yet they did not believe in him; 38 it was that the word spoken by the prophet Isaiah might be fulfilled: "Lord, who has believed our report, and to whom has the arm of the Lord been revealed?" [41–43] 41 Isaiah said this because he saw his glory and spoke of him. 42 Nevertheless many even of the authorities believed in him, but for fear of the Pharisees they did not confess it, lest they should be put out of the synagogue: 43 for they loved the praise of men more than the praise of God.

IN the picture Jesus is seen standing on the Chel, which was, as is well known, a terrace approached by twelve steps surrounding the sacred buildings in the enceinte of the temple. It was from 4½ to 5½ yards wide and the Gentiles were forbidden to set foot on it under pain of death, as announced in inscriptions on stones set up at regular intervals and rising above the ornate balustrade protecting it. Those on this terrace could look down into the Court of the Gentiles, the largest of the various Temple Courts, and all the people there assembled were witnesses of the extraordinary miracle related in the gospel. Judging from the comment made by the author of the sacred text, to the effect that some that stood by and heard it said that it thundered, we are, we think, justified in supposing that the sky was overcast as if threatening a storm. We see, however, from the words of Jesus himself, as quoted in the text, that he asserted the supernatural character of the incident, claiming the voice as a witness to his doctrine. "This voice," he said, "came not because of me but for your sakes," and further on the evangelist adds that on account of the many manifestations of the divine power which took place during the last few days of the Master's life on Earth among the chief rulers, etc., many believed on him, but, because of the Pharisees, they did not confess him, lest they should be put out of the synagogue.

The Ointment of Magdalene [G13]

MAGDALENE rose quietly from her seat among the holy women. She had around her a thin, bluish-white mantle, something like the material worn by the three holy kings, and her flowing hair was covered with a veil. Laying the ointment in a fold of her mantle, she passed through the walk that was planted with shrubbery, entered the hall, went up behind Jesus, and cast herself down at his feet, weeping bitterly. She bent her face low over the foot that was resting on the couch, while Jesus himself raised to her the other that was hanging a little toward the floor. Magdalene loosened the sandals and anointed Jesus's feet on the soles and upon the upper part. Then with both hands drawing her flowing hair from beneath her veil, she wiped the Lord's anointed feet, and replaced the sandals. Magdalene's action caused some interruption in Jesus's discourse. He had observed her approach, but the others were taken by surprise. Jesus said: "Be not scandalized at this woman!" and then addressed some words softly to her. She now arose, stepped behind him and poured over his head some costly water, and that so plentifully that it ran down upon his garments. Then with her hand she spread some of the ointment from the crown down the hind part of his head. The hall was filled with the delicious fragrance. The apostles whispered together and muttered their displeasure—even Peter was vexed at the interruption. Magdalene, weeping and veiled, withdrew around behind the table. When she was about to pass before Judas, he stretched forth his hand to stay her while he indignantly addressed to her some words on her extravagance, saying that the purchase money might have been given to the poor. Magdalene made no reply. She was weeping bitterly. Then Jesus spoke, bidding them let her pass, and saying that she had anointed him for his death, for later she would not be able to do it, and that wherever this gospel would be preached, her action and their murmuring would also be recounted. [10]

[MATTHEW 26:6–13] 6 Now when Jesus was at Bethany in the house of Simon the leper, 7 a woman came up to him with an alabaster flask of very expensive ointment, and she poured it on his head, as he sat at table. 8 But when the disciples saw it, they were indignant, saying, "Why this waste? 9 For this ointment might have been sold for a large sum, and given to the poor." 10 But Jesus, aware of this, said to them, "Why do you trouble the woman? For she has done a beautiful thing to me. 11 For you always have the poor with you, but you will not always have me. 12 In pouring this ointment on my body she has done it to prepare me for burial. 13 Truly, I say to you, wherever this gospel is preached in the whole world, what she has done will be told in memory of her."

IN connection with our account of the marriage at Cana we have already described how the rooms used at festivals were arranged in Palestine. The low table was generally of a horseshoe shape, and the guests reclined on the outer side of the circle, leaning on the left arm, so as to have the right arm free. The women did not eat with the men, but generally remained in an adjoining room or in a kind of extension of the arcades of the dining hall itself, separated from the men by a trellis-work partition. They could thus see all that was going on and if necessary give an opportune word of advice, as Mary the mother of Jesus did at Cana. With a room thus arranged and bearing in mind the ready hospitality of oriental houses, Magdalene could quite easily slip in unperceived behind the guests. Draped in her garments of penitence, which attracted no attention, she was able to pass like a shadow behind Jesus, break open the flask of perfumed ointment she had brought with her, which was no bigger than a fig, and pour a little of its contents on the head of her Master. Then, kneeling down, she spread the rest over his sacred feet, which she was able to reach without difficulty as they rested on the couch. Her anointing finished, she proceeded to wipe away the surplus ointment with her long hair, and the house was filled with the penetrating and medicinal odor of the spikenard, which was then much used in religious worship and at funerals. Her act of pious homage duly performed, Magdalene was for stealing quietly away, but the scent of the ointment betrayed her and gave rise to the disparaging remarks and murmurs against her of the guests, especially of Judas. This incident, in fact, seems to have given the final blow to the wavering fidelity of that disciple. He began boasting, talking about the necessity of economy and pretending to take a great interest in the poor, really, as John points out, only betraying his own avarice and dishonesty, which were already notorious. Jesus, having rebuked him before everyone by his high commendation of what Magdalene had done, the unfortunate Judas, wounded to the quick and already a traitor at heart rose from the table and went out to put his evil design into execution.

The Chief Priests Ask Jesus by What Right Does He Act in This Way [G14]

DURING his discourse today, some priests and scribes stepped up to him and inquired by what right he acted as he did. Jesus answered: "I too shall ask you something; and when you answer me, I shall tell you by what authority I do these things" (Matthew 21:23–32). Then he asked them by what authority John had baptized, and when they would not answer him, he replied that neither would he tell them by what authority he acted. [11]

[LUKE 20:1–8] 1 One day, as he was teaching the people in the temple and preaching the gospel, the chief priests and the scribes with the elders came up 2 and said to him, "Tell us by what authority you do these things, or who it is that gave you this authority." 3 He answered them, "I also will ask you a question; now tell me, 4 Was the baptism of John from heaven or from men?" 5 And they discussed it with one another, saying, "If we say, 'From heaven,' he will say, 'Why did you not believe him?' 6 But if we say, 'From men,' all the people will stone us; for they are convinced that John was a prophet." 7 So they answered that they did not know whence it was. 8 And Jesus said to them, "Neither will I tell you by what authority I do these things."

THE picture represents the scene as having taken place about eleven o'clock in the Court of the Gentiles. Many people are seated in the shade in the "Naos Basilica" of Herod. Jesus is going from group to group teaching. In the background behind him is the western portico and the gate leading to the town, corresponding with that now called the "Gate of the Chain." On the right is the terrace of the Chel; in this same building, surrounding the Court of the Women and itself in its turn encircled by the Chel, live the families engaged in the service of the temple.

In the same chapter as that just quoted we have a fresh proof of the great influence which had been exercised by John the Baptist, the forerunner of the Lord, and of the extent to which that influence had spread throughout the country. Challenged by Jesus to say in what name John had baptized and to tell him whether the baptism of John was from heaven or of men, the great men of the Jews, the scribes, the Pharisees, and the chief priests, formidable though their power was over the minds of their fellow-citizens, yet feared that the popular fury might turn upon them and that the people would stone them as blasphemers if they ventured even to throw a doubt on the divine mission of the son of Zechariah.

The Corner Stone [G15]

⊕

IN his afternoon instruction, Jesus introduced the similitude of the vine dresser, also that of the cornerstone rejected by the builders. [11]

[MATTHEW 21:42–46] 42 Jesus said to them, "Have you never read in the scriptures: 'The very stone which the builders rejected has become the head of the corner; this was the Lord's doing, and it is marvelous in our eyes'? 43 Therefore I tell you, the kingdom of God will be taken away from you and given to a nation producing the fruits of it." 44 [No text] 45 When the chief priests and the Pharisees heard his parables, they perceived that he was speaking about them. 46 But when they tried to arrest him, they feared the multitudes, because they held him to be a prophet.

THE more important buildings of the temple were built of Jerusalem limestone of a yellowish white color. The upper portion of the sanctuary was faced with white marble veined with blue, which, according to some who saw it, made it look like a mountain of snow, while others compared it to the waves of the sea. The supplementary buildings of the temple surrounding the Court of the Men and the Court of the Women were decorated in another fashion. According to the Talmud, they were faced with red and yellow stones, which had been hewn out of certain quarries near Jerusalem and which are, the red stones at least, peculiar to this one district. The stones, says the Talmud, were arranged in a net-like pattern, that is to say, in squares resembling those of the meshes of a net or, to express it somewhat differently, like a red and yellow chessboard.

In spite of their beautiful appearance, however, the stone we have just described crumbled away under the action of inclement weather, one or two blocks falling to pieces while the rest remained intact. No doubt, a reserve of stones was kept for replacing those thus destroyed, and some corner of one of the courts would be set apart as a work-yard for necessary repairs. There lay the beautiful stone left unused by the builders in the first instance and on the brink of rejection as an encumbrance, when, after a severe and damp winter, some cornerstone of the temple in a conspicuous and important portion of the building would become so disintegrated that it had to be taken out, leading to the substitution for it in a place of honor of the beautiful stone originally rejected.

This was the idea I have illustrated in my picture, taking it for granted that Jesus, according to his usual custom, took an actual and well-known fact to enforce his doctrine and render it more striking. We may, however, also suppose that our Lord merely turned to account a proverbial expression several times employed in the Bible, in Psalm 118:22, for instance, which is quoted word for word in the gospel narrative. In favor of the latter interpretation is the fact that Jesus would himself remember the words of the Old Testament, and it was from the very same psalm that the Jews took the exclamation with which they hailed the approach of Christ on Palm Sunday: "Blessed is he that cometh in the name of the Lord."

The Tribute Money [G16]

⊕

THEREUPON the Pharisees became so exasperated that they would willingly have arrested Jesus then and there but they dared not, as they saw how all the people clung to him. They determined, however, to set five of their confidential followers, who were relatives of some of the disciples, to spy on him, and they gave them orders to try to catch him by captious questions. These five men were some of them followers of the Pharisees; others, servants of Herod.

As Jesus mounted the teacher's chair next day in the circular hall of the temple, the five men appointed by the Pharisees pressed up through the aisle that ran from the door to the chair, the space all around being filled by the audience, and asked him whether they ought to pay tribute to Caesar. Jesus replied by telling them to show him the coin of the tribute; whereupon one of them drew from his breast pocket a yellow coin and pointed to the image of the Emperor. Then Jesus told them that they should render to Caesar the things that are Caesar's. [11]

[LUKE 20:20–26] 20 So they watched him, and sent spies, who pretended to be sincere, that they might take hold of what he said, so as to deliver him up to the authority and jurisdiction of the governor. 21 They asked him, "Teacher, we know that you speak and teach rightly, and show no partiality, but truly teach the way of God. 22 Is it lawful for us to give tribute to Caesar, or not?" 23 But he perceived their craftiness, and said to them, 24 "Show me a coin. Whose likeness and inscription has it?" They said, "Caesar's." 25 He said to them, "Then render to Caesar the things that are Caesar's, and to God the things that are God's." 26 And they were not able in the presence of the people to catch him by what he said; but marveling at his answer they were silent.

IT is morning, and in front of the Jewish notables rise the fifteen steps called the Psalms or the Degrees. On the left of these steps, beneath the green marble columns of the Court of Israel, can be seen the entrance to the rooms where the musicians keep their instruments. In the background, on the southwest, at the corner of the Court of the Women, where we now are, is the room or the pavilion, open to the sky, where the wine and oil were kept. We know that there were three other such pavilions, that of the Nazarites on the southeast, that where the wood to be used in the sacrifices was sorted, on the northeast, and, lastly, that on the northwest, reserved for the use of lepers.

At first sight, the way in which the enemies of Jesus endeavored to compromise him seems strange enough. They do not ask if they must pay tribute to Caesar, which, in case of a reply in the affirmative, might have made him odious in the eyes of the crowd, who were intensely irritated by the fiscal exactions of the Romans, but they asked "Is it lawful?" a truly singular enquiry when the very real suzerainty of the Roman Emperor over the Jewish people is borne in mind. Never throughout the whole course of the history of the Jews had they refused to pay tribute to the suzerain, whether that suzerain ruled from Nineveh, from Babylon, or from Persia. The Pharisees, however, had found means to arouse scruples on this point, and the people would evidently have been ready enough to adopt them. But Jesus, perceiving their craftiness, simply said, to put them to confusion, "Show me a coin." The current coin no longer bore the proud device engraved on that in use in the time of the Aesmonean or Maccabean princes: Jerusalem the Holy, but simply the effigy of the reigning Emperor Tiberius. The consequence was evident enough, the superscription convincing: they had to pay. For all that, however, the answer of Jesus did not prevent the Pharisees from saying later to Pilate: "he forbids the giving of tribute to Caesar."

The Pharisees Question Jesus [G17]

⊕

LATER in the day, seven of the Sadducees went to Jesus and questioned him upon the resurrection of the dead. They brought forward something about a woman that had already had seven husbands. Jesus answered that after the resurrection there would be no longer any sex or any marrying, and that God is a God of the living and not of the dead. I saw that his hearers were astounded at his teaching. The Pharisees left their seats and conferred together. One of them, named Manasseh, who held an office in the temple, very modestly asked Jesus which of the commandments was the greatest. Jesus answered the question, whereupon Manasseh heartily praised him. Then Jesus responded that the kingdom of God was not far from him, and he closed his discourse by some words on Christ (the Messiah) and David. [11]

[MARK 12:28–34] 28 And one of the scribes came up and heard them disputing with one another, and seeing that he answered them well, asked him, "Which commandment is the first of all?" 29 Jesus answered, "The first is, 'Hear, O Israel: The Lord our God, the Lord is one; 30 and you shall love the Lord your God with all your heart, and with all your soul, and with all your mind, and with all your strength.' 31 The second is this, 'You shall love your neighbor as yourself.' There is no other commandment greater than these." 32 And the scribe said to him, "You are right, Teacher; you have truly said that he is one, and there is no other but he; 33 and to love him with all the heart, and with all the understanding, and with all the strength, and to love one's neighbor as oneself, is much more than all whole burnt offerings and sacrifices." 34 And when Jesus saw that he answered wisely, he said to him, "You are not far from the kingdom of God." And after that no one dared to ask him any question.

Woe unto You, Scribes and Pharisees [G18]

ON the next day Jesus taught about six hours in the temple. After midday, the scribes and Pharisees crowded in such numbers around Jesus that the disciples were pushed to some distance from him. He spoke very severely against the Pharisees, and I heard him say once during this stern lecture: "You shall not now arrest me, because my hour has not yet come." [12]

[MATTHEW 23:1–16] 1 Then said Jesus to the crowds and to his disciples, 2 "The scribes and the Pharisees sit on Moses' seat; 3 so practice and observe whatever they tell you, but not what they do; for they preach, but do not practice. 4 They bind heavy burdens, hard to bear, and lay them on men's shoulders; but they themselves will not move them with their finger. 5 They do all their deeds to be seen by men; for they make their phylacteries broad and their fringes long, 6 and they love the place of honor at feasts and the best seats in the synagogues, 7 and salutations in the market places, and being called rabbi by men. 8 But you are not to be called rabbi, for you have one teacher, and you are all brethren. 9 And call no man your father on earth, for you have one Father, who is in heaven. 10 Neither be called masters, for you have one master, the Christ. 11 He who is greatest among you shall be your servant; 12 whoever exalts himself will be humbled, and whoever humbles himself will be exalted. 13 But woe to you, scribes and Pharisees, hypocrites! because you shut the kingdom of heaven against men; for you neither enter yourselves, nor allow those who would enter to go in.... 15 Woe to you, scribes and Pharisees, hypocrites! for you traverse sea and land to make a single proselyte, and when he becomes a proselyte, you make him twice as much a child of hell as yourselves. 16 Woe to you, blind guides, who say, 'If any one swears by the temple, it is nothing; but if any one swears by the gold of the temple, he is bound by his oath.' [33] You serpents, you brood of vipers, how are you to escape being sentenced to hell?"

THE Court of the Gentiles where Jesus was, was paved with polished stones which had been restored by Herod. It was washed, indeed flooded with water every morning, and to strangers visiting it for the first time it looked like a lake, so vividly did the polished floor reflect the surrounding buildings.

The Widow's Mite [G19]

⊕

JESUS today took the seat by the money box. It was an offering day for all that desired to purify themselves for the Passover feast. The Pharisees, on coming later, were greatly put out at finding Jesus there, but they declined his offer to yield to them his place. The apostles stood near him, two by two. The men came first to the money box, then the women, and after making their offering, they went out by another door to the left. The crowd stood without awaiting their turn, only five being allowed to enter at a time. Jesus sat there three hours. Toward midday, as a general thing, the offerings ended, but Jesus remained much longer, to the discontent of the Pharisees. This was the hall in which he had acquitted the woman taken in adultery. The last offering was made by a poor, timid widow. No one could see how much the offering was, but Jesus knew what she had given and he told his disciples that she had given more than all the rest, for she had put into the money box all that she had left to buy herself food for that day. He sent her word to wait for him near the house of John Mark. Then he mentioned the poor widow's offering. When toward evening he left the temple, he spoke to her on the way and told her that her son would follow him. His words greatly rejoiced the poor mother. Her son joined the disciples even before the crucifixion. The widow was very devout and strongly attached to the Jewish observances, though simple-minded and upright. [14]

[MARK 12:41–44] 41 And he sat down opposite the treasury, and watched the multitude putting money into the treasury. Many rich people put in large sums. 42 And a poor widow came, and put in two copper coins, which make a penny. 43 And he called his disciples to him, and said to them, "Truly, I say to you, this poor widow has put in more than all those who are contributing to the treasury. 44 For they all contributed out of their abundance; but she out of her poverty has put in everything she had, her whole living."

THE Greek name for the Court of the Women is Gazophylacium, or the Court of the Treasure, given to it on account of the thirteen chests placed at each of the five entrances in which were deposited the various offerings brought to the temple. These chests were of a curious and peculiar shape, and were made up of a collection of copper tubes of a greater or lesser length, according to the position they occupied in the general receptacle in which they were grouped. At the orifice of each tube was an inscription stating what kind of offerings were to be placed in it, and the pieces of money dropped into the openings went down the tube reserved for them into the interior of the chest, whence they were afterward removed by the priests. To prevent the clever contrivances by means of which thieves used to get at the money by introducing a stick or a line smeared with pitch, under pretence of putting their own offerings in, the tubes were made of a conical shape, broadening downward from the narrow opening. Thanks to this peculiarity, these collections of copper conduits looked very much like a group of trumpets, hence the popular name given to them.

Outside the entrance to the Gazophylacium was a kind of vestibule provided with seats against the walls affording a good position for watching the passers-by and noting the behavior of those who brought offerings. On this occasion Jesus too was seated there, resting after an exhausting day of teaching. He saw the various groups of pilgrims pass by who had come up to the temple for the festivals and had brought with them their voluntary offerings, and among them were many wealthy men who ostentatiously dropped in their generous gifts, while a widow also came in her turn and threw in two mites "all her living," equal to rather less than an English farthing. But for all that they represented "all her living," and this was why Jesus commended her so highly; and, anxious that the example should not be lost on his disciples, he called them together and praised the poor woman in their hearing, saying she "hath cast more in than all they which have cast into the treasury." It was this touching episode that ended a day which had been full of eager disputation. Just before Jesus had been reproaching the Pharisees with devouring widows' houses and for a pretence making long prayers; he now calls our attention to one of the poor widows ruined by the pretended worshippers of God, consecrating to the service of the Lord all that they had left to her.

The Disciples Admire the Buildings of the Temple [G20]

AS Jesus was walking along with his disciples, one of them pointed to the temple and made some remark on its beauty. Jesus replied that one stone of it would not remain upon another. [14]

[MARK 13:1–2] 1 And as he came out of the temple, one of his disciples said to him, "Look, Teacher, what wonderful stones and what wonderful buildings!" 2 And Jesus said to him, "Do you see these great buildings? There will not be left here one stone upon another, that will not be thrown down."

THE group of Jesus and his disciples are leaving the temple by the new gateway built by Herod the Great. It was the one which led to the Valley of Jehosaphat and to Bethany, whither Jesus was bound. It was low down in comparison with the platform of the Court of the Gentiles to which a flight of steps led up, and it opened on to a mass of houses occupied by the work-people employed at the temple. It was from this gateway that the high priest and his assistants issued on their way to the Mount of Olives to burn the red heifer.

In my picture can be seen the northern side of the temple buildings and the Chel, where can also be made out a pavilion or watchtower occupied by Levites, this part of the temple being but little frequented. On the right a glimpse is obtained of the northern portico, adjoining which are the outbuildings of the Antonia Citadel. It shows also the background beyond the watchtower of the Levites. Quite on the right can be seen the entrance to the buildings set apart for the attendants in charge of the animals for sacrifice, who from it could easily reach the Sheep-pool.

There was a striking peculiarity about the departure of Jesus from the temple on this occasion, for he was leaving it, never to return. It was the evening of Holy Tuesday, and on the Wednesday his death was to be decided on. Hence the terrible prophecy uttered by him which contrasts so ominously with the naïve admiration of his disciples and assumes the character of a malediction. "See what manner of stones and what buildings are here!" said the twelve. And truly from this point of view the temple walls did present a most imposing appearance, for Josephus asserts that most of the blocks which had been used in their construction measured twenty-five cubits in length by twelve in width and eight in height.

The Prophecy of the Destruction of the Temple [G21]

⊕

THEY were going to the Mount of Olives, upon one side of which was a kind of pleasure garden containing a chair for instruction and seats cut in the mossy banks. The priests were accustomed to come hither to rest at evening after a long day's work. Jesus seated himself in the chair, and some of the apostles asked when the destruction of the temple would take place. It was then that Jesus recounted the evils that were to fall upon the city, and ended with the words: "But he that shall persevere to the end, he shall be saved." He remained scarcely a quarter of an hour in this place.

Early on the following day Jesus returned to the resting-place on the Mount of Olives, and again spoke of the destruction of Jerusalem, illustrating with the similitude of a fig tree that was there standing. [14]

[MARK 13:3–14] 3 And as he sat on the Mount of Olives opposite the temple, Peter and James and John and Andrew asked him privately, 4 "Tell us, when will this be, and what will be the sign when these things are all to be accomplished?" 5 And Jesus began to say to them, "Take heed that no one leads you astray. 6 Many will come in my name, saying, 'I am he!' and they will lead many astray. 7 And when you hear of wars and rumors of wars, do not be alarmed; this must take place, but the end is not yet. 8 For nation will rise against nation, and kingdom against kingdom; there will be earthquakes in various places, there will be famines; this is but the beginning of the birth-pangs. 9 But take heed to yourselves; for they will deliver you up to councils; and you will be beaten in synagogues; and you will stand before governors and kings for my sake, to bear testimony before them. 10 And the gospel must first be preached to all nations. 11 And when they bring you to trial and deliver you up, do not be anxious beforehand what you are to say; but say whatever is given you in that hour, for it is not you who speak, but the Holy Spirit. 12 And brother will deliver up brother to death, and the father his child, and children will rise against parents and have them put to death; 13 and you will be hated by all for my name's sake. But he who endures to the end will be saved. 14 But when you see the desolating sacrilege set up where it ought not to be (let the reader understand), then let those who are in Judea flee to the mountains."

IN the valley of Jehosaphat, half way up the Mount of Olives, there were several resting-places for the use of the priests of the temple, planted with such trees as the terebinth or turpentine, the locust, mulberry, and cypress. When the wars came these resting-places were, of course, deserted and neglected, rapidly reverting to waste lands. They were, however, still the property of the Jews, though they were appropriated first by the Christians and later by the Muslims. They are now spoken of as belonging to the Mosques, that is to say, they are looked upon as municipal districts under the control of the religious authorities, embankments and excavations indicating very clearly the use to which they are put. Here it was that Jesus and the few apostles admitted to close intimacy with him went and sat down over against the temple after leaving it for the last time. Then, in full view of the imposing mass of the celebrated buildings, which looked as if they were destined to last forever, Jesus solemnly prophesied their destruction.

65

Conspiracy of the Jews [G22]

THE Pharisees were very greatly exasperated on Jesus's account. They held a council in the night and dispatched spies to watch him. They said, if Judas would only come to them again, otherwise they did not well know how to proceed in the affair. Judas had not been with them since that first evening. [14]

[MARK 14:1–2] 1 It was now two days before the Passover and the feast of Unleavened Bread. And the chief priests and the scribes were seeking how to arrest him by stealth, and kill him; 2 for they said, "Not during the feast, lest there be a tumult of the people."

THE *death of Jesus had long been decided on; indeed, ever since his miracles had grown so striking and his popularity had appeared to become a menace to the authority of the chief priests, the latter had determined to destroy him. The question now was not, therefore, as to his fate but as to the best means of securing his person without causing a tumult among the people. Once in their hands he could not escape, for, in the case of a judicial sentence being found impossible, these men would not have hesitated to assassinate him privately. In any case, however, they judged it prudent to put off the execution of Jesus until after the celebration of the feast, for fear of trouble with the assembled crowds. Under certain circumstances, the carrying out of legal sentences was put off until the concourse of pilgrims should add to the solemnity, but in this case the very sacredness of the time would have constituted a danger, more especially as the chief partisans of Jesus were among the turbulent and sturdy Galileans, ever ready for a conflict, and it was no rare thing in Judea for riots to take place during the great festivals. The postponement of the execution was therefore voted, but it was at the same time determined to watch for a favorable opportunity for an early arrest. After all, these resolutions came to naught, because Jesus was put to death just at the most solemn moment of the feast and therefore, with the greatest possible éclat. The Sanhedrin, in fact, doubtless perceived that the popularity of Jesus had not such deep root as they had thought, and the defection of one of the twelve confirmed them in this opinion. They therefore reverted to their original idea and determination to give to their victory all the noisy celebrity for which their hatred craved.*

Judas Goes to Find the Jews [G23]

⊕

JUDAS ran full speed to Jerusalem. I saw the devil with him all the time, red, thin-bodied, and angular. He was before him and behind him, as if lighting the way for him. Judas saw through the darkness. He stumbled not, but ran along in perfect safety. I saw him in Jerusalem running into the house in which, later on, Jesus was exposed to scorn and derision. The Pharisees and high priests were still together, but Judas did not enter their assembly. Two of them went out and spoke with him below in the courtyard. When he told them that he was ready to deliver Jesus and asked what they would give for him, they showed great joy, and returned to announce it to the rest of the council. After awhile, one came out again and made an offer of thirty pieces of silver. Judas wanted to receive them at once, but they would not give them to him. They said that he had once before been there, and then had absented himself for so long, that he should do his duty, and then they would pay him. I saw them offering hands as a pledge of the contract, and on both sides tearing something from their clothing. The Pharisees wanted Judas to stay awhile and tell them when and how the bargain would be completed. But he insisted upon going, that suspicion might not be excited. [22]

[MARK 14:10–1]1 10 Then Judas Iscariot, who was one of the twelve, went to the chief priests in order to betray him to them. 11 And when they heard it they were glad, and promised to give him money. And he sought an opportunity to betray him.

Angelic Dial of the Hours of the Passion

Whereas in the image of celestial duration above there is as yet no indication of passing time, as the events of the Passion—the intersection of Time and Eternity in the great and archetypal Mystical Fact—proceed, temporal markers will henceforward be indicated on the dial whenever Anne Catherine's detailed descriptions render this possible.

The Last Passover Supper

Thursday, April 2, AD 33 (*Nisan 13*)

Today, so-called Maundy Thursday, being Nisan 13 in the Jewish calendar, was the day prior to the Day of Preparation for the Passover. Shortly before daybreak Jesus called Peter and John and gave them instructions concerning the preparation for the Passover feast in the Cenacle (Luke 22:7–13). They went to Heli, the brother-in-law of the deceased Zechariah of Hebron, who had rented the Cenacle, which belonged to Nicodemus and Joseph of Arimathea. Heli showed Peter and John the room for the Last Supper. The two apostles then went to the house of the deceased priest Simeon, and one of Simeon's sons accompanied them to the marketplace, where they obtained four lambs to be sacrificed for the meal. They also went to Veronica's house and fetched the chalice to be used that evening by Jesus at the institution of the Holy Communion. Meanwhile Jesus spoke again to the disciples of his imminent death, and—in taking leave of her—talked at length alone with his mother, the holy Virgin Mary. In Jerusalem Judas met again with the Pharisees and made the final arrangements for the betrayal of Jesus. Around midday, after taking final leave of Mary, his mother, the other holy women, and Lazarus, Jesus went to Jerusalem with the remaining nine apostles and a group of seven disciples. The disciples went to the Cenacle to help with the preparations there, while Jesus walked with the nine apostles, teaching as he went, from the Mount of Olives to Mount Calvary and back again to the valley of Jehosaphat. Here they were met by Peter and John, who summoned them to the Passover feast. Judas arrived just before the meal began. Jesus dined with the twelve apostles in the main hall of the Cenacle; two groups of twelve disciples, each with a "house father," ate in separate side rooms. The house father of the first group, comprising older disciples, was Nathaniel, and that of the second group was Heliachim, a son of Cleophas and Mary Heli. All subsequent events on this evening of the Last Supper, and the following events that night on the Mount of Olives, are described in each of the four Gospels.

BEFORE BREAK OF DAY, Jesus, calling Peter and John, spoke to them at some length upon what they should order, what preparations they should make in Jerusalem for the eating of the paschal lamb. The disciples had questioned Jesus the day before upon where this supper was to be held. Jesus told the two apostles that they would, when ascending Mount Zion, meet a man carrying a water pitcher, one whom they already knew, as he was the same that had attended to the Passover meal for Jesus the year before at Bethany. They were to follow him into the house and say to him: "The Master bids us say to thee that his time is near at hand. He desires to celebrate Passover at thy house." They should then ask to see the supper room, which they would find prepared, and there they should make ready all that was needed. [H1]

I saw the two apostles going up to Jerusalem through a ravine that ran south of the temple and north of Zion. On the south side of the mount upon which the temple stood there were some rows of houses opposite which a rapid stream flowed down the height; on the other side of this stream ran the road by which the apostles ascended. On reaching a point of Zion higher than the temple mount, they turned toward the south and met the man designated by Jesus on a somewhat rising open space, and in the neighborhood of an old building surrounded by courts. They followed him and, when near the house, delivered to him Jesus's message. He showed great pleasure at seeing them and learning their errand. He told them that he had already been ordered to prepare a supper (probably by Nicodemus), though he knew not for whom, but now he greatly rejoiced that it was for Jesus. This man was Heli, the brother-in-law of Zechariah of Hebron, the same in whose house at Hebron Jesus had, after a certain sabbath of the preceding year, announced to the family the death of John. He had five unmarried daughters, but only one son, who was a Levite and who had been a friend of Luke before the latter joined the Lord. Heli went with his servants every year to the feast, hired a supper room, and prepared the Passover meal for people that had no friends in the city. On this occasion Heli had hired the dining hall of a spacious old house belonging to Nicodemus and Joseph of Arimathea.

ON the south side of Mount Zion, not far from the citadel of David and from the market, which was on the eastern ascent to the same, this old house stood in an open court surrounded by courtyards with massive walls, and between rows of shade trees.

To the right and left of the entrance and just inside the walls stood a couple of smaller buildings. In one of these the blessed Virgin and the other holy women celebrated

April 2, AD 33
Thursday, Before Dawn

the Passover supper, and there too after the crucifixion they frequently retired. The large building, that is, the principal one which contained the dining hall rented by Heli, stood a little back of the center of the court. It was in this house, in King David's time, that his valiant heroes and generals exercised themselves in arms; here too, before the building of the temple, had the Ark of the Covenant been deposited for a long time. Traces of its presence were still to be found in an underground apartment. I have seen also the prophet Malachi hidden in this vault. There it was that he wrote his prophecies of the most blessed sacrament and the Sacrifice of the New Law. Solomon also held this house in honor, and performed in it some symbolical action, but I now forget what. When a great part of Jerusalem was destroyed by the Babylonians, this house was spared. It was now the property of Nicodemus and Joseph of Arimathea, who arranged the principal building in a very suitable manner and let it as a guest house for strangers coming to Jerusalem for Passover. Moreover, the house and its dependencies served during the year as warehouses for tombstones, building stones, and as a place for stone-cutting in general, for Joseph of Arimathea owned an excellent quarry in his own country. He traded in monuments, architectural ornaments, and columns, which were here sculpted under his own eye. Nicodemus also was engaged in building, and devoted many of his leisure hours to sculpting. Excepting at the time of festivals, he often worked here either in the hall, or in the vault below, sculpting statues. It was owing to this art that he had formed a friendship for Joseph of Arimathea, and many of their transactions were undertaken together.

The principal edifice, the Cenacle proper, was a long, four-cornered building surrounded by a low colonnade, which could be thrown open and thus made one with the lofty hall beyond. The whole building rested on columns, or pillars, and was so constructed as to allow the gaze to penetrate in all directions, that is, when the portable screens generally in use were removed. The light fell through apertures near the top of the walls. In front (and this was the narrow side of the building), there was an anteroom, into which three entrances led. From it one stepped into the lofty and beautifully paved inner hall from whose roof several lamps were hanging. The halls had been decorated for the feast. They were hung half-way up with beautiful matting, or tapestry, and the aperture that had been opened in the ceiling was covered with blue gauze, shining and transparent. The rear end of the hall

April 2, AD 33
Thursday Morning

was cut off by a curtain of the same kind of gauze. The Cenacle, separated from the rest of the room, owing to this division into three parts, bore some resemblance to the temple, as it had a forecourt, a sanctuary, and the holy of holies. On either side in the last division were deposited dresses and other things necessary for the feast. In the center stood a kind of altar. Projecting from the wall and raised on three steps was a stone bench in form like a right-angled triangle whose sharp corner was fitted into the wall.

It must have been the upper side of the oven used for roasting the paschal lamb, for at the meal of today it was quite hot around the steps. On one side of this apartment there was an exit that led into the hall behind that projection, and from that hall there was a descent to the subterranean vaults and cellars, where it was warm. On the projection, or altar, lay different things in preparation for the feast, like chests, or drawers, that could be drawn out. On top were openings like a grating and a place for making a fire, as well as one for extinguishing it. I cannot describe it in detail. It appeared to be a kind of hearth for baking Passover bread and other kinds of pastry, for burning frankincense, or, at certain festivals, for consuming what remained of the sacrifice. It was like a paschal kitchen. Above this hearth, or altar, there was a kind of niche formed of projecting rafters and surmounted by a valve, probably for the escape of smoke. Suspended from the ceiling above the niche and hanging in front of it, I saw the figure of a paschal lamb. A knife was sticking in its throat, and its blood appeared to be dropping on the altar. I no longer remember exactly how this last was effected. In the back of the niche there were three little compartments, or cupboards, that turned like our tabernacles for opening or closing. In them I saw all kinds of vessels for Passover and deep oval dishes. Later on, the most blessed sacrament was kept there. In the side halls of the Cenacle here and there were built inclined couches, upon which lay heavy coverlets rolled together. These were the sleeping places. Fine cellars extended under the whole building. The resting place of the Ark of the Covenant was once in the back part, directly under the spot upon which the paschal hearth now stood. Below the cellars ran five gutters, which served to carry off the refuse to the slope of the hill on the top of which the house stood. At different times, I saw Jesus teaching and performing cures here. The disciples often lodged for the night in the side halls.

While Peter and John were speaking with Heli, I saw

Nicodemus in one of the buildings in the courtyard, whither the blocks of stone from the vicinity of the supper hall had been removed. For eight days previously I saw people busy cleaning the court and arranging the hall for the Passover feast. Some of the disciples themselves were among the workers.

WHEN Peter and John finished speaking with Heli, the latter passed through the courtyard and into the house. The two apostles, however, turned off to the right, went down the north side of the mountain through Zion, crossed a brook, proceeded by a path between hedges to the other side of the ravine that lay before the temple, and to the row of houses south of it. Here stood the house of old Simeon, now occupied by his sons, who were disciples in secret. The apostles entered and spoke with Obed, the elder, who served in the temple. Then they went with a tall, dark-complexioned man by the east side of the temple, through that part of Ophel by which Jesus on Palm Sunday entered Jerusalem, and thence to the cattle market in the city north of the temple. Here, on the south side of the market, I saw enclosures like little gardens, in which beautiful lambs were gamboling on the grass. On the occasion of Jesus's triumphal entrance I imagined these arrangements made in honor of that event, but now I found out that these were the paschal lambs here exposed for sale. I saw Simeon's son enter one of these enclosures, and the lambs leaping about him and butting him with their heads, as if they recognized him. He singled out four, which he took with him to the Cenacle, and that afternoon I again saw him there taking part in the preparation of the paschal lambs.

I still saw Peter and John traversing the city in all directions and giving orders for many things. I saw them also outside the door of a house to the north of Mount Calvary. It was the inn, on the northwest side of the city, in which many of the disciples were staying. This was the disciples' inn outside Jerusalem. It was under the care of Veronica, whose former name was Seraphia. From this inn, I saw them go to Veronica's own house, for they had many directions to give her. Veronica's husband was a member of the council. He was generally away from home attending to his business, and when he was in the house, his wife saw little of him. She was a woman of about the same age as the blessed Virgin. She had long known the holy family, for when the boy Jesus remained in Jerusalem after the feast, she it was who supplied him with food.

April 2, AD 33
Thursday, Later Morning

The two apostles got from Veronica all kinds of table service, which was carried by the disciples in covered baskets to the Cenacle. They took from here also the chalice of which Jesus made use in the institution of the blessed sacrament.

THIS chalice was a very wonderful and mysterious vessel that had lain in the temple for a long time among other old and precious things, whose use and origin even had been forgotten, just as with us many ancient, holy treasures have through the lapse of time fallen into oblivion. Frequently at the temple ancient vessels and precious ornaments whose use was no longer known were reset, made over anew, or sold. It was in this way, and by God's permission, that that holy vessel (whose unknown material prevented its being melted down, although frequent attempts had been made to do so) had been found by the young priests in the treasury of the temple. It was stowed away in a chest along with other objects no longer of use, and when discovered was sold to some antiquaries. The chalice and all the vessels belonging to it were afterward bought by Veronica. It had several times been made use of by Jesus in the celebration of festivals, and from today it became the exclusive possession of the holy community of Jesus Christ. It was not always the same as when used at the Last Supper. I no longer remember when the parts that composed it were put together; perhaps it was on the occasion of the Lord's using it at the Last Supper. It was now, however, along with all that was necessary for the institution of the blessed sacrament, put up in one portable case.

On a flat surface out of which a little board, or tablet, could be drawn, stood the large chalice surrounded by six small beakers. The chalice itself contained another smaller vase. I cannot remember whether the tablet held the holy thing or not. A little plate was laid upon the chalice, and over the whole was a convex cover. In the foot of the chalice was a place for keeping a spoon, which could be easily drawn out. All these vessels in fine linen coverings were protected by a cap, or case of leather, I think, which had a knob on top. The large chalice consisted of the cup and the foot, which latter must have been added at a later period, for it was of different material. The cup was pear-shaped, and of a brownish, highly polished metal, overlaid with gold. It had two small handles, by which it could be raised when its contents rendered it tolerably heavy. The foot was elaborately wrought of dark virgin gold, the edge encircled by a serpent. It was ornamented with a little bunch of grapes, and enriched with precious stones. The small spoon was concealed in the foot.

The large chalice was left to the church of Jerusalem under the care of James the Less. I see it still carefully preserved somewhere. It will again come to light as it did once before. The smaller cups that stood around it were distributed among the other churches: one to Antioch, another to Ephesus. These vessels enriched seven churches. The small beakers once belonged to the patriarchs, who drank some mysterious beverage out of them when they received or imparted the Blessing, as I have seen and already explained.

The large chalice once belonged to Abraham. Melchizedek brought it from the land of Semiramis, where it was lying neglected, to the land of Canaan, when he began to mark off settlements on the site afterward occupied by Jerusalem. He had used it at the sacrifice of bread and wine offered in Abraham's presence, and he afterward gave it to him. This same chalice was even in Noah's possession. It stood in the upper part of the ark. Moses also had it in his keeping. The cup was massive like a bell. It looked as if it had been shaped by nature, not formed by art. I have seen clear through it. Jesus alone knew of what it was made.

In the morning, while the two apostles in Jerusalem were engaged in the preparations for the Passover feast, Jesus took an affecting leave of the holy women, Lazarus, and his mother in Bethany, and gave them some final instructions and admonitions.

I saw him speaking alone with his blessed Mother, and I remember some of the words that passed between them. He had, he said, sent Peter the believing and John the loving to Jerusalem in order to prepare for Passover. Of Magdalene, who was quite out of herself from grief, he said: "She loves unspeakably, but her love is still encompassed by the body, therefore has she become like one quite out of her mind with pain." He spoke also of the treacherous scheming of Judas, and the blessed Virgin implored mercy for him.

Judas, under pretense of attending to different affairs and of discharging certain debts, had again left Bethany and hurried to Jerusalem. Jesus, although he well knew what he was after, questioned the nine apostles about him.

Judas spent the whole day in running around among the Pharisees and concerting his plans with them. The soldiers that were to apprehend Jesus were even shown him, and he so arranged his journey to and fro as to be able to account for his absence. Just before it was time for the Passover

April 2, AD 33
Thursday Noon

supper, he returned to the Lord. I have seen all his thoughts and plans. When Jesus spoke about him to Mary, I saw many things connected with his character and behavior. He was active and obliging, but full of avarice, ambition, and envy, which passions he struggled not to control. He had even performed miracles and, in Jesus's absence, healed the sick. When Jesus made known to the blessed Virgin what was about to happen to him, she besought him in touching terms to let her die with him. But he exhorted her to bear her grief more calmly than the other women, telling her at the same time that he would rise again, and he named the spot upon which he would appear to her. This time she did not shed so many tears, though she was sad beyond expression and there was something awe-inspiring in her deep gravity. Like a devoted Son, Jesus thanked her for all her love. He embraced her with his right arm and pressed her to his breast. He told her that he would celebrate his Last Supper with her in spirit, and named the hour at which she should receive his body and blood. He afterward took a very affecting leave of them all, and gave them instructions on many points.

Toward noon, Jesus and the nine apostles set out from Bethany for Jerusalem, followed by a band of seven disciples who, with the exception of Nathaniel and Silas, were principally from Jerusalem and its neighborhood. I remember that John Mark and the son of the poor widow who on the Thursday before, that is, just eight days ago, had offered her mite when Jesus was teaching by the alms box in the temple, were among them. Jesus had received the youth into the number of his disciples a few days previously. The holy women followed later.

Jesus and his companions walked here and there around the Mount of Olives, through the valley of Jehosaphat, and even as far as Mount Calvary. During the whole walk, Jesus gave uninterrupted instructions. Among other things he told the apostles that until now he had given them his bread and his wine, but that today he would give them his flesh and his blood. He would bestow upon them, he would make over to them, all that he had. While uttering these words, the countenance of the Lord wore a touching expression, as if he were pouring his whole soul out, as if he were languishing with love to give himself to man. His disciples did not comprehend his words—they thought that he was speaking of the paschal lamb. No words can say how affectionate, how patient Jesus was in his last instructions both at Bethany and on his way to Jerusalem. The holy women arrived later at the house of Mary Mark.

The seven disciples who had followed the Lord to Jerusalem did not make the journey with him. They carried in bundles to the Cenacle the robes necessary for the Passover ceremonies. After depositing them in the anteroom, they proceeded to the house of Mary Mark.

When Peter and John reached the Cenacle with the chalice, which they had brought from Seraphia's [that is, from Veronica's], the mantles of ceremony were already lying in the anteroom whither they had been carried by the seven disciples and some of their companions. They had also draped the walls of the supper room, opened the apertures in the roof, and prepared three hanging lamps. This done, Peter and John went out to the valley of Jehosaphat and summoned the Lord and the nine apostles. The disciples and friends who were also to eat their Passover feast in the Cenacle came later.

JESUS and his followers ate the paschal lamb in the Cenacle in three separate groups of twelve, each presided over by one who acted as host. Jesus and the twelve apostles ate in the hall itself; Nathaniel with as many of the oldest disciples, in one of the side rooms; and in another with twelve more sat Heliachim, son of Cleophas and Mary Heli, and the brother of Mary Cleophas. He had been a disciple of John the Baptist. In one of the side buildings near the entrance into the court of the Cenacle, the holy women took their meal.

Three lambs had been immolated and sprinkled for them in the temple. But the fourth was slaughtered and sprinkled in the Cenacle, and it was this that Jesus ate with the twelve. Judas was not aware of this circumstance. He had been engaged in various business affairs, among which was the plot to betray the Lord, and consequently had arrived only a few moments before the repast, and after the immolation of the lamb had taken place.

The slaughter of the lamb for Jesus and the apostles presented a scene most touching. It took place in the anteroom of the Cenacle, Simeon's son, the Levite, assisting at it. The apostles and disciples were present chanting the 118th Psalm. Jesus spoke of a new period then beginning, and said that the sacrifice of Moses and the signification of the paschal lamb were about to be fulfilled, that on this account the lamb was to be immolated as formerly in Egypt, and that now in reality were they to go forth from the house of bondage.

All the necessary vessels and instruments were now prepared. Then a beautiful little lamb was brought in, around its neck a garland which was taken off and sent to the blessed Virgin, who was at some distance with the other women. The lamb was then bound, its back to a little board, with a cord passed around the body. It reminded me of Jesus bound to the pillar. Simeon's son held the lamb's head up, and Jesus stuck it in the neck with a knife, which he then handed to Simeon's son that he might complete the slaughter. Jesus appeared timid in wounding the lamb, as if it cost him pain. His movement was quick, his manner grave. The blood was caught in a basin, and the attendants brought a branch of hyssop, which Jesus dipped into it. Then stepping to the door of the hall, he signed the two posts and the lock with the blood, and stuck the bloody branch above the lintel. He then uttered some solemn words, saying among other things: "The destroying angel shall pass by here. Without fear or anxiety, ye shall adore in this place when I, the true Paschal Lamb, shall have been immolated. A new era, a new sacrifice are now about to begin, and they shall last till the end of the world."

They then proceeded to the Passover hearth at the end of the hall where formerly the Ark of the Covenant reposed. There they found a fire already lighted. Jesus sprinkled the hearth with blood, and consecrated it as an altar. The rest of the blood, along with the fat, was thrown into the fire under the altar, after which, followed by the apostles, Jesus walked around the Cenacle singing psalms, and consecrated it as a new temple. During this ceremony, the doors were closed.

Meanwhile Simeon's son had prepared the lamb. It was fixed upon a spit, the forelegs fastened to a crosspiece, and the hind ones to the spit. Ah! It looked so much like Jesus on the cross! It was then, along with the three others that had been slaughtered in the temple, placed in the oven to be roasted.

All the paschal lambs of the Jews were immolated in the forecourt of the temple, in one of three different places, according as their owners were rich, or poor, or strangers.[†] That of Jesus was not slaughtered in the temple, though he observed all other points of the Law most strictly. That lamb was only a figure. Jesus himself would on the next day become the true Paschal Lamb.

Jesus next gave the apostles an instruction upon the paschal lamb and the fulfillment of what it symbolized, and as the time was drawing near and Judas had returned, they began to prepare the tables. After that they put on the traveling dresses of ceremony, which were in the anteroom, and changed their shoes. The dress consisted of a white tunic like a shirt, and over it a mantle, shorter in front than in the back. The tunic was tucked up into the girdle, and the wide sleeves were turned up. Thus equipped, each set went to its own table: the two bands of disciples into the

---

† Anne Catherine here explained the manner in which the families assembled together, and in what numbers, but Clemens Brentano says he had forgotten her words.

side halls, Jesus and the apostles into the Cenacle proper. Each took a staff in his hand, and then they walked in pairs to the table at which each stood in his place, his arms raised, and the staff resting upon one. Jesus stood in the center of the table. He had two small staves that the master of the feast had presented to him. They were somewhat crooked on top, and looked like short shepherd crooks. On one side they had a hook, like a cut-off branch. Jesus stuck them into his girdle crosswise on his breast, and when praying, supported his raised arms on the hooks. It was a most touching sight to see Jesus leaning on these staves as he moved. It was as if he had the cross, whose weight he would soon take upon his shoulders, now supporting him under the arms. Meanwhile all were chanting, "Blessed be the Lord God of Israel," "Praised be the Lord," etc. When the prayer was ended, Jesus gave one of the staves to Peter, the other to John. They put them aside, or passed them from hand to hand among the other apostles, but what this signified, I cannot now recall.

The table was narrow and only high enough to reach one-half foot above the knee of a man standing by it. In form it was like a horseshoe; and opposite Jesus, in the inner part of the half-circle, there was a space left free for the serving of the dishes. As far as I can remember, John, James the Greater, and James the Less stood on Jesus's right; then came Bartholomew, still on the right, but more toward the narrow end of the table; and round the corner at the inner side stood Thomas, and next to him Judas Iscariot. On Jesus's left were Peter, Andrew, and Thaddeus; then as on the opposite side, came Simon; and round at the inner side, Matthew and Philip. [H2]

In the center of the table lay the paschal lamb on a dish, its head resting on the crossed forefeet, the hind feet stretched out at full length. All around the edge of the dish were little bunches of garlic. Nearby was another dish with the Passover roast meat, and on either side a plate of green herbs. These latter were arranged in an upright position and so closely together that they looked as if they were growing. There was another plate with little bunches of bitter herbs that looked like aromatic herbs. Directly in front of Jesus's place stood a bowl of yellowish-green herbs, and another with some kind of a brownish sauce. Small round loaves served the guests for plates, and they made use of bone knives.

After the prayer, the master of the feast laid on the table in front of Jesus the knife for carving the paschal lamb, placed a cup of wine before him, and from a jug filled six

other cups, each of which he set between two of the apostles. Jesus blessed the wine and drank, the apostles drinking two by two from one cup. The Lord cut up the paschal lamb. The apostles in turn reached for their little loaves on some kind of an instrument that held them fast, and received each one a share. They ate it in haste, separating the flesh from the bone with their ivory knives, and the bones were afterward burned. They ate also, and that very quickly, the garlic and green herbs, first dipping them into the sauce. They ate the paschal lamb standing, leaning a little on the back of the seats. Jesus then broke one of the loaves of unleavened bread, covered up one part of it, and divided the other among the apostles. After that they ate the little loaves that had served as plates. Another cup of wine was brought. Jesus gave thanks, but drank not of it. He said: "Take this wine and divide it among you, for I shall henceforth drink no more wine, until the kingdom of God cometh." After the apostles had drunk, two by two, they chanted, and Jesus prayed and taught. After that they again washed their hands, and then reclined on the seats. During the preceding ceremony, they had been standing, or at least supporting themselves somewhat, and everything was done in haste. Jesus had also cut up another lamb, which was carried to the holy women in the side building where they were taking their meal. The apostles partook of the herbs, the salad, and the sauce. Jesus was exceedingly serene and recollected, more so than I ever before saw him. He bade the apostles forget their cares. Even the blessed Virgin was bright and cheerful as she sat at table with the women. It was very touching to see her turning so simply to the other women when, at times, they approached her and drew her attention by a little pull at her veil.

While the apostles were eating the herbs, Jesus continued to converse with them still quite lovingly, though he afterward became grave and sad. He said: "One among you will betray me—one whose hand is with me in the dish." [H3] He was at that moment distributing one of the vegetables, namely, the lettuce of which there was only one dish. He was passing it down his own side, and he had directed Judas, who was sitting crosswise from him, to distribute it on the other side. As Jesus made mention of a traitor, the apostles became very much alarmed. Then he repeated: "One whose hand is with me at table, or whose hand dips with me into the dish," which was as much as to say: "One of the twelve who are eating and drinking with me—one with whom I am breaking my bread." By these words, Jesus did not betray Judas to the others, for "to dip into the same dish" was a common expression significant of the most intimate friendship. Still Jesus intended by it to warn Judas, for he really was dipping his hand with him into the dish while distributing the lettuce. Later on, he said: "The Son of Man indeed goeth as it is written of him, but woe to that man by whom the Son of Man shall be betrayed! It were better for him had he never been born."

At these words the apostles became very much troubled, and asked in turn: "Lord, is it I?" for all knew well that they did not understand him perfectly. Peter meantime, leaning behind Jesus toward John, motioned to him to ask the Lord who it was, for having often received reproofs from Jesus, he was anxious lest it might be himself. Now, John was reclining at Jesus's right, and as all were leaning on the left arm in order to eat with the right hand, John lay with his head close to Jesus's breast. At the sign from Peter, John approached his head to Jesus's breast, and asked: "Lord, who is it?"—at which word he was interiorly admonished that Jesus referred to Judas. I did not see Jesus saying with his lips: "He to whom I shall give the morsel dipped," and I cannot say whether or not he said it softly to John. But John understood it when Jesus, having dipped into the sauce the morsel of bread folded in lettuce, offered it affectionately to Judas, who too was asking, "Lord, is it I?" Jesus looked at him lovingly and answered in general terms. To give bread dipped was a mark of love and confidence, and Jesus did it with heartfelt love, to warn Judas and to ward off the suspicions of the others. But Judas was interiorly inflamed with rage. During the whole meal I saw sitting at his feet a little monster, which frequently rose to his heart. I did not see John repeating to Peter what he had learned from Jesus, though I saw him setting his mind at rest by a glance.

The Washing of the Feet

THEY arose from table and, while putting on and arranging their robes, as was the custom before solemn prayer, the master of the feast with two servants came in to take away the table and put back the seats. While this was being done, Jesus ordered some water to be brought him in the anteroom, and the master again left the hall with his servants.

Jesus, standing in the midst of the apostles, spoke to them long and solemnly. But I have seen and heard so many things that it is not possible for me to give the Lord's discourse exactly. I remember that he spoke of his kingdom, of his going to his Father, and he told them that he would, before leaving them, give over to them all that he possessed. Then he gave them instructions upon penance, the knowledge and confession of sin, contrition, and just-

ification. I felt that this bore some reference to the washing of the feet, and I saw that all, with the exception of Judas, acknowledged their sins with sorrow. This discourse was long and solemn. When it was ended, Jesus sent John and James the Less to bring the water from the anteroom, and directed the others to place the seats in a half-circle. Meantime, he himself retired to the anteroom to lay aside his mantle, gird up his robe, and tie around him a towel, one end of which he allowed to hang.

While these preparations were being made, the apostles got into a kind of dispute as to who among them should have the first place, for as the Lord had expressly announced that he was about to leave them and that his kingdom was near, they were strengthened anew in their idea that he had somewhere a secret force in reserve, and that he would achieve some earthly triumph at the very last moment.

Jesus, still in the anteroom, commanded John to take a basin, and James the Less a leathern bottle of water. The latter carried the bottle before his breast, the spout resting on his arm. After he had poured some water from the bottle into the basin, Jesus bade the two follow him into the hall in the center of which the master of the feast had set another large, empty basin.

Entering the hall in this order, Jesus in a few words reproved the apostles for the strife that had arisen among them. He said among other things that he himself was their servant, and that they should take their places on the seats for him to wash their feet. They obeyed, observing the same order as at table. They sat on the backs of the seats, which were arranged in a half-circle, and rested their naked feet upon the seat itself. Jesus went from one to another and, from the basin held under them by John, with his hand scooped up water over the feet presented to him. Then taking in both hands the long end of the towel with which he was girded, he passed it over the feet to dry them, and then moved on with James to the next. John emptied the water after each one into the large basin in the center of the room, and then returned to the Lord with the empty one. Then Jesus again poured water from the bottle held by James over the feet of the next, and so on. [H4]

During the whole of the Passover Supper, the Lord's demeanor was most touching and gracious, and at this humble washing of his apostles' feet, he was full of love. He did not perform it as if it were a mere ceremony, but like a sacred act of love springing straight from the heart. By it he wanted to give expression to the love that burned within.

When he came to Peter, the latter, through humility, objected. He said: "Lord, dost thou wash my feet?" And the Lord answered: "What I do, thou knowest not now, but thou shalt know hereafter." And it appeared to me that he said to him in private: "Simon, thou hast deserved that my Father should reveal to thee who I am, whence I came, and whither I go. Thou alone hast known and confessed it, therefore I will build my church upon thee, and the gates of hell shall not prevail against it. My power shall continue with thy successors till the end of the world." Here Jesus pointed to Peter while saying to the others: "Peter shall be my representative with you when I shall have gone from among you. He shall direct you and make known to you your mission." Then said Peter: "Never shalt thou wash my feet!" And the Lord replied: "If I wash thee not, thou shalt have no part with me!" Thereupon, Peter exclaimed: "Lord, wash me—not only my feet, but also my hands and my head!" To which Jesus replied: "He that is washed needeth not but to wash his feet, but is clean wholly. And you are clean, but not all." At these last words, Jesus was thinking of Judas.

In his instruction, Jesus had spoken of the washing of the feet as of a purification from daily faults, because the feet, coming in continual contact with the earth in walking, are constantly liable to become soiled. This was a spiritual foot-washing, a kind of absolution. Peter, however, in his zeal, looked upon it as too great a humiliation for his Master. He knew not that to save him, Jesus would the next day humble himself for love of him to the shameful death of the cross.

When Jesus washed Judas's feet, it was in the most touching and loving manner. He pressed them to his cheek and in a low tone bade him enter into himself, for that he had been unfaithful and a traitor for the past year. But Judas appeared not to notice, and addressed some words to John. This roused Peter's anger, and he exclaimed: "Judas, the Master is speaking to thee!" Then Judas made some vague, evasive remark, such as: "Lord, far be it from me!" Jesus's words to Judas had passed unremarked by the other apostles, for he spoke softly, and they did not hear. They were, besides, busy putting on their sandals. Judas's treachery caused Jesus more pain than any other part of his Passion. Jesus then washed the feet of John and James; first those of the latter while Peter held the water bottle; then the former, for whom James held the basin.

Jesus next delivered an instruction upon humiliation. He told them that he who was the greatest among them should be the servant, and that for the future they should in humility wash one another's feet. Many other things he said bearing reference to their dispute as to who should be the greatest, as is recorded in the Gospel. Jesus now resumed the garments that he had laid aside, and the apos-

April 2, AD 33
Thursday, Later Afternoon

tles let down theirs that had been girded up for the eating of the paschal lamb.

The Institution of the Most Blessed Sacrament

AT the command of the Lord, the master of the feast again set out the table, which he raised a little higher. It was placed in the middle of the room and covered with a cloth, over which two others were spread, one red, and the other white and transparent. Then the master set two jugs, one of water, the other of wine, under the table.

Peter and John now brought from the back part of the hall, where was the paschal hearth, the chalice they had brought from Veronica's house. They carried it between them in its case, holding it on their hands, and it looked as if they were carrying a tabernacle. They placed the case on the table before Jesus. The plate with the ribbed Passover loaves, thin and whitish, stood near under a cover, and the other half of the loaf that had been cut at the Passover supper was also on the table. There was a wine and water vessel, also three boxes, one with thick oil, another with liquid oil, and a third empty. A spatula, or flat knife, lay near.

The breaking and distributing of bread and drinking out of the same cup were customary in olden times at feasts of welcome and farewell. They were used as signs of brotherly love and friendship. I think there must be something about it in the scriptures. Today Jesus elevated this custom to the dignity of the most holy Sacrament, for until now it was only a typical ceremony. One of the charges brought before Caiaphas on the occasion of Judas's treason was that Jesus had introduced something new into the Passover ceremonies, but Nicodemus proved from scripture that this was an ancient practice at farewell feasts.

Jesus's place was between Peter and John.[H5] The doors were closed, for everything was conducted with secrecy and solemnity. When the cover of the chalice had been removed and taken back to the recess in the rear of the Cenacle, Jesus prayed and uttered some very solemn words. I saw that he was explaining the Last Supper to the apostles, as also the ceremonies that were to accompany it. It reminded me of a priest teaching others the Holy Mass.

Jesus then drew from the flat board upon which the vessels stood a kind of shelf, took the white linen that was hanging over the chalice, and spread it on the shelf. I saw him next take a round, flat plate from the chalice and place it on the covered shelf. Then taking the loaves from the covered plate nearby, he laid them on the one before him. The loaves were four-cornered and oblong, in length sufficient to extend beyond the edge of the plate, though narrow enough to allow it to be seen at the sides.

Then he drew the chalice somewhat nearer to himself, took from it the little cup that it contained, and set to the right and left the six smaller vessels that stood around it.

He next blessed the Passover loaves and, I think, the oil also that was standing near, elevated the plate of bread with both hands, raised his eyes toward heaven, prayed, offered, set it down on the table, and again covered it. Then taking the chalice, he received into it wine and water, the former poured by Peter, and the latter by John. The water he blessed before it was poured into the chalice. He then added a little more water from the small spoon, blessed the chalice, raised it on high, praying and offering, and set it down again.

After that Jesus held his hands over the plate upon which the loaves had lain, while at his bidding Peter and John poured water on them; then with the spoon that he had taken from the foot of the chalice, he scooped up some of the water that had flowed over his own hands, and poured it upon theirs. Lastly, that same plate was passed around, and all the apostles washed their hands in it. I do not know whether these ceremonies were performed in this precise order, but these and all the others that reminded me so much of the Holy Mass, I looked upon with deep emotion.

During all this time Jesus was becoming more and more recollected. He said to the apostles that he was now about to give them all that he possessed, even his very self. He seemed to be pouring out his whole being in love, and I saw him becoming perfectly transparent. He looked like a luminous apparition.

In profound recollection and prayer, Jesus next broke the bread into several morsels and laid them one over another on the plate. With the tip of his finger he broke off a scrap from the first morsel and let it fall into the chalice, and at the same moment I saw, as it seemed to me, the blessed Virgin receiving the blessed sacrament, although she was not present in the Cenacle. It seemed to me that I saw her enter at the door and come before the Lord to receive the blessed sacrament, after which I saw her no more.

Again Jesus prayed and taught. His words, glowing with fire and light, came forth from his mouth and entered into all the apostles, excepting Judas. He took the plate with the morsels of bread (I do not remember whether he had placed it on the chalice or not) and said, "Take and eat.

April 2, Ap 33
Thursday, Early Evening

This is my body which is given for you." While saying these words, he stretched forth his right hand over it, as if giving a blessing, and as he did so, a brilliant light emanated from him. His words were luminous as also the bread, which as a body of light entered the mouth of the apostles. It was as if Jesus himself flowed into them. I saw all of them penetrated with light, bathed in light. Judas alone was in darkness. Jesus presented the bread first to Peter, then to John, and next made a sign to Judas, who was sitting diagonally from him, to approach. Thus Judas was the third to whom Jesus presented the blessed sacrament, but it seemed as if the word of the Lord turned back from the mouth of the traitor. I was so terrified at the sight that I cannot describe my feelings. Jesus said to Judas: "What thou art about to do, do quickly." The Lord then administered the blessed sacrament to the rest of the apostles, who came up two by two, each one holding for his neighbor a little, stiff cover with an ornamental edge that had lain over the chalice.

Jesus next raised the chalice by its two handles to a level with his face, and pronounced into it the words of consecration. While doing so, he was wholly transfigured and, as it were, transparent. He was as if passing over into what he was giving. He caused Peter and John to drink from the chalice while yet in his hands, and then he set it down. With the little spoon, John removed some of the sacred blood from the chalice to the small cups, which Peter handed to the apostles who, two by two, drank from the same cup. Judas also (though of this I am not quite certain) partook of the chalice, but he did not return to his place, for he immediately left the Cenacle. The others thought that Jesus had given him some commission to execute. He left without prayer or thanksgiving. [H6] And here we may see what an evil it is to fail to give thanks for our daily bread and for the Bread that endures to life eternal. During the whole meal I saw a little red monster with one foot like a bare bone sitting at Judas's feet and often rising up to his heart, but when outside the door, I saw three devils pressing around him. One entered into his mouth, one urged him on, and the third ran in front of him. It was night. They seemed to be lighting him as he hurried on like a madman.

The remains of the sacred blood in the chalice, the Lord poured into the small cup that fitted into it; then holding his fingers over the chalice, he bade Peter and John pour water and wine upon them. This ablution he gave to the two to drink from the chalice and, pouring what remained into the smaller cups, passed it down among the rest of the apostles. After that Jesus wiped out the chalice, put into it the little cup with what was left of the sacred blood, laid upon it the plate with the remains of the consecrated Passover bread, replaced the cover, wrapped the whole in the linen cloth, and deposited it in its case among the smaller cups. After the resurrection, I saw the apostles partaking of communion from this bread and wine consecrated by Jesus.

I do not remember having seen the Lord himself receive the sacred species. I must have let that pass unnoticed. When he administered his body and blood to the apostles, it appeared to me as if he emptied himself, as if he poured himself out in tender love. It is inexpressible. Neither did I see Melchizedek, when sacrificing bread and wine, receive it himself. It was given me to know why priests partake of the sacrifice, although Jesus did not.

(While uttering these words, Sister Emmerich glanced quickly around, as if listening to someone. She received an explanation on the above, but was able to communicate the following only:

Had angels been deputed to administer the Holy Eucharist, they would not receive it, but if priests did not partake of it, it would long since have been lost. It is by their participation that the sacrament is preserved.

Jesus's movements during the institution of the most blessed sacrament were measured and solemn, preceded and followed by explanations and instructions. I saw the apostles after each noting down some things in the little parchment rolls that they carried about them. Jesus's turning to the right and left was full of gravity, as he always was when engaged in prayer. Every action indicated the institution of the Holy Mass. I saw the apostles, when approaching one another and in other parts of it, bowing as priests are wont to do.)

Private Instructions and Consecrations

JESUS now gave to the apostles an instruction full of mystery. [H7] He told them how they were to preserve the blessed sacrament in memory of him until the end of the world, taught them the necessary forms for making use of and communicating it, and in what manner they were by degrees to teach and make known the mystery. He told them likewise when they were to receive what remained of the consecrated species, when to give some to the blessed Virgin, and how to consecrate it themselves after he should have sent them the Comforter.

Then he instructed them upon the priesthood, the sacred unction, and the preparation of the Chrism and the Holy Oils.[†] Three boxes, two with a mixture of balsam and oil, also some raw cotton, stood near the chalice case. They

were so formed as to admit being placed one on the other. Jesus taught many secret things concerning them: how to mix the ointment, what parts of the body to anoint, and upon what occasions. I remember among other things Jesus's mentioning a certain case in which the blessed sacrament could not be administered. Perhaps it was something bearing reference to extreme unction, though I do not now know clearly. He spoke of different kinds of anointing, among them that of kings. He said that even wicked kings who were anointed possessed a certain interior and mysterious power that was wanting to others. Then Jesus put some of the viscous ointment and oil into the empty box and mixed them together, but I cannot say whether it was at this moment or at the consecration of the bread and wine that the Lord blessed the oil.

After that I saw Jesus anointing Peter and John, on whose hands, at the institution of the blessed sacrament, he had poured the water that had flowed over his own, and who had drunk from the chalice in his hand.

From the center of the table, where he was standing, Jesus stepped a little to one side and imposed hands upon Peter and John, first on their shoulders and then on their head. During this action they joined their hands and crossed their thumbs. As they bowed low before him (and I am not sure that they did not kneel) the Lord anointed the thumb and forefinger of each of their hands with Chrism, and made the sign of the cross with it on their head. He told them that this anointing would remain with them to the end of the world. James the Less, Andrew, James the Greater, and Bartholomew, were likewise consecrated. I saw too that the Lord twisted crosswise over Peter's breast the narrow scarf that he wore around his neck, but that on the others he drew it across the breast over the right shoulder and under the left arm. Still I do not remember clearly whether this took place at the institution of the blessed sacrament, or not till the anointing.

Then I saw—but how, I cannot say—that Jesus at this anointing communicated to the apostles something essential, something supernatural. He told them also that after

---

† Earlier editions include at this point the following note: "It was not without surprise that the editor, some years after these things had been related by Anne Catherine, read, in the Latin edition of the Roman Catechism (Mayence, Muller), in reference to the sacrament of confirmation, that, according to the tradition of the holy Pope Fabian, Jesus taught his apostles in what manner they were to prepare the Holy Chrism, after the institution of the blessed sacrament. The Pope says this expressly, in the 54th paragraph of his Second Epistle to the Bishops of the East: 'Our predecessors received from the apostles and delivered to us that our Savior Jesus Christ, after having made the Last Supper with his apostles and washed their feet, taught them how to prepare the Holy Chrism.'"

they should have received the Holy Spirit they were to consecrate bread and wine for the first time, and anoint the other apostles. At these words of Jesus, I saw at a glance Peter and John, on the day of Pentecost and before the great baptism, imposing hands upon the other apostles, and eight days later upon several of the disciples. I saw also that John, after the resurrection, gave the most blessed sacrament to the blessed Virgin for the first time. This event used to be commemorated by the apostles as a feast. The church no longer keeps it, but in the Church Triumphant I see the day still celebrated. In the first days after Pentecost, I saw only Peter and John consecrating the most blessed sacrament; but later the others also consecrated.

The Lord blessed fire in a brass vessel. It burned ever after, even during the long absence of the apostles. It was kept near the spot in which the blessed sacrament was deposited, in one division of the ancient paschal hearth whence it was always removed for religious purposes.

April 2, AD 33
Thursday Night, 9 PM

All that Jesus did at the institution of the blessed Eucharist and the anointing of the apostles was done very secretly, and was later on taught as a mystery. It has to this day remained essentially in the church, though she has, under the inspiration of the Holy Spirit, developed it according to her needs.

During the preparing and consecrating of the Holy Chrism, the apostles lent their aid, and when Jesus anointed and imposed hands upon them, it was done with ceremony.

Whether Peter and John were both consecrated bishops, or Peter alone as bishop and John as priest, and what dignity the four others received, Sister Emmerich forgot to state. But the different way in which the Lord arranged the narrow scarf on Peter and the others seems to indicate different degrees of consecration.

When these holy ceremonies were concluded, the chalice, near which stood the consecrated Chrism, was recovered, and the blessed sacrament carried by Peter and John into the back part of the room. This portion of the hall was cut off from the rest by a curtain that opened in the middle, and it now became the Holy of Holies. The blessed sacrament was deposited back of and a little above the paschal oven. Joseph of Arimathea and Nicodemus always took care of the sanctuary and the Cenacle in the apostles' absence.

Jesus again delivered a long instruction and prayed several times with deep recollection. He often appeared to be conversing with his heavenly Father, and to be overflowing with love and enthusiasm. The apostles also were full of joy and zeal. They asked questions about different things, all of which Jesus answered. Of all this, I think many things are recorded in the holy scriptures. During this discourse Jesus addressed some words in private to Peter and John, who were sitting next to him, in reference to some of his earlier instructions. They were to communicate them to the other apostles, and these in turn to the disciples and holy women, according to the capacity of each for such knowledge. He spoke for some time to John alone. Of this I remember only that Jesus told him that his life would be longer than that of the others, and that he said something about seven churches, something about crowns and angels and similar significant symbols by which, as well as I know, he designated certain epochs. The other apostles felt slightly jealous at this special communication to John. Jesus alluded several times to his traitor, saying, "Now he is doing this, now he is doing that," and as he spoke, I saw Judas doing just what he said. When Peter vehemently protested that he would certainly remain faithful to him, Jesus said to him: "Simon, Simon! Behold Satan hath desired to have you that he may sift you as wheat. But I have prayed for you that your faith fail not; and you, being once converted, confirm your brethren." When Jesus said that whither he was going they could not follow, Peter again exclaimed that he would follow him even unto death. Jesus replied: "Amen, amen, I say to thee, before the cock crows twice, thou wilt deny me thrice!" When revealing to the apostles the trying times they were to encounter, Jesus asked, "When I sent you without purse or scrip or shoes, did you want any thing?" They answered: "No!" Then he replied: "But now he that hath a purse, let him take it, and likewise a scrip; and he that hath not, let him sell his coat and buy a sword. For I say to you, that this that is written must yet be fulfilled in me: And with the wicked was he reckoned. For the things concerning me have an end."

The apostles understood these words in a carnal sense, and Peter showed him two swords, short and broad like cleavers.

Jesus said: "It is enough. Let us go hence!" Then they recited the hymn of thanksgiving, put aside the table, and went into the anteroom.

Here Jesus met his mother, Mary Cleophas, and Magdalene, who besought him imploringly not to go to the Mount of Olives, for it was reported that he would there be arrested. Jesus comforted them in a few words, and stepped quickly past them. *It was then about nine o'clock.*

They went in haste down the road by which Peter and John had come up that morning to the Cenacle, and directed their steps to the Mount of Olives.

I have indeed always seen the Passover supper and the institution of the blessed sacrament take place as just related. But I have always been so deeply affected by it that I could remember only some part of the ceremony; now, however, I have seen it more distinctly. Such a sight exhausts beyond the power of words to say; for in it one beholds the recesses of hearts, one sees the love, the constancy of the Lord, and knows at the same time all that is to befall him. It is altogether impossible under such circumstances to observe external actions closely. One is dissolved in admiration, thanksgiving, and love. One cannot comprehend the errors of others, while the ingratitude of humankind and the thought of one's own sins weigh heavily. The eating of the paschal lamb was performed by Jesus in haste and in perfect conformity to the Law. The Pharisees interspersed the ceremony with some observances of their own.

Jesus on the Mount of Olives

Friday, April 3, AD 33 (Nisan 14)

As described by Anne Catherine, the moon was not quite full as Jesus, accompanied by the eleven apostles, walked through the valley of Jehosaphat up to the Mount of Olives. She recounted in detail the experiences undergone by Jesus in the Garden of Gethsemane, where his suffering began. Here he lived through, in his soul, all the future suffering of the apostles, disciples, and friends of the early church; and he also underwent the temptation which he overcame with the words: "Not my will, but thine, be done" (Luke 22:42). Around midnight Judas arrived at the Garden of Gethsemane accompanied by twenty soldiers and six officials. Judas went up to Jesus and kissed him, saying: "Hail, Master!" Jesus replied: "Judas, would you betray the Son of Man with a kiss?" (Luke 22:47–48).

There then took place the capture of Jesus. Thus began Good Friday, the last day in the earthly life of Jesus Christ. The sequence of events summarizing his suffering (Passion) and culminating in his death on the cross was described by Anne Catherine as follows:

The capture of Jesus shortly before midnight; Jesus presented to Annas around midnight; the trial by Caia-phas; Peter's denial; Jesus in the prison at Caiaphas's court; the sentencing of Jesus by Caiaphas; the suicide of Judas; Jesus presented to Pontius Pilate at around six o'clock that morning; Jesus presented to Herod Antipas; Jesus presented again to Pilate; the scourging of Jesus, which lasted about three-quarters of an hour and was over by about nine o'clock that morning; the crowning with thorns; Pilate handed over Jesus to be crucified and pronounced the death sentence upon him at about ten o'clock that morning; the carrying of the cross to Golgotha on Mount Calvary; after Jesus had fallen three times under the weight of the cross, Simon of Cyrene was compelled to help him carry the cross; Veronica came to mop the blood and sweat from the face of Jesus with her veil; Jesus fell to the ground for the fourth and fifth times—the fifth time in the presence of the "weeping daughters" of Jerusalem; Jesus, on his way up Mount Calvary, fell to the ground a sixth time, and then a seventh time shortly before reaching the summit—at this seventh time it was about 11:45 AM Jerusalem time; Jesus was disrobed for the crucifixion—at noon a reddish darkening appeared before the sun; Jesus was nailed to the cross at about 12:15 PM; then the cross was raised up; and at 12:30 PM the trumpets sounded forth from the temple announcing the slaying of the Passover lambs; the two criminals were cruc-ified—the repentant one to Jesus's right and the unrepentant one to his left; dice were cast for Jesus's clothes; Jesus, after being mocked, spoke the words: "Father, forgive them, for they know not what they do!"; shortly after 12:30 PM, a darkening of the sun took place, and the heavens grew darker and darker; the repentant criminal said: "Lord, let me come to a place where you may save me; remember me when you come into your kingdom," to which Jesus replied: "Truly, I say to you, today you will be with me in paradise!"; Jesus spoke the words to his mother, Mary, "Woman, behold, this is your son; he will be more your son than if you had given birth to him," and to John he said, "Behold! This is your mother!"; toward three o'clock that afternoon Jesus called out in a loud voice:

"Eli, Eli, lama sabachtani!" which means: "My God, my God, why hast thou forsaken me!"; Jesus spoke the words: "I thirst!"; the soldier Abenadar reached a sponge soaked in vinegar up to Jesus's mouth; Jesus spoke the words: "It is fulfilled!" followed by the words: "Father, into thy hands I commend my spirit!"; at these words Jesus died—it was just after three o'clock on that Good Friday afternoon, and an earthquake rent a gaping hole in the rock between Jesus's cross and that of the criminal to his left; the heavens were still darkened, and the radiant being of Jesus Christ descended into the gaping hole in the ground—thus began his descent into hell.

At the resurrection at dawn on Easter Sunday, April

5, AD 33 (Nisan 16), exactly 33½ years less 1⅓ days had elapsed since the birth of Jesus just before midnight on Saturday/Sunday, December 6/7, 2 BC.

WHEN Jesus left the Cenacle with the eleven, his soul was already troubled and his sadness on the increase. He led the eleven to the Mount of Olives by an unfrequented path through the valley of Jehosaphat. As they left the house, I saw the moon, which was not yet quite full, rising above the mountain. While walking in the valley of Jehosaphat with the apostles the Lord said that he would one day return hither, though not poor and powerless as he then was, to judge the world. Then would men tremble with fear and cry out: "Ye mountains, cover us!" But the disciples understood him not. They thought, as several times before during the evening, that from weakness and exhaustion he was wandering in speech. Sometimes they walked on, at others stood still talking to him. He said to them: "All of you shall be scandalized in me this night. For it is written: 'I will strike the shepherd, and the sheep of the flock will be dispersed.' But after I shall be risen again, I will go before you into Galilee."

The apostles were still full of the enthusiasm and devotion inspired by the reception of the most holy Sacrament, and the loving, solemn discourse of Jesus afterward. They crowded eagerly around him and expressed their love in different ways, protesting that they never could, they never would, abandon him. But as Jesus continued to speak in the same strain, Peter exclaimed: "Although all should be scandalized in thee, I will never be scandalized in thee!" The Lord replied: "Amen, I say to thee that in this night before the cock crows, thou wilt deny me thrice." "Yea, though I should die with thee, I will not deny thee." [H8] And so said all the others. They walked and paused alternately, and Jesus's sadness continued to increase. The apostles tried to dissipate it by human arguments, assuring him that just the opposite of what he dreaded would take place. But finding their efforts vain, they grew weary, and began already to doubt and fall into temptation.

They crossed the brook Kidron, but not by the bridge over which later on Jesus was led bound, for they had taken a byway. Gethsemane on the Mount of Olives, whither they were going, was in a direct line one-half hour from the Cenacle, for it was fifteen minutes from the Cenacle to the valley of Jehosaphat, and the same distance from the latter to Gethsemane. This spot, in which during his last days Jesus had sometimes passed the night with his apostles and instructed them, consisted of a large pleasure garden surrounded by a hedge. It contained some magnificent shrubbery and a great many fruit trees. Outside the garden were a few deserted houses, open for any that might wish to lodge there. Several persons, as well as the apostles, had keys to this garden, which was used both as a place of recreation and prayer. Oftentimes, too, people that had no gardens of their own gave there their feasts and entertainments. There were in it several arbors formed of dense foliage. The Garden of Olives was separated by a road from that of Gethsemane and was higher up the mountain. It was open, being surrounded by only a rampart of earth. It was smaller than the pleasure garden of Gethsemane, a retired corner of the mountain full of grottoes, terraces, and olive trees. One side of it was kept in better order. There were seats and benches and roomy caverns, cheerful and cool. Whoever wished, might find here a place suited to prayer and meditation. The spot chosen by Jesus was the wildest.

It was about nine o'clock when Jesus reached Gethsemane with the disciples. Darkness had fallen upon the earth, but the moon was lighting up the sky. Jesus was very sad. He announced to the apostles the approach of danger, and they became uneasy. Jesus bade eight of them to remain in the Garden of Gethsemane, where there was a kind of summerhouse built of branches and foliage. "Remain here," he said, "while I go to my own place to pray." He took Peter, John, and James the Greater with him, crossed the road, and went on for a few minutes, until he reached the Garden of Olives farther up the mountain. He was inexpressibly sad, for he felt his approaching agony and temptation. John asked how he, who had always consoled them, could now be so dejected. He replied: "My soul is sorrowful even unto death." [H9] He glanced around and on all sides saw anguish and temptation gathering about him like dense clouds filled with frightful pictures. It was at that moment he said to the three apostles: "Remain here and watch with me. Pray lest ye enter into temptation!" and they stayed in that place. Jesus went a few steps forward. But the frightful visions pressed around him to such a degree that, filled with alarm, he turned to the left from the apostles and plunged down into a grotto formed by an overhanging rock. The apostles remained in a hollow to the right above. The grotto in which Jesus concealed himself was about six feet deep. The earth sank gently toward the back, and plants and shrubs hanging from the rocks towering over the entrance made it a place into which no eye could penetrate.

April 2, AD 33
Thursday Night, 9–10 PM

When Jesus left the apostles, I saw a great number of frightful figures surrounding him in an ever-narrowing circle. His sorrow and anguish increased. He withdrew tremblingly into the back of the cave, like one seeking shelter from a violent tempest, and there he prayed. I saw the awful visions following him into the grotto, and becoming ever more and more distinct. Ah! It was as if that narrow cave encompassed the horrible, the agonizing vision of all the sins, with their delights and their punishments, committed from the Fall of our first parents till the end of the world; for it was here on the Mount of Olives that Adam and Eve, driven from Paradise, had first descended upon the inhospitable earth, and in that very grotto had they in fear and alarm bewailed their misery. I felt in a most lively manner that Jesus, in resigning himself to the sufferings that awaited him and sacrificing himself to divine Justice in satisfaction for the sins of the world, caused in a certain manner his divinity to return into the most holy Trinity. This he did in order—out of infinite love, in his most pure and sensitive, his most innocent and true humanity, supported by the love of his human heart alone—to devote himself to endure for the sins of the world the greatest excess of agony and pain. To make satisfaction for the origin and development of all kinds of sin and guilty pleasures, the most merciful Jesus, through love for us sinners, received into his own heart the root of all expiatory reconciliation and saving pains. He allowed those infinite sufferings in satisfaction for endless sins, like a thousand-branched tree of pain, to pierce through, to extend through all the members of his sacred body, all the faculties of his holy soul. Thus entirely given up to his humanity, he fell on his face, calling upon God in unspeakable sorrow and anguish. He saw in countless forms all the sins of the world with their innate hideousness. He took all upon himself and offered himself in his prayer to satisfy the justice of his heavenly Father for all that guilt by his own sufferings. But Satan who, under a frightful form and with furious mockery, moved around among all this abomination, became at each moment more violently enraged against him. He evoked before the eyes of his soul visions of the sins of men, one more frightful than the other, and constantly addressed to the sacred humanity of Jesus such words as, "What! Wilt thou take this also upon thyself? Art thou ready to endure its penalty? How canst thou satisfy for this?"

From that point in the heavens in which the sun appears between ten and eleven in the morning, a narrow path of light streamed toward Jesus, and on it I saw a file of angels coming down to him. They imparted to him fresh strength and vigor. The rest of the grotto was filled with the frightful and horrible visions of sin, and with the evil spirits mocking and tempting. Jesus took all upon himself. In the midst of this confusion of abomination, his heart, the only one that loved God and man perfectly, shrank in terror and anguish from the horror, the burden of all those sins. Ah, I saw there so many things! A whole year would not suffice to relate them!

When now this enormous mass of sin and iniquity had passed before the soul of Jesus in an ocean of horrible visions and he had offered himself as the expiatory sacrifice for all, had implored that all their punishment and chastisement might fall upon him, Satan, as once before in the desert, brought forward innumerable temptations; yes, he even dared to allege a crowd of accusations against the innocent Savior himself. "What!" said he to him, "wilt thou take all this upon thee, and thou art not pure thyself? See, here and here and here!" and he unfolded all kinds of forged bonds and notes before him, and with infernal impudence held them up under his eyes. He reproached him with all the faults of his disciples, all the scandal they had given, all the disturbances and disorder he had caused in the world by abolishing ancient customs. Satan acted like the most crafty and subtle Pharisee. He reproached Jesus with causing Herod's massacre of the Holy Innocents, with exposing his parents to want and danger in Egypt, with not having rescued John the Baptist from death, with bringing about disunion in many families, with having protected degraded people, refusing to cure certain sick persons, with injuring the Gergeseans by permitting the possessed to overturn their vats and their swine to rush into the sea. He accused him of the guilt of Mary Magdalene, since he had not prevented her relapse into sin; of neglecting his own family; of squandering the goods of others; and, in one word, all that the tempter would at the hour of death have brought to bear upon an ordinary mortal who, without a high and holy intention, had been mixed up in such affairs, Satan now suggested to the trembling soul of Jesus with the view of causing him to waver. It was hidden from him that Jesus was the Son of God, and he tempted him as merely the most righteous of men.

Yes, our divine Redeemer permitted, in a certain measure, his most holy humanity to veil his divinity, that he might endure those temptations that come upon the holiest souls at the hour of death respecting the intrinsic merit of their good works. That he might drain the chalice of suffering, he permitted the tempter, from whom his divinity was hidden, to upbraid him with his works of beneficence as so many sins incurring penalty and not yet blotted out by the grace of God. The tempter reproached him likewise for desiring to atone for the sins of others, although he was himself without merit and had not yet made satisfaction to God for the grace of many a so-called good work. The divinity of Jesus allowed the wicked fiend to tempt his sacred humanity just as he would tempt a man who might have ascribed his good works to some special merit of their own, independent of that which they can acquire by being united with the merits of the saving death of our Lord and Savior. Thus the tempter called up before Jesus all the works of his love as not only without merit for himself, but as so many crimes against God; and as their value was, in a certain measure, derived from the merits of his Passion not yet perfected and of whose worth Satan was ignorant, therefore for the grace by which he effected them he had not yet made satisfaction. For all his good works, Satan showed Jesus written bonds, telling him as he pointed to them: "For this action and for this also, hast thou incurred indebtedness." At last he unrolled before him a note that he had received from Lazarus for the sale of Magdalene's property in Magdalum, and the proceeds of which he had expended. Satan accompanied the action with these words: "How darest thou squander the property of others and thereby injure the family?" I saw in vision all those things for which the Lord offered himself in atonement, and with him I bore the burden of many of the accusations that the tempter made against him; for among those visions of the sins of the world that the Savior took upon himself I saw my own numerous transgressions. From the cloud of temptations that encircled Jesus, I saw a stream flow toward myself, and in it were shown me, to my great consternation, all my defects of omission and commission. Still, I kept my eyes turned toward my Lord, I struggled and prayed with him, and with him I turned to the consoling angels. Ah! The Lord writhed like a worm under the weight of his sorrow and agony.

It was with the greatest difficulty that I restrained myself while all these charges were brought against the innocent Savior. I was so enraged against Satan. But when he exhibited the note holding Jesus amenable for distributing the proceeds of Magdalene's property, I could no longer subdue my anger, and I exclaimed: "How canst thou charge Jesus with the sale of Magdalene's property as with a crime? I saw myself how the Lord devoted that sum received from Lazarus to works of mercy, how he released with it twenty-seven poor, abandoned creatures held prisoners for debt at Thirza."

At first Jesus knelt calmly in prayer, but after awhile his soul shrank in affright from the multitude and heinousness of man's sins and ingratitude against God. So over-

powering was the sadness, the agony of heart which fell upon him that, trembling and shuddering, he prayed imploringly: "Abba, Father, if it be possible, remove this chalice from me! My Father, all things are possible to thee. Take this chalice from me!" Then recovering himself, he added: "But not what I will, but what thou wilt." His will and the Father's were one. But now that through love he had delivered himself up to the weakness of his human nature, he shuddered at the thought of death.

I saw the grotto around him filled with frightful figures. I saw the sins, the wickedness, the vices, the torments, the ingratitude of men torturing and crushing him, and the horror of death, the terror that he experienced as man at the greatness of the expiatory sufferings soon to come upon him. I saw pressing around him and assailing him under the form of the most hideous specters. Wringing his hands, he swayed from side to side, and the sweat of agony covered him. He trembled and shuddered. He arose, but his trembling knees could scarcely support him. His countenance was quite disfigured and almost unrecognizable. His lips were white, and his hair stood on end. *It was about half-past ten o'clock* when he staggered to his feet and, bathed in sweat and often falling, tottered rather than walked to where the three disciples were awaiting him. He ascended to the left of the grotto and up to a terrace upon which they were resting near one another supported on their arm, the back of one turned toward the breast of his neighbor. Exhausted with fatigue, sorrow, and anxiety under temptation, they had fallen asleep. Jesus went to them like a man overwhelmed with sorrow whom terror drives to the company of his friends, and also like a faithful shepherd who, though himself trembling to the utmost, looks after his herd which he knows to be in danger, for he knew that they too were in anguish and temptation. All along this short distance, I saw that the frightful forms never left him. When he found the apostles sleeping, he clasped his hands and, sinking down by them from grief and exhaustion, he said: "Simon, sleepest thou?" At these words, they awoke and raised him up. In his spiritual dereliction, he said: "What! Could ye not watch one hour with me?" [H10] When they found him so terrified and disfigured, so pale, trembling, and saturated with sweat, shuddering and shaking, his voice feeble and stammering, they were altogether at a loss what to think. Had he not appeared surrounded by the light so well known to them, they would not have recognized him as Jesus. John said to him: "Master! What has befallen thee? Shall I call the other disciples?

April 2, AD 33
Thursday Night, 10:30 PM

85

Shall we take to flight?" Jesus answered: "Were I to live, teach, and work miracles for thirty-three years longer, it would not suffice for the accomplishment of what I have to fulfill before this time tomorrow. Do not call the eight! I have left them where they are because they could not see me in this suffering state without being scandalized at me. They would fall into temptation, forget many things that I have said to them, and lose confidence in me. But you who have seen the Son of Man transfigured, may also see him in this hour of darkness and complete derelic-tion of soul; nevertheless watch and pray, lest ye fall into temptation, for the spirit is willing, but the flesh is weak." These last words referred both to himself and to the apostles. Jesus wished by them to exhort his followers to perseverance, and to make known to them the struggle of his human nature against death, together with the cause of his weakness. In his overpowering sorrow, he said many other things to them, and remained with them about a quarter of an hour.

April 2, AD 33
Thursday Night, 10:30–11:15 PM

Jesus returned to the grotto, his anguish on the increase. The apostles, seeing him leave them thus, stretched out their hands after him, wept, threw themselves into one another's arms, and asked: "What does this mean? What is the matter with him? He is perfectly desolate!" And then covering their heads, they began in great anxiety to pray. All thus far related occupied about one hour and a half counting from Jesus's entrance into the Garden of Olives. In the scripture it does, indeed, say: "Could you not watch one hour with me?" But these words are not to be taken according to our measure of time. The three apostles who were with Jesus had prayed at first and then slept, for, owing to distrusted speeches, they had fallen into temptation. The eight however, who had remained at the entrance, did not sleep. The anxiety that marked all of Jesus's last actions on that evening greatly disquieted them, and they wandered around the Mount of Olives seeking a hiding place for themselves.

There was little bustle in Jerusalem on this evening. The Jews were in their homes busied with preparations for the feast. The lodgings for the Passover guests were not in the neighborhood of the Mount of Olives. As I went to and fro on the road, I saw here and there friends and disciples of Jesus walking together and conversing. They appeared to be uneasy and in expectation of something. The mother of the Lord, with Magdalene, Martha, Mary Cleophas, Mary Salome, and Salome had gone from the Cenacle to the house of Mary Mark. Alarmed at the reports that she had heard, Mary and her friends went on toward the city to get some news of Jesus. Here they were met by Lazarus, Nico-demus, Joseph of Arimathea, and some relatives from Hebron, who sought to comfort Mary in her great anxiety. These friends knew of Jesus's earnest discourse in the Cenacle, some from being themselves present in the side buildings, others from having been informed of it by the disciples; but although they questioned some Pharisees of their acquaintance, yet they heard of no immediate steps against our Lord. They said, therefore, "The danger is not so great. And besides, the enemies of Jesus would make no attempt against him so near to the feast." They did not know of Judas's treachery. Mary told them how restless he had been during the past few days, and of his sudden departure from the Cenacle. He had certainly gone with treacherous intentions, for, as she said, she had often warned him that he was a son of perdition. The holy women returned to the house of Mary Mark.

When Jesus went back into the grotto carrying his load of sadness with him, he cast himself face downward on the ground, his arms extended, and prayed to his heavenly Father. And now began for his soul a new struggle, which lasted three quar-ters of an hour. Angels came and showed him in a long series of visions and in all its extent what he would have to endure for the atonement of sin. [H11] They showed the beauty and excellence of man, the image of God, before the Fall, along with his deformity and corruption after the Fall. They showed how every sin originates from that first sin; they pointed out the essence and signification of con-cupiscence, its terrible effects upon the powers of the soul, as well as upon the physical well-being of man; also the essence and signification of all the sufferings entailed as chastisements by that same lusting after pleasure. They showed him, in the expiatory sufferings that awaited him, first a suffering that would reach to both body and soul, a punishment that would comprehend in its intensity all the penalty due to divine Justice for all the sins of the whole human race. Secondly, they showed him a suffering which, in order to be satisfactory, should chastise the crimes of the whole human race in that humanity which alone was sinless—namely, the most sacred humanity of the Son of God. That sacred humanity, through love, assumed all the guilt of humankind with the penalty due to it; conse-quently, it had also to gain the victory over man's abhor-rence of pain and death. All this the angels showed Jesus, sometimes appearing in whole choirs and exhibiting row after row of pictures, and sometimes displaying only the principal features of his suffering. I saw them pointing with raised finger to the visions as they appeared, and without hearing any voice, I understood what they said.

No tongue can express the horror, the anguish that overwhelmed the soul of Jesus at the sight of these visions of expiatory suffering. He understood not only the consequence of every species of concupiscence, but also its own peculiar expiatory chastisement, the significance of all the instruments of torture connected with it; so that not only the thought of the instrument made him shudder, but also the sinful rage of him that invented it, the fury and wickedness of all that had ever used it, and the impatience of all, whether innocent or guilty, who had been tortured with it. All these tortures and afflictions Jesus perceived in an interior contemplation, and the sight filled him with such horror that a bloody sweat started from the pores of his sacred body.

While the humanity of Christ so worthy of adoration was thus agonizing and writhing under this excess of suffering, I saw among the angels a feeling of compassion for him. There seemed to be a pause, in which they appeared desirous of giving him consolation, and I saw them praying to that effect before the throne of God. For an instant, there seemed to be a struggle between the mercy and the justice of God and that love which was sacrificing itself. I had also a vision of God not as before seated upon his throne, but in a less clearly defined, though luminous, figure. I saw the divine nature of the Son in the Person of the Father and, as it were, withdrawn into his bosom. The Person of the Holy Spirit was proceeding from the Father and the Son. He was, as it were, between them, and yet there was only one God. But who can speak of such things? I had more an interior perception of all this than a vision under human forms. In it I was shown that the divine will of Christ withdrew more into the Father in order to permit his most sacred humanity to suffer all those things for whose mitigation and warding off the human will struggled and prayed in agony; so that the Godhead of Christ being one with the Father, all that for whose removal his manhood prayed to the Father, should weigh upon his humanity alone. I saw all this at the instant of the angels' sympathetic emotion, when they conceived the desire to console Jesus, who did in fact, at that same moment, receive some alleviation. But now these visions disappeared, and the angels with their soothing compassion retired from the Lord, to whose soul a new sphere of agony more violent even than the last opened up.

When the Redeemer on the Mount of Olives, as a true and real human being, delivered himself to the temptation of human abhorrence against suffering and death; when he took upon himself also the vanquishing of that abhorrence the endurance of which forms a part of every suffer-

ing, the tempter was permitted to do to him what he does to every mortal who desires to offer himself a sacrifice in any holy cause. In the first part of the Lord's agony, Satan with furious mockery set before him the immensity of the debt that he was about assuming, and he carried the temptation so far as to represent the actions of the Redeemer himself as not free from faults. After that, in this second agony, there was displayed before Jesus in all its greatness and intrinsic bitterness the expiatory suffering necessary to discharge that immense debt. This was shown him by the angels, for it belongs not to Satan to show that expiation is possible. The Father of lies and despair never exhibits to men the works of divine mercy. But when Jesus, with heartfelt abandonment to the will of his heavenly Father, had victoriously resisted these assaults, a succession of new and terrifying visions passed before his soul. He experienced that uneasiness felt by every human heart on the point of making some great sacrifice. The questioning doubt: What advantage, what return shall I reap from this sacrifice? arose in the soul of the Lord, and the sight of the awful future overwhelmed his loving heart.

Upon the first man God sent a deep sleep, opened his side, took out one of his ribs, formed from it Eve, the first woman, the mother of all the living, and conducted her to Adam. Receiving her from God, Adam exclaimed: "This now is bone of my bones and flesh of my flesh. The man shall leave father and mother, and shall cleave to his wife; and they shall be two in one flesh." This is the marriage of which it is written: "This is a great sacrament, I speak in Christ and in the church." Christ, the new Adam, was pleased to permit a sleep, the sleep of death, to come upon him on the cross. He permitted, likewise, his side to be opened that the new Eve, his virginal Bride, the Church, the Mother of all the living, might be formed from it. He willed to give her the blood of Redemption, the water of purification, and his own Spirit, the three that render testimony upon earth. He willed to bestow upon her the holy Sacraments in order that she should be a Bride pure, holy, and undefiled. He willed to be her head and we the members, bone of his bone and flesh of his flesh. In taking human nature and willing to suffer death for us, he too left Father and Mother to cleave to his Bride, the Church. He has become one flesh with her, nourishing her with the most holy Sacrament of the Altar, in which he unceasingly espouses us. He wills to remain on earth with his Bride, the Church, until we shall all in her be united to him in heaven. He has said: "The gates of hell shall not prevail against her." To exercise this immeasurable love for sinners, the Lord became man and the brother of sinners, that he might thus take upon himself the punishment of all their guilt. He had indeed contemplated with anguish the immensity of that guilt and the greatness of the expiatory sufferings due to them, but at the same time he had offered himself joyfully as a victim of expiation to the will of his heavenly Father. Now, however, he beheld the sufferings, temptations, and wounds of the future Church, his Bride, which he had purchased at so dear a price, that of his own blood, and he saw the ingratitude of man.

Before the soul of the Lord there passed in review all the future sufferings of his apostles, disciples, and friends, and the small number of the primitive church. As her numbers increased, he saw heresies and schisms entering her fold, and the sin of Adam repeated by pride and disobedience in all forms of vanity and delusive self-righteousness. The tepidity, the malice, the wickedness of innumerable Christians; the manifold lies, the deceptive subtlety of all proud teachers; the sacrilegious crimes of all wicked priests with their frightful consequences; the abomination of desolation in the kingdom of God upon earth, in the sanctuary of the thankless human race whom, amid inexpressible sufferings, he was about to redeem with his blood and his life.

The scandals of the ages down to our own day and even to the end of the world, I saw pass before Jesus's soul in an immense succession of visions: all forms of error, proud fallacies, mad fanaticism, false prophecies, obstinate heresies, all kinds of wickedness. The apostates, the self-righteous, the teachers of error, the pretended reformers, the corrupters and the corrupted of all ages, mocked and tormented him for not having been crucified according to their ideas, for not having died comfortably on the cross according to their desires, according to their fancy or caprice. They tore and divided the seamless robe of the church. Each wanted to have a Redeemer other than he who had delivered himself through love. Countless numbers ill-treated him, mocked him, disowned him. He saw countless others who, disdainfully shrugging their shoulders and wagging their heads at him, avoided his arms stretched out to save them and hurried on to the abyss which swallowed them up. He saw innumerable others who dared not openly deny him, but who turned away in disgust from the wounds of his church, which they themselves had helped to inflict. They were like the Levite passing by the poor man that had fallen among robbers. Jesus saw them abandoning his wounded Bride like cowardly, faithless children who forsake their mother in the dead of night at the approach of the thieves and murderers to whom they themselves had opened the door. He saw them hastening after the booty that had been conveyed into the wilderness, the golden vessels and the broken necklaces. He saw them pitching their tents under the wild offshoots, far away from the true vine. He saw them like wandering

sheep becoming the prey of wolves, and led into unwholesome pasturage by base hirelings, instead of going into the sheepfold of the Good Shepherd who gave his life for his sheep. He saw them straying homeless, willfully closing their eyes to his city placed high upon a mountain, and which could not remain hid. He saw them scattered in the desert, driven hither and thither by changing winds among the sand drifts; but they would not see the house of his Bride, the Church, built upon a rock, with which he had promised to abide till the end of time, and against which the gates of hell shall never prevail. They would not enter through the narrow gate, because they were not willing to bend their neck. He saw them following leaders who would conduct them anywhere and everywhere, but not to the true door. They built upon the sand perishable huts of all kinds, without altar or sacrifice, the roofs surmounted by weathercocks, according to which their doctrines were ever changing; consequently they were ever in opposition to one another, they understood not one another, they had no fixed state. He saw them, time and again, pulling down their huts and hurling the fragments against the cornerstone of the church which, however, stood unshaken. He saw many among them, although darkness reigned in their dwellings, neglecting to go to the light that was placed on the candlestick in the house of the Bride. They wandered with closed eyes around the enclosed gardens of the church by whose perfumes alone they still lived. They stretched out their arms after shadowy forms and followed wandering stars that guided them to wells without water. When on the very brink of the precipice, they heeded not the voice of the Bride calling them and, though dying with hunger, proudly and pityingly derided the servants and messengers sent to invite them to the marriage feast. They would not enter the garden, for they feared the thorns of the hedge. The Lord saw them hungering and thirsting, but without wheat or wine. They were intoxicated with self-esteem and blinded by their own lights, wherefore they persisted in declaring that the church of the Word made flesh is invisible. Jesus beheld all, grieved over all, and longed to suffer for all, even for those that do not see him, that do not carry their cross after him in his Bride, to whom he gives himself in the most holy Sacrament; in his city built upon a mountain, and which cannot remain hidden; in his church founded upon a rock and against which the gates of hell cannot prevail.

All these innumerable visions upon the ingratitude of men and their abuse of the atoning death of my Lord I saw passing before his agonized soul, sometimes in changing pictures, and again in painful reproductions of the same. I saw Satan under many frightful forms, dragging away and strangling under the eyes of the Lord men redeemed by his blood; yes, even those anointed by his Sacrament. Jesus beheld with bitter anguish all the ingratitude, the corruption of Christendom past, present, and future. While these visions were passing before him, the voice of the tempter of his humanity was constantly heard whispering: "See! Canst thou undergo such sufferings in the sight of such ingratitude?" These words, added to the mockery and the abominations that he beheld in the rapidly changing visions, pressed with such violence upon him that his most sacred humanity was crushed under a weight of unspeakable agony. Christ, the Son of Man, writhed in anguish and wrung his hands. As if overwhelmed, he fell repeatedly on his knees, while so violent a struggle went on between his human will and his repugnance to suffer so much for so thankless a race, that the sweat poured from him in a stream of heavy drops of blood to the ground. Yes, he was so oppressed that he glanced around as if seeking help, as if calling upon heaven and earth and the stars of the firmament to witness his anguish. It seemed to me that I heard him crying out: "Ah, is it possible that such ingratitude can be endured! Witness ye my extreme affliction!"

At that moment, the moon and the stars appeared suddenly to draw nearer to the earth, and I felt in that same moment that the night became brighter. I noticed on the moon what I had not seen before. It looked quite different. It was not yet quite full, though it appeared to be larger than it does to us. In its center, I saw a dark spot. It looked like a flat disc lying before it. In the center of this disc, there appeared to be an opening through which streamed light to the moon not yet full. The dark spot was like a mountain, and all around the moon was a circle of light like a rainbow.

In his sore distress, Jesus raised his voice for some instants in loud cries of anguish. I saw that the three apostles sprang up in fright. With raised hands, they listened to Jesus's cries and were on the point of hastening to him. But Peter stopped James and John, saying: "Stay here! I will go to him." And I saw him hurrying forward and entering the grotto. "Master," he cried, "what has happened to thee?"—but he paused in terror at the sight of Jesus bathed in blood and trembling with fear. Jesus made no answer, and appeared not to notice Peter. Then Peter returned to the other two, and reported that Jesus had answered him only by sighs and groans. This news increased the sorrow and anxiety of the apostles. They covered their heads and sat weeping and praying with many tears.

I turned again to my Lord in his bitter agony. The frightful visions of the ingratitude and the misdeeds of future generations whose debt he was taking upon himself, whose chastisement he was about to endure, overwhelmed him with their ever-increasing multitude and horror. His struggle against the repugnance of his human nature for suffering continued, and several times I heard him cry out: "Father, is it possible to endure all this? O Father, if this chalice cannot pass from me, may thy will be done!"

Among this throng of apparitions typical of the outrages offered to divine Mercy, I saw Satan under various abominable forms, each bearing reference to the kind of guilt then exhibited. Sometimes he appeared as a great black figure in human shape, and again as a tiger, a fox, a wolf, a dragon, a serpent; not that he really took any of these forms, but he displayed the chief characteristics of their nature joined to other hideous appearances. There was nothing in them that perfectly resembled any creature. They were symbols of discord, of abomination, of contradiction, of horror, of sin—in a word, they were diabolical shapes. And by these hellish forms, Jesus beheld innumerable multitudes of men urged on, seduced, strangled, and torn to pieces—men for whose redemption from the power of Satan he was about to enter upon the way that led to the bitter death of the cross. At first I saw the serpent but seldom, but toward the last I beheld it in gigantic form, a crown upon its head. With terrible might and leading after it immense legions of human beings from every condition of life and of every race, it prepared to attack Jesus. Armed with all kinds of engines and destructive weapons, they struggled for some moments among themselves, and then with frightful fury turned the attack upon Jesus. It was an awful spectacle. Their weapons, their swords and spears, rose and fell like flails on a boundless threshing floor, and they raged against the heavenly grain of wheat that had come upon earth to die in order to feed humankind eternally with the bread of life.

I saw Jesus in the midst of these raging multitudes, many of whom appeared to me blind. He was as much affected by the sight as if their weapons really descended upon him. I saw him staggering from side to side, sometimes standing upright, and then falling to the ground. The serpent formed the central figure in this army, which it constantly led forward to new attacks. It lashed its tail around on all sides, and all whom it felled to the earth or enveloped in its coils it strangled, tore to pieces, or devoured. Upon this I received an instruction that these multitudes that were thus tearing Jesus to pieces represented the countless number of those that in diverse ways ill-treat him who, in his divinity and humanity, body and soul, flesh and blood under the forms of bread and wine in the most blessed sacrament, dwells ever present in that mystery as their Redeemer. Among these enemies of Jesus, I recognized the offences of all kinds committed against the blessed sacrament, that living pledge of his uninterrupted personal presence with the Catholic church. I saw with horror all the outrages springing from neglect, irreverence, and omission, as also those of abuse and the most awful sacrilege. I saw those that arose from the worship of the gods of this world, from spiritual darkness and false, superficial knowledge, from error, incredulity, fanaticism, hatred, and bloody persecution. I saw all kinds of people among these enemies: the blind and the lame, the deaf and the mute, and children. There were blind who would not see the truth; the lame through sloth, who would not follow it; the deaf who would not listen to its warnings or its threats; the mute who would never, with the sword of the word, take up their Lord's defense; and in fine, children spoiled by following worldly-minded and God-forgetting parents and teachers, who were fed on earthly pleasure, who were intoxicated with empty knowledge, and who loathed divine things, though starving without them. Among these children (the sight of whom grieved me especially, because Jesus so loved children), I noticed in particular many badly instructed, badly reared, and irreverent acolytes who do not honor Christ in the Holy Mass. Their guilt falls partly upon their teachers and the careless sacristans. But with terror I saw that many of the priests themselves, both of high and low degree, yes, even some that esteem themselves full of faith and piety—contribute their share toward outraging Jesus in the blessed sacrament. Of the many whom, to my great sorrow, I thus saw, I shall say a word of warning to one class only, and it is this: I saw numbers that believe, adore, and teach the presence of the living God in the most blessed sacrament, yet who do not sufficiently take it to heart. They forget, they neglect, the palace, the throne, the canopy, the seat, and the royal adornments of the king of heaven and earth, that is, the church, the altar, the tabernacle, the chalice, the monstrance of the living God, along with all the vessels, the furniture, the decorations, the festal robes, and all that is used in his worship, or the adornment of his house. All things were ignominiously covered with dust and rust, mouldering away and, through long years of neglect, falling to ruin. The service of the living God was shamefully neglected, and where it was not inwardly profaned, it was outwardly dishonored. Nor did all this arise from real poverty, but from indifference and sloth, from following old customs, from preoccupation of mind with vain, worldly affairs, and often too from self-seeking and spiritual death. I saw neglect of this kind in rich churches and in others tolerably well-off. Yes, I saw many in which worldly love of splendor and tinseled finery had replaced the magnificent and appropriate adornments of a more devout age. What the rich in ostentatious arrogance do, the poor foolishly aim at in their poverty and simplicity. This recalls to me our poor convent chapel in which the beautiful old stone altar had been covered with wood veined to imitate marble, a fact that always gave me sorrow.

These visions of the outrages offered to Jesus in the blessed sacrament I saw multiplied by innumerable church wardens who were totally deficient in their sense of equity, who failed to share at least what they had with their Redeemer present upon the altar, although he had delivered himself to death for them, although he remains for them hidden in the Sacrament. Even the poorest creatures are often better off than the Lord of heaven and earth in his churches. Ah, how deeply did the inhospitality of men trouble Jesus, who had given himself to them as food! Truly, riches are not necessary to entertain him who rewards a thousandfold the glass of cold water given to the thirsty! And how great is his thirst for us! Ought he not to complain when water swarming with worms is offered him in impure glasses? By such neglect I saw the weak scandalized, the sanctuary profaned, the churches abandoned, the ministers of religion despised. This state of impurity and negligence sometimes extended even to the souls of the faithful. They kept not the tabernacle of their hearts purer to receive therein the living God than was the tabernacle of the altar. For the fawning eye-service of princes and lords of the world, and to indulge their caprice and worldly designs, I saw every means carefully and actively resorted to by these unenlightened ecclesiastics, while the king of heaven and earth lay like another Lazarus outside the gate, vainly sighing after the crumbs of love denied him. He has nothing but the wounds which we have inflicted upon him and which the dogs lick, namely, ever-relapsing sinners who like dogs vomit and return to their food.

Were I to talk a whole year, it would not suffice to recount the different outrages committed against Jesus Christ in the blessed sacrament made known to me in this way. I saw the offenders in immense crowds with weapons corresponding to the varieties of crime perpetrated by them, assaulting the Lord and striking him to the ground. I saw irreverent sacristans of all centuries, light-minded, sinful, worthless priests offering the holy Sacrifice and distributing the blessed sacrament, and multitudes of tepid and unworthy communicants. I saw countless numbers to whom the source of all blessing, the mystery of the living God, had become an oath or a curse expressive of anger, and furious soldiers and servants of the devil who profaned the sacred vessels, who threw away the most blessed sacrament, who horribly outraged it, or who dishonored it in their frightful, hellish worship of false gods. Side by side with these hideous, barbarous cruelties, I saw innumerable other forms of godlessness more refined and subtle, but not less atrocious. I saw many souls, owing to bad example and perfidious teachers, losing their faith in Jesus's promises to remain always in the blessed sacrament, and no longer humbly adoring their Savior therein present. I saw in this multitude a great many sinful teachers who became teachers of error. They first struggled against one another, and then united against Jesus in the blessed sacrament of his church. I saw a great crowd of these apostate heresiarchs disdainfully rejecting the priesthood of the church, attacking and denying Jesus Christ's presence in the mystery of the blessed sacrament in the manner in which he himself gave this mystery to the church, which has truly preserved It. By their seductive words, they tore from the heart of Jesus countless numbers for whom he had shed his blood. Ah! It was fearful to look upon! For I saw the church as the body of Jesus, its scattered members all knitted together by him in his bitter Passion. I saw all those people, all those families with their descendants that had separated from the church, torn away from Jesus like entire pieces mangled and most painfully rent from his living flesh. Ah! He glanced at them so pitifully, he moaned so gently! He who, in order to unite to the body of his church, to the body of his bride, men so separated, so divided from one another, had given himself in the blessed sacrament to be their food, saw himself in this, his bride's body, torn and lacerated through the wicked fruit of the tree of disunion. The table of union in the blessed sacrament, Jesus's highest work of love, that in which he willed to remain forever among men, became through false teachers the boundary line of separation. And where alone it is good and beneficial that many should become one, namely, at the holy table, whereon the living God is himself the food, there must his children separate from infidels and heretics in order not to render themselves guilty of similar sins. I saw whole nations torn in this way from the heart of Jesus and deprived of participation in the treasures of grace left to the church. It was frightful to behold how at first only a few separated from Christ's church; and when, having increased to whole nations, they returned to her, they again attacked her and warred against one another on the question of what was holiest in her worship, namely, the blessed sacrament. But finally, I saw all who had separated from the church plunging into infidelity, superstition, heresy, darkness, and the false philosophy of the world. Perplexed and enraged, they united in large bodies to vent their anger against the church. They were urged on and destroyed by the serpent in the midst of them. Ah! It was as if Jesus felt himself torn into countless shreds. The Lord saw and felt in this distressing vision the whole weight of the poisonous tree of disunion with all its branches and fruits, which will continue to rend itself asunder until the end of time when the wheat will be gathered into the barn and the chaff cast into the fire.

The terror that I felt in beholding all this was so great, so dreadful, that our Lord appeared to me, and mercifully laying his hand on my breast, he said: "No one has ever before seen these things, and thy heart would break with fright, did I not sustain it."

I now saw the blood in thick, dark drops trickling down the pale face of the Lord. His once smoothly parted hair was matted with blood, tangled and bristling on his head, and his beard was bloody and torn. It was after that last vision, in which the armed bands had lacerated his flesh, that he turned as if fleeing out of the grotto, and went again to his disciples. But his step was far from secure. He walked bowed like one tottering under a great burden. He was covered with wounds, and he fell at every step. When he reached the three apostles, he did not, as on the first occasion, find them lying on their side asleep; they had sunk back on their knees with covered head, as I have often seen the people of that country sitting when in sorrow or in prayer. Worn out with grief, anxiety, and fatigue, they had fallen asleep; but when Jesus approached, trembling and groaning, they awoke. They gazed upon him with their weary eyes, but did not at once recognize him, for he was changed beyond the power of words to express. He was standing before them in the moonlight, his breast sunken, his form bent, his face pale and bloodstained, his hair in disorder, and his arms stretched out to them. He stood wringing his hands. The apostles sprang up, grasped him under the arms, and supported him tenderly. Then he spoke to them in deep affliction. On the morrow, he said, he was going to die. *In another hour*, his enemies would seize him, drag him before the courts of justice, abuse him, deride him, scourge him, and put him to death in the most horrible manner. He begged them to console his mother. He recounted to them in bitter anguish all that he would have to suffer until the evening of the next day, and again begged them to comfort his mother and Magdalene. He stood thus speaking for some moments, but the apostles kept silence, not knowing what to reply. They were so filled with grief and consternation at his words and appearance that they knew not what to say; indeed, they even thought that his mind was wandering. When he wanted to return to the grotto, he had not the power to do so. I saw that John and James had to lead him. When he

April 2, AD 33
Thursday Night, 11:15 PM

entered it, the apostles left him and went back to their own place. *It was then a quarter past eleven.*

During this agony of Jesus, I saw the blessed Virgin overwhelmed with sorrow and anguish in the house of Mary Mark. She was with Magdalene and Mary Mark in a garden adjoining the house. She had sunk on her knees on a stone slab. She was perfectly absorbed in her own interior, quite diverted in thought from everything around her, seeing only, feeling only the sufferings of her divine Son. She had sent messengers to obtain news of him, but unable to await their coming, in her anguish of heart she went with Magdalene and Salome out into the valley of Jehosaphat. I saw her walking along veiled, her arms often outstretched toward the Mount of Olives, where she saw in spirit Jesus agonizing and sweating blood. It seemed as if she would with her outstretched hands wipe his sacred face. In answer to these interior and vehement movements of her soul toward her Son, I saw that Jesus was stirred with thoughts of her. He turned his eyes in her direction as if seeking help from her. I saw this mutual sympathy under the appearance of rays of light passing to and fro between them. The Lord thought also of Magdalene and felt for her in her distress. He glanced toward her, and his soul was touched at sight of her. He therefore ordered the disciples to console her, for he knew that her love for him, after that of his mother, was greater than that of anyone else. He saw what she would have to suffer for him in the future, and also that she would never more offend him.

About this time, *perhaps a quarter after eleven*, the eight apostles were again in the arbor in the Garden of Gethsemane. They spoke together for awhile and then fell asleep. They were unusually faint-hearted, discouraged, and in sore temptation. Each had been looking out for a place of safety and anxiously asking: "What shall we do when he is dead? We have abandoned our friends, we have given up everything, we have become poor and objects of scorn to the world, we have devoted ourselves entirely to his service—and now, behold him crushed and helpless, with power to afford us no consolation!" The other disciples, after wandering about in various directions and hearing the reports of the awful prophecies to which Jesus had given utterance, nearly all retired to Bethphage.

Again I saw Jesus praying in the grotto. He had conquered the natural repugnance to suffer. Exhausted and trembling, he exclaimed: "My Father, if it be thy will, remove this chalice from me! Nevertheless, not my will but thine be done!"

And now the abyss opened before him and, as if on a pathway of light, he saw a long flight of steps leading down to Limbo. There he beheld Adam and Eve, all the patriarchs and prophets, the just of the Old Law, his mother's parents, and John the Baptist. They were with longing so intense awaiting his coming into that nether world that at the sight his loving heart grew strong and courageous. His death was to open heaven to these languishing captives! He was to deliver them from prison! For him they were sighing!

After Jesus had with deep emotion gazed upon those citizens of heaven belonging to former ages, the angels pointed out to him the multitudes of future saints who, joining their labors to the merits of his Passion, would through him be united to the heavenly Father. This vision was unspeakably beautiful and consoling. All passed before the Lord in their number, their race, and various degrees of dignity—all adorned with their sufferings and good works. Then did he behold the hidden and inexhaustible streams of salvation and sanctification that were to spring from the death that awaited him as Redeemer of humankind. The apostles, the disciples, virgins and holy women, martyrs, confessors, and hermits, popes and bishops, the future multitudes of religious men and women—in a word, the immense army of the blessed passed before him. All were adorned with crowns of victory won over passion and suffering. The flowers of their crowns differed in form, color, perfume, and vigor in accordance with the various sufferings, labors, and victories in which they had gloriously struggled. Their whole lives and actions, the peculiar worth and power of their combats and victories, as well as all the light, all the colors that symbolized their triumphs, came solely from their union with the merits of Jesus Christ. The reciprocal influence and relation of all these saints upon one another, their drinking out of one same fountain, namely, the most blessed sacrament and the Passion of the Lord, was a spectacle unspeakably wonderful and touching. Nothing connected with them happened by accident: their works and omissions, their martyrdom and victories, their apparel and appearance, though all so different, yet acted upon one another in unending unity and harmony. And this perfect unity in the most striking diversity sprang from the rays of light and sparkling colors of one single Sun, from the Passion of the Lord, the Word made flesh, in whom was life, the light of men, which shone in darkness, but which the darkness did not comprehend.

It was the army of future saints that passed before the soul of the Lord. Thus stood the Lord and Savior between the ardent desires of the patriarchs and the triumphant host of future saints, which reciprocally filling up and completing one another, so to say, surrounded the loving heart of the Redeemer like an immense crown of victory. This unspeakably touching spectacle afforded the soul of the Lord, who had allowed all kinds of human suffering to pass over him, some strength and consolation. Ah, he so dearly loved his brethren, his creatures, that willingly he would have suffered all for the purchase of one soul! As these visions referred to the future, they appeared hovering above the earth.

But now these consoling pictures disappeared, and the angels displayed before his eyes all the scenes of his approaching Passion. They appeared quite close to the earth, for the time was near at hand. There were many angelic actors in these scenes. I beheld everyone close to Jesus, from the kiss of Judas to his own last words upon the cross. I saw all, all there again, as I am accustomed to see it in my meditations upon the Passion. The treason of Judas, the flight of the disciples, the mockery and sufferings before Annas and Caiaphas, Peter's denial, Pilate's tribunal, Herod's derision, the scourging and crowning with thorns, the condemnation to death, the sinking under the weight of the cross, the meeting with the blessed Virgin and her swooning, the jeers of the executioners against her, Veronica's handkerchief, the cruel nailing to the cross and the raising of the same, the insults of the Pharisees, the sorrows of Mary, of Magdalene, and of John, and the piercing of his side—in a word, all, all, clearly, significantly, and in their minutest details passed before him. All the gestures, all the sentiments, and words of his future tormentors, I saw that the Lord beheld and heard in alarm and anguish of soul. He willingly accepted all, he willingly submitted to all through love for man. He was most painfully troubled at his shameful stripping on the cross, which he endured to atone for the immodesty of men, and he implored that he might retain a girdle at least upon the cross, but even this was not allowed him. I saw, however, that he was to receive help, not from the executioners, but from a certain good person.

Jesus saw and felt also his blessed Mother's sorrow and anguish of heart. With two holy women in the valley of Jehosaphat, she was in uninterrupted union with him by her interior participation in his sufferings and agony on the Mount of Olives.

At the close of these visions of the Passion, Jesus sank prostrate on his face like one in the throes of death. The angels and the visions disappeared, and the bloody sweat poured from him more copiously than before. I saw it soaking his yellowish garment and moistening the earth around. It was now dark in the grotto.

And now I saw an angel sweeping down toward him. In stature he was taller, in figure more distinct and more like a human being than any I had yet seen. He appeared in long, flowing robes, like those of a priest, ornamented with fringe. He carried in his hands, and before his breast, a small vessel shaped like the chalice used at the Last Sup-

per. Just above it floated a small oval morsel, about the size of a bean, which glowed with a reddish light. The angel hovered over the place where Jesus was lying and stretched forth his hand to him. When Jesus arose, he placed the shining morsel in his mouth and gave him to drink from the little luminous chalice. After that he disappeared.

Jesus had now voluntarily accepted the chalice of his Passion, and he received new strength. He remained in the grotto for a few minutes longer, absorbed in prayer and thanksgiving. He was indeed still under the pressure of mental suffering, but supernaturally strengthened to such a degree that, without fear or anxiety, he was able to walk with a firm step to his disciples. Though pale and exhausted, his bearing was erect and resolute. He had wiped his face with a linen cloth and with it smoothed down his hair which, moist with the blood and sweat of his agony, hung down in matted strands.

As he left the grotto, I saw the moon still with the remarkable-looking spot upon it and the circle around it; but its light, as well as that of the stars, was different from that which they gave forth during that great agony of Jesus. It seemed now to be more natural.

When Jesus returned to the disciples, he found them, as at first, lying on their side near the wall of the terrace, their heads covered, and asleep. The Lord said to them: "This is not the time to sleep. Ye should arise and pray, for behold the hour is at hand, and the Son of Man shall be betrayed into the hands of sinners. Arise, let us go! Behold, the traitor is approaching! Oh, it were better for him had he never been born!" The apostles sprang up affrighted and looked around anxiously. They had scarcely recovered themselves, when Peter exclaimed vehemently: "Master, I will call the others, that we may defend thee!" But Jesus pointed out to them at some distance in the valley, though still on the other side of the brook Kidron, a band of armed men approaching with torches. [H12] He told the apostles that one of that band had betrayed him. This they looked upon as impossible. Jesus repeated this and several other things with calm composure, again exhorted them to console his mother, and said: "Let us go to meet them! I shall deliver myself without resistance into the hands of my enemies." With these words, he left the Garden of Olives with the three apostles and went out to meet the soldiers on the road that separated it from the Garden of Gethsemane.

The blessed Virgin, Magdalene, and Salome, accompanied by some of the disciples who had seen the approach of the soldiers, left the valley of Jehosaphat and returned to the house of Mary Mark. Jesus's enemies came by a shorter route than that by which he had come from the Cenacle.

The grotto in which Jesus prayed that night was not the one in which he usually prayed on the Mount of Olives.

The latter was a more distant cavern of the mountain. It was there that he prayed on the day upon which he cursed the fig tree. He was then in great affliction of spirit, and he prayed with outstretched arms, leaning upon a rock. The impression of his form and hands remained upon the stone, and later on became objects of veneration, although it was not clearly known upon what occasion the marks were made. I have frequently beheld such impressions left upon stone by the prophets of the Old Law, by Jesus, Mary, some of the apostles, the body of St. Catherine of Alexandria on Mount Sinai, and by some other saints. They did not appear to be deep, nor were the lines very clearly defined. They resembled the marks that might be made by pressing upon a piece of solid dough.

Judas and His Band • The Wood of the Cross

AT the beginning of his treasonable career, Judas had really never looked forward to the result that followed upon it. He wanted to obtain the traitor's reward and please the Pharisees by pretending to deliver Jesus into their hands, but he had never counted on things going so far, he never dreamed of Jesus's being brought to judgment and crucified. He was thinking only of the money, and he had for a long time been in communication with some sneaking, spying Pharisees and Sadducees who by flattery were inciting him to treason. He was tired of the fatiguing, wandering, and persecuted life led by the apostles. For several months past he had begun this downward course by stealing the alms committed to his care; and his avarice, excited by Magdalene's lavish anointing of Jesus, urged him on to extremes. He had always counted upon Jesus's establishing a temporal kingdom in which he hoped for some brilliant and lucrative post. But as this was not forthcoming, he turned his thoughts to amassing a fortune. He saw that hardships and persecution were on the increase; and so he thought that before things came to the worst he would ingratiate himself with some of the powerful and distinguished among Jesus's enemies. He saw that Jesus did not become a king, whereas the high priests and prominent men of the temple were people very attractive in his eyes. And so he allowed himself to be drawn into closer communication with their agents, who flattered him in every way and told him in the greatest confidence that under any circumstances an end would soon be put to Jesus's career. During the last few days they followed him to Bethany, and thus he continued to sink deeper and deeper into depravity. He almost ran

his legs off to induce the high priests to come to some conclusion. But they would not come to terms and treated him with great contempt. They told him that the time now intervening before the feast was too short. If any action were taken now, it would create trouble and disturbance on the feast. The Sanhedrin alone paid some degree of attention to his proposals. After his sacrilegious reception of the sacrament, Satan took entire possession of him and he went off at once to complete his horrible crime. He first sought those agents who had until now constantly flattered him and received him with apparent friendship. Some others joined the party, among them Caiaphas and Annas, but the last-named treated him very rudely and scornfully. They were irresolute and mistrustful of the consequences, nor did they appear to place any confidence in Judas.

I saw the kingdom of hell divided against itself. Satan desired the crime of the Jews by the death of the most innocent; he longed for the death of Jesus, the converter of sinners, the holy teacher, the Savior, the just one, whom he hated. But at the same time he experienced a sentiment of fear at the thought of the guiltless death of Jesus, who would make no effort to conceal himself, who would not save himself; he envied him the power of suffering innocently. And so I saw the adversary on the one side stimulating the hatred and fury of Jesus's enemies assembled around the traitor; and on the other, insinuating to some of their number that Judas was a scamp, a knave, that the sentence could not be pronounced before the festival, nor could the requisite number of witnesses against Jesus be brought together.

They expressed opposite views upon the means to lay hold of Jesus, and some of them questioned Judas, saying, "Shall we be able to capture him? Has he not an armed band with him?" The base traitor answered: "No! He is alone with eleven disciples. He himself is greatly dejected and the eleven are quite faint-hearted." He told them also that now was their time to apprehend Jesus, now or never, for later he might not have it in his power to deliver him into their hands, and perhaps he would never return to them. For several days past, he said, and especially on that present day, the other disciples and Jesus himself aimed at him in their words; they appeared to divine what he was about, and if he returned to them again they would certainly murder him. He added that, if they did not seize Jesus now, he would slip away and, returning with a large army of followers, would cause himself to be proclaimed king. By such threats as these, Judas at last succeeded.

They yielded to his proposals to seize Jesus according to his directions, and he received the thirty pieces of silver, the price of his treason. These thirty pieces were of silver in plates, in shape like a tongue. In one end they were pierced with a hole, through which they were strung together with rings into a kind of chain. Each piece bore some impression.

Judas could not help feeling the marked and contemptuous mistrust with which the Pharisees were treating him. Pride and ostentation therefore urged him to present to them as an offering for the temple the money he had just received. By so doing, he thought to appear before them as an upright, disinterested man. But they rejected it as the price of blood, which could not be offered in the temple. Judas felt the cutting contempt, and he was filled with smothered rage. He had not expected such treatment. The consequences of his treachery were already assailing him even before his evil design was accomplished; but he was now too much entangled with his employers, he was in their hands and could not free himself. They watched him closely and would not allow him to leave their sight until he had laid before them the whole plan to be followed in apprehending Jesus. After that, three of the Pharisees went with the traitor down into a hall in which were the soldiers of the temple. None of them were of pure Jewish origin; they were of other and mixed nationalities. When all was agreed upon and the requisite number of soldiers gathered together, Judas, accompanied by a servant of the Pharisees, ran first to the Cenacle in order to see whether Jesus was still there; for if such were the case, they could easily have taken him by setting guards at the door. This information Judas had agreed to send the Pharisees by a messenger.

A short time before, after Judas had received the price of his treason, a Pharisee had gone down and dispatched seven slaves to procure the wood and get Christ's cross ready at once in case he should be judged, for next day, on account of the Passover feast, there would be no time to attend to it. They brought the wood from a distance of about three-quarters of an hour, where it lay near a long, high wall with a quantity of other wood belonging to the temple, and dragged it to a square behind the tribunal of Caiaphas. The trunk of the cross belonged to a tree that once grew in the valley of Jehosaphat near the brook Kidron. Having fallen across the stream, it had long served as a bridge. When Nehemiah hid the sacred fire and the holy vessels in the pool of Bethesda, with other pieces of wood it had been used as a covering; later on, it was again removed and thrown on the side of another wood pile. Partly with the view of deriding the royalty of Jesus, partly by apparent chance—but in reality because such was the

design of God—the cross was formed in a very peculiar way. Together with the inscription, it consisted of five different pieces. I have seen many facts, many different meanings in connection with the cross, but with the exception of what I have related, I have forgotten all.

Judas returned and reported that Jesus was no longer in the Cenacle. He must therefore be in his accustomed place of prayer on the Mount of Olives. Judas urged that only a small number of soldiers might be sent with him, lest the disciples, who were everywhere on the watch, should perceive something unusual and raise a protest. Three hundred men were to be stationed at the gates and in the streets of Ophel, a part of the city to the south of the temple, and along the valley of Millo as far as the house of Annas on Zion. They were to be in readiness to send reinforcements if necessary, for, as Judas reminded the Pharisees, Jesus counted all the rabble of Ophel among his followers. The infamous traitor told them also how careful they must be that he might not escape them, and recalled the fact of his often, by some mysterious means, suddenly becoming invisible and concealing himself in the mountains from his companions. He recommended them, moreover, to bind him with a chain and to make use of certain magical means to prevent his breaking his bonds. The Jews rejected his advice with scorn, saying: "We are not to be dictated to by you. When we get him, we shall hold him fast."

Judas arranged with the soldiers that he would enter the garden before them, kiss and salute Jesus as a friend and disciple coming to him on some business; then they were to step forward and take him into custody. He wanted to behave as if their coming coincided accidentally with his own, for he thought that after the betrayal he would take to flight like the other disciples and be heard of no more. He likewise thought that perhaps a tumult would ensue in which the apostles would defend themselves and Jesus would disappear as he had often done before. These thoughts especially occupied him now that he was thoroughly vexed at the contemptuous and distrustful manner of Jesus's enemies toward him, but not because his evil deed caused him remorse or the thought of Jesus touched him, for he had wholly given himself over to Satan.

He was very desirous also that the soldiers immediately following him should not carry chains and fetters, or that any notoriously infamous characters should appear in the party. The soldiers pretended to accede to his wishes, though in reality they regarded him as a dishonorable traitor of whom they had need, but who was not to be trusted and who was to be cast off when no longer of use. They had received special instructions to keep a close watch on him, and not to let him out of their sight and custody until they had taken Jesus and bound him; for he had received his pay and it was feared that the rascal would run off with the money and in the darkness of night they would either not capture Jesus at all, or else take another instead of him. In this case, nothing would come of their undertaking but disturbance and excitement on the Passover feast. The band that had been chosen for Jesus's apprehension was composed of about twenty soldiers, some of whom belonged to the temple guard, and others were in the employ of Annas and Caiaphas. Their dress was almost like that of the Roman soldiers. They wore helmets, and from their doublets hung leathern straps around their hips just like the Romans. The principal difference between them, however, was in their beard, for the Roman soldiers in Jerusalem wore whiskers only, their chin and upper lip being shaved. All of the twenty carried swords, and only a few were armed with spears also. Some bore lanterns mounted on long poles, while others carried torches of sticks smeared with pitch, but when they approached, only one of the lanterns was lighted. The Pharisees had intended sending a larger band with Judas, but he objected that so large a crowd would attract notice, since the Mount of Olives commanded a view of the whole valley. The greater part of them, therefore, remained in Ophel. Sentinels were stationed around here and there on the byroads, as well as in the city, in order to prevent a tumult or any attempt at rescue.

Judas went forward with the twenty soldiers, followed at some distance by four common executioners of the lowest grade, who carried ropes and fetters. Some steps behind these came those six agents with whom Judas had for a short time past been in communication. Of these one was a priest, a confidential friend of Annas; another was devoted to Caiaphas; the third and fourth were Pharisees; and the remaining two were agents of the Sadducees and at the same time Herodians. All were spies, sneaking fellows, cringing eye-servants of Annas and Caiaphas, and in secret the most malicious enemies of the Savior. The twenty soldiers accompanied Judas in a friendly manner until they reached the place where the road divided between the Garden of Gethsemane and that of Olives. Here they refused to allow him to advance alone. They adopted quite another tone, and acted toward him insolently and saucily.

The Arrest of the Lord

WHEN Jesus with the three apostles went out upon the road between Gethsemane and the Garden of Olives, there appeared at the entrance, about twenty paces ahead, Judas and the band of soldiers, between whom a quarrel had arisen. Judas wanted to separate from the soldiers and go forward alone to Jesus, as if he were a friend returning after an absence. They were to follow, and act in such a way as to make it appear that their coming was altogether unknown to him. But they would not agree to his proposal. They held him fast, exclaiming: "Not so, friend! Thou shalt not escape us, until we have the Galilean!" And when they caught sight of the eight apostles, who at sound of the noise came forth from the Garden of Gethsemane, they called up four of the soldiers to their assistance. But this Judas by no means assented to, and a lively dispute arose between him and the soldiers. When Jesus and the three apostles, by the light of the torches, distinguished the armed and wrangling band, Peter wished to repel them by force. He exclaimed: "Lord, the eight from Gethsemane are close at hand. Let us make an attack on the soldiers!" But Jesus told him to hold his peace, and took a few steps with them back on the road to a green plot. Judas, seeing his plans quite upset, was filled with rage and spite. Just at this moment, four of the disciples issued from the Garden of Gethsemane and inquired what was going on. Judas began to exchange words with them, and would fain have cleared himself by a lie, but the guards would not allow him to go on. These four last-comers were James the Less, Philip, Thomas, and Nathaniel. The last-named, who was a son of the aged Simeon, had along with several others been sent by Jesus's friends to the eight apostles in the Garden of Gethsemane to find out what was going on. They were actuated as much by anxiety as by curiosity.

With the exception of these four, all the disciples were straggling around in the distance, furtively on the lookout to discover what they could.

Jesus took some steps toward the band and said in a loud, distinct voice: "Whom seek ye?" The leaders answered: "Jesus of Nazareth," whereupon Jesus replied: "I am he." But scarcely had he uttered the words when, as if suddenly attacked by convulsions, they crowded back and fell to the ground one upon another. Judas, who was still standing by them, became more and more embarrassed. He looked as if desirous of approaching Jesus; consequently the Lord extended his hand, saying: "Friend, whereto art thou come?" Judas, confused and perplexed, stammered out something about a commission he had executed. Jesus in reply uttered some words like the following: "Oh, how much better it would have been for thee hadst thou never been born!"—I cannot remember the words distinctly. Meanwhile the soldiers had risen and approached the Lord and his apostles, awaiting the traitor's sign, the kiss.

Peter and the other disciples gathered around Judas, calling him a thief and a traitor. He tried to free himself by all kinds of excuses, but just at that moment up came the soldiers with offers of protection, thus openly witnessing against him.

Jesus again inquired: "Whom seek ye?" Turning toward him, they again answered: "Jesus of Nazareth." Jesus again replied: "I am he. I have already told you that I am he. If you seek me, let these go." At the words, "I am he," the soldiers fell to the ground a second time. [H13] They writhed as if struck with epilepsy, and Judas was again surrounded by the other apostles, for they were exasperated to a degree against him. Jesus now called out to the soldiers: "Arise"—and they arose, full of terror. Judas was still struggling with the apostles, who were pressing up against the guards. The latter turned upon them and freed the traitor, urging him anew to give them the sign agreed upon. They had been ordered to seize no one but him whom Judas would kiss. Judas now approached Jesus, embraced him and kissed him with the words: "Hail, Rabbi!" [H14] Jesus said: "Judas, dost thou betray the Son of Man with a kiss?" The soldiers instantly formed a circle around Jesus, and, drawing near, laid hands upon him. Judas wanted at once to flee, but the apostles would not allow him. They rushed upon the soldiers, crying out: "Lord, shall we strike with the sword?" Peter, more impetuous than the rest, seized the sword and struck at Malchus, the servant of the high priest, who was trying to drive them back, and cut off a piece of his ear. Malchus fell to the ground, thereby increasing the confusion. [H15]

At the moment of Peter's impetuous movement, the actors in the scene were situated as follows: Jesus was in the hands of the guard, who were about to bind him, and forming a circle around him at some little distance were the soldiers, one of whose number, Malchus, had been laid low by Peter. The other soldiers were engaged, some in driving back the disciples that were approaching too near, and some in pursuing those that had taken to flight. Four of the disciples were wandering around, timidly showing themselves only here and there in the distance. The soldiers were still too much alarmed by their late fall, and too much afraid of weakening the circle around Jesus, to make any very active pursuit. Judas, who immediately after his traitorous kiss wanted to make his escape, was met on his way by some of the disciples, who overwhelmed him with reproaches. Six official functionaries hastened to his rescue, while the four guards were busy around Jesus with cords and bands, being on the point of binding him.

This was the state of affairs when Peter struck down Malchus, and Jesus said: "Peter, put up thy sword, for whoever takes the sword shall perish by the sword. Thinkest thou that I cannot ask my Father to send me more than twelve legions of angels? Shall I not drink the chalice that

my Father has given me? How will the scriptures be fulfilled if it shall not thus be done?" Then he added: "Suffer me to heal the man!" And going to Malchus, he touched his ear and prayed, and at the same moment it was healed. [H16] The guard, the executioners, and the six officers surrounded Jesus. They mocked him, saying to the crowd: "He has dealings with the devil. It was by witchcraft that the ear appeared to be cut off, and now by witchcraft it appears to be healed."

Then Jesus addressed them: "Ye are come out with spears and clubs to apprehend me as if I were a murderer. I have daily taught among you in the temple, and ye dared not lay hands upon me; but this is your hour and the hour of darkness." They ordered him to be bound still more securely, and said to him deridingly: "Thou couldst not overthrow us by thy sorcery!" And the executioners said: "We shall deprive thee of thy skill!" Jesus made some reply that I cannot recall, and the disciples fled on all sides. The four executioners and the six Pharisees did not fall to the ground, nor did they in consequence rise again. The reason of this was revealed to me. They were in the same rank as Judas, that is, entirely in the power of Satan. Judas did not fall at the words of Jesus, although he was standing among the soldiers. All those that fell and rose up again were afterward converted and became Christians. Their falling and rising were symbolical of their conversion. They had not laid hands upon Jesus; they merely stood around him. Malchus was, after his healing, already converted to such a degree that he only kept up appearances in respect to the service he owed the high priest; and during the following hours, those of Jesus's Passion, he ran backward and forward to Mary and the other friends, giving them news of all that was taking place.

The executioners bound Jesus with the greatest rudeness and barbarous brutality, the Pharisees meanwhile uttering insolent and scornful words. The executioners were pagans of the very lowest class. Their necks, legs, and arms were naked; their loins were girded with a sort of bandage, and they wore a short jerkin without sleeves, fastened at the sides with straps. They were short, stout, very active, with a brownish-red complexion like the Egyptian slaves.

They bound Jesus's hands upon his breast in a cruel manner. With sharp new cords, they pitilessly fastened the wrist of the right hand to the left forearm just below the elbow and that of the left hand to the right forearm. They put around his waist a broad girdle armed with sharp points, and bound his hands again with links of willow, or osier, which were fixed to the girdle. Around his neck they laid a collar in which were points and other instruments to wound, and from it depended two straps, which like a stole were crossed over the breast and bound down to the girdle so tightly that the neck was not free to move. At four points of this girdle were fastened four long ropes, by means of which the executioners could drag our Lord hither and thither according to their wicked will. All the fetters were perfectly new. They appeared to have been especially prepared, when the plan was formed of apprehending Jesus, for the purpose to which they were now being put.

And now, after several more torches had been lighted, the pitiable procession was set in motion. First went ten of the guard, then followed the executioners dragging Jesus by the ropes; next came the scoffing Pharisees, and the ten other soldiers closed the procession. The disciples were still straying about wailing and lamenting, as if bereft of their senses. John, however, was following rather closely behind the last of the guards. The Pharisees, seeing him, ordered him to be seized. At this command, some of the guard turned and hurried after him. But he fled from them, and when they laid hold of the linen scarf he wore around his neck, he loosened it quickly and thus effected his escape. He had laid aside his mantle, retaining nothing but a short, sleeveless undergarment, that he might be able to flee more easily. Around his neck, head, and arms, however, he was enveloped in that long, narrow scarf which the Jews were accustomed to wear.

The executioners dragged and ill-used Jesus in the most cruel manner. They exercised upon him all kinds of malice, and this principally from a base deference and desire to please the six officials, who were full of rage and venom against him. They led him along the roughest roads, over ruts and stones and mire, keeping the long ropes stretched while they themselves sought good paths. In this way Jesus had to go wherever the ropes would allow him. His tormentors carried in their hands knotted cords with which they struck him, as a butcher might do the animal he was leading to slaughter. All this they accompanied with mockery and insult so low and indecent that the repetition of it would be revolting.

Jesus was barefoot. Besides the usual undergarment, he wore a seamless, woollen shirt, or blouse, and over that an outside robe. The undergarment of the disciples, like that of the Jews in general, consisted of a scapular that fell before and behind over the breast and shoulders. It was made of two pieces fastened together on the shoulder by straps, but open at the sides. The lower part of the body was covered with a girdle from which hung four lappets which, after being wound around the loins, formed a sort of trousers. I must not forget to say that, at the apprehension of the Lord, I saw no written order. His enemies went to work as if he were an outlaw, a person beyond the pale of the law.

Narrow Village Street

The procession moved on at a hurried pace. When it left the road between the Garden of Olives and the pleasure garden of Gethsemane, it turned for a short distance to the right on the west side of Gethsemane, until it reached a bridge that there crossed the brook Kidron. When Jesus was coming with the apostles to the Mount of Olives, he did not cross that bridge. He took a round-about way through the valley of Jehosaphat and crossed the brook over a bridge farther to the south. That over which he was now led in fetters was very long, since it spanned not only the Kidron, which flowed here close to the mount, but also a part of the uneven heights of the valley, thus forming a paved highway for transportation. Even before the procession reached the bridge, I saw Jesus fall to the earth twice, owing to the pitiless manner in which he was dragged along and the jerking of the executioners at the ropes. But when they reached the middle of the bridge, they exercised their villainy upon him with still greater malice. The executioners pushed poor, fettered Jesus, whom they held fast with ropes, from the bridge into the brook Kidron, about the height of a man below, [H17] accompanying their brutality with abusive words, as for instance: "Now he can drink his fill!" Were it not for divine assistance, Jesus would have been killed by the fall. He fell first on his knees and then on his face, so that he would have been severely wounded on the stony bed of the brook, which was here very shallow, if he had not saved himself a little by stretching out his previously tightly bound hands. They had been loosened from the girdle, I know not whether by divine help or whether by the executioners before they thrust him down. The marks of his knees, feet, elbows, and fingers were, by God's will, impressed upon the places that they touched, which later on became objects of veneration. Such things are no longer believed, but similar impressions in stone, made by the feet, the hands, and the knees of the patriarchs and prophets, made by Jesus, the blessed Virgin, and some of the saints, have often been shown me in historical visions. The rocks were softer and more believing than the hearts of men; they bore witness at this terrible moment to the divine Truth that had thus impressed them.

I had not seen Jesus take anything to drink in the vehement thirst that consumed him after his awful agony in the Garden of Olives. But when pushed into the Kidron, I saw him drinking with difficulty and, at the same time, I heard him murmuring that thereby was fulfilled a prophetic verse from the Psalms, which bore reference to drinking from the torrent by the way (Ps. cviii).

Meanwhile the executioners relaxed not their hold on the long ropes that bound Jesus; and since it would have been difficult for them to draw him up again, and a wall on the opposite shore rendered it impossible for them to allow him to wade across, they dragged him by means of the ropes back through the Kidron. Then they went down

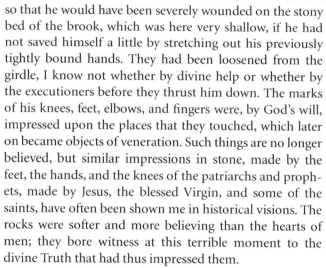

April 2, A.D. 33
Thursday Night 11:45 PM

themselves and hauled him up backwards over the high bank. And now, amid mocking and cursing, kicking and striking, those miserable wretches dragged poor Jesus forward with the ropes, a second time over the long bridge. His long, woollen garment, heavy with water, clung so closely around his limbs that he could scarcely walk; and when he reached the opposite end of the bridge, he sank once more to the earth. They pulled him up again, striking him with the cords and, with shameful and mocking words, tucked up his wet garment into the girdle. They said, for example, something about his girding himself for the eating of the paschal lamb, and similar mockery.

It was not yet midnight when I saw the four executioners dragging Jesus over a rugged, narrow road, along which ran only an uneven footpath. They dragged him over sharp stones and fragments of rocks, through thorns and thistles, inhumanly hurrying him on with curses and blows. The six brutal Pharisees were, wherever the road permitted it, always in his vicinity. Each carried in his hand a different kind of torturing stick, with which he tormented him, thrusting him, goading him on, or beating him with it.

While the executioners were dragging Jesus, his naked feet bleeding, over sharp stones, thorns, and thistles, the scornful satirical speeches of the six Pharisees were piercing his loving heart. It was at these moments they made use of such mockery as: "His precursor, the Baptist, did not prepare a good way for him here!" or: "Why does he not raise John from the dead that he may prepare the way for him?" Such were the taunts uttered by these ignominious creatures and received with rude shouts of laughter. They were caught up in turn by the executioners, who were incited thus to load poor Jesus with fresh ill-usage.

After the soldiers had driven the Lord forward for some time, they noticed several persons lurking around here and there in the distance. They were disciples who, upon the report of Jesus's arrest, had come from Bethphage and other hiding places, to spy around and see how it was faring with their Master. At sight of them, Jesus's enemies became anxious, lest they should make a sudden attack and rescue him; therefore they signalled by a call to Ophel, a little place in the environs of Jerusalem, to send a reinforcement, as had been agreed upon.

The procession was still distant some minutes from the entrance which, to the south of the temple, led through Ophel to Mount Zion, upon which Annas and Caiaphas dwelt, when I saw a band of fifty soldiers issuing from the gate, in order to reinforce their companions. They came forward in three groups: the first was ten strong; the last, fifteen, for I counted them; and the middle group, five and twenty. They bore several torches. They were bold and wanton in their bearing, and they shouted and hurrahed as they came along, as if to announce themselves to the approaching band and to congratulate them on their success. Their coming was a noisy one. At the moment in which the foremost band joined Jesus's escort, a slight confusion arose, and I saw Malchus and several others drop out of the rear and slip off in the direction of the Mount of Olives.

When this shouting band hurried from Ophel by torchlight to meet the approaching procession, the disciples lurking around dispersed in all directions. [H18] I saw that the blessed Virgin, in her trouble and anguish, with Martha, Magdalene, Mary Cleophas, Mary Salome, Mary Mark, Susanna, Johanna Chusa, Veronica, and Salome, again directed her steps to the valley of Jehosaphat. They were to the south of Gethsemane, opposite that part of the Mount of Olives where was another grotto in which Jesus had formerly been accustomed to pray. I saw Lazarus, John Mark, Veronica's son, and Simeon's son with them. The last-named, along with Nathaniel, had been in Gethsemane with the eight apostles, and had fled across when the tumult began. They brought news to the blessed Virgin. Meanwhile they heard the cries and saw the torches of the two bands as they met. The blessed Virgin was in uninterrupted contemplation of Jesus's torments and sympathetic suffering with her divine Son. She allowed the holy women to lead her back part of the way so that, when the tumultuous procession should have passed, she might again return to the house of Mary Mark.

The fifty soldiers belonged to a company of three hundred men who had been sent at once to guard the gates and streets of Ophel and its surroundings, for Judas the traitor had drawn the high priest's attention to the fact that the inhabitants of Ophel, who were mostly poor artisans, day laborers, and carriers of wood and water to the temple, were the most attached partisans of Jesus. It might easily be feared therefore that some attempt would be made to free him as he passed through. The traitor knew very well that Jesus had here bestowed upon many of the poor laborers consolation, instruction, healing, and alms. It was also here in Ophel that Jesus had tarried when, after the murder of John the Baptist in Machaerus, he was journeying back from Bethany to Hebron. He had paused awhile to console John's friends, and he had healed many of the poor day laborers and brick carriers who had been wounded at the overthrow of the great building and the tower of Siloam. Most of these people, after the descent of the Holy Spirit, joined the Christian community, and

when the separation of the Christians from the Jews took place and several settlements of the former were erected, they pitched their tents and built their huts across the valley as far as the Mount of Olives. Stephen resided there at that time. Ophel was on a hill south of the temple. It was surrounded by walls and inhabited principally by day laborers. It appeared to me to be not much smaller than Dulmen.†

The good inhabitants of Ophel were roused by the shouts of the garrison as their companions entered. They hurried from their houses and pressed to the streets and gates held by the soldiers, asking the cause of the uproar. But here they met with a rough reception. The military rabble, made up of a mixture of low, insolent slaves, roughly and jeeringly drove them back to their dwellings. But as here and there they heard such remarks as these: "Jesus, the evildoer, your false prophet, is about to be led in a prisoner. The high priests will put an end to his proceedings. He will have to pay the penalty of the cross," the whole place was roused from sleep by the loud cries and lamentations of the people. The poor creatures, men and women, ran about wailing or, with outstretched arms, cast themselves on their knees, crying to heaven and lauding Jesus's good deeds. The soldiers, thrusting them and dealing blows on all sides, drove them back to their homes, at the same time insulting Jesus, and saying: "Here is an evident proof that he is an agitator of the people!" They were, however, a little cautious in acting with the populace, through fear of rousing them by greater violence to open insurrection; consequently, they aimed only at clearing the streets by which the procession was to pass through Ophel.

Meanwhile the ill-used Jesus and his barbarous escort came nearer and nearer to the gates of Ophel. Our Lord had repeatedly fallen to the earth, and he now appeared utterly unable to proceed farther. Taking advantage of this, a compassionate soldier said: "You see for yourselves that the poor man can go no farther. If we are to take him alive before the high priests, we must loosen the cords that bind his hands, that he may be able to support himself when he falls." While the procession halted for the executioners to loosen the cords, another good-hearted soldier brought him a drink of water from a neighboring well. He scooped it up in a vessel made of bark formed into the shape of a cone, such as soldiers and travelers carried about them in that country as drinking vessels. When Jesus said to this man a few words of acknowledgment, uttering at the same time some prophetic expressions about "drinking from

† A small town in Westphalia, where Anne Catherine lived at this time.

living fountains," and "the streams of living waters," the Pharisees mocked and reviled him, accusing him of vain boasting and blasphemy. He ought, they said, to give up his empty talk. He should never again give drink to a beast, much less to a human being. It was shown me that the two compassionate soldiers, through whose intervention his bands had been loosened and he had received a drink, were suddenly illuminated by grace. After Jesus's

with ropes, urged on with blows, like a poor, fainting animal driven to sacrifice by insolent, half-naked executioners and overbearing soldiers. The latter were busy keeping off the crowd of lamenting and grateful people who were making their way to see Jesus, who were stretching out to him hands that he had cured of lameness, who were crying after him in supplicating tones with tongues that he had loosened from muteness, who were gazing after him with

Valley of Kidron (Mar Saba)

death they were converted, and later on joined the community in the capacity of disciples. I once knew their names, also those that they afterward bore as disciples, and their whole history, but it would be impossible to remember all that. It is too much.

The procession again started forward, Jesus being illtreated as before, and crossed a height up to the gates of Ophel. Here it was received by the heartrending cries and lamentations of the inhabitants, who were bound to Jesus by a debt of gratitude. Only with great difficulty could the soldiers keep back the crowds of men and women pressing from all sides. They rushed forward wringing their hands, falling on their knees and, with outstretched arms, crying aloud: "Release unto us this man! Who will help us? Who will heal us? Who will console us? Release unto us this man!" It was a heartrending spectacle—Jesus pale, bruised, and disfigured, his hair torn, his robe wet and soiled, tucked up into his girdle, he himself dragged

eyes to which he had restored vision and which were now streaming with tears.

Already in the Valley of Kidron numbers of filthy, ragged creatures from the lowest classes, excited by the soldiers and urged on by the followers of Annas, Caiaphas, and other enemies of Jesus, joined the procession with cries of mockery and derision. These newcomers now added their share of jeers and insults against the good people of Ophel. Ophel was built on a hill, for I saw in the center of it the highest point. It was an open place, and on it were all kinds of beams and rafters for building, like piles of wood in a carpenter yard. The procession now reached another gate in the wall through which it wound somewhat downward.

The people were prevented from following it beyond the city limits. The road now led somewhat into a valley. On the right stood a large building, I think the remains of Solomon's works, and to the left lay the pool of Bethesda.

After passing these, they kept on in a westerly direction down a steep street called Millo and then, turning a little to the south, they ascended a flight of high steps to the Mount of Zion, upon which was the house of Annas. Along the way our Lord was abused and reviled, while the rabble that kept pouring from the city incited his vile custodians to multiplied cruelties. From the Mount of Olives to this point, Jesus fell to the ground seven times.

The inhabitants of Ophel were still full of terror and distress when a new scene excited their compassion. The blessed Mother was, by the holy women and their friends, led through Ophel from the Valley of Kidron to the house of Mary Mark, which stood at the foot of Mount Zion. When the good people recognized her, their compassion was aroused and they sent up a wail of anguish. So great a crowd pressed around Mary and her companions that the mother of Jesus was almost carried in their arms.

Mary was speechless with grief. She did not open her lips after she reached the house of Mary Mark until the arrival of John. Then she began to ask questions and to give vent to her grief. John related to her everything that he had seen happen to Jesus from the moment that they left the Cenacle up to the present. A little later she was conducted to Martha's house near that of Lazarus at the west side of the city. They led her along unfrequented routes, in order to shun those by which Jesus was being dragged, and thus spare her the anguish of a meeting with him.

Peter and John, who were following the procession at some distance, [H19] ran hurriedly when it entered the city to some of the good acquaintances whom John had among the servants of the high priests, to find in some way an opportunity of entering the judgment hall into which their Master would soon be brought. These acquaintances of John were messengers attached to the court. They had now to scour the whole town in order to awaken the ancients of different ranks and many other personages, and call them to the council. They desired very much to please the two apostles, but could think of no other means of doing so than by supplying them with mantles such as they themselves wore and letting hem assist in calling the members of the council; then under cover of the mantle they might enter with them into the judgment hall of Caiaphas, from which all were to be excluded but the bribed rabble, the soldiers, and false witnesses. Nicodemus, Joseph of Arimathea, and other well-disposed individuals belonged to the council, so that the apostles were able to deliver the summons to their Master's friends, the only ones whom the Pharisees had perhaps designedly omitted from the list of the invited. Judas meanwhile, the devil at his side, like a frantic malefactor was wandering around the steep, wild prec-ipices south of Jerusalem where all the filth of the city was thrown.

Means Taken by Jesus's Enemies for Carrying Out Their Designs

AS soon as Jesus was taken into custody, Annas and Caiaphas were informed of the fact and they began actively to arrange their plans. The courts were lighted up and all the entrances provided with guards. Messengers were dispatched to all parts of the city to summon the members of the council, the scribes, and all those that had anything to do with the trial. Many of them, however, as soon as the compact with Judas was completed, had already assembled at the house of Caiaphas and were there awaiting the result. The ancients from the three classes of citizens were also called; and as the Pharisees, the Sadducees and the Herodians from all parts of the country had been for some days gathered in Jerusalem for the feast, they discussed among themselves and before the High Council the design of seizing Jesus. The high priests now selected from the lists in their possession those whom they knew to be his most bitter enemies. These they summoned with the command to gather up, each in his own circle, all the evidence and proofs against Jesus they possibly could, and to bring them to the judgment court. Just at this time, all the Pharisees and Sadducees and other wicked people from Nazareth, Capernaum, Thirza, Gabara, Jotopata, Shiloh, and other places, whom Jesus had so often, by exposing the truth, put to shame before the people, were assembled in Jerusalem. They were filled with rage and vengeance. Each hunted up some scoundrel among the Passover guests from his own country, and bribed him with money to cry out against and calumniate Jesus. These guests were gathered in bands, according to their respective districts. But with the exception of some evident lies and bitter invectives, nothing could be brought forward but those accusations upon which in their own synagogues Jesus had so often silenced them.

All these now gathered, one after another, in the judgment hall of Caiaphas. There, too, assembled the mass of Jesus's enemies from among the haughty Pharisees and scribes, along with their suborned witnesses from Jerusalem itself. Many of those exasperated vendors whom he had driven from the temple; many a puffed-up doctor whom he had there silenced before the people; and perhaps many a one who had not yet forgotten that he had been instructed and put to shame by him when, as a boy of twelve, he had taught for the first time in the temple, were now here arrayed against him. Among his enemies were also impenitent sinners whom he had refused to heal; relapsing sinners who had again become sick; conceited youths whom he would not receive as disciples; wicked avaricious persons who were exasperated at his distributing to the poor the money that they were in hopes of getting for themselves; rascals whose companions he had converted; debauchees and adulterers whose victims he had won over to virtue; covetous heirs who had been disappointed in their expectations by the cure of those from whom they expected to inherit; and many venal time-servers ever ready to pander to wickedness. These emissaries of Satan were brimful of rage against everything holy, and consequently against the Holy of Holies. This scum of the Jewish people assembled for the feast, urged on by the chief enemies of Jesus, pressed forward from all sides and rushed in a continuous stream to the palace of Caiaphas in order falsely to accuse the true Paschal Lamb of God, the spotless one, who had taken upon himself the sins of the world; and to cast upon him their foul consequences which, indeed, he had really assumed, which he was then enduring, and for which he was atoning.

While this miserable Jewish rabble was seeking after some way by which to sully the pure Savior, many devout souls and friends of Jesus were going around in trouble and anguish of heart (for they were ignorant of the mystery about to be accomplished), sighing and listening to all that they could hear. If they uttered a word, they were repulsed by the bystanders; and if they kept silence, they were regarded as disaffected. Many well-meaning, but weak, simple-minded people were scandalized at what they saw and heard. They yielded to temptation and fell away from their faith. The number of those that persevered was not great. Things were then as they are now. Many a one was willing to bear the semblance of a good Christian so long as no inconvenience resulted from it, but became ashamed of the cross when they saw it held in contempt. Still, many in the beginning of these unfounded, these unjust proceedings whose fury and base cruelty cried to heaven for vengeance, seeing the uncomplaining patience of the Savior, were touched at heart, and they walked away silent and dejected.

Glance at Jerusalem at this Hour

THE LARGE and densely populated city, now increased in extent by the numerous camps of the Passover guests stretching out around it, was, after the multiplied private and public prayers, religious exercises, and other preparations for the feast, sunk in sleep, when the news of the arrest roused alike the foes and friends of the Lord. Numbers immediately responded to the summons of the high priests, and the various points of the city began to present a lively scene. They hurried, some by moonlight, others with torches, through the streets—which in Jerusalem were generally dismal and desolate at night, for the windows and doors of most of the houses opened into their inner courts. All turned their steps in the direction of Zion, from whose height glimmered the light of torches. The report of what had just taken place soon spread around, and here and there might be heard knocking at courtyard gates to rouse the sleepers within. Bustle, talking, and confusion were going on in many sections of the city. Servants and newsmongers were hurrying to and fro in search of news, which they hastened to report to those by whom they had been sent. Heavy bars and bolts were shoved with a clang before many a gate, for the people were full of anxiety and in dread of a revolt. Here and there they stepped to the doors and called out to some acquaintance who was passing for news; or the latter, as he hurried by, shouted the desired information. Then were heard malicious speeches, such as are made nowadays on similar occasions. They said: "Now will Lazarus and his sisters see with whom they have been dealing. Johanna Chusa, Susanna, Mary Mark, and Salome will now regret their conduct, but too late! And how humbled will Sirach's wife Seraphia [Veronica] appear before her husband, who so often forbade her having anything to do with the Galilean! The followers of this seditious leader, this visionary, always looked with pity upon those that entertained views other than their own—and now many a one of them will not know where to hide his head. Who would now be seen strewing palm branches and spreading mantles and veils under the feet of the animal he rides? Those hypocrites, who always wanted to be better than others, will now receive their due. They too will be brought up to trial, for they are all implicated in the affairs of the Galilean. The matter is more deeply rooted than is generally thought. I am anxious to see how Nicodemus and Joseph of Arimathea will comport themselves. They have long been looked upon with a mistrustful eye, for they make common cause with Lazarus, but they are very cunning. Now all will come to light." Many were heard to speak in this way. They were persons embittered against certain families, and especially against those women who up till now had borne public witness to Jesus and his followers. In other places, the news was received in a very different way. Some were frightened at it, some bewailed it in private, while others timidly hunted up a friend in sympathy with themselves in order to pour out their heart. But only a few ventured to express such sympathy openly and decidedly.

All quarters of the city, however, were not aroused, only those parts to which the messengers had brought the invitation to the trial and those in which the Pharisees sought

1. Bethlehem Gate
2. Citadel
3. Hippicus Tower
4. Phasael Tower
5. Mirianne Tower
6. A Palace of Herod
7. Jesus's Grave
8. Ephraim Gate
9. Way of the Cross
10. Golgotha
11. Herod Agrippa's Wall
12. Damascus Gate
13. Benjamin Gate
14. To Citadel of David
15. Suburb of David
16. Suburb of Akra
17. House of Veronica
18. House of Caiphas
19. Suburb of Bezetha
20. A Palace of Herod
21. Forum
22. Cattle Market
23. Pool of Bethesda
24. Sheep Gate
25. Sepulchers
26. Citadel of Antonia
27. House of Worship
28. Temple Courtyard
29. Nicanor's Gate
30. Priests' Quarters
31. Women's Courtyard
32. Synedrion
33. Assembly Hall
34. Golden Gate?
35. Hall of Solomon
36. Golden Gate?
37. Pinnacle of Temple
38. Court of Gentiles
39. Royal Hall
40. Hulda Double-Gate
41. Hulda Triple-Gate
42. Temple Hill Ophel
43. Siloah Tower
44. Hippodrome
45. Houses, Lower City
46. Zion Suburb
47. Lower City
48. Brook Kidron
49. Road to Bethany
50. Water Gate
51. Well of Mary
52. Way to Pool
    of Bethesda
53. Bridge to Upper City

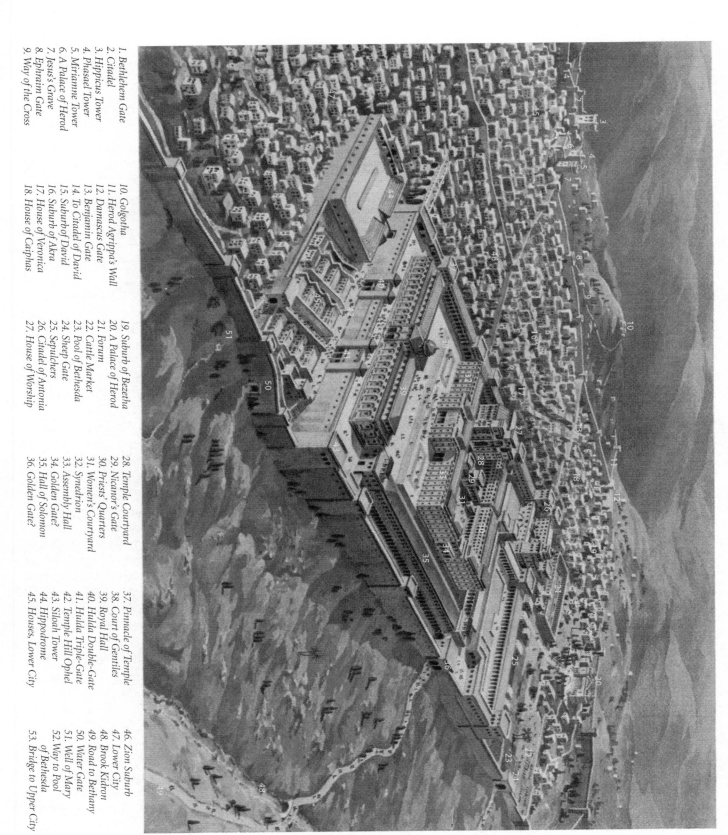

The Temple and its Environs at the Time of Christ

104

their false witnesses. The streets in the direction of Zion were of all others the most alive. It seemed as if one saw in different parts of Jerusalem sparks of hatred and fury bursting forth, flames rushing along the streets, uniting with others, becoming stronger and more powerful until at last, like a whirlwind of lurid fire, they flashed up Mount Zion and into the judgment hall of Caiaphas. In some quarters all was still at peace, but there too, by degrees, things became stirring.

The Roman soldiers took no part in what was going on, but their posts were strengthened and their cohorts drawn up together. They kept a sharp lookout on all sides. This indeed they always did at the Passover time, on account of the great multitude come together to the feast. They were quiet, and self-possessed, but at the same time very much on their guard. The people who were now hurrying forward shunned the points at which the sentinels were stationed, for it was always vexatious to the Pharisaical Jews to be accosted by them. The high priests had sent a message to Pilate telling him why they had stationed soldiers around Ophel and one quarter of Zion, but he and they were full of mutual distrust. Pilate slept not. He passed the night listening to reports and issuing orders. His wife, however, lay stretched upon her couch. Her sleep, though heavy, was disturbed. She sighed and wept as if in troubled dreams.

In no part of the city was sympathy with Jesus so touching as in Ophel among the poor temple slaves and day laborers who dwelt on that hill. Terror came upon them so suddenly in the stillness of the night, and the violence of the proceedings roused them from sleep. There they saw their holy teacher, their benefactor, who had healed and nourished them, torn and ill-used, passing like a fearful vision before them. Their sympathy and grief gathered fresh strength upon beholding his afflicted mother wandering about with her friends. Ah, what a sad sight to see that mother pierced with anguish hurrying through the streets at midnight with the holy women, the friends of Jesus, from one acquaintance's house to another, their hearts beating with fear at being out at so unusual an hour! They were often obliged to hide in corners from some rude band that was passing; frequently were they insulted as women of bad character; more than once they heard bitter, malicious speeches against Jesus, and rarely a compassionate word. Reaching at last their place of refuge, they sank down completely exhausted, shedding tears and wringing their hands. They were all equally distressed; and yet each tried to support her fainting neighbor in her arms, or else sat apart in deep affliction, her head enveloped and resting on her knees. And now came a knock at the door. The women heard it anxiously. The rap was gentle and timid.

No enemy raps in that manner. The holy women open the door, though not without some feeling of dread, and welcome a friend or the servant of some friend of their Lord and Master. They gather round him with questions, and hear what fills them with fresh sorrow. They can no longer remain quiet, and so they again hurry out into the streets to seek for news of Jesus, though soon to return with renewed grief.

Most of the apostles and disciples were now timidly wandering in the valleys near and around Jerusalem, and hiding in the caves on the Mount of Olives. They started at one another's approach, asked in low tones for news, and the sound of every footstep interrupted their anxious communications. They often changed their place of concealment, and some of them ventured to approach the city. Others stole away to the camps of the Passover guests, there to inquire for news from acquaintances belonging to their own part of the country, or to send scouts into the city for a similar purpose. Others again climbed to the top of Mount Zion and gazed anxiously at the torches moving to and fro on Zion, listened to the distant sounds, formed a thousand conjectures as to the cause, and then hurried down into the valley with the hope of getting some certain intelligence.

The stillness of the night began to be more and more interrupted by the din and bustle around the court of Caiaphas. This quarter was brilliantly lighted up with torches and burning pitch lamps, while from all around the city sounded the bellowing of the numerous beasts of burden and animals for sacrifice belonging to the multitudes of strangers now in the Passover quarters. Ah, how touching was the sound of the bleating of the gentle, innocent, helpless lambs! It was heard throughout the night from countless little victims which were next morning to be slaughtered in the temple. One alone was offered because he himself willed it. Like a sheep led to the slaughter, he opened not his mouth; and like a lamb mute before the shearers, he opened not his mouth. That pure, spotless Paschal Lamb was Jesus Christ!

Above these scenes on earth was spread a sky whose appearance was strikingly dark and lowering. The moon sailed on with a threatening aspect, red, her disc covered with spots. She appeared, as it were, sick and in dread, as if shuddering at the prospect of becoming full, for then it was that Jesus was to be put to death. Outside the city to the south, in the steep, wild, and dismal Valley of Hinnom, wandering companionless through accursed, swampy places filled with ordure and refuse, lashed by his guilty conscience, fleeing from his own shadow, hunted by Satan, was Judas Iscariot, the traitor—while thousands of evil spirits were hurrying around on all sides urging men on to wickedness and entangling them in sin. Hell was let loose, and everywhere were its inmates tempting humankind to evil. The burden of the Lamb grew heavier, and the fury of Satan, taking a twofold increase, became blind and insane in its effects. The Lamb took all the burden upon himself, but Satan wills the sin. And although the righteous one sins not, although this vainly tempted one falls not, yet let his enemies perish in their own sin.

The angels were wavering between grief and joy. They were longing to entreat at the throne of God for help to be sent down to Jesus, but at the same time they were able only to adore in deepest amazement that wonder of divine justice and mercy which the Holy of Holies in the heights of heaven had contemplated from all eternity, and which was now about to be accomplished in time upon earth, for the angels believe in God the Father, the almighty Creator of heaven and earth, and in Jesus Christ, his only Son, our Lord, who was conceived by the Holy Spirit, born of the Virgin Mary, who began that night to suffer under Pontius Pilate, who would the next morning be crucified, who would die, and who would be buried; who would descend into hell, and who would rise from the dead on the third day; who would ascend into heaven, there to sit at the right hand of God, the Father almighty, whence he should come to judge the living and the dead. They believe too in the Holy Spirit, the holy Catholic church, the communion of saints, the forgiveness of sins, the resurrection of the body, and life everlasting. Amen!

All this is only a small portion of the impression which must fill even to bursting a poor sinful heart with anguish, contrition, consolation, and compassion, if, seeking some relief as it were from these terrible scenes, it turns its gaze for a few minutes from the cruel arrest of our Savior and glances over Jerusalem at that solemn midnight of time created, and looks into that hour in which the everlasting justice and infinite mercy of God meeting, embracing, and penetrating each other, began the most holy work of divine and human love, to chastise the sins of men assumed by the God-Man, and to atone for them by that same God-Man. Such was the aspect of Jerusalem when the dear Savior was led to Annas.

April 2, AD 33
Thursday, Midnight

Jesus before Annas

It was toward midnight when Jesus was led through the brilliantly lighted courtyard into the palace of Annas. He was conducted to a hall as large as a small church. At the upper end opposite the entrance on a high gallery, or platform, under which people could come and go, sat Annas surrounded by twenty-eight counselors. A flight of steps broken here and there by landings, or resting places, led up to the front of his tribunal, or judgment seat, which was entered from behind, thus communicating with the inner part of the building.

Jesus, still surrounded by a body of the soldiers by whom he had been arrested, was dragged forward several steps by the executioners that held the cords. [H20] The hall was crowded with soldiers, the rabble, the slandering Jews, the servants of Annas, and some of the witnesses whom Annas had gathered together, and who later on made their appearance at the house of Caiaphas.

Annas could scarcely wait for the arrival of the poor Savior. He was beaming with mischievous joy; cunning and mockery were in his glance. He was at this time the president of a certain tribunal, and he sat here with his committee authorized to examine into false doctrines and to hand over the accused to the high priest.

Jesus stood before Annas pale, exhausted, silent, his head bowed, his garments wet and spattered with mud, his hands fettered, his waist bound by ropes the ends of which the executioners held. Annas, that lean, old villain, with a scraggy beard, was full of irony and freezing Jewish pride. He put on a half-laughing appearance, as if he knew nothing at all of what had taken place, and as if he were greatly surprised to find Jesus in the person of the prisoner brought before him. His address to him, which, however, I cannot reproduce in his own words, was in sense something like the following: "Ha, look there! Jesus of Nazareth! It is thou! Where now are thy disciples, thy crowds of followers? Where is thy kingdom? It appears that things have taken another turn with thee! Thy slanders have come to an end! People have had quite enough of thy blasphemy, thy calumny against priests, and thy sabbath-breaking. Who are thy disciples? Where are they? Now, art thou silent? Speak, seditious man! Speak, seducer! Didst thou not eat the paschal lamb in an unlawful place? Thou dost wish to introduce a new doctrine. Who has given thee authority to teach? Where hast thou studied? Speak! What is thy doctrine which throws everything into confusion? Speak! Speak! What is thy doctrine?"

At these words, Jesus raised his weary head, looked at Annas, and replied: "I have spoken openly before all the world where the Jews were gathered together. In secret I have spoken nothing. Why questionest thou me? Ask those that have heard what I have spoken unto them. Behold! They know what I have said."

The countenance of Annas during this reply of Jesus betrayed rage and scorn. A base menial standing near Jesus remarked this, and the villain struck the Lord with his open, mailed hand. The blow fell full upon the mouth and cheek of the Lord, while the scoundrel uttered the words: "Answerest thou the high priest so?" Jesus, trembling under the violence of the blow and jerked at the same time by the executioners, one pulling this way, another that, fell sideways on the steps, the blood flowing from his face. The hall resounded with jeers and laughter, mockery, muttering, and abusive words. With renewed ill-usage, they dragged Jesus up. He said quietly: "If I have spoken evil, give testimony of the evil; but if well, why strikest thou me?"

Annas, still more enraged by Jesus's calm demeanor, summoned the witnesses (because Jesus himself so willed it) to come forward and declare whatever they had heard him say. Thereupon the rabble set up a storm of cries and abuse. [H21] "He has said," they cried, "that he is a king, that God is his Father, that the Pharisees are adulterers. He stirs up the people, he heals on the sabbath day and by the power of the devil. The inhabitants of Ophel have gone crazy over him, calling him their deliverer, their prophet. He allows himself to be called the Son of God. He speaks of himself as one sent by God. He cries woe to Jerusalem, and alludes in his instructions to the destruction of the city. He observes not the fasts. He goes about with a crowd of followers. He eats with the unclean, with pagans, publicans, and sinners, and saunters around with adulteresses and women of bad character. Just now, outside the gate of Ophel, he said to a man who gave him a drink that he would give to him the waters of eternal life and that he should never thirst again. He seduces the people with words of double meaning. He squanders the money and property of others. He tells people all kinds of lies about his kingdom and such like things."

These accusations were brought forward against the Lord without regard to order or propriety. The witnesses stepped up to him and made their charges, derisively gesticulating in his face, while the executioners jerked him first to one side, then to the other, saying: "Speak! Answer!" Annas and his counselors, laughing scornfully, insulted him during the pauses made by the witnesses; for instance, they would exclaim: "Now, there! We hear the fine doctrine! What hast thou to answer? That, also, would be public teaching. The whole country is full of it! Canst thou produce nothing here? Why dost thou not issue some command, O King thou Son of God—show now thy mission!"

These expressions on the part of the judges were fol-lowed by pulling, pushing, and mocking on that of the executioners and bystanders, who would all have been glad to imitate the insolent fellow that struck Jesus in the face.

Jesus staggered from side to side. With freezing irony, Annas again addressed him: "Who art thou? What kind of a king art thou? What kind of an envoy art thou? I think that thou art only an obscure carpenter's son. Or art thou Elijah who was taken up to heaven in a fiery chariot? They say that he is still living. Thou too canst render thyself invisible, for thou hast often disappeared. Or perhaps thou art Malachi? Thou hast always vaunted thyself upon this prophet, and thou didst love to apply his words to thyself. It is also reported of him that he had no father, that he was an angel, and that he is not yet dead. What a fine opportunity for an imposter to give himself out for him! Say, what kind of a king art thou? Thou art greater than Solomon! That too is one of thy speeches. Come on! I shall not longer withhold from thee the title of thy kingdom!"

Annas now called for writing materials. Taking a strip of parchment about three feet long and three fingers in breadth, he laid it upon a table before him, and with a reed pen wrote a list of words in large letters, each of which contained some accusation against the Lord. Then he rolled the parchment and stuck it into a little hollow gourd, which he closed with a stopper. This he next fastened to a reed and, sending the mock scepter to Jesus, scornfully addressed him in such words as the following: "Here, take the scepter of thy kingdom! In it are enclosed all thy titles, thy rights, and thy honors. Carry them hence to the high priest, that he may recognize thy mission and thy kingdom, and treat thee accordingly." Then turning to the soldiers, he said: "Bind his hands and conduct this king to the high priest."

Some time previously they had loosened Jesus's hands. They now bound them again crosswise on his breast after they had fastened in them the accusations of Annas against him, and thus amid shouts of laughter, mocking cries, and all kinds of ill-usage, Jesus was dragged from the tribunal of Annas to that of Caiaphas.

Jesus Led from Annas to Caiaphas

WHEN Jesus was being led to Annas, he had passed the house of Caiaphas. He was now conducted back to it by a road that ran diagonally between the two. They were scarcely three hundred paces apart. The road, which ran between high walls and rows of small houses belonging to the judgment hall of Caiaphas, was lighted up by torches and lanterns, and filled with clamoring, boisterous Jews. It was with difficulty that the soldiers could keep back the crowd. Those that had outraged Jesus before Annas continued their jibes and jests and ill-treatment before the crowd, abusing and ill-treating him the whole way. I saw armed men of all kinds belonging to the tribunal driving away little parties of wailing people who were compassionate toward Jesus, while to some that had distinguished themselves by reviling and accusing him, they gave money, and admitted them with their companions into the court of Caiaphas.

To reach the judgment hall of Caiaphas, one had to pass through a gateway into a spacious exterior court, then through a second gateway into another which, with its walls, surrounded the whole house. (This we shall call the inner court.) A kind of open vestibule surrounded on three sides by a covered colonnade formed the front of the house, which was more than twice as long as it was broad and before which was a level, open square. This vestibule, or forecourt, was called the atrium, into which entrances led from the three sides, the principal one being from the rear, that is, from the house itself. Entering from this side, one proceeded to the left under the open sky to a pit lined with masonry, wherein fire was kept burning; then turning to the right, he would come upon a covered space back of a row of columns higher than any yet described. This formed the fourth side of the atrium and was about half its size. Here upon a semicircular platform up to which led several steps, were the seats for the members of the council. That of the high priest was elevated and in the center. The prisoner, surrounded by the guard, stood for trial in the middle of the semicircle. Upon either side and behind him down into the atrium were places for the witnesses and accusers. Three doors at the back of the judges' seats led into a large, circular hall, around whose wall seats were ranged. This room was used for secret consultations. On leaving the judges' seats and coming out into this hall, one found doors right and left. They opened upon flights of several steps, leading down into the inner court which here following the shape of the house, ran off into a circular form. On leaving the hall by the door on the right and turning to the left in the court, one found himself at the entrance of a dark, subterranean vault containing prison cells. They lay under the rear halls which, like the open tribunal, were higher than the atrium, and consequently afforded space for underground vaults. There were many prisons in this round part of the court. In one of them after Pentecost, I saw John and Peter sitting a whole night. This was when they were imprisoned after Peter had cured the lame man at the Beautiful Gate of the temple.

April 3, AD 33
Friday, Very Early Morning

In and around the building were numberless lamps and torches. All was as bright as day. In the center of the atrium, besides, shone the great pit of fire. It was like a furnace sunk in the earth, but open on top. The fuel was, I think, peat, and it was thrown in from above. Rising from the sides to above the height of a man were pipes in the shape of horns for carrying off the smoke. In the center, however, one could see the fire. Soldiers, servants, the rabble, most of whom were bribed witnesses, were crowding around the fire. There were some females among them, girls of doubtful fame, who sold to the soldiers a reddish beverage by the glass and, on receipt of a trifling sum, baked cakes for them. This scene of disorder and merriment reminded me of carnival time.

Most of those that had been summoned were already assembled around the high priest Caiaphas on the semicircular platform, while here and there others were coming in. The accusers and false witnesses almost filled the atrium; others were trying to force their way in, and it was only with difficulty that they were kept back.

Shortly before the arrival of the procession with Jesus, Peter and John, still enveloped in the messenger mantles, entered the outer court of the house. Through the influence of one of the servants known to him, John was fortunate enough to make his way through the gate of the inner court which, however, on account of the great crowd, was at once closed behind him. When Peter, who had been kept back a little by the crowd, reached the closed gate, the maidservant in charge would not let him pass. John interposed, but Peter would not have got in had not Nicodemus and Joseph of Arimathea, who just then sought admittance, said a good word for him. Once inside they laid off the mantles, which they gave back to the servants, and then took their place to the right among the crowd in the atrium where they could see the judges' seats. Caiaphas was already seated in his elevated tribunal in the center of the raised semicircular platform, and around him were sitting about seventy members of the Sanhedrin. Public officers, the scribes, and the ancients were sitting or standing on either side, and around them ranged many of the witnesses and rabble. Guards were stationed below the platform, under the entrance colonnade, and through the atrium as far as the door by which the procession was expected. This door was not the one directly opposite the tribunal, but that to the left of the atrium.

Caiaphas was a man of great gravity, his countenance florid and fierce. He wore a long, dull red mantle ornamented with golden flowers and tassels. It was fastened on the shoulders, the breast, and down the front with shining buckles of various form. On his head was a cap, the top of which resembled a low episcopal miter. [H22] The pieces front and back were bent so as to meet on top, thus leaving openings at the side, from which hung ribbons. From either side of the head lappets fell upon the shoulders. Caiaphas and his counselors were already a long time assembled; many of them had even remained since the departure of Judas and his gang. The rage and impatience of Caiaphas had reached such a pitch that, magnificently attired as he was, he descended from his lofty tribunal and went into the outer court asking angrily whether Jesus would soon come. At last the procession was seen approaching, and Caiaphas returned to his seat.

Jesus before Caiaphas

AMID frantic cries of mockery, with pushing and dragging and casting of mud, Jesus was led into the atrium, where, instead of the unbridled rage of the mob, were heard the dull muttering and whispering of restrained rage. Turning to the right on entering, the procession faced the tribunal. When Jesus passed Peter and John, he glanced at them lovingly, though without turning his head, for fear of betraying them. Scarcely had he passed through the colonnaded entrance and appeared before the council, when Caiaphas cried out to him: "Hast thou come, thou blasphemer of God, thou that dost disturb this our sacred night!" The tube containing Annas's accusations against Jesus was now drawn from the mock scepter. When the writing which it contained was read, Caiaphas poured forth a stream of reproaches and abusive epithets against Jesus, while the soldiers and wretches standing near dragged and pulled him about. They had in their hands little iron rods, some of them capped with sharp goads, others with pear-shaped knobs, with which they drove him from side to side, crying: "Answer! Open thy mouth! Canst thou not speak!" All this went on while Caiaphas, even more enraged than Annas, hurled question after question to Jesus who, calm and suffering, kept his eyes lowered, not even glancing at him. The wretches, in their efforts to force him to speak, struck him on the neck and sides, hit him with their fists, and goaded him with their puncheons. And more than this, a cruel lad, with his thumb, pressed Jesus's underlip upon his teeth, saying: "Here, now, bite!"

And now came the interrogation of the witnesses. It consisted of nothing but the disorderly cries, the enraged shouts of the bribed populace, or the deposition of some of Jesus's enemies belonging to the exasperated Pharisees and Sadducees. A certain number of them had been selected as representatives of their party on this feast. They brought forward all those points that Jesus had answered a hundred times before: for instance, they said that he wrought cures and drove out devils through the devil himself; that he violated the sabbath, kept not the prescribed fasts; that his disciples ate with unwashed hands; that he incited the people, called the Pharisees a brood of vipers and an adulterous generation; predicted the destruction of Jerusalem; and associated with pagans, publicans, sinners, and women of ill-repute; that he went around with a great crowd of followers, gave himself out as a king, a prophet, yes, even as the Son of God; and that he was constantly talking about his kingdom. They advanced, moreover, that he attacked the liberty of divorce, that he had cried woe upon Jerusalem, that he called himself the bread of life and put forward the unheard-of doctrine that whoever did not eat his flesh and drink his blood would not have eternal life.

In this way were all his words, his instructions, and his parables misrepresented and perverted, mixed up with words of abuse and outrage, and attributed to him as crimes. The witnesses, however, contradicted and confused one another. One said: "He gives himself out for a king"; another cried, "No! He only allows himself to be so styled, for when they wanted to proclaim him king, he fled." Then one of them shouted: "He says he is the Son of God," to which someone else retorted: "No, that's not so! He calls himself a son only because he fulfills his father's will." Some declared that those whom he had healed fell sick again, so that his healing power was nothing but the effect of magic. On the charge of sorcery principally, many accusations were lodged against him, and numbers of witnesses came forward. The cure of the man at the pool of Bethesda was brought up in a distorted light and falsely represented. The Pharisees of Sepphoris, with whom Jesus had once disputed upon the subject of divorce, accused him now of teaching false doctrine, and that young man of Nazareth whom he had refused to receive as a disciple was base enough to step forward and witness against him. They accused him also of acquitting at the temple the woman taken in adultery, of taxing the Pharisees with crime, and of many other things.

Notwithstanding all their efforts, they were unable to prove any one of their charges. The crowd of witnesses seemed to come forward more for the purpose of deriding Jesus to his face than to render testimony. They contended hotly among themselves, while Caiaphas and some of the counselors ceased not their raillery and taunting expressions. They cried out: "What a king thou art! Show thy power! Call the angelic legions of which thou spokest in the Garden of Olives! Where hast thou hidden the money thou didst receive from widows and simpletons? Thou hast squandered whole estates, and what hast thou to show for it? Answer! Speak! Now that thou shouldst speak before the judges, thou art mute; but where it would have been better to be silent, that is, before the mob and female rabble, thou didst have words enough," etc.

All these speeches were accompanied by renewed ill-usage from the servants, who tried with cuffs and blows to force Jesus to answer. Through God's help alone was he enabled longer to live, that he might bear the sins of the world. Some of the vile witnesses declared the Lord to be an illegitimate son, which charge others contradicted with the words: "That is false! His mother was a pious virgin belonging to the temple, and we were present at her marriage to a most God-fearing man." And then followed a hot dispute among these last witnesses.

They next accused Jesus and his disciples of not offering sacrifice in the temple. True it is that I never saw Jesus or the apostles, after they began to follow him, bringing any sacrifice to the temple excepting the paschal lamb, though Joseph and Anne frequently during their lifetime offered sacrifice for Jesus. But these accusations were of no account, for the Essenes never offered sacrifice, and no one thought of subjecting them to punishment for the omission. The charge of sorcery was frequently repeated, and more than once Caiaphas declared that the confusion of the witnesses in their statements was due to witchcraft.

Some now said that Jesus had, contrary to the law, eaten the paschal lamb on the previous day, and that the year before he had sanctioned other irregularities at the same feast. This testimony gave rise to new expressions of rage and derision from the vile crowd. But the witnesses had so perplexed and contradicted one another that, mortified and exasperated, Caiaphas and the assembled counselors found that not one of the accusations against Jesus could be substantiated. Nicodemus and Joseph of Arimathea were then called up to explain how it happened that they had allowed Jesus to eat the paschal lamb in a supper room belonging to the last-named. Having taken their places before Caiaphas, they proved from written documents that the Galileans, according to an ancient custom, were permitted to eat the paschal lamb one day earlier than the other Jews. They added that everything else pertaining to the ceremony had been carefully observed, for that persons belonging to the temple were present at it. This last assertion greatly puzzled the witnesses, and the enemies of Jesus were particularly exasperated when Nico-

April 3, AD 33
Friday Morning, 2:30 AM

demus sent for the writings and pointed out the passages containing this right of the Galileans. Besides several other reasons for this privilege, which I have forgotten, there was this: the immense crowds congregated at the same time and for the same purpose in the temple rendered it impossible for all to get through the ceremonies at a given hour; and again, if all were to return home at the same time, the roads would be so thronged as to render them impassable. Now, although the Galileans did not always make use of their privilege, yet Nicodemus incontestably proved its existence from written documents. The rage of the Pharisees against Nicodemus became still greater when the latter closed his remarks by saying that the members of the council must feel greatly aggrieved at being called upon to preside over a trial instituted by prejudice so evident, carried on with haste so violent on the night preceding the most solemn of their festivals; and that the gross contradictions of all the witnesses in their presence and before the assembled multitude were to them a positive insult. The Pharisees glanced wrathfully at Nicodemus and, with barefaced insolence, hurriedly continued to question the base witnesses. After much shameful, perverse, lying evidence, two witnesses at last came forward and said: "Jesus declared that he would destroy the temple made by hands, and in three days build up another not made by human hands." But these two also wrangled over their words. One said: "Jesus was going to build up a new temple; therefore it was that he had celebrated a new Passover in another building, for he was going to destroy the old temple." The other retorted: "The building in which he ate the paschal lamb was built by human hands, consequently he did not mean that."

Caiaphas was now thoroughly exasperated, for the ill-treatment bestowed upon Jesus, the contradictory statements of the witnesses, and the incomprehensibly silent patience of the accused were beginning to make a very deep impression upon many of those present, and some of the witnesses were laughed to scorn. The silence of Jesus roused the conscience of many, and about ten of the soldiers were so touched by it that, under pretext of indisposition, they left the court. As they passed Peter and John, they said to them: "The silence of Jesus the Galilean in the midst of treatment so shameful is heart-rending. It is a wonder the earth does not swallow his persecutors alive. But tell us, whither shall we go?" The two apostles, however, perhaps because they did not trust the soldiers or feared to be recognized by them or the bystanders as Jesus's disciples, answered sadly and in general terms: "If truth calls you, follow it; the rest will take care of itself." Thereupon these men left the outer court of Caiaphas's house, and hurried from the city. They met some persons who directed them to caves on the other side of Mount Zion to the south of Jerusalem. Here they found hidden several of the apostles, who at first shrank from them in alarm. But their fears were dispelled on receiving news of Jesus and upon hearing that the soldiers were themselves in danger. They soon after separated and scattered to different places.

Caiaphas, infuriated by the wrangling of the last two witnesses, rose from his seat, went down a couple of steps to Jesus, and said: "Answerest thou nothing to this testimony against thee?" He was vexed that Jesus would not look at him. At this the executioners pulled our Lord's head back by the hair, and with their fist gave him blows under his chin. But his glance was still downcast. Caiaphas angrily raised his hands and said in a tone full of rage: "I adjure thee by the living God that thou tell us whether thou be Christ, the Messiah, the Son of the most blessed God."

A solemn silence fell upon the clamoring crowd. Jesus, strengthened by God, said in a voice inexpressibly majestic, a voice that struck awe into all hearts, the voice of the Eternal Word: "I am! Thou sayest it! And I say to you, soon you shall see the Son of Man sitting on the right hand of the power of God, and coming in the clouds of heaven!"

While Jesus was pronouncing these words, I saw him shining with light. The heavens were open above him and, in an inexpressible manner, I saw God, the Father almighty. I saw the angels and the prayers of the just crying, as it were, and pleading for Jesus. I saw, besides, the divinity as if speaking from the Father and from Jesus at the same time: "If it were possible for me to suffer, I would do so, but because I am merciful, I have taken flesh in the Person of my Son, in order that the Son of Man may suffer. I am just—but behold! He is carrying the sins of these men, the sins of the whole world!"

I saw yawning below Caiaphas the whole abyss of hell, a lurid, fiery sphere full of horrible shapes. I saw Caiaphas standing above it, separated from it by only a thin crust. I saw him penetrated with diabolical rage. The whole house now appeared to be one with the open abyss of hell below. When the Lord solemnly declared that he was Christ, the Son of God, it was as if hell grew terror-stricken before him, as if it launched the whole force of its rage against him by means of those gathered in the tribunal of Caiaphas.

As all these things were shown me in forms and pictures, I saw hell's despair and fury in numberless horrible shapes coming up in many places out of the earth. Among them I remember to have seen crowds of little, dark figures like dogs with short paws and great, long claws, but I do not now recall what species of wickedness was symbolized in them. I remember only the figures. I saw frightful-looking shadows similar to those moving among most of those present, or sitting upon the head or shoulders of many. The assembly was full of them, and they excited the people to fury and wickedness. I saw also at this moment, from the graves on the other side of Zion, hideous figures hurriedly rising. I think they were evil spirits. In the vicinity of the temple, likewise, I saw many apparitions rising out of the earth. Some of them appeared to be captives, for they moved along slowly in fetters. I do not now know whether these last were demons, or souls banished to certain places on the earth and who were perhaps now going to Purgatory, which the Lord was about to open to them by his condemnation to death. One can never fully express such things for fear of scandalizing the ignorant, but when one sees these things, one feels them, and they make the hair stand on end. This moment was full of horror. I think that John too must have seen something of it, for I heard him afterward speaking about it. The few who were not entirely abandoned to evil felt with deep dismay the horror of this moment, but the wicked experienced only a wild outburst of rage.

Caiaphas, as if inspired by hell, seized the hem of his magnificent mantle, clipped it with a knife and, with a whizzing noise, tore it [H23] as he exclaimed in a loud voice: "He has blasphemed! What need have we of further witnesses? Behold now ye have heard the blasphemy, what think ye?" At these words, the whole assembly rose and cried out in a horrid voice: "He is guilty of death! He is guilty of death!"

During these shouts, that sinister rage of hell was most frightful in the house of Caiaphas. Jesus's enemies appeared to be possessed by Satan, as did also their partisans and fawning servants. It was as if the powers of darkness were proclaiming their triumph over light. Such a sense of horror fell upon all present in whom there was still some little connection with good, that many of them drew their mantles closer around them and slipped away. The witnesses belonging to the better classes, as their presence was no longer necessary, also left the judgment hall, their conscience racked by remorse. The rabble, however, gathered around the fire in the forecourt where, having received the price of their perfidy, they ate and drank to excess.

The high priest, addressing the executioners, said: "I deliver this king to you. Render to the blasphemer the honors due him!" After these words, he retired with his council to the round hall back of the tribunal, into which no one could see from the vestibule.

John, in his deep affection, thought only of the blessed

Virgin. He feared that the dreadful news might be communicated to her suddenly by some enemy; so casting at Jesus, the Holy of Holies, a glance that said: "Master, thou knowest well why I am going," he hurried from the judgment hall to seek the blessed Virgin as sent to her by Jesus himself. Peter, quite consumed by anxiety and pain and, on account of his bodily exhaustion, feeling keenly the sensible chilliness of the coming morning, concealed his deep trouble as well as he could, and timidly approached the fire in the atrium, around which all kinds of low-lived wretches were warming themselves. He knew not what he was doing, but he could not leave his Master.

Jesus Mocked and Insulted

As soon as Caiaphas, having delivered Jesus to the soldiers, left the judgment hall with his council, the very scum of the miscreants present fell like a swarm of infuriated wasps upon our Lord, [H24] who until then had been held fast by two of the four executioners that guided the ropes with which he was bound. Two of them had retired before the sentence, in order to make their escape with the others. Even during the trial, the executioners and other wretches had cruelly torn whole handfuls of hair from the head and beard of Jesus. Some good persons secretly picked up the locks of hair from the ground and slipped away with them, but after a little while it disappeared from their possession. During the trial also the miscreants had spat upon Jesus, struck him again and again with their fists, goaded him with cudgels whose rounded ends were armed with sharp points, and had even run needles into his body. But now they exercised their villainy upon him in a manner altogether frantic and irrational. They put upon him, one after the other, several crowns of straw and bark plaited in various ludicrous forms which, with wicked words of mockery, they afterward struck from his head. Sometimes they cried: "Behold the Son of David crowned with the crown of his Father!" Or again: "Behold, here is more than Solomon!" Or: "This is the king who is preparing a marriage feast for his son!" And thus they turned to ridicule all the eternal truths which, for the salvation of humankind, he had in truth and parables taught. They struck him with their fists and sticks, threw him from side to side, and spat upon him. At last they plaited a crown of coarse wheat straw, such as grows in that country, put upon him a high cap, almost similar to the high miters of the present day; and, after stripping him of his knitted robe, placed over the miter the straw crown. There, now, stood poor Jesus clothed only in his nether-bandage and the scapular that fell on his breast and back; but this last they soon tore from him, and he never recovered it. They threw around him an old, tattered mantle too short in front to cover the knees, and put around his neck a long iron chain which, like a stole, hung from the shoulders across the breast and down to the knees. The ends of the chain were furnished with two great, heavy rings studded with sharp points which, as he walked, struck against his knees and wounded them severely. They pinioned anew his hands upon his breast, placed in them a reed, and covered his disfigured countenance with the spittle of their impure mouths. His torn hair and beard, his breast, and the whole of the upper part of the mantle of derision were laden with filth in every degree of loathsomeness. They tied a rag across his eyes, struck him with their fists and sticks, and cried out: "Great prophet! Prophesy, who has struck thee?" But Jesus answered not. He prayed interiorly, sighed, and bore their blows. Thus ill-used, blindfolded, and covered with filth, they dragged him by the chain into the rear council hall. They kicked him and drove him forward with their clubs, while uttering such derisive cries as, "Forward, O king of straw! He must show himself to the council in the regal insignia which we have bestowed upon him!" When they entered the council hall wherein many of the members were still sitting with Caiaphas on the elevated, semicircular platform, a new scene of outrage began; and with an utterly base meaning and purely sacrilegious violation, sacred customs and ceremonies were imitated. As, for instance, when they covered Jesus with mud and spittle, the vile miscreants exclaimed: "Here now is thy royal unction, thy prophetic unction!" It was thus they mockingly alluded to Magdalene's anointing and to baptism. "What!" they cried jeeringly, "art thou going to appear before the Sanhedrin in this unclean trim? Thou wast wont to purify others, and yet thou art not clean thyself. But we will now purify thee." Thereupon, they brought a basin full of foul, muddy water in which lay a coarse rag; and amid pushes, jests, and mockery mingled with ironical bows and salutations, with sticking out the tongue at him or turning up to him their hinder parts, they passed the wet smeary rag over his face and shoulders as if cleansing him, though in reality rendering him more filthy than before. Finally, they poured the whole contents of the basin over his face with the mocking words: "There, now, is precious balm for thee! There now, thou hast had water at a cost of three hundred pence! Now, thou hast thy baptism of the pool of Bethesda!"

This last outrage showed forth, though without their intending it, the likeness between Jesus and the paschal lamb, for on this day the lambs slaughtered for sacrifice were first washed in the pond near the sheep gate and then in the pool of Bethesda to the south of the temple. They were then solemnly sprinkled with water before being slaughtered in the temple for the Passover. The enemies of Jesus were alluding to the paralytic who for thirty-eight years had been sick, and who had been cured by him at the pool of Bethesda, for I afterward saw that same man washed or baptized in its waters. I say "washed or baptized," because at this moment the action with its circumstances does not recur clearly to my mind.

Now they dragged and pulled Jesus around with kicks and blows in the circle formed by the members of the council, all of whom greeted him with raillery and abuse. I saw the whole assembly filled with raging, diabolical figures. It was a scene of horrible gloom and confusion. But around the ill-treated Jesus, since the moment in which he said that he was the Son of God, I frequently saw a glory, a splendor. Many of those present seemed to have an interior perception of the same, some more, others less; they experienced, at least, a feeling of dread upon seeing that, in spite of the scorn and ignominy with which he was laden, the indescribable majesty of his bearing remained unchanged. The halo around him seemed to incite his enemies to a higher degree of fury. But to me that glory appeared so remarkable that I am of opinion that they veiled Jesus's countenance on that account, because since the words: "I am he," the high priest could no longer endure his glance.

*April 3, AD 33
Friday Morning, 4:45 AM*

Peter's Denial

WHEN Jesus solemnly uttered the words: "I am he," and Caiaphas rent his garments crying out: "He is guilty of death"—when the hall resounded with the mocking cries and furious shouts of the rabble—when the heavens opened above Jesus—when hell gave free vent to its rage—when the graves gave up their captive spirits—when all was horror and consternation—then were Peter and John, who had suffered much from having to witness silently and passively the frightful abuse to which Jesus was subjected, no longer able to remain. John went out with many of the crowd and some of the witnesses who were leaving the hall, and hurried off to the mother of Jesus, who was staying at Martha's, not far from the corner gate, where Lazarus owned a beautiful house in Jerusalem. But Peter could not go—he loved Jesus too much. He could scarcely contain himself. He wept bitterly, though trying to hide his tears as well as he could.

He could not remain standing any longer in the judgment hall, for his deep emotion would have betrayed him, nor could he leave without attracting notice. So, he retired to the atrium and took a place in the corner near the fire, around which soldiers and people of all kinds were standing in groups. They went out occasionally to mock Jesus and then came back to make their low, vulgar remarks upon what they had done. Peter kept silence; but already the interest he manifested in the proceedings, joined to the expression of deep grief depicted on his countenance, drew upon him the attention of Jesus's enemies. Just at this moment, the portress approached the fire; and as all were prating and jesting at Jesus's expense and that of his disciples, she, like a bold woman, saucily put in her word and, fixing her eyes upon Peter, said: "Thou too art one of the Galilean's disciples!" Peter, startled and alarmed, and fearing rough treatment from the rude crowd, answered: "Woman, I know him not! I know not what thou meanest. I do not understand thee!" [H25] With these words, wishing to free himself from further remark, he arose and left the atrium. *At that moment, a cock somewhere outside the city crowed.* I do not remember having *heard* it, but I *felt* that it was crowing outside the city. As Peter was making his way out, another maidservant caught sight of him, and said to the bystanders: "This man, also, was with Jesus of Nazareth." They at once questioned him: "Art thou not also one of his disciples?" Peter, greatly troubled and perplexed, answered with an oath: "Truly, I am not! I do not even know the man!" [H26] And he hurried through the inner to the exterior court, to warn some of his acquaintances whom he saw looking over the wall. He was weeping and so full of grief and anxiety on Jesus's account that he hardly gave his denial a thought. In the other court were many people, among them some of Jesus's friends, who not being able to get nearer to the scene of action had climbed on the wall to be better able to hear. Peter, being allowed to go out, found among them a number of disciples whom anxiety had forced hither from their caves on Mount Hinnom. They went straight up to Peter, and with many tears questioned him about Jesus. But he was so excited and so fearful of betraying himself that he advised them in a few words to go away, as there was danger for them where they were. Then he turned off and wandered gloomily about, while they, acting on his word, hastened to leave the city. I recognized about sixteen of the first disciples, among them: Bartholomew, Nathaniel, Saturnin, Joseph Barsabbas, Simeon (later on, bishop of Jerusalem), Zacchaeus, and Manahem, the youth endowed with the gift of prophecy but born blind, to whom Jesus had restored sight.

Peter could not rest anywhere. His love for Jesus drove him back into the inner court that surrounded the house. They let him in again, on account of Nicodemus and Joseph of Arimathea, who had in the first instance procured his admittance. He did not, however, return to the court of the judgment hall, but turning went along to the right until he reached the entrance of the circular hall back of the tribunal. In that hall Jesus was being dragged about and abused by the vile rabble. Peter drew near trembling, and although he felt himself an object of remark, yet his anxiety for Jesus drove him through the doorway, which was beset by the crowd watching the outrages heaped upon Jesus. Just then they were dragging him, crowned with straw, around the circle. Jesus cast a glance full of earnest warning upon Peter, a glance that pierced him to the soul. But when, still struggling with fear, he heard from some of the bystanders the words: "What fellow is that?" He re-entered the court. There, sad and distracted with compassion for Jesus and anxiety for his own safety, he wandered about with loitering steps. At last seeing that he was attracting notice upon himself, he went again into the atrium and took a seat by the fire. He had sat there a considerable time when some that had seen him outside and noticed his preoccupied and excited manner re-entered and again directed their attention to him, while referring in slighting terms to Jesus and his affairs. One of them said: "Truly, thou also dost belong to his adherents! Thou art a Galilean. Thy speech betrays thee." Peter began to evade the remark [H27] and to make his way out of the hall, when a brother of Malchus stepped up to him and said: "What! Did I not see thee with him in the Garden of Olives? Didst thou not wound my brother's ear?"

Peter became like one beside himself with terror. While trying to free himself, he began in his impetuous way to curse and swear that he knew not the man, and ended by running out of the atrium into the court that surrounded the house. *The cock again crowed.* Just at that moment, Jesus was being led from the circular hall and across this court down into a prison under it. He turned toward Peter and cast upon him a glance of mingled pity and sadness. Forcibly and with a terrifying power, the word of Jesus fell upon his heart: "Before the cock crows twice, thou wilt deny me thrice!" Worn out with grief and anxiety, Peter had entirely forgotten his presumptuous protestation on the Mount of Olives, rather to die with his Master than to deny him, as also the warning he had then received from Jesus. But at that glance, the enormity of his fault rose up before him and well-nigh broke his heart. He had sinned. He had sinned against his ill-treated, unjustly condemned Savior, who was silently enduring the most horrible outrages, who had so truly warned him to be on his guard.

Filled with remorse and sorrow, he covered his head with his mantle and hurried into the other court, weeping bitterly. [H28] He no longer feared being accosted. To everyone he met he would willingly have proclaimed who he was, and how great was the crime that rested on him. Who would presume to say that in such danger, affliction, anxiety, and perplexity, in such a struggle between love and fear, worn out with fatigue, consumed by watching, pursued by dread, half-crazed from pain of mind caused by the overwhelming sorrows of this most pitiful night, with a temperament at once so childlike and so ardent, he would have been stronger than Peter? The Lord left Peter to his own strength, therefore did he become so weak, just as they always do that lose sight of the words: "Pray and watch, that ye enter not into temptation."

Mary in the Judgment Hall of Caiaphas

THE BLESSED Virgin, united in constant, interior compassion with Jesus, knew and experienced in her soul all that happened to him. She suffered everything with him in spiritual contemplation, and like him she was absorbed in continual prayer for his executioners. But at the same time, her mother-heart cried uninterruptedly to God that He might not suffer these crimes to be enacted, that He might ward off these sufferings from her most blessed Son, and she irresistibly longed to be near her poor, outraged Jesus. When then John, after the frightful cry: "He is guilty of death!" left the court of Caiaphas and went to her at Lazarus's in Jerusalem, not far from the corner gate; and when, by his account of the terrible sufferings of her Son, he confirmed what she already well knew from interior contemplation, she ardently desired to be conducted together with Magdalene (who was almost crazed from grief), and some others of the holy women, to where she might be near her suffering Jesus. John, who had left the presence of his divine Master only to console her who was next to Jesus with him, accompanied the blessed Virgin when led by the holy women from the house. Magdalene, wringing her hands, staggered with the others along the moonlit streets, which were alive with people returning to their homes. The holy women were veiled. But their little party, closely clinging to one another, their occasional sobs and expressions of grief, which could not be restrained, drew upon them the notice of the passersby, many of whom were Jesus's enemies; and the bitter, abusive words which they heard uttered against the Lord added to their pain. The most afflicted mother suffered in constant, interior contemplation the torments of Jesus, which, however, like all other things, she quietly kept in her heart; for, like him, she suffered with him in silence.

The holy women supported her in their arms. When passing under an arched gateway of the inner city, through which their way led, they were met by some well-disposed people returning from Caiaphas's judgment hall and lamenting the scenes they had witnessed. They approached the holy women and, recognizing the mother of Jesus, paused a moment to salute her with heartfelt compassion: "O thou most unhappy mother! Thou most afflicted mother! O thou most distressed mother of the Holy One of Israel!" Mary thanked them earnestly, and the holy women with hurried steps continued their sorrowful way.

As they drew near to Caiaphas's, the route led to the side opposite the entrance where there was only one surrounding wall, while on the side of the entrance itself, it ran through two courts. Here a fresh and bitter sorrow was in store for the mother of Jesus and her companions. They had to pass a high, level place upon which, under a light awning, the cross of Christ was being constructed by torchlight. The enemies of Jesus had already, as soon as Judas went out to betray him, commanded the cross to be prepared for him just as soon as he should be seized, for then Pilate would have no cause for delay. They thought they would deliver the Lord very early to him for sentence of death; they did not expect it to be so long delayed. The Romans had already prepared the crosses for the two robbers. The workmen, full of chagrin at being obliged to labor during the night, uttered horrible curses and abusive epithets which, with every stroke of the hammer, pierced the heart of the most afflicted mother. Still she prayed for those blind wretches who, cursing and swearing, were putting together the instrument for their own redemption, and the cruel martyrdom of her Son.

When now they reached the outer court of the house, Mary, in the midst of the holy women and accompanied by John, withdrew into a corner under the gateway leading into the inner court. Her soul, filled with inexpressible sufferings, was with Jesus. She sighed for the door to be opened, and hoped, through John's intervention, to be allowed admittance. She felt that this door alone separated her from her Son *who, at the second crowing of the cock,* was to be led out of the house and into the prison below. At last the door opened and Peter, weeping bitterly, his head covered and his hands outstretched, rushed to meet the crowd issuing forth. The glare of the torches, added to the light shed by the moon, enabled him at once to recognize John and the blessed Virgin. It seemed to him that conscience, which the glance of the Son had roused and terrified, stood before him in the person of the mother. Oh, how the soul of poor Peter quivered when Mary accosted him with: "O Simon, what about my Son, what about Jesus?" Unable to speak or to support the glance of Mary's eyes, Peter turned away wringing his hands. But Mary would not desist. She approached him and said in a voice full of emotion: "O Simon, son of Cephas, thou answerest me not?" Thereupon in the deepest woe, Peter exclaimed: "O Mother, speak not to me! Thy Son is suffering cruelly. Speak not to me! They have condemned him to death, and I have shamefully denied him thrice!" And when John drew near to speak to him, Peter, like one crazed by grief, hurried out of the court and fled from the city. He paused not until he reached that cave on the Mount of Olives upon whose stones were impressed the marks of Jesus's hands while he prayed. In that same cave our first father Adam did penance, for it was here that he first reached the curse-laden earth.

The blessed Virgin, in compassion for Jesus in this new pain, that of being denied by the disciple who had been the first to acknowledge him the Son of the Living God, at these words of Peter sank down upon the stone pavement upon which she was standing by the pillar of the gateway. The marks of her hand or foot remained impressed upon the stone, which is still in existence, though I do not now remember where I have seen it. Most of the crowd had dispersed after Jesus was imprisoned, and the gate of the court was still standing open. Rising from where she had fallen and longing to be nearer her beloved Son, John conducted the blessed Virgin and the holy women to the front of the Lord's prison. Mary was indeed with Jesus in spirit and knew all that was happening to him, and he too was with her. But this most faithful mother wished to hear with her bodily ears the sighs of her Son. She could in her present position hear both the sighs of Jesus and the insults heaped upon him. The little group could not here remain long unobserved. Magdalene was too greatly agitated to conquer the vehemence of her grief, and though the blessed Virgin by a special grace appeared wonderfully dignified and venerable in her exterior manifestation of her exceedingly great suffering, yet even while going this short distance she was obliged to listen to words of bitter import, such as: "Is not this the Galilean's mother? Her Son will certainly be crucified, though not before the festival, unless indeed he is the greatest of criminals." The blessed Virgin turned and, guided by the Spirit that enlightened her interiorly, went to the fireplace in the atrium where only a few of the rabble were still standing. Her companions followed in speechless grief. In this place of horror, where Jesus had declared that he was the Son of God and where the brood of Satan had cried out: "He is guilty of death," the most afflicted mother's anguish was so great that she appeared more like a dying than a living person. John and the holy women led her away from the spot.

The lookers-on became silent, as if stupefied. The effect produced by Mary's presence was what might be caused by a pure spirit passing through hell.

The little party proceeded along a way that ran back of the house and passed that mournful spot upon which the cross was being prepared. As it was found difficult to pronounce sentence upon Jesus, so was it hard to get ready his cross. The workmen were obliged frequently to bring fresh wood, because this or that piece proved a misfit or broke under their hands. It was in this way that the various kinds of wood were employed that God willed to be used. I have had many visions on this subject, and I have seen the angels hindering the laborers in their work until they recommenced and finished it as God would have it done. But as I do not clearly remember the several circumstances, I shall pass them over.

Jesus Imprisoned

THE PRISON cell into which Jesus was introduced lay under the judgment hall of Caiaphas. It was a small, circular vault. A part of it I see in existence even now. Only two of the four executioners remained with Jesus. After a short interval they exchanged places with two others, and these again were soon relieved. They had not given the Lord his own garments again. He was clothed with only the filthy mantle of mockery, and his hands were still bound. [H29]

When the Lord entered the prison, he prayed his heavenly Father to accept all the scorn and ill-treatment that he had endured up to that moment and all that he had still to suffer in atonement for the sins of his executioners and for all those that, in future ages, might be in danger of sinning through impatience and anger.

Even in this prison the executioners allowed Jesus no rest. They bound him to a low pillar that stood in the center of the prison, though they would not permit him to lean against it. He was obliged to stagger from side to side on his tired feet, which were wounded and swollen from frequent falls and the strokes of the chain that hung to his knees. They ceased not to mock and outrage him, and when the two executioners in charge were wearied, two others replaced them, and new scenes of villainy were enacted.

It is not possible for me to repeat all the acts of wickedness performed against the purest and the holiest. I am too sick. I am almost dying from compassion. Ah, how ashamed we should be that through effeminacy and fastidiousness we cannot bear to talk of or listen to the details of all that the innocent Redeemer patiently suffered for us. Horror seizes upon us on such occasions, similar to that of a murderer forced to lay his hands upon the wounds of his victim. Jesus endured all without opening his lips; and it was man, sinful man, who thus raged against his Brother, his Redeemer, and his God. I too am a poor, sinful creature, and it was for my sake that all this suffering fell upon him. On the Day of Judgment all things will be laid open. Then shall we see how, in the ill-treatment of the Son of God, when as the Son of Man he appeared in time, we have had a share by the sins we so frequently commit, and which are indeed a kind of continuation of and participation in the outrages offered to Jesus by those diabolical miscreants. Ah! If we rightly reflected upon this, we should more earnestly than ever repeat the words found in so many of our prayer books: "Lord, let me rather die than ever outrage thee again by sin!"

Standing in his prison, Jesus prayed uninterruptedly for his tormentors. When at last they grew tired of their cruel sport and became somewhat quiet, I saw Jesus leaning against the pillar and surrounded by light. *Day was dawning*, the day of his infinite sufferings and atonement. The day of our Redemption glanced faintly through an opening overhead in the prison wall and shone upon our holy, ill-used Paschal Lamb, who had taken upon himself all the sins of the world. Jesus raised his manacled hands to greet the dawning light and clearly and audibly pronounced a most touching prayer to his Father in heaven. In it he thanked him for sending this day after which the patriarchs had sighed, after which he too, since his coming upon earth, had longed so ardently as to break forth into the cry: "I have a baptism wherewith I am to be baptized, and how am I straitened until it be accomplished!" How touchingly the Lord thanked for this day, which was to accomplish the aim of his life, our salvation; which was to unlock heaven, subdue hell, open the source of blessings to humankind, and fulfill the will of his Father!

I repeated that prayer after Jesus, but I cannot now recall it. I was so sick from compassion, and I had to weep over his pains. As he continued to thank for all the terrible sufferings which he bore for me, I desisted not from imploring: "Ah, give me, give me thy pains! They are mine by right, they are all for my crimes!"

In streamed the light, and Jesus greeted the day in a prayer of thanksgiving so touching that, quite overcome with love and compassion, I repeated his words after him like a child. It was a scene indescribably sad, sacred, and solemn, a scene full of love—to see Jesus after the horrible turmoil of the night standing radiant with light by that low pillar in the center of his narrow prison cell, and *hailing with thanksgiving the first ray of dawn* on that great day of his propitiatory sacrifice. Ah! That ray of light came to Jesus as a judge might visit a criminal in prison to be reconciled to him before the execution of the sentence. Jesus thanked it so lovingly. The executioners, worn out, appeared to be dozing. Suddenly they looked up in wonder, but did not disturb Jesus. They appeared frightened and amazed. *Jesus may have been something over an hour in this prison.*

Judas at the Judgment Hall

WHILE Jesus was in prison, Judas, who until then—like one in despair and driven by the demon—was wandering around the Valley of Hinnom, on the steep southern side of Jerusalem, where lay naught but refuse, bones, and carrion, approached the precincts of Caiaphas's judgment hall. He stole around with the bundle of silver pieces, the price of his treachery, still hanging to the girdle at his side. The pieces were linked together by a little chain. All was silent. Judas, unrecognized, asked the guard what was going to happen to the Galilean. They replied: "He has been condemned to death, and he will be crucified." He heard some persons telling one another how dreadfully Jesus had been treated and how patient he was, while others said that at daybreak he was to appear again before the High Council to receive solemn condemnation. While the traitor, in order to escape recognition, gathered up this news here and there, day dawned and things began to be astir both in and around the hall. Judas, to escape being seen, slipped off behind the house. Like Cain, he fled the sight of men. Despair was taking possession of his soul. But what did he meet here? This was the place where the cross had been put together.

The several pieces lay in order side by side, and the workmen, wrapped in their mantles, were lying asleep. The sky glistened with a white light above the Mount of Olives, as if shuddering at sight of the instrument of our Redemption. Judas glanced at it in horror, and fled. He had seen the gibbet to which he had sold the Lord! He fled from the spot and hid, resolved to await the result of the morning trial.

The Morning Trial

As soon as it was clear daylight, Caiaphas, Annas, the ancients and scribes assembled in the great hall to hold a trial perfectly lawful. [H30] Trial by night was not legal. That of the preceding night had been held only because time pressed on account of the feast, and that some of the preparatory attestations might be taken. Most of the members had passed the rest of the night in side chambers in Caiaphas's house, or on couches prepared for them above the judgment hall; but many, such as Nicodemus and Joseph of Arimathea, went away and *returned at daybreak*. It was a large assembly, and business was conducted in a very hurried manner. When now they held council against Jesus in order to condemn him to death, Nicodemus, Joseph of Arimathea, and a few others opposed his enemies. They demanded that the case should be postponed till after the festival in order not to give rise to a tumult among the people. They argued also that no just sentence could be rendered upon the charges as yet brought forward, since all the witnesses had contradicted one another. The high priests and their large party became exasperated by this opposition, and they told their opponents in plain terms that they understood clearly why this trial was so repugnant to them since, perhaps, they themselves were not quite innocent of having taken part in the doctrines of the Galilean.

The high priests even went so far as to exclude from the council all those that were in any way well-disposed toward Jesus. These members protested against taking any part in its proceedings, left the judgment hall, and betook themselves to the temple. From that time forward they never sat in the council. Caiaphas now ordered poor, abused Jesus, who was consumed from want of rest, to be brought from the prison and presented before the council, so that after the sentence he might without delay be taken to Pilate. The servants hurried tumultuously into the prison, overwhelmed Jesus with words of abuse, loosened his hands, dragged the old tattered mantle from his shoulders, put on him his own long, woven robe, which was still covered with all kinds of filth, fastened the ropes again around his waist, and led him forth from the prison. All this was accompanied with blows, by way of hastening the operation, for now as before all took place with violent hurry and horrible barbarity. Like a poor animal for sacrifice, with blows and mockery, Jesus was dragged by the executioners into the judgment hall through the rows of soldiers assembled in front of the house. And as through ill-treatment and exhaustion he presented so unsightly an appearance, his only covering being his torn and soiled undergarment, the disgust of his enemies filled them with still greater rage. Compassion found no place in any one of those hardened hearts.

Caiaphas, full of scorn and fury for Jesus standing before him in so miserable a plight, thus addressed him: "If thou be the anointed of the Lord, the Messiah, tell us!" Then Jesus raised his head and with divine forbearance and solemn dignity said: "If I shall tell you, you will not believe me. And if I shall also ask you, you will not answer me, nor let me go. But hereafter the Son of Man shall be sitting on the right hand of the power of God." The members of the council glanced from one to another and, smiling scornfully, said to Jesus with disdain: "So then, thou! *Thou* art the Son of God?" With the voice of eternal truth, Jesus answered: "Yes, it is as ye say. I am he!" At this word of the Lord all looked at one another, saying: "What need we any further testimony? For we ourselves have heard it from his own mouth."

Then all rose up with abusive words against Jesus, "the poor, wandering, miserable, destitute creature of low degree, who was their Messiah, and who would one day sit upon the right hand of God!" They ordered the executioners to bind him anew, to place the chain around his neck, and to lead him as a condemned criminal to Pilate. A messenger had already been dispatched to notify Pilate to hold himself in readiness to judge a malefactor at an early hour, because on account of the coming festival there was no time to be lost. Some words of dissatisfaction passed among them with regard to the Roman governor; they were vexed at having to send Jesus first to him. But they dared not themselves pronounce sentence of death in cases that concerned other than their religious laws and those of the temple; and as they wanted to bring Jesus to death with a greater appearance of justice, they desired that he should be judged as an offender against the Emperor, and that the condemnation should come principally from the Roman governor. Soldiers were ranged in the outer court and in front of the house, and many of Jesus's enemies and others of the rabble were already gathered outside. The high priest and some other members of the council walked first, then followed the poor Savior among the executioners and a crowd of soldiers, and lastly came the mob. In this order they descended Zion into the lower city, and proceeded to Pilate's palace. Many of the priests that had assisted at the late trial now went to the temple, where there was much to be done today.

The Despair of Judas

JUDAS, the traitor, lurking at no great distance, heard the noise of the advancing procession, and words such as these dropped by stragglers hurrying after it: "They are taking him to Pilate. The Sanhedrin has condemned the Galilean to death. He has to die on the cross. He cannot live much longer, for they have already handled him shockingly. He is patient as one beside himself with horror. He speaks not, excepting to say that he is the Messiah and that he will one day sit at the right hand of God. That is all that he says,

April 3, AD 33
Friday, Early Morning's Light

therefore he must be crucified. If he had not said that, they could have brought no cause of death against him, but now he must hang on the cross. The wretch that sold him was one of his own disciples and he had only a short time previously eaten the paschal lamb with him. I should not like to have a share in that deed. Whatever the Galilean may be, he has never delivered a friend to death for money. In truth, the wretch that sold him deserves to hang!" Then anguish, despair, and remorse began to struggle in the soul of Judas, but all too late. Satan instigated him to flee. The bag of silver pieces hanging from his girdle under his mantle was for him like a hellish spur. He grasped it tightly in his hand, to prevent its rattling and striking him at every step. On he ran at full speed, not after the procession, not to cast himself in Jesus's path to implore mercy and forgiveness, not to die with Jesus. No, not to confess with contrition before God his awful crime, but to disburden himself of his guilt and the price of his treachery before men. Like one bereft of his senses, he rushed into the temple, whither several of the council, as superintendents of the priests whose duty it was to serve, also some of the elders, had gone directly after the condemnation of Jesus. They glanced wonderingly at one another, and then fixed their gaze with a proud and scornful smile upon Judas, who stood before them, his countenance distorted by despairing grief. He tore the bag of silver pieces from his girdle and held it toward them with the right hand, while in a voice of agony he cried: "Take back your money! By it ye have led me to betray the just one. Take back your money! Release Jesus! I recall my contract. I have sinned grievously by betraying innocent blood!" The priests poured out upon him the whole measure of their contempt. Raising their hands, they stepped back before the offered silver, as if to preserve themselves from pollution, and said: "What is it to us that thou hast sinned? Thinkest thou to have sold innocent blood? Look thou to it! It is thine own affair! We know what we have bought from thee, and we find him deserving of death. Thou hast thy money. We want none of it!" With these and similar words spoken quickly and in the manner of men that have business on hand and that wish to get away from an importunate visitor, they turned from Judas. Their treatment inspired him with such rage and despair that he became like one insane. His hair stood on end, with both hands he rent asunder the chain that held the silver pieces together, scattered them in the temple, and fled from the city. [H31]

I saw him again running like a maniac in the Valley of

Hinnom with Satan under a horrible form at his side. The evil one, to drive him to despair, was whispering into his ear all the curses the prophets had ever invoked upon this valley, wherein the Jews had once sacrificed their own children to idols. It seemed to him that all those maledictions were directed against himself; as, for instance, "They shall go forth, and behold the carcasses of those that have sinned against me, whose worm dieth not, and whose fire shall never be extinguished." Then sounded again in his ears: "Cain, where is Abel, thy brother? What hast thou done? His blood cries to me. Cursed be thou upon the earth, a wanderer and a fugitive!" And when, reaching the brook Kidron, he gazed over at the Mount of Olives, he shuddered and turned his eyes away, while in his ears rang the words: "Friend, whereto hast thou come? Judas, dost thou betray the Son of Man with a kiss?"

Oh, then horror filled his soul! His mind began to wander, and the fiend again whispered into his ear: "It was here that David crossed the Kidron when fleeing from Absalom. Absalom died hanging on a tree. David also sang of thee when he said: 'And they repaid me evil for good. May he have a hard judge! May Satan stand at his right hand, and may every tribunal of justice condemn him! Let his days be few, and his bishopric let another take! May the iniquity of his father be remembered in the sight of the Lord, and let not the sin of his mother be blotted out, because he persecuted the poor without mercy and put to death the broken in heart! He has loved cursing, and it shall come unto him. And he put on cursing like a garment, and like water it went into his entrails, like oil into his bones. May it be unto him like a garment which covereth him, and like a girdle may it enclose him forever!' Amid these frightful torments of conscience, Judas reached a desolate spot full of rubbish, refuse, and swampy water southeast of Jerusalem, at the foot of the Mount of Scandals where no one could see him. From the city came repeated sounds of noisy tumult, and Satan whispered again: "Now he is being led to death! Thou hast sold him! Knowest thou not how the law runs: 'he who sells a soul among his brethren, and receives the price of it, let him die the death'? Put an end to thyself, thou wretched one! Put an end to thyself!" Overcome by despair, Judas took his girdle and hung himself on a tree. The tree was one that consisted of several trunks, and rose out of a hollow in the ground. [H32] As he hung, his body burst asunder, and his bowels poured out upon the earth.

Jesus is Taken to Pilate

THE INHUMAN crowd that conducted Jesus from Caiaphas to Pilate passed through the most populous part of the city, [H33] which was now swarming with Passover guests and countless strangers from all parts of the country.

The procession proceeded northward from Mount Zion, down through a closely built street that crossed the valley, then through a section of the city called Acre, along the west side of the temple to the palace and tribunal of Pilate, which stood at the northwest corner of the temple opposite the great forum, or market.

Caiaphas and Annas, with a large number of the chief council in robes of state, stalked on in advance of the procession. After them were carried rolls of writing. They were followed by numerous scribes and other Jews, among them all the false witnesses and the exasperated Pharisees who had been particularly active at the preceding accusation of the Lord. Then after a short intervening distance, surrounded by a crowd of soldiers and those six functionaries who had been present at the capture, came our dear Lord Jesus bound as before with ropes which were held by the executioners. The mob came streaming from all sides and joined the procession with shouts and cries of mockery. Crowds of people were standing along the way.

Jesus was now clothed in his woven undergarment, which was covered with dirt and mud. From his neck hung the heavy, rough chain that struck his knees painfully as he walked. His hands were fettered as on the day before, and the four executioners dragged him again by the cords fastened to his girdle. By the frightful ill-treatment of the preceding night, he was perfectly disfigured. He tottered along, a picture of utter misery—haggard, his hair and beard torn, his face livid and swollen with blows. Amid fresh outrage and mockery he was driven onward. Many of the mob had been instigated by those in power to scoff in this procession at Jesus's royal entrance into Jerusalem on Palm Sunday. They saluted him in mockery with all kinds of regal titles; cast on the road at his feet stones, clubs, pieces of wood, and filthy rags; and in all kinds of satirical songs and shouts reproached him with his solemn entrance. The executioners pushed him and dragged him by the cords over the objects that impeded his path, so that the whole way was one of uninterrupted maltreatment.

Not very far from the house of Caiaphas, crowded together in the corner of a building, and waiting for the coming procession, were the blessed and afflicted mother of Jesus, Magdalene, and John. Mary's soul was always with Jesus, but wherever she could approach him in body also, her love gave her no rest. It drove her out upon his path and into his footsteps. After her midnight visit to Caiaphas's tribunal, she had in speechless grief tarried only a short time in the Cenacle; for scarcely was Jesus led forth from prison for the morning trial when she too arose. Enveloped in mantle and veil, and taking the lead of John and Magdalene, she said: "Let us follow my Son to Pilate. My eyes must again behold him." Taking a bypath, they got in advance of the procession, and here the blessed Virgin stood and waited along with the others. The mother of Jesus knew how things were going with her Son. Her soul had him always before her eyes, but that interior view could never have depicted him so disfigured and maltreated as he really was by the wickedness of human creatures. She did, in truth, see constantly his frightful sufferings, but all aglow with the light of his love and his sanctity, with the glory of that patient endurance with which he was accomplishing his sacrifice. But now passed before her gaze the frightful reality in all its ignoble significance. The proud and enraged enemies of Jesus, the high priests of the true God, in their robes of ceremony, full of malice, fraud, falsehood, and blasphemy, passed before her, revolving deicidal designs. The priests of God had become priests of Satan. Oh, terrible spectacle! And then that uproar, those cries of the populace! And lastly, Jesus, the Son of God, the Son of Man, Mary's own Son, disfigured and maltreated, fettered and covered with blows, driven along by the executioners, tottering rather than walking, jerked forward by the barbarous executioners who held the ropes that bound him, and overwhelmed by a storm of mockery and malediction! Ah! Had he not been the most wretched, the most miserable in that tempest of hell unchained, had he not been the only one calm and in loving prayer, Mary would never have known him, so terribly was he disfigured. He had, besides, only his undergarment on, and that had been covered with dirt by the malicious executioners. As he approached her, she lamented as any mother might have done: "Alas! Is this my Son? Ah! Is this my Son! O Jesus, my Jesus!" The procession hurried by. Jesus cast upon his mother a side glance full of emotion. She became unconscious of all around, and John and Magdalene bore her away. But scarcely had she somewhat recovered herself when she requested John to accompany her again to Pilate's palace.

That friends abandon us in our hour of need, Jesus likewise experienced on this journey, for the inhabitants of Ophel were all assembled at a certain point on the way. But when they beheld Jesus so despised and disfigured, led forward in the midst of the executioners, they too wavered in their faith. They could not imagine that the king, the prophet, the Messiah, the Son of God could possibly be in such a situation. They heard their attachment to Jesus jeered at by the Pharisees as they passed. "There, look at your fine king!" they cried. "Salute him! Ah, now you hang your head when he is going to his coronation, when he will so soon mount his throne! It is all over with his prodigies. The high priest has put an end to his witchcraft." The poor people, who had received so many cures and favors from Jesus, were shaken in their faith by the frightful spectacle exhibited before them by the most venerable personages of the land, the high priest and the members of the Sanhedrin. The best of them turned away in doubt, while the viciously inclined, with scoffs and jeers, joined the procession wherever they could, for the avenues of approach were here and there occupied by guards appointed by the Pharisees in order to prevent a tumult.

The Palace of Pilate and its Surroundings

AT the foot of the northwestern corner of the temple mount stood the palace of Pilate, the Roman governor. It was on somewhat of an elevation, and was reached by a long flight of marble steps. It overlooked a spacious square surrounded by a colonnade under which vendors sat to sell their wares. A guardhouse and four entrances on the north, south, east, and west sides, respectively, broke the uniformity of the colonnade enclosing the square, which was called the forum, and which on the east stretched over the northwest corner of the temple mount. From this end of the forum, one could see as far as Mount Zion. Pilate's palace lay to the south. The forum was somewhat higher than the surrounding streets, which sloped down from it. On the outer side of the colonnade the houses of the neighboring streets adjoined it in some places. Pilate's palace did not adjoin the forum—a spacious court separated the two. On the eastern side of this court was a high arched gateway, which opened into a street that led to the sheep gate on the road to the Mount of Olives. On the western side was another gateway like the first, which led to the west of the city through the section Acre and up to Zion.

TISSOT ILLUSTRATIONS
[SECTION H]

The Passion and Death of Jesus Christ

⊕

The Man Bearing a Pitcher · · · · · · · · · · · · · · · 122

The Last Supper · 124

Judas Dipping His Hand in the Dish · · · · · · · · · 126

The Washing of the Feet · · · · · · · · · · · · · · · · 128

The Communion of the Apostles · · · · · · · · · · · 130

Judas Leaves the Cenacle · · · · · · · · · · · · · · · · 132

The Last Sermon of Our Lord · · · · · · · · · · · · · 134

Address to Philip · 136

The Protestations of Peter · · · · · · · · · · · · · · · 138

My Soul is Sorrowful unto Death · · · · · · · · · · · 140

You Could Not Watch with Me for One Hour · · 142

The Grotto of the Agony · · · · · · · · · · · · · · · · 144

The Procession of Judas · · · · · · · · · · · · · · · · · 146

The Guards Falling Backward · · · · · · · · · · · · · 148

The Kiss of Judas · 150

The Ear of Malchus · 152

The Healing of Malchus · · · · · · · · · · · · · · · · · 154

The Bridge of Kidron · · · · · · · · · · · · · · · · · · 156

The Flight of the Apostles · · · · · · · · · · · · · · · 158

Peter and John Follow from Afar · · · · · · · · · · · 160

The Tribunal of Annas · · · · · · · · · · · · · · · · · · 162

The False Witnesses · 164

Annas and Caiaphas · 166

The Torn Cloak—Jesus Condemned to Death · · 168

Maltreatments in the House of Caiaphas · · · · · · 170

The First Denial of Peter · · · · · · · · · · · · · · · · 172

The Second Denial of Peter · · · · · · · · · · · · · · 174

The Third Denial: Jesus's Look of Reproach · · · · 176

The Sorrow of Peter · · · · · · · · · · · · · · · · · · · 178

The Apostles' Hiding Place · · · · · · · · · · · · · · · 180

Good Friday Morning: Jesus in Prison · · · · · · · · 182

The Morning Judgment · · · · · · · · · · · · · · · · · 184

Judas Returns the Money · · · · · · · · · · · · · · · · 186

Judas Hangs Himself · · · · · · · · · · · · · · · · · · · 188

Jesus Led from Caiaphas to Pilate · · · · · · · · · · · 190

The Man Bearing a Pitcher [H1]

BEFORE break of day, Jesus, calling Peter and John, spoke to them at some length upon what they should order, what preparations they should make in Jerusalem for the eating of the paschal lamb. The disciples had questioned Jesus the day before upon where this supper was to be held. Jesus told the two apostles that they would, when ascending Mount Zion, meet a man carrying a water pitcher, one whom they already knew, as he was the same that had attended to the Passover meal for Jesus the year before at Bethany. They were to follow him into the house and say to him: "The Master bids us say to thee that his time is near at hand. He desires to celebrate Passover at thy house." They should then ask to see the supper room, which they would find prepared, and there they should make ready all that was needed.

I saw the two apostles going up to Jerusalem through a ravine that ran south of the temple and north of Zion. On the south side of the mount upon which the temple stood there were some rows of houses opposite which a rapid stream flowed down the height; on the other side of this stream ran the road by which the apostles ascended. On reaching a point of Zion higher than the temple mount, they turned toward the south and met the man designated by Jesus on a somewhat rising open space, and in the neighborhood of an old building surrounded by courts. They followed him and, when near the house, delivered to him Jesus's message. He showed great pleasure at seeing them and learning their errand. He told them that he had already been ordered to prepare a supper (probably by Nicodemus), though he knew not for whom, but now he greatly rejoiced that it was for Jesus. This man was Heli, the brother-in-law of Zechariah of Hebron, the same in whose house at Hebron Jesus had, after a certain sabbath of the preceding year, announced to the family the death of John. He had five unmarried daughters, but only one son, who was a Levite and who had been a friend of Luke before the latter joined the Lord. Heli went with his servants every year to the feast, hired a supper room, and prepared the Passover meal for people that had no friends in the city. [71]

[MARK 14:12–17] 12 And on the first day of Unleavened Bread, when they sacrificed the passover lamb, his disciples said to him, "Where will you have us go and prepare for you to eat the passover?" 13 And he sent two of his disciples, and said to them, "Go into the city, and a man carrying a jar of water will meet you; follow him, 14 and wherever he enters, say to the householder, 'The Teacher says, Where is my guest room, where I am to eat the passover with my disciples?' 15 And he will show you a large upper room furnished and ready; there prepare for us." 16 And the disciples set out and went to the city, and found it as he had told them; and they prepared the passover. 17 And when it was evening he came with the twelve.

THE disciples had asked the Savior to give them his instructions about the Passover, and he had chosen Peter and John to go and prepare everything, and first of all to find the place described by him. They are represented in my picture watching for the man passing bearing a pitcher, of whom the Master had spoken, having for this purpose taken up their posts against the wall of the Zion quarter, where the street leads down by way of the Ophel suburb to the well now known as the Fountain of the Virgin, the ancient En-Rogel. The water of this well being the purest in Jerusalem was the best suited for making the unleavened bread used at the Passover. Men and women bearing pitchers pass along this street, the women in greater numbers than the men, for the fetching of water is generally their business. It would therefore be easy to observe the few men who returned from the well, slowly climbing up the hill, laden as they are with their heavy loads. Many have already passed, but not yet the one designated by the Master. When he comes, it is John, the beloved and trusted friend of Jesus, who recognizes him immediately, and the disciples at once prepare to follow him. They have scarcely a hundred steps to go, for they are already far up the street and quite close to the ancient Zion, which looks down upon the mountain on which Jerusalem is built. The precise and homely details here given to us by the Evangelist, with those supplied throughout the whole history of the successive scenes of the Passion, enable us to obtain a wonderfully vivid and truthful idea of all the facts connected with this deeply interesting period. We feel that eye-witnesses are speaking, or at least that eye-witnesses inspired the writer even in his most minute shades of expression. John saw everything, the other apostles were in the very best possible position for obtaining trustworthy testimony; so that in reading the divine record, the whole tragic story is lived through again, as it were before our very eyes, the two thousand years which have passed roll away as though they had never been, and we receive just such a vivid impression as we should in reading a contemporary journal.

The Last Supper [H2]

JESUS next gave the apostles an instruction upon the paschal lamb and the fulfillment of what it symbolized, and as the time was drawing near and Judas had returned, they began to prepare the tables. After that they put on the traveling dresses of ceremony, which were in the anteroom, and changed their shoes. The dress consisted of a white tunic like a shirt, and over it a mantle, shorter in front than in the back. The tunic was tucked up into the girdle, and the wide sleeves were turned up. Thus equipped, each set went to its own table: the two bands of disciples into the side halls, Jesus and the apostles into the Cenacle proper. Each took a staff in his hand, and then they walked in pairs to the table at which each stood in his place, his arms raised, and the staff resting upon one. Jesus stood in the center of the table. The table was narrow and only high enough to reach one-half foot above the knee of a man standing by it. In form it was like a horseshoe. [76]

[MATTHEW 26:20] 20 When it was evening, he sat at table with the twelve disciples.

THE room is prepared for the Passover; the draperies, decorated with festoons of foliage, hang as usual between the pillars; the lamp is lit, for it is already night. The twelve apostles, with Christ in the midst of them, are beginning the ceremonial of the feast in accordance with the ancient ritual: with robes tucked up, loins girt, sandals on the feet, and the staff in the hand, in a word, in traveling dress in remembrance of the Exodus from Egypt. Thus must be accomplished the solemn ceremony every Jew was bound to perform and of which the principal rite was the eating of the Paschal Lamb.

Judas Dipping His Hand in the Dish [H3]

IN the inner part of the half-circle, there was a space left free for the serving of the dishes. As far as I can remember, John, James the Greater, and James the Less stood on Jesus's right; then came Bartholomew, still on the right, but more toward the narrow end of the table; and round the corner at the inner side stood Thomas, and next to him Judas Iscariot. On Jesus's left were Peter, Andrew, and Thaddeus; then as on the opposite side, came Simon; and round at the inner side, Matthew and Philip. While the apostles were eating the herbs, Jesus continued to converse with them still quite lovingly, though he afterward became grave and sad. He said: "One among you will betray me—one whose hand is with me in the dish." He was at that moment distributing one of the vegetables, namely the lettuce, of which there was only one dish. He was passing it down his own side, and he had directed Judas, who was sitting crosswise from him, to distribute it on the other side. [76]

[MARK 14:17–20] 17 And when it was evening he came with the twelve. 18 And as they were at table eating, Jesus said, "Truly, I say to you, one of you will betray me, one who is eating with me." 19 They began to be sorrowful, and to say to him one after another, "Is it I?" 20 He said to them, "It is one of the twelve, one who is dipping bread into the dish with me." [JOHN 13:21–27] 21 When Jesus had thus spoken, he was troubled in spirit, and testified, "Truly, truly, I say to you, one of you will betray me." 22 The disciples looked at one another, uncertain of whom he spoke. 23 One of his disciples, whom Jesus loved, was lying close to the breast of Jesus; 24 so Simon Peter beckoned to him and said, "Tell us who it is of whom he speaks." 25 So lying thus, close to the breast of Jesus, he said to him, "Lord, who is it?" 26 Jesus answered, "It is he to whom I shall give this morsel when I have dipped it." So when he had dipped the morsel, he gave it to Judas, the son of Simon Iscariot. 27 Then after the morsel, Satan entered into him. Jesus said to him, "What you are going to do, do quickly."

WE have already described the way in which the guests were placed at meals. After having removed the sandals, they ate their food reposing on couches, as indicated in the verse of the gospel quoted above by the Latin word discumbens. This couch was a sort of divan sloping slightly toward the feet and provided with a headrest at the upper end. Long cushions were placed on the couches so that those using them could recline comfortably on the left side, leaving the right arm and hand free. There was generally room enough on each couch for two people, except on the couches at the end of the table or on the inside of the horseshoe it formed. The servants in waiting stood in the center and the couches radiated all round it, each at right angles with the table. This arrangement explains how it was that John, placed on the right hand of Jesus, could easily lean his head upon the breast of the Lord and speak to him in a low voice without being heard, while Peter, placed on the left side, had next to him the arm on which Jesus was reclining, so that it would be much more difficult for him to communicate with the Master. As for the place occupied by Judas, that is to a certain extent necessarily determined by the incident itself; for, to be able to dip his hand in the same dish as Jesus, he would have to occupy a seat in the center of the horseshoe nearly opposite to him.

In the gospel account quoted above, it will be noticed how full of melancholy reproach is the insistence with which the Master speaks of the treason about to be committed. "One of the twelve," he says emphatically, so that no one may suppose he is speaking of one of the many disciples who were less familiar with his person, and on whom he had not showered so many fatherly benefits. "One of you that dippeth with me in the dish" he insists; the fact of eating out of one dish being indeed considered among the Jews and throughout the whole of the East as a kind of covenant, which, in case of injury inflicted by one of the parties to it on the other, aggravated the heinousness of the offence. With regard to Judas the remark had the greater weight inasmuch as he and the Lord had not taken this one meal only together, but he had long been admitted to close and constant intimacy with Jesus.

The Washing of the Feet [H4]

THEY arose from table and, while putting on and arranging their robes, as was the custom before solemn prayer, the master of the feast with two servants came in to take away the table and put back the seats. While this was being done, Jesus ordered some water to be brought him in the anteroom, and the master again left the hall with his servants. Jesus, standing in the midst of the apostles, spoke to them long and solemnly. When it was ended, he sent John and James the Less to bring the water from the anteroom, and directed the others to place the seats in a half-circle. Meantime, he himself retired to the anteroom to lay aside his mantle, gird up his robe, and tie around him a towel, one end of which he allowed to hang. Jesus, still in the anteroom, commanded John to take a basin, and James the Less a leathern bottle of water. The latter carried the bottle before his breast, the spout resting on his arm. After he had poured some water from the bottle into the basin, Jesus bade the two follow him into the hall in the center of which the master of the feast had set another large, empty basin. Entering the hall in this order, Jesus in a few words reproved the apostles for the strife that had arisen among them. He said among other things that he himself was their servant, and that they should take their places on the seats for him to wash their feet. They obeyed, observing the same order as at table. They sat on the backs of the seats, which were arranged in a half-circle, and rested their naked feet upon the seat itself.

Jesus went from one to another and, from the basin held under them by John, with his hand scooped up water over the feet presented to him. Then taking in both hands the long end of the towel with which he was girded, he passed it over the feet to dry them, and then moved on with James to the next. John emptied the water after each one into the large basin in the center of the room, and then returned to the Lord with the empty one. Then Jesus again poured water from the bottle held by James over the feet of the next, and so on. When he came to Peter, the latter, through humility, objected. He said: "Lord, dost thou wash my feet?" And the Lord answered: "What I do, thou knowest not now, but thou shalt know hereafter." When Jesus washed Judas's feet, it was in the most touching and loving manner. He pressed them to his cheek and in a low tone bade him enter into himself, for that he had been unfaithful and a traitor for the past year. Jesus's words to Judas passed unremarked by the other apostles, for he spoke softly, and they did not hear. They were, besides, busy putting on their sandals. Judas's treachery caused Jesus more pain than any other part of his Passion. Jesus then washed the feet of John and James; first those of the latter while Peter held the water bottle; then the former, for whom James held the basin. [77]

[JOHN 13:4–11] 4 [Jesus] rose from supper, laid aside his garments, and girded himself with a towel. 5 Then he poured water into a basin, and began to wash the disciples' feet, and to wipe them with the towel with which he was girded. 6 He came to Simon Peter; and Peter said to him, "Lord, do you wash my feet?" 7 Jesus answered him, "What I am doing you do not know now, but afterward you will understand." 8 Peter said to him, "You shall never wash my feet." Jesus answered him, "If I do not wash you, you have no part in me." 9 Simon Peter said to him, "Lord, not my feet only but also my hands and my head!" 10 Jesus said to him, "He who has bathed does not need to wash, except for his feet, but he is clean all over; and you are clean, but not every one of you." 11 For he knew who was to betray him; that was why he said, "You are not all clean."

THEIR Passover duties performed in accordance with the requirements of the Jewish law, and before the inauguration of the new rite which Jesus was about to institute, the Lord and his disciples left the room in which they had kept the Passover, to repair to another divided into two parts by a curtain, on one side of which seats were provided for the new ceremony. The apostles were seated in the same order as before, for already the Christian hierarchy may be said to have been founded. On the left, at the edge of the table, is Judas, succeeded by Thomas, Bartholomew, James the Less, who is bringing the water, James the Greater, and then John, who is looking down at the basin in which the feet are to be washed. Jesus has taken up his position in the center of the group, having on his left, that is to say on the right of the picture, Peter, Andrew, Thaddeus, Simon, Matthew, and Philip. Jesus has begun with Philip, who is putting on his sandals again; the scene with Peter, described in the sacred text, will take place in the center, and the ceremony will conclude with the washing of the feet of Judas.

The Communion of the Apostles [H5]

⊕

AT the command of the Lord, the master of the feast again set out the table, which he raised a little higher. It was placed in the middle of the room and covered with a cloth, over which two others were spread, one red, and the other white and transparent. Then the master set two jugs, one of water, the other of wine, under the table. Peter and John now brought from the back part of the hall, where was the paschal hearth, the chalice they had brought from Veronica's house. Jesus's place was between Peter and John. The doors were closed, for everything was conducted with secrecy and solemnity. When the cover of the chalice had been removed and taken back to the recess in the rear of the Cenacle, Jesus prayed and uttered some very solemn words. Then, taking the chalice, he received into it wine and water, the former poured by Peter, and the latter by John.

During all this time Jesus was becoming more and more recollected. He said to the apostles that he was now about to give them all that he possessed, even his very self. He took the plate with the morsels of bread (I do not remember whether he had placed it on the chalice or not) and said, "Take and eat. This is my body which is given for you." While saying these words, he stretched forth his right hand over it, as if giving a blessing, and as he did so, a brilliant light emanated from him. His words were luminous as also the bread, which as a body of light entered the mouth of the apostles. It was as if Jesus himself flowed into them. I saw all of them penetrated with light, bathed in light. Judas alone was in darkness.

Jesus presented the bread first to Peter, then to John, and next made a sign to Judas, who was sitting diagonally from him, to approach. Thus Judas was the third to whom Jesus presented the blessed sacrament, but it seemed as if the word of the Lord turned back from the mouth of the traitor. I was so terrified at the sight that I cannot describe my feelings. Jesus said to Judas: "What thou art about to do, do quickly." The Lord then administered the blessed sacrament to the rest of the apostles, who came up two by two. [78]

[LUKE 22:19–20] 19 And he took bread, and when he had given thanks he broke it and gave it to them, saying, "This is my body which is given for you. Do this in remembrance of me." 20 And likewise the cup after supper, saying, "This cup which is poured out for you is the new covenant in my blood."

THE disciples had already been profoundly moved by the washing of their feet by the Lord, and the mysterious words Jesus had just pronounced over the bread and wine had put the finishing touch to their emotion. At heart, in spite of all the comforting words their Master had lavished upon them, they are anxious and saddened by their presentiment of the events about to take place, and they are all silent. Jesus alone says a few words in a low voice; he breaks the sacred bread and distributes it among the disciples, who reverently approach to receive it in their hands. I have therefore supposed, as indeed the sacred text seems to suggest, that John and Peter, placed on the right and left hand of Jesus, were the first to communicate, and that the other apostles came in turn one by one, with feelings suitable to a moment so supreme, to receive the same great privilege.

The Church was now founded, and it was, therefore, fitting to inaugurate a ceremony, which was to be repeated throughout all future centuries, in such a manner as to impress all who were present with the solemnity of the sacred rite and enable them ever to retain undimmed their memory of it.

Judas Leaves the Cenacle [H6]

⊕

JESUS next raised the chalice by its two handles to a level with his face, and pronounced into it the words of consecration. While doing so, he was wholly transfigured and, as it were, transparent. He was as if passing over into what he was giving. He caused Peter and John to drink from the chalice while yet in his hands, and then he set it down. With the little spoon, John removed some of the sacred blood from the chalice to the small cups, which Peter handed to the apostles who, two by two, drank from the same cup.

Judas also (though of this I am not quite certain) partook of the chalice, but he did not return to his place, for he immediately left the Cenacle. The others thought that Jesus had given him some commission to execute. He left without prayer or thanksgiving. And here we may see what an evil it is to fail to give thanks for our daily bread and for the Bread that endures to life eternal. During the whole meal I saw a little red monster with one foot like a bare bone sitting at Judas's feet and often rising up to his heart, but when outside the door, I saw three devils pressing around him. One entered into his mouth, one urged him on, and the third ran in front of him. It was night. They seemed to be lighting him as he hurried on like a madman. [79]

[JOHN 13:30] 30 So, after receiving the morsel, he immediately went out; and it was night.

JUDAS, *impatient to execute his designs, and annoyed, moreover, at the words of Jesus: "That thou doest, do quickly," left the guest-chamber and hurried away, after having, no doubt, himself taken part in the celebration of the second Passover and received a portion of the sacred bread. It was already night and the moon was rising, casting deep shadows in the narrow streets and thus intensifying the gloom. The ninth hour was approaching, and Judas was impatiently expected. Many were those who would not go to bed that night, the gratification of their hatred would have to serve instead of repose. Complete silence reigned in the town except for the occasional barking of dogs, breaking the stillness at irregular intervals. Judas glided along the walls and went down into the city, approaching the temple, where he expected to find the soldiers of the escort which was to go with him to take Jesus. There were some bridges to cross, and the silence seemed deeper than ever down in the valleys separating the temple from the town. Perhaps an occasional cry may for a moment have added to the betrayer's distress: a sentinel may have fallen asleep in some porch and an officer of the night patrol may have set fire to his gibbeh or upper garment to wake him, according to the requirements of the law.*

The Last Sermon of Our Lord [H7]

JESUS now gave to the apostles an instruction full of mystery. He told them how they were to preserve the blessed sacrament in memory of him until the end of the world, taught them the necessary forms for making use of and communicating it, and in what manner they were by degrees to teach and make known the mystery. Then he instructed them upon the priesthood, the sacred unction, and the preparation of the chrism and the holy oils. After that I saw Jesus anointing Peter and John, on whose hands, at the institution of the blessed sacrament, he had poured the water that had flowed over his own, and who had drunk from the chalice in his hand.

From the center of the table, where he was standing, Jesus stepped a little to one side and imposed hands upon Peter and John, first on their shoulders and then on their head. During this action they joined their hands and crossed their thumbs. As they bowed low before him (and I am not sure that they did not kneel) the Lord anointed the thumb and forefinger of each of their hands with chrism, and made the sign of the cross with it on their head. He told them that this anointing would remain with them to the end of the world. James the Less, Andrew, James the Greater, and Bartholomew were likewise consecrated. All that Jesus did at the institution of the blessed Eucharist and the anointing of the apostles was done very secretly, and was later on taught as a mystery.

Jesus again delivered a long instruction and prayed several times with deep recollection. He often appeared to be conversing with his heavenly Father, and to be overflowing with love and enthusiasm. The apostles also were full of joy and zeal. They asked questions about different things, all of which Jesus answered. During this discourse Jesus addressed some words in private to Peter and John, who were sitting next to him, in reference to some of his earlier instructions. They were to communicate them to the other apostles, and these in turn to the disciples and holy women, according to the capacity of each for such knowledge. He spoke for some time to John alone. Of this I remember only that Jesus told him that his life would be longer than that of the others, and that he said something about seven churches, something about crowns and angels and similar significant symbols by which, as well as I know, he designated certain epochs. [80]

[JOHN 13:31–35] 31 When he had gone out, Jesus said, "Now is the Son of man glorified, and in him God is glorified; 32 if God is glorified in him, God will also glorify him in himself, and glorify him at once. 33 Little children, yet a little while I am with you. You will seek me; and as I said to the Jews so now I say to you, 'Where I am going you cannot come.' 34 A new commandment I give to you, that you love one another; even as I have loved you, that you also love one another. 35 By this all men will know that you are my disciples, if you have love for one another." [JOHN 14:1–4] 1 "Let not your hearts be troubled; believe in God, believe also in me. 2 In my Father's house are many rooms; if it were not so, would I have told you that I go to prepare a place for you? 3 And when I go and prepare a place for you, I will come again and will take you to myself, that where I am you may be also. 4 And you know the way where I am going."

THE new order had begun: the old order had already given place to it. Henceforth every act of Jesus, every gesture however slight, takes a new and, in a certain sense, a sacramental signification; it is, so to speak, the liturgical initiation of the apostles, and it behoves them to remember in order that they may communicate to their spiritual heirs everything the Savior did and said on this his last night on earth. In our engraving, Jesus is represented wearing his prophet's mantle, in which we see the origin of the cope, or tallity, a wide garment fastened at the neck, which falls in a very different manner from an ordinary mantle. The apostles are very sure to have worn the tallith with the four tassels at the feast of the Passover, and this is why I have represented them in it in the picture illustrating the last discourse of the Lord. They are not grouped accidentally, but in strictly hierarchal order, in order to shadow forth the organization of the church, which from this time may be looked upon as an accomplished fact. Jesus standing in the midst of his disciples, and as it were officiating for them, pronounces his last words, his farewell discourse. Reading the account of it in the gospel of John, we cannot fail to be impressed with the deep solemnity of the occasion, indeed, the whole night seems to have been passed in the observance of an uninterrupted series of sacred rites.

Address to Philip

⊕

[JOHN 14:5–20] 5 Thomas said to him, "Lord, we do not know where you are going; how can we know the way?" 6 Jesus said to him, "I am the way, and the truth, and the life; no one comes to the Father, but by me. 7 If you had known me, you would have known my Father also; henceforth you know him and have seen him." 8 Philip said to him, "Lord, show us the Father, and we shall be satisfied." 9 Jesus said to him, "Have I been with you so long, and yet you do not know me, Philip? He who has seen me has seen the Father; how can you say, 'Show us the Father'? 10 Do you not believe that I am in the Father and the Father in me? The words that I say to you I do not speak on my own authority; but the Father who dwells in me does his works. 11 Believe me that I am in the Father and the Father in me; or else believe me for the sake of the works themselves. 12 Truly, truly, I say to you, he who believes in me will also do the works that I do; and greater works than these will he do, because I go to the Father. 13 Whatever you ask in my name, I will do it, that the Father may be glorified in the Son; 14 if you ask anything in my name, I will do it. 15 If you love me, you will keep my commandments. 16 And I will pray the Father, and he will give you another Counselor, to be with you for ever, 17 even the Spirit of truth, whom the world cannot receive, because it neither sees him nor knows him; you know him, for he dwells with you, and will be in you. 18 I will not leave you desolate; I will come to you. 19 Yet a little while, and the world will see me no more, but you will see me; because I live, you will live also. 20 In that day you will know that I am in my Father, and you in me, and I in you."

The Protestations of Peter [H8]

THE apostles were still full of the enthusiasm and devotion inspired by the reception of the most holy Sacrament, and the loving, solemn discourse of Jesus afterward. They crowded eagerly around him and expressed their love in different ways, protesting that they never could, they never would, abandon him. But as Jesus continued to speak in the same strain, Peter exclaimed: "Although all should be scandalized in thee, I will never be scandalized in thee!" The Lord replied: "Amen, I say to thee that in this night before the cock crows, thou wilt deny me thrice." [83]

[MATTHEW 26:30–35] 30 And when they had sung a hymn, they went out to the Mount of Olives. 31 Then Jesus said to them, "You will all fall away because of me this night; for it is written, 'I will strike the shepherd, and the sheep of the flock will be scattered.' 32 But after I am raised up, I will go before you to Galilee." 33 Peter declared to him, "Though they all fall away because of you, I will never fall away." 34 Jesus said to him, "Truly, I say to you, this very night, before the cock crows, you will deny me three times." 35 Peter said to him, "Even if I must die with you, I will not deny you." And so said all the disciples.

THE mysterious ceremonies are now accomplished; the disciples must leave the guest-chamber and follow Jesus, who, as is his custom, is going forth to pray. It is a very dark night; the moon appears now and then only to disappear directly, obscured by the clouds which drift across it, driven onward by the west wind from the sea. No sooner are they in the open air than the apostles are seized with anxious forebodings, the gloomy prophecies of the Master haunt them and they feel that the terrible moment foretold is not far off.

In order to reach the Garden of Gethsemane from Zion, where the guest-chamber was situated, they had to leave the town and pass the ruins of the Tower of Shiloh, but recently destroyed, and the gate by which the refuse from the town was removed. The southern wall of the town was then skirted and, passing the Ophel Gate, they would find themselves on the slope of the mountain from which rose the huge buildings erected by Herod. In the distance, wrapt in shadow, was the bed of the Kidron torrent, at that time of year almost dried up, which was reached by a somewhat steep path dangerous at night to foot-passengers who had to cross the Kidron by a bridge. Several tombs, which still exist at the present day, were passed on the right, including those named after Absalom, Zachariah, and Saint James.

The whole scene is melancholy and gloomy in the extreme, for, in addition to the tombs on the left, the traveler has on the right the mighty walls of the temple, which tower above him and almost overwhelm him with their solemn majesty. At last Jesus and his followers reach Gethsemane, the name of which means wine-press, and which was a farm or oil-press surrounded by gardens or, more strictly speaking, by orchards sacred to the cultivation of fruit trees such as the olive, the fig, and the mulberry. As they made their way thither, the anxiety of the apostles was ever on the increase as the moment of danger drew nearer, for the triple influence of the gloom of the city and of the mountain, with the growing intensity of the darkness of the night, combined to weigh down their spirits. When about half-way on the road, Peter, in the enthusiasm of his faith and in his confidence in himself for the future, began to make all manner of rash protestations of fidelity, little dreaming how soon he would break his promises. As for the other disciples, they were all thoroughly unnerved by terror and they were sure to flee at the very first alarm. It is now half past ten at night.

My Soul is Sorrowful unto Death [H9]

⊕

IT was about nine o'clock when Jesus reached Gethsemane with the disciples. Darkness had fallen upon the earth, but the moon was lighting up the sky. Jesus was very sad. He announced to the apostles the approach of danger, and they became uneasy. Jesus bade eight of them remain in the Garden of Gethsemane, where there was a kind of summerhouse built of branches and foliage. "Remain here," he said, "while I go to my own place to pray." He took Peter, John, and James the Greater with him, crossed the road, and went on for a few minutes, until he reached the Garden of Olives farther up the mountain. He was inexpressibly sad, for he felt his approaching agony and temptation. John asked how he, who had always consoled them, could now be so dejected. He replied: "My soul is sorrowful even unto death." He glanced around and on all sides saw anguish and temptation gathering about him like dense clouds filled with frightful pictures. It was at that moment he said to the three apostles: "Remain here and watch with me. Pray lest ye enter into temptation!" and they stayed in that place. [83]

[MARK 14:34] 34 And he said to them, "My soul is very sorrowful, even to death; remain here, and watch."

WE have just explained that the Garden of Gethsemane is situated in the lower part of the valley, where begin the slopes of the Mount of Olives. Near to it are certain caves which have been converted into family tombs, some of which, as yet unoccupied, afford places of retirement for solitary prayer and meditation. After having entered the Garden with Jesus, the apostles divided into two groups; three of them following the Master at a little distance, the rest dispersing about the mountain slopes so as to watch from a somewhat higher position the approaches to the Garden. From thence, in fact, they could look down upon the various paths leading up to the temple and no one could pass along them unnoticed. The three chosen companions of Jesus: Peter, James, and John, accompanied him in the direction of the cave to which he proposed retiring, and, having reached a rock with a level surface about a stone's cast from it and a little above the path by way of which Judas and the soldiers led by him would presently appear, they halted in obedience to the command of the Savior, while he himself went slowly forward, his soul exceeding sorrowful unto death, to wrestle alone with the temptation assailing him.

You Could Not Watch with Me for One Hour [H10]

⊕

I SAW the grotto around him filled with frightful figures. I saw the sins, the wickedness, the vices, the torments, the ingratitude of men torturing and crushing him, and the horror of death, the terror that he experienced as man at the greatness of the expiatory sufferings soon to come upon him, I saw pressing around him and assailing him under the form of the most hideous specters. Wringing his hands, he swayed from side to side, and the sweat of agony covered him. He trembled and shuddered. He arose, but his trembling knees could scarcely support him. His countenance was quite disfigured and almost unrecognizable. His lips were white, and his hair stood on end.

It was about half-past ten o'clock when he staggered to his feet and, bathed in sweat and often falling, tottered rather than walked to where the three disciples were awaiting him. He ascended to the left of the grotto and up to a terrace upon which they were resting near one another supported on their arm, the back of one turned toward the breast of his neighbor. Exhausted with fatigue, sorrow, and anxiety under temptation, they had fallen asleep. Jesus went to them like a man overwhelmed with sorrow whom terror drives to the company of his friends, and also like a faithful shepherd who, though himself trembling to the utmost, looks after his herd which he knows to be in danger, for he knew that they too were in anguish and temptation. All along this short distance, I saw that the frightful forms never left him. When he found the apostles sleeping, he clasped his hands and, sinking down by them from grief and exhaustion, he said: "Simon, sleepest thou?" At these words, they awoke and raised him up. In his spiritual dereliction, he said: "What! Could ye not watch one hour with me?" [85]

[MATTHEW 26:40–42] 40 And he came to the disciples and found them sleeping; and he said to Peter, "So, could you not watch with me one hour? 41 Watch and pray that you may not enter into temptation; the spirit indeed is willing, but the flesh is weak." 42 Again, for the second time, he went away and prayed, "My Father, if this cannot pass unless I drink it, thy will be done."

AFTER the first paroxysm of agony had subsided Jesus went to his disciples to seek for some little consolation from them. They are his dearest friends; he will tell them all he is going through, and, when they have prayed together, the force of the temptation by which he is assailed will perhaps abate. The Savior, therefore, approaches the place where he had left them. His garments in disorder, his hair still wet with the bloody sweat, bearing witness to the awful suffering he has gone through; his whole bearing betraying the dejection in which his agony has left him. The apostles, worn out with sorrow and fatigue, have fallen asleep upon the rock, Peter still armed with the two swords with which he had provided himself before starting for Gethsemane.

Not long ago we quoted the protestations of devotion made by the chief of the apostles in the extremity of his zeal; his enthusiastic ardor had, however, been damped by the sad prediction of Jesus, and he had come to the garden not knowing what to think, keeping concealed under his abayeh the two cutlasses or swords he had brought with him in case there should be a struggle. The silence and the terrors of this awful night have overcome him too now and he lies asleep, until he is roused by the gentle reproach of Jesus.

The Grotto of the Agony [H11]

⊕

WHEN Jesus went back into the grotto carrying his load of sadness with him, he cast himself face downward on the ground, his arms extended, and prayed to his heavenly Father. And now began for his soul a new struggle, which lasted three quarters of an hour. Angels came and showed him in a long series of visions and in all its extent what he would have to endure for the atonement of sin. They showed the beauty and excellence of man, the image of God, before the Fall, along with his deformity and corruption after the Fall. They showed how every sin originates from that first sin. They showed him the expiatory sufferings that awaited him. All this the angels showed Jesus, sometimes appearing in whole choirs and exhibiting row after row of pictures, and sometimes displaying only the principal features of his suffering. I saw them pointing with raised finger to the visions as they appeared, and without hearing any voice, I understood what they said. All these tortures and afflictions Jesus perceived in an interior contemplation, and the sight filled him with such horror that a bloody sweat started from the pores of his sacred body. [86]

[LUKE 22:41] 41 And he withdrew from them about a stone's throw, and knelt down and prayed, 42 "Father, if thou art willing, remove this cup from me; nevertheless not my will, but thine, be done."

WHEN Jesus had reached the cave, his anguish became even greater than before, reaching an intensity which the evangelists describe by the expression "being in an agony." In my picture the Savior is represented at the culminating moment when all the approaching sufferings of his Passion and death, aggravated by the ingratitude of humankind, rise up before him in all their awful reality. Angels now appeared to him, each one bringing vividly before him some one particular agony which he would have to endure; the circles they form as they move slowly about his prostrate figure shadow forth one anguish after another with cruel relentlessness. This is the cup which Jesus prays his Father "if it be possible to remove from him"; but all the time he knows full well that he must drink it and that to the very last drop; his soul shudders at the thought; his heart is breaking; the tears gush forth abundantly, and in the extremity of his anguish he falls prostrate upon the ground, while his features, his limbs, and his garments, with the rock on which he lies, are stained with his sweat, which is "as it were great drops of blood."

The Procession of Judas [H12]

⊕

WHEN Jesus returned to the disciples, he found them, as at first, lying on their side near the wall of the terrace, their heads covered, and asleep. The Lord said to them: "This is not the time to sleep. Ye should arise and pray, for behold the hour is at hand, and the Son of Man shall be betrayed into the hands of sinners. Arise, let us go! Behold, the traitor is approaching! Oh, it were better for him had he never been born!" The apostles sprang up affrighted and looked around anxiously. They had scarcely recovered themselves, when Peter exclaimed vehemently: "Master, I will call the others, that we may defend thee!" But Jesus pointed out to them at some distance in the valley, though still on the other side of the brook Kidron, a band of armed men approaching with torches. He told the apostles that one of that band had betrayed him. [93]

[MATTHEW 26:47] 47 While he was still speaking, Judas came, one of the twelve, and with him a great crowd with swords and clubs, from the chief priests and the elders of the people.

ISCARIOT, *the surname of Judas, has given rise to many different opinions. Some, among others Eusebius and Saint Jerome, think that the traitor was born in the town of Iscariot belonging to the tribe of Ephraim and that he took his second name from it. Others affirm that he was of the tribe of Issachar and on that account was called Issachariotes or, abbreviated, Ischariots: but the more universally received, and certainly the most probable, explanation is that the name of the betrayer was made up of the two Hebrew words:* ish *and* carioth *or* Kerioth. *Now Kerioth is a small town belonging to the tribe of Judah, so that the traitor was the only one of the apostles of Judean extraction, the others being all from Galilee, and related more or less nearly to one family.*

The traitor and those who were with him left Jerusalem by the same gate as Jesus himself had done, that of Ophel; then, going down the rapid descent leading to the brook Kidron, they crossed the bridge spanning it and went on to the Garden of Gethsemane. Judas was accompanied by numerous scribes and Pharisees, and he now again exhorted them to take every possible precaution to prevent the escape of Jesus. If he attempted to slip away unperceived, as had happened before on the brow of the hill above Nazareth, or still more recently in the temple, they must be prepared to stone him at once! Then, however, the Master had said: "Mine hour is not yet come," whereas now the hour had come and Judas perhaps secretly wished, though he appeared to fear, the frustration of the plot his avarice had led him to engage in, but which could yield him no further advantage now. Judas was, however, to achieve complete success, and it may be that the ease with which his crime was accomplished was not the least count in his subsequent despair.

The Guards Falling Backward [H13]

⊕

JESUS took some steps toward the band and said in a loud, distinct voice: "Whom seek ye?" The leaders answered: "Jesus of Nazareth," whereupon Jesus replied: "I am he." But scarcely had he uttered the words when, as if suddenly attacked by convulsions, they crowded back and fell to the ground one upon another. Jesus again inquired: "Whom seek ye?" Turning toward him, they again answered: "Jesus of Nazareth." Jesus again replied: "I am he. I have already told you that I am he. If you seek me, let these go." At the words, "I am he," the soldiers fell to the ground a second time. [97]

[JOHN 18:3–9] 3 So Judas, procuring a band of soldiers and some officers from the chief priests and the Pharisees, went there with lanterns and torches and weapons. 4 Then Jesus, knowing all that was to befall him, came forward and said to them, "Whom do you seek?" 5 They answered him, "Jesus of Nazareth." Jesus said to them, "I am he." Judas, who betrayed him, was standing with them. 6 When he said to them, "I am he," they drew back and fell to the ground. 7 Again he asked them, "Whom do you seek?" And they said, "Jesus of Nazareth." 8 Jesus answered, "I told you that I am he; so, if you seek me, let these men go." 9 This was to fulfil the word which he had spoken, "Of those whom thou gavest me I lost not one."

THE treason is accomplished now, and from the shadows of the trees issue the accomplices forming the escort of Judas, who press forward in disorder to seize the person of the Lord. The Master, seeing that they were arresting the apostles also, exclaimed: "I am he!" and, anxious to have it fully understood that he surrendered voluntarily, he, almost for the last time before his death, availed himself of his supernatural power. As he pronounced the simple words: "I am he!" the soldiers were all flung backward by an irresistible force and fell to the ground.

The Kiss of Judas [H14]

⊕

JUDAS was still struggling with the apostles, who were pressing up against the guards. The latter turned upon them and freed the traitor, urging him anew to give them the sign agreed upon. They had been ordered to seize no one but him whom Judas would kiss. Judas now approached Jesus, embraced him and kissed him with the words: "Hail, Rabbi!" Jesus said: "Judas, dost thou betray the Son of Man with a kiss?" The soldiers instantly formed a circle around Jesus, and, drawing near, laid hands upon him. [97]

[MARK 14:44–46] 44 Now the betrayer had given them a sign, saying, "The one I shall kiss is the man; seize him and lead him away under guard." 45 And when he came, he went up to him at once, and said, "Master!" And he kissed him. 46 And they laid hands on him and seized him. [MATTHEW 26:49–50] 49 And he came up to Jesus at once and said, "Hail, Master!" And he kissed him. 50 Jesus said to him, "Friend, why are you here?" Then they came up and laid hands on Jesus and seized him.

ACCORDING to a tradition quoted by Saint Ignatius in a letter to John the Evangelist, James the Less, who was in the garden with Jesus, resembled him so much that one might well have been taken for the other. It was, perhaps, for this reason that the Jews required of Judas that he should identify Jesus with a kiss. In my picture, Judas is seen rising on tip-toe to reach the face of his Master. Peter, seeing the treacherous embrace and anticipating the scuffle which is about to ensue, asks the Lord if he shall call the other eight apostles, who have remained in the garden at some little distance off. The scene of the tragic incident is on the path between the Garden of Gethsemane and the Mount of Olives.

The Ear of Malchus [H15]

⊕

THE soldiers instantly formed a circle around Jesus, and, drawing near, laid hands upon him. Judas wanted at once to flee, but the apostles would not allow him. They rushed upon the soldiers, crying out: "Lord, shall we strike with the sword?" Peter, more impetuous than the rest, seized the sword and struck at Malchus, the servant of the high priest, who was trying to drive them back, and cut off a piece of his ear. Malchus fell to the ground, thereby increasing the confusion, and Jesus said: "Peter, put up thy sword, for whoever takes the sword shall perish by the sword. Thinkest thou that I cannot ask my Father to send me more than twelve legions of angels? Shall I not drink the chalice that my Father has given me? How will the scriptures be fulfilled if it shall not thus be done?" [97]

[JOHN 18:10–11] 10 Then Simon Peter, having a sword, drew it and struck the high priest's slave and cut off his right ear. The slave's name was Malchus. 11 Jesus said to Peter, "Put your sword into its sheath; shall I not drink the cup which the Father has given me?"

The Healing of Malchus [H16]

⊕

THEN he added: "Suffer me to heal the man!" And going to Malchus, he touched his ear and prayed, and at the same moment it was healed. The guard, the executioners, and the six officers surrounded Jesus. They mocked him, saying to the crowd: "He has dealings with the devil. It was by witchcraft that the ear appeared to be cut off, and now by witchcraft it appears to be healed." Then Jesus addressed them: "Ye are come out with spears and clubs to apprehend me as if I were a murderer. I have daily taught among you in the temple, and ye dared not lay hands upon me; but this is your hour and the hour of darkness." [97]

[LUKE 22:51–53] 51 But Jesus said, "No more of this!" And he touched his ear and healed him. 52 Then Jesus said to the chief priests and officers of the temple and elders, who had come out against him, "Have you come out as against a robber, with swords and clubs? 53 When I was with you day after day in the temple, you did not lay hands on me. But this is your hour, and the power of darkness."

JESUS had just been nearly strangled with barbarous brutality, and Peter, in his zeal for his Master, had used his sword, cutting off the ear of Malchus, which, covered with blood, hangs down from the head of the luckless soldier. But Jesus was there; he rebuked the too eager apostle, and, turning to the wounded man, expressed his willingness to heal him. No doubt, think the bystanders, he is going to be guilty of some fresh act of sorcery; what a good thing it will be to have some fresh charge to add to the indictment which is being drawn up against him whom they characterize as a deceiver. Did he not, only the other day, heal a blind man in the temple by merely anointing his eyes with a clay made of earth mixed with his own spittle? Had he not restored to health at the Pool of Bethesda the cripple who had had an infirmity of thirty-eight years' standing? Jesus, however, troubled himself not at all about their perverse thoughts, he touched the ear of the wounded man, and thus consecrated his last moment of liberty to the healing of one of his enemies.

The Bridge of Kidron [H17]

⊕

THE procession moved on at a hurried pace. When it left the road between the Garden of Olives and the pleasure garden of Gethsemane, it turned for a short distance to the right on the west side of Gethsemane, until it reached a bridge that there crossed the brook Kidron. Even before the procession reached the bridge, I saw Jesus fall to the earth twice, owing to the pitiless manner in which he was dragged along and the jerking of the executioners at the ropes. But when they reached the middle of the bridge, they exercised their villainy upon him with still greater malice. The executioners pushed poor, fettered Jesus, whom they held fast with ropes, from the bridge into the brook Kidron, about the height of a man below, accompanying their brutality with abusive words. [99]

[PSALM 110:7] 7 He will drink from the brook by the way; therefore he will lift up his head.

ACCORDING to an ancient tradition, which reappears in the visions of Anne Catherine Emmerich, Jesus, as he was passing over the Kidron bridge, on the south side of the valley, received a treacherous push by order of the Pharisees, and was flung into the torrent. The words: De torrente in via bibet *were thus literally fulfilled. It is somewhat difficult to understand what object the Jews can have had in inflicting this cruel indignity on the Lord. But they meant to bring about the death of Jesus, no matter at what cost, and, as the bridge they were crossing had no parapet, it seemed a good opportunity to get rid of him without any noise or fuss. Had they succeeded they would have avoided a double danger. To begin with they would have averted a popular tumult, the fear of which had so much troubled the Sanhedrin at their last meeting. And then, would it not be more prudent to finish the matter off while the Jews had Jesus in their own power? Once let him come into the hands of Pilate and who could say what would happen? Perhaps the false charges brought against the prisoner would seem of no account to the indifferent Roman procurator. Suppose he should set at liberty the man who was so fatally undermining their influence? At this thought they became capable of anything, and there would have been nothing surprising if they had bribed one of the guards, who would, of course, have had no scruples in obeying, to put their captive quietly out of the way, in such a manner that no suspicion of murder should fall upon the instigators of the crime.*

However that may be, the brutal action must have made a vivid impression upon the mind of the traitor who was still present, already tortured as he was by remorse. We may well believe that the sad and dignified bearing of the Master as he called him "Friend" when he received the kiss, succeeded by the miracle of the healing of the ear of Malchus and the supernatural falling back of the guards, must have given Judas plenty of food for reflection.

The Flight of the Apostles [H18]

⊕

WHEN this shouting band hurried from Ophel by torchlight to meet the approaching procession, the disciples lurking around dispersed in all directions. I saw that the blessed Virgin, in her trouble and anguish, with Martha, Magdalene, Mary Cleophas, Mary Salome, Mary Mark, Susanna, Johanna Chusa, Veronica, and Salome, again directed her steps to the valley of Jehosaphat. They were to the south of Gethsemane, opposite that part of the Mount of Olives where was another grotto in which Jesus had formerly been accustomed to pray. I saw Lazarus, John Mark, Veronica's son, and Simeon's son with them. The last-named, along with Nathaniel, had been in Gethsemane with the eight apostles, and had fled across when the tumult began. [100]

[MARK 14:50] 50 And they all forsook him, and fled. [MATTHEW 26:56] 56 But all this has taken place, that the scriptures of the prophets might be fulfilled. Then all the disciples forsook him and fled.

Peter and John Follow from Afar [H19]

⊕

PETER and John, who were following the procession at some distance, ran hurriedly when it entered the city to some of the good acquaintances whom John had among the servants of the high priests, to find in some way an opportunity of entering the judgment hall into which their Master would soon be brought. [102]

[JOHN 18:15] 15 Simon Peter followed Jesus, and so did another disciple. As this disciple was known to the high priest, he entered the court of the high priest along with Jesus.

THE intervention of Jesus on behalf of the apostles at the moment of his own arrest had been successful. "If therefore ye seek me," he had said, "let these go their way." The fact was the enemies of the Savior knew full well that the presence of the apostles at the trial would only embarrass the accusers, and that what they needed to support a really compromising indictment against their prisoner were trusty witnesses of a very different stamp. One disciple, however, probably Mark, for he is the only evangelist who relates the incident, and he lived at Jerusalem, was seized by the sbirri. Mark tells us that the young man in question wore "a linen cloth cast about his naked body," leading us to suppose that, disturbed by the noise of the arrest and the flaring of the torches, he had run out of his house in haste just as he was. No doubt the soldiers caught hold of him by this linen cloth, and he would have been arrested had he not slipped nimbly out of it and fled from them naked, leaving the garment in the hands of his astonished captors.

Not one of his friends, therefore, shared the fate of Jesus; in the very first hour, indeed, in the first moment, they all forsook him and fled, as related in the sacred text. Not until the fatal procession had started on its way to the house of the high priest did two of the disciples, Peter and John, regain something of their presence of mind and follow their Master afar off. Peter, no doubt, now remembered all the fine promises he had made and which he was so very soon to forget and break. As for John, the beloved disciple of Jesus, he at least was quite ready to follow him and if need were to interfere on his behalf. Moreover, he was on good terms with the people in the house of Caiaphas, and he might well hope to be able to get in there without danger, so as to send tidings of how things were going to the other apostles and to the mother of Jesus, whom he had left in all the anguish of her sad forebodings. He therefore followed at some distance the multitude escorting the Master, hiding behind the low wall of the path which was very steep at that part of the way.

The Tribunal of Annas [H20]

IT was toward midnight when Jesus was led through the brilliantly lighted courtyard into the palace of Annas. He was conducted to a hall as large as a small church. At the upper end opposite the entrance on a high gallery, or platform, under which people could come and go, sat Annas surrounded by twenty-eight counselors. A flight of steps broken here and there by landings, or resting places, led up to the front of his tribunal, or judgment seat, which was entered from behind, thus communicating with the inner part of the building. Jesus, still surrounded by a body of the soldiers by whom he had been arrested, was dragged forward several steps by the executioners that held the cords. The hall was crowded with soldiers, the rabble, the slandering Jews, the servants of Annas, and some of the witnesses whom Annas had gathered together, and who later on made their appearance at the house of Caiaphas.

Jesus stood before Annas pale, exhausted, silent, his head bowed, his garments wet and spattered with mud, his hands fettered, his waist bound by ropes the ends of which the executioners held. Annas, still more enraged by Jesus's calm demeanor, summoned the witnesses (because Jesus himself so willed it) to come forward and declare whatever they had heard him say. These accusations were brought forward against the Lord without regard to order or propriety. The witnesses stepped up to him and made their charges, derisively gesticulating in his face, while the executioners jerked him first to one side, then to the other, saying: "Speak! Answer!" [106]

[JOHN 18:13] 13 First they led him to Annas; for he was the father-in-law of Caiaphas, who was high priest that year.

THE first halt made by the captors of Jesus was at the house of Annas, father-in-law of Caiaphas, whose tribunal was situated in the part of the city overlooking the so-called Millo, which they reached soon after passing through the gate. The crowd had now increased, and the populace, bribed perhaps to some extent at least by the enemies of Jesus, are already beginning to get up a tumult. All the judges have been summoned to attend and most of them are assembled in the house of Annas, a man of more importance than Caiaphas, but the law required that the case should be heard by the high priest of the year, and it was now decided to take Jesus to him. The procession, therefore, resumed its march and, going through an ancient gateway in the outer walls of the city, entered a network of narrow streets, where groups of hostile or merely curious spectators had already gathered. John is the only one of the evangelists who mentions the incident of the halt at the house of Annas; the others only speak of the prisoner having been brought before Caiaphas, where the actual judgment was pronounced; they evidently considered the first pause on the road as an episode of no consequence, not worth introducing into their narrative.

The False Witnesses [H21]

AFTER much shameful, perverse, lying evidence, two witnesses at last came forward and said: "Jesus declared that he would destroy the temple made by hands, and in three days build up another not made by human hands." But these two also wrangled over their words. Caiaphas was now thoroughly exasperated, for the ill-treatment bestowed upon Jesus, the contradictory statements of the witnesses, and the incomprehensibly silent patience of the accused were beginning to make a very deep impression upon many of those present, and some of the witnesses were laughed to scorn. [107]

[MARK 14:55–61] 55 Now the chief priests and the whole council sought testimony against Jesus to put him to death; but they found none. 56 For many bore false witness against him, and their witness did not agree. 57 And some stood up and bore false witness against him, saying, 58 "We heard him say, 'I will destroy this temple that is made with hands, and in three days I will build another, not made with hands.'" 59 Yet not even so did their testimony agree. 60 And the high priest stood up in the midst, and asked Jesus, "Have you no answer to make? What is it that these men testify against you?" 61 But he was silent and made no answer. Again the high priest asked him, "Are you the Christ, the Son of the Blessed?"

THE crowd is increasing rapidly, swelled by the dregs of the populace of Jerusalem. A stone parapet, however, protects the Judgment Hall itself from being invaded. The latter is full: Caiaphas as president occupies an armchair in the center, while the other judges, who have been purposely chosen from among the enemies of Jesus, are ranged in the semicircle of seats on either side. Opposite to the presidential chair, in the entrance indicated by two columns supporting lamps, stands Jesus bound, his hands tied together with cords, the ends of which are held by his guards. He is, in fact, quite at the mercy of the people, for the gospel tells us that "one of the officers that stood by struck him with the palm of the hand" at the very beginning of the trial, and neither the judges nor the Savior's guards interfered to protect him.

The false witnesses, who have been bribed to testify against him, can be seen rising up here and there among the crowd, coming to the aid of the painfully embarrassed judges, who have no accusation to bring against the pretended criminal but their own unbridled hatred. The tumult is now at its height. The air is heavy with the smoke from the lamps and the emanations from the over-excited and frenzied crowd. The judges, raising their voices, endeavor to make themselves heard above the noise, but it is just all they can do to get a hearing. Jesus alone is calm, his dignified bearing and the touching gentleness of his demeanor exasperate his enemies. He is assailed from every side, jostled about and buffeted, insulted in every possible way; he replies but with a few words full of nobility, the striking justice of which puts the finishing touch to the rage of his accusers. At the back of the room the men crowded together in the narrow court and looking on through the open doors, stand on tip-toe or cling to the columns to get a better view.

Annas and Caiaphas [H22]

⊕

CAIAPHAS was a man of great gravity, his countenance florid and fierce. He wore a long, dull red mantle ornamented with golden flowers and tassels. It was fastened on the shoulders, the breast, and down the front with shining buckles of various form. On his head was a cap, the top of which resembled a low episcopal miter. The pieces front and back were bent so as to meet on top, thus leaving openings at the side, from which hung ribbons. From either side of the head lappets fell upon the shoulders. Caiaphas and his counselors were already a long time assembled; many of them had even remained since the departure of Judas and his gang. The rage and impatience of Caiaphas had reached such a pitch that, magnificently attired as he was, he descended from his lofty tribunal and went into the outer court asking angrily whether Jesus would soon come. At last the procession was seen approaching, and Caiaphas returned to his seat. [109]

The Torn Cloak—Jesus Condemned to Death by the Jews [H23]

⊕

CAIAPHAS, infuriated by the wrangling of the last two witnesses, rose from his seat, went down a couple of steps to Jesus, and said: "Answerest thou nothing to this testimony against thee?" He was vexed that Jesus would not look at him. At this the executioners pulled our Lord's head back by the hair, and with their fist gave him blows under his chin. But his glance was still downcast. Caiaphas angrily raised his hands and said in a tone full of rage: "I adjure thee by the living God that thou tell us whether thou be Christ, the Messiah, the Son of the most blessed God." A solemn silence fell upon the clamoring crowd. Jesus, strengthened by God, said in a voice inexpressibly majestic, a voice that struck awe into all hearts, the voice of the Eternal Word: "I am! Thou sayest it! And I say to you, soon you shall see the Son of Man sitting on the right hand of the power of God, and coming in the clouds of heaven!" Caiaphas, as if inspired by hell, seized the hem of his magnificent mantle, clipped it with a knife and, with a whizzing noise, tore it as he exclaimed in a loud voice: "He has blasphemed! What need have we of further witnesses? Behold now ye have heard the blasphemy, what think ye?" At these words, the whole assembly rose and cried out in a horrid voice: "He is guilty of death! He is guilty of death!" [111]

[MATTHEW 26:63–66] 63 But Jesus was silent. And the high priest said to him, "I adjure you by the living God, tell us if you are the Christ, the Son of God." 64 Jesus said to him, "You have said so. But I tell you, hereafter you will see the Son of man seated at the right hand of Power, and coming on the clouds of heaven." 65 Then the high priest tore his robes, and said, "He has uttered blasphemy. Why do we still need witnesses? You have now heard his blasphemy. 66 What is your judgment?" They answered, "He deserves death."

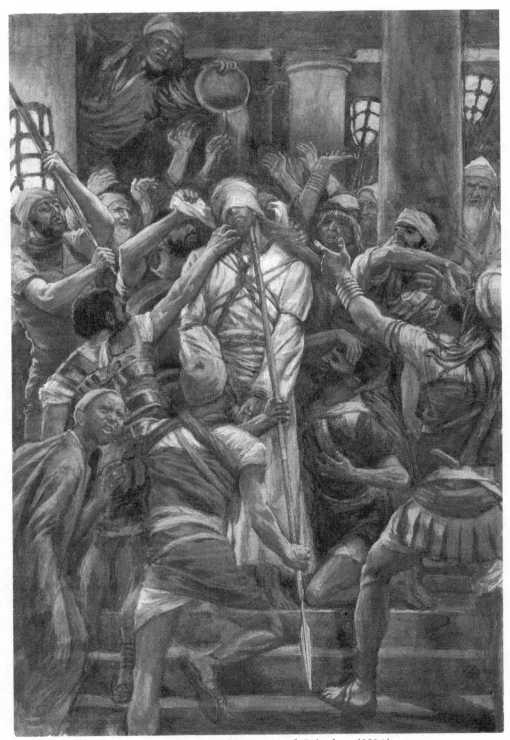

Maltreatments in the House of Caiaphas [H24]

AS soon as Caiaphas, having delivered Jesus to the soldiers, left the judgment hall with his council, the very scum of the miscreants present fell like a swarm of infuriated wasps upon our Lord. They struck him with their fists and sticks, threw him from side to side, and spat upon him. Here, now, stood poor Jesus clothed only in his nether-bandage and the scapular that fell on his breast and back; but this last they soon tore from him, and he never recovered it. They threw around him an old, tattered mantle and put around his neck a long iron chain which, like a stole, hung from the shoulders across the breast and down to the knees. They tied a rag across his eyes, struck him with their fists and sticks, and cried out: "Great prophet! Prophesy, who has struck thee?" But Jesus answered not. He prayed interiorly, sighed, and bore their blows. Thus ill-used, blindfolded, and covered with filth, they dragged him by the chain into the rear council hall. Thereupon, they brought a basin full of foul, muddy water in which lay a coarse rag; and amid pushes, jests, and mockery mingled with ironical bows and salutations, with sticking out the tongue at him or turning up to him their hinder parts, they passed the wet smeary rag over his face and shoulders as if cleansing him, though in reality rendering him more filthy than before. Finally, they poured the whole contents of the basin over his face with mocking words. It was a scene of horrible gloom and confusion.

But around the ill-treated Jesus, since the moment in which he said that he was the Son of God, I frequently saw a glory, a splendor. Many of those present seemed to have an interior perception of the same, some more, others less; they experienced, at least, a feeling of dread upon seeing that, in spite of the scorn and ignominy with which he was laden, the indescribable majesty of his bearing remained unchanged. [112]

[MATTHEW 26:67] 67 Then they spat in his face, and struck him; and some slapped him. [MARK 14:65] 65 And some began to spit on him, and to cover his face, and to strike him, saying to him, "Prophesy!" And the guards received him with blows. [LUKE 22:63–65] 63 Now the men who were holding Jesus mocked him and beat him; 64 they also blindfolded him and asked him, "Prophesy! Who is it that struck you?" 65 And they spoke many other words against him, reviling him.

THE subject now represented takes us back to a little before the third denial of Peter, or at least to before the Lord turned and looked at him, for we assume that the look was given on the way to prison. Jesus, once condemned by acclamation on the suggestion of the high priest himself, a nameless scene of horror began. The Sanhedrin, instead of protecting him from the crowd, as in such a case it was the duty of the legal authorities to do, abandoned him to their mercy and thus sanctioned the worst outrages. It is true that the members of the supreme council did not themselves take any part in the insults heaped on Jesus, but there is not the slightest doubt that they were as responsible as if they had, for they certainly could have prevented them. His persecutors flung themselves upon the prisoner with a positively diabolical fury, raining blows upon him, "spitting in his face, buffeting him and smiting him with the palms of their hands." They blindfolded him with a dirty rag, and as they struck him they mocked him, saying: "Prophesy unto us, thou Christ, who is he that smote thee?"

Truly the unfortunate victim paid dearly enough now for his brief triumph on Palm Sunday, for the homage paid to him at Bethany, for the precious ointment of Mary Magdalene, and for his few short moments of joy, which he must now expiate with all this agony and humiliation. The enemies of the Prophet cannot but have been intoxicated with the thought of having him, who had previously caused them so much anxiety, in their hands under such conditions. But the night was far spent, even the tormentors were getting weary, and there was no longer any danger of the escape of their victim. The crowd now melted away and the guards led Jesus, with soiled garments, bleeding face, and limbs bruised by the blows he had received and galled by his fetters, as he had now been bound some four hours, it being already three o'clock in the morning, that is to say, eleven hours since he was taken prisoner. Long before, Job had said, and his words were perhaps prophetic of the sufferings of Christ: "They have gaped upon me with their mouth, they have smitten me upon the cheek reproachfully; they have gathered themselves together against me." These words were literally fulfilled in the scene we have just described, and yet more remarkably true was the beautifully worded prophecy of Isaiah, when he glorified beforehand the divine gentleness of the insulted Messiah, saying: "I gave my back to the smiters, and my cheeks to them that plucked off the hair; I hid not my face from shame and spitting."

The First Denial of Peter [H25]

⊕

PETER kept silence; but already the interest he manifested in the proceedings, joined to the expression of deep grief depicted on his countenance, drew upon him the attention of Jesus's enemies. Just at this moment, the portress approached the fire; and as all were prating and jesting at Jesus's expense and that of his disciples, she, like a bold woman, saucily put in her word and, fixing her eyes upon Peter, said: "Thou too art one of the Galilean's disciples!" Peter, startled and alarmed, and fearing rough treatment from the rude crowd, answered: "Woman, I know him not! I know not what thou meanest. I do not understand thee!" With these words, wishing to free himself from further remark, he arose and left the atrium. At that moment, a cock somewhere outside the city crowed. I do not remember having heard it, but I felt that it was crowing outside the city. [113]

[JOHN 18:15–18] 15 Simon Peter followed Jesus, and so did another disciple. As this disciple was known to the high priest, he entered the court of the high priest along with Jesus, 16 while Peter stood outside at the door. So the other disciple, who was known to the high priest, went out and spoke to the maid who kept the door, and brought Peter in. 17 The maid who kept the door said to Peter, "Are not you also one of this man's disciples?" He said, "I am not." 18 Now the servants and officers had made a charcoal fire, because it was cold, and they were standing and warming themselves; Peter also was with them, standing and warming himself.

The Second Denial of Peter [H26]

AS Peter was making his way out, another maidservant caught sight of him, and said to the bystanders: "This man, also, was with Jesus of Nazareth." They at once questioned him: "Art thou not also one of his disciples?" Peter, greatly troubled and perplexed, answered with an oath: "Truly, I am not! I do not even know the man!" And he hurried through the inner to the exterior court, to warn some of his acquaintances whom he saw looking over the wall. He was weeping and so full of grief and anxiety on Jesus's account that he hardly gave his denial a thought. [113]

[JOHN 18:25] 25 Now Simon Peter was standing and warming himself. They said to him, "Are not you also one of his disciples?" He denied it and said, "I am not." [LUKE 22:56–58] 56 Then a maid, seeing him as he sat in the light and gazing at him, said, "This man also was with him." 57 But he denied it, saying, "Woman, I do not know him." 58 And a little later some one else saw him and said, "You also are one of them." But Peter said, "Man, I am not."

The Third Denial of Peter: Jesus's Look of Reproach [H27]

⊕

PETER could not rest anywhere. His love for Jesus drove him back into the inner court that surrounded the house. They let him in again, on account of Nicodemus and Joseph of Arimathea, who had in the first instance procured his admittance. He did not, however, return to the court of the judgment hall, but turning went along to the right until he reached the entrance of the circular hall back of the tribunal. In that hall Jesus was being dragged about and abused by the vile rabble. Peter drew near trembling, and although he felt himself an object of remark, yet his anxiety for Jesus drove him through the doorway, which was beset by the crowd watching the outrages heaped upon Jesus. Just then they were dragging him, crowned with straw, around the circle. Jesus cast a glance full of earnest warning upon Peter, a glance that pierced him to the soul. [114]

[LUKE 22:59–61] 59 And after an interval of about an hour still another insisted, saying, "Certainly this man also was with him; for he is a Galilean." 60 But Peter said, "Man, I do not know what you are saying." And immediately, while he was still speaking, the cock crowed. 61 And the Lord turned and looked at Peter. And Peter remembered the word of the Lord, how he had said to him, "Before the cock crows today, you will deny me three times."

IN spite of his repeated denials, Peter approached the judgment hall to try to see what was going on, while John thus left to himself had availed himself of his own special facilities to secure a place as near as possible to Jesus. Peter, finding himself surrounded on all sides by strangers, for as a Galilean he was, of course, a foreigner, and attracted the constant notice of the guards by his peculiar accent, became nervous, lost his presence of mind and, getting more and more over-excited, he denied his Master for the third time. The man referred to by Luke, though he does not mention his name, was perhaps the kinsman of Malchus, of whom John speaks in his account of the same scene; or it may even have been the same person who Matthew relates said to Peter "thou also art one of them, for thy speech betrayeth thee." It is, however, very possible that each of the three men mentioned was a different person, and that Peter did not utter his false oaths until he was absolutely driven to do so by the harassing attacks made on him from every side.

When the scene represented in my picture took place, the trial was over, the sentence had been pronounced, and the judges were retiring. It is late, about three o'clock, and the cock crows again. Jesus is leaving the judgment hall, given over for a few moments to the tumultuous mob, intoxicated with fury against him, which has been surging about the scene of the trial for nearly four hours. He is being taken, subjected the while to the most cruel treatment, to a small prison adjoining the judgment hall where he is to be kept in sight by his guards for the rest of the night, and it is in this short transit that Jesus turns round and looks upon Peter. It would indeed be difficult to analyze all that look expressed; but Peter himself understood it all too well, that rapid glance lights up his troubled conscience like a flash of lightning in the night, and suddenly everything comes back to his memory: his protestations on the way to Gethsemane, the warnings of Jesus, his own thrice-repeated denial and the crowing of the cock.

The Sorrow of Peter [H28]

WORN out with grief and anxiety, Peter had entirely forgotten his presumptuous protestation on the Mount of Olives, rather to die with his Master than to deny him, as also the warning he had then received from Jesus. But at that glance, the enormity of his fault rose up before him and well-nigh broke his heart. He had sinned. He had sinned against his ill-treated, unjustly condemned Savior, who was silently enduring the most horrible outrages, who had so truly warned him to be on his guard. Filled with remorse and sorrow, he covered his head with his mantle and hurried into the other court, weeping bitterly. He no longer feared being accosted. To everyone he met he would willingly have proclaimed who he was, and how great was the crime that rested on him. Who would presume to say that in such danger, affliction, anxiety, and perplexity, in such a struggle between love and fear, worn out with fatigue, consumed by watching, pursued by dread, half-crazed from pain of mind caused by the overwhelming sorrows of this most pitiful night, with a temperament at once so childlike and so ardent, he would have been stronger than Peter? The Lord left Peter to his own strength, therefore did he become so weak, just as they always do that lose sight of the words: "Pray and watch, that ye enter not into temptation." [114]

[LUKE 22:62] 62 And he went out and wept bitterly. [MATTHEW 26:75] 75 And Peter remembered the saying of Jesus, "Before the cock crows, you will deny me three times." And he went out and wept bitterly.

IN Syria the cocks are heard crowing for the first time between eleven o'clock and midnight, they crow the second time between one and two o'clock, and that with the punctuality of a clock, while the third crowing takes place about three o'clock in the morning. Now it was about the third watch of the night, that is to say, toward three o'clock in the morning, that Jesus left the judgment hall to be taken to prison where he was to remain until daybreak, waiting for the second judgment, which was to endorse officially the one already pronounced upon the prisoner during the night. It came about, therefore, quite naturally for the third and last crowing of the cock to coincide with the look of reproach from Jesus and combine to trouble the soul of Peter and produce an agonized burst of remorseful repentance.

Outside the judgment hall groups of bystanders had probably collected at the beginning of the remarkable scenes which had taken place. In Eastern countries, where neighbors visit each other so readily, the news of what was going on would spread round about with great rapidity, and everyone from far and near would hasten to see what was going to happen. Moreover, the friends of Jesus, the holy women especially, could not have been indifferent to his fate; they are very sure to have been there, anxiously on the watch in the hope of some chance occurring of seeing him, hearing him speak and getting some idea, if only from a distance, of how things were going with him. No doubt they were aware of the presence in the palace of Caiaphas of Peter and of John, and they must indeed have impatiently waited for them to come out to give them some account of what had happened.

Presently the uproar within became greater than ever, the yelling of the crowd could be more distinctly heard; for the sitting of the council was coming to an end. Then the door opened quite suddenly, and Peter, beside himself with grief, rushed out weeping bitterly. The friends of the Lord surrounded him, asking questions and trying to find out from him what was to become of Jesus. Through his sobs Peter manages to make them understand that the Master is condemned to death, and that he, the chief of his apostles, has denied him three times. Then Peter left them, to take his way with tottering steps down into the valley, and, leaving the town, to join the rest of the disciples, who were no doubt still hidden in the caves of the Valley of Hinnom.

The Apostles' Hiding Place

TRADITION *justifies us in forming a very distinct picture of how the apostles behaved after they had left their Master. It appears pretty certain that they left Gethsemane by way of the lower portion of the valley, keeping alongside of the bed of the Kidron torrent, passing the tombs which rose up on their right and then, finding that they were not pursued, they halted to consult together as to where they should go, deciding in the end to direct their steps toward the sepulchral caves of the Valley of Hinnom. There they would be quite safe from surprise, not too far from the town, and at the same time they would be not so very distant from Zion, so that they might hope to receive news of their Master.*

This Valley of Hinnom, on the south of Jerusalem, separates the tribes of Benjamin and of Judah from each other. On the west it becomes merged in the Valley of Gihon and on the south it adjoined the King's Garden, watered by the Pool of Siloam. In former times, under the earlier kings who reigned before Josiah, sacrifices were offered up to Moloch in this valley, and it was called the Valley of Tophet or of the Drums, because those musical instruments were beaten to drown the cries of the unfortunate children offered up to the god. "Therefore," to quote the Prophet Jeremiah (7:32), "behold the days shall come, saith the Lord, that it shall no more be called Tophet nor the valley of the son of Hinnom but the valley of slaughter, for they shall bury in Tophet till there be no place." As a matter of fact the southern side of this valley is full of tombs hewn in the living rock, and it is among them that tradition tells us the apostles took refuge after Jesus had been arrested in the Garden of Gethsemane. One of these isolated tombs, which is among the first the traveler comes to at the bottom of the valley, is in fairly good preservation, and from it we may gain an idea of the original appearance of the tomb of our blessed Lord. It is entered by a vestibule in the same manner as is the Church of the Holy Sepulchre, and part of it is detached from the mountain, while the rest is hollowed out beneath it.

The style of the various tombs corresponds with that of most of the architecture of the country; that is to say, with Greek architecture in its decadence, with an Egyptian moulding surmounting the whole. The cornice is generally enriched with triglyphs which separate from each other medallions and bunches of grapes, the latter a very favorite ornament with Jewish architects. The limestone rock of which the mountain is here built up lends itself very readily to the excavation of these tombs, and the fine grain of the stone is at the same time suitable for the carving of the various decorative details. Though it is easily worked when it is being hewn or carved it rapidly becomes sufficiently hardened on exposure to the action of the air and light to give to the sculptures produced in it considerable durability.

Good Friday Morning: Jesus in Prison [H29]

⊕

THE prison cell into which Jesus was introduced lay under the judgment hall of Caiaphas. It was a small, circular vault. A part of it I see in existence even now. Only two of the four executioners remained with Jesus. After a short interval they exchanged places with two others, and these again were soon relieved. They had not given the Lord his own garments again. He was clothed with only the filthy mantle of mockery, and his hands were still bound.

When the Lord entered the prison, he prayed his heavenly Father to accept all the scorn and ill-treatment that he had endured up to that moment and all that he had still to suffer in atonement for the sins of his executioners and for all those that, in future ages, might be in danger of sinning through impatience and anger.

Even in this prison the executioners allowed Jesus no rest. They bound him to a low pillar that stood in the center of the prison, though they would not permit him to lean against it. He was obliged to stagger from side to side on his tired feet, which were wounded and swollen from frequent falls and the strokes of the chain that hung to his knees. They ceased not to mock and outrage him, and when the two executioners in charge were wearied, two others replaced them, and new scenes of villainy were enacted. [116]

[MARK 15:1] 1 And as soon as it was morning the chief priests, with the elders and scribes, and the whole council held a consultation; and they bound Jesus and led him away and delivered him to Pilate.

THE tumult is over now for a time and Jesus, still bound, is alone in prison. The pale white light of the dawn already heralds the opening of the much longed-for day. The Savior is engaged in prayer, and is offering up to his Father the day which is to be so pregnant of results and for which, to quote his own words, he is come.

We have represented him bound to a short column, and certain slight marks on it lead us to suppose that that column is the very one still preserved in the Church of Saint Praxedes at Rome. Every court of justice had its scourging column, but probably the form differed considerably. Saint Jerome tells us that he saw the column of the scourging in the porch of a church at Zion; some fragments of this column are reverently preserved in the Church of the Holy Sepulchre at Jerusalem and others in various sanctuaries of Europe: at Madrid, Venice, and elsewhere. The column, which is now at Rome, was taken there six hundred years after the time of Jerome, that is to say, in the tenth century, a fact which must be borne in mind in considering the authenticity of the various relics. As for us, we have come to the conclusion after due consideration of the facts we have to judge by, that Jesus was bound at different times to three different columns: that connected with the judgment hall of Caiaphas; that of the actual scourging; and that of the crowning with thorns. We have already said where the first two now are and add here that the third is the Church of the Holy Sepulcher at Jerusalem.

The Morning Judgment [H30]

⊕

AS soon as it was clear daylight, Caiaphas, Annas, the ancients and scribes assembled in the great hall to hold a trial perfectly lawful. Trial by night was not legal. That of the preceding night had been held only because time pressed on account of the feast, and that some of the preparatory attestations might be taken. Caiaphas now ordered poor, abused Jesus, who was consumed from want of rest, to be brought from the prison and presented before the council, so that after the sentence he might without delay be taken to Pilate.

Like a poor animal for sacrifice, with blows and mockery, Jesus was dragged by the executioners into the judgment hall through the rows of soldiers assembled in front of the house. Caiaphas, full of scorn and fury for Jesus standing before him in so miserable a plight, thus addressed him: "If thou be the anointed of the Lord, the Messiah, tell us!" Then Jesus raised his head and with divine forbearance and solemn dignity said: "If I shall tell you, you will not believe me. And if I shall also ask you, you will not answer me, nor let me go. But hereafter the Son of Man shall be sitting on the right hand of the power of God." The members of the council glanced from one to another and, smiling scornfully, said to Jesus with disdain: "So then, thou! Thou art the Son of God?" With the voice of eternal truth, Jesus answered: "Yes, it is as ye say. I am he!" At this word of the Lord all looked at one another, saying: "What need we any further testimony? For we ourselves have heard it from his own mouth." [117]

[LUKE 22:66–71] 66 When day came, the assembly of the elders of the people gathered together, both chief priests and scribes; and they led him away to their council, and they said, 67 "If you are the Christ, tell us." But he said to them, "If I tell you, you will not believe; 68 and if I ask you, you will not answer. 69 But from now on the Son of man shall be seated at the right hand of the power of God." 70 And they all said, "Are you the Son of God, then?" And he said to them, "You say that I am." 71 And they said, "What further testimony do we need? We have heard it ourselves from his own lips."

Judas Returns the Money [H31]

⊕

THEN anguish, despair, and remorse began to struggle in the soul of Judas, but all too late. Satan instigated him to flee. The bag of silver pieces hanging from his girdle under his mantle was for him like a hellish spur. He grasped it tightly in his hand, to prevent its rattling and striking him at every step. On he ran at full speed, not after the procession, not to cast himself in Jesus's path to implore mercy and forgiveness, not to die with Jesus. No, not to confess with contrition before God his awful crime, but to disburden himself of his guilt and the price of his treachery before men.

Like one bereft of his senses, he rushed into the temple, whither several of the council, as superintendents of the priests whose duty it was to serve, also some of the elders, had gone directly after the condemnation of Jesus. They glanced wonderingly at one another, and then fixed their gaze with a proud and scornful smile upon Judas, who stood before them, his countenance distorted by despairing grief. He tore the bag of silver pieces from his girdle and held it toward them with the right hand, while in a voice of agony he cried: "Take back your money! By it ye have led me to betray the just one. Take back your money! Release Jesus! I recall my contract. I have sinned grievously by betraying innocent blood!"

The priests poured out upon him the whole measure of their contempt. Raising their hands, they stepped back before the offered silver, as if to preserve themselves from pollution, and said: "What is it to us that thou hast sinned? Thinkest thou to have sold innocent blood? Look thou to it! It is thine own affair! We know what we have bought from thee, and we find him deserving of death. Thou hast thy money. We want none of it!" With these and similar words spoken quickly and in the manner of men that have business on hand and that wish to get away from an importunate visitor, they turned from Judas. Their treatment inspired him with such rage and despair that he became like one insane. His hair stood on end, with both hands he rent asunder the chain that held the silver pieces together, scattered them in the temple, and fled from the city. [118]

[MATTHEW 27:2–10] 2 And they bound him and led him away and delivered him to Pilate the governor. 3 When Judas, his betrayer, saw that he was condemned, he repented and brought back the thirty pieces of silver to the chief priests and the elders, 4 saying, "I have sinned in betraying innocent blood." They said, "What is that to us? See to it yourself." 5 And throwing down the pieces of silver in the temple, he departed; and he went and hanged himself. 6 But the chief priests, taking the pieces of silver, said, "It is not lawful to put them into the treasury, since they are blood money." 7 So they took counsel, and bought with them the potter's field, to bury strangers in. 8 Therefore that field has been called the Field of Blood to this day. 9 Then was fulfilled what had been spoken by the prophet Jeremiah, saying, "And they took the thirty pieces of silver, the price of him on whom a price had been set by some of the sons of Israel, 10 and they gave them for the potter's field, as the Lord directed me."

IT *is still early morning. Jesus has just heard the ratification of his sentence and that it was decided he should be taken before the Roman governor. Then Judas, "which had betrayed him," when he sees that his victim cannot possibly escape death, realizes at last the full extent of his treacherous wrongdoing, and his soul is seized with remorse. He repents, but his repentance is the repentance of despair, and, eager to get rid of the torture which overwhelms him, he hastens to the temple, determined to confess his crime and to give back the money he had received on the evening of the day before.*

The Jews are in the temple, wearing on their foreheads the phylacteries always put on for morning prayer. If, however, the miserable man had had any hope that the step he was about to take would save Jesus, the revolting reply he received must very quickly have convinced him of his mistake. Then his despair reaches its height, he flings down the pieces of silver in a great hurry and rushes away to go and kill himself. We have laid the scene of this tragic incident in the Court of the Jews in the lower part of the temple.

Judas Hangs Himself [H32]

⊕

I SAW him again running like a maniac in the Valley of Hinnom with Satan under a horrible form at his side. The evil one, to drive him to despair, was whispering into his ear all the curses the prophets had ever invoked upon this valley, wherein the Jews had once sacrificed their own children to idols. And when, reaching the brook Kidron, he gazed over at the Mount of Olives, he shuddered and turned his eyes away, while in his ears rang the words: "Friend, whereto hast thou come? Judas, dost thou betray the Son of Man with a kiss?"

Oh, then horror filled his soul! His mind began to wander, and the fiend again whispered into his ear: "It was here that David crossed the Kidron when fleeing from Absalom. Absalom died hanging on a tree. " Amid these frightful torments of conscience, Judas reached a desolate spot full of rubbish, refuse, and swampy water southeast of Jerusalem, at the foot of the Mount of Scandals, where no one could see him. From the city came repeated sounds of noisy tumult, and Satan whispered again: "Now he is being led to death! Thou hast sold him! Knowest thou not how the law runs 'he who sells a soul among his brethren, and receives the price of it, let him die the death'? Put an end to thyself, thou wretched one! Put an end to thyself!" Overcome by despair, Judas took his girdle and hung himself on a tree. The tree was one that consisted of several trunks, and rose out of a hollow in the ground. As he hung, his body burst asunder, and his bowels poured out upon the earth. [119]

[MATTHEW 27:5] 5 And throwing down the pieces of silver in the temple, he departed; and he went and hanged himself. [ACTS OF THE APOSTLES 1:16–18] 16 "Brethren, the scripture had to be fulfilled, which the Holy Spirit spoke beforehand by the mouth of David, concerning Judas who was guide to those who arrested Jesus. 17 For he was numbered among us, and was allotted his share in this ministry. 18 (Now this man bought a field with the reward of his wickedness; and falling headlong he burst open in the middle and all his bowels gushed out.)

Jesus Led from Caiaphas to Pilate [H33]

THE inhuman crowd that conducted Jesus from Caiaphas to Pilate passed through the most populous part of the city, which was now swarming with Passover guests and countless strangers from all parts of the country. The procession proceeded northward from Mount Zion, down through a closely built street that crossed the valley, then through a section of the city called Acre, along the west side of the temple to the palace and tribunal of Pilate, which stood at the northwest corner of the temple opposite the great forum, or market.

Caiaphas and Annas, with a large number of the chief council in robes of state, stalked on in advance of the procession. After them were carried rolls of writing. They were followed by numerous scribes and other Jews, among them all the false witnesses and the exasperated Pharisees who had been particularly active at the preceding accusation of the Lord. Then after a short intervening distance, surrounded by a crowd of soldiers and those six functionaries who had been present at the capture, came our dear Lord Jesus bound as before with ropes which were held by the executioners. The mob came streaming from all sides and joined the procession with shouts and cries of mockery. Crowds of people were standing along the way.

Jesus was now clothed in his woven undergarment, which was covered with dirt and mud. From his neck hung the heavy, rough chain that struck his knees painfully as he walked. His hands were fettered as on the day before, and the four executioners dragged him again by the cords fastened to his girdle. By the frightful ill-treatment of the preceding night, he was perfectly disfigured. He tottered along, a picture of utter misery—haggard, his hair and beard torn, his face livid and swollen with blows. Amid fresh outrage and mockery he was driven onward. [119]

[MATTHEW 27:2] 2 and they bound him and led him away and delivered him to Pilate the governor. [JOHN 18:28] 28 Then they led Jesus from the house of Caiaphas to the praetorium. It was early. They themselves did not enter the praetorium, so that they might not be defiled, but might eat the passover.

THE *crowds accompanying Jesus now all hastened down the steep streets leading from the Zion to the Roman quarter of the town where the praetorium was situated. There, in the Antonia Citadel, dwelt Pilate the governor, and in it also were the barracks of the Roman garrison. Jesus has been stripped of the garments he had worn when he had left the guest-chamber the evening before. They were much soiled, and bore witness all too clearly to the cruel treatment to which their wearer had been subjected during the night; if the governor had seen them he might have turned their condition to the advantage of the prisoner, for he might have chosen to consider the state they were in as an insult to his own dignity, as well as an outrage on humanity. Jesus therefore wore nothing now but his seamless undergarment and the rest of his clothes, which were of a reddish color, were not restored to him until just before he was compelled to carry his cross.*

The procession went down the Tyropeon valley which was crossed by means of bridges. It was then a very deep depression, completely separating the temple from the town, but it became filled up in the various subsequent sieges. The crowds which had collected the evening before were now augmented by a fresh concourse of people; the judges before whom Jesus had been taken in the morning were hastening along on their asses with their scribes to be present at the examination by the governor. They stand in great dread of the Roman representative, for the contempt with which he treats them on every fresh opportunity does not tend to inspire them with confidence, and they feel that they must be on the spot to accuse Jesus and if need be to rouse up the people and incite them to demand the death of him they have themselves already condemned.

The weather is now overcast, a slight rain fell in the morning and still continues to fall at intervals, the road is slippery and many fall by the way. Jesus himself is wet through. In the lower quarters of the town where the people had been aroused during the night by the tumult which had been going on, the excitement and disorder have begun, and everyone is already flocking in the direction of the Antonia Citadel, where the events of the new day are to be inaugurated.

From Pilate's steps one could see across the court and into the forum, which lay to the north, and whose entrance at that point was furnished with columns and stone seats, the latter resting against the courtyard wall. As far as these seats and no farther would the Jewish priests approach the judgment hall of Pilate in order not to incur defilement; a line was even drawn across the pavement of the court to indicate the precise boundary. Near the western gateway of the court was erected in the precincts of the square a large guardhouse, which extending to the forum on the north, and on the south connecting by means of the gateway with the praetorium of Pilate, formed a forecourt and an atrium from the forum to the praetorium. That part of Pilate's palace used as a judgment hall was called the praetorium. The guardhouse was surrounded by columns. It had an open court in the center, under which were the prisons in which the two robbers were confined. This court was alive with Roman soldiers. In the forum, not far from this guardhouse and near the colonnade that surrounded it, stood the whipping pillar. Several others were standing in the enclosure of the square. The nearest were used for corporal punishment; to the most distant were fastened the beasts for sale. On the forum in front of the guardhouse was a terrace, level and beautiful, something like a place of execution, furnished with stone seats and reached by a flight of stone steps. From this place, which was called Gabbatha, Pilate was accustomed to pronounce solemn sentence. The marble steps that gave access to Pilate's palace led to an open terrace from which the governor listened to the plaintiffs, who sat opposite on the stone benches next the entrance to the forum. By speaking in a loud voice from the terrace, one could easily be heard in the forum.

Back of Pilate's palace rose still higher terraces with gardens and summerhouses. By these gardens, the palace was connected with the dwelling of Pilate's wife, whose name was Claudia Procula. A moat separated these buildings from the mountain on which the temple was built.

Adjoining the eastern side of Pilate's palace was that council house or judgment hall of Herod the Elder, in whose inner court many innocent children were once upon a time murdered. Its appearance was now somewhat changed, owing to the addition of new buildings; the entrance was from the eastern side, although there was still one from Pilate's hall.

Four streets ran hither from the eastern section of the city, three toward Pilate's palace and the forum; the fourth passed the northern side of the latter toward the gate that led to Bethzur. Near this gate and on this street stood the beautiful house owned by Lazarus in Jerusalem, and not far from it a dwelling belonging to Martha.

Of these four streets, the one that was nearest to the temple extended from the sheep gate. On entering the latter, one found on his right the Probatica, or pool in which the sheep were washed. It was built so close to the wall that the arches above it were constructed in that same wall. It had a drain outside the wall down into the valley of Jehosaphat, on which account this place, just before the gate, was marshy. Some buildings surrounded the pool. The paschal lambs were, before being taken to the temple, washed here for the first time; but at the pool of Bethesda, south of the temple, they afterward received a more solemn purification. In the second street stood a house and courtyard that once belonged to Mary's mother, St. Anne. She and her family used to put up there with their cattle for sacrifice when they went to Jerusalem for the festival days. In this house also, if I remember rightly, Joseph and Mary's wedding was celebrated.

The forum, as I have said, stood higher than the surrounding streets, through which ran gutters down to the sheep pool. On Mount Zion, opposite the ancient citadel of David, stood a similar forum; to the southeast and in its vicinity lay the Cenacle; and to the north were the judgment halls of Annas and Caiaphas. The citadel of David was now a deserted, dilapidated fortress full of empty courts, stables, and chambers, which were hired as resting places to caravans and travelers with their beasts of burden. This building had already long lain deserted. Even at the birth of Christ, I saw it in its present condition. The retinue of the three holy kings with its numerous beasts of burden put up at it.

Jesus before Pilate

ACCORDING to our reckoning of time, it was *about six in the morning* when the procession of the high priests and Pharisees, with the frightfully maltreated Savior, reached the palace of Pilate. Between the large square and the entrance into the praetorium were seats on either side of the road where Annas, Caiaphas, and the members of the council that had accompanied them placed themselves. Jesus, however, still bound by cords, was dragged forward by the executioners to the foot of the steps that led up to Pilate's judgment seat. At the moment of their arrival, Pilate was reclining on a kind of easy-chair upon the projecting terrace. A small, three-legged table was standing by him, upon which lay the insignia of his office and some other things, which I do not now recall. Officers and soldiers surrounded him, and they too wore badges indicative of Roman dominion.

The high priests and Jews kept far from the tribunal because, according to their Law, to approach it would have defiled them. They would not step over a certain boundary line.

When Pilate saw the mob hurrying forward with great tumult and clamor, and the maltreated Jesus led to the foot of his steps, he arose and addressed them with a scornful air. His manner was something like that of a haughty French marshal treating with the deputies of a poor little city. "What have you come about so early? Why have you handled the poor man so roughly? You began early to flay him, to slaughter him." But they cried out to the executioners: "Onward with him into the judgment hall!" Then turning to Pilate, they said: "Listen to our accusation against this malefactor. We cannot, for fear of defilement, enter the judgment hall."

Scarcely had this outcry died away when a tall, powerful, venerable-looking man from the crowd, pressing behind in the forum, cried out: "True, indeed, ye dare not enter that judgment hall, for it has been consecrated with innocent blood! Only he dares enter! Only he among all the Jews is pure as the Innocents!" After uttering these words with great emotion, he disappeared in the crowd. His name was Zadoch. He was a wealthy man and a cousin of the husband of Seraphia, who was afterward called Veronica. Two of his little boys had, at Herod's command, been slaughtered among the innocent children in the court of the judgment hall. Since that time he had entirely withdrawn from the world and, like an Essene, lived with his wife in continency. He had once seen Jesus at Lazarus's and listened to his teaching. At this moment, in which he beheld the innocent Jesus dragged in so pitiable a manner up the steps, the painful recollection of his murdered babes tore his heart, and he uttered that cry as a testimony to the Lord's innocence. The enemies of Jesus were, however, too urgent in their demands and too exasperated at Pilate's manner toward them and their own humbled position before him, to pay particular attention to the cry.

Jesus was dragged by the executioners up the lofty flight of marble steps and placed in the rear of the terrace, from which Pilate could speak with his accusers below. When Pilate beheld before him Jesus, of whom he had heard so many reports, so shockingly abused and disfigured, and still with that dignity of bearing which no ill-treatment could change, his loathing contempt for the Jewish priests and council increased. These latter had sent word to him at an early hour that they were going to hand over to him

Jesus of Nazareth, who was guilty of death, that he might pronounce sentence upon him. Pilate, however, let them see that he was not going to condemn him without some well-proved accusation. In an imperious and scornful manner, therefore, he addressed the high priests: "What accusation do you bring against this man?" To which they answered angrily: "If we did not know him to be a malefactor, we should not have delivered him to you." "Take him," replied Pilate, "and judge him according to your Law." "Thou knowest," they retorted, "that it is not lawful for us to condemn any man to death."

The enemies of Jesus were full of rage and fury. Their whole desire seemed to be to put an end to him before the legal festival, that they might then slaughter the paschal lamb. For this end they wished to proceed in the most violent hurry. They knew not that he was the true Paschal Lamb, he whom they themselves had dragged before the tribunal of an idolatrous judge, over whose threshold they did not dare to pass for fear of defiling themselves and thus being unable to eat the typical paschal lamb.

As the governor summoned them to bring forward their accusations, this they now proceeded to do. They laid three principal charges against him, for each of which they produced ten witnesses. They worded them in such a way that Jesus might be made to appear as an offender against the Emperor, and Pilate be forced to condemn him. It was only in cases pertaining to the laws of religion and the temple that they had a right to take things into their own hands. The first charge they alleged was: "Jesus is a seducer of the people, a disturber of the peace, an agitator," and then they brought forth some witnesses to substantiate the charge. Next they said: "He goes about holding great meetings, breaking the sabbath, and healing on the sabbath." Here Pilate interrupted them scornfully: "It is easily seen that none of you were sick, else you would not be scandalized at healing on the sabbath." They continued: "He seduces the people by horrible teaching, for he says that to have eternal life, they must eat his flesh and blood." Pilate was provoked at the furious hate with which they uttered this charge. He glanced at his officers and with a smile said sharply to the Jews: "It would almost appear that you yourselves are following his teaching and are aiming at eternal life, since you, too, seem so desirous of eating his flesh and his blood."

Their second accusation was: "Jesus stirs up the people not to pay tribute to the Emperor." Here Pilate interrupted them angrily. As one whose office it was to know about such things, he retorted with emphasis: "That is a great lie! I know better than that!" Then the Jews shouted out their third accusation: "Let it be so! This man of low, obscure, and doubtful origin, puts himself at the head of a large party and cries woe to Jerusalem. He scatters also among the people parables of double meaning of a king who is preparing a wedding feast for his son. The people gathered in great crowds around him on a mountain, and once they wanted to make him king; but it was sooner than he wished, and so he hid himself. During the last few days he came forward more boldly. He made a tumultuous entrance into Jerusalem, causing regal honors to be shown him, while the people, by his orders, cried: 'Hosanna to the son of David! Blessed be the reign of our father David which is now come!' Besides this, he teaches that he is the Christ, the anointed of the Lord, the Messiah, the promised king of the Jews, and allows himself so to be called." This third charge, like the two preceding, was supported by ten witnesses.

At the word that Jesus caused himself to be called the Christ, the king of the Jews, Pilate became somewhat thoughtful. He went from the open terrace into the adjoining apartment, casting as he passed him a scrutinizing glance upon Jesus, and ordered the guard to bring the Lord into the judgment chamber. [J1]

Caravan Resting Place

Pilate was a fickle, weak-minded, superstitious pagan. He had all kinds of dark forebodings concerning the sons of his gods who had lived upon earth, and he was not ignorant of the fact that the Jewish prophets had long ago foretold one who was to be the anointed of God, a redeemer, a deliverer, a king, and that many of the Jews were looking for his coming. He knew also that kings from the East had come to Herod the Elder, inquiring after a newborn king, that they might honor him; and that after this many children were put to death at Herod's order. He knew indeed the traditions relating to a Messiah, a king of the Jews; but zealous idolater that he was, he put no faith in them, he could not fancy what kind of a king was meant. Most likely he thought with the liberal-minded

Jews and Herodians of his day, who dreamed but of a powerful, victorious ruler. So the accusation that Jesus, standing before him so poor, so miserable, so disfigured, should give himself out for that anointed of the Lord, for that king, appeared to him truly ridiculous. But because the enemies of Jesus had brought forward the charge as injurious to the rights of the Emperor, Pilate caused the Savior to be conducted to his presence for an examination.

Pilate regarded Jesus with astonishment as he addressed him: "Art thou the king of the Jews?" And Jesus made answer: "Sayest thou this thing of thyself, or have others told it thee of me?" Pilate, a little offended that Jesus should esteem him so foolish as, of his own accord, to ask so poor and miserable a creature whether he was a king, answered evasively something to this effect: "Am I a Jew, that I should know about things so nonsensical? Thy people and their priests have delivered thee to me for condemnation as one deserving of death. Tell me, what hast thou done?" Jesus answered solemnly: "My kingdom is not of this world. If my kingdom were of this world, I should certainly have servants who would combat for me, that I should not be delivered to the Jews. But my kingdom is not here below." Pilate heard these earnest words of Jesus with a kind of shudder, and said to him thoughtfully: "Art thou then indeed a king?" And Jesus answered: "As thou sayest! Yes, I am the king. I was born, and I came into this world, to bear witness to the truth. Everyone that is of the truth, heareth my voice." Pilate cast a glance on him and, rising, said: "Truth! What is truth?" Some other words were then exchanged, whose purport I do not now remember.

Pilate went out again to the terrace. He could not comprehend Jesus, but he knew this much about him, that he was not a king who would prove mischievous to the Emperor, and that he laid no claim to any kingdom of this world. As to a kingdom belonging to another world, the Emperor troubled himself little about that. Pilate therefore called down from the terrace to the high priests below: "I find no kind of crime in this man!"

Thereupon the enemies of Jesus were seized with new fury. They launched out into a torrent of accusations against him, while Jesus stood in silence praying for the poor creatures. Pilate turned to him and asked: "Hast thou nothing to say to all these charges?" But Jesus answered not a word. Pilate regarded him in amazement as he said: "I see plainly that they are acting falsely against thee!" (He used some expression for the word lie that I cannot remember.) But the accusers, whose rage was on the increase, cried out: "What! Thou findest no guilt in him? Is it no crime to stir up the people? He has spread his doctrine throughout the whole country, from Galilee up to these parts."

When Pilate caught the word *Galilee*, he reflected a

moment and then called down: "Is this man from Galilee a subject of Herod?" The accusers answered: "Yes. His parents once lived in Nazareth, and now his own dwelling is near Capernaum." Pilate then said: "Since he is a Galilean and subject to Herod, take him to Herod. He is here for the feast, and can judge him at once." He then caused Jesus to be taken from the judgment chamber and led down again to his enemies, while at the same time he sent an officer to inform Herod that one of his subjects, a Galilean, Jesus of Nazareth, was being brought to him to be judged. Pilate was rejoiced to be able in this way to escape passing sentence on Jesus, for the whole affair made him feel uncomfortable. At the same time, he had a motive of policy in showing this act of courtesy to Herod, between whom and himself there was an estrangement, for he knew that Herod was very desirous of seeing Jesus.

Jesus's enemies were in the highest degree exasperated at being thus dismissed before the populace, at being thus obliged to lead Jesus away to another tribunal; consequently, they vented their rage upon him. With renewed fury they surrounded him, bound him anew and, along with the clamoring soldiers, drove him in furious haste with cuffs and blows across the crowded forum and through the street that led to the palace of Herod not far off. Some Roman soldiers accompanied them.

Claudia Procula, the lawful wife of Pilate, had while Pilate was treating with the Jews sent a servant to tell her husband that she was very anxious to speak with him. As Jesus was now being led to Herod, she stood concealed upon an elevated balcony, and with deep anxiety and trouble of mind watched him being led across the forum.

Origin of the Devotion of the "Holy Way of the Cross"

THE BLESSED Virgin, standing with Magdalene and John in a corner of the forum hall, had with unspeakable pain beheld the whole of the dreadful scene just described, had heard the clamorous shouts and cries. And now when Jesus was taken to Herod, she begged to be conducted by John and Magdalene back over the whole way of suffering trodden by her divine Son since his arrest the preceding evening. They went over the whole route—to the judgment hall of Caiaphas, to the palace of Annas, and thence through Ophel to Gethsemane on the Mount of Olives. On many places where Jesus had suffered outrage and injury, they paused in heartfelt grief and compassion, and wherever he had fallen to the ground the blessed Mother fell on her knees and kissed the earth. Magdalene wrung her hands, while John in tears assisted the afflicted mother to rise, and led her on further. This was the origin of that devotion of the church, the Holy Way of the Cross, the origin of that sympathetic meditation upon the bitter Passion of our divine Redeemer even before it was fully accomplished by him. Even then, when Jesus was traversing that most painful way of suffering, did his pure and immaculate mother, in her undying, holy love, seek to share the inward and outward pains of her Son and her God, venerate and weep over his footsteps as he went to die for us, and offer all to the heavenly Father for the salvation of the world.

Thus, at every step of the blessed Redeemer, did she gather the infinite merits that he acquired for us, and lay them up in her most holy and compassionate heart, that unique and venerable treasury of all the gifts of salvation, out of which and through which, according to the eternal degree of the triune God, every fruit and effect of the mystery of Redemption perfected in the fullness of time should be bestowed upon fallen man. From the most pure blood of this most holy heart was formed by the Holy Spirit that body which today was, from a thousand wounds, pouring forth Its precious blood as the price of our Redemption. For nine months had Jesus dwelt under that heart full of grace. As a virgin inviolate had Mary brought him forth, cared for him, watched over him, and nourished him at her breast, in order to give him over today for us to the most cruel death on the tree of the cross. Just as the Eternal Father spared not his Only-Begotten Son, but delivered him up for us, so the blessed Mother, the Mother of God, spared not the blessed Fruit of her womb, but consented that he, as the true Paschal Lamb, should be sacrificed for us upon the cross. And so Mary is, in her Son and next to him, the concurrent cause of our salvation, our redemption, our mediatrix and powerful advocate with God, the Mother of grace and of mercy.

All the just of olden times from our penitent first parents down to the last soul that had entered into Abraham's bosom, lamented, prayed, and offered sacrifice on this day in the holy heart of the divine Mother, the queen of patriarchs and prophets. So too, till the end of time, will it belong only to a childlike love for Mary to practice the devotion of the Holy Way of the Cross, a devotion originated by her and by her bequeathed to the church. By this devotion so rich in blessings, so pleasing to God, will the soul advance in faith and in love to the most holy Redeemer. It is an extremely significant fact, though unfortunately one too little appreciated, that wherever the love of Mary grows cold and devotion to the mysteries of the rosary becomes extinct, there too dies out the devotion of the Holy Way of the Cross yes, even faith in the infinite value of the precious blood is lost.

Magdalene in her grief was like an insane person. Immeasurable as her love was her repentance. When, in her love, she longed to pour out her soul at the feet of Jesus, as once the precious balm upon his head, full of horror she descried between her and the Redeemer the abyss of her crimes; then was the pain of repentance in all its bitterness renewed in her heart. When, in her gratitude, she longed to send up like a cloud of incense her thanksgiving for forgiveness received, she saw him, full of pains and torments, led to death. With unspeakable grief she comprehended that Jesus was undergoing all this on account of her sins, which he had taken upon himself in order to atone for them with his own blood. This thought plunged her deeper and deeper into an abyss of repentant sorrow. Her soul was, as it were, dissolved in gratitude and love, in sorrow and bitterness, in sadness and lamentation, for she saw and felt the ingratitude, the capital crime of her nation, in delivering its Savior to the ignominious death of the cross. All this was expressed in her whole appearance, in her words and gestures.

John suffered and loved not less than Magdalene, but the untroubled innocence of his pure heart lent a higher degree of peace to his soul.

Pilate and his Wife

WHILE Jesus was being taken to Herod and while he was enduring mockery at his tribunal, I saw Pilate going to his wife, Claudia Procula. They met at a summerhouse in a terraced garden behind Pilate's palace. Claudia was trembling and agitated. She was a tall, fine-looking woman, though rather pale. She wore a veil that fell gracefully in the back, but without concealing her hair, which was wound round her head and adorned with ornaments. She wore earrings and necklace, and her long, plaited robe was fastened on her bosom by a clasp. She conversed long with Pilate and conjured him by all that was sacred to him not to injure Jesus, the prophet, the Holy of Holies, and then she related some things from the dreams, or visions, which she had had of Jesus the night before.

I remember that she saw the annunciation to Mary, the birth of Christ, the adoration of the shepherds and the kings, the prophecies of Simeon and Anna, the flight into Egypt, the massacre of the Holy Innocents, the temptation in the desert, and other scenes from the holy life of Jesus. She saw him always environed with light, while the malice and wickedness of his enemies appeared under the most terrible pictures. She saw the sanctity and anguish of his mother and his own infinite sufferings under symbols of unchanging love and patience. She endured unspeakable anguish and sadness, for these visions, besides being something very unusual for her, were irresistibly impressive and convincing. Some of them, as for instance, the massacre of the Innocents and Simeon's prophecy in the temple, she beheld as taking place even in the neighborhood of her own house.

When next morning, alarmed by the uproar of the tumultuous mob, she looked out upon the forum, she recognized in the Lord the one shown her in vision the night before. She saw him now the object of all kinds of abuse and ill-treatment, while being led by his enemies across the forum to Herod. In terrible anguish, she sent at once for Pilate to whom, frightened and anxious, she related the visions she had seen in her dreams as far as she could make herself understood. She entreated and implored, and clung to Pilate in the most touching manner. [J2]

Pilate was greatly astonished, and somewhat troubled at what she related. He compared it with all that he had heard of Jesus, with the fury of the Jews, with Jesus's silence, and with his dignified and wonderful answers to all the questions he had put to him. He wavered uneasily in his own mind, but soon yielded to his wife's representations and said: "I have already declared that I find no guilt in Jesus. I shall not condemn him, for I know the utter wickedness of the Jews." He spoke at length of Jesus's bearing toward himself, quieted his wife's fears, and even went so far as to give her a pledge of assurance that he would not condemn him. I do not remember what kind of a jewel, whether a ring or a seal, Pilate gave as a sign of his promise. With this understanding they parted.

I saw Pilate as a crack-brained, covetous, proud, vacillating man, with a great fund of meanness in his character. He was deterred by no high fear of God from working out his own ends, could give himself to the meanest actions, and at the same time practiced the lowest, the most dastardly kind of superstitious idolatry and divination when he found himself in any difficulty. So now, off he hurried to his gods, before whom in a retired apartment of his house he burned incense and demanded of them all kinds of signs. He afterward watched the sacred chickens eating, and Satan whispered to him sometimes one thing, sometimes another. At one time he thought that Jesus ought to be released as innocent; again, he feared that his own gods would take vengeance on him if he saved the life of a man who exercised so singular an influence upon him that he believed him some kind of demigod, for Jesus might do much harm to his divinities. "Perhaps," thought he, "he is indeed a kind of Jewish god. There are so many prophecies that point to a king of the Jews who shall conquer all things. Kings from the star worshippers of the East have already been here seeking such a king in this country. He might, perhaps, elevate himself above my gods and my Emperor, and so I should have much to answer for, if he does not die. Perhaps his death would be a triumph for my gods." Then came before him the remembrance of the wonderful dreams of his wife, who had never seen Jesus, and this remembrance weighed heavily in favor of Jesus's release in the wavering scales held by Pilate. It looked now as if he were resolved to release him. He wanted to be just, but he attained not his aim for the same reason that he had not waited for an answer from Jesus to his own question, "What is truth?"

Jesus before Herod

ON the forum and in the streets through which Jesus was led to Herod, a constantly increasing crowd was gathered, composed of the inhabitants from the neighboring places and the whole country around, come up for the feast. The most hostile Pharisees in the whole land had taken their places with their own people in order to stir up the fickle mob against Jesus. Before the Roman guardhouse near Pilate's palace, the Roman soldiers were drawn up in strong numbers, and many other important points of the city were occupied by them.

Herod's palace was situated in the new city to the north of the forum, not far from that of Pilate. An escort of Roman soldiers from the country between Switzerland and Italy joined the procession. Jesus's enemies were greatly enraged at this going backward and forward, and they ceased not to insult him and encourage the executioners to drag him and push him about. Pilate's messenger had announced the coming procession, consequently Herod was awaiting it. He was seated in a large hall on a cushioned throne, surrounded by courtiers and soldiers. The high priests went in through the colonnade and ranged on either side, while Jesus stood in the entrance. Herod was very much flattered that Pilate had openly, before the high priests, accorded to him the right of judgment upon a Galilean; so he put on a very arrogant air and made a great show of business. He was well-pleased also at seeing Jesus before him in so sorry a plight, since he had always disdained to appear in his presence. John had spoken of Jesus in terms so solemn, and he had heard so much of him from his spies and tale-bearers, that Herod was exceedingly curious about him. He was in an extraordinarily good humor at the thought of being able to institute, before his courtiers and the high priests, a grand judicial inquiry concerning Jesus, in which he might show off his knowledge before both parties. He had also been informed that Pilate could find no guilt in Jesus, and that was to his cringing mind a hint that he was to treat the accusers with some reserve, a proceeding that only increased their fury. As soon as they entered his presence, they began to vociferate their complaints. Herod however looked inquisitively at Jesus, and when he saw him so mis-

erable, so ill-treated, his garments bespattered with filth, his hair torn and dishevelled, his face covered with blood and dirt, a feeling of loathsome compassion stole over the effeminate, voluptuous king. He uttered God's name (it was something like "Jehovah"), turned his face away with an air of disgust and said to the priests: "Take him away! Clean him! How could you bring before my eyes so unclean, so maltreated a creature!" At these words the servants led Jesus into the vestibule, brought a basin of water and an old rag with which they removed some of the dirt, ill-treating him all the while. Their rough manner of acting opened the wounds on his disfigured face. Herod meantime reproached the priests with their brutality. He appeared to wish to imitate Pilate's manner of acting toward them, for he said: "It is very evident that he has fallen into the hands of butchers. You are beginning your work today before the time." The high priests replied only by vehemently alleging their complaints and accusations. When Jesus was again led in, Herod, who wanted to play the agreeable toward him, ordered a glass of wine to be brought to him that he might regain a little strength. But Jesus shook his head, and would not accept the drink.

Herod was very affable to Jesus; he even flattered him and repeated all that he knew of him. At first he asked him several questions, and wanted to see a sign from him. But Jesus answered not a syllable, and quietly kept his eyes cast down. Herod became very much vexed and ashamed before those present. Wishing, however, to conceal his embarrassment, he poured forth a torrent of questions and empty words. "I am very sorry," he said, "to see thee so gravely accused. I have heard many things of thee. Dost thou know that thou didst offend me in Thirza when, without my permission, thou didst release the prisoners whom I had confined there? But perhaps thy intentions were good. Thou hast now been delivered to me by the Roman governor that I may judge thee. What sayest thou to all these charges? Thou art silent? They have often told me of thy great wisdom in speaking and teaching—I should like to hear thee refute thy accusers. What sayest thou? Is it true that thou art the king of the Jews? Art thou the Son of God? Who art thou? I hear that thou hast performed great miracles. Prove it to me by giving me some sign. It belongs to me to release thee. Is it true that thou hast given sight to men born blind? Didst thou raise Lazarus from the dead? Didst thou feed several thousand people with a few loaves? Why dost thou not answer! I conjure thee to perform one of thy miracles! It will be to thy own advantage." But Jesus was silent. Herod, with increasing volubility, went on: "Who art thou? What is the matter with thee? Who has given thee power? Why canst thou no longer exercise it? Art thou he of whose birth things so extraordinary are told? Once some kings came from the East to my father, to inquire after a newborn king of the Jews, to whom they wanted to do homage. Now, they say that this child is no other than thyself. Is this true? Didst thou escape the death which at that time fell upon so many children? How did that happen? Why didst thou remain so long in retirement? Or do they relate those events of thee only in order to make thee a king? Answer me! What kind of a king art thou? Truly, I see nothing royal about thee! They have, as I have heard, celebrated for thee lately a triumphant procession, to the temple. What does that mean? Speak! How comes it that such popularity ends in this way?" To all these questions Herod received no answer from Jesus. It was revealed to me that Jesus would not speak with him because, by his adulterous connection with Herodias and the murder of the Baptist, Herod was under excommunication.

Annas and Caiaphas took advantage of Herod's displeasure at Jesus's silence in order to renew their charges. Among others, they brought forward the following: Jesus had called Herod a fox, and for a long time he had been laboring to overthrow his whole family; he wanted to establish a new religion, and he had already eaten the Passover yesterday. This last accusation had been lodged with Caiaphas at the time of Judas's treason, but some of Jesus's friends had brought forth writings to show that that was allowed under certain circumstances.

Herod, although greatly vexed at Jesus's silence, did not permit himself to lose sight of his political ends. He did not wish to condemn Jesus, partly because of his own secret fear of him and the remorse he felt for John's murder, and partly again because the high priests were odious to him, because they would never palliate his adultery and on account of it had excluded him from the sacrifices. But the chief reason for Herod's not condemning Jesus was that he would not pass sentence on one whom Pilate had declared to be without guilt. He had political views also in thus acting; he wanted to show Pilate an act of courtesy in presence of the high priests. He ended by overwhelming Jesus with words of scorn and contempt, and said to his servants and bodyguard (of whom there were about two hundred in his palace): "Take this fool away, and show the honor due to so ridiculous a king. He is more fool than malefactor!"

The Savior was now led out into a large court and treated with unspeakable outrage and mockery. The court was surrounded by the wings of the palace, and Herod, standing on a flat roof, gazed for a considerable time upon the ill-treatment offered to Jesus. [J3] Annas and Caiaphas were at his back, trying by all means in their power to induce him to pass sentence upon Jesus. Herod, however, would not yield. He replied in a tone loud enough to be heard by the Roman soldiers: "It would be for me the greatest sin, did I condemn him." He meant probably the greatest sin against Pilate's decision, who had been so gracious as to send Jesus to him.

When the high priests and enemies of Jesus saw that Herod would in no way comply with their wishes, they dispatched some of their number with money to Acre, a section of the city where at present many Pharisees were stopping. The messengers were directed to summon them to be in attendance at once with all their people in the vicinity of Pilate's palace. A large sum of money was put into the hands of these Pharisees for distribution among the people as bribes, that with furious and vehement clamoring they might demand Jesus's death. Other messengers were sent to spread among the people threats of God's vengeance if they did not insist upon the death of the blasphemer. They gave out the report also that if Jesus were not put to death, he would go over to the Romans, that this was what he meant by the kingdom of which he had so constantly spoken. Then, indeed, would the Jews be utterly ruined. On other sides they spread the report that Herod had condemned Jesus, but that the people must express their will on the subject; that his followers were to be feared, for if Jesus were freed in any way, the feast would be altogether upset, and then would the Romans and his followers unite in taking vengeance. Thus were scattered abroad confused and alarming rumors in order to rouse and exasperate the populace. At the same time, Jesus's enemies caused money to be distributed among Herod's soldiers, that they might grossly maltreat Jesus, yes, even hasten his death, for they would rather see him die in that way than live to be freed by Pilate's sentence.

From this insolent, godless rabble, our Lord had to suffer the most shameful mockery, the most barbarous ill-treatment. When they led him out into the court, a soldier brought from the lodge at the gate a large white sack in which cotton had been packed. They cut a hole in the bottom of the sack and, amid shouts of derisive laughter from all present, threw it over Jesus's head. It hung in wide folds over his feet. Another soldier laid a red rag like a collar around his neck. And now they bowed before him, pushed him here and there, insulted him, spat upon him, struck him in the face because he had refused to answer their king, and rendered him a thousand acts of mock homage. They threw filth upon him, pulled him about as if he were dancing, forced him in the wide, trailing mantle of derision to fall to the earth, and dragged him through a gutter which ran around the court the whole length of the buildings, so that his sacred head struck against the pillars and stones at the corners. Then they jerked him to his feet and set up fresh shouting, began new outrages. Among the two hundred soldiers and servants of Herod's court were people from regions most widely separated, and every wicked miscreant in that crowd wanted, by some special, infamous act toward Jesus, to do honor to himself and his province. They carried on their brutality with violent haste and mocking shouts. Those that had received money from the Pharisees took advantage of the confusion to strike the sacred head of Jesus with their clubs. He looked at them with compassion, sighed and groaned from pain. But they, in whining voices, mocked his moaning, and at every fresh outrage broke out into derisive shouts of laughter. There was not one to pity Jesus. I saw the blood running down from his head in the most pitiable manner, and three times did I see him sink to the earth under the blows from their clubs. At the same time, I saw weeping angels hovering over him, anointing his head. It was made known to me that these blows would have proved fatal, were it not for the divine assistance. The Philistines who, in the racecourse at Gaza, hunted blind Samson to death, were not so violent and cruel as these wretches.

April 3, AD 33
Friday, 8:15 AM

But time pressed. The high priests must soon appear in the temple and, as they had received the assurance that all their instructions would be attended to, they made one more effort to obtain Jesus's condemnation from Herod. But he was deaf to their prayers. He still turned his thoughts toward Pilate alone, to whom he now sent back Jesus in his garment of derision.

Jesus Taken from Herod to Pilate

WITH renewed irritation, the high priests and the enemies of Jesus made their way back with him from Herod to Pilate. They were mortified at being forced to return, without his condemnation, to a tribunal at which he had already been pronounced innocent. They took therefore another and longer route in order to exhibit him in his ignominy to another portion of the city, also that they might have longer to abuse him, and give their emissaries more time to stir up the populace against him.

The way they now took was very rough and uneven. The executioners by whom Jesus was led left him no moment of peace, and the long garment impeded his steps. It trailed in the mud and sometimes threw him down, on which occasions he was, with blows on the head and kicks, dragged up again by the cords. He was on this journey subjected to indescribable scorn and outrage both from his conductors and the populace, but he prayed the while

that he might not die until he had consummated his Passion for us.

It was a quarter after eight in the morning when the procession with the maltreated Jesus again crossed the forum (though from another side, probably the eastern) to Pilate's palace. The crowd was very great. The people were standing in groups, those from the same places and regions together. The Pharisees were running around among them, stirring them up. Remembering the insurrection of the Galilean zealots at the last Passover, Pilate had assembled upwards of a thousand men whom he distributed in the praetorium and its surroundings, and at the various entrances of the forum, and his own palace.

The blessed Virgin, her elder sister Mary Heli with her daughter Mary Cleophas, Magdalene, and several other holy women—in all about twenty—were, while the following events were taking place, standing in a hall from which they could hear everything, and where they could slip in and out. John was with them in the beginning.

Jesus, in his garments of derision, was led through the jeering crowd. The most audacious were everywhere pushed forward by the Pharisees, and they surpassed the others in mockery and insults. One of Herod's court officers, who had reached the place before the procession, announced to Pilate how very much he appreciated his attention, but that he found the Galilean, so famed for his wisdom, nothing better than a silent fool, that he had treated him as such and sent him back to him. Pilate was very glad that Herod had not acted in opposition to himself and condemned Jesus. He sent his salutations to him in return, and thus they today were made friends who, since the fall of the aqueduct, had been enemies.

Jesus was led again through the street before Pilate's house and up the steps to the elevated platform. The executioners dragged him in the most brutal manner, the long garment tripped him, and he fell so often on the white marble steps that they were stained with blood from his sacred head. His enemies, who had retaken their seats on the side of the forum, and the rude mob, broke out into jeers and laughter at his every fall, while the executioners drove him up with kicks.

Pilate was reclining on a chair something like a small couch, a little table by his side. [J4] As on the preceding occasion, he was attended by officers and men holding rolls of written parchment. Stepping out upon the terrace from which he was accustomed to address the multitude, he thus spoke to Jesus's accusers: "You have presented unto me this man as one that perverteth the people, and behold I, having examined him before you, find no cause in him in those things wherein you accuse him. No, nor Herod neither. For I sent you to him and behold, nothing worthy of death is brought against him. I will chastise him therefore and let him go." At these words, loud murmurs and shouts of disapprobation arose among the Pharisees, who began still more energetically to stir up the people and distribute money among them. Pilate treated them with the utmost contempt. Among other cutting remarks, he let fall the following sarcastic words: "You will not see enough innocent blood flow at the slaughtering today without this man's!"

It was customary for the people to go to Pilate just before Passover and, according to an ancient custom, demand the release of some one prisoner. It was now time for this. The Pharisees, while at Herod's palace, had dispatched emissaries to Acre—a section of the city west of the temple—to bribe the assembled multitude to demand, not Jesus's liberation, but his crucifixion. Pilate was hoping that the people would ask that Jesus should be released, and he thought by proposing along with him a miserable miscreant, who had already been condemned to death, he was leaving to them no choice. That notorious malefactor was called Barabbas, and was hated by the whole nation. He had in an insurrection committed murder; and besides that, I saw all kinds of horrible things connected with him. He was given to sorcery and, in its practice, had even cut open the womb of pregnant women.

And now there arose a stir among the people in the forum. A crowd pressed forward, their speaker at their head. Raising their voice so as to be heard on Pilate's terrace, they cried out: "Pilate, grant us what is customary on this feast!" For this demand Pilate had been waiting, so he at once addressed them. "It is your custom that I should deliver to you one prisoner on your festival day. Whom will you that I release to you, Barabbas or Jesus, the king of the Jews—Jesus, the anointed of the Lord?"

Pilate was quite perplexed concerning Jesus. He called him the "king of Jews," partly in character of an arrogant Roman who despised the Jews for having so miserable a king, between whom and a murderer the choice rested; and partly from a kind of conviction that he might really be that wonderful king promised to the Jews, the anointed of the Lord, the Messiah. His presentiment of the truth was also half-feigned. He mentioned these titles of the Lord because he felt that envy was the principal motive that excited the high priests against Jesus, whom he himself esteemed innocent.

A moment of hesitation and deliberation on the part of the populace followed upon Pilate's question, and then only a few voices shouted loudly: "Barabbas!" At that instant, Pilate was called for by one of his wife's servants, who showed him the pledge he had given her that morning, and said: "Claudia Procula bids thee remember thy promise." The Pharisees and high priests were greatly excited. They ran among the crowd, threatening and commanding. They had, however, no great trouble in making the mob carry out their wishes.

Mary, Magdalene, John, and the holy women, trembling and weeping, were standing in a corner of the hall. Although the mother of Jesus knew that there was no help for humankind excepting by his death, yet she was, as the mother of the most holy Son, full of anxiety, full of longing for the preservation of his life. Jesus had become man voluntarily to undergo crucifixion; still, when led to death, though innocent, he suffered all the pangs and torments of his frightful ill-treatment just as any human being would have suffered. And in the same way did Mary suffer all the affliction and anguish of an ordinary mother whose most innocent child should have to endure such things from the thankless multitude. She trembled, she shuddered with fear, and still she hoped. John went frequently to a little distance in the hope of being able to bring back some good news. Mary prayed that so great a crime might not be perpetrated. She prayed like Jesus on the Mount of Olives: "If it be possible, let this chalice pass!" And thus the loving mother continued to hope, for while the words and efforts of the Pharisees to stir up the people ran from mouth to mouth, the rumor also reached her that Pilate was trying to release Jesus. Not far from her stood a group of people from Capernaum, and among them many whom Jesus had healed and taught. They feigned not to recognize John and the veiled women standing so sorrowfully apart, and cast toward them furtive glances. Mary, like all the rest, thought they would surely not choose Barabbas in preference to their benefactor and Savior, but in this she was disappointed.

Pilate had returned to his wife, as a sign that his promise still held good, the pledge he had given her early that morning. He again went out on the terrace and seated himself on the chair by the little table. The high priests also were seated. Pilate called out again: "Which of the two shall I release unto you?" Thereupon arose from the whole forum and from all sides one unanimous shout: "Away with this man! Give us Barabbas!" Pilate again cried: "But what shall I do with Jesus, the Christ, the king of the Jews?" With tumultuous violence, all yelled: "Crucify him! Crucify him!" Pilate asked for the third time: "Why, what evil hath he done? I find not the least cause of death in him. I will scourge him and then let him go." But the shout: "Crucify him! Crucify him!" burst from the crowd like a roar from hell, while the high priests and Pharisees, frantic with rage, were vociferating violently. Then poor, irresolute Pilate freed the wretch Barabbas and condemned Jesus to be scourged!

The Scourging of Jesus

PILATE, the base, pusillanimous judge, had several times repeated the cowardly words: "I find no guilt in him, therefore will I chastise him and let him go!" To which the Jews shouted no other response than, "Crucify him! Crucify him!" But Pilate, still hoping to carry out his first resolve not to condemn Jesus to death, commanded him to be scourged after the manner of the Romans. Then the executioners, striking and pushing Jesus with their short staves, led him through the raging multitude on the forum to the whipping pillar, which stood in front of one of the halls that surrounded the great square to the north of Pilate's palace and not far from the guardhouse.

And now came forward to meet Jesus the executioners' servants with their whips, rods, and cords, which they threw down near the pillar. There were six of them, swarthy men all somewhat shorter than Jesus, with coarse, crisp hair, to whom nature had denied a beard other than a thin, short growth like stubble. Their loins were girded and the rest of their clothing consisted of a jacket of leather, or some other wretched stuff, open at the sides, and covering the upper part of the body like a scapular. Their arms were naked, and their feet encased in tattered sandals. They were vile malefactors from the frontiers of Egypt who, as slaves and culprits, were here employed on buildings and canals. The most wicked, the most abject among them were always chosen for the punishment of criminals in the praetorium.

These barbarous men had often scourged poor offenders to death at this same pillar. There was something beastly, even devilish, in their appearance, and they were half-intoxicated. Although the Lord was offering no resistance whatever, yet they struck him with their fists and ropes and with frantic rage dragged him to the pillar, which stood alone and did not serve as a support to any part of the building. It was not very high, for a tall man with outstretched arms could reach the top, which was provided with an iron ring. Toward the middle of it on one side were other rings, or hooks. It is impossible to express

the barbarity with which those furious hounds outraged Jesus on that short walk to the pillar. They tore from him Herod's mantle of derision, and almost threw the poor Savior to the ground.

Jesus trembled and shuddered before the pillar. With his own hands, swollen and bloody from the tight cords, and in tremulous haste, he laid aside his garments, while the executioners struck and abused him. He prayed and implored so touchingly and, for one instant, turned his head toward his most afflicted mother, who was standing

Pilate's House

with the holy women in a corner of one of the porches around the square, not far from the scourging place. Turning to the pillar, as if to cover himself by it, Jesus said: "Turn thine eyes from me!" I know not whether he said these words vocally or mentally, but I saw how Mary took them, for at the same moment, I beheld her turning away and sinking into the arms of the holy women who surrounded her, closely veiled.

And now Jesus clasped the pillar in his arms. The executioners, with horrible imprecations and barbarous pulling, fastened his sacred, upraised hands, by means of a wooden peg, behind the iron ring on top. In thus doing, they so stretched his whole body, that his feet, tightly bound below at the base, scarcely touched the ground.

There stood the Holy of Holies, divested of clothing, laden with untold anguish and ignominy, stretched upon the pillar of criminals, while two of the bloodhounds, with sanguinary rage, began to tear with their whips the sacred back from head to foot. [J5] The first rods, or scourges, that they used looked as if made of flexible white wood, or they might have been bunches of ox sinews, or strips of hard, white leather.

Our Lord and Savior, the Son of God, true God and true Man, quivered and writhed like a poor worm under the strokes of the criminals' rods. He cried in a suppressed voice, and a clear, sweet-sounding wailing, like a loving prayer under excruciating torture, formed a touching accompaniment to the hissing strokes of his tormentors. Now and then the cries of the populace and the Pharisees mingled with those pitiful, holy, blessed, plaintive tones like frightful peals of thunder from an angry storm cloud. Many voices cried out together: "Away with him! Crucify him!" for Pilate was still negotiating with the people. The uproar was so great that, when he wanted to utter a few words, silence had to be enforced by the flourish of a trumpet. At such moments could be heard the strokes of the rods, the moans of Jesus, the blasphemy of the executioners, and the bleating of the paschal lambs, which were being washed in the pool near the sheep gate to the east. After this first purification, that they might not again soil themselves, their jaws were muzzled and they were carried by their owners along the clean road to the temple. They were then driven around toward the western side, where they were subjected to another ceremonial washing. The helpless bleating of the lambs had in it something indescribably touching. They were the only sounds in unison with the Savior's sighs.

The Jewish mob kept at some distance, about the breadth of a street, from the place of scourging. Roman soldiers were standing here and there, but chiefly around the guardhouse. All kinds of loungers were loitering near the pillar itself, some in silence, others with expressions of contempt. I saw many of them suddenly roused to sympathy, and at such moments it seemed as if a sudden ray of light shot from Jesus to them.

I saw infamous, scantily clad youths at one side of the guardhouse preparing fresh rods, and others going off to seek thorn branches. Some executioners of the high priests went up to the scourgers and slipped them money, and a large jug of thick, red juice was brought to them, from which they guzzled until they became perfectly furious from intoxication. *They had been at work about a quarter of an hour* when they ceased to strike, and joined two of the others in drinking. Jesus's body was livid, brown, blue, and red, and entirely covered with swollen cuts. His sacred blood was running down on the ground. He trembled and shuddered. Derision and mockery assailed him on all sides.

The night before had been cold. All the morning until now the sky was overcast, and a shower of hail had for a few moments fallen on the wondering multitude. Toward noon, however, the sky cleared and the sun shone out.

The second pair of scourgers now fell upon Jesus with fresh fury. They made use of different rods, rough, as if set with thorns, and here and there provided with knots and splinters. Under their furious blows, the swollen welts on Jesus's sacred body were torn and rent; his blood spurted around so that the arms of his tormentors were sprinkled with it. Jesus moaned and prayed and shuddered in his agony.

Just at this time, a numerous band of strangers on camels were riding past the forum. They gazed with fright and horror while some of the bystanders explained to them what was going on. They were travelers, some of whom had received baptism, and others had been present at Jesus's Sermon on the Mount. The shouts and uproar of the populace became still greater in the vicinity of Pilate's palace.

The last two scourgers struck Jesus with whips consisting of small chains, or straps, fastened to an iron handle, the ends furnished with iron points, or hooks. They tore off whole pieces of skin and flesh from his ribs. Oh, who can describe the awful barbarity of that spectacle!

But those monsters had not yet satiated their cruelty. They loosened the cords that bound Jesus and turned his back to the pillar and, because he was so exhausted as to be no longer able to stand, they bound him to it with fine cords passed under his arms across his breast, and below the knees. [J6] His hands they fastened to the ring in the middle of the opposite side. Only blood and wounds, only barbarously mangled flesh could be seen on the most sacred, most venerable body of the Son of God. Like furious bloodhounds raged the scourgers with their strokes. One held a slender rod in his left hand, and with it struck the face of Jesus. There was no longer a sound spot on the Lord's body. He glanced, with eyes swimming in blood, at his torturers, and sued for mercy; but they became only the more enraged. He moaned in fainting tones: "Woe! Woe!"

The terrible scourging had lasted fully three-quarters of an hour when an obscure man, a stranger and relative of

April 3, AD 33
Friday, 8:30 AM

that blind Ctesiphon whom Jesus had restored to sight, rushed indignantly to the back of the pillar, a sickle-shaped knife in his hand, and cried out: "Hold on! Do not beat the innocent man to death!" The drunken executioners, startled for a moment, paused, while with one stroke the stranger quickly cut the cords that bound Jesus. They were all knotted together, and fastened to a great iron nail at the back of the pillar. The man then fled back and disappeared in the crowd. Jesus sank, covered with blood and wounds, at the foot of the pillar and lay unconscious in his own blood. The executioners left him lying there and went to drink and call to their villainous companions, who were weaving the crown of thorns.

Jesus quivered in agony as, with bleeding wounds, he lay at the foot of the pillar. I saw just then some bold girls passing by. They paused in silence before him, holding one another by the hand, and looked at him in feminine disgust, which renewed the pain of all his wounds. He raised his bleeding head, and turned his sorrowful face in pity toward them. They passed on, while the executioners and soldiers laughed and shouted some scandalous expressions after them.

Several times during the scourging I saw weeping angels around Jesus and, during the whole of that bitter, ignominious punishment that fell upon him like a shower of hail, I heard him offering his prayer to his Father for the sins of humankind. But now, as he lay in his own blood at the foot of the pillar, I saw an angel strengthening him. It seemed as if the angel gave him a luminous morsel.

The executioners again drew near and, pushing Jesus with their feet, bade him rise, for they had not yet finished with the king. They struck at him while he crept after his linen band, which the infamous wretches kicked with shouts of derision from side to side, so that Jesus, in this his dire necessity, had most painfully to crawl around the ground in his own blood like a worm trodden underfoot, in order to reach his girdle and with it cover his lacerated loins. Then with blows and kicks they forced him to his tottering feet, but allowed him no time to put on his robe, which they threw about him with the sleeves over his shoulders. They hurried him to the guardhouse by a roundabout way, all along which he wiped the blood from his face with his robe. They were able to proceed quickly from the place of scourging because the porches around the building were open toward the forum; one could see through to the covered way under which the robbers and Barabbas lay imprisoned. As Jesus was led past the seats of

the high priests, the latter cried out: "Away with him! Away with him!" and in disgust turned from him into the inner court of the guardhouse. There were no soldiers in it when Jesus entered, but all kinds of slaves, executioners, and vagrants, the very scum of the populace.

As the mob had become so excited, Pilate had sent to the fortress Antonia for a reinforcement of Roman guards, and these he now ordered to surround the guardhouse. They were permitted to talk and laugh and ridicule Jesus, though they had to keep their ranks. Pilate wanted thus to restrain the people and keep them in awe. There were upwards of a thousand men assembled.

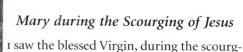

April 3, AD 33
Friday, 8:45 AM

Mary during the Scourging of Jesus

I saw the blessed Virgin, during the scourging of our Redeemer, in a state of uninterrupted ecstasy. She saw and suffered in an indescribable manner all that her Son was enduring. Her punishment, her martyrdom, was as inconceivably great as her most holy love. Low moans frequently burst from her lips, and her eyes were inflamed with weeping. Mary Heli, her elder and very aged sister, who bore a great resemblance to St. Anne, supported her in her arms. Mary Cleophas, Mary Heli's daughter, was likewise present, and she too for the most part leaned on her mother's arm. The other holy women were trembling with sorrow and anxiety. They were pressing with low cries of grief around the blessed Virgin, as if expecting their own sentence of death. Mary wore a long robe, almost sky-blue, and over it a long, white, woollen mantle, and a veil of creamy white. Magdalene was very much disturbed, indeed quite distracted by grief; her hair hung loose under her veil.

When, after the scourging, Jesus fell at the foot of the pillar, I saw that Claudia Procula, Pilate's wife, sent to the Mother of God a bundle of large linen cloths. I do not now know whether she thought that Jesus would be released, and then the mother of the Lord could bind up his wounds with them, or whether the compassionate pagan sent the linens for the use to which the blessed Virgin afterward put them.

Mary saw her lacerated Son driven past her by the executioners. With his garment he wiped the blood from his eyes in order to see his mother. She raised her hands in agony toward him and gazed upon his blood-stained footprints. Then, as the mob moved over to another side, I saw the blessed Virgin and Magdalene approaching the place of scourging. Surrounded and hidden by the other holy women and some well-disposed people standing by, they cast themselves on their knees and soaked up the sacred blood of Jesus with the linens until not a trace of it could be found.

The holy women were about twenty in number, but I did not see John with them at that time. Simeon's son Obed, Veronica's son, and Aram and Themeni, the two nephews of Joseph of Arimathea were, though sad and full of sorrow, busied in the temple.

It was about nine o'clock in the morning when the scourging was over.

Personal Appearance of Mary and of Magdalene

I SAW the blessed Virgin with cheeks pale and haggard, her nose pinched and long, her eyes almost bloodshot from weeping. It is astonishing, as well as indescribable, how plain, straightforward, and simple she was in appearance. Although since yesterday evening and even during the whole night, she had in fright, in anguish, and in tears, been wandering through the valley of Jehosaphat and the crowded streets of Jerusalem, still was her dress in perfect order, her whole appearance marked by extreme propriety. There was not even a fold of her garments that did not bespeak sanctity. Everything about her was so upright and simple, so dignified, so pure, and so innocent. Her look as she gazed around was so noble, and as she turned her head a little, her veil fell in soft and graceful folds. Her movements were not eager and, though under the influ-ence of the most grievous anguish, all her actions were performed simply and gently. Her garments were damp with the dew of the night and her own innumerable tears, but they were spotless and in perfect order. Her beauty was indescribable and altogether superhuman, for beauty in her was made up of immaculate purity, truth, simplicity, dignity, and holiness.

Magdalene, on the contrary, was just the reverse. She was taller and, both in figure and carriage, exhibited much more style. Her beauty, however, was now destroyed, owing to her violent repentance and intense grief. She was, if not decidedly ugly, at least painful to look upon, on account of the unrestrained fury of her passions. Her garments, wet and stained with mud, hung torn and dis-ordered around her; her long hair floated loose and dishevelled under her wet, tossed veil. She was perfectly changed in appearance. She thought of nothing but her grief, and looked almost like one bereft of sense. There were many people here from Magdalum and the surrounding country who had known her in her early splendor, who

had seen her in her wasting life of sin, and who had lost sight of her in her long retirement. Now they pointed her out with the finger and mocked at her forlorn appearance. Yes, there were some from Magdalum base enough even to throw mud at her as she passed along. But she did not notice it, so absorbed was she in her own sorrow.

Jesus Crowned with Thorns and Mocked

April 3, AD 33
Friday, 9:15 AM

WHILE JESUS WAS being scourged, Pilate had several times addressed the multitude, and again had the shout gone up: "He shall be executed, even if we die for it!" And when Jesus was led to the crowning, they cried again: "Away with him! Away!" New bands of Jews were constantly arriving, and as they came, they were instigated by the runners of the high priests to raise that cry.

Now followed a short interval of rest. Pilate gave some orders to his soldiers. The high priests and council meanwhile, seated on elevated benches on either side of the street in front of Pilate's terrace, shaded by trees and awnings, ordered food and drink to be brought them by their servants. I saw Pilate again perplexed and doubting. Yielding to his superstition, he retired alone to burn incense before his gods and to busy himself in all kinds of divination.

I saw the blessed Virgin and her companions, when they had dried up Jesus's blood after the scourging, leaving the forum. I saw them with the bloody linens in a small house built in a wall in the neighborhood. I do not now recall to whom it belonged, nor do I remember having seen John at the scourging.

The crowning and mocking of Jesus took place in the inner court of the guardhouse, which stood in the forum over the prisons. It was surrounded with pillars, and the entrance was open. There were about fifty low-lived wretches belonging to the army, jailer's servants, executioners, lads, slaves, and whipping servants, who took an active part in this maltreatment of Jesus. [J7] The mob at first crowded in eagerly, but was soon displaced by the thousand Roman soldiers who surrounded the building. They stood in rank and order, jeering and laughing, thereby giving to Jesus's tormentors new inducement to multiply his sufferings. Their jokes and laughter encouraged them as applause does the actor.

There was a hole in the middle of the court, and to this they had rolled the base of an old column, which may once have stood there. On that base they placed a low, round stool with an upright at the back by which to raise it, and maliciously covered it with sharp stones and potsherds.

Once more they tore Jesus's clothing from his wounded body, and threw over him instead an old red military cloak tattered and so short that it did not reach to the knees. Shreds of yellow tassels hung on it here and there. It was kept in a corner of the executioners' room and used to throw around criminals after their scourging, either to dry the blood or to turn them into derision. Now they dragged Jesus to the stool covered with stones and potsherds, and violently forced his wounded, naked body down upon them. Then they put upon him the crown of thorns. It was two hands high, thick, and skillfully plaited, with a projecting edge on top. They laid it like a binder round his brow and fastened it tightly in the back, thus forming it into a crown. It was woven from thorn branches three fingers thick, the thorns of which grew straight out. In plaiting the crown, as many of them as possible had been designedly pressed inward. There were three kinds of thorns, such as with us are called buckthorn, blackthorn, and hawthorn. The projecting edge on top was formed of one kind, which we call blackberry, and it was by this the torturer fastened it on and moved it in order to produce new sufferings. I have seen the spot whence the miscreants brought the thorns.

Next they placed in Jesus's hand a thick reed with a tufted top. All this was done with mock solemnity, as if they were really crowning him king. Then they snatched the reed from his hand and with it struck the crown violently, until his eyes filled with blood. They bent the knee before him, stuck out their tongue at him, struck and spat in his face, and cried out: "Hail, king of the Jews!" With shouts of mocking laughter, they upset him along with the stool, in order to force him violently down upon it again.

I am not able to repeat all the base inventions employed by those wretches to insult the poor Savior. Ah! His thirst was horrible, for he was consumed with the fever of his wounds, the laceration caused by the inhuman scourging. He quivered. The flesh on his sides was in many places torn even to the ribs. His tongue contracted convulsively. Only the sacred blood trickling down from his head laved, as it were in pity, his parched lips which hung languishingly open. Those horrible monsters, seeing this, turned his mouth into a receptacle for their own disgusting filth. Jesus underwent this maltreatment for ab*out half an hour*, during which time the cohort surrounding the praetorium in rank and order kept up an uninterrupted jeering and laughing.[†]

"Ecce Homo!"

AND now they again led Jeus, the crown of thorns upon his head, the mock scepter in his fettered hands, the purple mantle thrown around him, into Pilate's palace. He was unrecognizable on account of the blood that filled his eyes and ran down into his mouth and beard. His body, covered with swollen welts and wounds, resembled a cloth dipped in blood, and his gait was bowed down and tottering. The mantle was so short that he had to stoop in order to cover himself with it, for at the crowning they had again torn off all his clothing. When he reached the lowest step of the flight that led up to Pilate, even that hard-hearted being was seized with a shudder of compassion and disgust. He leaned on one of his officers, and as the priests and the people kept up their shouts and mockery, he exclaimed: "If the devil were as cruel as the Jews, one could not live with him in hell!" Jesus was wearily dragged up the steps, and while he stood a little back, Pilate stepped to the front of the balcony. The trumpet sounded to command attention, for Pilate was going to speak. Addressing the high priests and the people, he said: "Behold! I bring him forth to you, that you may know that I find no cause in him!"

Then Jesus was led forward by the executioners to the front of the balcony where Pilate was standing, so that he could be seen by all the people in the forum. Oh, what a terrible, heart-rending spectacle! Silence, awful and gloomy, fell upon the multitude as the inhumanly treated Jesus, the sacred, martyrized figure of the Son of God, covered with blood and wounds, wearing the frightful crown of thorns, appeared and, from his eyes swimming in blood, cast a glance upon the surging crowd! Nearby stood Pilate, pointing to him with his finger and crying to the Jews: "Behold the man!" [J8]

While Jesus, the scarlet cloak of derision thrown around his lacerated body, his pierced head sinking under the weight of the thorny crown, his fettered hands holding the mock scepter, was standing thus before Pilate's palace, in infinite sadness and benignity, pain and love, like a bloody phantom, exposed to the raging cries of both priests and people, a band of strangers, men and women, their gar-

---

† These meditations on the sufferings of Jesus filled Anne Catherine with such feelings of compassion that she begged of God to allow her to suffer as he had done. She instantly became feverish and parched with thirst, and, by morning, was speechless from the contraction of her tongue and of her lips. She was in this state when her friend came to her in the morning, and she looked like a victim which had just been sacrificed. Those around succeeded, with some difficulty, in moistening her mouth with a little water, but it was long before she could give any further details concerning her meditations on the Passion. Even then, she was so exhausted that it was not without great difficulty, and after many intervals of rest, that she narrated all which our Lord suffered in this crowning with thorns. She was scarcely able to speak, because she herself felt every sensation which she described in this account.

ments girded, crossed the forum and went down to the sheep pool. They were going to help in the washing of the paschal lambs, whose gentle bleating was still mingling with the sanguinary shouts of the multitude, as if wishing to bear witness to the silent truth. Now it was that the true Paschal Lamb of God, the revealed though unrecognized mystery of this holy day, fulfilled the prophecies and stretched himself in silence on the slaughtering bench.

The high priests and judges were perfectly infuriated at the sight of Jesus, the dread mirror of their own conscience, and they vociferated: "Away with him! Crucify him!" Pilate called out: "Are you not yet satisfied? He has been handled so roughly that he will never more want to be a king." But they and all the people, as if beside themselves with fury, cried out violently: "Away with him! To the cross with him!" Again did Pilate order the trumpet to be sounded, and again did he cry out: "Take him you and crucify him, for I find no cause in him!" To this the high priests shouted: "We have a law, and according to it he must die, for he has made himself the Son of God!" Pilate responded: "If you have such a law, that a man like this one must die, then may I never be a Jew!" The words, however, "He has made himself the Son of God," renewed Pilate's anxiety, aroused again his superstitious fears. He caused Jesus therefore to be brought before him into the judgment hall, where he spoke to him alone. [J9] He began by asking: "Whence art thou?" But Jesus gave him no answer. "Dost thou not answer me?" said Pilate. "Knowest thou not that I have power to crucify thee and power to release thee?" "Thou shouldst not have any power," answered Jesus, "unless it were given thee from above; therefore he that hath delivered me to thee hath the greater sin."

Just at this moment, Claudia Procula, Pilate's wife, anxious at seeing his irresolution, sent again to him, directing the messenger to show him once more the pledge he had given her of his promise. But he returned a vague, superstitious reply in which he appealed to his gods.

Undecided and perplexed as before, Pilate again went forth and addressed the people, telling them that he could find no guilt in Jesus. They meanwhile had been stirred up by the report spread by the high priests and Pharisees, namely, that "Jesus's followers had bribed Pilate's wife; that if Jesus were set free, he would unite with the Romans and then they would all be put to death." This so roused the multitude that they clamored more vehemently than ever for his death. Pilate, desirous of obtaining in some way an answer to his questions, went back again to Jesus in the judgment hall. When alone with him, he glanced at him almost in fear, and thought in a confused sort of a way: "What if this man should indeed be a god?" And then with an oath he at once began adjuring Jesus to say whether he was a god and not a human being, whether he was that king promised to the Jews. How far did his kingdom extend? To what rank did his divinity belong? and ended by declaring that, if Jesus would answer his questions, he would set him free. What Jesus said to Pilate in answer, I can repeat only in substance, not in words. The Lord spoke words of terrible import. He gave Pilate to understand what kind of a king he was, over what kind of a kingdom he reigned, and what was the truth, for he told him the truth. He laid before him the abominable state of his own conscience, foretold the fate in store for him—exile in misery and a horrible end. He told him, moreover, that he would one day come to pass sentence upon him in just judgment.

Frightened and vexed at Jesus's words, Pilate again went out upon the balcony and proclaimed his intention of freeing Jesus. Then arose the cry: "If thou release this man, thou art not Caesar's friend, for whosoever maketh himself a king, speaketh against Caesar!" Others shouted: "We will denounce thee to Caesar as a disturber of our feast. Make up thy mind at once, for under pain of punishment we must be in the temple by ten tonight." And the cry: "To the cross with him! Away with him!" [J10] resounded furiously on all sides, even from the flat roofs of the houses near the forum, upon which some of the mob had clambered.

Pilate now saw that he could do nothing with the raging multitude. There was something truly frightful in the confusion and uproar. The whole mass of people collected before the palace was in such a state of rage and excitement that a violent insurrection was to be feared. Then Pilate called for water. The servant that brought it poured it from a vase over his hands before the people, while Pilate called down from the balcony: "I am innocent of the blood of this just man! Look ye to it!" [J11] Then went up from the assembled multitude, among whom were people from all parts of Palestine, the horrible, the unanimous cry: "His blood be upon us and upon our children!"

Jesus Condemned to the Death of the Cross

PILATE, who was not seeking the truth but a way out of difficulty, now became more undecided than ever. His conscience reproached him: "Jesus is innocent." His wife said: "Jesus is holy." His superstition whispered: "He is an enemy of thy gods." His cowardice cried out: "He is himself a god, and he will avenge himself." Then did he again anxiously and solemnly question Jesus, and then did Jesus make known to him his secret transgressions, his future career and miserable end, and warned him that he would come one day sitting on the clouds to pronounce a just sentence upon him. And now came a new weight to be cast into the false scales of his justice against Jesus's release. He was offended at having to stand before Jesus, whom he could not fathom, with his ignominious conscience unveiled under his gaze; and that the man whom he had caused to be scourged and whom he had power to crucify, should predict for him a miserable end; yes, that the lips to which no lie had ever been imputed, which had uttered no word of self justification, should, even in this moment of dire distress, summon him on that day to a just judgment. All this roused his pride. But as no one sentiment ruled supreme in this miserable, irresolute creature, he was seized with anxiety at the remembrance of the Lord's warning, and so he determined to make a last effort to free him. At the threats of the Jews, however, to denounce him to the Emperor, another cowardly fear took possession of Pilate. The fear of an earthly sovereign overruled the fear of the king whose kingdom was not of this world. The cowardly, irresolute wretch thought: "If he dies, so die with him also what he knows of me and what he has predicted of me." At the threat of the Emperor, Pilate yielded to the will of the multitude, although against the promise he had pledged to his wife, against right and justice and his own conscience. Through fear of the Emperor, he delivered to the Jews the blood of Jesus; for his own conscience he had naught but the water which he ordered to be poured over his hands while he cried out: "I am innocent of the blood of this just man. Look ye to it!" No, Pilate! But do thou thyself look to it! Thou knowest him to be just, and yet thou dost shed his blood! Thou art an unjust, an unprincipled judge! And that same blood, which Pilate sought to wash from his hands and which he could not wash from his soul, the bloodthirsty Jews invoked as a malediction upon themselves and upon their children. The blood of Jesus, which cries for pardon for us, they invoke as vengeance upon themselves: They cry: "His blood be upon us and our children!"

While this terrible cry was resounding on all sides, Pilate ordered preparations to be made for pronouncing the sentence. His robes of ceremony were brought to him. A crown, in which sparkled a precious stone, was placed on his head, another mantle was thrown around him, and a staff was borne before him. A number of soldiers surrounded him, officers of the tribunal went before him carrying something, and scribes with parchment rolls and little tablets followed him. The whole party was preceded by a man sounding a trumpet. Thus did Pilate leave his palace and proceed to the forum where, opposite the scourging place, there was a high, beautifully constructed judgment seat. Only when delivered from that seat had the sentence full weight. It was called Gabbatha. It consisted of a circular balcony, and up to it there were several flights of steps. It contained a seat for Pilate, and behind it a bench for others connected with the tribunal. [J12] The balcony was surrounded and the steps occupied by soldiers. Many of the Pharisees had already left the palace and gone to the temple. Only Annas, Caiaphas, and about twenty-eight others went at once to the judgment seat in the forum, while Pilate was putting on his robes of ceremony. The two thieves had been taken thither when Pilate presented the Lord to the people with the words, "*Ecce Homo.*" Pilate's seat was covered with red, and on it lay a blue cushion bordered with yellow.

And now Jesus in the scarlet cloak, the crown of thorns upon his head, his hands bound, [J13] was led by the soldiers and executioners through the mocking crowd and placed between the two thieves in front of the judgment seat. [J14] From this seat of state Pilate once more said aloud to the enemies of Jesus: "Behold there your king!" But they yelled: "Away, away with this man! Crucify him!" "Shall I crucify your king?" said Pilate. "We have no king but Caesar!" responded the high priests.

From that moment Pilate spoke no word for nor with Jesus. He began the sentence of condemnation. The two thieves had been already sentenced to the cross, but their execution, at the request of the high priests, had been postponed till today. They thought to outrage Jesus the more by having him crucified with two infamous murderers. The crosses of the thieves were already lying near them, brought by the executioners' assistants. Our Lord's was not yet there, probably because his death sentence had not yet been pronounced.

The blessed Virgin, who had withdrawn to some distance when Pilate presented Jesus to the Jews and when he was greeted by them with that bloodthirsty cry, now, surrounded by several women, again pressed through the crowd to be present at the death sentence of her Son and her God. Jesus, encircled by the executioners and greeted with rage and derisive laughter by his enemies, was standing at the foot of the steps before Pilate. The trumpet commanded silence, and with dastardly rage Pilate pronounced the sentence of death.

The sight of that base double-tongued wretch; the triumph of the bloodthirsty but now satisfied Pharisees who had so cruelly hunted down their prey; the innumerable sufferings of the most blessed Savior; the inexpressible affliction and anguish of his blessed Mother and the holy women; the eager listening of the furious Jews; the cold, proud demeanor of the soldiers; and the apparitions of all those horrible, diabolical forms among the crowd, quite overpowered me. Ah! I felt that I should have been standing there instead of my beloved Lord. Then truly would the sentence have been just!

Pilate first spoke some words in which, with high-sounding titles, he named the Emperor Claudius Tiberius. Then he set forth the accusation against Jesus; that, as a seditious character, a disturber and violator of the Jewish laws, who had allowed himself to be called the Son of God and the king of the Jews, he had been sentenced to death by the high priests, and by the unanimous voice of the people given over to be crucified. Furthermore Pilate, that iniquitous judge, who had in these last hours so frequently and publicly asserted the innocence of Jesus, now proclaimed that he found the sentence of the high priests just, and ended with the words: "I also condemn Jesus of Nazareth, king of the Jews, to be nailed to the cross." Then he ordered the executioners to bring the cross. I have also some indistinct recollection of his taking a long stick, the center of which was full of pith, breaking it, and throwing the pieces at Jesus's feet.

The most afflicted mother of Jesus, the Son of God, on hearing Pilate's words became like one in a dying state, for now was the cruel, frightful, ignominious death of her holy and beloved Son and Savior certain. John and the holy women took her away from the scene, that the blinded multitude might not render themselves still more guilty by jeering at the sorrow of the mother of their Savior. But Mary could not rest. She longed to visit every spot marked by Jesus's sufferings. Her companions had once more to accompany her from place to place, for the mystical sacrifice that she was offering to God by her most holy compassion urged her to pour out the sacrifice of her tears wherever the Redeemer born of her had suffered for the sins of humankind, his brethren. And so the mother of the Lord, by the consecration of her tears, took possession of all the sacred places upon earth for the future veneration of the church, the mother of us all, just as Jacob set up the memorial stone and consecrated it with oil that it should witness to the promise made him.

Pilate next seated himself on the judgment seat and wrote out the sentence, which was copied by several officials standing behind him. Messengers were dispatched with the copies, for some of them had to be signed by others. I do not know whether this formality was requisite for the sentence, or whether it included other commissions, but some of the writings were certainly sent to certain dis-

tant places. Pilate's written condemnation against Jesus clearly showed his deceit, for its purport was altogether different from that which he had pronounced orally. I saw that he was writing against his will, in painful perplexity of mind, and as if an angel of wrath were guiding his hand. The written sentence was about as follows:

"Urged by the high priests, and the Sanhedrin, and fearing an insurrection of the people who accuse Jesus of Nazareth of sedition, blasphemy, and infraction of the laws, and who demand that he should be put to death, I have (though indeed without being able to substantiate their accusations) delivered him to be crucified along with two other condemned criminals whose execution was postponed through the influence of the high priests because they wanted Jesus to suffer with them. I have condemned Jesus because I do not wish to be accused to the Emperor as an unjust judge of the Jews and as an abettor of insurrections; and I have condemned him as a criminal who has acted against the laws, and whose death has been violently demanded by the Jews."

Pilate caused many copies of this sentence to be made and sent to different places. The high priests, however, were not at all satisfied with the written sentence, especially because Pilate wrote that they had requested the crucifixion of the thieves to be postponed in order that Jesus might be executed with them. They quarreled with Pilate about it at the judgment seat. And when with varnish he wrote on a little dark brown board the three lines of the inscription for the cross, they disputed again with him concerning the title, and demanded that it should not be "king of the Jews," but "He called himself the king of the Jews." Pilate, however, had become quite impatient and insulting, and he replied roughly: "What I have written, I have written." [J15]

They wanted likewise the cross of Jesus not to rise higher above his head than those of the two thieves. But it had to be so, for it was at first too short to allow the title written by Pilate to be placed over Jesus's head. They consequently opposed its being made higher by an addition, thus hoping to prevent the title so ignominious to themselves from being put up. But Pilate would not yield. They had to raise the height by fastening on the trunk a piece upon which the title could be placed. And it was thus the cross received that form so full of significance, in which I have always seen it.

Claudia Procula sent back to Pilate his pledge and declared herself released from him. I saw her that same evening secretly leaving his palace and fleeing to the holy women, by whom she was concealed in Lazarus's house. Later on, she followed Paul and became his special friend. On a greenish stone in the rear side of Gabbatha, I afterward saw a man engraving two lines with a sharp iron instrument. In them were the words, *Judex injustus*, "Unjust judge," and also the name of Claudia Procula. I see this stone still in existence, though unknown, in the foundation of a building that occupies the site upon which Gabbatha once stood.

After the proclamation of the sentence, the most holy Redeemer again fell a prey to the savage executioners. They brought him his own clothes, [J16] which had been taken from him at the mocking before Caiaphas. They had been safely kept and, I think, some compassionate people must have washed them, for they were clean. It was also, I think, customary among the Romans thus to lead the condemned to execution. Now was Jesus again stripped by the infamous ruffians, who loosened his hands that they might be able to clothe him anew. They dragged the red woollen mantle of derision from his lacerated body, and in so doing tore open many of his wounds. Tremblingly, he himself put on the undergarment about his loins, after which they threw his woollen scapular over his neck. But as they could not put on over the broad crown of thorns the brown, seamless tunic which his blessed Mother had woven, they snatched the crown from his head, causing the blood to gush anew from all the wounds with unspeakable pain. When they had put the woven tunic upon his wounded body, they threw over it his loose white, woollen robe, his broad girdle, and lastly his mantle. Then they bound around his waist the fetter girdle, by whose long cords they led him. All this took place with horrible barbarity, amid kicks and blows.

The two thieves were standing on the right and left of Jesus, their hands bound. When before the tribunal, they had, like Jesus, a chain hanging around their neck. They had a covering around their loins, and a kind of sleeveless scapular jacket made of some old stuff and open at the sides. On their head was a cap of twisted straw around which was a roll, or pad, shaped almost like the hats worn by children. The thieves were of a dirty brown complexion, and were covered with the welts left by their scourging. The one that was afterward converted was now quiet and recollected in himself, but the other was furious and insolent. He joined the executioners in cursing and deriding Jesus who, sighing for their salvation, cast upon them looks of love and bore all his sufferings for them. The executioners meanwhile were busy gathering together their tools. All things were made ready for this, the saddest, the most cruel journey, upon which the loving, the most sorely afflicted Redeemer was to carry for us ingrates the burden of our sins, and at the end of which he was to pour out from the chalice of his body, pierced by the outcasts of the human race, the atoning torrent of his precious blood.

At last Annas and Caiaphas, angry and wrangling, finished with Pilate. Taking with them the couple of long, narrow scrolls, or parchment rolls, that they had received, copies of the sentence, they hurried off to the temple. They had need of haste to arrive in time.

Here the high priests parted from the true Paschal Lamb. They hurried to the temple of stone, to slaughter and eat the type, while allowing its realization, the true Lamb of God, to be led to the altar of the cross by infamous executioners. Here did the way divide—one road leading to the veiled, the other to the accomplished sacrifice. They delivered the pure, expiating Paschal Lamb of God, whom they had outwardly attacked with their atrocious barbarity, whom they had striven to defile, to impure and inhuman executioners, while they themselves hastened to the stone temple, there to sacrifice the lambs that had been washed, purified, and blessed. They had, with timid care, provided against contracting outward legal impurity themselves, while sullying their soul with inward wickedness, which was boiling over in rage, envy, and scorn. "His blood be upon us and upon our children!" With these words they had fulfilled the ceremony, had laid the hand of the sacrificer upon the head of the victim. Here again, the road branched into two: the one to the Altar of the Law, the other to the Altar of Grace. But Pilate, that proud, irresolute pagan, who trembled in the presence of the true God and who nevertheless paid worship to his idols and courted the favor of the world—Pilate, a slave of death, ruling for a short time and on his way to the ignominious term of eternal death—goes with his assistants, and surrounded by his guard, along a path running between those two roads of his own palace, preceded by his trumpeters. *The unjust sentence was pronounced at about ten o'clock in the morning according to our time.*

Jesus Carries His Cross to Golgotha

WHEN Pilate left the judgment seat, part of the soldiers followed him and drew up in file before the palace. A small band remained near the condemned. Twenty-eight armed Pharisees, among them those six furious enemies of Jesus who had assisted at his arrest on the Mount of Olives, came on horseback to the forum in order to accompany the procession. The executioners led Jesus in to the center. Several slaves, dragging the wood of the cross, entered through the gate on the western side, and threw it down noisily at his feet. The two arms, which were lighter and provided with tenons, were bound with cords to the trunk, which was broader and heavier. The wedges, the little foot-block, and the board just finished for the inscription were carried along with other things by boys who were learning the executioners' trade.

As soon as the cross was thrown on the ground before him, Jesus fell on his knees, put his arms around it, and kissed it three times while softly uttering a prayer of thanksgiving to his heavenly Father for the redemption of humankind now begun. Pagan priests were accustomed to embrace a newly erected altar, and in like manner the Lord embraced his cross, the eternal altar of the bloody sacrifice of expiation. But the executioners dragged Jesus up to a kneeling posture; and with difficulty and little help (and that of the most barbarous kind) he was forced to take the heavy beams upon his right shoulder and hold them fast with his right arm. [117] I saw invisible angels helping him, otherwise he would have been unable to lift the cross from the ground. As he knelt, he bent under the weight. While Jesus was praying, some of the other executioners placed on the back of the two thieves the arms of their crosses (not yet fastened to the trunk), and tied their upraised hands upon them by means of a stick around which they twisted the cord. These crosspieces were not quite straight, but somewhat curved. At the moment of crucifixion they were fastened to the upper end of the trunk, which trunk—along with the other implements of execution—was carried after the condemned by slaves. Pilate's horsemen were now ready to start, and the trumpet sounded. Just then one of the mounted Pharisees approached Jesus, who was still kneeling under his load, and exclaimed: "It is all over with fine speeches now! Hurry up, that we may get rid of him! Forward! Forward!" They jerked him to his feet, and then fell upon his shoulder the whole weight of the cross, of that cross which, according to his own sacred words of eternal truth, we must carry after him. And now that blessed triumphal procession of the king of kings, so ignominious upon earth, so glorious in the sight of heaven, began. Two cords were tied to the end of the cross, and by them two of the executioners held it up, so that it could not be dragged on the ground. Around Jesus, though at some distance, walked the four executioners holding the cords fastened to the fetter-girdle that bound his waist. His mantle was tied up under his arms. Jesus, with the wood of the cross bound on his shoulder, reminded me in a striking manner of Isaac carrying the wood for his own sacrifice on the mountain. Pilate's trumpeter gave the signal for starting, for Pilate himself with a detachment of soldiers intended to go into the city, in order to prevent the possibility of an insurrection. He was armed and on horseback, surrounded by his officers and a troop of cavalry. A company of about three hundred foot soldiers followed, all from the frontier between Switzerland and Italy.

The procession of the crucifixion was headed by a trumpeter, who sounded his trumpet at every street corner and proclaimed the execution. Some paces behind him came a crowd of boys and other rude fellows, carrying drink, cords, nails, wedges, and baskets of tools of all kinds, while sturdy servant men bore poles, ladders, and the trunks belonging to the crosses of the thieves. The ladders consisted of mere poles, through which long wooden pegs were run. Then followed some of the mounted Pharisees, after whom came a lad bearing on his breast the inscription Pilate had written for the cross. The crown of thorns, which it was impossible to leave on during the carriage of the cross, was taken from Christ's head and placed on the end of a pole, which this lad now carried over his shoulder. This boy was not very wicked.

And next came our Lord and Redeemer, bowed down under the heavy weight of the cross, bruised, torn with scourges, exhausted, and tottering. Since the Last Supper of the preceding evening, without food, drink, and sleep, under continual ill-treatment that might of itself have ended in death, consumed by loss of blood, wounds, fever, thirst, and unutterable interior pain and horror, Jesus walked with tottering steps, his back bent low, his feet naked and bleeding. With his right hand he grasped the heavy load on his right shoulder, and with the left he wearily tried to raise the flowing garment constantly impeding his uncertain steps. The four executioners held at some distance the cords fastened to his fetter girdle. The two in front dragged him forward, while the two behind urged him on. In this way he was not sure of one step, and the tugging cords constantly prevented his lifting his robe. His hands were bruised and swollen from the cords that had tightly bound them, his face was covered with blood and swellings, his hair and beard were torn and matted with blood, the burden he carried and the fetters pressed the coarse woollen garment into the wounds of his body and the wool stuck fast to those that had been reopened by the tearing off of his clothes. Jeers and malicious words resounded on all sides. He looked unspeakably wretched and tormented, though lovingly resigned. His lips moved in prayer, his glance was supplicating, forgiving, and suffering. The two executioners behind him, who held up the end of the cross by means of ropes fastened to it, increased the toil of Jesus, for they jerked the ropes or let them lie slack, thus moving his burden from side to side. The procession was flanked by soldiers bearing lances.

Then came the two thieves, each led by two executioners holding cords fastened to their girdles. They had the curved crosspieces belonging to the trunk of their crosses fastened on their backs, with their outstretched arms bound to the ends of them. They wore only a short tunic around their loins; the upper part of their body was covered with a loose, sleeveless jacket open at the sides, and on their head was the cap of twisted straw. They were partly intoxicated by the drink that had been given them. The good thief, however, was very quiet; but the bad one was insolent and furious, and he cursed continually. The executioners were dark complexioned, short, thickset fellows, with short, black hair, crisp and scrubby. Their beard was sparse, a few little tufts scattered over the chin. The shape of their face was not Jewish. They were canal laborers, and belonged to a race of Egyptian slaves. They wore only a short tunic like an apron, and on their breast was a leathern covering without sleeves. They were, in every sense of the word, beastly. Behind the thieves rode one-half of the Pharisees, closing the procession. Sometimes they rode together, and again singly along the whole line of the procession, urging them on and keeping order. Among the mob that led the way, carrying the implements of execution, were some lowborn Jewish lads who, of their own accord, had pushed themselves into the crowd.

At a considerable distance followed Pilate, his party preceded by a trumpeter on horseback. Pilate, in military costume, rode among his officers followed by a troop of cavalry and three hundred foot soldiers. His train crossed the forum, and then passed out into a broad street.

The procession formed for Jesus wound through a very narrow back street, in order not to obstruct the way of the people going to the temple, as well as to prove no hindrance to Pilate and his escort.

Most of the people had dispersed immediately after the sentence was pronounced, either to return to their own homes or to go to the temple. *They had already lost a great part of the morning*, and so they had to hurry their preparations for the slaughtering of the paschal lamb. The crowd of loiterers was nevertheless very great. It was a mixed company consisting of strangers, slaves, workmen, boys, women, and all kinds of rough people. They rushed headlong through the streets and byways, in order here and there to catch a glimpse of the mournful procession. The Roman soldiers in the rear kept them from swelling its numbers, and they were obliged consequently to plunge down the next bystreet and head off the procession again. Most of them, however, made straight for Golgotha. The narrow alley through which Jesus was first conducted was scarcely two paces wide, and it was full of filth thrown from the gates of the

houses on either side. He had much to suffer here. The executioners were brought into closer contact with him and from the gates and windows the servants and slaves there employed threw after him mud and kitchen refuse. Malicious rascals poured black, filthy, bad-smelling water on him; yes, even children, running out of their houses, were incited by the rabble to gather stones in their aprons and, darting through the crowd, throw them at his feet with words of mockery and reviling. Thus did children do unto him who had pronounced the children beloved, blessed, and happy.

Jesus's First Fall under the Cross

TOWARD the end of that narrow street or alley, the way turned again to the left, becoming broader and somewhat steep. Under it was a subterranean aqueduct extending from Mount Zion. I think it ran along the forum, where flowed a covered gutter down to the sheep pool near the sheep gate. I could hear the gurgling and rippling of the water in the pipes. Just here where the street begins to ascend, there was a hollow place often filled, after a rain, with mud and water. In it, as in many such places in the streets of Jerusalem, lay a large stone to facilitate crossing. Poor Jesus, on reaching this spot with his heavy burden, could go no farther. The executioners pulled him by the cords and pushed him unmercifully. Then did the divine cross-bearer fall full length on the ground by the projecting stone, his burden at his side. [J18] The drivers, with curses, pulled him and kicked him. This brought the procession to a halt, and a tumult arose around Jesus. In vain did he stretch out his hand for someone to help him. "Ah! It will soon be over!" He exclaimed, and continued to pray. The Pharisees yelled: "Up! Raise him up! Otherwise he'll die in our hands." Here and there on the wayside weeping women might be seen, and children whimpering from fear. With the aid of supernatural help, Jesus raised his head, and the terrible, the diabolical wretches, instead of alleviating his sufferings, put the crown of thorns again upon him. When at last, with all kinds of ill-treatment, they dragged him up again, they laid the cross once more upon his shoulder. And now with the greatest difficulty he had to hang his poor head, racked with thorns, to one side in order to be able to carry his heavy load on his shoulder, for the crown was broad. Thus Jesus tottered, with increased torture, up the steep and gradually widening street.

April 3, AD 33
Friday, 11 AM

Jesus, Carrying His Cross,
Meets His Most Holy and Afflicted
Mother • His Second Fall under the Cross

THE BLESSED Mother of Jesus, who shared every suffering of her Son, had about an hour previously—when the unjust sentence was pronounced upon him—left the forum with John and the holy women to venerate the places consecrated by his cruel suffering. But now when the running crowd, the sounding trumpets, and the approach of the soldiers and Pilate's cavalcade announced the commencement of the bitter Way of the Cross, Mary could no longer remain at a distance. She must behold her divine Son in his sufferings, and she begged John to take her to some place that Jesus would pass. They left, in consequence, the vicinity of Zion, passed the judgment seat, and went through gates and shady walks which were open just now to the people streaming hither and thither, to the western side of a palace which had an arched gateway on the street into which the procession turned after Jesus's first fall. The palace was the residence of Caiaphas; the house on Zion was his official tribunal. John obtained from the compassionate porter the privilege of passing through and of opening the opposite gate. I was terrified when I saw the blessed Virgin so pale, her eyes red with weeping, wrapped from head to foot in a bluish-green mantle, trembling and shuddering, going through this house with the holy women, John, and one of the nephews of Joseph of Arimathea. They could already distinguish the tumult and uproar of the approaching multitude only some houses off, the sound of the trumpet and the proclamation at the corners that a criminal was being led to execution. When the servant opened the gate, the noise became more distinct and alarming. Mary was in prayer. She said to John: "Shall I stay to behold it, or shall I hurry away? Oh, how shall I be able to endure it?" John replied: "If thou dost not remain, it will always be to thee a cruel regret." They stepped out under the gateway and looked to the right down the street, which was here somewhat rising, but which became level again at the spot upon which Mary was standing. The procession at this moment may not have been more than eighty paces distant from them. It was preceded by none of the rabble, though they were still following on the side and in the rear. Many of them, as I have said, were running through the neighboring street, to get other places from which they could obtain a look.

And now came on the executioner's servants, insolent and triumphant, with their instruments of torture, at sight of which the blessed Mother trembled, sobbed, and wrung her hands. One of the men said to the bystanders: "Who is that woman in such distress?" And someone answered: "She is the mother of the Galilean." When the miscreants heard this, they jeered at the sorrowing mother in words of scorn, pointed at her with their fingers; and one of the base wretches, snatching up the nails intended for the crucifixion, held them up mockingly before her face. Wringing her hands, she gazed upon Jesus and, in her anguish, leaned for support against one of the pillars of the gate. She was pale as a corpse, her lips livid. The Pharisees came riding forward, then came the boy with the inscription—and oh! a couple of steps behind him, the Son of God, her own Son, the Holy One, the Redeemer! Tottering, bowed down, his thorn-crowned head painfully bent over to one shoulder on account of the heavy cross he was carrying, Jesus staggered on. The executioners pulled him forward with the ropes. His face was pale, wounded, and bloodstained, his beard pointed and matted with blood. From his sunken eyes full of blood he cast, from under the tangled and twisted thorns of his crown, frightful to behold, a look full of earnest tenderness upon his afflicted mother, and for the second time tottered under the weight of the cross and sank on his hands and knees to the ground. The most sorrowful mother, in vehemence of her love and anguish, saw neither soldiers nor executioners—saw only her beloved, suffering, maltreated Son. Wringing her hands, she sprang over the couple of steps between the gateway and the executioners in advance, and rushing to Jesus, fell on her knees with her arms around him. [J19] I heard, but I know not whether spoken with the lips or in spirit, the words: "My Son!"— "My Mother!"

The executioners insulted and mocked. One of them said: "Woman, what dost thou want here? If thou hadst reared him better, he would not now be in our hands." I perceived, however, that some of the soldiers were touched. They obliged the blessed Virgin to retire, but not one of them laid a finger on her. John and the women led her away, and she sank, like one paralyzed in the knees by pain, on one of the cornerstones that supported the wall near the gateway. Her back was turned toward the procession, and her hands came in contact with the obliquely projecting stone upon which she sank. It was a green veined stone. Where Mary's knees touched it, shallow hollow places were left, and where her hands rested, the impression remained. They were not very distinct impressions, but such as might be made by a stroke upon a surface like dough, for the stone was very hard. I saw that, under Bishop James the Less, it was removed into the first Catholic church, the church near the pool of Bethesda. As I have before said, I have more than once seen similar impressions in stone made by the touch of holy persons on great and remarkable occasions. This verifies the saying: "It would move the heart of a stone," and this other: "This makes an impression." The Eternal Wisdom, in his mercy, needed not the art of printing in order to leave to posterity a witness to holy things.

When the soldiers flanking the procession drove it forward with their lances, John took the blessed Mother in through the gate, which was then closed.

The executioners meanwhile had dragged our Lord up again, and laid the cross upon his shoulder in another position. The arms of the cross had become loose from the trunk to which they had at first been bound, and one had slipped down and become entangled in the ropes. Jesus now took them in his arms, and the trunk dragged behind a little more on the ground.

Here and there among the rabble following the procession with jeers and laughter, I saw the veiled figures of weeping women moving along with uneven steps.

Simon of Cyrene • Jesus's Third Fall under the Cross

AFTER going some distance up the broad street, the procession passed through a gateway in an old inner wall of the city. In front of this gate was a wide open space at which three streets met. There was a large stepping stone here, over which Jesus staggered and fell, the cross by his side. He lay on the ground, leaning against the stone, unable to rise. Just at this instant, a crowd of well-dressed people came along on their way to the temple. They cried out in compassion: "Alas! The poor creature is dying!" Confusion arose among the rabble, for they could not succeed in making Jesus rise. The Pharisees leading the procession cried out to the soldiers: "We shall not get him to Golgotha alive. You must hunt up someone to help him carry the cross." Just then appeared, coming straight down the middle of the street, Simon of Cyrene, a pagan, followed by his three sons. He was carrying a bundle of sprigs under his arm, for he was a gardener, and he had been working in the gardens toward the eastern wall of the city. Every year about the time of the feast, he was accustomed to come up to Jerusalem with his wife and children, to trim the hedges. Many other laborers used to come for the same purpose. The crowd was so great that he could not escape, and as soon as the soldiers saw by his dress that he was a poor pagan laborer, they laid hold on him and dragged him forward to help carry the Galilean's cross. He resisted and showed great unwillingness, but they forcibly constrained him. [J20] His little boys screamed and cried, and some women that knew the man took charge of them. Simon was filled with disgust and repugnance for the task imposed upon him. Poor Jesus looked so horribly misera-

ble, so awfully disfigured, and his garments were covered with mud; but he was weeping, and he cast upon Simon a glance that roused his compassion. He had to help him up. Then the executioners tied one arm of the cross toward the end of the trunk, made a loop of the cords, and passed it over Simon's shoulder. He walked close behind Jesus, thus greatly lightening his burden. They rearranged the crown of thorns, and at last the dolorous procession resumed its march.

Simon was a vigorous man of forty years. He had no covering on his head. He wore a short, close-fitting jacket; his loins were bound with lappets, his legs with leathern straps, and his sandals turned up in sharp beaks at the toes. His little boys were dressed in tunics of colored stripes. Two of them were almost grown. They were named Rufus and Alexander, and later on they joined the disciples. The third was younger, and I have seen him still as a child with Stephen. Simon had not borne the cross long after Jesus when he felt his heart deeply touched.

Veronica and her Veil

THE STREET through which Jesus was now going was long and somewhat winding, and into it several side streets ran. From all quarters respectable-looking people were on their way to the temple. They stepped back, some from a pharisaical fear of becoming legally impure, others moved by a feeling of compassion. Simon had assisted the Lord with his burden almost two hundred paces when, from a handsome house on the left side of the street, up to whose forecourt (which was enclosed by a low, broad wall surmounted by a railing of some kind of shining metal) a flight of terraced steps led, there issued a tall, elegant-looking woman, holding a little girl by the hand, and rushed forward to meet the procession. It was Seraphia, the wife of Sirach, one of the members of the council belonging to the temple. Owing to her action of this day, she received the name of Veronica from *vera* (true) and *icon* (picture, or image).

Seraphia had prepared some costly spiced wine with the pious design of refreshing the Lord on his dolorous journey. She had been waiting in anxious expectation and had already hurried out once before to meet the procession. I saw her veiled, a little girl (whom she had adopted as her own child) by the hand, hurrying forward at the moment in which Jesus met his blessed Mother. But in the disturbance that followed, she found no opportunity to carry out her design, and so she hastened back to her house to await the Lord's coming.

As the procession drew near, she stepped out into the street veiled, a linen cloth hanging over her shoulder. The little girl, who was about nine years old, was standing by her with a mug of wine hidden under her little mantle. Those at the head of the procession tried in vain to keep her back. Transported with love and compassion, with the child holding fast to her dress, she pressed through the mob running at the side of the procession, in through the soldiers and executioners, stepped before Jesus, fell on her knees, and held up to him the outspread end of the linen kerchief, with these words of entreaty: "Permit me to wipe the face of my Lord!" [J21] Jesus seized the kerchief with his left hand and, with the flat, open palm, pressed it against his bloodstained face. Then passing it still with the left hand toward the right, which was grasping the arm of the cross, he pressed it between both palms and handed it back to Seraphia with thanks. She kissed it, hid it beneath her mantle, where she pressed it to her heart, and arose to her feet. Then the little girl timidly held up the mug of wine, but the brutal soldiers and executioners would not permit her to refresh Jesus with it. This sudden and daring act of Seraphia caused a stoppage in the procession of hardly two minutes, of which she made use to present the kerchief. The mounted Pharisees, as well as the executioners, were enraged at the delay, and still more at this public homage rendered to the Lord. They began, in consequence, to beat and pull Jesus. Veronica meanwhile fled back with the child to her house.

Scarcely had she reached her own apartment when, laying the kerchief on a table, she sank down unconscious. The little girl, still holding the mug of wine, knelt whimpering by her. A friend of the family, entering the room, found her in this condition. She glanced at the outspread kerchief and beheld upon it the bloody face of Jesus frightfully, but with wonderful distinctness, impressed. [J22] It looked like the face of a corpse. She roused Seraphia and showed her the Lord's image. It filled her with grief and consolation, and casting herself on her knees before the kerchief, she exclaimed: "Now will I leave all, for the Lord has given to me a memento!"

This kerchief was a strip of fine fabric about three times as long as wide. It was usually worn around the neck, and sometimes a second was thrown over the shoulder. It was customary upon meeting one in sorrow, in tears, in misery, in sickness, or in fatigue, to present it to wipe the face. It was a sign of mourning and sympathy. In hot countries, friends presented them to one another. Seraphia ever after kept this kerchief hanging at the head of her bed. After her death, it was given by the holy women to the Mother of God, and through the apostles at last came into the possession of the church.

Seraphia was a cousin of John the Baptist, her father being the son of Zechariah's brother. She was from Jerus-

alem. When Mary, a little girl of four years, was placed among the young girls at the temple, I saw Joachim, Anne, and some that had accompanied them going into Zechariah's paternal house not far from the fish market. A very old relative of the family now occupied it, Zechariah's uncle, perhaps, and Seraphia's grandfather. At the time of Mary's espousals with Joseph, I saw that Seraphia was older than the blessed Virgin. She was related also to the aged Simeon who had prophesied at Jesus's presentation in the temple, and from early youth she was brought up with his sons. Simeon had inspired these young people with a longing after the Messiah. This waiting for salvation was, for a long time, like a secret affection among many good people; others at that time had no idea of such things. When Jesus at the age of twelve remained behind in Jerusalem to teach in the temple, I saw Seraphia older than the mother of Jesus and still unmarried. She sent Jesus food to a little inn outside of Jerusalem, where he put up when he was not in the temple. It was at this same inn, a quarter of an hour from Jerusalem and on the road to Bethlehem, that Mary and Joseph, when going to present Jesus in the temple after his birth, spent one day and two nights with the two old people. They were Essenes, and the wife was related to Johanna Chusa. They were acquainted with the holy family and Jesus. Their inn was an establishment for the poor. Jesus and the disciples often took shelter there; and in his last days, when he was preaching in the temple, I often saw food sent thither by Seraphia. But at that time there were other occupants in it. Seraphia married late in life. Her husband Sirach, a descendant of the chaste Susanna, was a member of the council belonging to the temple. He was at first very much opposed to Jesus, and Seraphia, on account of her intimate connection with Jesus and the holy women, had much to suffer from him. He had even on several different occasions confined her for a long time in a prison cell. Converted at last by Joseph of Arimathea and Nicodemus, he became more lenient, and allowed his wife to follow Jesus. At Jesus's trial before Caiaphas, both last night and this morning, he had, in company with Nicodemus, Joseph of Arimathea, and all well-disposed people, declared himself for our Lord, and with them left the Sanhedrin. Seraphia was still a beautiful, majestic woman, although she must have been over fifty years old. At the triumphant entrance of Jesus into Jerusalem, which we celebrate on Palm Sunday, I saw her among the other women with a child on her arm. She took her veil from her head and spread it joyfully and reverently in the Lord's path. It was this same veil with which she now went forward to meet the Lord in his dolorous, but victorious and triumphant procession, and remove in part the traces of his sufferings—this same veil that gave to its possessor the new and triumphant name of Veronica, and this same veil that is now held in public veneration by the church.

In the third year after Christ's ascension, the Roman Emperor sent officials to Jerusalem to collect proofs of the rumors afloat in connection with Jesus's death and resurrection. One of these officials took back with him to Rome Nicodemus, Seraphia, and a relative of Johanna Chusa, the disciple Epaphras. This last-named was merely a simple servant of the disciples, having formerly been engaged in the temple as a servant and messenger of the priests. He was with the apostles in the Cenacle during the first days after Jesus's resurrection, when he saw Jesus as he frequently did afterward. I saw Veronica with the Emperor, who was sick. His couch was elevated a couple of steps, and concealed by a large curtain. The room was four-cornered, and not very large. I saw no window in it, but light entered from the roof in which there were valves that could be opened or closed by means of hanging cords. The Emperor was alone, his attendants in the antechamber. I saw that Veronica had brought with her, besides the veil, one of the linens from Jesus's tomb. She unfolded the former before the Emperor. It was a long, narrow strip of stuff, which she had once worn as a veil around her head and neck. The impression of Jesus's face was on one end of it, and when she held it up before the Emperor, she grasped the whole length of the veil in one hand. The face of Jesus was not a clean, distinct portrait, for it was impressed on the veil in blood; it was also broader than a painted likeness would have been, for Jesus had pressed the veil all around his face. On the other cloth that Veronica had with her, I saw the impression of Jesus's scourged body. I think it was one of the cloths upon which Jesus had been washed for burial. I did not see that these cloths made any impression on the Emperor, or that he touched them, but he was cured by merely looking upon them. He wanted to keep Veronica in Rome, and to give her as a reward a house, goods, and faithful servants, but she longed for nothing but to return to Jerusalem and to die where Jesus had died. I saw that she did return, with the companions of her journey. I saw in the persecution of the Christians in Jerusalem, when Lazarus and his sisters were driven into exile, that Seraphia fled with some other women. But being overtaken, she was cast into prison where, as a martyr for the truth, for Jesus, whom she had so often fed with earthly bread, and who with his own flesh and blood had nourished her to eternal life, she died of starvation.

The Weeping Daughters of Jerusalem • Jesus's Fourth and Fifth Falls beneath the Cross

THE PROCESSION had still a good distance to go before reaching the gate, and the street in that direction was somewhat declining. The gate was strong and high. To reach it, one had to go first through a vaulted arch, then across a bridge, then through another archway. The gate opened in a southwesterly direction. The city wall at this point of egress ran for a short distance, perhaps for some minutes, southward, then turned a little toward the west, and, finally, took a southerly direction once more around Mount Zion. On the right of the gate, the wall extended northward to the corner gate, and then turned eastward along the northern side of Jerusalem.

As the procession neared the gate, the executioners pressed on more violently. Close to the gate there was a large puddle of muddy water in the uneven road, cut up by vehicles. The barbarous executioners jerked Jesus forward; the crowd pressed. Simon of Cyrene tried to step sideways for the sake of convenience, thereby moving the cross out of its place, and poor Jesus for the fourth time fell so heavily under his burden into the muddy pool that Simon could scarcely support the cross. Jesus then, in a voice interrupted by sighs, though still high and clear, cried out: "Woe! Woe, Jerusalem! How often would I have gathered together thy children as the hen doth gather her chickens under her wings, and thou dost cast me so cruelly out of thy gate!" The Lord was troubled and in sorrow. The Pharisees turned toward him and said mockingly: "The disturber of the peace has not yet had enough. He still holds forth in unintelligible speeches," etc. They beat him and pushed him, and raising him to his feet, dragged him out of the rut. Simon of Cyrene meanwhile had become very much exasperated at the barbarity of the executioners, and he exclaimed: "If you do not cease your villainy, I will throw down this cross even if you kill me also!"

Just outside the gate there branched from the highroad northward to Golgotha a rough, narrow road several minutes in length. Some distance farther, the highroad itself divided in three directions: on the left to the southwest through the Valley of Gihon toward Bethlehem; westward toward Emmaus and Joppa; and on the right, off to the northwest and running around Mount Calvary toward the corner gate which led to Bethzur. Through this gate by which Jesus was led out, one could see off toward the southwest and to the left the Bethlehem gate. These two gates of Jerusalem were next to each other.

In the center of the highroad and opposite the gate where the way branched off to Mount Calvary, stood a post supporting a board upon which, in white raised letters that looked as if they were done in haste, was written the death sentence of our Savior and the two thieves. Not far from this spot, at the corner of the road, a large number of women might be seen weeping and lamenting. Some were young maidens, others poor married women, who had run out from Jerusalem to meet the procession; others were from Bethlehem, Hebron, and the neighboring places, who, coming up for the feast, had here joined the women of Jerusalem.

Jesus again sank fainting. He did not fall to the ground, because Simon, resting the end of the cross upon the earth, drew nearer and supported his bowed form. The Lord leaned on him. This was the fifth fall of Jesus while carrying his cross. At sight of his countenance so utterly wretched, the women raised a loud cry of sorrow and pity and, after the Jewish manner of showing compassion, extended toward him kerchiefs with which to wipe off the perspiration. At this Jesus turned to them and said: "Daughters of Jerusalem" (which meant, also, people from other Jewish cities), "weep not over me, but weep for yourselves and for your children. For behold, the days shall come wherein they will say: 'Blessed are the barren and the wombs that have not borne, and the paps that have not given suck!' Then shall they begin to say to the mountains: 'Fall upon us!' and to the hills: 'Cover us!' For if in the green wood they do these things, what shall be done in the dry?" [J23] Jesus said some other beautiful words to the women, but I have forgotten them. Among them, however, I remember these: "Your tears shall be rewarded. Henceforth, ye shall tread another path," etc.

There was a pause here, for the procession halted awhile. The rabble bearing the instruments of torture went on ahead to Mount Calvary, followed by a hundred Roman soldiers detached from Pilate's corps. He himself had, at some distance, accompanied the procession as far as the gateway, but there he turned back into the city.

Jesus on Golgotha • The Sixth and the Seventh Falls of Jesus • His Imprisonment

THE PROCESSION again moved onward. With blows and violent jerking at the cords that bound him, Jesus was driven up the rough, uneven path between the city wall and Mount Calvary toward the north. At a spot where the winding path in its ascent turned toward the south, poor Jesus fell again for the sixth time. But his tormentors beat him and drove him on more rudely than ever until he reached the top of the rock, the place of execution, when with the cross he fell heavily to the earth for the seventh time.

Simon of Cyrene, himself fatigued and ill-treated, was altogether worn out with indignation and compassion. He wanted to help poor Jesus up again, but the executioners with cuffs and insults drove him down the path. He soon after joined the disciples. All the lads and workmen that had come up with the procession, but whose presence was no longer necessary, were driven down also. The mounted Pharisees had ridden up by the smooth and easy winding path on the western side of Mount Calvary, from whose top one could see even over the city wall.

The place of execution, which was on the level top of the mount, was circular, and of a size that could be enclosed in the cemetery of our own parish church. It was like a tolerably large riding ground, and was surrounded by a low wall of earth, through which five pathways were cut. [J24, 25] Five paths, or entrances, of this kind seemed to be peculiar to this country in the laying out of different places; for instance, bathing places, baptismal pools, and the pool of Bethesda. Many of the cities also were built with five gates. This arrangement is found in all designs belonging to the olden times, and also in those of more modern date built in the spirit of pious imitation. As with all other things in the Holy Land, it breathed a deeply prophetic signification, which on this day received its realization in the opening of those five ways to salvation, the five sacred wounds of Jesus.

The Pharisees on horseback drew up on the western side beyond the circle, where the mountain sloped gently; that toward the city, up which the criminals were brought, was steep and rough. About one hundred Roman soldiers from the confines of Switzerland were stationed, some on the mountain, some around the circular wall of the place of execution. Some, too, were standing on guard around the two thieves. As space was needed, they were not at once brought up to the top of the mount, but with their arms still bound to the crosspieces were left lying on a slope where the road turned off to the south, and at some distance below the place of execution. A great crowd, mostly of the vulgar class, who had no fear of defilement, strangers, servants, slaves, pagans, and numbers of women, were standing around the circle. Some were on the neighboring heights, and these were being constantly joined by others on their way to the city. Toward evening there had gathered on Mount Gihon a whole encampment of Passover guests, many of whom gazed from a distance at the scene on Mount Calvary, and at times pressed nearer to get a better view.

It was about a quarter to twelve when Jesus, laden with the cross, was dragged into the place of execution, [J26] thrown on the ground, and Simon driven off. The executioners then pulled Jesus up by the cords, took the sections of the cross apart, and put them together again in proper form. Ah! How sad and miserable, what a terribly lacerated, pale and bloodstained figure was that of poor Jesus as he stood on that place of martyrdom! The executioners threw him down again with words of mockery such as these: "We must take the measure of thy throne for thee, O king!" But Jesus laid himself willingly upon the cross. Had it been possible for him, in his state of exhaustion, to do it more quickly, they would have had no necessity to drag him down. Then they stretched him out and marked the length for his hands and feet. The Pharisees were standing around, jeering and mocking. The executioners now dragged Jesus up again and led him, bound, about seventy steps northward down to a cave cut in the rock. It looked as if intended for a cellar, or cistern. They raised the door and pushed him down so unmercifully that, without a miracle, his knees would have been crushed on the rough stone floor. I heard his loud, sharp cries of pain. The executioners closed the door above him, and set guards before it. I accompanied Jesus on those seventy steps, and I think that I saw angels helping him, supporting him a little, that his knees should not be crushed. The stone under them became soft.

April 3, AD 33
Friday, 11:45 AM

And now the executioners began their preparations. In the center of the place of execution, the highest point of Golgotha's rocky height, was a circular elevation, about two feet high, with a few steps leading to it. After taking the measure of the lower part of each of the three crosses, the executioners chiselled out holes in that little elevation to receive them. Those for the thieves were raised to the right and left of the eminence. Their trunks were rough, shorter than that of Jesus, and sawed off obliquely at the upper end. The crosspieces, to which their hands were still fastened, were at the moment of crucifixion attached tightly to the upper end of the cross. The executioners next laid Christ's cross on the spot upon which they intended to crucify him, so that it could be conveniently raised and deposited in the hole made to receive it. They fitted the tenons of the two arms into the mortises made for them in the trunk, nailed on the foot-block, bored the holes for the nails and also for the title written by Pilate, hammered in the wedges under the mortised arms, and made hollow places here and there down the trunk. These were intended to receive the crown of thorns and Jesus's back, so that his body might rather stand than hang, thus preventing the hands from being torn by the weight and hastening death. In the earth behind the little eminence they sank a post with a crossbeam around which the ropes for raising

the cross could be wound. They made several other preparations of a similar nature.

Mary and the Holy Women Go to Golgotha

AFTER that most painful meeting with her divine Son carrying his cross before the dwelling of Caiaphas, the most afflicted mother was conducted by John and the holy women, Johanna Chusa, Susanna, and Salome, to the house of Nazareth in the vicinity of the corner gate.

Here the other holy women, in tears and lamentations, were gathered around Magdalene and Martha. Some children were with them. They now went all together, in number seventeen, with the blessed Virgin, careless of the jeers of the mob, grave and resolute, and by their tears awe-inspiring, across the forum, where they kissed the spot upon which Jesus had taken up the burden of the cross. Thence they proceeded along the whole of the sorrowful way trodden by him and venerated the places marked by special sufferings. The blessed Virgin saw and recognized the footprints of her divine Son, she numbered his steps, pointed out to the holy women all the places consecrated by his sufferings, regulated their halting and going forward on this Way of the Cross, which with all its details was deeply imprinted in her soul.

In this manner, that most touching devotion of the early church, first written by the sword of Simeon's prophecy on the loving mother-heart of Mary, was transmitted from her lips to the companions of her sorrows, and from them passed down to us. It is the sacred gift of God to the heart of the Mother whence it has descended from heart to heart among her children. Thus is the tradition of the church propagated. If people could see as I do, such gifts would appear to them more replete with life and holiness than any other. To the Jews, all places in which holy events, events dear to the heart happened, were thenceforth sacred. They forgot no spot remarkable for some great occurrence. They raised upon it a monument of stones, and went thither at times to pray. And so arose the devotion of the Holy Way of the Cross, not from any afterthought, but from the nature of man himself and the designs of God over his people, and from the truest mother-love which, so to speak, first trod that way under the very feet of Jesus himself.

The holy band of mourners now arrived at Veronica's dwelling, which they entered, for Pilate with his riders and two hundred soldiers, having turned back at the city gate, was coming along the street. Here with tears and expressions of sorrow, the holy women gazed upon the face of Jesus impressed upon Veronica's veil, and glorified his goodness toward his faithful friend. Taking the vessel of aromatic wine which Veronica had not been permitted to present to Jesus, they went to the gate nearby and out to Golgotha. Their number was increased on the way by the addition of many well-disposed people who traversed the streets with a demeanor at once orderly and deeply impressed. This procession was almost greater than that which followed Jesus, inclusive of the rabble running after it.

The sufferings of the most afflicted Mother of Sorrows on this journey, at the sight of the place of execution and her ascent to it, cannot be expressed. They were twofold: the pains of Jesus suffered interiorly and the sense of being left behind. Magdalene was perfectly distracted, intoxicated and reeling, as it were, with grief, precipitated from agony to agony. From silence long maintained she fell to lamenting, from listlessness to wringing her hands, from moaning to threatening the authors of her misery. She had to be continually supported, protected, admonished to silence, and concealed by the other women.

They went up the hill by the gently sloping western side and stood in three groups, one behind the other, outside the wall enclosing the circle. [J27] The mother of Jesus, her niece Mary Cleophas, Salome, and John stood close to the circle. Martha, Mary Heli, Veronica, Johanna Chusa, Susanna, and Mary Mark stood a little distance back around Magdalene, who could no longer restrain herself. Still farther back were about seven others, and between these groups were some well-disposed individuals who carried messages backward and forward. The mounted Pharisees were stationed in groups at various points around the circle, and the five entrances were guarded by Roman soldiers.

What a spectacle for Mary! The place of execution, the hill of crucifixion, the terrible cross outstretched before her, the hammers, the ropes, the dreadful nails! And all around, the brutal, drunken executioners, with curses completing their preparations! The crucifixion stakes of the thieves were already raised, and to facilitate ascent, plugs were stuck in the holes bored to receive them. The absence of Jesus intensified the mother's martyrdom. She knew that he was still alive, she longed to see him, and yet she shuddered at the thought, for when she should again behold him it would be in suffering unutterable.

Toward ten in the morning, when the sentence had been pronounced, a little hail fell at intervals. At the time of Jesus's journey to Golgotha, the sky cleared and the sun shone out, but toward twelve it was partially obscured by a lurid, reddish fog.

Jesus Stripped for Crucifixion and Drenched with Vinegar

FOUR executioners now went to the prison cave, seventy steps northward, and dragged Jesus out. [J28] He was imploring God for strength and offering himself once more for the sins of his enemies. They dragged him with pushes, blows, and insults over these last steps of his Passion. The people stared and jeered; the soldiers, cold and grave, stood proudly erect keeping order; the executioners furiously snatched him from the hands of his guards and dragged him violently into the circle.

The holy women gave a man some money to take to the executioners together with the vessel of spiced wine and beg them to allow Jesus to drink it. The wretches took the wine but, instead of giving it to Jesus, they drank it themselves. There were two brown jugs standing near.

In one was a mixture of vinegar and gall, and in the other, a kind of vinegar yeast. It may have been wine mingled with wormwood and myrrh. Some of this last-mentioned they held in a brown cup to the lips of the Savior, who was still bound in fetters. He tasted it, but would not drink. [J29] There were eighteen executioners in the circle: the six scourgers, the four that led Jesus, the two that held the ropes, and six crucifiers. Some were busied around Jesus, some with the thieves, and they worked and drank alternately. They were short, powerfully built fellows, filthy in appearance, cruel and beastly. Their features denoted foreign origin; their hair was bushy, their beard scrubby. They served the Romans and Jews for pay.

The sight of all this was rendered still more frightful to me, since I saw what others did not see, namely, the evil one in his proper form. I saw, too, great, frightful-looking demons at work among those barbarous men, handing them what they needed, making suggestions, and helping them in every way. Besides these, I saw numberless little figures of toads, serpents, clawed dragons, and noxious insects, which entered into the mouth of some, darted into the bosom of others, and sat on the shoulders of others. They upon whom I saw these evil spirits were those that indulged in wicked thoughts of rage, or that uttered words of mockery and malediction. But above the Lord I frequently saw during the crucifixion great figures of weeping angels and, in a halo of glory, little angelic faces. I saw similar angels of compassion and consolation hovering above the blessed Virgin and all others well-disposed to Jesus, strengthening and supporting them.

And now the executioners tore from our Lord the mantle they had flung around his shoulders. [J30] They next removed the fetter-girdle along with his own, and dragged the white woollen tunic over his head. Down the breast it had a slit bound with leather. When they wanted to remove the brown, seamless robe that his blessed Mother had knit for him, they could not draw it over his head, on account of the projecting crown of thorns. They consequently tore the crown again from his head, opening all the wounds afresh, tucked up the woven tunic and, with words of imprecation and insult, pulled it over his wounded and bleeding head.

There stood the Son of Man, trembling in every limb, covered with blood and welts; covered with wounds, some closed, some bleeding; covered with scars and bruises! He still retained the short woollen scapular over his breast and back, and the tunic about his loins. The wool of the scapular was dried fast in his wounds and cemented with blood into the new and deep one made by the heavy cross upon his shoulder. This last wound caused Jesus unspeakable suffering. The scapular was now torn ruthlessly from his frightfully lacerated and swollen breast. His shoulder and back were torn to the bone, the white wool of the scapular adhering to the crusts of his wounds and the dried blood on his breast. At last, they tore off his girdle and Jesus, our sweetest Savior, our inexpressibly maltreated Savior, bent over as if trying to hide himself. As he appeared about to swoon in their hands, they set him upon a stone that had been rolled nearby, thrust the crown of thorns again upon his head, and offered him a drink from that other vessel of gall and vinegar. But Jesus turned his head away in silence. And now, when the executioners seized him by the arms and raised him in order to throw him upon the cross, a cry of indignation, loud murmurs and lamentations arose from all his friends. His blessed Mother prayed earnestly, and was on the point of tearing off her veil and reaching it to him for a covering. God heard her prayer. At that same instant a man, who had run from the city gate and up through the crowd thronging the way, rushed breathless, his garments girded, into the circle among the executioners, and handed Jesus a strip of linen, which he accepted with thanks and wound around himself.

There was something authoritative in the impetuosity of this benefactor of his Redeemer, obtained from God by the prayer of the blessed Virgin. With an imperious wave of the hand toward the executioners, he said only the words: "Allow the poor man to cover himself with this!" and, without further word to any other, hurried away as quickly as he came. It was Jonadab, the nephew of Joseph, from the region of Bethlehem. He was the son of that

*April 3, AD 33
Friday, 12:15 PM*

brother to whom, after the birth of Christ, Joseph had pawned the ass that was no longer necessary. He was not one of Jesus's courageous followers, and today he had been keeping at a distance and spying around everywhere. Already, on hearing of the stripping for the scourging, he was filled with sorrow; and when the time for the crucifixion was drawing near, he was seized in the temple by extraordinary anxiety. While the blessed Mother on Golgotha was crying to God, a sudden and irresistible impulse took possession of Jonadab, drove him out of the temple, and up to Mount Calvary. He indignantly felt in his soul the ignominy of Ham, who mocked at his father Noah intoxicated with wine, and like another Shem, he hurried to cover his blessed Redeemer. The executioners who crucified Jesus were Hamites, that is, descendants of Ham. Jesus was treading the bloody wine press of the new wine of Redemption when Jonadab covered him. Jonadab's action was the fulfillment of a prefiguring type, and it was rewarded.

Jesus Nailed to the Cross

JESUS was now stretched on the cross by the executioners. He had lain himself upon it; but they pushed him lower down into the hollow places, rudely drew his right hand to the hole for the nail in the right arm of the cross, and tied his wrist fast. One knelt on his sacred breast and another held the closing hand flat; another placed the long, thick nail, which had been filed to a sharp point, upon the palm of his sacred hand, and struck furious blows with the iron hammer. [J31] A sweet, clear, spasmodic cry of anguish broke from the Lord's lips, and his blood spurted out upon the arms of the executioners. The muscles and ligaments of the hand had been torn and, by the three-edged nail, driven into the narrow hole. I counted the strokes of the hammer, but my anguish made me forget their number. The blessed Virgin sobbed in a low voice, but Magdalene was perfectly crazed.

The hand auger was a large piece of iron like a Latin T, and there was no wood at all about it. The large hammer also was, handle and all, of one piece of iron, and almost of the same shape as the wooden mallet we see used by a joiner when striking on a chisel.

The nails, at the sight of which Jesus shuddered, were so long that when the executioners grasped them in their fists, they projected about an inch at either end. The head consisted of a little plate with a knob, and it covered as much of the palm of the hand as a crown-piece would do. They were three-edged, thick near the head as a moderate sized thumb, then tapered to the thickness of a little finger, and lastly were filed to a point. When hammered in, the point could be seen projecting a little on the opposite side of the cross.

After nailing our Lord's right hand, the crucifiers found that his left, which also was fastened to the cross-piece, did not reach to the hole made for the nail, for they had bored a good two inches from the fingertips. They consequently unbound Jesus's arm from the cross, wound cords around it and, with their feet supported firmly against the cross, pulled it forward until the hand reached the hole. Now, kneeling on the arm and breast of the Lord, they fastened the arm again on the beam, and hammered the second nail through the left hand. The blood spurted up and Jesus's sweet, clear cry of agony sounded above the strokes of the heavy hammer. Both arms had been torn from their sockets, the shoulders were distended and hollow, and at the elbows one could see the disjointed bones. Jesus's breast heaved, and his legs were drawn up doubled to his body. His arms were stretched out in so straight a line that they no longer covered the obliquely rising crosspieces. One could see through the space thus made between them and his armpits.

The blessed Virgin endured all this torture with Jesus. She was pale as a corpse, and low moans of agony sounded from her lips. The Pharisees were mocking and jesting at the side of the low wall by which she was standing, therefore John led her to the other holy women at a still greater distance from the circle. Magdalene was like one out of her mind. She tore her face with her fingernails, till her eyes and cheeks were covered with blood.

About a third of its height from below, there was fixed to the cross by an immense spike a projecting block to which Jesus's feet were to be nailed, so that he should be rather standing than hanging; otherwise his hands would have been torn, and his feet could not have been nailed without breaking the bones. A hole for the nail had been bored in the block, and a little hollow place was made for his heels. Similar cavities had been made all down the trunk of the cross, in order to prolong his sufferings, for without them the hands would have been torn open and the body would have fallen violently by its own weight.

The whole body of our blessed Redeemer had been contracted by the violent stretching of the arms to the holes for the nails, and his knees were forcibly drawn up. The executioners now fell furiously upon them and, winding ropes around them, fastened them down to the cross; but on account of the mistake made in the holes in the cross-piece, the sacred feet of Jesus did not reach even to the block. When the executioners saw this, they gave vent to curses and insults. Some thought they would have to bore

new holes in the transverse arm, for that would be far less difficult than moving the footblock. Others with horrible scoffing cried out: "He will not stretch himself out, but we will help him!" Then they tied ropes around the right leg and, with horrible violence and terrible torture to Jesus, pulled the foot down to the block, and tied the leg fast with cords. [J32] Jesus's body was thus most horribly distended. His chest gave way with a cracking sound, and he moaned aloud: "O God! O God!" They had tied down his arms and his breast also that his hands might not be torn away from the nails. The abdomen was entirely displaced, and it seemed as if the ribs broke away from the breastbone. The suffering was horrible.

With similar violence the left foot was drawn and fastened tightly with cords over the right; and because it did not rest firmly enough over the right one for nailing, the instep was bored with a fine, flathead piercer, much finer than the one used for the hands. It was like an auger with a puncher attached. Then seizing the most frightful-looking nail of all, which was much longer than the others, they drove it with great effort through the wounded instep of the left foot and that of the right foot resting below. With a cracking sound, it passed through Jesus's feet into the hole prepared for it in the footblock, and through that again back into the trunk of the cross. I have seen, when standing at the side of the cross, one nail passing through both feet.

The nailing of the feet was the most horrible of all, on account of the distension of the whole body. I counted thirty-six strokes of the hammer amid the poor Redeemer's moans, which sounded to me so sweet, so pure, so clear.

The blessed Virgin had returned to the place of execution. At the sound of the tearing and cracking and moaning that accompanied the nailing of the feet, in her most holy compassion she became like one dying, and the holy women, supporting her in their arms, led her again from the circle just as the jeering Pharisees were drawing nearer. During the nailing and the raising of the cross which followed, there arose here and there, especially among the women, such cries of compassion as: "Oh, that the earth would swallow those wretches! Oh, that fire from heaven would consume them!" But these expressions of love were answered with scorn and insult by Jesus's enemies.

Jesus's moans were purely cries of pain. Mingled with them were uninterrupted prayers, passages from the Psalms and Prophecies, whose predictions he was now fulfilling. During the whole time of his bitter Passion and until the moment of death, he was engaged in this kind of prayer, and in the uninterrupted fulfillment of the prophecies. I heard all the passages he made use of and repeated them with him, and when I say the Psalms, I always remember the verses that Jesus used. But now I am so crushed by the tortures of my Lord that I cannot recall them. I saw weeping angels hovering over Jesus during this terrible torture.

At the beginning of the crucifixion, the commander of the Roman guard ordered the title written by Pilate to be fastened on its tablet at the head of the cross. This irritated the Pharisees, for the Romans laughed loudly at the words: "King of the Jews." After consulting as to what measures they should take to procure a new title, some of the Pharisees rode back to the city, once more to beg Pilate for another inscription.

While the work of crucifixion was going on, some of the executioners were still chiselling at the hole on the little elevation into which the cross was to be raised, for it was too small and the rock very hard. Some others, having drunk the spiced wine which they had received from the holy women, but which they had not given to Jesus, became quite intoxicated, and they felt such a burning and griping in their intestines that they became like men insane. They called Jesus a sorcerer, railed furiously at his patience, and ran more than once down the mount to gulp down asses' milk. Near the encampment of the Passover guests were women with she-asses, whose milk they sold.

The position of the sun at the time of Jesus's crucifixion showed it to be about a quarter past twelve, and at the moment the cross was lifted, the trumpet of the temple resounded. The paschal lamb had been slaughtered.

The Raising of the Cross

AFTER the crucifixion of our Lord, the executioners passed ropes through a ring at the back of the cross, and drew it by the upper part to the elevation in the center of the circle. Then they threw the ropes over the transverse beam, or derrick, raised on the opposite side. Several of the executioners, by means of these ropes, lifted the cross upright, while others supported it with blocks around the trunk, and guided the foot to the hole prepared for it. [J33] They shoved the top somewhat forward, until it came into a perpendicular line, and its whole weight with a tremulous thud shot down into the hole. The cross vibrated under the shock. Jesus moaned aloud. The weight of the outstretched body fell lower, the wounds were opened wider, the blood ran more profusely, and the dislocated bones struck against one another. The executioners now shook the cross again in their efforts to steady it, and hammered

five wedges into the hole around it: one in front, one to the right, another to the left, and two at the back, which was somewhat rounded. [J34]

A feeling of terror and, at the same time, one akin to deep emotion, was felt by Jesus's friends on beholding the cross swaying in the air and, at last, plunging into place with a heavy crash, amid the jeering shouts of the executioners, the Pharisees, and the distant crowd, whom Jesus could now see. But along with those shouts of derision, there arose other sounds at that dreadful moment—sounds of love and compassion from his devout followers. In touching expressions of pity, the holiest voices on earth, that of his afflicted mother, of the holy women, the beloved disciple, and all the pure of heart, saluted the "Eternal Word made flesh" elevated upon the cross. Loving hands were anxiously stretched forth as if to help the Holy of Holies, the Bridegroom of souls, nailed alive to the cross, quivering on high in the hands of raging sinners. But when the upraised cross fell with a loud crash into the hole prepared for it, a moment of deep silence ensued. It seemed as if a new feeling, one never before experienced, fell upon every heart. Hell itself felt with terror the shock of the falling cross and, with cries of rage and blasphemy, rose up again against the Lord in its instruments, the cruel executioners and Pharisees. Among the poor souls and in Limbo, there arose the joy of anxious expectation about to be realized. They listened to that crash with longing hope. It sounded to them like the rap of the coming victor at the door of redemption. For the first time, the holy cross stood erect upon the earth, like another tree of life in Paradise, and from the wounds of Jesus, enlarged by the shock, trickled four sacred streams down upon the earth, to wash away the curse resting upon it and to make it bear for himself, the new Adam, fruits of salvation.

While our Savior was thus standing upright upon the cross, and the cries of derision had for a few minutes been reduced to sudden silence, the flourish of trumpets and trombones sounded from the temple. It announced that the slaughter of the types, the paschal lambs, had begun; and at the same time, with solemn foreboding, it broke in upon the shouts of mockery and the loud cries of lamentation around the true, slaughtered Lamb of God. Many a hard heart shuddered and thought of the Baptist's words: "Behold the Lamb of God, who hath taken upon himself the sins of the world!"

The little eminence upon which the cross was raised was about two feet high. When the foot of the cross was placed

April 3, AD 33
Friday, 12—12:30 PM

near the hole, the feet of Jesus were about the height of a man above the ground; but when it was sunk into it, his friends could embrace and kiss his feet. A sloping path led up to it. Jesus's face was turned toward the northwest.

The Crucifixion of the Thieves

WHILE Jesus was being nailed to the cross, the thieves were still lying on the eastern side of the mount, their hands bound to the crosspiece fastened on their shoulders, and guards keeping watch over them. Both were suspected of the murder of a Jewish woman who, with her children, was traveling from Jerusalem to Joppa. They were arrested under the disguise of wealthy merchants at a castle in that neighborhood. Pilate often made this castle his stopping place when he was engaged in military affairs. The thieves had been imprisoned a long time before being brought to trial and condemnation, but I have forgotten the details. The one commonly called "the left thief" was older than the other and a great miscreant. He was the master and seducer of the converted one. They are usually called Dismas and Gesmas. I have forgotten their right names, so I shall call them the good Dismas and the bad Gesmas.

Both belonged to that band of robbers on the Egyptian frontiers from whom the holy family, on the flight to Egypt with the child Jesus, received shelter for the night. Dismas was that leprous boy who, on Mary's advice, was washed by his mother in the water used for bathing the child Jesus and instantly healed by it. The charity and protection which his mother, in spite of her companions, then bestowed upon the holy family, was rewarded by that outward, symbolical purification, which received its realization at the time of the crucifixion when, through the blood of Jesus, her son was inwardly cleansed from sin. Dismas had gone to ruin and he knew not Jesus; still he was not utterly bad, and the patience of the Lord had touched him. While lying on the mount, he spoke constantly of Jesus to his companion, Gesmas. He said: "They are dealing frightfully with the Galilean. The evil he has done by his new laws must be much greater than ours. But he has great patience, as well as great power, above all men." To which Gesmas responded: "Come now, what kind of power has he? Were he as powerful as they say, he could help us and himself too." And thus they bandied words. When Jesus's cross was raised, the executioners dragged the thieves up to it with the words: "Now it's your turn." They unbound them from the crosspiece and proceeded with great hurry, for the sun was clouding over and all things betokened a storm.

The executioners placed ladders against the upright trunks and fastened the curved crosspieces to the top of them. Two ladders were now placed against each of the two crosses, and executioners mounted them. Meanwhile the mixture of myrrh and vinegar was given them to drink, their old doublets were taken off, and by means of ropes passed under their arms and thrown up over those of the cross, they were drawn up to their places. Their ascent was rendered the more painful by the shocks they received and the striking against the wooden pegs that were stuck through the holes in the trunk of the cross. On the crossbeam and the trunk, ropes of twisted bark were knotted. The arms of the thieves were bent and twisted over the crosspieces; and around the wrists and elbows, the knees and ankles, cords were wound and twisted so tightly by means of those long wooden pegs that blood burst from the veins and the joints cracked. The poor creatures uttered frightful shrieks of pain. The good thief Dismas said to the executioners as they were drawing him up the cross: "Had you treated us as you did the poor Galilean, this trouble would have been spared you."

The Executioners Cast Lots for Jesus's Garments

AT the place outside the circle upon which the thieves had lain, the crucifiers had meanwhile gathered Jesus's garments and divided them into several parts, in order to cast lots for them. [J35] The mantle was narrow at the top and wide at the bottom. It had several folds, and the breast was lined, thus forming pockets. The executioners tore it up into long strips, which they distributed among themselves. They did the same to the long white garment, which was closed at the opening on the breast with straps. Then they divided the long linen scarf, the girdle, the breast scapular, and the linen that was worn around the loins, all of which were soaked with the Lord's blood. But because they could not agree concerning the brown woven robe, which would have been useless to them if torn up, they brought out a board with numbers on it and some bean-shaped stones marked with certain signs. They threw the stones on the board in order to decide by lot whose the robe should be. Just at this point of the proceedings a messenger, sent by Nicodemus and Joseph of Arimathea, came running toward them to say that a purchaser had been found for the clothes of Jesus. So they bundled them up, ran down the mount, and sold them. It was in this way that these sacred relics came into the possession of the Christians.

Jesus Crucified · The Two Thieves

THE TERRIBLE concussion caused by the shock when the cross was let fall into the hole prepared for it drove the precious blood in rich streams from Jesus's thorn-crowned head, and from the wounds of his sacred feet and hands. The executioners now mounted ladders and loosened the cords with which they had bound the sacred body to the trunk of the cross, in order to prevent its tearing away from the nails when raised. The blood, whose circulation had been checked by the tightly bound cords and the horizontal position of the body, now with new force, owing to the loosening of the cords and the upright position, resumed its course. Jesus's torments were, in consequence, redoubled. For seven minutes he hung in silence as if dead, sunk in an abyss of untold pain, and for some moments unbroken stillness reigned around the cross. Under the weight of the thorny crown, the sacred head had sunk upon the breast, and from its countless wounds the trickling blood had filled the eyes, the hair, the beard, and the mouth—open, parched, and languishing. The sacred face, on account of the immense crown, could be uplifted only with unspeakable pain. The breast was widely distended and violently torn upward; the shoulders were hollow and frightfully stretched; the elbows and wrists, dislocated; and the blood was streaming down the arms from the now enlarged wounds of the hands. Below the contracted breast there was a deep hollow place, and the entire abdomen was sunken and collapsed, as if shrunken away from the frame. Like the arms, the loins and legs were most horribly disjointed. Jesus's limbs had been so violently distended, his muscles and the torn skin so pitifully stretched, that his bones could be counted one by one. The blood trickled down the cross from under the terrible nail that pierced his sacred feet. The whole of the sacred body was covered with wounds, red swellings and scars, with bruises and boils, blue, brown and yellow, and with bloody places from which the skin had been peeled. All these wounds had been reopened by the violent tension of the cords, and were again pouring forth red blood. Later the stream became whitish and watery, and the sacred body paler. When the crusts fell off, the wounds looked like flesh drained of blood. In spite of its frightful disfigurement, our Lord's sacred body presented upon the cross an appearance at once noble and touching. Yes, the Son of God, the Eternal sacrificing himself in time, was beautiful, holy, and pure in the shattered body of the dying Paschal Lamb laden with the sins of the whole human race.

Mary's complexion was a beautiful bright olive tinged

April 3, AD 33
Friday, 12–12:30 PM

with red; and such, also, was that of her divine Son. By the journeys and fatigue of his later years, his cheeks below the eyes and the bridge of his nose were somewhat tanned. His chest, high and broad, was free from hair, unlike that of John the Baptist, which was like a skin quite covered with hair. Jesus had broad shoulders and strong, muscular arms. His thighs also were provided with powerful, well-marked sinews, and his knees were large and strong, like those of a man that had traveled much on foot and knelt long in prayer. His limbs were long, the muscles of the calves strongly developed by frequent journeying and climbing of mountains. His feet were very beautiful and perfect in form, though from walking barefoot over rough roads the soles were covered with great welts. His hands, too, were beautiful, his fingers long and tapering. Though not effeminate, they were not like those of a man accustomed to hard work. His neck was not short, though firm and muscular. His head was beautifully proportioned and not too large, his forehead high and frank, his whole face a pure and perfect oval. His hair, not exceedingly thick, and of a golden brown, was parted in the middle and fell in soft tresses down his neck. His beard, which was rather short, was pointed and parted on his chin.

But now his hair was almost all torn off, and what was left was matted with blood, his body was wound upon wound, his breast was crushed and there was a cavity visible below it. His body had been stretched asunder, and the ribs appeared here and there through the torn skin. Over the projecting bones of the pelvis the sacred body was so stretched in length that it did not entirely cover the beam of the cross.

The cross was somewhat rounded in the back, but flat in front, and hollowed out in the necessary places. The trunk was about as wide as it was thick. The several pieces of which the cross was formed were of different colored wood: some brown, some yellow, the trunk darker than the rest, like wood that had lain a long time in water.

The crosses of the thieves were rougher. They stood on the edge of the little eminence, to the right and left of Jesus's cross, and far enough from it for a man to ride on horseback between them. They were somewhat turned toward each other, and not so high as the Lord's. The thieves looked up to Jesus, one praying, the other jeering, and Jesus said something down from his cross to Dismas. The aspect of the thieves on the cross was hideous, especially that of the one to the left, who was a ferocious, drunken reprobate. They hung there distorted, shattered, swollen, and bound fast with cords. Their faces were livid, their lips brown from drink and confined blood, their eyes red, swollen, and starting from their sockets. They yelled and shrieked under the pressure of the cords. Gesmas cursed and reviled. The nails in the crosspiece forced their heads forward. They writhed convulsively, and in spite of the hard twisting around the wooden peg of the cords that bound their legs, one of them worked his foot up so that the bent knee stood out.

Jesus Mocked •
His First Saying on the Cross

AFTER the crucifixion of the thieves and the distribution of the Lord's garments, the executioners gathered up their tools, addressed some mocking and insulting words to Jesus, and went their way. The Pharisees still present spurred up their horses, rode around the circle in front of Jesus, outraged him in many abusive words, and then rode off. The hundred Roman soldiers with their commander also descended the mount and left the neighborhood, for fifty others had come up to take their place. The captain of this new detachment was Abenadar, an Arab by birth, who was later on baptized as Ctesiphon. The subaltern officer was Cassius. He was a kind of petty agent of Pilate, and at a subsequent period he received the name of Longinus. Twelve Pharisees, twelve Sadducees, twelve scribes, and some of the Ancients likewise rode up the mount. Among the last-named were those Jews that had in vain requested of Pilate another inscription for the title of the cross. They were furious, for Pilate would not allow them even to appear in his presence. They rode around the circle and drove away the blessed Virgin, calling her a dissolute woman. John took her to the women who were standing back. Magdalene and Martha supported her in their arms.

When the Pharisees and their companions, in making the rounds of the circle, came before Jesus, they wagged their heads contemptuously, saying: "Fie upon thee, liar! How dost thou destroy the temple, and buildest it again in three days?" "He always wanted to help others, and he cannot help himself! Art thou the Son of God? Then, come down from the cross!" "Is he the king of Israel? Then let him come down from the cross, and we will believe in him." "He trusted in God. Let him help him now!" The soldiers, in like manner, mocked and said: "If thou art the king of the Jews, help thyself now!"

At the sight of the Redeemer's silently abandoning himself to the full of his immeasurable sufferings, the thief on the left exclaimed: "His demon has now deserted him"; and a soldier stuck a sponge filled with vinegar on a stick and held it before Jesus's face. He appeared to suck a little of it. The mocking went on, and the soldier said: "If thou art the king of the Jews, help thyself!" All this took place while the first detachment of soldiers was being relieved by that under Abenadar.

And now Jesus, raising his head a little, exclaimed: "Father, forgive them, for they know not what they do!" and then he prayed in a low tone. Gesmas cried out: "If thou art the Christ, help thyself and us!" The mocking continued. Dismas, the thief on the right, was deeply touched at hearing Jesus pray for his enemies. When Mary heard the voice of her child, she could no longer be restrained, but pressed forward into the circle, followed by John, Salome, and Mary Cleophas. The captain of the guard did not prevent her.

Dismas, the thief on the right, received by virtue of Jesus's prayer an interior enlightenment. When the blessed Virgin came hurrying forward, he suddenly remembered that Jesus and his mother had helped him when a child. He raised his voice and cried in a clear and commanding tone: "How is it possible that ye can revile him when he is praying for you! He has kept silence and patience, he prays for you, and you outrage him! He is a prophet! He is our king! He is the Son of God!" At this unexpected reproof out of the mouth of the murderer hanging there in misery, a tumult arose among the scoffers. They picked up stones to stone him on the cross. The centurion Abenadar, however, repulsed their attack, caused them to be dispersed, and restored order and quiet.

The blessed Virgin felt herself strengthened by that prayer of Jesus. Gesmas was again crying to Jesus: "If thou be the Christ, help thyself and us!" when Dismas thus addressed him: "Neither dost thou fear God, seeing thou art under the same condemnation. And we indeed justly, for we receive the due reward of our deeds, but this man had done no evil. Oh, bethink thee of thy sins, and change thy sentiments!" Thoroughly enlightened and touched, he then confessed his crime to Jesus, saying: "Lord, if thou dost condemn me, it will be just. But have mercy on me!" Jesus replied: "Thou shalt experience my mercy." At these words Dismas received the grace of deep contrition, *which he indulged for the next quarter of an hour.* [136]

All the foregoing incidents took place, either simultaneously or one after the other, between twelve and half-past, as indicated by the sun, and a few moments after the raising of the cross. A great change was rapidly taking place in the souls of most of the spectators, for even while the penitent thief was speaking, fearful signs were beheld in nature, and all present were filled with anxiety.

TISSOT ILLUSTRATIONS
[SECTION J]

The Passion and Death of Jesus Christ

⊕

Jesus Before Pilate, First Interview · · · · · · · · · · · 226
The Message of Pilate's Wife, Claudia · · · · · · · · 228
Jesus Before Herod · · · · · · · · · · · · · 230
Jesus Led from Herod to Pilate · · · · · · · · · · · · · 232
The Scourging of the Back · · · · · · · · · · · · · · · 234
The Scourging of the Front · · · · · · · · · · · · · · 236
The Crowning with Thorns · · · · · · · · · · · · · · 238
Ecce Homo: "Behold the Man!" · · · · · · · · · · · · 240
Jesus Before Pilate, Second Interview · · · · · · · · 242
Let Him be Crucified · · · · · · · · · · · · · · · · · · 244
Pilate Washes his Hands · · · · · · · · · · · · · · · 246
Jesus Falls Down the Steps · · · · · · · · · · · · · · 248
Jesus Hears His Death Sentence · · · · · · · · · · · 250
Jesus Leaves the Praetorium in Scarlet Cloak · · · 252
The Judgment on the Gabbatha · · · · · · · · · · · · 254
The Title on the Cross · · · · · · · · · · · · · · · · · · 256
They Dressed Him in His Own Garments · · · · · · 258
Jesus Bearing the Cross · · · · · · · · · · · · · · · · · 260
Jesus Falls Beneath the Cross · · · · · · · · · · · · · 262

Jesus Meets His Mother · · · · · · · · · · · · · · · · · 264
Simon the Cyrenian Carries Cross with Jesus · · · 266
Seraphia Wipes the Face of Jesus · · · · · · · · · · · 268
The Holy Face · 270
The Daughters of Jerusalem · · · · · · · · · · · · · · 272
Golgotha Seen from Walls of Judicial Gate · · · · · 274
Golgotha Seen from Walls of Herod's Palace · · · · 276
The Procession Nearing Golgotha · · · · · · · · · · · 278
The Holy Women Watch from Afar · · · · · · · · · · 280
Jesus Taken from the Cistern · · · · · · · · · · · · · 282
The Vase of Myrrh and Gall · · · · · · · · · · · · · · 284
Jesus Stripped of His Clothing · · · · · · · · · · · · 286
The First Nail · 288
The Nail for the Feet · · · · · · · · · · · · · · · · · · 290
The Raising of the Cross · · · · · · · · · · · · · · · · 292
The Five Wedges · 294
The Garments Divided by Cast Lots · · · · · · · · · 296
The Pardon of the Good Thief · · · · · · · · · · · · · 298

Jesus before Pilate, First Interview [J1]

JESUS was dragged by the executioners up the lofty flight of marble steps and placed in the rear of the terrace, from which Pilate could speak with his accusers below. When Pilate beheld before him Jesus, of whom he had heard so many reports, so shockingly abused and disfigured, and still with that dignity of bearing which no ill-treatment could change, his loathing contempt for the Jewish priests and council increased. In an imperious and scornful manner, therefore, he addressed the high priests: "What accusation do you bring against this man?" To which they answered angrily: "If we did not know him to be a malefactor, we should not have delivered him to you." "Take him," replied Pilate, "and judge him according to your Law." "Thou knowest," they retorted, "that it is not lawful for us to condemn any man to death." Besides this, he teaches that he is the Christ, the anointed of the Lord, the Messiah, the promised king of the Jews, and allows himself so to be called." At the word that Jesus caused himself to be called the Christ, the king of the Jews, Pilate became somewhat thoughtful. He went from the open terrace into the adjoining apartment, casting as he passed him a scrutinizing glance upon Jesus, and ordered the guard to bring the Lord into the judgment chamber. Pilate regarded Jesus with astonishment as he addressed him: "Art thou the king of the Jews?" And Jesus made answer: "Sayest thou this thing of thyself, or have others told it thee of me?" Pilate, a little offended that Jesus should esteem him so foolish as, of his own accord, to ask so poor and miserable a creature whether he was a king, answered evasively something to this effect: "Am I a Jew, that I should know about things so nonsensical? Thy people and their priests have delivered thee to me for condemnation as one deserving of death. Tell me, what hast thou done?" Jesus answered solemnly: "My kingdom is not of this world. If my kingdom were of this world, I should certainly have servants who would combat for me, that I should not be delivered to the Jews. But my kingdom is not here below." Pilate heard these earnest words of Jesus with a kind of shudder, and said to him thoughtfully: "Art thou then indeed a king?" And Jesus answered: "As thou sayest! Yes, I am the king. I was born, and I came into this world, to bear witness to the truth. Everyone that is of the truth, heareth my voice." Pilate cast a glance on him and, rising, said: "Truth! What is truth?" Some other words were then exchanged, whose purport I do not now remember. [194]

[JOHN 18:29–38] 29 So Pilate went out to them and said, "What accusation do you bring against this man?" 30 They answered him, "If this man were not an evildoer, we would not have handed him over." 31 Pilate said to them, "Take him yourselves and judge him by your own law." The Jews said to him, "It is not lawful for us to put any man to death." 32 This was to fulfill the word which Jesus had spoken to show by what death he was to die. 33 Pilate entered the praetorium again and called Jesus, and said to him, "Are you the King of the Jews?" 34 Jesus answered, "Do you say this of your own accord, or did others say it to you about me?" 35 Pilate answered, "Am I a Jew? Your own nation and the chief priests have handed you over to me; what have you done?" 36 Jesus answered, "My kingship is not of this world; if my kingship were of this world, my servants would fight, that I might not be handed over to the Jews; but my kingship is not from the world." 37 Pilate said to him, "So you are a king?" Jesus answered, "You say that I am a king. For this I was born, and for this I have come into the world, to bear witness to the truth. Every one who is of the truth hears my voice." 38 Pilate said to him, "What is truth?" After he had said this, he went out to the Jews again, and told them, "I find no crime in him."

IN the Gospel of Saint John (18:28), it is written that the Jews went not themselves into the judgment hall, lest they should be defiled and be thereby prevented from eating the Passover. This explains how it was that when Pilate wished to confer with the Jews he "went forth" to speak to them, returning again to Jesus, with whom he thus found himself alone. The hall of audience in the Praetorium was on the first floor, and its height can still be exactly estimated by means of the twenty-eight white marble steps which led up to it and were carried away by Saint Helena, to be eventually preserved in the Church of Santa Croce di Gerusalemme, at Rome. The room in question adjoined a loggia which served as a kind of tribune to the governor, when, as sometimes happened, he took it into his head to harangue the people. To go backward and forward from it to the room in which Jesus was involved, therefore, the taking by Pilate of but a very few steps. All the local arrangements represented in my various pictures were suggested to me by one or another passage in the gospel narrative, which throws a very vivid light on the subject for those who read it attentively.

The Message of Pilate's Wife, Claudia Procula [J2]

⊕

WHILE Jesus was being taken to Herod and while he was enduring mockery at his tribunal, I saw Pilate going to his wife, Claudia Procula. They met at a summerhouse in a terraced garden behind Pilate's palace. Claudia was trembling and agitated. She conversed long with Pilate and conjured him by all that was sacred to him not to injure Jesus, the prophet, the Holy of Holies, and then she related some things from the dreams, or visions, which she had had of Jesus the night before.

The next day, alarmed by the uproar of the tumultuous mob, she looked out upon the forum and recognized in the Lord the one shown her in vision the night before. She saw him now the object of all kinds of abuse and ill-treatment, while being led by his enemies across the forum to Herod. In terrible anguish, she sent at once for Pilate to whom, frightened and anxious, she related the visions she had seen in her dreams as far as she could make herself understood. She entreated and implored, and clung to Pilate in the most touching manner.

Pilate was greatly astonished, and somewhat troubled at what she related. He compared it with all that he had heard of Jesus, with the fury of the Jews, with Jesus's silence, and with his dignified and wonderful answers to all the questions he had put to him. He wavered uneasily in his own mind, but soon yielded to his wife's representations and said: "I have already declared that I find no guilt in Jesus. I shall not condemn him, for I know the utter wickedness of the Jews." He spoke at length of Jesus's bearing toward himself, quieted his wife's fears, and even went so far as to give her a pledge of assurance that he would not condemn him. I do not remember what kind of a jewel, whether a ring or a seal, Pilate gave as a sign of his promise. With this understanding they parted. [196]

[MATTHEW 27:19] 19 Besides, while he was sitting on the judgment seat, his wife sent word to him, "Have nothing to do with that righteous man, for I have suffered much over him today in a dream."

PILATE *has left the Praetorium to parley with the Jews who are waiting below opposite the loggia. He is seated in a movable chair of state raised on several steps as a sign of his high rank and power. A servant hastens in, bringing a message from his wife, whose name, according to tradition, was Claudia Procula or Procla. The servant brings with her the ring of her mistress as a proof of the authenticity of the message. The noble, touching tenor of this message shows that Claudia has a soul worthy of conversion to Christianity; so that it is by no means difficult to believe that she did become as tradition relates, a follower of the Savior. The Greek menology even goes so far as to place her in the rank of the saints, and certain legends relate that Pilate, who was always alike ambitious and irresolute, persecuted her to such an extent that she left him to join the Christian community.*

Jesus Before Herod [J3]

JESUS was now led out into a large court and treated with unspeakable outrage and mockery. The court was surrounded by the wings of the palace, and Herod, standing on a flat roof, gazed for a considerable time upon the ill-treatment offered to Jesus. Annas and Caiaphas were at his back, trying by all means in their power to induce him to pass sentence upon Jesus. At the same time, Jesus's enemies caused money to be distributed among Herod's soldiers, that they might grossly maltreat Jesus, yes, even hasten his death, for they would rather see him die in that way than live to be freed by Pilate's sentence. From this insolent, godless rabble, our Lord had to suffer the most shameful mockery, the most barbarous ill-treatment. When they led him out into the court, a soldier brought from the lodge at the gate a large white sack in which cotton had been packed. They cut a hole in the bottom of the sack and, amid shouts of derisive laughter from all present, threw it over Jesus's head. [198]

[LUKE 23:4–11] 4 And Pilate said to the chief priests and the multitudes, "I find no crime in this man." 5 But they were urgent, saying, "He stirs up the people, teaching throughout all Judea, from Galilee even to this place." 6 When Pilate heard this, he asked whether the man was a Galilean. 7 And when he learned that he belonged to Herod's jurisdiction, he sent him over to Herod, who was himself in Jerusalem at that time. 8 When Herod saw Jesus, he was very glad, for he had long desired to see him, because he had heard about him, and he was hoping to see some sign done by him. 9 So he questioned him at some length; but he made no answer. 10 The chief priests and the scribes stood by, vehemently accusing him. 11 And Herod with his soldiers treated him with contempt and mocked him; then, arraying him in gorgeous apparel, he sent him back to Pilate.

THE decision of Pilate to send Jesus back to Herod appears to have had a twofold motive; in the first place he wished to get rid of a galling responsibility, and in the second he wished to pay his court to Herod, with whom, as the sacred text implies, he was at enmity. There were in fact many causes of friction between the governor of Judea and the tetrarch of Galilee. The various feasts which took place at Jerusalem often led to risings in which the men of Galilee always took the most prominent part; they were, therefore, generally the first to fall victims to the vengeance of the pro-consul, and more often than not their own sovereign may have considered the means of repression resorted to excessive.

Herod Antipas, for it is of him we are now speaking, generally lived at his capital, Tiberias, but, on the occasion of the great festivals, he would naturally be at Jerusalem, possibly staying in the palace of his father, Herod the Great. In setting himself to curry favor with Herod, Pilate little expected how well he would succeed: the tetrarch, blasé as he was from self-indulgence, anticipated a new pleasure in witnessing the marvelous works with which he hoped Jesus would entertain him. He no doubt took the Savior for a kind of Simon the magician, who would be only too glad to win his liberty and the favor of the king by performing some wonderful feats of jugglery. But Herod was very quickly undeceived, for, at the very first glance, the sight of the Nazarene must have affected him disagreeably; Jesus, it must be remembered, having been at the mercy of the populace since the morning. He had nothing on but his seamless garment, and he was in far too wretched and miserable a plight for his appearance to have given any pleasure to the effeminate sensualist, who delighted in the dancing of Salome and was given over to adultery. For all that, however, he received the prisoner with a certain amount of empressement, overwhelming him with a great flow of words and asking him many questions, to all of which Jesus answered only with a silence full of majesty.

It was a humiliating lesson for Herod; for this so-called king of the Jews seemed to take his title seriously and to look upon the tetrarch with absolute disdain. Herod was deeply wounded. The members of the Sanhedrin were there, vehemently accusing Jesus. Herod, though he does not believe all their angry accusations, means to have his revenge for the wound inflicted on his own self-love, and with this end in view he begins to set at naught and mock the prisoner. This pretended king who has been brought before him, is really too carelessly dressed, his royal purple is in too bad a condition, let us give him a gorgeous robe more worthy of his sovereign dignity! Some old rags of white stuff are therefore hunted up from some neglected corner of the palace, some comic-looking, tattered garment in which holes can easily be made for the head and arms, and behold there is Jesus arrayed in fitting guise for a pretender to the throne! A white garment was in fact worn by candidates for a crown, and this garment resembled the gala dress of the wealthy and highly born. Thus arrayed, Jesus was sent back to Pilate before whom he had already been brought, Herod abandoning his rights.

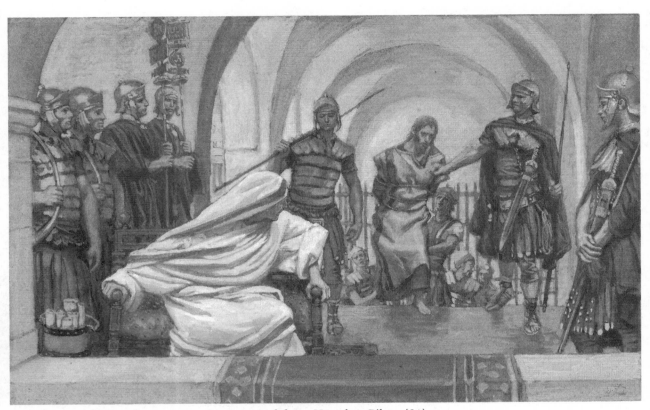

Jesus Led from Herod to Pilate [J4]

⊕

JESUS was led again through the street before Pilate's house and up the steps to the elevated platform. The executioners dragged him in the most brutal manner, the long garment tripped him, and he fell so often on the white marble steps that they were stained with blood from his sacred head. His enemies, who had retaken their seats on the side of the forum, and the rude mob, broke out into jeers and laughter at his every fall, while the executioners drove him up with kicks.

Pilate was reclining on a chair something like a small couch, a little table by his side. As on the preceding occasion, he was attended by officers and men holding rolls of written parchment. Stepping out upon the terrace from which he was accustomed to address the multitude, he thus spoke to Jesus's accusers: "You have presented unto me this man as one that perverteth the people, and behold, I, having examined him before you, find no cause in him in those things wherein you accuse him. No, nor Herod neither. For I sent you to him and behold, nothing worthy of death is brought against him. I will chastise him therefore and let him go." [199]

[LUKE 23:11–16] 11 And Herod with his soldiers treated him with contempt and mocked him; then, arraying him in gorgeous apparel, he sent him back to Pilate. 12 And Herod and Pilate became friends with each other that very day, for before this they had been at enmity with each other. 13 Pilate then called together the chief priests and the rulers and the people, 14 and said to them, "You brought me this man as one who was perverting the people; and after examining him before you, behold, I did not find this man guilty of any of your charges against him; 15 neither did Herod, for he sent him back to us. Behold, nothing deserving death has been done by him; 16 I will therefore chastise him and release him."

PILATE, *warned of the return of Jesus, again appears upon the judgment seat to harangue the Jews and to tell them that he has examined the accused and found him innocent, thus convicting his hearers of hypocrisy and untruth. But in spite of all this, the governor's fear of the people makes him yield one iniquitous concession after another, until at last the death of the Just One is brought about. Already, although Pilate has "found no fault" in the prisoner, he permits him to be scourged.*

The Scourging of the Back [J5]

PILATE, the base, pusillanimous judge, had several times repeated the cowardly words: "I find no guilt in him, therefore will I chastise him and let him go!" To which the Jews shouted no other response than, "Crucify him! Crucify him!" But Pilate, still hoping to carry out his first resolve not to condemn Jesus to death, commanded him to be scourged after the manner of the Romans. Then the executioners, striking and pushing Jesus with their short staves, led him through the raging multitude on the forum to the whipping pillar, which stood in front of one of the halls that surrounded the great square to the north of Pilate's palace and not far from the guardhouse.

And now came forward to meet Jesus the executioners' servants with their whips, rods, and cords, which they threw down near the pillar. There were six of them, swarthy men all somewhat shorter than Jesus, with coarse, crisp hair, to whom nature had denied a beard other than a thin, short growth like stubble. Their loins were girded and the rest of their clothing consisted of a jacket of leather, or some other wretched stuff, open at the sides, and covering the upper part of the body like a scapular. Their arms were naked, and their feet encased in tattered sandals. They were vile malefactors from the frontiers of Egypt who, as slaves and culprits, were here employed on buildings and canals. The most wicked, the most abject among them were always chosen for the punishment of criminals in the praetorium.

Although the Lord was offering no resistance whatever, yet they struck him with their fists and ropes and with frantic rage dragged him to the pillar, which stood alone and did not serve as a support to any part of the building. It was not very high, for a tall man with outstretched arms could reach the top, which was provided with an iron ring. Toward the middle of it on one side were other rings, or hooks. It is impossible to express the barbarity with which those furious hounds outraged Jesus on that short walk to the pillar. They tore from him Herod's mantle of derision, and almost threw the poor Savior to the ground. Jesus trembled and shuddered before the pillar. With his own hands, swollen and bloody from the tight cords, and in tremulous haste, he laid aside his garments, while the executioners struck and abused him. He prayed and implored so touchingly and, for one instant, turned his head toward his most afflicted mother, who was standing with the holy women in a corner of one of the porches around the square, not far from the scourging place. Turning to the pillar, as if to cover himself by it, Jesus said: "Turn thine eyes from me!" I know not whether he said these words vocally or mentally, but I saw how Mary took them, for at the same moment, I beheld her turning away and sinking into the arms of the holy women who surrounded her, closely veiled.

And now Jesus clasped the pillar in his arms. The executioners, with horrible imprecations and barbarous pulling, fastened his sacred, upraised hands, by means of a wooden peg, behind the iron ring on top. In thus doing, they so stretched his whole body, that his feet, tightly bound below at the base, scarcely touched the ground. There stood the Holy of Holies, divested of clothing, laden with untold anguish and ignominy, stretched upon the pillar of criminals, while two of the bloodhounds, with sanguinary rage, began to tear with their whips the sacred back from head to foot. [202]

[MATTHEW 27:26] 26 Then he released for them Barabbas, and having scourged Jesus, delivered him to be crucified.

WE have already said that the column to which Jesus was bound during the scourging to which he was subjected is probably the one alluded to by Saint Jerome, and which he and Saint Paul alike venerated. It upheld the portico of a church in the Zion quarter, to which it had been removed by Saint Helena. In every court of justice there was, in fact, a scourging column, and the one in question was probably originally in the forum or public square opposite the Praetorium. There was also, most likely in the court of the guardhouse, another short column to which Jesus was fastened when he was crowned with thorns; this, which was called the Column of Reproach, and is still held in high honor in the Church of Saint Praxedes, might perhaps be the column from the tribunal of Caiaphas to which our Lord was bound during the night of Holy Thursday preceding Good Friday. In our picture we have represented the forum with a number of shops at the farther end, closed just now on account of the crowds which have collected. We have supposed, in accordance with certain traditions which have come down to us, that John, who had accompanied the blessed Virgin, may have secured a place in one of these shops from which he was able to watch all the sufferings of his divine Master. From this vantage point, when Jesus had been compelled to carry his cross and had started for Golgotha laden with it, his divine Mother was able to follow the melancholy procession, and, guided by John, to take a short cut so as to meet her Son again on the Via Dolorosa a little farther on.

The Scourging of the Front [J6]

⊕

BUT those monsters had not yet satiated their cruelty. They loosened the cords that bound Jesus and turned his back to the pillar and, because he was so exhausted as to be no longer able to stand, they bound him to it with fine cords passed under his arms across his breast, and below the knees. His hands they fastened to the ring in the middle of the opposite side. Only blood and wounds, only barbarously mangled flesh could be seen on the most sacred, most venerable body of the Son of God. Like furious bloodhounds raged the scourgers with their strokes. One held a slender rod in his left hand, and with it struck the face of Jesus. There was no longer a sound spot on the Lord's body. He glanced, with eyes swimming in blood, at his torturers, and sued for mercy; but they became only the more enraged. He moaned in fainting tones: "Woe! Woe!" Several times during the scourging I saw weeping angels around Jesus, and during the whole of that bitter, ignominious punishment that fell upon him like a shower of hail, I heard him offering his prayer to his Father for the sins of humankind. But now, as he lay in his own blood at the foot of the pillar, I saw an angel strengthening him. It seemed as if the angel gave him a luminous morsel. [202]

[JOHN 19:1] 1 Then Pilate took Jesus and scourged him.

SEVERAL different modes of scourging were practiced in the time of our Savior. The rabbis tell us that in some cases the victim was fastened to a column lofty enough for him to be almost suspended by the hands, which were fastened together uplifted above the head, while the feet, also bound together, were fastened to the base of the column, so as to keep the body in position. The executioners then inflicted thirteen blows on each shoulder and on the loins with a rod, thus making the legal forty stripes save one. The scourging inflicted by the Romans was far more terrible. In fact, instead of rods they used cords, to the end of which they fastened little square bits of bone or pellets of metal. To which of these modes of torture was our Savior subjected? We ourselves are inclined to believe that he was treated in the Jewish way, just as a slave would have been. If our interpretation be correct, Jesus would have been given over to the four executioners, who, in accordance with the Jewish law, were to inflict on him the forty stripes save one. The men who performed this revolting task were Syrian or Idumean recruits, in the service of the governor, not Roman soldiers. Every blow brought blood and tore away a portion of the skin and flesh, till at last the very bones were laid bare, thus literally fulfilling the prophecy: "The plowers plowed upon my back, they made long their furrows." (Psalm 129:3)

The Crowning with Thorns [J7]

THE crowning and mocking of Jesus took place in the inner court of the guardhouse, which stood in the forum over the prisons. It was surrounded with pillars, and the entrance was open. There were about fifty low-lived wretches belonging to the army, jailer's servants, executioners, lads, slaves, and whipping servants, who took an active part in this maltreatment of Jesus. The mob at first crowded in eagerly, but was soon displaced by the thousand Roman soldiers who surrounded the building. They stood in rank and order, jeering and laughing, thereby giving to Jesus's tormentors new inducement to multiply his sufferings. Their jokes and laughter encouraged them as applause does the actor. There was a hole in the middle of the court, and to this they had rolled the base of an old column, which may once have stood there. On that base they placed a low, round stool with an upright at the back by which to raise it, and maliciously covered it with sharp stones and potsherds. Once more they tore Jesus's clothing from his wounded body, and threw over him instead an old red military cloak tattered and so short that it did not reach to the knees. Then they put upon him the crown of thorns. It was two hands high, thick, and skillfully plaited, with a projecting edge on top. They laid it like a binder round his brow and fastened it tightly in the back, thus forming it into a crown. It was woven from thorn branches three fingers thick, the thorns of which grew straight out. In plaiting the crown, as many of them as possible had been designedly pressed inward. Next they placed in Jesus's hand a thick reed with a tufted top. All this was done with mock solemnity, as if they were really crowning him king. [204]

[MATTHEW 27:27–30] 27 Then the soldiers of the governor took Jesus into the praetorium, and they gathered the whole battalion before him. 28 And they stripped him and put a scarlet robe upon him, 29 and plaiting a crown of thorns they put it on his head, and put a reed in his right hand. And kneeling before him they mocked him, saying, "Hail, King of the Jews!" 30 And they spat upon him, and took the reed and struck him on the head.

THE cloak or mantle worn by Jesus on his way to death was a short military cloak, and not really, as is generally supposed, a purple robe properly so called. The text of Matthew is perfectly clear on this point. The scarlet robe referred to in 27:28, was very evidently just a loose garment of coarse wool dyed red, such as the Roman soldiers wore over their armor. It was a piece of stuff cut into a circular form, which was fastened on the left shoulder or at the neck with a clasp, and the wearer could drape it in many different ways. It was of the color of cochineal and rather more pink than what is now known as madder red. It will be remembered that among the Jews this color was symbolic of sin and, in the remoter days of antiquity, it symbolized Typhon, the spirit of the earth, who represents physical evil. Jesus, with the scarlet robe upon his shoulders, was thus marked out as the victim of the whole world, laden with the sins of the human race, even as the scapegoat with its bands and fringes of red wool was sent adrift by the Jewish priests carrying with it the sins of the people. . . . The color of purple, on the other hand, was among the ancients typical of royalty. It was a kind of red richly shot with blue, and the dye producing it was obtained from a shell found in considerable numbers off the coast of Tyre.

The crown of thorns is supposed to have consisted of a band of rushes from the seashore, strengthened with twigs of a prickly thorn twisted in and out. The appearance of the whole must have been rather that of a domed crown than of a simple wreath, which would merely have rested on the forehead, leaving the head itself uncovered. The expression of Mark, 15:19: "And they smote him on the head with a reed," as if to force the crown down on his brow, would appear to lend color to our idea that it covered the head entirely, the twigs of thorns going all the way round the edge of the crown. The band formed of rushes, which was the foundation of the sacred crown of thorns, is still to be seen in the Cathedral of Notre Dame at Paris, and the single thorns and twigs which made up the rest of the instrument of torture, preserved in other sanctuaries, are in a sufficiently good state of preservation and would evidently fit well on to the band, so that it is possible to form a very accurate idea of what the crown must have been as a whole. This precious relic passed into the hands of Saint Louis while almost intact, after having belonged for many centuries to the Byzantine Emperors. Later, the thorns were taken off and distributed among the various sanctuaries where they are still to be seen.

Ecce Homo: "Behold the Man!" [J8]

AND now they again led Jesus, the crown of thorns upon his head, the mock scepter in his fettered hands, the purple mantle thrown around him, into Pilate's palace. He was unrecognizable on account of the blood that filled his eyes and ran down into his mouth and beard. His body, covered with swollen welts and wounds, resembled a cloth dipped in blood, and his gait was bowed down and tottering. The mantle was so short that he had to stoop in order to cover himself with it, for at the crowning they had again torn off all his clothing. Then Jesus was led forward by the executioners to the front of the balcony where Pilate was standing, so that he could be seen by all the people in the forum. Oh, what a terrible, heart-rending spectacle! Silence, awful and gloomy, fell upon the multitude as the inhumanly treated Jesus, the sacred, martyrized figure of the Son of God, covered with blood and wounds, wearing the frightful crown of thorns, appeared and, from his eyes swimming in blood, cast a glance upon the surging crowd! Nearby stood Pilate, pointing to him with his finger and crying to the Jews: "Behold the man!" [205]

]JOHN 19:4–7] 4 Pilate went out again, and said to them, "See, I am bringing him out to you, that you may know that I find no crime in him." 5 So Jesus came out, wearing the crown of thorns and the purple robe. Pilate said to them, "Behold the man!" 6 When the chief priests and the officers saw him, they cried out, "Crucify him, crucify him!" Pilate said to them, "Take him yourselves and crucify him, for I find no crime in him." 7 The Jews answered him, "We have a law, and by that law he ought to die, because he has made himself the Son of God." [MATTHEW 27:28] 28 And they stripped him and put a scarlet robe upon him.

AFTER *the agony of the scourging and the mocking ceremony of the crowning with thorns, Jesus was again taken before Pilate. The latter, who had once more taken his place in the loggia of the court of justice, seeing the lamentable condition to which the prisoner was reduced, thought it would be enough to show him thus attired and bleeding, to excite the pity of the spectators and to appease the hatred of his enemies. He led him, therefore, to the front of the judgment hall and presented him to the people with the words: Ecce Homo! Behold the man!*

In our picture we have endeavored to depict as nearly as possible the exact spot from which Pilate addressed the people. We can tell what was the approximate height of the story in which the praetorium and the adjoining loggia were situated, from that of the Scala Sancta of twenty-eight steps which led up to them and which was taken to Rome by Saint Helena. What is now called the Ecce Homo Arch is too far from the praetorium to have been the spot from which Jesus was pointed out to the people by Pilate; but the stones of which the arch is composed were probably silent witnesses of the scene, the arch being near enough for that. The restricted space in which the crowd is shown represents the street leading to the Sheep Gate and the Sheep Pool, and the steps leading up to the praetorium are kept clear of the populace by the bodyguard of the Roman garrison, while the entrance to the forum on the other side is shut in by the tribunal called Gabbatha. Between these two points the angry populace is closely packed, yelling and howling, their hatred ever on the increase; the farther off the brawlers are, the louder do they shout; they brandish their arms and their fingers twitch as if eager to seize their enemy. Jesus, his hands bound, yet holding in them his reed scepter, looks down upon the Gehenna into which he is doomed to descend again ere long, standing there motionless and calm in spite of the pain he must be suffering from his many wounds.

Jesus Before Pilate, Second Interview [J9]

$\oplus$

THE words, however, "He has made himself the Son of God," renewed Pilate's anxiety, aroused again his superstitious fears. He caused Jesus therefore to be brought before him into the judgment hall, where he spoke to him alone. He began by asking: "Whence art thou?" But Jesus gave him no answer. "Dost thou not answer me?" said Pilate. "Knowest thou not that I have power to crucify thee and power to release thee?" "Thou shouldst not have any power," answered Jesus, "unless it were given thee from above; therefore he that hath delivered me to thee hath the greater sin." [206]

[JOHN 19:8–12] 8 When Pilate heard these words, he was the more afraid; 9 he entered the praetorium again and said to Jesus, "Where are you from?" But Jesus gave no answer. 10 Pilate therefore said to him, "You will not speak to me? Do you not know that I have power to release you, and power to crucify you?" 11 Jesus answered him, "You would have no power over me unless it had been given you from above; therefore he who delivered me to you has the greater sin." 12 Upon this Pilate sought to release him, but the Jews cried out, "If you release this man, you are not Caesar's friend; every one who makes himself a king sets himself against Caesar."

ALL *the efforts of Pilate to save Jesus have proved vain, and he can no longer shut his eyes to what the Jews are aiming at. He goes back once more to the praetorium, where he finds himself alone with the accused. Now the more Jesus suffers the more wonderful does his silent self-possession appear to the Roman governor, and the greater becomes the uneasiness of Pilate, the more painful are the reproaches of his conscience. He wants to talk with the prisoner, to penetrate into the mystery in which his personality is shrouded, and he tries to enter into conversation with him by asking him where he came from, saying: "Whence art thou?" But Jesus gave him no answer, and when Pilate tried to intimidate him by saying: "Speakest thou not unto me? Knowest thou not that I have power to crucify thee and have power to release thee?" he received a reply so lofty that his admiration was excited to the highest point, and he felt compelled to do his very utmost to rescue the dignified sufferer from the hands of his enemies.*

Let Him be Crucified [J10]

FRIGHTENED and vexed at Jesus's words, Pilate again went out upon the balcony and proclaimed his intention of freeing Jesus. Then arose the cry: "If thou release this man, thou art not Caesar's friend, for whosoever maketh himself a king, speaketh against Caesar!" Others shouted: "We will denounce thee to Caesar as a disturber of our feast. Make up thy mind at once, for under pain of punishment we must be in the temple by ten tonight." And the cry: "To the cross with him! Away with him!" resounded furiously on all sides, even from the flat roofs of the houses near the forum, upon which some of the mob had clambered. [206]

[MATTHEW 27:23] 23 And he said, "Why, what evil has he done?" But they shouted all the more, "Let him be crucified." [27:25] And all the people answered, "His blood be on us and on our children!"

THE crowd now occupies the place where Jesus had been scourged, with the column by which he had suffered rising up in the midst. On the left is the bodyguard opposite the judgment hall of Pilate with its adjoining loggia; on the right the Gabbatha, called in Greek Lithostrotos, an open tribunal paved with yellow and red stones forming a kind of rostrum where judgment was given; the name of which, as stated by Saint John (19:13), means pavement. The crowd, which was often considerable, could go up to the forum, which was reached by a few steps, and from thence could look on at the ceremony of giving judgment and hear announced the decisions of the presiding judge. On the right and left were the arches upholding the palace of the governor, one of which still exists, walled into the chapel of the convent of the nuns of Zion.

As we have seen, Pilate had hoped that the dramatic effect of his Ecce homo, with the sight of Jesus in his suffering condition, would have aroused the compassion of the mob and saved him from the odium of pronouncing a judgment for which his own conscience reproached him. Who, he had thought, could resist the effect of the sudden apparition of that bleeding specter? that head crowned with thorns, that face wounded by repeated blows, that lacerated body drooping with fatigue, covered with sweat and displaying terrible, bleeding wounds, those bound hands in which quivered the reed scepter, was not all this enough to rouse the pity of the most hardened and most barbarous hearts? He was mistaken. He had reckoned without making due allowance for the thirst for blood natural to an excited mob and without remembering the intrigues of the Sanhedrin, who were circulating among the crowds, like the perjured counselors that they were, suggesting the cry raised all too soon for the death of Jesus. In spite of his benevolent intentions, which became more decided after the message from his wife Claudia, Pilate, thanks to his weakness and successive concessions to the clamor of the people, only succeeded in adding to the sufferings of Jesus.

Pilate Washes his Hands [J11]

PILATE now saw that he could do nothing with the raging multitude. There was something truly frightful in the confusion and uproar. The whole mass of people collected before the palace was in such a state of rage and excitement that a violent insurrection was to be feared. Then Pilate called for water. The servant that brought it poured it from a vase over his hands before the people, while Pilate called down from the balcony: "I am innocent of the blood of this just man! Look ye to it!" Then went up from the assembled multitude, among whom were people from all parts of Palestine, the horrible, the unanimous cry: "His blood be upon us and upon our children!" [206]

[MATTHEW 27:24–25] 24 So when Pilate saw that he was gaining nothing, but rather that a riot was beginning, he took water and washed his hands before the crowd, saying, "I am innocent of this man's blood; see to it yourselves." 25 And all the people answered, "His blood be on us and on our children!"

THE sacred text does not seem to imply that Pilate left the spot where he had washed his hands in the presence of the assembled people. It follows, therefore, that it was not at the Gabbatha or Lithostrotos that the scene described took place, but in the so-called Ecce homo loggia, and it is there that we have chosen to represent it.

Jesus Falls Down the Steps

⊕

THE flight of steps to which the name of La Scala Santa or the Holy Stair has been given is still to be seen at Rome, to which city it was removed by Saint Helena. It is of white marble veined with grey, and it led up to the Roman praetorium, so that nothing which has been preserved to us connected with the Passion of our Lord is more worthy of the veneration of the pilgrim than are these steps, which were actually trodden by his sacred feet. Even the Via Dolorosa is less exactly what it was at the time when Christ passed along it and his blood stained the ground; for, of course, the level of the soil has been raised and modified, whereas in the sanctuaries enshrining the more enduring relics, marble facings keep worshippers to some extent at a distance. Pilgrims to the Scala Santa touch the very steps down which, according to tradition, Jesus, whose feet slipped at the top, rolled all bruised and bleeding. For this reason the Holy Stair is always climbed on the knees.

Bird's Eye View of the Forum: Jesus Hears His Death Sentence [J12]

WHILE this terrible cry was resounding on all sides, Pilate ordered preparations to be made for pronouncing the sentence. He left his palace and proceeded to the forum where, opposite the scourging place, there was a high, beautifully constructed judgment seat. Only when delivered from that seat had the sentence full weight. It was called Gabbatha. It consisted of a circular balcony, and up to it there were several flights of steps. It contained a seat for Pilate, and behind it a bench for others connected with the tribunal. The balcony was surrounded and the steps occupied by soldiers. Only Annas, Caiaphas, and about twenty-eight others went at once to the judgment seat in the forum, while Pilate was putting on his robes of ceremony. The two thieves had been taken thither when Pilate presented Jesus to the people with the words, "Ecce Homo." Pilate's seat was covered with red, and on it lay a blue cushion bordered with yellow.

And now Jesus in the scarlet cloak, the crown of thorns upon his head, his hands bound, was led by the soldiers and executioners through the mocking crowd and placed between the two murderers in front of the judgment seat. The crosses of the thieves were already lying near them, brought by the executioners' assistants. [207]

[JOHN 19:13] 13 When Pilate heard these words, he brought Jesus out and sat down on the judgment seat at a place called The Pavement, and in Hebrew, Gabbatha.

THE accompanying engraving gives an impression of a wider open space than that of the forum, and this fact must be borne in mind in reading the following notes. The large buildings in brown stone in the background are the lower portion of the massive Antonia Citadel. In it, as is well known, were situated the praetorium and the palace of the governor, Pontius Pilate; while the loggia from which he looked down as he stood beside Jesus and cried Ecce homo! can be clearly seen and is to be identified by the red carpet hanging from it. Skirting along the palace is the narrow street already referred to, leading from the Tyropeon to the Sheep Gate. Beyond this street and opposite to the gateway of the palace is the narrow entrance to the public square or forum, with a portico consisting of three columns, an architectural feature much in vogue at Jerusalem. On the left of this portico a few steps lead up to the guardhouse, in which were stationed the Roman soldiers whose business it was, under the orders of the governor, to watch over the country, nip in the bud any incipient revolt, and restore order in case of disturbance. The precaution was very far from needless, for it is a notorious fact that risings were of very frequent occurrence, especially at the great Jewish festivals. It was in the inner court of the guardhouse that, as we have already said, the crowning with thorns probably took place. In front of the portico and on the left of the guardhouse is the column at which Jesus was scourged, still all red with his blood. On the other side, that is to say on the right, is the Gabbatha or Lithostrotos to which Pilate repaired to announce the condemnation of Jesus. The Master is accompanied by the two thieves bearing their crosses; his own cross is already being prepared behind him, while lying near it is the bundle of his clothes shortly to be restored to him. The forum is filled with the Roman soldiers forming the escort of the prisoners and with the chief Jews accompanying the victim, some on horseback, some riding donkeys, and others on foot. Here and there are posted Roman sentinels to keep back the crowd. The flat roofs of the neighboring houses, belonging to the Bethesda quarter, are covered with spectators. Farther to the right at one corner of the forum, a slope leads down to the Ecce homo Arch, which marks the limit of the property belonging to the governor's palace. The town stretches far away on the left, dominated by the Zion quarter, which is reached by crossing the lower town known as the Acre quarter and the Tyropeon valley.

Jesus Leaves the Praetorium in a Scarlet Cloak [J13]

⊕

AND now Jesus in the scarlet cloak, the crown of thorns upon his head, his hands bound, was led by the soldiers and executioners through the mocking crowd and placed between the two murderers in front of the judgment seat. [207]

THE trial of Jesus is at last completed; his fate is decided, there is nothing now left to do but to pronounce the sentence from the Gabbatha. This was a formality required by the Roman law; sentence of death was always proclaimed in broad daylight and from some lofty spot. Pilate was sure to omit none of the requisite formalities, so fearful was he of compromising himself with the superior authority from whom he held his office. This dread of the Roman governor is well illustrated by the words of the Jews: "If thou let this man go, thou art not Caesar's friend." If Pilate is ready to abandon an innocent man for political reasons, still more cause is there for him to observe in the most minute particulars all the petty rules of Roman legal procedure.

The victim comes forth from the judgment hall with wounds still bleeding, the blue weals left by the scourging are still visible, his knees and elbows are grazed through many a fall, and his wrists, tightly bound with ropes and chains, are black and swollen with congested blood. Jesus is still wearing the scarlet robe which had been put upon him in mockery, and the woollen stuff sticks to the wounds on his shoulders, which are all torn and bleeding from the terrible scourging to which he has been subjected. Presently, when his own garments are returned to the divine victim, the tearing off of this "scarlet robe" will open all the wounds afresh and his blood will flow copiously yet again. It is now half past eleven, or, according to Jewish time, to quote the words of John, "near the sixth hour," and the agony of the Savior was not yet nearly over, indeed, it was now to become more terrible every moment.

The Judgment on the Gabbatha [J14]

⊕

JESUS, encircled by the executioners and greeted with rage and derisive laughter by his enemies, was standing at the foot of the steps before Pilate. The trumpet commanded silence, and with dastardly rage Pilate pronounced the sentence of death. He first spoke some words in which, with high-sounding titles, he named the Emperor Claudius Tiberius. Then he set forth the accusation against Jesus; that, as a seditious character, a disturber and violator of the Jewish laws, who had allowed himself to be called the Son of God and the king of the Jews, he had been sentenced to death by the high priests, and by the unanimous voice of the people given over to be crucified. Furthermore Pilate, that iniquitous judge, who had in these last hours so frequently and publicly asserted the innocence of Jesus, now proclaimed that he found the sentence of the high priests just, and ended with the words: "I also condemn Jesus of Nazareth, king of the Jews, to be nailed to the cross." Then he ordered the executioners to bring the cross. [207]

[JOHN 19:13] 13 When Pilate heard these words, he brought Jesus out and sat down on the judgment seat at a place called The Pavement, and in Hebrew, Gabbatha.

The Title on the Cross [J15]

PILATE next seated himself on the judgment seat and wrote out the sentence, which was copied by several officials standing behind him. Messengers were dispatched with the copies, for some of them had to be signed by others. Pilate's written condemnation against Jesus clearly showed his deceit, for its purport was altogether different from that which he had pronounced orally. I saw that he was writing against his will, in painful perplexity of mind, and as if an angel of wrath were guiding his hand. The written sentence was about as follows: "Urged by the high priests, and the Sanhedrin, and fearing an insurrection of the people who accuse Jesus of Nazareth of sedition, blasphemy, and infraction of the laws, and who demand that he should be put to death, I have (though indeed without being able to substantiate their accusations) delivered him to be crucified along with two other condemned criminals whose execution was postponed through the influence of the high priests because they wanted Jesus to suffer with them. I have condemned Jesus because I do not wish to be accused to the Emperor as an unjust judge of the Jews and as an abettor of insurrections; and I have condemned him as a criminal who has acted against the laws, and whose death has been violently demanded by the Jews."

Pilate caused many copies of this sentence to be made and sent to different places. The high priests, however, were not at all satisfied with the written sentence, especially because Pilate wrote that they had requested the crucifixion of the thieves to be postponed in order that Jesus might be executed with them. They quarrelled with Pilate about it at the judgment seat. And when with varnish he wrote on a little dark brown board the three lines of the inscription for the cross, they disputed again with him concerning the title, and demanded that it should not be "king of the Jews," but "He called himself the king of the Jews." Pilate, however, had become quite impatient and insulting, and he replied roughly: "What I have written, I have written!" [208]

[JOHN 19:19–22] 19 Pilate also wrote a title and put it on the cross; it read, "Jesus of Nazareth, the King of the Jews." 20 Many of the Jews read this title, for the place where Jesus was crucified was near the city; and it was written in Hebrew, in Latin, and in Greek. 21 The chief priests of the Jews then said to Pilate, "Do not write, 'The King of the Jews,' but, 'This man said, I am King of the Jews.'" 22 Pilate answered, "What I have written I have written."

AN *important fragment of the title which was placed above the Savior on the cross is preserved in the Church of Santa Croce de Gerusalemme at Rome. It was repeated three times, the top line being written in Hebrew, the middle line in Greek, and the bottom line in Latin; each sentence signifying exactly the same thing: Jesus of Nazareth the King of the Jews.*

As is well known, the Hebrew characters are read from right to left and the whole superscription was in red ink on a white ground. Such tablets as that employed in this instance were called tituli or tabulæ, which illustrates the fact that it was customary to write sentences of condemnation and laws on white tablets. The circlet of twisted rushes seen in our illustration was that forming the foundation of the crown of thorns, and is now preserved in the Cathedral of Notre Dame at Paris; it was brought from the East by Saint Louis, who obtained it from the Byzantine Emperor then on the throne. The thorns which accompanied this wreath are now distributed in various sanctuaries and abbeys. The roundheaded nail shown in the drawing is the one now to be seen in Rome, in the same church as the tablet on which the title is written.

They Dressed Him in His Own Garments [J16]

⊕

AFTER the proclamation of the sentence, the most holy Redeemer again fell a prey to the savage executioners. They brought him his own clothes, which had been taken from him at the mocking before Caiaphas. They had been safely kept and, I think, some compassionate people must have washed them, for they were clean. It was also, I think, customary among the Romans thus to lead the condemned to execution. Now was Jesus again stripped by the infamous ruffians, who loosened his hands that they might be able to clothe him anew. They dragged the red woollen mantle of derision from his lacerated body, and in so doing tore open many of his wounds. Tremblingly, he himself put on the undergarment about his loins, after which they threw his woollen scapular over his neck. But as they could not put on over the broad crown of thorns the brown, seamless tunic which his blessed Mother had woven, they snatched the crown from his head, causing the blood to gush anew from all the wounds with unspeakable pain. When they had put the woven tunic upon his wounded body, they threw over it his loose white, woollen robe, his broad girdle, and lastly his mantle. Then they bound around his waist the fetter girdle, by whose long cords they led him. All this took place with horrible barbarity, amid kicks and blows. [209]

[MATTHEW 27:31] 31 And when they had mocked him, they stripped him of the robe, and put his own clothes on him, and led him away to crucify him.

PILATE *and his assistants had now left the Gabbatha; the scarlet military cloak in which Jesus had been put to derision is taken off his shoulders; the blood flows afresh as the wounds are reopened and the crown of thorns is torn from the victim's brow, in order to pass over his head the seamless vesture for which lots will be cast on Golgotha. The Savior's white robe is then restored to him, together probably with his sash, sandals, and lastly his cloak. According to tradition, certain pious believers had taken charge of the garments of the Master when they were taken off after the ill-treatment he had received in the house of Caiaphas. There had been time to have them cleaned and mended. We are, we think, justified in supposing that all through his Passion Jesus was allowed to retain the undergarment of linen which Jews then wore about the loins next the skin and which was fashioned something like the underdrawers of the present day. If so, he was never perfectly naked even on Golgotha, but I feel bound to add that few agree with me on this point. There is, in fact, a tradition to the effect that when Jesus was stripped before the crucifixion his modesty was saved from being put to the blush by the charity of one of the holy women standing by. Nothing, however, confirms this touching story, which is probably after all only a pious fiction, and it is infinitely more likely that Jesus wore the light garment referred to above until the end.*

259

Jesus Bearing the Cross [J17]

⊕

AS soon as the cross was thrown on the ground before him, Jesus fell on his knees, put his arms around it, and kissed it three times while softly uttering a prayer of thanksgiving to his heavenly Father for the redemption of humankind now begun. Pagan priests were accustomed to embrace a newly erected altar, and in like manner the Lord embraced his cross, the eternal altar of the bloody sacrifice of expiation. But the executioners dragged Jesus up to a kneeling posture; and with difficulty and little help (and that of the most barbarous kind) he was forced to take the heavy beams upon his right shoulder and hold them fast with his right arm. I saw invisible angels helping him, otherwise he would have been unable to lift the cross from the ground. As he knelt, he bent under the weight. While Jesus was praying, some of the other executioners placed on the back of the two thieves the arms of their crosses (not yet fastened to the trunk), and tied their upraised hands upon them by means of a stick around which they twisted the cord. These crosspieces were not quite straight, but somewhat curved. . . . They jerked Jesus to his feet, and then fell upon his shoulder the whole weight of the cross, of that cross which, according to his own sacred words of eternal truth, we must carry after him. [210]

[JOHN 19:17] 17 So they took Jesus, and he went out, bearing his own cross, to the place called the place of a skull, which is called in Hebrew Golgotha.

CRUCIFIXION, *as is well known, is a very ancient mode of execution, and the form of the cross varied greatly. It seems to have been at first a mere stake to which the condemned was either bound or nailed, modified later by the addition of a transverse beam or branch. The name of the cross was determined by the way in which this transverse piece of wood was fastened on. If it sloped much, it was called a crus decussata, literally, an oblique cross. This was the form now called Saint Andrew's cross, and it resembled the Greek letter X. If the second branch or beam was placed across the top of the main stake the cross became a crux commissa, now often called Saint Anthony's cross, but when the central beam rose somewhat above the transverse one it formed a crux immissa, which is now known by the name of the Latin cross. To which of these three types the cross on which Jesus suffered belonged it is difficult to determine. It certainly was not that now known as Saint Andrew's; but with regard to the other two forms choice is difficult. Many authorities consider it certain that the Latin form was used, relying upon the way in which the early Fathers of the Church speak of it, comparing it to the Roman standard, to a man swimming, to a bird in flight, to the four cardinal points, to Moses praying with outstretched arms, all expressions which may be said justly to apply to the traditional form. Still, this does not really prove anything finally, for figures of rhetoric and popular similes are never particularly exact. Something far more precise in the way of evidence is needed. Moreover, it must be observed that whatever was the form of the cross when it was laid upon the shoulders of Jesus and he was compelled to carry it, it must necessarily have been converted into a crux immissa by the addition of the tablet bearing the superscription which so enraged the Jews. As for the examples of Early Christian art which have come down to us, neither do they prove anything finally, for sometimes the Latin cross and sometimes that forming the Greek letter T is introduced.*

Jesus Falls Beneath the Cross [J18]

THE procession of the crucifixion was headed by a trumpeter. Some paces behind him came a crowd of boys and other rude fellows, carrying drink, cords, nails, wedges, and baskets of tools of all kinds, while sturdy servant men bore poles, ladders, and the trunks belonging to the crosses of the thieves. Then followed some of the mounted Pharisees, after whom came a lad bearing on his breast the inscription Pilate had written for the cross. And next came our Lord and Redeemer, bowed down under the heavy weight of the cross, bruised, torn with scourges, exhausted, and tottering. The four executioners held at some distance the cords fastened to his fetter girdle. The two in front dragged him forward, while the two behind urged him on. Then came the two thieves, each led by two executioners holding cords fastened to their girdles. They had the curved crosspieces belonging to the trunk of their crosses fastened on their backs, with their outstretched arms bound to the ends of them, and on their head a cap of twisted straw. The executioners wore only a short tunic like an apron, and on their breast was a leathern covering without sleeves.

The procession formed for Jesus wound through a very narrow back street. Toward the end of that street, or alley, the way turned again to the left, becoming broader and somewhat steep. Just here where the street begins to ascend there was a hollow place often filled, after a rain, with mud and water. In it, as in many such places in the streets of Jerusalem, lay a large stone to facilitate crossing. Poor Jesus, on reaching this spot with his heavy burden, could go no farther. The executioners pulled him by the cords and pushed him unmercifully. Then did the divine cross-bearer fall full length on the ground by the projecting stone, his burden at his side. The drivers, with curses, pulled him and kicked him. This brought the procession to a halt, and a tumult arose around Jesus. In vain did he stretch out his hand for someone to help him. "Ah! It will soon be over!" He exclaimed, and continued to pray. [211]

[LUKE 23:27] 27 And there followed him a great multitude of the people, and of women who bewailed and lamented him.

THE street is terribly steep and the big stones with which it is paved are slippery, so that Jesus, exhausted with fatigue, falls beneath his burden. Those in attendance on him are in no mood to give him any assistance, they only jeer at and insult him, pouring out opprobrious epithets upon him. All around, however, are crowds whose attitude is rather noisy and excited than positively hostile. "A great company of people followed him," says Luke, and there was nothing surprising in the numbers which had come together, for executions always attract a concourse of people. Moreover, it was the time of the Passover and, as is well known, that festival was always attended by vast multitudes, all of whom had been from the commencement of the trial deeply interested in the fate of the prophet about whom there had been so much discussion. Jesus as he falls seems in my picture to be appealing to the bystanders for a little help in his need. Shall we not do well to remember that it was for us that the Savior suffered so long ago as well as for those living at the time?

Jesus Meets His Mother [J19]

⊕

MARY could no longer remain at a distance. She must behold her divine Son in his sufferings, and she begged John to take her to some place that Jesus would pass. They left, in consequence, the vicinity of Zion, passed the judgment seat, and went through gates and shady walks which were open just now to the people streaming hither and thither, to the western side of a palace which had an arched gateway on the street into which the procession turned after Jesus's first fall. When the servant opened the gate, the noise became more distinct and alarming.

Mary was in prayer. She said to John: "Shall I stay to behold it, or shall I hurry away? Oh, how shall I be able to endure it?" John replied: "If thou dost not remain, it will always be to thee a cruel regret."

And now came on the executioner's servants, insolent and triumphant, with their instruments of torture, at sight of which the blessed Mother trembled, sobbed, and wrung her hands. One of the men said to the bystanders: "Who is that woman in such distress?" And someone answered: "She is the mother of the Galilean." When the miscreants heard this, they jeered at the sorrowing mother in words of scorn, pointed at her with their fingers; and one of the base wretches, snatching up the nails intended for the crucifixion, held them up mockingly before her face.

Tottering, bowed down, his thorn-crowned head painfully bent over to one shoulder on account of the heavy cross he was carrying, Jesus staggered on. The executioners pulled him forward with the ropes. His face was pale, wounded, and bloodstained, his beard pointed and matted with blood. From his sunken eyes full of blood he cast, from under the tangled and twisted thorns of his crown, frightful to behold, a look full of earnest tenderness upon his afflicted mother, and for the second time tottered under the weight of the cross and sank on his hands and knees to the ground.

The most sorrowful mother, in vehemence of her love and anguish, saw neither soldiers nor executioners—saw only her beloved, suffering, maltreated Son. Wringing her hands, she sprang over the couple of steps between the gateway and the executioners in advance, and rushing to Jesus, fell on her knees with her arms around him. I heard, but I know not whether spoken with the lips or in spirit, the words: "My Son!"—"My Mother!" [212]

THE meeting of Jesus with his mother is not referred to in the gospel narrative, but tradition is unanimous in asserting that it took place at the fourth station of the Via Dolorosa. Mary was accompanied by John, Mary Magdalene, and Mary Salome, with other holy women, who, the evangelists tell us, followed the Master to Golgotha.

It was very natural that the mother of the Lord should have been present in the forum at the scourging, though at a distance, and should have witnessed from afar the Ecce Homo incident; in fact, that she should have seen all that the rest of the crowd did. When the procession began to move off on its way to Golgotha, Mary, who had just heard the sentence of death passed upon her son from the Gabbatha and who had seen the cross placed upon his shoulders, tried to get near enough to him to help him with his burden, but it was impossible, for the narrow street was already blocked up with soldiers and the crowds accompanying the victim. The Virgin was, therefore, compelled to take another route. A tradition tells us that in the angle formed by the street leading to the Sheep Gate and the Tyropoeon Valley, or Valley of the Cheese Merchants, there was a house with courtyards and out-buildings belonging to Caiaphas, who, as we know, had his judgment hall in the Zion quarter. Now John, as already stated above, had relations among the attendants of the high priest, and it was thanks to this circumstance that he was able to go into the judgment hall and to secure the admittance of Peter. He would thus also be able to let the blessed Virgin and her companions pass through the courts and gardens of this house and, cutting diagonally across from one street to another, he managed for the little party of friends of Jesus to arrive at the fourth station of the cross in time to meet him without having to go up the steep ascent climbed by the procession. It is generally supposed that the fall of Jesus occurred at the very moment of the touching meeting.

Simon the Cyrenian Compelled to Carry the Cross with Jesus [J20]

⊕

AFTER going some distance up the broad street, the procession passed through a gateway in an old inner wall of the city. In front of this gate was a wide open space at which three streets met. There was a large stepping stone here, over which Jesus staggered and fell, the cross by his side. He lay on the ground, leaning against the stone, unable to rise. Just then appeared, coming straight down the middle of the street, Simon of Cyrene, a pagan, followed by his three sons. He was carrying a bundle of sprigs under his arm, for he was a gardener, and he had been working in the gardens toward the eastern wall of the city. Every year about the time of the feast, he was accustomed to come up to Jerusalem with his wife and children, to trim the hedges. Many other laborers used to come for the same purpose. The crowd was so great that he could not escape, and as soon as the soldiers saw by his dress that he was a poor pagan laborer, they laid hold on him and dragged him forward to help carry the Galilean's cross. He resisted and showed great unwillingness, but they forcibly constrained him.

Simon was filled with disgust and repugnance for the task imposed upon him. Poor Jesus looked so horribly miserable, so awfully disfigured, and his garments were covered with mud; but he was weeping, and he cast upon Simon a glance that roused his compassion. He had to help him up. Then the executioners tied one arm of the cross toward the end of the trunk, made a loop of the cords, and passed it over Simon's shoulder. He walked close behind Jesus, thus greatly lightening his burden. They rearranged the crown of thorns, and at last the dolorous procession resumed its march. [213]

[MARK 15:21] 21 And they compelled a passerby, Simon of Cyrene, who was coming in from the country, the father of Alexander and Rufus, to carry his cross.

WHEN Jesus fell the second time, his enemies began to be uneasy. He would never, they feared, get up the ascent to Golgotha without help. They therefore resolved to let him have a little assistance, and the man named Simon happening to be at hand, they compelled him to carry the cross. This Simon came from Cyrene, a province situated on the northern coast of Africa, where there was then a very numerous colony of Jews. It would appear that he was domiciled at Jerusalem, for the gospel narrative says he was passing by "coming out of the country." He was, adds Mark, the father of Alexander and Rufus, which proves that all three were known to the evangelists at the time of the compilation of the sacred text. It is, in fact, supposed that these sons of Simon, Alexander and Rufus, were converted to Christianity later and became deacons of the early Church. In the Epistle of Paul to the Romans occur the words: "Salute Rufus chosen in the Lord," and the Roman martyrology includes Simon of Cyrene among the saints. Some even say that he become bishop of Bostra in the Syrian Desert, and that he was burnt to death by the heathen authorities. There is a point of dispute as to whether the Cyrenian carried the cross the rest of the way alone or whether he merely shared the burden with Jesus. The gospel narrative would appear to favor the former interpretation of the incident, but it might also be taken to mean the latter, which was the most prevalent belief among the early Christians, and as a result was generally adopted by painters. We think, therefore, that we are fairly justified in assuming that Jesus bore the upper part of the cross with the transverse beam and that Simon merely upheld the long heavy central beam, the dragging weight of which added so greatly to the burden of the victim. Another very natural suggestion has been made and that is that we owe to Simon and his two sons the account of all that passed until the arrival of the Master at Calvary. As a matter of fact, they were of course able to see and hear everything; they were indeed the only witnesses who could do so, for none of the apostles were near; John, the blessed Virgin, and the other holy women were unable to follow Jesus except afar off, on account of the crowds and the narrowness of the streets. They did not all meet again until they got to Golgotha itself.

Seraphia (Veronica) Wipes the Face of Jesus [J21]

⊕

THE street through which Jesus was now going was long and somewhat winding, and into it several side streets ran. From all quarters respectable-looking people were on their way to the temple. They stepped back, some from a pharisaical fear of becoming legally impure, others moved by a feeling of compassion. Simon had assisted the Lord with his burden almost two hundred paces when, from a handsome house on the left side of the street, up to whose forecourt (which was enclosed by a low, broad wall surmounted by a railing of some kind of shining metal) a flight of terraced steps led, there issued a tall, elegant-looking woman, holding a little girl by the hand, and rushed forward to meet the procession. It was Seraphia, the wife of Sirach, one of the members of the council belonging to the temple. Owing to her action of this day, she received the name of Veronica from *vera* (true) and *icon* (picture, or image).

As the procession drew near, she stepped out into the street veiled, a linen cloth hanging over her shoulder. A little girl, who was about nine years old, was standing by her with a mug of wine hidden under her little mantle. Those at the head of the procession tried in vain to keep her back. Transported with love and compassion, with the child holding fast to her dress, she pressed through the mob running at the side of the procession, in through the soldiers and executioners, stepped before Jesus, fell on her knees, and held up to him the outspread end of the linen kerchief, with these words of entreaty: "Permit me to wipe the face of my Lord!" Jesus seized the kerchief with his left hand and, with the flat, open palm, pressed it against his bloodstained face. Then passing it still with the left hand toward the right, which was grasping the arm of the cross, he pressed it between both palms and handed it back to Seraphia with thanks. She kissed it, hid it beneath her mantle, where she pressed it to her heart, and arose to her feet. Then the little girl timidly held up the mug of wine, but the brutal soldiers and executioners would not permit her to refresh Jesus with it.

This sudden and daring act of Seraphia caused a stoppage in the procession of hardly two minutes, of which she made use to present the kerchief. The mounted Pharisees, as well as the executioners, were enraged at the delay, and still more at this public homage rendered to the Lord. They began, in consequence, to beat and pull Jesus. Veronica meanwhile fled back with the child to her house. [214]

JESUS is still painfully toiling up the long narrow street skirting along one of the inner walls of the town and leading up to Golgotha. The higher he climbs the more slowly he goes. He is panting for breath beneath his load, in spite of the help of the Cyrenian. From time to time he is compelled to pause altogether, overwhelmed with fatigue and exhausted from the loss of so much blood. Tradition now intervenes with a touching story of how a lady of Jerusalem, a great lady connected with many of the chief Jewish families and, moreover, secretly in intimate relations with the family and friends of Jesus, approached the sufferer, eager to do something to console him. According to some accounts, her name was Berenice, but Anne Catherine Emmerich speaks of her as Seraphia, the wife of Sirach, a member of the Sanhedrin. Whatever her original name may have been, however, she has ever since been known in Catholic tradition by the symbolic title of Veronica, from the words vera icon, *signifying true portrait, and referring to the miracle said to have been affected by her means. Learning that the procession would pass her house this good woman determined to seize the opportunity of showing yet once more her reverence and compassion for Jesus. She had prepared a cordial which should restore his strength, and, just as the group of which the Lord was the central figure was passing her door, she issued from her house, which was on the left side of the street, so as to meet him face to face.*

The Holy Face [J22]

⊕

SCARCELY had Seraphia reached her own apartment when, laying the kerchief on a table, she sank down unconscious. The little girl, still holding the mug of wine, knelt whimpering by her. A friend of the family, entering the room, found her in this condition. She glanced at the outspread kerchief and beheld upon it the bloody face of Jesus frightfully, but with wonderful distinctness, impressed. It looked like the face of a corpse. She roused Seraphia and showed her the Lord's image. It filled her with grief and consolation, and casting herself on her knees before the kerchief, she exclaimed: "Now will I leave all, for the Lord has given to me a memento!" This kerchief was a strip of fine wool about three times as long as wide. It was usually worn around the neck, and sometimes a second was thrown over the shoulder. It was customary upon meeting one in sorrow, in tears, in misery, in sickness, or in fatigue, to present it to wipe the face. It was a sign of mourning and sympathy. Seraphia ever after kept this kerchief hanging at the head of her bed. After her death, it was given by the holy women to the Mother of God, and through the apostles at last came into the possession of the church. [214]

NOW Jesus, wishing to recompense Seraphia for this act of pious pity, so used the linen cloth that, with the blood from his wounds which filled all the hollows of his face, his beard, his eyebrows, and his nostrils, he produced a perfect likeness of his features upon the surface of the cloth. No doubt the linen was in this case a kind of veil of very fine material such as Jewish women were in the habit of wearing on the head and shoulders. Veronica treasured it up with pious reverence, handing it over later to the care of the church, and it is now preserved and shown to the faithful at Rome.

The Daughters of Jerusalem [J23]

THE procession had still a good distance to go before reaching the gate, and the street in that direction was somewhat declining. The gate was strong and high. To reach it, one had to go first through a vaulted arch, then across a bridge, then through another archway. As the procession neared the gate, the executioners pressed on more violently. Close to the gate there was a large puddle of muddy water in the uneven road, cut up by vehicles. The barbarous executioners jerked Jesus forward; the crowd pressed. Simon of Cyrene tried to step sideways for the sake of convenience, thereby moving the cross out of its place, and poor Jesus for the fourth time fell so heavily under his burden into the muddy pool that Simon could scarcely support the cross.

In the center of the highroad and opposite the gate where the way branched off to Mount Calvary, stood a post supporting a board upon which, in white raised letters that looked as if they were done in paste, was written the death sentence of our Savior and the two thieves. Not far from this spot, at the corner of the road, a large number of women might be seen weeping and lamenting. Some were young maidens, others poor married women, who had run out from Jerusalem to meet the procession; others were from Bethlehem, Hebron, and the neighboring places, who, coming up for the feast, had here joined the women of Jerusalem.

Jesus again sank fainting. He did not fall to the ground, because Simon, resting the end of the cross upon the earth, drew nearer and supported his bowed form. The Lord leaned on him. This was the fifth fall of Jesus while carrying his cross. At sight of his countenance so utterly wretched, the women raised a loud cry of sorrow and pity and, after the Jewish manner of showing compassion, extended toward him kerchiefs with which to wipe off the perspiration. At this Jesus turned to them and said: "Daughters of Jerusalem" (which meant, also, people from other Jewish cities), "weep not over me, but weep for yourselves and for your children. For behold, the days shall come wherein they will say: 'Blessed are the barren and the wombs that have not borne, and the paps that have not given suck!' Then shall they begin to say to the mountains: 'Fall upon us!' and to the hills: 'Cover us!' For if in the green wood they do these things, what shall be done in the dry?" Jesus said some other beautiful words to the women, but I have forgotten them. Among them, however, I remember these: "Your tears shall be rewarded. Henceforth, ye shall tread another path," etc. [216]

[LUKE 23:27–31] 27 And there followed him a great multitude of the people, and of women who bewailed and lamented him. 28 But Jesus turning to them said, "Daughters of Jerusalem, do not weep for me, but weep for yourselves and for your children. 29 For behold, the days are coming when they will say, 'Blessed are the barren, and the wombs that never bore, and the breasts that never gave suck!' 30 Then they will begin to say to the mountains, 'Fall on us'; and to the hills, 'Cover us.' 31 For if they do this when the wood is green, what will happen when it is dry?"

THE procession has passed through the gate of judgment and now halts beyond it for the coming up of the rearguard, which has been delayed by the necessity of keeping back the crowds. At the small gateway itself the pressure has become immense and the people are wedged together in dense masses; the procession itself, on the other hand, has now emerged from the narrow streets and the precautions against surprise must be redoubled, for the governor is still anxious, there being always some fear of a revolt. The many women who have followed at a distance are now able to approach Jesus, with others who happened just then to be in the neighborhood of the well of Amygdalum or of Hezekiah. Their wailing and sobs add yet more to the pathos of the scene of which the exhausted and tottering victim is the central figure. Jesus, availing himself of the brief halt at the foot of Mount Golgotha, which he has soon to climb, turns to the weeping women and answers their compassionate outcry with a few solemn words which are his last exhortation before his death: "Weep not for me but for yourselves and for your children." There is now but one more effort to be made, and, still with the aid of Simon of Cyrene, Jesus resumes the painful march. It is now about half past twelve.

Golgotha and Holy Sepulcher, Seen from Walls of the Judicial Gate [J24]

THE procession again moved onward. With blows and violent jerking at the cords that bound him, Jesus was driven up the rough, uneven path between the city wall and Mount Calvary toward the north. At a spot where the winding path in its ascent turned toward the south, poor Jesus fell again for the sixth time. But his tormentors beat him and drove him on more rudely than ever until he reached the top of the rock, the place of execution, when with the cross he fell heavily to the earth for the seventh time. The place of execution, which was on the level top of the mount, was circular, and of a size that could be enclosed in the cemetery of our own parish church. It was like a tolerably large riding ground, and was surrounded by a low wall of earth, through which five pathways were cut. Five paths, or entrances, of this kind seemed to be peculiar to this country in the laying out of different places; for instance, bathing places, baptismal pools, and the pool of Bethesda. Many of the cities also were built with five gates. This arrangement is found in all designs belonging to the olden times, and also in those of more modern date built in the spirit of pious imitation. As with all other things in the Holy Land, it breathed a deeply prophetic signification, which on this day received its realization in the opening of those five ways to salvation, the five sacred wounds of Jesus. [216]

WITH a view to helping the reader to form an accurate idea of the scene of the crucifixion, which is of so much importance for all who would follow the gospel narrative, we have done our beset to give a faithful restoration of Golgotha and the districts surrounding it, as they were two thousand years ago. At the present day all the sacred sites are covered over with buildings: temples, chapels, galleries, courts, domes, etc., enshrining them like relics in a reliquary, and these various structures at first sight appear very complicated and confusing, too much so, perhaps. As a matter of fact, the erection of these various works necessitated a very considerable leveling of the soil, and the slopes of the little mountain have been constantly tampered with from early Christian times until the present day. Our plans will serve to give some idea of the original appearance of the district.

To begin with, there is the elevation known as Calvary or Golgotha which was but a few feet high. The first of these names is the Latin translation of the second, which signifies "the place of a skull," or merely a skull. According to an old legend, the hill was called the "place of a skull" because the skull of Adam, which had been preserved by Noah, was buried in it.

On the summit of Golgotha can be seen the holes in which the three crosses were placed, a low wall encircling the sacred spot. In the foreground a ruin will be noticed, at the bottom of which is a pit into which the beams which had formed the instruments of the execution, that is to say, the crosses of the Savior and of the two thieves, were thrown after the crucifixion. It was Saint Helena who in the first instance discovered them, when she was having some excavations made under the guidance of an old Jew who knew the tradition relating to the site. At the top of the slope leading down to this pit is the spot where the soldiers cast lots for the garments of Jesus, and a little lower down is the cistern to which the Master is said to have been allowed to retire while the cross was got ready for his execution. Beyond Golgotha, on the slope to the right, can be seen the entrance to the Garden of Joseph of Arimathea, surrounded by a low wall, above which is seen the top of the Holy Sepulcher, while in the background rises the palace of Herod, with its towers standing out against the landscape between Jerusalem and Bethlehem.

Golgotha and Holy Sepulcher, Seen from Walls of Herod's Palace [J25]

IN this restoration the three holes in which the crosses were placed can be seen again in their little enclosure, while behind them are the walls of the town and the gate of judgment. In the distance, beyond the massive buildings of the temple and the Antonia Tower, rises the Mount of Olives with Mount Scopus on the left, where Titus encamped when he besieged Jerusalem. Below the summit of Golgotha is the cave named after Melchizedek.

According to the legend relating to the skull of Adam, that skull was placed in this cave by Shem, who received it from Noah as a special privilege, on account of his having been the founder of the favored race which was to give birth to the Messiah. And Shem, actuated by prophetic insight, deposited the skull on the very spot on which he knew that the Messiah was to die, and, continues the legend, when the Savior died and the rocks were rent in twain, the blood which flowed from the cross ran down through the fissures of the cave till some of it reached the skull and washed away the sins of the first man. The words of Paul (Ephesians 5:14): "Awake thou that sleepest, and arise from the dead, and Christ shall give thee light" are by some critics supposed to refer to this incident. Hence Saint Ambrose, commenting on the Gospel of Luke, teaches that Christ was crucified on Golgotha because it was fitting that the life which we should receive through the Redeemer should begin where he through whom death first entered the world was buried.

In front of the cave is a flat stone called the Stone of Anointing, on which the body of Jesus was placed after the deposition from the cross, to be washed and anointed with spices. Nearer to the spectator is another flat stone of considerable size, on which it is said some of the Holy Women stood at the beginning of the crucifixion. Later, the Blessed Virgin, with Mary Magdalene and Mary Salome, approached the platform of Golgotha on the right, to look on from thence at the execution. On the left can still be seen the wall of the garden of Joseph of Arimathea, which is partly hewn out of the living rock. Still farther to the left is a suburb of Jerusalem with its numerous houses. [216]

The Procession Nearing Golgotha [J26]

⊕

THE Pharisees on horseback drew up on the western side beyond the circle, where the mountain sloped gently; that toward the city, up which the criminals were brought, was steep and rough. A great crowd, mostly of the vulgar class, who had no fear of defilement, strangers, servants, slaves, pagans, and numbers of women, were standing around the circle. It was about a quarter to twelve when Jesus, laden with the cross, was dragged into the place of execution, thrown on the ground, and Simon driven off. The executioners then pulled Jesus up by the cords, took the sections of the cross apart, and put them together again in proper form. [216]

[MARK 15:22] 22 And they brought him to the place called Golgotha (which means the place of a skull).

MANY *paths led up the slopes of Golgotha, and Jesus is compelled to take the shortest, which is also the steepest. Simon the Cyrenian, with his two sons, Alexander and Rufus, at a little distance behind, come to help him to rise as he falls for the last few times. The thieves follow him, each bearing the upper portion of his own cross, called in Latin the* patibulum, *which, according to Plautus, condemned criminals were compelled to carry all round the town before their execution. The assistants bring up the rear laden with everything which will be required for the erection of the crosses and for the carrying out of all the legal formalities; one has the nails, hammers, and ropes, another the vinegar and the wine mixed with myrrh, etc. The Pharisees and the chief priests, mounted on horses or asses, take an easier path, which makes more of a detour, to reach the platform of Golgotha, where they look forward to gloating on all the terrible details of the execution. On the left can be seen the wall enclosing the garden of Joseph of Arimathea in which is a sepulcher hewn out of the living rock, where Jesus was soon to be buried.*

The Holy Women Watch from Afar [J27]

⊕

AFTER that most painful meeting with her divine Son carrying his cross before the dwelling of Caiaphas, the most afflicted mother was conducted by John and the holy women, Johanna Chusa, Susanna, and Salome, to the house of Nazareth in the vicinity of the corner gate. Here the other holy women, in tears and lamentations, were gathered around Magdalene and Martha. Some children were with them. They now went all together, in number seventeen, with the blessed Virgin, careless of the jeers of the mob, grave and resolute, and by their tears awe-inspiring, across the forum, where they kissed the spot upon which Jesus had taken up the burden of the cross. Thence they proceeded along the whole of the sorrowful way trodden by him and venerated the places marked by special sufferings.

The holy band of mourners now arrived at Veronica's dwelling, which they entered, for Pilate with his riders and two hundred soldiers, having turned back at the city gate, was coming along the street. Here with tears and expressions of sorrow, the holy women gazed upon the face of Jesus impressed upon Veronica's veil, and glorified his goodness toward his faithful friend. Taking the vessel of aromatic wine which Veronica had not been permitted to present to Jesus, they went to the gate nearby and out to Golgotha. They went up the hill by the gently sloping western side and stood in three groups, one behind the other, outside the wall enclosing the circle. The mother of Jesus, her niece Mary Cleophas, Salome, and John stood close to the circle. Martha, Mary Heli, Veronica, Johanna Chusa, Susanna, and Mary Mark stood a little distance back around Magdalene, who could no longer restrain herself. Still farther back were about seven others, and between these groups were some well-disposed individuals who carried messages backward and forward. The mounted Pharisees were stationed in groups at various points around the circle, and the five entrances were guarded by Roman soldiers. [218]

[LUKE 23:49] 49 And all his acquaintances and the women who had followed him from Galilee stood at a distance and saw these things.

THE crowd had now been driven away from the scene of the approaching crucifixion by the soldiers on guard. The cross was being made ready and had assumed its final form by the addition of the title set up above it, which had been carried thus far by the herald. The enemies of Jesus tried to cause a tumult on account of the tenor of this description: "Jesus of Nazareth the King of the Jews." They understood well enough that Pilate, in inscribing such a title as this, intended to mock them by a covert allusion to their dependence on Rome, and they had tried to make him alter it by saying, "Write not the King of the Jews; but that he said: I am the King of the Jews"; to which Pilate had replied haughtily enough: "What I have written, I have written."

The holes for the nails were made beforehand by piercing the wood so as to save trouble at the end. The nails were, in fact, used like pegs, and of course preliminary measurements had to be taken, which occupied a good deal of time. While the men whose duty it was to prepare the cross were going to and fro, a cordon of sentinels, chosen from among the Roman soldiers, surrounded the little hill.

According to certain traditions which have come down to us, the legion then on duty at Jerusalem consisted of men from Switzerland and Gaul. They dispersed the spectators and kept them at a distance, so that Mary the Mother of Jesus and the other holy women were not able to approach near to Jesus. Among the holy women were Mary, the wife of Cleophas and sister of the Blessed Virgin; the mother of James the Less and of John Salome with Mary Magdalene. From the distance they could only see the general stir of preparation for the execution; but no doubt John, who, as already stated, could circulate freely among the authorities, came to them now and then with the news of such details as he observed. According to tradition also, it was not until Jesus was laid upon the cross and the first moans were wrung from him by the anguish caused by the driving of the nails into his hands, that the loving watchers, unable any longer to refrain themselves, forced their way on to Mount Golgotha, the sentinels letting the mother of the condemned victim pass, and with her her immediate attendants. They are said to have taken up their stand at the edge of the platform, on a spot overlooking the rock above a natural excavation which had there been hollowed out.

281

Jesus Taken from the Cistern [J28]

⊕

THE executioners now dragged Jesus up again and led him, bound, about seventy steps northward down to a cave cut in the rock. It looked as if intended for a cellar, or cistern. They raised the door and pushed him down so unmercifully that, without a miracle, his knees would have been crushed on the rough stone floor. I heard his loud, sharp cries of pain. The executioners closed the door above him, and set guards before it.

Four executioners now went to the prison cave, seventy steps northward, and dragged Jesus out. He was imploring God for strength and offering himself once more for the sins of his enemies. They dragged him with pushes, blows, and insults over these last steps of his Passion. The people stared and jeered; the soldiers, cold and grave, stood proudly erect keeping order; the executioners furiously snatched him from the hands of his guards and dragged him violently into the circle. [218]

ACCORDING to an old Greek tradition, this is what happened between the arrival at Golgotha and the crucifixion on a certain spot now enclosed within the Church of the Holy Sepulcher and there venerated by the Christian believer. Some of the escorts of Jesus were engaged in preparing the wood for the cross, while others put the pieces together and placed in the right position the cord for raising the instrument of death when the victim should be bound to it. While all this was going on in the very restricted space at the disposal of the executioners, it was only natural that the guards should have cleared the ground as much as possible and have put the prisoners out of the way for the time being. Jesus, says the tradition referred to above, was therefore removed to an old excavation in the rock, rather like the cistern of a well, situated a few paces off, on the northwest of the platform of Golgotha. The guards pushed him roughly along, making him fall on his knees more than once in the short distance, and then flinging him into the cave all bleeding and bruised. There his feet were passed through two holes in a stone and fastened together with a chain, and thus bound the sufferer was left in the pit with a guard on watch. The two thieves, still bound to the cross-beams of their respective crosses, had to lie on the ground, for in that position they were less likely to be able to make any attempt at escape. The preparations meanwhile went briskly forward, and, when they were on the point of completion, the soldiers went to fetch the chief victim and drew him forth from the pit to lead him to the platform of Golgotha.

The Vase of Myrrh and Gall [J29]

AT last, they tore off his girdle and Jesus bent over as if trying to hide himself. As he appeared about to swoon in their hands, they set him upon a stone that had been rolled nearby, thrust the crown of thorns again upon his head, and offered him a drink from that other vessel of gall and vinegar. But Jesus turned his head away in silence. [218]

[MATTHEW 27:34] 34 they offered him wine to drink, mingled with gall; but when he tasted it, he would not drink it. [MARK 15:23] 23 And they offered him wine mingled with myrrh; but he did not take it.

JESUS, then, has been deprived of his garments. After the toilsome assent to Golgotha, his body is doubtless covered with sweat. Exposed as he now is to the chill air on the summit of the hill and to the drizzling rain which is falling, he shivers with cold. The "darkness over all the land," which was to mark the hours of his dying anguish, was already heralded by a sinister gloom resulting from the gathering together of masses of cloud. He turns pale and sinks exhausted on to the cross laid on the ground ready to receive him. Seeing him so weak, his enemies fear that his strength will give way utterly, that he will swoon or faint, and thus retard or even prevent the execution by dying before its accomplishment. Their desire is that he should be crucified in the full possession of all his faculties, and not in an unconscious state. They want to hear his cries of anguish; they want to gaze on his features all distorted with pain; they long to see his limbs convulsed under the long drawn out torture of the cross. They have a ready-prepared cordial at hand and they offer it to him to drink. It consists of wine mixed with myrrh, intended to revive the victim for a time and make him keenly alive to every pang. This was not, however, in accordance with the generally received idea of the purpose of beverages of this kind; in the opinion of the populace they were intended to mitigate the sufferings of those condemned to death, and this thought was suggested by a passage in the book of Proverbs (31: 6–7): "Give strong drink unto him that is ready to perish, and wine unto those that be of heavy hearts. Let him drink and forget his poverty, and remember his misery no more." Among the Romans a drink of this kind was called sopor, *on account of its power to benumb and in some cases to deaden the senses entirely. The task of preparing this beverage was reserved to ladies of the highest rank, and it was no doubt to them that Matthew referred in the present instance. There is, however, a divergence between his account and that of Mark. The latter speaks very distinctly of wine mingled with myrrh, while the former says: "they gave him vinegar to drink mingled with gall." We may perhaps suppose that Matthew heard a bitter drink spoken of, and if so, the beverage might be taken to be composed of vinegar and myrrh, or of vinegar and some such substance as bitter apple, which, on account of its extreme bitterness, was called gall by the Jews. "When Jesus," adds the evangelist, "had tasted thereof he would not drink"; he needed neither to dull his senses to give himself courage nor did he want a stimulant to aid him to rally his forces; his momentary rest had restored to him all his strength of endurance. After the first shock was over, his blood flowed freely again, and he gave himself up to his executioners, who flung him brutally down upon the cross.*

Jesus Stripped of His Clothing [J30]

⊕

THE executioners next laid Christ's cross on the spot upon which they intended to crucify him, so that it could be conveniently raised and deposited in the hole made to receive it. They fitted the tenons of the two arms into the mortises made for them in the trunk, nailed on the foot-block, bored the holes for the nails and also for the title written by Pilate, hammered in the wedges under the mortised arms, and made hollow places here and there down the trunk. These were intended to receive the crown of thorns and Jesus's back, so that his body might rather stand than hang, thus preventing the hands from being torn by the weight and hastening death. In the earth behind the little eminence they sank a post with a crossbeam around which the ropes for raising the cross could be wound. They made several other preparations of a similar nature. And now the executioners tore from our Lord the mantle they had flung around his shoulders. They next removed the fetter-girdle along with his own, and dragged the white woollen tunic over his head. Down the breast it had a slit bound with leather. When they wanted to remove the brown, seamless robe that his blessed mother had knit for him, they could not draw it over his head, on account of the projecting crown of thorns. They consequently tore the crown again from his head, opening all the wounds afresh, tucked up the woven tunic and, with words of imprecation and insult, pulled it over his wounded and bleeding head. [218]

ALL is now ready; the wood of the cross has been screwed together and made perfectly strong and firm; the ropes for raising it are in their places, the holes for the nails are bored. Time presses, not a moment must be lost! Jesus is now led forth and the stripping off of his garments begins. Of course the crown of thorns is the first thing taken off, as "the vesture that is without seam" could only be removed by dragging it over the head of the Savior. That "vesture" was soaked with the blood of the sufferer and stuck to the unhealed wounds inflicted on him in the scourging, so that when it was torn off much fresh suffering must have been caused by the pulling away with it of portions of lacerated flesh. The seamless garment removed, nothing was left but the short linen drawers such as are worn by all Jews. Certain critics assert that even these were taken off so as to make the victim drink the very dregs of shame, and that one of the holy women, some say the blessed Virgin herself, came forward to offer to the Savior a garment to cover his nudity. Yet others claim that it was a young man who arrived in the very nick of time to supply the sufferer's need. However that may be, there is little doubt that when on the cross Jesus was girt about the loins with linen drapery. It would indeed have been a most extraordinary exception had it been otherwise in a Jewish country. Nevertheless, a certain number of the Fathers of the Church have asserted their belief in the complete nudity of the Savior at his execution, seeing in it many beautiful mystic meanings, such as the parallel which will naturally occur to every one, between the nudity of the first man and that of the second Adam.

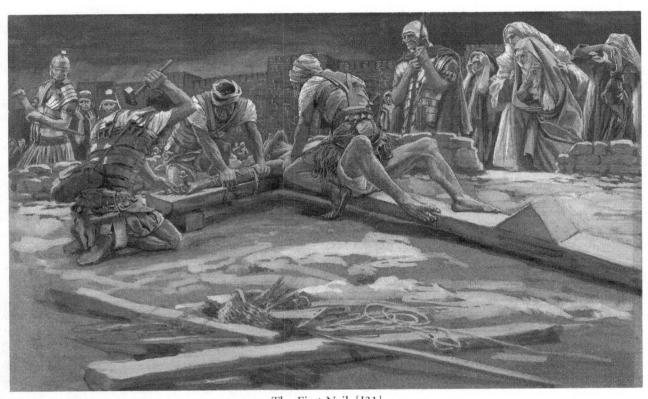

The First Nail [J31]

⊕

JESUS was now stretched on the cross by the executioners. He had lain himself upon it; but they pushed him lower down into the hollow places, rudely drew his right hand to the hole for the nail in the right arm of the cross, and tied his wrist fast. One knelt on his sacred breast and another held the closing hand flat; another placed the long, thick nail, which had been filed to a sharp point, upon the palm of his sacred hand, and struck furious blows with the iron hammer. [219]

[MARK 15:25] 25 And it was the third hour, when they crucified him.

IT was, of course, with the hands that the horribly painful operation of the nailing began; but, as there was a danger that the weight of the body would tear away the flesh, the probability is that the limbs were first bound to the cross with cords. It is evident that but for some such precaution the work could not have been properly done. The upper part of the body was also kept in place by a whole series of ligatures, which must indeed have added in a very marked degree to the sufferings of the condemned, for, if they were drawn tight enough to be of any use in binding the victim to the instrument of death, they must have eaten into the flesh, and by compressing the chest, have made respiration horribly painful, while the free circulation of the blood was also checked. Without these cords supporting the body by being passed under the armpits, the victim could not long have retained his position, for on the slightest slipping of the limbs, or the first swoon of the sufferer, the knees would have bent, the head would have fallen forward and the body would have followed it, drawn out of the perpendicular by its own weight. Then the hands would have dragged away from the nails and a horrible fall would have broken the legs, which were held in position by the nail in the feet. Such skilled workmen as the executioners in the service of Pilate, accustomed for a long time to their sinister task of crucifying malefactors, were not at all likely to risk any such accident; they are very sure to have bound Jesus securely before they drove in the nails.

Jesus, then, lies extended on the cross, the body placed in the right position for his martyrdom; one arm is bound down to begin with, the hand extended so that the palm comes over the hole already pierced in the wood. Then one of the executioners drives the point of the huge nail in with vigorous blows from his hammer. As the first blow rings out, a groan escapes the lips of the victim, and from a little distance a cry replies to it, for Mary, the mother of the sufferer, is standing with the other holy women at the foot of the mount, and she rushes forward as if to succor her divine Son.

The first nail driven home, the upper part of the body is stretched out horizontally and the second arm is made fast with ropes. Another nail is driven in, and one of the executioners flings himself astride upon the sufferer to hold him down. The next step is to bind the head and shoulders to the cross, and then the legs, all quivering with anguish, are drawn down while the executioners put out all their strength to drive the third nail through both feet.

All this time the friends of Jesus are bewailing his terrible sufferings; they cling to each other and huddle together, wild with compassion and misery, as they listen to his moans, while at each stroke of the hammer they shudder afresh. They have gradually approached the scene of the awful drama. They had at first been arrested at the foot of the hill, but now they have managed to advance as far as the southern corner of Golgotha to a small space just at the edge of the platform. The crowd meanwhile has been pressing nearer; the chief priests and the leading Jews are close at hand, eager to witness everything; the sentinels have hard work to keep the space reserved for the execution clear of the curious crowds, and clear it must be kept if the difficult operation of the elevation of the cross is to be successfully accomplished.

The Nail for the Feet [J32]

⊕

ABOUT a third of its height from below, there was fixed to the cross by an immense spike a projecting block to which Jesus's feet were to be nailed, so that he should be rather standing than hanging; otherwise his hands would have been torn, and his feet could not have been nailed without breaking the bones. A hole for the nail had been bored in the block, and a little hollow place was made for his heels. Similar cavities had been made all down the trunk of the cross, in order to prolong his sufferings, for without them the hands would have been torn open and the body would have fallen violently by its own weight.

The whole body of our blessed Redeemer had been contracted by the violent stretching of the arms to the holes for the nails, and his knees were forcibly drawn up. The executioners now fell furiously upon them and, winding ropes around them, fastened them down to the cross; but on account of the mistake made in the holes in the crosspiece, the sacred feet of Jesus did not reach even to the block. When the executioners saw this, they gave vent to curses and insults. Some thought they would have to bore new holes in the transverse arm, for that would be far less difficult than moving the foot-block. Others with horrible scoffing cried out: "He will not stretch himself out, but we will help him!" Then they tied ropes around the right leg and, with horrible violence and terrible torture to Jesus, pulled the foot down to the block, and tied the leg fast with cords. With similar violence the left foot was drawn and fastened tightly with cords over the right; and because it did not rest firmly enough over the right one for nailing, the instep was bored with a fine, flathead piercer, much finer than the one used for the hands. It was like an auger with a puncher attached. Then seizing the most frightful-looking nail of all, which was much longer than the others, they drove it with great effort through the wounded instep of the left foot and that of the right foot resting below. With a cracking sound, it passed through Jesus's feet into the hole prepared for it in the footblock, and through that again back into the trunk of the cross. I have seen, when standing at the side of the cross, one nail passing through both feet. [220]

ON *the subject of the cross and the nails, many suggestions have been made as to the symbolic meaning of their numerical combinations. To begin with, the cross with its four corners might be taken to represent the altar of sacrifice, and the fact that these four corners did as a matter of course point to the four cardinal points of the compass, has been taken to show forth in the clearest way the catholicity of the Christian faith. Moreover, the victim being fastened to the altar of sacrifice by three nails, we get the symbolic figure three, which is the emblem of the trinity, or the divine triangle, and, when it is combined with the number four, represented by the four corners of the cross, we get the deeply significant number of seven, which is everywhere that signifying completed production. Lastly, the sacrifice of the divine victim was brought about by the infliction of five deep wounds, two in the hands, two in the feet, and one in the side. This new number of five, added to that of the three nails and the four corners, gives a total of twelve. Now there are twelve hours in the day, twelve months in the year, and the number twelve is, therefore, that which represents the grand cycle of nature, of the eternal, ever-recurring year, and at the same time, the work of our Lord Jesus Christ, carried on by the twelve apostles. By changing a single one of these figures it is very evident that the whole superstructure will be overturned, and this may possibly be the reason why the idea that only three nails were used in the crucifixion was in the first instance adopted. If, on the other hand, we suppose that as many as four nails were employed, the total number obtained would be thirteen, a number which everywhere symbolizes defeat, death, and all their consequences. It is for our readers to decide what value they will attach to the remarks made above: those who accept them start from the principle that all numbers have their meaning, a symbolism of their own.*

The Raising of the Cross [J33]

⊕

AFTER the crucifixion of our Lord, the executioners passed ropes through a ring at the back of the cross, and drew it by the upper part to the elevation in the center of the circle. Then they threw the ropes over the transverse beam, or derrick, raised on the opposite side. Several of the executioners, by means of these ropes, lifted the cross upright, while others supported it with blocks around the trunk, and guided the foot to the hole prepared for it. [221]

THE elevation of the cross with the victim upon it was a delicate operation hedged about with more than one difficulty. The body of the sufferer, held in place as it was by the nails in the hands and feet, was, of course, high up on the cross, so that all the weight was concentrated above the center, and the slightest slip on the part of those whose duty it was to set up the instrument of execution would have resulted in a horrible accident.

One of the most ancient traditions attributes to the cross a length of no less than fifteen feet, while the crossbeam was nearly half that length. All that we concede is that the feet of our Lord were near enough to the ground to be embraced by anyone standing at the foot of the cross, and that Mary Magdalene did so embrace them is affirmed by all traditions.

The necessary precautions must therefore be taken; time was pressing; everything must be done in such a manner as to prevent accident, for the sabbath would begin at sunset, and it was not lawful to put to death on that day. The upright pieces of wood which were to serve as gibbets for the two thieves were already in position, and it was therefore a comparatively simple thing to prepare for their execution, all that was left to be done being to bind each of them with his transverse beam to the post which had been fixed in the ground beforehand.

These remarks bring us to the moment before the elevation of the cross. The upright beams of the crosses for the thieves being firmly fixed in the ground, it was easy to connect them at the top with a horizontal beam, over which could be drawn without difficulty the ropes fastened to the ends of the transverse beam of the cross of Jesus. Some of the assistants have now only to push the cross from behind, while it is slowly drawn up by others with the aid of the ropes, care being taken to keep it properly balanced and in the right position with regard to the beam at the top and the upright supports, as, with the aid of levers, the lower extremity is placed in the hole in the ground already prepared for it. The whole operation is really accomplished in the twinkling of an eye, and, through the darkness and gloom, which are ever on the increase, the body of Jesus, of the bluish-white color of marble, dashed with the red blood from his wounds, is seen to rise up through the air before the spectators who look on in a silence weighted with tragedy. Mary, the mother of the sufferer, and the friends who have been with her from the first are still there, following all that the beloved victim goes through with eyes full of anguish; their hearts are crucified with him, they feel as if their own last hour had come.

The Five Wedges [J34]

THEY shoved the top somewhat forward, until it came into a perpendicular line, and its whole weight with a tremulous thud shot down into the hole. The cross vibrated under the shock. Jesus moaned aloud. The executioners now shook the cross again in their efforts to steady it, and hammered five wedges into the hole around it: one in front, one to the right, another to the left, and two at the back, which was somewhat rounded. A feeling of terror and, at the same time, one akin to deep emotion, was felt by Jesus's friends on beholding the cross swaying in the air and, at last, plunging into place with a heavy crash, amid the jeering shouts of the executioners, the Pharisees, and the distant crowd, whom Jesus could now see. But along with those shouts of derision, there arose other sounds at that dreadful moment—sounds of love and compassion from his devout followers. In touching expressions of pity, the holiest voices on earth, that of his afflicted mother, of the holy women, the beloved disciple, and all the pure of heart, saluted the "Eternal Word made flesh" elevated upon the cross. Loving hands were anxiously stretched forth as if to help the Holy of Holies, the Bridegroom of souls, nailed alive to the cross, quivering on high in the hands of raging sinners.

But when the upraised cross fell with a loud crash into the hole prepared for it, a moment of deep silence ensued. It seemed as if a new feeling, one never before experienced, fell upon every heart. Hell itself felt with terror the shock of the falling cross and, with cries of rage and blasphemy, rose up again against the Lord in its instruments, the cruel executioners and Pharisees. Among the poor souls and in Limbo, there arose the joy of anxious expectation about to be realized. They listened to that crash with longing hope. It sounded to them like the rap of the coming victor at the door of redemption. For the first time, the holy cross stood erect upon the earth, like another tree of life in Paradise, and from the wounds of Jesus, enlarged by the shock, trickled four sacred streams down upon the earth, to wash away the curse resting upon it and to make it bear for himself, the new Adam, fruits of salvation. [221]

ONE of the most acute pangs of the death by crucifixion must have been the shock caused by the falling of the cross into the hole in the ground prepared for it. The cross once set up in its place, it had still to be wedged firmly in, and to do this it was not enough to fill in the hole, which was, of course, much too big for it, with the earth that had been removed; it would be sure to rock about unsteadily in the newly-disturbed soil. In fact, wedges would be required, and the probability is that they were introduced as represented in my picture. This done, the horizontal bar of wood with the aid of which the ropes had done their part of the work was removed, and the cross stood upright in all its dignity with the Son of Man, all bleeding from his wounds, crucified upon it. The awful task is completed at last; the platform is cleared of the debris encumbering it: the ropes, the ladders, the tools. The clothes of the divine victim, which are to be divided among the four chief executioners as their perquisite, are done up into a bundle and laid aside for the time being. The executioners now withdraw to a distance, leaving the space around the cross vacant, and in a moment it becomes crowded with Pharisees, influential Jews, in a word, with all those who have brought about the death of the Master. They are eager to watch closely the agony of him who has for so long a time rendered them anxious. They begin to give vent to their rage by all manner of insulting epithets; the sight of his blood, instead of appeasing, intoxicates them. With them the crowd surrounding Golgotha also surges nearer; there is no longer any need to keep the people at a distance; no rescue is possible now, and these dregs of the populace are free to come and gloat over the awful spectacle.

The Garments Divided by Cast Lots [J35]

⊕

AT the place outside the circle upon which the thieves had lain, the crucifiers had meanwhile gathered Jesus's garments and divided them into several parts, in order to cast lots for them. The mantle was narrow at the top and wide at the bottom. It had several folds, and the breast was lined, thus forming pockets. The executioners tore it up into long strips, which they distributed among themselves. They did the same to the long white garment, which was closed at the opening on the breast with straps. Then they divided the long linen scarf, the girdle, the breast scapular, and the linen that was worn around the loins, all of which were soaked with the Lord's blood. But because they could not agree concerning the brown woven robe, which would have been useless to them if torn up, they brought out a board with numbers on it and some bean-shaped stones marked with certain signs. They threw the stones on the board in order to decide by lot whose the robe should be. Just at this point of the proceedings a messenger, sent by Nicodemus and Joseph of Arimathea, came running toward them to say that a purchaser had been found for the clothes of Jesus. So they bundled them up, ran down the mount, and sold them. It was in this way that these sacred relics came into the possession of the Christians. [222]

[JOHN 19:23–24] 23 When the soldiers had crucified Jesus they took his garments and made four parts, one for each soldier; also his tunic. But the tunic was without seam, woven from top to bottom; 24 so they said to one another, "Let us not tear it, but cast lots for it to see whose it shall be." This was to fulfil the scripture, "They parted my garments among them, and for my clothing they cast lots."

NOW that the crowd has dispersed, the four hardened executioners are able to give their minds to their own affairs. The law gave them the garments of those put to death; they had not the slightest intention of renouncing their claim, and, as they were careful fellows, they also resolved not to injure their booty. They therefore refrained from cutting the seamless vesture, which would have made it of no use to anyone, but decided to begin by dividing the clothes into four equal parts and then to draw lots for them.

The Pardon of the Good Thief [J36]

THE crosses of the thieves were somewhat turned toward each other, and not so high as the Lord's. The thieves looked up to Jesus, one praying, the other jeering, and Jesus said something from his cross to Dismas. And now Jesus, raising his head a little, exclaimed: "Father, forgive them, for they know not what they do!" and then he prayed in a low tone. Gesmas cried out: "If thou art the Christ, help thyself and us!" The mocking continued. Dismas, the thief on the right, was deeply touched at hearing Jesus pray for his enemies. When Mary heard the voice of her child, she could no longer be restrained, but pressed forward into the circle, followed by John, Salome, and Mary Cleophas. The captain of the guard did not prevent her. Dismas, the thief on the right, received by virtue of Jesus's prayer an interior enlightenment. When the blessed Virgin came hurrying forward, he suddenly remembered that Jesus and his mother had helped him when a child. He raised his voice and cried in a clear and commanding tone: "How is it possible that ye can revile him when he is praying for you! He has kept silence and patience, he prays for you, and you outrage him! He is a prophet! He is our king! He is the Son of God!" The blessed Virgin felt herself strengthened by that prayer of Jesus. Gesmas was again crying to Jesus: "If thou be the Christ, help thyself and us!" when Dismas thus addressed him: "Neither dost thou fear God, seeing thou art under the same condemnation. And we indeed justly, for we receive the due reward of our deeds, but this man had done no evil. Oh, bethink thee of thy sins, and change thy sentiments!" Enlightened and touched, he then confessed his crime to Jesus, saying: "Lord, if thou dost condemn me, it will be just. But have mercy on me!" Jesus replied: "Thou shalt experience my mercy." At these words Dismas received the grace of deep contrition, which he indulged for the next quarter of an hour.

While the darkness was on the increase, the spectators gazing up at the sky and the cross deserted by all excepting Jesus's mother and his nearest friends, Dismas, in deepest contrition and humble hope, raised his head to Jesus and said: "Lord, let me go to some place whence thou mayest rescue me! Remember me when thou shalt come into thy kingdom!" Jesus replied to him: "Amen, I say to thee, this day thou shalt be with me in Paradise!" [224]

[LUKE 23:39–43] 39 One of the criminals who were hanged railed at him, saying, "Are you not the Christ? Save yourself and us!" 40 But the other rebuked him, saying, "Do you not fear God, since you are under the same sentence of condemnation? 41 And we indeed justly; for we are receiving the due reward of our deeds; but this man has done nothing wrong." 42 And he said, "Jesus, remember me when you come into your kingdom." 43 And he said to him, "Truly, I say to you, today you will be with me in Paradise."

THE tumult on Golgotha is at its height. Meanwhile, the sun is becoming obscured in an unusual manner; an unprecedented darkness is spreading through the town, and many of the spectators withdraw. The result of this thinning of the crowd is that there is more room at the foot of the cross, and the faithful followers of Jesus are able to draw nearer. The devoted group at last succeed in getting quite close to the beloved sufferer and can actually touch his feet. Mary Magdalene, who is quite beside herself with grief, will not leave the post she has taken up until the end. The two thieves hang one on either side of the Savior, but their attitude towards him differs very much. One of them joins eagerly in the insults heaped on the principal sufferer, his heart is filled with impotent rage. The other malefactor, however, is touched by the divine gentleness of the crucified Savior, and when he finds that he remains silent, this second malefactor takes up his defence. There is something alike daring and grand in the intervention of this dying thief in the midst of his own agony on behalf of the crucified Redeemer. "Dost thou not fear God," he says to his companion, "seeing thou art in the same condemnation?" But what follows is still more admirable. "And we indeed justly," the penitent thief goes on, "for we receive the due reward of our deeds: but this man hath done nothing amiss." He therefore proclaims from his own cross his belief in the innocence of the victim, and, this confession made, he has but to turn toward that victim to share in the benefits won by the sacrifice. This is why, addressing the Savior himself, he appeals to him in the humble yet sublime prayer: "Lord, remember me when thou comest into thy kingdom." The prayer of the penitent thief was soon answered. Jesus, who held his peace in the midst of all the insults of his enemies, would not leave such an act of faith without response. "Verily I say unto thee, today shalt thou be with me in Paradise." The soul of the sinner, thus so suddenly redeemed, and finding itself so near to God, enters into a kind of ecstasy with his eyes fixed upon the face of his Master. In the various pictures which follow he will be seen still wearing that same expression, and nothing will again trouble the peace of this ransomed soul about to enter into the eternal life.

The Sun Obscured • The Second and the Third Sayings of Jesus on the Cross

Until ten that morning at which hour Pilate pronounced the sentence, hail had fallen at intervals, but from that time until twelve o'clock the sky was clear and the sun shone. *At twelve, however, the sun became obscured by a murky red fog. About the sixth hour (but, as I saw, about half-past by the sun, for the Jewish mode of reckoning varied from the sun) that luminary began to be obscured in a manner altogether wonderful.* I saw the celestial bodies, the stars and the planets, circling in their orbits and passing one another. I descried the moon on the opposite side of the earth and then, by a sudden run or bound, looking like a hanging globe of fire, it flashed up full and pale above the Mount of Olives. The sun was enveloped in fog, and the moon came sweeping up before it from the east. At first, I saw to the east of the sun something like a dark mountain, which soon entirely hid it. The center appeared pale yellow, and around it was a red circle like a ring of fire. The sky became perfectly dark, and the stars shone out with a reddish gleam. Terror seized upon man and beast. The cattle bellowed and ran wildly about; the birds sought their hiding places, and lighted in flocks on the hills around Mount Calvary. One could catch them in his hands. The scoffers were silenced, while the Pharisees tried to explain these signs as natural phenomena, but they succeeded badly, and soon they, too, were seized with terror. All eyes were raised to the sky. Many beat their breast, wrung their hands, and cried: "His blood be upon his murderers!" Others far and near fell on their knees and implored Jesus's forgiveness, and Jesus, notwithstanding his agony, turned his eyes toward them. While the darkness was on the increase, the spectators gazing up at the sky and the cross deserted by all excepting Jesus's mother and his nearest friends, Dismas, in deepest contrition and humble hope, raised his head to Jesus and said: "Lord, let me go to some place whence thou mayest rescue me! Remember me when thou shalt come into thy kingdom!" Jesus replied to him: "Amen, I say to thee, this day thou shalt be with me in Paradise!"

The mother of Jesus, Mary Cleophas, Mary Magdalene, and John were standing around Jesus's cross, between it and those of the thieves, and looking up at the Lord. The blessed Virgin, overcome by maternal love, was in her heart fervently imploring Jesus to let her die with him. At that moment, the Lord cast an earnest and compassionate glance down upon his mother and, turning his eyes toward John, said to her: "Woman, behold, this is thy son! He will be thy son more truly than if thou hadst given him birth." [K1]

Then he praised John, and said: "He has always been innocent and full of simple faith. He was never scandalized, excepting when his mother wanted to have him elevated to a high position." To John, he said: "Behold, this is thy mother!" and John reverently and like a filial son embraced beneath the cross of the dying Redeemer Jesus's mother, who had now become his mother also. After this solemn bequest of her dying Son, the blessed Virgin was so deeply affected by her own sorrow and the gravity of the scene that the holy women, supporting her in their arms, seated her for a few moments on the earthen rampart opposite the cross, and then took her away from the circle to the rest of the holy women.

I do not know whether Jesus spoke all those words aloud with his sacred lips or not, but I perceived them interiorly when, before his death, he gave his blessed Mother to John as his mother and John to her as a son. In such contemplations many things are understood that are not set down in writing, and one can relate the least part of them only in ordinary language. What is seen in such visions is so clear that one believes and understands it at once, but it is impossible to clothe it in intelligible words. So on such an occasion one is not at all surprised to hear Jesus addressing the blessed Virgin, not as "Mother," but as "Woman"; for one feels that in this hour in which, by the sacrificial death of the Son of Man, her own Son, the Promise was realized. Mary stood in her dignity as the Woman who was to crush the serpent's head. Nor is one then surprised that Jesus gave to her, whom the angel saluted: "Hail, full of grace!" John as a son, for everyone knows that his name is a name of grace, for there, all are what they are called. John was become a child of God and Christ lived in him. I felt that by these words Jesus gave to Mary, as to their mother, all those that, like John, receiving him and believing in his name, become the sons of God, and who are born not of blood, nor of the will of the flesh, nor of the will of man, but of God. I felt that the purest, the humblest, the most obedient of creatures, she who said to the angel: "Behold the handmaid of the Lord! Be it done to me according to thy word!"—she who had become the Mother of the Eternal Word Incarnate, now that she understood from her dying Son that she was to be the spiritual mother of another son, in the midst of her grief at parting and still humbly obedient, again pronounced, though in her heart, the words: "Behold the handmaid of the Lord! Be it done to me according to thy word!" I felt that she took at that moment for her own children all the children of God, all the brethren of Jesus. These things appear in vision so simple, so necessarily following as a consequence, though out of vision so manifold and complex, that they are more easily felt by the grace of God than expressed in words.

Fear Felt by the Inhabitants of Jerusalem

It was about half-past one o'clock when I was taken into Jerusalem to see what was going on there. Fear and consternation filled Jerusalem. Fog and gloomy darkness hung over its streets. Many lay with covered heads in corners, striking their breasts. Others, standing on the roofs of the houses, gazed up at the sky and uttered lamentations. Animals were bellowing and hiding, birds were flying low and falling to the ground. Pilate had made a visit to Herod, and both were now looking in terror at the sky from that terrace upon which Herod had that morning, with so much state, watched Jesus insulted and maltreated by the mob. "This is not natural," they said. "Too much has certainly been done to Jesus." Then they went across the forum to Pilate's palace. Both were very uneasy, and they walked with rapid strides surrounded by their guards. Pilate turned away his head from Gabbatha, the judgment seat, from which he had sentenced Jesus to death. The forum was deserted. The people had hurried to their homes, though some few were still running about with mournful cries, and several small groups were gathered in the public places. Pilate sent for some of the Jewish elders to come to his palace, and asked them what they thought the darkness meant. As for himself, he said, he looked upon it as a sign of wrath. Their God appeared to be angry at their desiring to put the Galilean to so violent a death, for he certainly was a prophet and a king, but that he himself washed his hands, etc. But the elders, hardened in their obstinacy, explained it as a natural phenomenon not at all uncommon. Many were converted, also those soldiers that, at the arrest of Jesus on the Mount of Olives, had fallen and again risen.

By degrees a crowd gathered before Pilate's palace. On the same spot upon which they had in the morning cried: "Crucify him! Away with him!" they now cried: "Unjust judge! His blood be upon his murderers!" Pilate had to surround himself with soldiers. That Zadoch who, in the morning, when Jesus was taken into the judgment hall, had loudly proclaimed his innocence, cried and shouted

*April 3, AD 33
Friday, 1:30 PM*

in such a way that Pilate was on the point of arresting him. Pilate sternly reproached the Jews. He had, he said, no part whatever in the affair. Jesus was their king, their prophet, their holy one whom they, and not he, had put to death. It was nothing to him (Pilate), for they themselves had brought about his death.

Anxiety and terror reached their height in the temple. The slaughtering of the paschal lamb had just begun when the darkness of night suddenly fell upon Jerusalem. All were filled with consternation, while here and there broke forth loud cries of woe. The high priests did all they could to maintain peace and order. The lamps were lighted, making the sacred precincts as bright as day, but the consternation became only the greater. Annas, terribly tormented, ran from corner to corner in his desire to hide himself. The screens and lattices before the windows of the houses were shaken, and yet there was no storm. The darkness was on the increase. In distant quarters of the city, the northwest section toward the walls, where there were numerous gardens and sepulchers, some of the latter fell in, as if the ground were shaken.

Jesus Abandoned • His Fourth Saying on the Cross

AFTER Jesus's third word to his blessed Mother and John, an interval of gloomy silence reigned upon Golgotha, and many of the onlookers fled back to the city. The malicious revilings of the Pharisees ceased. The horses and asses of the riders huddled close to one another and drooped their heads. Vapor and fog hung over everything.

Jesus, in unspeakable torture, endured on the cross extreme abandonment and desolation of soul. He prayed to his heavenly Father in those passages of the Psalms that were now being fulfilled in himself. I saw around him angelic figures. He endured in infinite torment all that a poor, crushed, tortured creature, in the greatest abandonment, without consolation human or divine, suffers when faith, hope, and love stand alone in the desert of tribulation, without prospect of return, without taste or sentiment, without a ray of light, left there to live alone. No words can express this pain. By this suffering Jesus gained for us the strength, by uniting our abandonment to the merits of his own upon the cross, victoriously to conquer at our last hour, when all ties and relations with this life and mode of existence, with this world and its laws, cease; and when therefore the ideas which we form in this life of the other world also cease. He gained for us merit to stand firm in our own last struggle when we too shall feel ourselves entirely abandoned. He offered his misery, his poverty, his pains, his desolation for us miserable sinners, so that whoever is united with Jesus in the body of the church must not despair at that last hour even if, light and consolation being withdrawn, he is left in darkness. Into this desert of interior night we are no longer necessitated to plunge alone and exposed to danger. Jesus has let down into the abyss of the bitter sea of desolation his own interior and exterior abandonment upon the cross, thus leaving the Christian not alone in the dereliction of death, when the light of heavenly consolation burns dim. For the Christian in that last hour of peril, there is no longer any dark and unknown region, any loneliness, any abandonment, any despair; for Jesus, the Light, the Truth, and the Way, blessed the dark way by traversing it himself, and by planting his cross upon it, chased from it all that is frightful.

April 3, AD 33
Friday, just after 3 PM

Jesus wholly abandoned, wholly deprived of all things, and utterly helpless, sacrificed himself in infinite love. Yes, he turned his abandonment itself into a rich treasure by offering to his heavenly Father his life, labors, love, and sufferings, along with the bitter sense of our ingratitude that thereby he might strengthen our weakness and enrich our poverty. He made before God his last testament, by which he gave over all his merits to the church and to sinners. He thought of everyone. In his abandonment he was with every single soul until the end of time. He prayed too for those heretics who believe that being God, he did not feel his sufferings, and that as man he felt them only a little, or at least far less than another would have done. But while I was sharing in and sympathizing with Jesus's prayer, I heard these words as if coming from his lips: "We should, by all means, teach the people that Jesus, more keenly than any human being can conceive, endured this pain of utter abandonment, because he was hypostatically united with the divinity, because he was truly God and man. Being in his sacred humanity wholly abandoned by the Father, he felt most perfectly that bereavement, he drained to the dregs the bitter cup of dereliction, he experienced for the time what a soul endures that has lost its God forever.

And so when in his agony he cried out with a loud voice, he meant not only to make known his dereliction, but also to publish to all afflicted souls who acknowledge God as their Father that the privilege of recurring to him in filial confidence he merited for them then and there. Toward the third hour, Jesus cried in a loud voice: "Eli, Eli, lama sabachthani!" which means: "My God! My God! Why hast thou forsaken me!" [K2]

When this clear cry of our Lord broke the fearful stillness around the cross, the scoffers turned toward it and one said: "He is calling Elijah"; and another: "Let us see whether Elijah will come to deliver him." When the most afflicted mother heard the voice of her Son, she could no longer restrain herself. She again pressed forward to the cross, followed by John, Mary Cleophas, Magdalene, and Salome. [K3]

While the people around were lamenting and trembling with fear, a troop of about thirty distinguished men from Judea and the neighborhood of Joppa came riding up on horseback. They were on their way to Jerusalem for the celebration of the feast. When they beheld the frightful treatment to which Jesus had been subjected and the threatening appearances in nature, they expressed their horror aloud and cried out: "Were it not that the temple of God is in it, this cruel city should be burned to the ground for having charged itself with such a crime."

Such expressions from strangers evidently of high rank encouraged the people. Loud murmurs and cries of grief resounded everywhere, and many of those similarly impressed retired together from the scene. The remaining spectators were now divided into two parties: one gave utterance to sorrow and indignation; the other continued to insult Jesus and rage against him. The Pharisees, however, were disheartened. They feared a rising of the populace, since great disturbance was even then prevailing in Jerusalem. They deliberated with the centurion Abenadar, whereupon an order was given to close the city gate in the neighborhood of Mount Calvary, that communication with the city might thus be cut off. A messenger was sent to Pilate and Herod for a bodyguard of five hundred men to prevent an insurrection. In the meantime, the centurion Abenadar did all in his power to secure peace and order. He forbade the Pharisees to insult Jesus, lest the people might be infuriated.

Soon after three o'clock the sky brightened a little, and the moon began to recede from the sun in an opposite direction. The sun, red and rayless, appeared surrounded by a mist, and the moon sank suddenly as if falling to the opposite side. By degrees the sunbeams shone out again, and the stars disappeared, but the sky still looked lowering. With returning light, the scoffers on Golgotha again became bold and triumphant. Then it was that they said: "He is calling Elijah." Abenadar commanded quiet and order.

The Death of Jesus • Fifth, Sixth, and Seventh Sayings on the Cross

AS it grew light, the body of Jesus could be seen on the cross, pale, weak, perfectly exhausted, becoming whiter from the great loss of blood. He said, I know not whether praying in voice audible to me alone, or half-aloud: "I am pressed like the wine which was once trodden here in the wine press. I must pour out all my blood until water cometh, and the shell becometh white, but wine shall here be made no more." I afterward had a vision relating to these words, and in it I saw Japhet making wine in this place.[†]

Jesus was now completely exhausted. With his parched tongue he uttered the words: "I thirst!" And when his friends looked up at him sadly, he said to them: "Could you not have given me a drink of water?" He meant that during the darkness no one would have prevented their doing so. John was troubled at Jesus's words, and he replied: "O Lord, we forgot it!" Jesus continued to speak in words such as these: "My nearest friends must forget me and offer me no drink, that the scriptures may be fulfilled." This forgetfulness was very bitter to him. Hearing Jesus's complaint, his friends begged the soldiers and offered them money if they would reach to him a drink of water. They would not do it, but instead they dipped a pear-shaped sponge into vinegar, a little bark keg of which was standing near, and poured upon it some drops of gall. But the centurion Abenadar, whose heart was touched by Jesus, took the sponge from the soldiers, pressed it out, and filled it with pure vinegar. Then he stuck into it a sprig of hyssop, which served as a mouthpiece for sucking, and fastened the whole to the point of his lance. He raised it in such a way that the tube should incline to Jesus's mouth and through it he might be able to suck the vinegar from the sponge. [K4]

Of some of the words that I heard the Lord speaking in admonition to the people, I remember only that he said: "And when I shall no longer have voice, the mouth of the dead shall speak"; whereupon some of the bystanders cried out: "He still blasphemes!" But Abenadar commanded peace.

The hour of the Lord was now come. He was struggling with death, and a cold sweat burst out on every limb. John was standing by the cross and wiping Jesus's feet with his handkerchief. Magdalene, utterly crushed with grief, was leaning at the back of the cross. The blessed Virgin, supported in the arms of Mary Cleophas and Salome, was standing between Jesus and the cross of the good thief, her gaze fixed upon her dying Son. [K5] Jesus spoke: "It is consummated!" and raising his head he cried with a loud voice: "Father, into thy hands I commend my Spirit!" The sweet, loud cry rang through heaven and earth. [K6] Then he bowed his head and gave up the spirit. I saw his soul like a luminous phantom descending through the earth near the cross down to the sphere of Limbo. John and the holy women sank, face downward, prostrate on the earth.

Abenadar the centurion, an Arab by birth, and a disciple baptized later on as Ctesiphon, had, since the moment in which he had given Jesus the vinegar to drink, remained seated on his horse close to the eminence upon which the

---

† Of this vision, Anne Catherine related what follows: I saw on Mount Calvary after the Deluge the patriarch Japhet, a tall, dark-skinned old man, encamping with numerous flocks and descendants. Their huts were sunk in the earth, the roofs covered with sods upon which plants and flowers were growing. Grapevines were everywhere flourishing, and wine was made on Mount Calvary in a new way, over which Japhet himself presided. I saw also the various ways in which wine was formerly prepared and used, and many circumstances connected with the wine itself, of which I remember only the following: at first, the grapes were merely eaten; later on, they were pressed in stone troughs by means of wooden blocks, and lastly huge wooden cylinders and pestles were employed for the same end. But in the time of Japhet, I saw that a new kind of press was invented, in form very like the holy cross. The trunk of a tree, hollow and large in diameter, was placed upright, and in it were suspended the grapes in a sack through which the juice could run. Upon the sack pressed a pestle and block. On either side of the hollow trunk and directed toward the sack were arms which, on being worked up and down, crushed the grapes. The juice thus expressed flowed through five holes bored in the hollow trunk down into a vat cut in the rock. From this it ran into a vessel formed of two pieces of bark, each taken from a tree cut in half from top to bottom. The two halves, being put together, were then overlaid with thin wooden rods, and the cracks cemented with pitch. From this last vessel, the grape juice flowed into that rocky cellar-like cave into which the Lord Jesus was thrust before his crucifixion. At the time of Japhet it was a pure cistern. I saw that the cracks of the wooden vat were covered with sods and stones for greater protection. At the foot of the press and that of the stone vat, haircloth was laid before an opening in one of the cracks, to catch the skins which were always disposed of on that side. When the press was ready to receive them, the workmen filled the sack with grapes (which until wanted were stored away in the cistern), hung it in the hollow upright, nailed it fast, placed the heavy pestle with its block in the open mouth of the sack, and began to work the levers in and out, thus making them strike against the sack of grapes, from which the wine flowed. I saw another workman busy at the top of the press, keeping the contents of the sack from making their way up above the block. These particulars reminded me of Jesus's crucifixion, on account of the striking similarity between the press and the cross. They had also a long tube with a prickly head, like a hedgehog (perhaps it was a large thistlehead), and this they pushed through the crack and the upright press whenever they became stopped up. This tube recalled the lance and sponge. I saw, standing around, leathern bottles and vessels of bark smeared with pitch. I saw many youths and boys, with girdles such as Jesus used to wear, working here. Japhet was very old. He was clothed in the skins of beasts and wore a long beard.

He regarded the new wine press with great satisfaction. There was celebrated a festival, and on a stone altar animals that had been allowed to run in the vineyard, young asses, goats, and sheep, were sacrificed.

cross was raised, the forefeet of the animal planted near it and, consequently, higher than the hindfeet. Deeply affected, he gazed long, earnestly and fixedly into the thorn-crowned countenance of Jesus. The horse hung his head as if in fear, and Abenadar, whose pride was humbled, let the reins hang loose. When the Lord in a clear, strong voice uttered those last words, when he died with that loud cry that rang through heaven, earth, and hell, the earth quaked and the rock between him and the thief on his left

deemed, after his public homage to the Son of God would no longer remain in the service of his enemies. He turned his horse toward Cassius, the subaltern officer, known under the name of Longinus, dismounted, picked up his lance, presented it to him and addressed a few words both to him and the soldiers. Cassius mounted the horse and assumed the command. Abenadar next hurried down Mount Calvary and through the Valley of Gihon to the caves in the Valley of Hinnom, where he announced to the

Tombs in the Valley of Hinnom

was rent asunder with a crashing sound. [K7] That loud cry, that witness of God, resounded like a warning, arousing terror and shuddering in mourning nature. It was consummated! The soul of our Lord had left the body! The death cry of the dying Redeemer had roused all that heard it; even the earth, by its undulations, seemed to recognize the Savior, and a sharp sword of sorrow pierced the hearts of those that loved him. Then it was that grace penetrated the soul of Abenadar. The horse trembled under his rider, who was reeling with emotion; then it was that grace conquered that proud mind, hard as the rock of Golgotha. He threw his lance to the ground and, with his great clenched fist, struck his breast vigorous blows, crying aloud in the voice of a changed man: "Blessed be God the almighty, the God of Abraham and Jacob! This was a just man! Truly, he is the Son of God!" [K8] And many of the soldiers, deeply affected by his words, followed his example.

Abenadar, who was now a changed being, a man re-

disciples hidden therein the death of the Lord, after which he hastened into the city and went straight to Pilate.

Terror fell upon all at the sound of Jesus's death cry, when the earth quaked and the rock beneath the cross was split asunder. A feeling of dread pervaded the whole universe. The veil of the temple was on the instant rent in twain, the dead arose from their graves, the walls in the temple fell, while mountains and buildings were overturned in many parts of the world.

Abenadar rendered public testimony to his belief in Jesus, and his example was followed by many of the soldiers. Numbers of those present, and some of the Pharisees last come to the scene, were converted. Many struck their breast, wept, and returned home, while others rent their garments and sprinkled their head with dust. All were filled with fear and dread. [K9]

John at last arose. Some of the holy women, who until then were standing at a distance, now pressed into the circle, raised the mother of Jesus and her companions, and led them away.

When the loving Lord of life, by a death full of torture, paid for sinners their debt, as man he commended his soul to his God and Father, and gave his body over to the tomb. Then the pale, chill pallor of death overspread that sacred vessel now so terribly bruised and quivering with pain. It became perfectly white, and the streams of blood running down from the numerous wounds grew darker and more perceptible. His face was elongated, his cheeks sunken, his nose sharp and pinched. His underjaw fell, and his eyes, which had been closed and full of blood, opened halfway. For a few instants he raised his thorn-crowned head for the last time and then let it sink on his breast under the burden of pain. His lips, blue and parted, disclosed the bloody tongue in his open mouth. His fingers, which had been contracted around the heads of the nails, now relaxed and fell a little forward while the arms stretched out to their natural size. His back straightened itself against the cross, and the whole weight of his sacred body fell upon the feet. His knees bent and fell to one side, and his feet twisted a little around the nail that pierced them.

April 3, AD 33
Friday, just after 3 PM

When Jesus's hands became stiff, his mother's eyes grew dim, the paleness of death overspread her countenance, her feet tottered, and she sank to the earth. Magdalene, John, and the others, yielding to their grief, fell also with veiled faces.

When that most loving, that most afflicted mother arose from the ground, she beheld the sacred body of her Son, whom she had conceived by the Holy Spirit, the flesh of her flesh, the bone of her bone, the heart of her heart, the holy vessel formed by the divine overshadowing in her own blessed womb, now deprived of all its beauty and comeliness and even of its most holy soul, given up to the laws of that nature which he had himself created and which man had by sin abused and disfigured. She beheld that beloved Son crushed, maltreated, disfigured, and put to death by the hands of those whom he had come in the flesh to restore to grace and life. Ah! She beheld that sacred body thrust from among men, despised, derided, emptied, as it were, of all that was beautiful, truthful, and lovely, hanging like a leper, mangled on the cross between two murderers! Who can conceive the sorrow of the mother of Jesus, of the queen of martyrs!

The sun was still obscured by fog. During the earthquake the air was close and oppressive, but afterward there was a sensible decrease in temperature. The appearance of

our Lord's corpse on the cross was exceedingly awful and impressive. The thieves were hanging in frightful contortions, and seemingly intoxicated with liquor. At last both became silent. Dismas was in prayer.

It was just after three o'clock when Jesus expired. When the first alarm produced by the earthquake was over, some of the Pharisees grew bolder. They approached the chasm made by it in the rock of Golgotha, threw stones into it, fastened ropes together, and let them down; but as they could not reach the bottom of the abyss, they became a little more thoughtful and, comprehending in some degree why people were lamenting and beating their breast, they rode off from the scene. [K10] Some were entirely changed in their ideas. The people soon dispersed and went in fear and anxiety through the valley in the direction of the city, many of them being converted. [K11] Part of the band of fifty Roman soldiers strengthened the guard at the city gate until the arrival of the five hundred that had been asked for. The gate was locked. Other posts around were occupied by soldiers, to prevent a concourse of people and confusion. Cassius (Longinus) and about five of his soldiers remained inside the circle and lying around on the rampart. Jesus's relatives were near the cross. They sat in front of it, lamenting and weeping. Several of the holy women had returned to the city. All was lonely, still, and sad. Off in the distance, here and there, in the valley and on the remote heights, a disciple might be descried peering timidly and inquiringly toward the cross, and retiring quickly on the approach of anyone. [K12]

The Earthquake • Apparitions of the Dead in Jerusalem

WHEN Jesus with a loud cry gave up his spirit into the hands of his heavenly Father, I saw his soul, like a luminous figure, penetrating the earth at the foot of the cross, accompanied by a band of luminous angels, among whom was Gabriel. I saw a great multitude of evil spirits driven by those angels from the earth into the abyss.

Jesus sent many souls from Limbo to reenter their body, in order to frighten and warn the impenitent, as well as to bear witness to himself.

By the earthquake at Jesus's death, when the rock of Golgotha was split, many portions of the earth were upheaved while others sank, and this was especially the case in Palestine and Jerusalem. In the temple and throughout the city, the inhabitants were just recovering somewhat from the fright caused by the darkness when the heaving of the earth, the crash of falling buildings in many quarters, gave rise to still more general consternation; and, to crown their terror, the trembling and wailing crowd, hurrying hither and thither in dire confusion, encountered here and there the corpses raised from the dead, as they walked about uttering their warnings in hollow voices.

The high priests in the temple had recommenced the slaughtering of the lambs, which had been interrupted by the frightful darkness. They were rejoicing triumphantly over the returning light when suddenly the ground began to quake, a hollow rumbling was heard, and the crash of toppling walls, accompanied by the hissing noise made by the rending of the veil, produced for the moment in the vast assemblage speechless terror broken only by an occasional cry of woe. But the crowd was so well-ordered, the immense edifice so full, the going and coming of the great number engaged in slaughtering so perfectly regulated— the act of slaughtering, the draining of blood, the sprinkling of the altars with it by the long row of countless priests amid the sound of canticles and trumpets—all this was done with so great accord, so great harmony of action, that the fright did not lead to general confusion and dispersion. The temple was so large, there were so many different halls and apartments, that the sacrifices went on quietly in some, while fright and horror were pervading others, and in others still the priests managed to keep order. It was not till the dead made their appearance in different parts of the temple that the ceremonies were entirely interrupted and the sacrifices discontinued, as if the temple had become polluted. [K13] Still even this did not come so suddenly upon the multitude as to cause them in their flight to rush precipitously down the numerous steps of the temple. They dispersed by degrees, hurrying down one group at a time, while in some quarters of the building the priests were able to bring back the frightened worshippers and keep them together. Still, however, the anxiety, the fright of all, though different in degree, was something quite indescribable.

The appearance of the temple at this moment may be pictured to oneself by comparing it to a great anthill in full and well-ordered activity. Let a stone be thrown into it or a stick introduced among the little creatures here and there, and confusion will reign around the immediate scene of disturbance, though activity may continue uninterruptedly in other groups, and soon the damaged places are covered and repaired.

The high priest Caiaphas and his followers, owing to their desperate insolence, did not lose presence of mind. Like the sagacious magistrate of a seditious city, by threats, by the separation of parties, by persuasion, and all kinds of deceitful arguments, Caiaphas warded off the danger.

By his demoniacal obstinacy especially, and his own apparent calmness, he prevented not only a general panic, so destructive in its consequences, but likewise hindered the people from construing those frightful warnings into a testimony of the innocent death of Jesus. The Roman garrison on the fortress Antonia did all that could be done to maintain order, and although the confusion and consternation were great and caused a discontinuance of the festal ceremonies, yet there was no insurrection. The blaze was reduced to a glimmering spark of anxiety, which the people, separating by degrees, carried with them to their homes, and which was there for the most part by the activity of the Pharisees finally extinguished.

And so it was in general. I remember the following striking incidents: The two great columns at the entrance of the Holy of Holies in the temple, between which hung a magnificent curtain, fell in opposite directions, the left-hand one to the south, the right-hand to the north. The beam which they supported gave way and the great curtain was, with a hissing noise, rent from top to bottom so that, opening on either side, it fell. This curtain was red, blue, white, and yellow. Many celestial spheres were described upon it, also figures like the brazen serpent. The people could now see into the Holy of Holies. In the northern wall near it was the little cell in which Simeon used to pray. A great stone was hurled upon it, and the roof fell in. In some of the halls the floor sank here and there, beams were displaced, and pillars gave way.

In the Holy of Holies, between the porch and the altar, an apparition of the murdered high priest Zechariah was seen. He uttered threatening words, spoke of the death of the other Zechariah,[†] also that of John, denominating the high priests the murderers of the prophets. He came from the opening made by the falling stone near Simeon's place of prayer, and addressed the priests in the Holy of Holies. Simon Justus was a pious high priest, an ancestor of the aged priest Simeon who had prophesied on the occasion of Jesus's presentation in the temple. His two prematurely deceased sons now appeared as tall phantoms near the principal chair of instruction, and in menacing terms spoke of the murder of the prophets, of the sacrifice of the Old Law, which was now at an end, and admonished all present to embrace the doctrine of the crucified.

Jeremiah appeared at the altar and uttered words of denunciation. The sacrifice of the Old Law was ended, he said, and a new one had begun. These speeches and appa-

---

† The Zechariah here referred to was the father of John the Baptist, who was tortured and afterwards put to death by Herod, because he would not betray John into the hands of the tyrant. He was buried by his friends within the precincts of the temple.

ritions in places to which Caiaphas or the priests alone had access were hushed up and denied. It was forbidden to speak of them under penalty of excommunication. And now there arose a great clamor, the doors of the sanctuary sprang open, a voice cried out: "Let us go hence!" and I saw the angels departing from the temple. The altar of incense was elevated to some height and a vessel of incense tilted over. The shelf that held the rolls of scripture fell in, and the rolls were scattered around. The confusion increased to such a degree that the time of day was forgotten. Nicodemus, Joseph of Arimathea, and many others left the temple and went away. Corpses were lying here and there, others were wandering through the halls and uttering warning words to the people. At the sound of the voice of the angels fleeing from the temple, the dead returned to their graves. The teacher's chair in the outer porch fell to pieces. Many of the thirty-two Pharisees who had ridden to Golgotha just before Jesus expired, returned in the midst of this confusion to the temple. As they had been converted at the foot of the cross, they looked upon all these signs with still greater consternation and, addressing some stern reproaches to Annas and Caiaphas, they quickly retired.

*April 3, AD 33
Friday, just after 3 PM*

Annas, who was really, though in secret, Jesus's principal enemy, who for a long time had headed all the hidden intrigues against him and the disciples, and who had also instructed the false witnesses as to what they were to say, was so terrified that he became like one bereft of reason. He fled from corner to corner through the most retired apartments of the temple. I saw him moaning and crying, his muscles contracted as if in convulsions, conveyed to a secret room where he was surrounded by several of his followers. Once Caiaphas clasped him tightly in his arms in order to raise his courage, but in vain. The apparition of the dead cast him into utter despair. Caiaphas, although excessively alarmed, had in him so proud and obstinate a devil that he would not allow his terror to be seen. He bade defiance to all and, with a bold front, set his rage and pride against the warning signs of God and his own secret fright. But as he could no longer continue the sacred ceremonies, he hid and commanded others to hide all the events and apparitions not already known to the people. He gave out, and caused others to do the same, that these apparitions, indicative of God's anger, were due to the followers of the crucified Galilean, for their coming to the temple had polluted it. Only the enemies of the sacred Law, he said, which Jesus had tried to overturn, had experienced any alarm, and many of the things that had happened could be ascribed to the witchcraft of the Galilean who, in death as in life, had disturbed the peace of the temple. And so it came to pass that he silenced some by such words, and frightened others with threats. Many, however, were deeply impressed, though they concealed their sentiments. The feast was postponed until the temple could be purified. Many of the lambs were not slaughtered, and the people dispersed by degrees.

The tomb of Zechariah under the temple wall was sunken and destroyed, and in consequence, some stones fell out of the wall. Zechariah left it, but did not again return to it. I know not where he again laid off his body. Simon Justus's sons, who had arisen from their graves, laid theirs down again in the vault under the temple mount, when Jesus's body was being prepared for burial.

While all these things were going on in the temple, a similar panic was experienced in many other quarters of Jerusalem. *Just after three o'clock*, many tombs were violently shattered, especially in the northwestern section of the city where there were numerous gardens. I saw here and there the dead lying in their winding sheets. In other places, there were only masses of rottenness, in others skeletons, and from many proceeded an intolerable stench.

At Caiaphas's tribunal, the steps upon which Jesus stood when exposed to the mockery of the rabble were overturned, also a portion of the fireplace in the hall in which Peter's first denial took place. The destruction here was so great that a new entrance had to be made. It was in this place that the corpse of the high priest Simon Justus appeared, to whose race belonged Simeon who had prophesied at Jesus's presentation in the temple. His apparition uttered some menacing words upon the unjust sentence that had here been pronounced. Several members of the Sanhedrin were present. The individuals that on the preceding night had given entrance to Peter and John, were converted. They fled to the caves in which the disciples were concealed. At Pilate's palace, the stone was shattered and the whole place upon which Pilate had exhibited Jesus to the multitude fell in. All things reeled under the powerful shaking-up they got, and in the court of the neighboring judgment hall the place in which the bodies of the innocents murdered by Herod's orders were interred fell in. In many other parts of the city walls were overturned and others cracked, but no edifices were entirely destroyed. Pilate, perplexed and superstitious, was in the greatest consternation and wholly incapable of discharging the duties of his charge. The earthquake shook his palace. It rocked and trembled under him as he fled from room to room. The dead from the court below proclaimed to him his false judgment and contradictory sentence. He thought that those voices proceeded from the gods of Jesus the prophet, so he locked himself up in a secret corner of his palace, where he burned incense and sacrificed to his own deities, to whom he also made a vow, that they might render those of the Galilean innocuous to him. Herod too was in his own palace and, like one crazed from fear, he ordered every entrance to be bolted and barred.

There were about one hundred deceased belonging to all periods of time who arose in body from their shattered tombs both in Jerusalem and its environs. They went mostly in couples to certain parts of the city, encountering the frightened inhabitants in their flight, and testifying to Jesus in denunciatory words, few but vigorous. [K14] Most of the sepulchers stood solitary in the valleys, though there were many in the newly laid out portions of the city, especially among the gardens toward the northwest, between the corner gate and that leading to the place of crucifixion. There were besides, around and under the temple, many secret graves long since forgotten.

Not all the dead whose corpses were exposed to view by the falling of their tombs arose. Many a one became merely visible, because the graves were in common. But many others, whose souls Jesus sent to earth from Limbo, arose, threw off the covering from their face and went, not walking, but as if floating, along the streets of Jerusalem to their friends and relatives. They entered the houses of their posterity, and rebuked them severely for the part they had taken in the murder of Jesus. I saw some of them meeting, as if they were friends or relatives, and going in couples through the streets of the city. I could see no movement of their feet under their long winding sheets. They passed along as if lightly hovering above the ground. The hands of some were enfolded in broad bands of linen, others hung down under the large sleeves that bound the arms. The covering of the face was thrown up over the head, and the pale, yellow countenance with its long beard looked dried and withered. Their voices sounded strange and unearthly, and these voices, joined to their incessant moving from place to place, unconcerned about all around, was their only external expression; indeed they seemed almost nothing but voice. They were clothed somewhat differently, each according to the custom at the time of his death, his position in society, and his age. On the crossways upon which Jesus's punishment was trumpeted as the procession moved on to Golgotha, they stood still and proclaimed glory to Jesus and woe to his murderers. The people standing afar hearkened, shuddered, and fled, as the dead floated toward them. I heard them on the

forum in front of Pilate's palace crying aloud in threatening terms. I remember the words: "Cruel Judge!" The people fled into the most secret corners of their houses and hid. Intense fear pervaded the whole city. About four o'clock, the dead returned to their graves. Many other spirits appeared in different quarters after Christ's resurrection. The sacrifice was interrupted and everything thrown into confusion. Only a very few of the people ate the paschal lamb that evening.

Among the dead who arose on this occasion in and around Jerusalem (and there were at least one hundred), no relative of Jesus was found. The tombs in the northwestern section of Jerusalem were once beyond the precincts of the city, but when it was enlarged they were included in its limits. I had also a glimpse of other deceased persons who arose here and there in different parts of the Holy Land, appeared to their relatives, and bore witness to Jesus Christ's mission. I saw, for instance, Zadoch, a very pious man, who divided all his wealth between the poor and the temple and founded an Essene community near Hebron. He was one of the last prophets before Christ. He had waited very earnestly for the appearance of the Messiah, he had many revelations upon the same, and communication with the ancestors of the holy family. This Zadoch, who lived about one hundred years before Jesus, I saw arise and appear to several persons in the region of Hebron. I saw once that his soul was among the first to return to his body, and then I saw all those souls walking around with Jesus, as if they had again laid their body down. I saw also various deceased persons appearing to the disciples of the Lord in their hiding places, and addressing to them words of admonition.

I saw that the darkness and earthquake were not confined to Jerusalem and its environs. They extended throughout other regions of the country, yes, even in far distant places they spread terror and destruction. In Thirza, the towers of the prison from which Jesus had released the captives were overthrown, as well as other buildings. In the land of Cabul I saw that a great many places suffered injury. Throughout Galilee, where chiefly Jesus had journeyed, I saw isolated buildings in many places, and especially numerous houses belonging to the Pharisees who had persecuted the Lord most violently, toppling down over wife and child, while they themselves were away at the feast. The destruction around the Sea of Galilee was very remarkable. In Capernaum many buildings were overturned. The place between Tiberias and the garden of Zorobabel, the centurion of Capernaum, was almost demolished. The entire rocky projection belonging to the centurion's beautiful gardens near Capernaum was torn away. The lake rushed into the valley and its waters flowed near to Capernaum, which, before that, was fully half an hour's distance from it. Peter's house and the dwelling of the blessed Virgin outside Capernaum and toward the lake remained unharmed.

The Sea of Galilee was greatly disturbed. In some places its banks caved in, and in others they seemed to be pushed out, its shape thereby being notably changed. It began to assume that which it has at the present day, and, especially in its near surroundings, it can no longer be readily recognized. The change was particularly great at the southwest end of the sea, just below Tarichea, where the long dike of black stone which separated the marsh from the sea and gave a fixed direction to the course of the Jordan entirely gave way and occasioned great destruction.

On the eastern side of the sea, where the swine of the Gerasens plunged into the marsh, many places sank in; the same happened likewise in Gergesa, Gerasa, and throughout the entire district of Chorazin. The mountain upon which Jesus had twice multiplied the loaves sustained a great shaking, and the stone upon which the bread was multiplied was rent in twain. In and around Paneas, many things were overturned. In the Decapolis half of the cities sank, and many places in Asia sustained severe damage: for instance, Nicaea, but chiefly many situated east and northeast of Paneas. In Upper Galilee too I saw great destruction. Most of the Pharisees found, on their return from the feast, dire distress in their homes, and news of it reached others while yet in Jerusalem. It was on this account that the enemies of Jesus were so dejected, and that they ventured not until Pentecost to molest his followers in any notable way.

On Mount Garizim I saw many objects belonging to the temple tumbling down. Above a well, which was protected by a little temple, stood an idol. Both idol and roof were precipitated into the well. At Nazareth, one half of the synagogue out of which his enemies had thrust Jesus, fell; and that part of the mountain down which they wanted to cast him was torn away.

Many a mountain, valley, and city sustained great damage, and several changes were made in the bed of the Jordan. By the shocks upon the seashore and the inflowing of little streams, obstacles arose against the rushing water, so that the course of the river was in many places considerably turned aside. In Machaerus and the other cities under Herod's jurisdiction, the earthquake was not felt. They were situated outside the circle of warning and repentance, like those men who did not fall in the Garden of Olives and who consequently did not rise again.

In many regions, the sojourn of evil spirits, I saw those spirits falling in great crowds with the toppling buildings and mountains. The quaking of the earth reminded me then of the convulsions of the possessed when the evil one felt that he had to depart. When, near Gerasa, a portion of that mountain from which the demon with the herd of swine had plunged into the swamp by the seashore rolled down into that same swamp, I saw rushing with it into the abyss, like an angry cloud, an immense multitude of evil spirits.

I think it was in Nicaea that I saw something of which I still remember, although imperfectly, the details. I saw a harbor in which lay many ships, and nearby a house from which rose a great tower. I saw there a man, a pagan, the custodian of the ships. It was his duty to climb up into the tower from time to time and gaze out over the sea, to find out whether ships were coming or if any assistance was needed. Hearing a roaring noise among the ships in the harbor, he became apprehensive of an enemy's approach. Hurrying quickly up into the watchtower, and looking out upon the ships, he beheld floating over them numerous dark figures that cried out to him in mournful tones: "If you desire to save these ships, steer them away from here, for we have to go into the abyss! Great Pan is dead." These are the only words that I distinctly remember of the apparitions. But they told him other things, and gave him many directions as to where and how, on a voyage which he was destined to take, he should make known what they now imparted to him. They exhorted him also when messengers would come and announce the doctrine of him who had just died, to receive them well.

Through the power of the Lord, the evil spirits were forced to warn that good man and proclaim their own disgrace. Then a violent storm arose, but the ships had already been secured. I saw at the same time the devils plunging with loud bellowing into the sea, and one half of the city swallowed up by the earthquake. The good man's house remained standing. Soon after that he sailed around in his ship for a long time, executing his commissions and making known the death of "The great Pan," as they called the Lord. Later on he went to Rome, where his statements excited intense wonder. I saw many other things connected with this man, but I have forgotten them. Among other things, I saw that one of the narratives of his travels became in repetition mixed up with what I had seen, and it was very far-spread, but I do not clearly recollect how they were connected. I think the man's name sounded like Thamus, or Tramus.

Joseph of Arimathea Requests the Body of Jesus from Pilate

QUIET was scarcely restored to Jerusalem after all those frightful events, when Pilate, already so terrified, was assailed on all sides with accounts of what had occurred. The council of the Jews also, as they had determined to do that morning, sent to him for permission to break the legs of the crucified, and thus put an end to their life, for they wanted to take them down from the cross, that they might not hang thereon upon the sabbath. Pilate dispatched some executioners to Golgotha for this purpose.

Just after that I saw Joseph of Arimathea, a member of the council, going to Pilate. [K15] He had already heard of Jesus's death, and with Nicodemus had concluded to bury the Lord's body in the new sepulcher hewn out of a rock in his own garden, not very far from Golgotha. I think I saw him outside the gate as if examining, or reconnoitering, the premises. Some few of his servants were already in the garden, cleaning it and arranging things inside the sepulcher. Nicodemus had gone to buy linen and spices for preparing the body for burial, and he was now waiting for Joseph.

Joseph found Pilate very anxious and perplexed. He begged openly and fearlessly that he might be allowed to take the body of Jesus, the king of the Jews, down from the cross, as he wanted to lay it in his own sepulcher. Pilate's anxiety increased on beholding so distinguished a man begging so earnestly to be permitted to honor the body of Jesus, whom he himself had caused to be ignominiously crucified. The innocence of Jesus recurred to him, making him still more uneasy, but he overcame himself, and asked: "Is he, then, already dead?" for only a few moments had elapsed since he sent executioners out to break the bones of the crucified, and thus end their life. He summoned the centurion Abenadar, who was returned from the caves where he had spoken with some of the disciples, and asked him whether the king of the Jews was already dead. Abenadar in reply related to him the death of the Lord about three o'clock, his last words, and his loud cry, the quaking of the earth and the rending of the rock. Outwardly Pilate appeared merely to be surprised, since the crucified generally lived longer, but inwardly he was filled with trouble and alarm at the coincidence of those signs with Jesus's death. He wished perhaps to palliate in some measure his cruelty by at once expediting an order for Joseph of Arimathea, by which he gave him the body of the king of the Jews with permission to take it down from the cross and bury it. He was glad by so doing to be able to annoy the high priests, who would rather have had Jesus dishonorably buried along with the two thieves. It was probably Abenadar himself whom Pilate dispatched to see the order executed, for I saw him present at the taking down of Jesus from the cross.

Joseph of Arimathea took leave of Pilate and went to meet Nicodemus, who was awaiting him at the house of a well-disposed woman. She lived on the broad street near that narrow alley in which our Lord, just at the commencement of his bitter Way of the Cross, was made to endure such ignominy. Nicodemus had purchased here a lot of aromatic plants and herbs for the embalming, for the woman was a vendor of such things. She procured elsewhere many kinds of spices that she herself did not have, also linen and bandages for the same purpose, all of which she rolled together into a package that could be easily carried. Joseph of Arimathea went himself and bought a winding sheet of cotton, very fine and beautiful, six ells long and several wide. His servants collected under a shed near the house of Nicodemus ladders, hammers, strong iron nails, water bottles, vessels, sponges, and all that was necessary for the work before them. The smaller objects they packed on a light litter, or handbarrow, almost like that upon which the disciples carried the body of John the Baptist from Herod's citadel of Machaerus.

The Side of Jesus Opened • The Legs of the Thieves Broken

MEANWHILE all was silent and mournful on Golgotha. The crowd had timidly dispersed to their homes. The mother of Jesus, John, Magdalene, Mary Cleophas, and Salome were standing or sitting with veiled heads and in deep sadness opposite the cross. Some soldiers were seated on the earthen wall, their spears stuck in the ground near them. Cassius was riding around, and the soldiers were interchanging words with their companions posted at some distance below. The sky was lowering; all nature appeared to be in mourning. Things were in this position when six executioners were seen ascending the mount with ladders, spades, ropes, and heavy, triangular iron bars used for breaking the bones of malefactors.

When they entered the circle, the friends of Jesus drew back a little. New fear seized upon the heart of the blessed Virgin lest the body of Jesus was to be still further outraged, for the executioners mounted up the cross, roughly felt the sacred body, and declared that he was pretending to be dead. Although they felt that he was quite cold and stiff, yet they were not convinced that he was already dead. John, at the entreaty of the blessed Virgin, turned to the soldiers, to draw them off for a while from the body of the Lord. The executioners next mounted the ladders to the crosses of the thieves. Two of them with their sharp clubs broke the bones of their arms above and below the elbows, while a third did the same above the knees and ankles. [K16] Gesmas roared frightfully, consequently the executioner finished him by three blows of the club on the breast. Dismas moaned feebly, and expired under the torture. He was the first mortal to look again upon his Redeemer. The executioners untwisted the cords and allowed the bodies to fall heavily to the earth. Then tying ropes around them, they dragged them down into the valley between the mount and the city wall, and there buried them.

The executioners appeared still to have some doubts as to the death of the Lord, and his friends, after witnessing the terrible scene just described, were more anxious than ever for them to withdraw. Cassius, the subaltern officer, afterward known as Longinus, a somewhat hasty, impetuous man of twenty-five, whose airs of importance and officiousness joined to his weak, squinting eyes often exposed him to the ridicule of his inferiors, was suddenly seized by wonderful ardor. The barbarity, the base fury of the executioners, the anguish of the blessed Virgin, and the grace accorded him in that sudden and supernatural impulse of zeal, all combined to make of him the fulfiller of a prophecy. His lance, which was shortened by having one section run into another, he drew out to its full length, stuck the point upon it, turned his horse's head, and drove him boldly up to the narrow space on top of the eminence upon which the cross was planted. There was scarcely room for the animal to turn, and I saw Cassius reining him up in front of the chasm made by the cleft rock. He halted between Jesus's cross and that of the good thief, on the right of our Savior's body, grasped the lance with both hands, and drove it upward with such violence into the hollow, distended right side of the sacred body, through the entrails and the heart, that its point opened a little wound in the left breast. [K17] When with all his force he drew the blessed lance from the wide wound it had made in the right side of Jesus, a copious stream of blood and water rushed forth and flowed over his upraised face, bedewing him with grace and salvation. He sprang quickly from his horse, fell upon his knees, struck his breast, and before all present proclaimed aloud his belief in Jesus. [K18]

The blessed Virgin, John, and the holy women, whose eyes were riveted upon Jesus, witnessed with terror the sudden action, accompanied the thrust of the lance with a cry of woe, and rushed up to the cross. Mary, as if the thrust had transfixed her own heart, felt the sharp point piercing her through and through. She sank into the arms of her friends, while Cassius, still on his knees, was loudly confessing the Lord and joyfully praising God. He was enlightened; he now saw plainly and distinctly. The eyes of his body, like those of his soul, were healed and opened. All were seized with a sentiment of the deepest reverence at sight of the Redeemer's blood which, mixed with water, fell

in a foamy stream into a hollow in the rock at the foot of the cross. Mary, Cassius, the holy women, and John scooped it up in the drinking cups they had with them, poured it into flasks, and dried the hollow with linen cloths. †

Cassius was entirely changed, deeply touched and humbled. He had received perfect sight. The soldiers present, touched also by the miracle they had witnessed, fell on their knees, striking their breast and confessing Jesus, from the wide opening of whose right side blood and water were copiously streaming. It fell upon the clean stone, and lay there foaming and bubbling. The friends of Jesus gathered it up with loving care, Mary and Magdalene mingling with it their tears. The executioners who meanwhile had received Pilate's order not to touch the body of Jesus, as he had given it to Joseph of Arimathea for burial, did not return.

The lance of Cassius was in several sections that slipped one into the other. When not drawn out, it looked like a stout staff of moderate length. The part that inflicted a wound was of iron, smooth and pear-shaped, on the top of which a point could be stuck, and from the lower part two sharp, curved blades could be drawn when needed.

All the above took place around the cross of Jesus soon after four o'clock, while Joseph of Arimathea and Nicodemus were making the purchase necessary for the burial of Christ. When the friends of Jesus on Golgotha were informed by Joseph of Arimathea's servants, who were come from cleaning and arranging the sepulcher, that their master had Pilate's permission to take down the sacred body and lay it in his own new tomb, John and the holy women returned at once to the city, to the quarter on Mount Zion, that the blessed Virgin might take a little rest. [K19] They wanted also to get some things still necessary for the burial. The blessed Virgin had a little dwelling among the buildings belonging to the Cenacle. They did not go by the nearest gate, for that was closed and guarded on the other side by the soldiers that the Pharisees had called for when they feared an uprising of the populace. They went by one more to the south, the one that led to Bethlehem.

---

† Anne Catherine added: "Cassius was baptized by the name of Longinus; and was ordained deacon, and preached the faith. He always kept some of the blood of Christ—it dried up, but was found in his coffin in Italy. He was buried in a town at no great distance from the locality where St. Clare passed her life. There is a lake with an island upon it near this town, and the body of Longinus must have been taken there." Anne Catherine appears to designate Mantua by this description, and there is a tradition preserved in that town to the effect. I do not know which St. Clare lived in the neighborhood.

Some Localities of Ancient Jerusalem

ON the eastern side of Jerusalem was the first gate south of the southeast angle of the temple, which led into that quarter of the city called Ophel. The one to the north of the northeast corner was the sheep gate. Between these two gates was a third (though not as yet long in existence) that led to some streets which ran one above another on the east side of the temple mount, and in which principally stonecutters and other laborers resided. Their dwellings adjoined the foundation walls of the temple. Almost all the houses of these two streets belonged to Nicodemus, who had had them built. The stonecutters that occupied them either paid him rent or worked for him, for they had business relations with him and his friend, Joseph of Arimathea. The last-named owned large quarries in his native place, and carried on an active trade in marble. Nicodemus had not long before built a beautiful new gate for these streets; it is now called the gate of Moriah. As it was just finished, Jesus was the first to pass through it on Palm Sunday. He went through Nicodemus's new gate, through which no one before him had passed, and he was buried in Joseph of Arimathea's new sepulcher, in which before him no one had rested. Later on, this gate was walled up, and there is a saying that the Christians will once again enter the city through it. Even in the present day, there is a walled-up gate in this region, called by the Turks "the Golden Gate."

If there were no walls to obstruct the course, a straight road from the sheep gate toward the west would strike almost between the northwest end of Mount Zion and through the center of Golgotha. From this gate to Golgotha in a straight line the distance was perhaps three-quarters of an hour, but from Pilate's house to Golgotha it was in a straight line about five-eighths of an hour. The fortress Antonia rose from a projecting rock on the northwest of the temple mount. When one turned to the left from Pilate's palace and passed westward through the arch, the fortress lay on his left. On one of its walls was an elevated platform that overlooked the forum, and from it Pilate was accustomed to address the populace, to publish new laws, for instance. When Jesus was carrying his cross inside the city, he often had Mount Calvary on his right. (Jesus's journey must have been made partly in a southwesterly direction). It led through the gate of an inner wall which ran off toward Zion, which quarter of the city stood very high. Beyond this wall and to the west there was another quarter that contained more gardens than houses. Toward the outer wall of the city there were magnificent sepulchers with beautifully sculptured entrances, and above many of them pretty little gardens. In this quarter stood the house owned by Lazarus. It has beautiful gardens that extended toward where the outer western wall turned off to the south. There was, I think, near the great sheep gate a little private entrance through the city wall into those gardens. Jesus and his disciples, with Lazarus's permission, often made use of it in coming and going. The gate on the northwest corner opened in the direction of Bethzur, which lay more to the north than Emmaus and Joppa. Several royal tombs stood to the north of the outer wall. This western and sparsely built portion of the city was the lowest of all. It sloped gently toward the city wall and then as gently rose again before reaching it. This second slope was covered with beautiful gardens and vineyards. Back of this ran a broad paved road inside the walls with paths leading to them and to the towers. The latter were not like ours, which have their stairs inside. On the other side of the wall outside the city there was a declivity toward the valley, so that the walls around this lower quarter looked as if built on a raised terrace. Here too were found gardens and vineyards. Jesus's way to Golgotha did not run through these gardens, for the quarter in which they were lay at the end of his journey northward to the right. It was thence Simon of Cyrene was coming when he met Jesus. The gate through which Jesus was led out of the city was not directly toward the west, but rather facing the southwest. On passing out of that gate and turning to the left, one found the city wall running southward for a short distance when it made a sharp turn to the west, and then ran again to the south around Mount Zion. On this left side of the wall and on the way to Zion rose a very strong tower like a fortress. On this same side and very near the gate that led to the place of execution, opened another. Of all the city gates, these two were nearest each other. The distance between them was not greater than that between the castle gate and Luding's gate here in Dulmen. This last-mentioned gate of Jerusalem opened westward into the valley, and from it the road ran to the left and a little southward toward Bethlehem. Somewhat beyond the gate of execution the road turned northward and ran straight to Golgotha, which faced the city on the east and was very steep, but which on the west sloped gradually. Looking from this side toward the west, one could see for some distance along the road leading to Emmaus. There was a field on the roadside, and there I saw Luke gathering herbs when, after the resurrection, he and Cleophas on their way to Emmaus were met by Jesus. Toward ten o'clock on the morning of the crucifixion, Jesus's face was turned to the northwest, that is, in the direction of the cross erected for him on Golgotha. When hanging on the cross, if he turned his head to the right, he could catch a glimpse of the fortress Antonia. All along the city wall, both north and east of Golgotha, lay gardens, vineyards, and sepulchers. The cross of Jesus was buried on the northeast side and at the foot of Mount Calvary. Opposite the spot upon which the crosses were afterward discovered and to the northeast there were beautiful terraces covered with vines. Looking southward from the point upon which the cross stood on Golgotha, one could see the house of Caiaphas away below the fortress of David.

Garden and Tomb Belonging to Joseph of Arimathea

THE GARDEN of Joseph of Arimathea was at least seven minute's distance from Mount Calvary, near the Bethlehem gate, and on the height that sloped down to the city wall. It was very beautiful with its tall trees, its seats, and its shady nooks. On one side it extended up to the height upon which rose the city wall. A person coming down into the valley from the northern side would perceive on entering the garden that the ground rose on his left up to the city wall. To the right and at the end of the garden lay a detached rock, in which was the sepulcher. Turning to the right, he would come to the entrance of the grotto which was facing the east, on rising ground and against the city wall. In either end of the same rock, north and south, there were two smaller grottoes with low entrances. A narrow pathway ran around its western side. The ground in front of the grotto was higher than that of the entrance itself, so that to reach the door, one had to descend some steps, just as in another little tomb on the eastern side of the rock. The outer entrance was closed with lattice-work. The space inside the grotto was sufficiently great for four men to stand against the wall to the right and as many to the left, and yet permit the body to be carried between them by the bearers. The walls of the grotto rounded at the western side until they formed, just opposite the door, a broad but not very high niche. The rocky wall here formed an arching roof over the tomb, which was about two feet above the level of the ground, with space hollowed out on top to receive a corpse in its winding sheet. The tomb projected like an altar, being connected with the rock only on one side. There was room for one person to stand at the head, another at the foot, and still a third before the tomb even when the doors of the niche were closed. The doors were of copper, or some other metal, and opened to both sides, where there was space for them against the walls. They did not stand perpendicularly, but lay a little obliquely before the niche, and reached low enough to the ground for a stone laid against them to prevent their being opened. The stone intended for this purpose was now lying outside the entrance of the grotto.

After the burial of the Lord it was brought in for the first time and laid before the closed doors of the tomb. It was large and somewhat rounded on the side that was to lie next the doors, because the wall near them was not at right angles. To open the doors, the immense stone was not first rolled out of the vault, for that, owing to the confined space, would have been attended with the greatest difficulty. But a chain let down from the roof was fastened to rings fixed in the stone. Then the chain being drawn up by the aid of several men exerting all their strength, the stone was swung to one side of the grotto, leaving the doors of the tomb free.

In the garden opposite the entrance to the grotto there was a stone bench. If one mounted to the roof of the grotto, which was covered with grass, he could descry the heights of Zion and some of the towers above the city walls. The Bethlehem gate, an aqueduct, and the well of Gihon also could be seen from here. The rock inside was white veined with red and brown. The grotto was finished very neatly.

We must here remark that, in the four years during which Anne Catherine related her visions, she described many changes connected with the holy places profaned and laid waste, yet always venerated either secretly or openly. She herself venerated them in vision. She saw many stones and fragments of rock, the witnesses of the Passion and Resurrection of the Lord, placed by St. Helena, after her discovery of the holy places, in the Church of the Holy Sepulcher built by her. They were placed in a narrow space near one another, and put under the protection of the city. Anne Catherine honored in vision the Church of the Crucifixion, that of the Holy Sepulcher, and several parts of the Sepulcher itself over which chapels are now raised. But sometimes, when she venerated not so much the tomb itself as the site upon which the sepulcher stood, it seemed to her that she saw it in the vicinity, though still somewhat removed from the spot upon which the cross had stood.

The Descent from the Cross

WHILE there were only a few guards around the cross, I saw about five men coming through the valley from Bethany. They drew near the place of execution, looked up to the cross, and then stole away again. I think they must have been disciples. Three times I saw two men in the vicinity as if making examinations and anxiously deliberating together. They were Joseph of Arimathea and Nicodemus. The first time was during the crucifixion. (Perhaps it was then that they sent to buy Jesus's garments from the soldiers). The second was when they came to see whether the crowd had dispersed. After looking around, they went to the tomb to make some preparations. The third time was when they returned from the tomb. They went right up to the cross, looked up and all around, as if watching for a good opportunity, consulted as to the best plan of action for the task before them, and then went back to the city.

And now began the transport to Golgotha of all that was necessary for the embalming. Besides the instruments to be used in taking the sacred body down from the cross, the servants took with them two ladders from a shed near Nicodemus's dwelling. Each of these ladders consisted of a single pole in which pieces of thick plank were so fitted as to form steps. They were provided with hooks, which could be hung higher or lower at pleasure, either to steady the ladder itself in some particular position or to hang on it the tools and other articles necessary for the work that was being done.

The good women from whom they had received the spices for the embalming packed everything nicely for them. Nicodemus had brought one hundred pounds of spices, equal to thirty-seven pounds of our weight, as has more than once been explained to me. They carried these spices around the neck in little kegs made of bark. One of the kegs contained some kind of powder. In bags made of parchment, or leather, were bunches of aromatic herbs. Joseph had with him also a box of ointment. Of what the box was composed I know not, but it was red with a blue rim. The servants, as already mentioned, carried in a handbarrow various kinds of vessels, leathern bottles, sponges, and tools. They took with them likewise fire in a closed lantern.

The servants left the city before their master and by another gate (I think the Bethlehem Gate) and went out to Golgotha. On their way through the city, they passed a house to which the blessed Virgin with the other women and John had retired, in order to make some preparations for the Lord's burial. They joined the servants, whom they followed at a little distance. There were about five women, some of whom carried large bundles of linen under their mantles. It was a custom among the women, whenever they went out toward evening or upon any secret mission of piety, to envelop their whole person in a long strip of linen at least a yard in width. This they did very skillfully. They began with one arm, and then wound the linen so closely about the lower limbs that they could not take a long step. I have seen them entirely enveloped in this way, the linen brought up cleverly around the other arm and even enveloping the head. On this occasion there was something striking in the dress, for it looked to me like a robe of mourning.

Joseph and Nicodemus also were in mourning attire: false sleeves, maniples, and wide girdles of black, and their long and flowing mantles which they had drawn over their head were of a dark gray color. Their wide mantles covered all that they were carrying. Both directed their steps toward the gate of execution.

The streets were quiet and lonely. General terror kept the inhabitants in their homes. Many were prostrate in penance, and only a few were observing the prescriptions for the festival. When Joseph and Nicodemus arrived at the gate, they found it closed, and the streets and walls around beset by soldiers. *They were those for whom the Pharisees asked after two o'clock when they were fearing a tumult,* and they had not yet been remanded. Joseph presented them Pilate's written order to be allowed to pass. The soldiers expressed their readiness to comply with it, but explained at the same time that they had already vainly tried to open the gate, that probably it had received some damage from the earthquake shock, and that the executioners sent out to break the bones of the crucified had to return through the corner gate. But as soon as Joseph and Nicodemus grasped the bolt, the gate opened of itself with perfect ease.

It was still cloudy and foggy when they reached Golgotha, where they found their servants and the holy women, the latter sitting in front of the cross and in tears. Cassius and several converted soldiers stood like changed men, timidly and reverently, at some distance. Joseph and Nicodemus told the holy women and John of all that they had done to save Jesus from the ignominious death inflicted upon the thieves, and heard from them in return with what difficulty they had warded off the breaking of the Lord's bones, and how the prophecy had been fulfilled. They told also of how Cassius had pierced the sacred body with his lance. As soon as the centurion Abenadar arrived, they began sadly and reverently that most holy labor of love, the taking down from the cross and preparing for burial of the sacred body of their Master, their Lord, their Redeemer.

The most holy Virgin and Magdalene were seated upon the right side of the little mound between the cross of Dismas and that of Jesus. The other women were busied arranging the spices and linens, the water, the sponges, and the vessels. Cassius also drew near when he saw Abenadar approaching, and imparted to him the miracle wrought on his eyes. All were extremely touched. Their movements were marked by an air of solemn sadness and gravity. They worked with hearts full of love, but without many words. Sometimes the silence in which the sacred duties were quickly and carefully being rendered was broken by a deep sigh or a vehement exclamation of woe. Magdalene gave way unrestrainedly to her grief. Her emotion was violent. No consideration, not even the presence of so many around her, could make her repress it.

Nicodemus and Joseph placed the ladders behind the cross and mounted, carrying with them a very long strip of linen, to which three broad straps were fastened. They bound the body of Jesus under the arms and knees to the trunk of the cross, and the arms they fastened in the same way at the wrists. Then by striking upon strong pegs fixed against the points of the nails at the back of the cross, they forced out the nails from Jesus's hands, which were not very much shaken by the blows. The nails fell easily out of the wounds, for they had been enlarged by the weight of the body which, supported now by means of the linen band, no longer rested upon them. The lower part of the body, which in death had sunk down on the knees, rested now in a sitting posture upon a linen band that was bound up around the hands on the arms of the cross. While Joseph was striking out the left nail and allowing the left arm to sink down gently on the body, Nicodemus was binding the right arm in the same way to the cross, also the thorn-crowned head, which had fallen upon the right shoulder. The right nail was then forced out, and the arm allowed to sink into the band that supported the body. Abenadar the centurion had meanwhile, though with great effort, been driving out the enormous nail from the feet.

Cassius reverently picked up the nails as they fell out, and laid them down together by the blessed Virgin. Next, removing the ladders to the front of the cross and close to the sacred body, they loosened the upper band from the trunk of the cross, and hung it on one of the hooks of the ladder. They did the same to the two other bands, which they hung on two of the lower hooks. Thus with the gently lowered bands, the sacred body sank by degrees to where the centurion Abenadar, mounted on portable steps, was waiting to receive it. He clasped the limbs below the knees in his arms and descended slowly, while Nicodemus and Joseph, holding the upper part in their arms, gently and cautiously, as if carrying a beloved and very severely wounded friend, came down the ladders step by step. In this way did that most sacred, that most terribly maltreated body of the Redeemer reach the ground. [K20]

This taking down of Jesus from the cross was inexpressibly touching. Everything was done with so much precaution, so much tenderness, as if fearing to cause the Lord pain. Those engaged in it were penetrated with all the love and reverence for the sacred body that they had felt for the Holy of Holies during his life. All were looking up with eyes riveted, and accompanying every movement with raising of hands, tears, and gestures of pain and grief. But no word was uttered. When the men engaged in the sacred task gave expression to their reverent emotion it was as if involuntary, as if they were performing some solemn function; and when necessary to communicate directions to one another, they did it in few words and a low tone. When the blows of the hammer by which the nails were driven out resounded, Mary and Magdalene, as well as all that had been present at the crucifixion, were pierced with fresh grief, for the sound reminded them of that most cruel nailing of Jesus to the cross. They shuddered, as if expecting again to hear his piercing cries, and grieved anew over his death proclaimed by the silence of those blessed lips. As soon as the sacred body was taken down, the men wrapped it in linen from the knees to the waist and laid it on a sheet in his mother's arms which, in anguish of heart and ardent longing, were stretched out to receive it. [K21]

The Body of Jesus Prepared for Burial

THE BLESSED Virgin was seated upon a large cover spread upon the ground, her right knee raised a little, and her back supported by a kind of cushion made, perhaps, of mantles rolled together. There sat the poor mother, exhausted by grief and fatigue, in the position best suited for rendering love's last, sad duties to the remains of her murdered Son. The men laid the sacred body on a sheet spread upon the mother's lap. The venerable head of Jesus rested upon her slightly raised knee, and his body lay outstretched upon the sheet. Love and grief in equal degrees struggled in the breast of the blessed Mother. She held in her arms the body of her beloved Son, whose long martyrdom she had been able to soothe by no loving ministrations; and at the same time she beheld the frightful maltreatment exercised upon it, she gazed upon its wounds now close under her eyes. She pressed her lips to his bloodstained cheeks, while Magdalene knelt with her face bowed upon his feet.

The men meanwhile had retired to a little cave that lay deep on the southwestern side of the mount. There they completed their preparations for the burial and set all things in order. Cassius and a number of soldiers who had been converted to the Lord remained standing at a respectful distance. All the ill-disposed had returned to the city, and those now present served as a guard to prevent the approach of anyone likely to interrupt the last honors being shown to Jesus. Some of them, when called upon, rendered assistance here and there by handing different articles.

The holy women helped in various ways, presenting when necessary vessels of water, sponges, towels, ointments, and spices. When not so engaged, they remained at a little distance attentively watching what was going on. Among them were Mary Cleophas, Salome, and Veronica, but Magdalene was always busied around the sacred body. Mary Heli, the blessed Virgin's elder sister, who was already an aged matron, was sitting apart on the earthwall of the circle, silently looking on. John lent constant assistance to the blessed Virgin. He went to and fro between the women and the men, now helping the former in their task of love, and afterward assisting the latter in every way to prepare all things for the burial. Everything was thought of. The women had leathern water bottles, which they opened, and pressed the sides together to pour out their contents, also a vessel nearby on burning coals. They gave Mary and Magdalene clear water and fresh sponges as required, squeezing into leathern bottles those that had been used. I think the round lumps that I saw them squeezing out must have been sponges.

The blessed Virgin's courage and fortitude, in the midst of her inexpressible anguish, were unshaken. Her sorrow was not such as could cause her to permit the marks of outrage and torture to remain upon the sacred body, and so she immediately began earnestly and carefully to wash and purify it from every trace of ill-usage. With great care she opened the crown of thorns in the back and, with the assistance of others, removed it from Jesus's head. Some of the thorns had penetrated deeply, and that the removal of the crown might not by disturbing them enlarge the wounds, they had first to be cut off. The crown was deposited near the nails. Then with a pair of round, yellow pincers,[†] Mary drew from the wounds the long splinters and sharp thorns still sunken in the Lord's head, and showed them sadly to the compassionate friends standing around. The thorns were laid by the crown, though some of them may have been kept as tokens of remembrance.

The face of the Lord was hardly recognizable, so greatly was it disfigured by blood and wounds. The torn hair of the head and beard was clotted with blood. Mary washed the head and face and soaked the dried blood from the hair with sponges. As the washing proceeded, the awful cruelties to which Jesus had been subjected became more apparent, and roused emotions of compassion, sorrow, and tenderness as she went from wound to wound. With a sponge and a little linen over the fingers of her right hand, she washed the blood from the wounds of the head, from the broken eyes, the nostrils, and the ears. With the little piece of linen on the forefinger, she purified the half-opened mouth, the tongue, the teeth, and the lips. She divided into three parts the little that remained of his hair. One part fell on either side of the head, and the third over the back. The front hair, after disengaging and cleansing it, she smoothed behind his ears.[††]

When the sacred head had been thoroughly cleansed, the blessed Virgin kissed the cheeks and covered it. Her care was next directed to the neck, the shoulders, the breast, and the back of the sacred body, the arms and the torn hands filled with blood. Ah, then was the terrible condition to which it had been reduced displayed in all its horror! The bones of the breast, as well as all the nerves, were dislocated and strained and thereby become stiff and inflexible. The shoulder upon which Jesus had borne the heavy cross was so lacerated that it had become one great wound, and the whole of the upper part of the body was full of welts and cuts from the scourges. There was a small wound in the left breast where the point of Cassius's lance had come out, and in the right side was opened that great, wide wound made by the lance, which had pierced his heart through and through. Mary washed and purified all these wounds, while Magdalene, kneeling before her, frequently lent assistance, though for the most part she remained at Jesus's feet, bathing them for the last time, more with her tears than with water, and wiping them with her hair.

The head, the upper part of the body, and the feet of the Lord had now been cleansed from blood. The sacred body still lay in Mary's lap, bluish white, glistening like flesh drained of blood, with here and there brown stains of coagulated blood that looked like red moles, and red places where the skin had been torn off. The blessed Virgin

---

[†] Anne Catherine said that the shape of these pincers reminded her of the scissors with which Samson's hair was cut off. In her visions of the third year of the public life of Jesus she had seen our Lord keep the sabbath-day at Misael—a town belonging to the Levites, of the tribe of Asher—and as a portion of the Book of Judges was read in the synagogue, had beheld upon that occasion the life of Samson.

[††] Anne Catherine was accustomed, when speaking of persons of historical importance, to explain how they divided their hair. "Eve," she said, "divided her hair in two parts, but Mary into three." And she appeared to attach importance to these words. No opportunity presented itself for her to give any explanation upon the subject, which probably would have shown what was done with the hair in sacrifices, funerals, consecrations, or vows, etc. She once said of Samson: "His fair hair, which was long and thick, was gathered up on his head in seven tresses, like a helmet, and the ends of these tresses were fastened upon his forehead and temples. His hair was not in itself the source of his strength, but only as the witness to the vow which he had made to let it grow in God's honor. The powers that depended upon these seven tresses were the seven gifts of the Holy Spirit. He must have already broken his vows and lost many graces, when he allowed this sign of being a Nazarene to be cut off. I did not see Delilah cut off all his hair, and I think one lock remained on his forehead. He retained the grace to do penance and of that repentance by which he recovered strength sufficient to destroy his enemies. The life of Samson is figurative and prophetic."

covered the parts as they were washed, and began to embalm the wounds, commencing with those of the head. The holy women knelt by her in turn, presenting to her a box from which, with the forefinger and thumb of the right hand, she took out something like salve, or precious ointment, with which she filled and anointed all the wounds. She put some upon the hair also, and I saw her taking the hands of Jesus in her own left hand, reverently kissing them, and then filling the wide wounds made by the nails with the ointment, or sweet spices. The ears, nostrils, and wound of Jesus's side, she likewise filled with the same. Magdalene was busied principally with the feet of Jesus. She repeatedly wiped and anointed them, but only to bedew them again with her tears, and she often knelt long with her face pressed upon them.

I saw that the water used was not thrown away, but poured into the leathern bottles into which the sponges had been squeezed. More than once I saw fresh water brought by some of the men, Cassius or some other soldier, in the leathern bottles and jugs that the women had brought with them. They procured it at the well of Gihon, which was so near that it could be seen from the garden of the sepulcher.

When the blessed Virgin had anointed all the wounds, she bound up the sacred head in linen, but the covering for the face, attached to that of the head, she did not as yet draw down. With a gentle pressure, she closed the half-broken eyes of Jesus, and kept her hand upon them for a little while. Then she closed the mouth, embraced the sacred body of her Son, and weeping bitter tears, allowed her face to rest upon his. Magdalene's reverence for Jesus did not permit her to approach her face to his. She pressed it to his feet only.

Joseph and Nicodemus had already been standing awhile at some distance waiting, when John drew near the blessed Virgin with the request that she would permit them to take the body of Jesus, that they might proceed in their preparations for the burial, as the sabbath was near. Once more Mary closely embraced Jesus, and in touching words took leave of him. The men raised the most sacred body in the sheet upon which it was resting in the lap of his mother, and carried it down to the place where the burial preparations were to be made. [K22] Mary's grief, which had been somewhat assuaged by her loving ministrations to Jesus, now burst forth anew, and, quite overcome, she rested with covered head in the arms of the women. Magdalene, as if fearing that they wanted to rob her of her Beloved, with outstretched hands ran some steps after the sacred body, but soon she turned back again to the blessed Virgin.

They carried the body of Jesus a little distance down from Golgotha's summit to a cave on the side of the mount in which there was a beautiful flat rock. It was here that the men had prepared the place for embalming. I saw first a linen cloth, open-worked something like a net. It looked as if it had been pierced with a sharp instrument, and was like the large so-called hunger cloth (*Hungertuch*) that is hung up in our churches during Lent. When as a child I saw that cloth hanging up, I used to think it was the same that I had seen at the preparations for the Lord's burial. Perhaps it was pierced like a net in order to allow the water used in washing to flow through it. I saw another large cloth opened out. They laid the body of the Lord on the open-worked one, and some of them held the other over it. Nicodemus and Joseph knelt down and, under cover of this upper cloth, loosened from the lower part of Jesus's body the bandage that they had bound around it from the knees to the hips when taken down from the cross. They removed likewise that other covering which Jonadab, the nephew of his foster father Joseph, had given him before the crucifixion. Thus with great regard to modesty, they sponged, under cover of the sheet held over it, the lower part of the Lord's body.

Then, linen bands being stretched under the upper part of the sacred body and the knees, it was raised, still under cover of the sheet, and the back treated in the same way without turning the body over. They washed it until the water squeezed from the sponges ran clean and clear. After that they poured water of myrrh over the whole body, and I saw them laying it down and reverently, with their hands, stretching it out at full length, for it had stiffened in the position in which, when in death it had sunk down upon the cross, the knees bent. Under the hips they laid a linen strip, four feet in width and about twelve feet in length, almost filled the lap with bunches of herbs and fine, crisp threadlike plants, like saffron, and then sprinkled over all a powder, which Nicodemus had brought with him in a box. The bunches of herbs were such as I have often seen on the celestial tables laid upon little green and gold plates with blue rims. Next they tightly bound the linen strip around the whole, drew the end up between the sacred limbs, and stuck it under the band that encircled the waist, thus fastening it securely. After this they anointed the wounds of the thighs, scattered sweet spices over them, laid bunches of herbs between the limbs all the way down to the feet, and bound the whole in linen from the feet up.

John once more conducted the blessed Virgin and the other holy women to the sacred remains of Jesus. Mary knelt down by Jesus's head, took a fine linen scarf that hung around her neck under her mantle and which she had received from Claudia Procula, Pilate's wife, and laid it under the head of her Son. Then she and the other holy women filled in the spaces between the shoulders and the head, around the whole neck and up as far as the cheeks with herbs, some of those fine threadlike plants, and the costly powder mentioned before, all of which the blessed Virgin bound up carefully in the fine linen scarf. Magdalene poured the entire contents of a little flask of precious balm into the wound of Jesus's side, while the holy women placed aromatic herbs in the hands and all around and under the feet. Then the men covered the pit of the stomach and filled up the armpits and all other parts of the body with sweet spices, crossed the stiffened arms over the bosom, and closely wrapped the whole in the large white sheet as far as the breast, just as a child is swathed. Then, having fastened under one of the armpits the end of a broad linen band, they wound it round the arms, the hands, the head, and down again around the whole of the sacred body until it presented the appearance of a mummy. Lastly, they laid the Lord's body on the large sheet, twelve feet long, that Joseph of Arimathea had bought, and wrapped it closely around it. The sacred body was laid on it crosswise. Then one corner was drawn up from the feet to the breast, the opposite one was folded down over the head and shoulders, and the sides were doubled round the whole person. [K23]

While all were kneeling around the Lord's body, taking leave of it with many tears, a touching miracle was exhibited before their eyes: the entire form of Jesus's sacred body with all its wounds appeared, as if drawn in brown and reddish colors, on the cloth that covered it. It was as if he wished gratefully to reward their loving care of him, gratefully to acknowledge their sorrow, and leave to them an image of himself imprinted through all the coverings that enveloped him. Weeping and lamenting, they embraced the sacred body, and reverently kissed the miraculous portrait. Their astonishment was so great that they opened the outside wrapping, and it became still greater when they found all the linen bands around the sacred body white as before and only the uppermost cloth marked with the Lord's figure.

The cloth on the side upon which the body lay received the imprint of the whole back of the Lord; the ends that covered it were marked with the front likeness. The parts of this latter, to produce the perfect form, had to be laid together, because the corners of the cloth were all crossed over the body in front. The picture was not a mere impression formed by bleeding wounds, for the whole body had been tightly wrapped in spices and numerous linen bands. It was a miraculous picture, a witness to the creative Godhead in the body of Jesus.

I have seen many things connected with the subsequent history of this holy winding sheet, but I cannot recall them in their precise order. After the resurrection it, along with the other linens, came into the possession of Jesus's friends. Once I saw a man carrying it off with him under his arm when he was starting on a journey. I saw it a second time in the hands of the Jews, and I saw it long in veneration among the Christians of different places. Once a dispute arose about it, and for its settlement, the holy winding sheet was thrown into the fire; but rising miraculously above the flames, it flew into the hands of the Christians.

At the prayer of holy men, three impressions of the holy image were taken off, both the back and the picture formed on the folds of the front. These impressions were consecrated by contact with the original and the solemn intention of the church. They have even effected great miracles. I have seen the original, somewhat damaged, somewhat torn, held in veneration by some non-Catholic Christians of Asia. I have forgotten the name of the city, but it is situated in a large country near the home of the three kings. In those visions I also saw something connected with Turin and France and Pope Clement I, as well as something about the Emperor Tiberius, who died five years after the death of Christ, but I have forgotten it.

The Sepulcher

THE MEN now laid the sacred body on the leathern litter, placed over it a brown cover, and ran two poles along the sides. I thought right away of the Ark of the Covenant. Nicodemus and Joseph carried the front ends on their shoulders; Abenadar and John, the others. There followed the blessed Virgin, her elder sister Mary Heli, Magdalene, and Mary Cleophas. [K24] Then the group of women that had been seated at some distance; Veronica, Johanna Chusa, Mary Mark; Salome, the wife of Zebedee; Mary Salome, Salome of Jerusalem, Susanna, and Anna, a niece of Joseph. She was the daughter of one of his brothers, and had been reared in Jerusalem. Cassius and his soldiers closed the procession. The other women, namely, Maroni of Nain, Dinah the Samaritan, and Mara the Suphanite were at the time with Martha and Lazarus in Bethany.

Two soldiers with twisted torches walked on ahead, for light was needed in the grotto of the sepulcher. The procession moved on for a distance of about seven minutes singing Psalms in a low, plaintive tone, through the valley to the garden of the tomb. I saw on a hill on the other side of the valley James the Greater, the brother of John, looking at the procession, and then going off to tell the other disciples, who were hiding in the caves.

The garden of the sepulcher was not laid out with any view to regularity. The rock in which the sepulcher was cut lay at one end, entirely overgrown with verdure. The front of the garden was protected by a quickset hedge, inside of which at the entrance was a little enclosure formed of stakes, upon which rested long poles held in place by iron pegs. Outside the garden and also to the right of the sepulcher stood some palm trees; the other vegetation consisted chiefly of bushes, flowers, and aromatic plants.

I saw the procession halt at the entrance of the garden. It was opened by removing some of the poles, which were afterward used as levers for rolling away the stone from the door of the grotto. Before reaching the rock, they took the cover from the litter, raised the sacred body, and placed it upon a narrow board which had previously been covered with a linen cloth. Nicodemus and Joseph took one end of the board; the other two, the upper end, which was covered. The grotto, which was perfectly new, had been cleaned out and fumigated by Nicodemus's servants. It was very neat inside and was ornamented by a beautifully carved coping. The funereal couch was broader at the head than at the foot. It was cut out in the form of a body swathed in its bands and winding sheet, and slightly elevated at the head and foot.

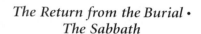

April 3, AD 33
Friday, Sunset to Late Evening

The holy women sat down upon a seat opposite the entrance of the grotto. [K25] The four men carried the Lord's body down into it, set it down, strewed the stone couch with sweet spices, spread over it a linen cloth, and deposited the sacred remains upon it. The cloth hung down over the couch. Then, having with tears and embraces given expression to their love for Jesus, they left the cave. The blessed Virgin now went in, and I saw her sitting on the head of the tomb, which was about two feet from the ground. She was bending low over the corpse of her child and weeping. When she left the cave, Magdalene hurried in with flowers and branches, which she had gathered in the garden and which she now scattered over the sacred body. She wrung her hands, and with tears and sighs embraced the feet of Jesus. When the men outside gave warning that it was time to close the doors, she went back to where the women were sitting. The men raised the cloth that was hanging over the side of the tomb, folded it around the sacred body, and then threw the brown cover over the whole. Lastly, they closed the brown doors, probably of copper or bronze, which had a perpendicular bar on the outside crossed by a transverse one. It looked like a cross.

The great stone, intended for securing the doors and which was still lying outside the cave, was in shape almost like a chest[†] or tomb, and was large enough for a man to lie at full length upon it. It was very heavy. By means of the poles brought from the garden entrance, the men rolled it into place before the closed doors of the tomb. The outside entrance was secured by a light door of wickerwork.

All that took place in the grotto was by torchlight, for it was dark in there. [K26] I saw during the burial several men lurking around in the neighborhood of the garden and of Mount Calvary. They looked timid and sorrowful. I think they were disciples who, in consequence of Abenadar's account of what was going on, had ventured forth from their caves and come hither. They now appeared to be returning.

The Return from the Burial • The Sabbath

It was now the hour at which the sabbath began. Nicodemus and Joseph returned to the city by a little private gate which, by special permission I think, Joseph had been allowed to make in the city wall near the garden. They had previously informed the blessed Virgin, Magdalene, John, and some of the women, who wanted to return to Golgotha to pray and to get some things they had left there, that this gate, as well as that of the Cenacle, would be opened to them whenever they would knock. Mary Heli, the blessed Virgin's aged sister, was conducted back to the city by Mary Mark and some other women. The servants of Nicodemus and Joseph went back to Golgotha for the tools and things they had left here.

The soldiers went to join the guard at the gate of execution, while Cassius rode to Pilate with the lance. He related all that had happened to him, and promised to bring him an exact account of all that might still take place, if he would give him command of the guard which the Jews, as had already been reported, would not fail to ask of him. Pilate listened with secret dismay, but treated Cassius as an enthusiast, and impelled by disgust and superstition, ordered him to put the lance outside the door.

When the blessed Virgin and her companions were returning with their vessels and other things from Golgotha, where they had again poured out their tears and prayers, they espied coming toward them a troop of soldiers headed by a torchbearer. The women halted on both

† Apparently Anne Catherine here spoke of the ancient cases in which her poor countrymen keep their clothes. The lower part of these cases is smaller than the upper, and this gives them some likeness to a tomb. She had one of these cases, which she called her chest. She often described the stone by this comparison, but her descriptions have not, nevertheless, given us a very clear idea of its shape.

sides of the road until the crowd passed. The soldiers were going up to Golgotha, perhaps to take away and bury the crosses before the sabbath. When they had passed, the holy women continued their way to the little private gate.

Peter, James the Greater, and James the Less met Joseph and Nicodemus in the city. All wept. Peter was especially vehement in his expressions of grief. He embraced Joseph and Nicodemus with tears, accused himself, lamented that he had not been present at the death of the Lord, and thanked them for bestowing upon him a tomb. All were quite beside themselves with sorrow. They agreed that the door of the Cenacle should be opened upon their knocking, and then separated, in order to seek the other disciples who were scattered in various directions.

Later I saw the blessed Virgin and her companions knocking at the Cenacle and being admitted, then Abenadar, and by degrees most of the apostles and several of the disciples entered. The holy women retired to the apartments occupied by the blessed Virgin. They took some refreshment and spent some moments in tears and mourning, relating to one another all that had happened. The men changed their garments, and I saw them standing under the lamp celebrating the sabbath. Then they ate lambs at the different tables around the Cenacle, but without any ceremony. It was not the paschal lamb. They had already eaten that yesterday. All were in great trouble and sadness. The holy women also prayed with Mary under a lamp. Later, when it had grown quite dark, Lazarus, Martha, the widow Maroni of Nain, Dinah the Samaritan, and Mara the Suphanite were admitted. They were come from Bethany to keep the sabbath. Once more was sorrow renewed by the narrations of each.

The Imprisonment of Joseph of Arimathea • The Holy Sepulcher Guarded

JOSEPH of Arimathea *left the Cenacle at a late hour* and, with some of the disciples and holy women, started for his home. They were proceeding sadly and timidly along the streets of Zion when an armed band dashed suddenly from their place of concealment in the neighborhood of Caiaphas's judgment hall and laid hands upon Joseph of Arimathea. His companions fled with cries of terror. I saw that they imprisoned the good Joseph in a tower of the city wall not very far from the judgment hall. Caiaphas had committed the care of this seizure to pagan soldiers, who celebrated no sabbath. The intention was to let Joseph die of starvation, and to keep his disappearance secret.

April 3, AD 33
Late Friday Night

On the night between Friday and Saturday, Caiaphas and some of the chief men among the Jews held a consultation upon what ought to be done with regard to the extraordinary events that had just taken place, and their effect upon the people. *It was far in the night* when they went to Pilate to tell him that as that seducer said, while he was still alive, "After three days I will rise again," it would be right "to command the sepulcher to be guarded until the third day; otherwise his disciples might come and steal him away, and say to the people, 'He is risen from the dead,' and the last error would be worse than the first."

Pilate wanted to have nothing more to do with the affair, so he said to them: "You have a guard. Go, guard it as you know." He, however, appointed Cassius to keep watch and give him an account of all that he observed. Thereupon *I saw twelve men leaving the city before sunrise*. They were accompanied by soldiers not dressed in the Roman uniform. They were temple soldiers, and looked to me like halbadiers, or life-guardsmen. They took with them lanterns on long poles, in order to be able to distinguish things clearly in the dark, and also to have light in the gloomy sepulcher.

When, on their arrival, they assured themselves that the sacred body was safe, they fastened a string across the doors of the tomb proper and another from that to the stone lying before them. Then they sealed the two together with a seal in the form of a half-moon. The twelve men returned afterward to the city, and the guard took up a position opposite the outer door of the sepulcher. Five or six took turns in watching, [K27] while some others presented themselves occasionally with provisions from the city. Cassius never left his post. He remained most of the time in the sepulcher itself, sitting or standing before the entrance to the tomb, and in such a position that he could see that side at which rested the feet of the Lord. He had received great interior graces and had been admitted to the clear understanding of many mysteries. As such a condition, being almost all the time in a state of wonderful interior enlightenment, was something so new to him, he was, as it were, transported out of himself, wholly regardless of external things. He here became entirely changed, a new man. He spent the day in penance, thanksgiving, and adoration.

The Friends of Jesus on Holy Saturday

AS I HAVE SAID, *I saw yesterday evening the men in the Cenacle celebrating the sabbath and then taking a repast*. They were about twenty in number. They were clothed in long white garments girdled at the waist, and were gathered together under a hanging lamp. When they separated after the repast, some went to take their rest in adjoining apartments, others to their own homes. *Today* I saw most of them remaining quietly in the house, assembling at intervals for prayer and reading, and occasionally admitting some newcomer.

In the house occupied by the blessed Virgin there was a large hall with several little recesses cut off by hangings and movable partitions. These were private sleeping places. When the holy women returned from the sepulcher, they put everything they brought back again into its place, and lighted the lamp that was hanging from the center of the ceiling. Then they gathered under it around the blessed Virgin, and took turns in praying most devoutly. They were all in deep sorrow. After that they partook of some refreshment, and were soon joined by Martha, Maroni, Dinah, and Mary who, after celebrating the sabbath in Bethany, had come hither with Lazarus. The last-named went to the men in the Cenacle. When, with tears on both sides, the death and burial of the Lord had been recounted to the newly arrived, and *the hour was far advanced*, some of the men, among them Joseph of Arimathea, left the supper room, called for the women that wanted to return to their homes in the city, and took their leave. It was on the way that that armed band seized Joseph near the judgment hall of Caiaphas, and cast him into the tower.

The women who had remained with the blessed Virgin now retired, each to her own screened sleeping place. They veiled their heads in long linen scarves, and sat for a little while in silent grief on the ground, leaning on the sleeping covers that were rolled up against the wall. After some moments, they arose, spread out the covers, laid aside their sandals, girdles, and some articles of dress, enveloped themselves from head to foot, as they were accustomed to do on retiring to rest, and lay down on their couches for a short sleep. *At midnight* they rose again, dressed, folded the couch together, assembled once more under the lamp around the blessed Virgin, and prayed in turn.

When the blessed Virgin and the holy women, notwithstanding their great suffering, had discharged this duty of nocturnal prayer (which I have frequently seen practiced since by the faithful children of God and holy persons, either urged thereto by special grace, or in obedience to a rule laid down by God and his church), John and some of the disciples knocked at the door of the women's hall. He and the other men had previously prayed, like the women,

April 4, AD 33 Saturday, 3 AM

under the lamp in the Cenacle. The holy women at once enveloped themselves in their mantles and, along with the blessed Virgin, followed them to the temple.

It was about the same time that *the tomb was sealed, that is, about three o'clock in the morning*, that I saw the blessed Virgin with the other holy women, John, and several of the disciples, going to the temple. It was customary among many of the Jews to visit the temple at daybreak the morning after the eating of the paschal lamb. It was in consequence opened about midnight, because the sacrifices on that morning began very early. But today, on account of the disturbance of the feast and the defilement of the temple, everything had been neglected, and it seemed to me as if the blessed Virgin, with her friends, wanted to take leave of it. It was there that she had been reared, there she had adored the holy mystery, until she herself bore in her womb that same holy mystery, that holy one who, as the true Paschal Lamb, had been so barbarously immolated the day before. The temple was, according to the custom of this day, open, the lamps lighted, and even the vestibule of the priests (a privilege granted to this day) was thrown open to the people. But the sacred edifice, with the exception of a few guards and servants, was quite deserted; marks of yesterday's disorder and confusion lay everywhere around. It had been defiled by the presence of the dead, and at the sight of it, the thought arose in my mind: "How will it ever be restored?"

Simeon's sons and Joseph of Arimathea's nephews, the latter of whom were very much grieved at the news of their uncle's arrest, welcomed the blessed Virgin and her companions and conducted them everywhere, for they had the care of the temple. Silently they gazed, with mingled feelings of awe and adoration, at the work of destruction, the visible marks of God's anger. Only here and there were a few words spoken, to recount the events of the preceding day.

Yesterday's destruction was evidenced in many different ways, for no attempt at repair had yet been made. Where the vestibule joined the sanctuary, the wall had so given way that a person could easily creep through the fissure, and the whole threatened to fall. The beam above the rent curtain before the sanctuary had sunk; the pillars that supported it had declined from each other at the top; and the curtain, torn in two, hung down at the sides. So great an opening was made in the wall of the vestibule by the huge stone that had been precipitated from the north side of the temple near Simeon's oratory upon the spot on which

Zechariah appeared, that the blessed Virgin could pass through without difficulty. This brought her to the great teacher's chair, from which the boy Jesus had taught, and from this spot she could see through the torn curtain into the Holy of Holies, something that would not have been possible before. Here and there, likewise, walls were cracked, portions of the floor sunk in, beams displaced, and pillars leaning out of their proper direction.

The blessed Virgin visited with her companions all places rendered sacred to her by the presence of Jesus. Kneeling down, she kissed them, recalling with tears and in a few touching words the particular remembrances connected with each. Her companions imitated her example, kneeling and kissing the hallowed spots.

The Jews regarded with extraordinary reverence all places in which anything held sacred by them had happened. They touched and kissed them, prostrating with their faces upon them, and I could never feel surprised at such manifestations. When one knows and believes and feels that the God of Abraham, Isaac, and Jacob is a living God, who dwelt among his people in his temple, his house, at Jerusalem, the wonder would be if they did not venerate such places. Whoever believes in a living God, in a Father and Redeemer and Sanctifier of humankind, His children, wonders not that, impelled by love, He is still living among the living. He feels that he owes to Him and to everything connected with him more love, honor, and reverence than to earthly parents, friends, teachers, superiors, and princes. The temple and the holy places were to the Jews what the most blessed sacrament is to Christians. But there were among them some blind and some enlightened, just as there are amongst us some that, adoring not the living God in our midst, are fallen into the superstitious service of the gods of the world. They reflect not upon these words of Jesus: "Whoever denies me before men, him also will I deny before my heavenly Father." People that unceasingly serve the spirit and falsehood of the world in thoughts and words and works, that cast aside all exterior worship of God, say indeed, if perchance they have not cast off God himself as altogether too exterior for them: "We adore God in spirit and in truth." But they do not know that these words mean in the Holy Spirit and in the Son, who took flesh from Mary, the Virgin, and who bore witness to the truth; who lived amongst us, who died for us on earth, and who will be with his church in the blessed sacrament until the end of time.

The blessed Virgin and her companions thus reverently visited many parts of the temple. She showed them where, as a little girl, she had first entered the sacred edifice, and where on the south side she had been educated until her espousals with Joseph. She pointed out to them the scene of her marriage, that of Jesus's presentation, and that of Simeon's and Anna's prophecies. At this point she wept bitterly, for the prophecy had been fulfilled, the sword had pierced her soul. She showed where she had found Jesus when a boy teaching in the temple, and she reverently kissed the teacher's chair. They went also to the offering box into which the widow had put her mite, and to the spot upon which the Lord forgave the woman taken in adultery. After they had thus with reverential touching, tears, prayers, and recalling of reminiscences, honored all the places rendered venerable by Jesus's presence, they returned to Zion.

The blessed Virgin did not leave the temple without many tears and deep grief, for its ruins and its desolate aspect on that day, once so sacred, bore witness to the sins of her people. She thought of Jesus weeping over it, and of his prophecy: "Destroy this temple, and in three days I will build it up again." She thought of how the enemies of Jesus had destroyed the temple of his body, and she longed for the third day upon which that word of Eternal Truth would be fulfilled.

Returned to the Cenacle on Zion at daybreak, the blessed Virgin retired with her companions to her own dwelling on the right of the courtyard. At the entrance John left them and joined the men in the Cenacle, upwards of twenty in number, who spent the whole sabbath in the supper room, mourning the death of their Master and praying by turns under the lamp. I saw them occasionally and very cautiously admitting newcomers, and conferring with them in tears. All experienced an inward reverence for John and a feeling of confusion in his presence, since he had been at the death of the Lord. But John was full of love and sympathy toward them, and, simple and ingenuous as a child, he gave place to everyone. Once I saw them eating. They remained very silently together, and the house was closed. They were safe from attack, for the house belonged to Nicodemus, and they had hired it for the Passover supper.

Again *I saw the holy women assembled until evening* in the hall which was lighted by a lamp, the doors being closed and the windows covered. Sometimes they ranged round the blessed Virgin under the lamp for prayer; or sometimes they retired alone to their several recesses, enveloped their heads in mourning veils, and sat on flat

April 4, AD 33
Saturday, Daybreak

boxes strewn with ashes (the sign of grief), or prayed with the face turned to the wall. Before they assembled under the lamp for prayer, they always laid aside their mourning veils and left them in the little recesses. I saw also that the weak among them took a little nourishment, but the others fasted.

More than once my gaze was directed to the holy women, and I always saw them as just described, praying or mourning in a darkened hall. When my meditation turned to the blessed Virgin dwelling in thought upon our Savior, I sometimes saw the holy tomb and about seven guards sitting or standing opposite the entrance. Close to the doors of the rocky cave, in which was the real tomb, the tomb proper, stood Cassius. He moved not from the spot, he was silent and recollected. I saw the closed doors of the tomb and the stone lying before them. But through the doors, I could see the body of the Lord lying just as it had been left. It was environed with light and splendor, and rested between two adoring angels, one at the head, the other at the foot. When my thoughts turned to the holy soul of our Redeemer, there was vouchsafed me a vision of his descent into hell so great, so extended, that I have been able to retain only a very small portion. I shall, however, relate what I can of it.

Some Words on Christ's Descent into Hell

WHEN Jesus with a loud cry gave up his most holy soul, I saw it as a luminous figure surrounded by angels, among them Gabriel, penetrating the earth at the foot of the holy cross. I saw his divinity united with his soul, while at the same time, it remained united to his body hanging on the cross. I cannot express how this was. I saw the place whither the soul of Jesus went. It seemed to be divided into three parts. It was like three worlds, and I had a feeling that it was round, and that each one of those places was a kind of locality, a sphere separated from the others.

Just in front of Limbo, there was a bright, cheerful tract of country clothed in verdure. It is into this that I always see the souls released from Purgatory entering before being conducted to heaven. The Limbo in which were the souls awaiting Redemption was encompassed by a gray, foggy atmosphere, and divided into different circles. The Savior, resplendent and conducted in triumph by angels, pressed on between two of these circles. The one on the left contained the souls of the leaders of the people down to Abraham, that on the right, the souls from Abraham to John the Baptist. Jesus went on between these two circles. They knew him not, but all were filled with joy and ardent desire. It was as if this place of anxious, distressed longing was suddenly enlarged. The Redeemer passed through

them like a refreshing breeze, like light, like dew, quickly like the sighing of the wind. The Lord passed quickly between these two circles to a dimly lighted place in which were our first parents, Adam and Eve. He addressed them, and they adored him in unspeakable rapture. The procession of the Lord, accompanied by the first human beings, now turned to the left, to the Limbo of the leaders of God's people before the time of Abraham. This was a species of Purgatory, for here and there were evil spirits, who in manifold ways worried and distressed some of those souls. The angels knocked and demanded admittance. There was an entrance, because there was a *going in*; a gate, because there was an *unlocking*; and a *knocking*, because the one that was coming had to be announced. It seemed to me that I heard the angel call out: "Open the gates! Open the doors!" Jesus entered in triumph, while the wicked spirits retired, crying out: "What hast thou to do with us? What dost thou want here? Art thou now going to crucify us?" and so on. The angels bound them and drove them before them. The souls in this place had only a vague idea of Jesus, they knew him only slightly; but when he told them clearly who he was, they broke forth into songs of praise and thanksgiving. And now the soul of the Lord turned to the circle on the right, to Limbo proper. There he met the soul of the good thief going under the escort of angels into Abraham's bosom, while the bad thief, encompassed by demons, was being dragged down into hell. The soul of Jesus addressed some words to both and then, accompanied by a multitude of angels, of the redeemed, and by those demons that were driven out of the first circle, went likewise into the bosom of Abraham.

This space, or circle, appeared to me to lie higher than the other. It was as if a person climbed from the earth under the churchyard up into the church itself. The evil spirits struggled in their chains, and wanted not to enter, but the angels forced them on. In this second circle were all the holy Israelites to the left, the patriarchs, Moses, the judges, the kings; on the right, the prophets and all the ancestors of Jesus, as also his relatives down to Joachim, Anne, Joseph, Zechariah, Elizabeth, and John. There were no demons in this circle, no pain nor torment, only the ardent longing for the fulfillment of the Promise now realized. Unspeakable felicity and rapture inundated these souls as they saluted and adored the Redeemer, and the demons in their fetters were forced to confess before them their ignominious defeat. Many of the souls were sent up to resuscitate their bodies from the tomb and in them to render visible testimony to the Lord. This was the moment in which so many dead came forth from their tombs in Jerusalem. They looked to me like walking corpses. They laid their bodies again upon the earth, just as a messenger of justice lays aside his mantle of office after having fulfilled his superior's commands.

I now saw the Savior's triumphant procession entering another sphere lower than the last. It was the abiding place of pious pagans who, having had some presentiment of truth, had ardently sighed after it. It was a kind of Purgatory, a place of purification. There were evil spirits here, for I saw some idols. I saw the evil spirits compelled to confess the deception they had practiced. I saw the blessed spirits rendering homage to the Savior with touching expressions of joy. Here, too, the demons were chained by the angels and driven forward before them.

And thus I saw the Redeemer passing rapidly through these numerous abodes and freeing the souls therein confined. He did a great many other things, but in my present miserable state I am unable to relate them.

At last I saw him, his countenance grave and severe, approaching the center of the abyss, namely, hell itself. In shape it looked to me like an immeasurably vast, frightful, black stone building that shone with a metallic luster. Its entrance was guarded by immense, awful-looking doors, black like the rest of the building, and furnished with bolts and locks that inspired feelings of terror. Roaring and yelling most horrible could plainly be heard, and when the doors were pushed open, a frightful, gloomy world was disclosed to view.

As I am accustomed to see the Heavenly Jerusalem under the form of a city, and the abodes of the blessed therein under various kinds of palaces and gardens full of wonderful fruits and flowers, all according to the different degrees of glory, so here I saw everything under the appearance of a world whose buildings, open spaces, and various regions were all closely connected. But all proceeded from the opposite of happiness, all was pain and torment. As in the sojourns of the blessed all appears formed upon motives and conditions of infinite peace, eternal harmony and satisfaction, so here are the disorder, the malformation of eternal wrath, disunion, and despair.

As in heaven there are innumerable abodes of joy and worship, unspeakably beautiful in their glittering transparency, so here in hell are gloomy prisons without number, caves of torment, of cursing, and despair. As in heaven there are gardens most wonderful to behold, filled with fruits that afford divine nourishment, so here in hell there are horrible wildernesses and swamps full of torture and pain and of all that can give birth to feelings of detestation, of loathing, and of horror. I saw here temples, altars, palaces, thrones, gardens, lakes, streams, all formed of blasphemy, hatred, cruelty, despair, confusion, pain, and torture, while in heaven all is built up of benedictions, of love, harmony, joy, and delight. *Here* is the rending, eternal disunion of the damned; *there* is the blissful communion of the saints. All the roots of perversity and untruth are here cultivated in countless forms and deeds of punishment and affliction. Nothing here is right, no thought brings peace, for the terrible remembrance of divine justice casts every damned soul into the pain and torment that his own guilt has planted for him. All that is terrible here, both in appearance and reality, is the nature, the form, the fury of sin unmasked, the serpent that now turns against those in whose bosom it was once nourished. I saw there also frightful columns erected for the sole purpose of creating feelings of horror and terror, just as in the kingdom of God they are intended to inspire peace and the sentiment of blissful rest, etc. All this is easily understood, but cannot be expressed in detail.

When the gates were swung open by the angels, one beheld before him a struggling, blaspheming, mocking, howling, and lamenting throng. I saw that Jesus spoke some words to the soul of Judas. Some of the angels forced that multitude of evil spirits to prostrate before Jesus, for all had to acknowledge and adore him. This was for them the most terrible torment. A great number were chained in a circle around others who were in turn bound down by them. In the center was an abyss of darkness. Lucifer was cast into it, chained, and thick black vapor mounted up around him. This took place by the divine decree. I heard that Lucifer (if I do not mistake) will be freed again for awhile fifty or sixty years before the year AD 2000. I have forgotten many other dates that were told me. Some other demons are to be freed before Lucifer, in order to chastise and tempt humankind. I think that some are let loose now in our own day, and others will be freed shortly after our time.

It is impossible for me to relate all that was shown me. It is too much. I cannot reduce it to order, I cannot arrange it. I am also so dreadfully sick. When I try to speak of these things, they rise up before my eyes, and the sight is enough to make one die.

I saw too the redeemed souls in countless numbers leaving the places of their purification, leaving Limbo, and accompanying the soul of the Lord to a place of bliss below the Heavenly Jerusalem. It was there that some time ago I saw a deceased friend of mine. The soul of the good thief entered with the rest and again saw the Lord, according to his promise, in Paradise. I saw prepared here for the delight and refreshment of the souls celestial tables such as were often shown me in visions vouchsafed for my consolation.

I cannot say exactly the time of these events, nor their duration, neither can I repeat all that I saw and heard, because some things were incomprehensible even to myself, and others would be misunderstood. I saw the Lord in many different places, even on the seas. It seemed as if he sanctified and delivered every creature; everywhere the evil spirits fled before him into the abyss. Then I saw the soul of the Lord visiting many places on the earth. I saw him in Adam's tomb under Golgotha. The souls of Adam and Eve came again to him there. He conversed with them, and I saw him as if under the earth, going with them in many directions, visiting tomb after tomb of the prophets. Their souls entered their bodies, and Jesus explained many mysteries to them. Then I saw him with this chosen band, among whom was David, visiting many scenes of his own life and Passion, explaining to them the typical events that had there taken place, and with inexpressible love pointing out to them their fulfillment.

Among other places, I saw him with these souls at that of his baptism, where numerous figurative events had happened. He explained them all and, deeply touched, I beheld the everlasting mercy of Jesus in permitting the grace of his own holy baptism to flow upon them for their greater advantage.

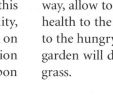

April 4, AD 33
Saturday, Sunset

It was unspeakably touching to see the soul of the Lord encompassed by those happy, blessed spirits shining through the dark earth, through rocks, through the water and the air, and lightly floating over the surface of the ground.

These are the few points that I can remember of my meditations, so full, so extended, upon the descent of the Lord into hell after his death, and of his releasing the souls of the just patriarchs of the earliest times. But besides this vision relating to time, I saw one connected with eternity, in which I was shown his mercy toward the poor souls on this day. I saw that, every year on the solemn celebration of this day (Good Friday) by the church, he casts upon Purgatory a glance by which many souls are released. I saw that even today, Holy Saturday, upon which day I had this contemplation, he released from their place of purification some souls that had sinned at the time of his crucifixion. I saw today the release of many souls, some unknown and others known to me, though I cannot name any of them.

(Being in a state of ecstasy today, Sister Emmerich related what follows):

The first descent of Jesus into Limbo was the fulfillment of early types, and in itself a type whose fulfillment is effected by today's releasing of the poor souls. The descent into hell that I saw was a vision of time past, but the freeing of the souls today is a lasting truth. The descent of Jesus into hell was the planting of the tree of grace, the tree of his own sacred merits, for the poor souls; and the constant recurrence of today's releasing of those souls is the fruit brought forth by that tree of grace in the spiritual garden of the ecclesiastical year. The Church Militant must cultivate the tree and gather the fruits, in which the Church Suffering must be allowed to share, since it can do nothing for itself. So it is with all the merits of the Lord. We must labor with him, in order to share in them. We must eat our bread in the sweat of our brow. All that Jesus did for us in time brings forth fruit for eternity, but we must in time cultivate and gather that fruit, otherwise we shall not enjoy it in eternity. The church is a most provident mother. Her year is in time the most complete garden of fruits for eternity. Her year contains a supply sufficient for the wants of all. Woe to the slothful and faithless laborers in that garden who, in any way, allow to go to waste a grace that might have restored health to the sick, strength to the weak, or furnished food to the hungry! On the Day of Judgment, the Master of the garden will demand an account of even the least blade of grass.

Our Lord Jesus Christ

TISSOT ILLUSTRATIONS
[SECTION K]

The Passion and Death of Jesus Christ

⊕

The Four Guards Sat Down and Watched Him·· 328
What Jesus Saw from the Cross · · · · · · · · · · · · · 330
Stabat Mater: Woman, Behold Thy Son · · · · · · · 332
My God, Why Hast Thou Forsaken Me? · · · · · · · 334
Mater Dolorosa: The Sorrowful Mother · · · · · · · 336
I Thirst: The Vinegar Given to Jesus · · · · · · · · · · 338
The Death of Jesus · 340
Consummatum Est: It is Finished · · · · · · · · · · · · 342
The Earthquake · 344
The Confession of the Centurion · · · · · · · · · · · · 346
The Centurion Abenadar · · · · · · · · · · · · · · · · · 348
The Chasm in the Cave beneath Golgotha · · · · · 350
The Crowd Left Golgotha Beating their Breasts· 352
The Disciples Watch from Afar in Agony · · · · · · 354
The Dead Appear in the Temple · · · · · · · · · · · · 356

The Dead Appear in Jerusalem · · · · · · · · · · · · · 358
Joseph of Arimathea Begs for Body of Jesus · · · · 360
The Thieves' Legs are Broken · · · · · · · · · · · · · · 362
The Strike of the Lance · · · · · · · · · · · · · · · · · · 364
The Confession of Longinus · · · · · · · · · · · · · · · 366
Jesus Alone on the Cross· · · · · · · · · · · · · · · · · · 368
The Descent from the Cross · · · · · · · · · · · · · · · 370
The Holy Virgin Receives the Body of Jesus · · · · 372
The Body of Jesus Carried to Anointing Stone · · 374
The Holy Virgin Kisses the Face of Jesus · · · · · · 376
Jesus Carried to the Tomb · · · · · · · · · · · · · · · · 378
The Two Marys Watch the Tomb · · · · · · · · · · · · 380
Jesus in the Sepulcher · · · · · · · · · · · · · · · · · · · 382
The Watch over the Tomb · · · · · · · · · · · · · · · · · 384

The Four Guards Sat Down and Watched Him

⊕

[MATTHEW 27:36] 36 Then they sat down and kept watch over him there.

As the mysterious and awful darkness became deeper and deeper, the crowd melted away altogether, until at last Golgotha was deserted by all but those immediately concerned in the tragedy going on. According to tradition, it was now that one of the servants of Joseph of Arimathea, who was watching the division of the sacred garments, seized a favorable moment to offer a large sum of money to the executioners for their spoil. This was how it came about that these priceless relics came into the possession of the early Christians, and from their hands passed into the care of different sanctuaries, where some of them have been preserved to our own day.

The bargain having been struck to their satisfaction, the four executioners, having nothing else to do, came and sat down in the four corners of the platform of Golgotha, and, weary and worn out as they were after the fatigue of their long and horrible task, they took their ease, watching the cross on which Jesus still hung. It was indeed the custom, as we are told by various writers of antiquity, to mount guard over those undergoing crucifixion, for death was not always certain or speedy. If the friends of the victim were able to take him down and tend him, their efforts to restore him might very often have been successful. The hemorrhage which, at the beginning of the long anguish, was very abundant, is said to have been arrested at an early stage by the swelling caused by the nails which had been driven through the hands and feet, so that the victim might linger for a very long time before he yielded up his last breath. Flavius Josephus relates how one of his friends, who had been taken down from the cross before it was too late, had been brought back to life. To guard against any such rescue from the full penalty, or attempt at rescue, guards were posted on the spot and forbidden to lose sight of the victim for a single instant.

What Jesus Saw from the Cross

⊕

THIS is the idea I wish to express in my engraving: a momentary lull has occurred in the midst of the shouts and insults of the spectators, who are alarmed by the threatening signs in the sky and by the ever-increasing darkness. Now, from the top of the cross on the summit of Golgotha, which dominates the town of Jerusalem, Jesus looks down on those beneath him. The eyes of all, those eyes which are the windows of the soul, are fixed on him; he sees every one who has aided in his condemnation, including the judge himself. Down at his still bleeding feet he sees, as he bends his head, the weeping Magdalene, consumed with the fervor of her love and penitence; while beyond her stands his mother, gazing up at him with an expression of ineffable tenderness; with John, that most devoted of all the disciples, and Mary Salome, the latter weeping bitterly. Farther away are the blasphemers, surfeited at last with the gratification of their malice, but on them, in the very midst of their triumph, has fallen fear and astonishment. In some cases, perhaps, faith in the Redeemer may be already nascent, and stubborn hearts may be touched with the all-powerful grace of God. Yet a little farther off, beyond the wall of the garden of Joseph of Arimathea, is the sepulcher which that same evening is to receive the body of the Savior. Beyond the trees, again, the dying sufferer can make out groups of the more timid of his followers, the disciples who, in spite of their love for the Master, dare not approach nearer until the darkness shall be so great that there will be no danger of their being recognized.

So profound is the silence that even the distant murmur of voices from the city and the blasts of the trumpets from the temple can faintly be heard. Far away down below rises up a great column of dense smoke from the altar of burnt sacrifice. The wind is in the east and comes from the direction of the Dead Sea, laden with the mixed fumes of incense, burning meat, and melting fat; the air is heavy and oppressive, while all around is wrapped in a mantle of the deepest gloom.

We have thus far refrained from relating certain legends about the wood of which the cross was made. These various suppositions are, of course, altogether gratuitous and optional, such as the following story, according to which the Queen of Sheba, when she went into the Palace of Solomon, which was called the House of the Forest of Lebanon, noticed a beam in it and predicted that that beam would be used in the execution of a man who would cause the ruin of all Israel. Solomon, continues this strange legend, anxious to guard against the fulfillment of the sinister prophecy, had the beam buried in the very spot where the Troubled Pool, or Pool of Bethesda, spoken of by John, was afterward situated. At the time of the Passion of our Lord, this beam is said to have been discovered, dug up and used to form the cross of the Savior. Here is another story of a similar kind: Seth, third son of Adam, having obtained entrance to the terrestrial Paradise, from which his parents had been expelled, obtained from the angel who guarded the tree of life three of its seeds, which he planted on the grave of his father. From these three seeds grew three small stems, which, being joined together, formed the beam just alluded to as having been used by Solomon and hidden by him.

Stabat Mater: Woman, Behold Thy Son [K1]

⊕

THE mother of Jesus, Mary Cleophas, Mary Magdalene, and John were standing around the cross of Jesus, between it and those of the thieves, and looking up at the Lord. The blessed Virgin, overcome by maternal love, was in her heart fervently imploring Jesus to let her die with him. At that moment, the Lord cast an earnest and compassionate glance down upon his mother and, turning his eyes toward John, said to her: "Woman, behold, this is thy son! He will be thy son more truly than if thou hadst given him birth." Then he praised John, and said: "He has always been innocent and full of simple faith. He was never scandalized, excepting when his mother wanted to have him elevated to a high position." To John, he said: "Behold, this is thy mother!" and John reverently and like a filial son embraced beneath the cross of the dying Redeemer Jesus's mother, who had now become his mother also. After this solemn bequest of her dying Son, the blessed Virgin was so deeply affected by her own sorrow and the gravity of the scene that the holy women, supporting her in their arms, seated her for a few moments on the earthen rampart opposite the cross, and then took her away from the circle to the rest of the holy women. [300]

[JOHN 19:25–27] 25 So the soldiers did this. But standing by the cross of Jesus were his mother, and his mother's sister, Mary the wife of Cleophas, and Mary Magdalene. 26 When Jesus saw his mother, and the disciple whom he loved standing near, he said to his mother, "Woman, behold, your son!" 27 Then he said to the disciple, "Behold, your mother!" And from that hour the disciple took her to his own home.

WHEN the tumult had abated, Jesus was able to make himself heard. His mother was standing opposite to him with John beside her, and it was to them that he addressed himself. His voice was ineffably sad, and scarcely reached their ears as the words painfully succeeded each other with all the solemnity of a last testament. Jesus was anxious that Mary should not be left alone after his death, and therefore placed her under the care of John, who was to be to her a son when he himself was gone. By this touching act of solicitude he made sure that Mary should have a home to go to and some one to take care of her; moreover, she would have a new object for the tenderness with which she had hedged about the Master during his life. As only natural, it is John himself who relates this beautiful incident, which reflects such honor upon him and must have made such a profound impression upon him.

My God, My God, Why Hast Thou Forsaken Me? [K2]

⊕

JESUS, wholly abandoned, wholly deprived of all things, and utterly helpless, sacrificed himself in infinite love. Yes, he turned his abandonment itself into a rich treasure by offering to his heavenly Father his life, labors, love, and sufferings, along with the bitter sense of our ingratitude that thereby he might strengthen our weakness and enrich our poverty. He made before God his last testament, by which he gave over all his merits to the church and to sinners. He thought of everyone. In his abandonment he was with every single soul until the end of time. He prayed too for those heretics who believe that, being God, he did not feel his sufferings, and that as man he felt them only a little, or at least far less than another would have done. But while I was sharing in and sympathizing with Jesus's prayer, I heard these words as if coming from his lips: "We should, by all means, teach the people that Jesus, more keenly than any human being can conceive, endured this pain of utter abandonment, because he was hypostatically united with the divinity, because he was truly God and man. Being in his sacred humanity wholly abandoned by the Father, he felt most perfectly that bereavement, he drained to the dregs the bitter cup of dereliction, he experienced for the time what a soul endures that has lost its God forever. And so when in his agony he cried out with a loud voice, he meant not only to make known his dereliction, but also to publish to all afflicted souls who acknowledge God as their Father that the privilege of recurring to him in filial confidence he merited for them then and there. Toward the third hour, Jesus cried in a loud voice: "*Eli, Eli, lama sabachthani!*" which means: "My God! My God! Why hast thou forsaken me!" When this clear cry of our Lord broke the fearful stillness around the cross, the scoffers turned toward it and one said: "He is calling Elijah"; and another: "Let us see whether Elijah will come to deliver him." [302]

[MARK 15:34–35] 34 And at the ninth hour Jesus cried with a loud voice, "Eloi, Eloi, lama sabachthani?" which means, "My God, my God, why hast thou forsaken me?" 35 And some of the bystanders hearing it said, "Behold, he is calling Elijah."

IT is the ninth hour, that is to say, three o'clock in the afternoon, and the Jews, fancying that the death of their victim will be delayed for some time longer, are beginning to withdraw one after the other. All of a sudden, under stress of a supreme agony, convulsing alike body and soul, Jesus gives utterance to that cry of anguish, the most heartrending which ever resounded upon this earth: "My God! My God! why hast thou forsaken me?" Mary flings herself forward toward her dying Son and all the other mourners resume their places; Mary Magdalene is still at the feet of the Lord. It is worthy of notice that this dying cry of Jesus is a quotation from the 22nd Psalm, the whole of the first part of which—so extremely precise is the prophecy it contains—might be an actual description of the tragic drama which culminated on Golgotha.

Mater Dolorosa: The Sorrowful Mother [K3]

⊕

WHEN the most afflicted mother heard the voice of her Son, she could no longer restrain herself. She again pressed forward to the cross, followed by John, Mary Cleophas, Magdalene, and Salome. [302]

MANY know the beautiful hymn dedicated by the medieval church to the virgin Mother: "At the cross her station keeping, stood the mournful mother weeping, close to Jesus to the last. Through her soul his sorrow sharing, all his bitter anguish bearing, now at length the sword had passed. Oh! how sad and sore distressèd was that mother highly blessèd, of the sole begotten one! Christ above in torment hangs; she beneath beholds the pangs of her dying glorious Son. Is there one who would not weep, whelmed in miseries so deep, Christ's dear mother to behold? Can the human heart refrain from partaking in her pain, in that mother's pain untold? Bruised, derided, cursed, defiled, she beheld her tender child with the cruel scourges rent; Saw him hang in desolation, for the sins of his own nation, till his spirit forth he sent. O thou, mother, fount of love, touch my spirit from above, in my heart each wound renew, of my Savior crucified. Let me share with thee his pain, who for love of me was slain, who for me in torments died. Let me mingle tears with thee, mourning him who died for me, all the days that I may live. By the cross with thee to stay, there with thee to weep and pray, this I thee entreat to give."

The first strophe of this hymn has decided once for all in the popular imagination the attitude of Mary at Golgotha: Stabat, it says, or, 'she stood.' It is, however, difficult to believe that she really maintained a stoical attitude. Mary was a woman, and the fact of the strength given her from above would not save her, any more than it did her divine Son, from the shrinking from suffering natural to humanity. Jesus had prostrated himself upon the ground at Gethsemane, and Mary doubtless sunk down more than once on Golgotha, and needed the ministrations of John and the holy women to support and restore her. It is even said that once she was led by them away from the platform, quite overcome and trembling with anguish. But for this absence of his mother, temporary though it was, it would have seemed as if Jesus would have been spared one terrible ordeal: that of finding himself alone, forsaken alike, apparently, by heaven and earth.

I Thirst: The Vinegar Given to Jesus [K4]

JESUS was now completely exhausted. With his parched tongue he uttered the words: "I thirst!" And when his friends looked up at him sadly, he said to them: "Could you not have given me a drink of water?" He meant that during the darkness no one would have prevented their doing so. John was troubled at Jesus's words, and he replied: "O Lord, we forgot it!" Jesus continued to speak in words such as these: "My nearest friends must forget me and offer me no drink, that the scriptures may be fulfilled." This forgetfulness was very bitter to him. Hearing Jesus's complaint, his friends begged the soldiers and offered them money if they would reach to him a drink of water. They would not do it, but instead they dipped a pear-shaped sponge into vinegar, a little bark keg of which was standing near, and poured upon it some drops of gall. But the centurion Abenadar, whose heart was touched by Jesus, took the sponge from the soldiers, pressed it out, and filled it with pure vinegar. Then he stuck into it a sprig of hyssop, which served as a mouthpiece for sucking, and fastened the whole to the point of his lance. He raised it in such a way that the tube should incline to Jesus's mouth and through it he might be able to suck the vinegar from the sponge. [303]

[JOHN 19:28–29] 28 After this Jesus, knowing that all was now finished, said (to fulfil the scripture), "I thirst." 29 A bowl full of vinegar stood there; so they put a sponge full of the vinegar on hyssop and held it to his mouth.

ALMOST at the same moment as he made his touching appeal to his Father, Jesus uttered that other cry recorded: "I thirst!" "Now," says John, "there was set a vessel full of vinegar." This vinegar, or acidulated drink, was called posca by the Romans. Sometimes it was merely wine which had turned sour, often called vinegar in Greek, but sometimes it was really vinegar mixed with water, and it was customary for soldiers to take some with them with which to quench their thirst when they were on guard for any length of time. Some man standing by then, moved to compassion by the touching complaint of Jesus, ran and soaked a sponge in this vinegar and offered it to him to drink. The sponge thus used had no doubt been brought with them by the executioners to wipe off the blood with which they were covered after the crucifixion. The man put this sponge, saturated with the vinegar, upon a branch of hyssop. It is John, who was an eyewitness of all that occurred, who mentions what kind of branch was used; the other evangelists merely say a reed. Now the stem of the hyssop, though it resembles a reed in general appearance, is really not nearly so strong. The very thickest that could possibly be found would not be able to bear the weight of a sponge full of liquid. On the other hand, the stem in question forms a perfect tube, in every way suitable for sucking up liquid or for ejecting it. In our engraving, therefore, we have represented the sponge alluded to in the gospel narrative as having been placed, not at the top but at the lower end of the stem of hyssop, in such a manner that the liquid with which it was saturated could be made to ascend the hollow tube by the pressing of the sponge, while Jesus sucked the vinegar through the upper opening. Any other plan than that here suggested, however small and round the sponge may have been could have achieved nothing but the smearing of the face of the sufferer, which, under pretence of soothing his sufferings, would really only have added to them, for his body was everywhere covered with wounds. The cheeks, the nose and the lips of the sufferer must have been grazed in his many falls. Now it was no doubt a compassionate man who ran to give the divine Master drink when he cried: "I thirst!" and we feel that we are justified in supposing him to have acted in the manner represented in our engraving. John goes on to say that Jesus accepted the proffered beverage. As we already remarked, he had refused the narcotic offered to him at the beginning of his martyrdom on the cross, but he was willing to receive the refreshment offered to him at the end by the compassionate soldier.

The Death of Jesus [K5]

ONE *last cry was uttered by Jesus before his death, as related in the accounts given of the final scene by Matthew and Luke. Matthew adds nothing to the fact that that cry was uttered, but Luke has preserved for us the last words of Jesus. "And when Jesus had cried with a loud voice, he said: Father, into thy hands I commend my spirit." It is John who gives us the last details with regard to the death of Christ. "He bowed his head," says that evangelist. Hitherto he had held his head erect, but now that his work is finished, he bends it gently and yields up his spirit.*

In our picture John is seen approaching to kiss the feet of his divine Master; Mary Magdalene, who has never left her post, is still on her knees, while the mother of the Lord stretches out her arms towards her Son, as if she would fain follow him. Very few spectators are now left about the cross, for the death of the divine victim has taken place sooner than was expected, and, as a matter of fact, it ensued with a rapidity unusual in cases of crucifixion. Pilate was, indeed, so surprised at hearing that the end was come that he sent a centurion to make sure that the victim was really dead, thus affording a guarantee to posterity that he who was to rise again on the third day had indeed suffered death. [303]

Consummatum Est: It is Finished [K6]

⊕

THE hour of the Lord was now come. He was struggling with death, and a cold sweat burst out on every limb. John was standing by the cross and wiping Jesus's feet with his handkerchief. Magdalene, utterly crushed with grief, was leaning at the back of the cross. The blessed Virgin, supported in the arms of Mary Cleophas and Salome, was standing between Jesus and the cross of the good thief, her gaze fixed upon her dying Son. Jesus spoke: "It is consummated!" and raising his head he cried with a loud voice: "Father, into thy hands I commend my Spirit!" The sweet, loud cry rang through heaven and earth. Then he bowed his head and gave up the spirit. I saw his soul like a luminous phantom descending through the earth near the cross down to the sphere of Limbo. John and the holy women sank, face downward, prostrate on the earth. [303]

[LUKE 23:46] 46 Then Jesus, crying with a loud voice, said, "Father, into thy hands I commit my spirit!" And having said this he breathed his last. [JOHN 19:30] 30 When Jesus had received the vinegar, he said, "It is finished"; and he bowed his head and gave up his spirit.

THIS last cry was one alike of obedient submission and of triumph. In one brief, telling sentence it summed up the whole of the work of Jesus Christ as foreshadowed by the various types and foretold by the prophecies of the Old Testament now fulfilled. It is the final completion of the covenant between the Son of Man and God the Father, and between them and the human race. All is finished now! The work is done; the prophecies are accomplished. There are no more insults to be submitted to now, no more tortures to endure; the Man of Sorrows has gone through all the suffering to which he was foredoomed, and, humanity being through his sacrifice reconciled to God, there is nothing left for him to do but to die. It is, then, at this supreme moment that he rallies his strength for an instant to proclaim to the world in a thrilling voice: "It is finished."

The Earthquake [K7]

⊕

WHEN the Lord in a clear, strong voice uttered those last words, when he died with that loud cry that rang through heaven, earth, and hell, the earth quaked and the rock between him and the thief on his left was rent asunder with a crashing sound. That loud cry, that witness of God, resounded like a warning, arousing terror and shuddering in mourning nature. It was consummated! The soul of our Lord had left the body! The death cry of the dying Redeemer had roused all that heard it; even the earth, by its undulations, seemed to recognize the Savior, and a sharp sword of sorrow pierced the hearts of those that loved him. [304]

[MATTHEW 27:51] 51 And behold, the curtain of the temple was torn in two, from top to bottom; and the earth shook, and the rocks were split.

EXTRAORDINARY phenomena accompanied the death of Jesus Christ. In the temple the Babylonian veil, was "rent in twain from the top to the bottom," symbolizing in a truly dramatic manner the way in which heaven was thrown open and access to it rendered possible to man by the fact of the death of Christ. Then "the earth did quake and the rocks rent" on Golgotha and in the city of Jerusalem. This manifestation of superhuman power of course overwhelms with terror the few witnesses who still remain on Golgotha. Their hearts are full of anxious fears, awaiting the occurrence of still more awful phenomena. Following the example of the mother of the divine sufferer, they prostrate themselves upon the rock, all wet with the blood of the Redeemer. The Roman centurion and the soldiers, greatly agitated, also kneel. The alarm spreads; in fact, similar shocks have been felt and similar reports heard in the town; walls are cracking, monuments are being overturned, the ground is heaving convulsively and here and there is rent open. The earth beneath, like the heaven above, each in its own way, is manifesting its sorrow, and the death of a God for those he himself created is not to take place unperceived or unmarked.

The Confession of the Centurion [K8]

⊕

THEN it was that grace penetrated the soul of Abenadar. The horse trembled under his rider, who was reeling with emotion; then it was that grace conquered that proud mind, hard as the rock of Golgotha. He threw his lance to the ground and, with his great clenched fist, struck his breast vigorous blows, crying aloud in the voice of a changed man: "Blessed be God the almighty, the God of Abraham and Jacob! This was a just man! Truly, he is the Son of God!" And many of the soldiers, deeply affected by his words, followed his example. [304]

[LUKE 23:47] 47 Now when the centurion saw what had taken place, he praised God, and said, "Certainly this man was innocent!"

THE centurion here referred to was the Roman captain who had charge of the triple execution on Golgotha. He was in command of the soldiers who formed the escort of the condemned and who were on guard throughout the execution to keep back the crowds. He had to hold himself in readiness to meet any emergency, such as a rising among the people or an attempt at rescue. "Now when the centurion saw what was done," says the sacred text, that is to say, when he noted the supernatural darkness spreading over all the land, when he heard the last loud cry of Jesus, felt the earthquake, heard the splitting of the rock, and perhaps was told of the rending of the veil in the temple, for the rumor of that significant phenomenon may already have spread, he glorified God, saying: "Certainly this was a righteous man."

The Centurion Abenadar [K9]

⊕

ABENADAR, who was now a changed being, a man redeemed, after his public homage to the Son of God would no longer remain in the service of his enemies. He turned his horse toward Cassius, the subaltern officer, known under the name of Longinus, dismounted, picked up his lance, presented it to him and addressed a few words both to him and the soldiers. Cassius mounted the horse and assumed the command. Abenadar next hurried down Mount Calvary and through the Valley of Gihon to the caves in the Valley of Hinnom, where he announced to the disciples hidden therein the death of the Lord, after which he hastened into the city and went straight to Pilate. Abenadar rendered public testimony to his belief in Jesus, and his example was followed by many of the soldiers. Numbers of those present, and some of the Pharisees last come to the scene, were converted. Many struck their breast, wept, and returned home, while others rent their garments and sprinkled their head with dust. All were filled with fear and dread. [304]

LUKE gives us a few details which are as picturesque as they are interesting. To begin with, he implies that the centurion was standing opposite to the cross as we have represented him in our pictures, that is to say, in a good position for seeing and hearing all that went on, so that nothing could escape him. In the second place, Luke seems to suggest that it was the loud cry of Jesus which made the soldier come to the conclusion that he did. Accustomed as he no doubt had been for many years to witnessing the carrying out of capital punishments, he had never before been witness to a similar incident, for those who suffered crucifixion generally died from exhaustion, and, as a matter of course, were quite unable to utter a cry so loud as that of Jesus. The centurion, therefore, recognized the supernatural character of that cry, which, taken in connection with all that he already knew of the Master, with what he had himself noticed in his bearing throughout his sufferings and with the signs and tokens which succeeded his death, converted him to belief in the Savior and wrung from him the confession quoted above.

The Chasm in the Rock in the Cave beneath Golgotha [K10]

THE sun was still obscured by fog. During the earthquake the air was close and oppressive, but afterward there was a sensible decrease in temperature. The appearance of our Lord's corpse on the cross was exceedingly awful and impressive. The thieves were hanging in frightful contortions, and seemingly intoxicated with liquor. At last both became silent. Dismas was in prayer. It was just after three o'clock when Jesus expired. When the first alarm produced by the earthquake was over, some of the Pharisees grew bolder. They approached the chasm made by it in the rock of Golgotha, threw stones into it, fastened ropes together, and let them down; but as they could not reach the bottom of the abyss, they became a little more thoughtful and, comprehending in some degree why people were lamenting and beating their breast, they rode off from the scene. [305]

[MATTHEW 27:51] 51 And behold, the curtain of the temple was torn in two, from top to bottom; and the earth shook, and the rocks were split.

THE rock is rent open and the subsoil is laid bare, the numerous cracks across it proving how widespread and extraordinary has been the phenomenon which has just taken place. The widest of these cracks is a regular chasm which has opened between the cross of Jesus and that of the impenitent thief. It appears to be deep as well as wide, and the Jews wish to examine its dimensions, which are such as to astonish them. To be able to ascertain better the effect produced by the convulsion, they penetrate into the cave named after Adam, where, according to a tradition, the skull of the first man had been buried, and which had also served as the grave of Melchizedek. As this cave is hewn out of the very rock from which rises the cross with the Redeemer upon it and the rent can be clearly seen from it, some of the spectators put their hands into that rent, and, to their intense horror, when they draw them back they find that they are covered with blood.

If we are to believe certain tales [Tissot refers here to Anne Catherine Emmerich], similar phenomena occurred throughout the rest of Palestine at the same time as the one just described. Secular buildings and temples fell down here and there, while the whole of Egypt was the scene of disasters, nearly all the temples being much injured, their massive columns, enshrined though they were in the cyclopean masses of the living rock, their architraves and cornices were flung to the ground, bearing witness to the mighty event which had just been accomplished. In the crowded seaports and on the deserted coasts alike the mighty cry was heard in the night: "Great Pan is dead!" as if paganism, its very existence threatened by the sacrifice offered up on Golgotha, was condemned to proclaim the efficacy of that sacrifice before its own extinction. And we are all well acquainted with the celebrated sentence of Dionysius the Areopagite, said to have been uttered at the very moment when these awful events were occurring: "Either the God of nature is suffering or the framework of the world is falling to pieces." It probably was a darkness spreading over all the earth which led Dionysius to pronounce these remarkable words. Moreover, Tertullian, in his "Apology," did not hesitate, in addressing the Roman authorities, to refer to the phenomena in question as well-known facts recorded in the public archives. These phenomena did not all take place simultaneously: "Now from the sixth hour," says Matthew, that is to say from the middle of the day, or three hours before the death of Jesus, "there was darkness over all the land unto the ninth hour," this darkness continuing throughout and rendering more awful and terrible the other manifestations of Almighty power: the rending in twain of the veil of the temple, the earthquake, the opening of the chasm in the rock, and the apparition of the dead, all of which phenomena, as is well known, took place immediately after the Savior yielded up his last breath.

The Crowd Left Golgotha While Beating Their Breasts [K11]

⊕

PEOPLE were lamenting and beating their breast, they rode off from the scene. Some were entirely changed in their ideas. The people soon dispersed and went in fear and anxiety through the valley in the direction of the city, many of them being converted. [305]

[LUKE 23:48] 48 And all the multitudes who assembled to see the sight, when they saw what had taken place, returned home beating their breasts.

The Disciples Watch from Afar in Agony [K12]

⊕

OFF in the distance, here and there, in the valley and on the remote heights, a disciple might be descried peering timidly and inquiringly toward the cross, and retiring quickly on the approach of anyone. [305]

[LUKE 23:49] 49 And all his acquaintances and the women who had followed him from Galilee stood at a distance and saw these things.

THE time wears on, the hours of this fateful Friday pass slowly by, in suffering for Jesus, in anxiety for his disciples. After their first moment of terror they have come forth from their hiding place in the tombs of Hinnom. They climb up the Valley of Gihon and cautiously advance under cover of the walls of Herod's Palace and can see the crowd surrounding Golgotha. Step by step they creep along, deeply moved by what they rightly imagine to be going on. By skirting along the height on the northwest of the town, they can look on from a distance at the gradual development of the mighty drama of the cross.

The Dead Appear in the Temple [K13]

⊕

WHEN Jesus with a loud cry gave up his spirit into the hands of his heavenly Father, I saw his soul, like a luminous figure, penetrating the earth at the foot of the cross, accompanied by a band of luminous angels, among whom was Gabriel. I saw a great multitude of evil spirits driven by those angels from the earth into the abyss. Jesus sent many souls from Limbo to reenter their body, in order to frighten and warn the impenitent, as well as to bear witness to himself.

By the earthquake at Jesus's death, when the rock of Golgotha was split, many portions of the earth were upheaved while others sank, and this was especially the case in Palestine and Jerusalem. In the temple and throughout the city, the inhabitants were just recovering somewhat from the fright caused by the darkness when the heaving of the earth, the crash of falling buildings in many quarters, gave rise to still more general consternation; and, to crown their terror, the trembling and wailing crowd, hurrying hither and thither in dire confusion, encountered here and there the corpses raised from the dead, as they walked about uttering their warnings in hollow voices.

The temple was so large, there were so many different halls and apartments, that the sacrifices went on quietly in some, while fright and horror were pervading others, and in others still the priests managed to keep order. It was not till the dead made their appearance in different parts of the temple that the ceremonies were entirely interrupted and the sacrifices discontinued, as if the temple had become polluted. Still, even this did not come so suddenly upon the multitude as to cause them in their flight to rush precipitously down the numerous steps of the temple. They dispersed by degrees, hurrying down one group at a time, while in some quarters of the building the priests were able to bring back the frightened worshippers and keep them together. Still, however, the anxiety, the fright of all, though different in degree, was something quite indescribable. And now there arose a great clamor, the doors of the sanctuary sprang open, a voice cried out: "Let us go hence!" and I saw the angels departing from the temple. The altar of incense was elevated to some height and a vessel of incense tilted over. The shelf that held the rolls of scripture fell in, and the rolls were scattered around. The confusion increased to such a degree that the time of day was forgotten. Nicodemus, Joseph of Arimathea, and many others left the temple and went away. Corpses were lying here and there, others were wandering through the halls and uttering warning words to the people. At the sound of the voice of the angels fleeing from the temple, the dead returned to their graves. [306]

[MATTHEW 27:52] 52 The tombs also were opened, and many bodies of the saints who had fallen asleep were raised.

THE apparition in the temple of the departed must have produced a profound impression of dismay upon the consciences of the Jews, for as is well known, those who came in contact with the dead were rendered impure, and such contact must, according to the Jewish belief, neutralize the efficacy of the Passover sacrifices. This is why the Levites are running away alike shocked and terrified.

The Dead Appear in Jerusalem [K14]

WHILE all these things were going on in the temple, a similar panic was experienced in many other quarters of Jerusalem. Just after three o'clock, many tombs were violently shattered, especially in the northwestern section of the city where there were numerous gardens. I saw here and there the dead lying in their winding sheets. In other places, there were only masses of rottenness, in others skeletons, and from many proceeded an intolerable stench. There were about one hundred deceased belonging to all periods of time who arose in body from their shattered tombs both in Jerusalem and its environs. They went mostly in couples to certain parts of the city, encountering the frightened inhabitants in their flight, and testifying to Jesus in denunciatory words, few but vigorous. Not all the dead whose corpses were exposed to view by the falling of their tombs arose. Many a one became merely visible, because the graves were in common. But many others, whose souls Jesus sent to earth from Limbo, arose, threw off the covering from their face and went, not walking, but as if floating, along the streets of Jerusalem to their friends and relatives. They entered the houses of their posterity, and rebuked them severely for the part they had taken in the murder of Jesus. I saw some of them meeting, as if they were friends or relatives, and going in couples through the streets of the city. I could see no movement of their feet under their long winding sheets. They passed along as if lightly hovering above the ground. The hands of some were enfolded in broad bands of linen, others hung down under the large sleeves that bound the arms. The covering of the face was thrown up over the head, and the pale, yellow countenance with its long beard looked dried and withered. Their voices sounded strange and unearthly, and these voices, joined to their incessant moving from place to place, unconcerned about all around, was their only external expression; indeed they seemed almost nothing but voice. They were clothed somewhat differently, each according to the custom at the time of his death, his position in society, and his age. The people standing afar hearkened, shuddered, and fled, as the dead floated toward them. Intense fear pervaded the whole city. About four o'clock, the dead returned to their graves. Many other spirits appeared in different quarters after Christ's resurrection. [308]

[MATTHEW 27:53] 53 And coming out of the tombs after his resurrection they went into the holy city and appeared to many.

IT was not only in the sacred precincts that the dead appeared; they were also seen in the streets of the city, gliding like shades over the surface of the ground and spreading horror and dread before them wherever they went. Matthew is the only one of the evangelists who relates this last marvel, the greatest of all the portents which accompanied the death of the Master. Does he mean to describe the actual resurrection of dead bodies or merely phantom-like semblances of the departed which "appeared unto many?" The text certainly says "bodies of the saints" and not the semblance of bodies, but there seems to be no need to strain the sense of the words used, and it would certainly appear that those who rose from the dead in this instance did not rise in the sense in which Lazarus did. On the other hand, we may ask, who were those who had the honor of being associated in a certain way with the resurrection of the Savior? We do not know. Adam, Noah, Abraham, David, and others have been suggested, or, again, Joseph and John the Baptist. In the verse quoted on the preceding page the evangelist Matthew says: Multa corpora sanctorum qui dormierant, *or, "many bodies of the saints which slept arose." From the very earliest days of Christianity the word sleep has been used as a touching euphemism for death. Hence the name cemetery, which is taken from a Greek word signifying sleeping-place and is now given to Christian burial-places where the remains of whole generations await the awaking of the Resurrection morn.*

Joseph of Arimathea Begs Permission to Remove the Body of Jesus [K15]

JUST after that I saw Joseph of Arimathea, a member of the council, going to Pilate. He had already heard of Jesus's death, and with Nicodemus had concluded to bury the Lord's body in the new sepulcher hewn out of a rock in his own garden, not very far from Golgotha. I think I saw him outside the gate as if examining, or reconnoitering, the premises. Some few of his servants were already in the garden, cleaning it and arranging things inside the sepulcher. Nicodemus had gone to buy linen and spices for preparing the body for burial, and he was now waiting for Joseph.

Joseph found Pilate very anxious and perplexed. He begged openly and fearlessly that he might be allowed to take the body of Jesus, the king of the Jews, down from the cross, as he wanted to lay it in his own sepulcher. Pilate's anxiety increased on beholding so distinguished a man begging so earnestly to be permitted to honor the body of Jesus, whom he himself had caused to be ignominiously crucified. The innocence of Jesus recurred to him, making him still more uneasy, but he overcame himself, and asked: "Is he, then, already dead?" for only a few moments had elapsed since he sent executioners out to break the bones of the crucified, and thus end their life. He summoned the centurion Abenadar, who was returned from the caves where he had spoken with some of the disciples, and asked him whether the king of the Jews was already dead. Abenadar in reply related to him the death of the Lord about three o'clock, his last words, and his loud cry, the quaking of the earth and the rending of the rock. Outwardly Pilate appeared merely to be surprised, since the crucified generally lived longer, but inwardly he was filled with trouble and alarm at the coincidence of those signs with Jesus's death. He wished perhaps to palliate in some measure his cruelty by at once expediting an order for Joseph of Arimathea, by which he gave him the body of the king of the Jews with permission to take it down from the cross and bury it. He was glad by so doing to be able to annoy the high priests, who would rather have had Jesus dishonorably buried along with the two thieves. It was probably Abenadar himself whom Pilate dispatched to see the order executed, for I saw him present at the taking down of Jesus from the cross. [310]

[MARK 15:43–45] 43 Joseph of Arimathea, a respected member of the council, who was also himself looking for the kingdom of God, took courage and went to Pilate, and asked for the body of Jesus. 44 And Pilate wondered if he were already dead; and summoning the centurion, he asked him whether he was already dead. 45 And when he learned from the centurion that he was dead, he granted the body to Joseph.

EVEN Pilate must have been greatly troubled by the events of this terrible day. The dream of his wife Claudia, on which he has had time to think quietly since the iniquitous condemnation, the awful phenomena of which he has been a witness, and above all, his memory of the bearing of the Master, of his words so pregnant with meaning, of his look so calm yet so penetrating, with his superhuman silence later, all combine to fill with alarm the guilty conscience of the governor, who has sacrificed an innocent victim to fear for himself. All of a sudden, however, a member of the Sanhedrin comes to him, "went in boldly," says Mark, and truly courage was needed to proffer such a request as his! He came to crave as a favor that the body of the victim should be given to him, thereby denouncing himself as a disciple of that victim. His boldness was indeed something quite new in Joseph the "honorable counselor," for hitherto he had been, it is true, a disciple "but secretly for fear of the Jews." It was Jesus on the cross who had changed him. He is no longer afraid of anything; he goes boldly to claim the body of the Master. And Pilate, full of marvel at so speedy a death, "called unto him the centurion" to learn the truth from his mouth. The latter, as we know, himself full of emotion and excitement, told what he knew and withdrew. Joseph of Arimathea then repeated his request and Pilate granted it without demur. Would not showing a little benevolence now soothe his own conscience, full of remorse as it was for the crime of the morning? He therefore gave the body of Jesus to Joseph. This free giving was by no means usual, for many a time did the procurators refuse to restore to their families the bodies of the dead unless they were paid to do so. Pilate, however, in this case is bent on being generous. He has no heart to make a bargain. Joseph of Arimathea, therefore, leaves at once and disappears in the streets of the city to seek a shroud.

The Thieves' Legs are Broken [K16]

QUIET was scarcely restored to Jerusalem after all those frightful events, when Pilate, already so terrified, was assailed on all sides with accounts of what had occurred. The council of the Jews also, as they had determined to do that morning, sent to him for permission to break the legs of the crucified, and thus put an end to their life, for they wanted to take them down from the cross, that they might not hang thereon upon the sabbath. Pilate dispatched some executioners to Golgotha for this purpose. Meanwhile all was silent and mournful on Golgotha. The crowd had timidly dispersed to their homes. The mother of Jesus, John, Magdalene, Mary Cleophas, and Salome were standing or sitting with veiled heads and in deep sadness opposite the cross. Some soldiers were seated on the earthen wall, their spears stuck in the ground near them. Cassius was riding around, and the soldiers were interchanging words with their companions posted at some distance below. The sky was lowering; all nature appeared to be in mourning.

Things were in this position when six executioners were seen ascending the mount with ladders, spades, ropes, and heavy, triangular iron bars used for breaking the bones of malefactors. When they entered the circle, the friends of Jesus drew back a little. New fear seized upon the heart of the blessed Virgin lest the body of Jesus was to be still further outraged, for the executioners mounted up the cross, roughly felt the sacred body, and declared that he was pretending to be dead. Although they felt that he was quite cold and stiff, yet they were not convinced that he was already dead. John, at the entreaty of the blessed Virgin, turned to the soldiers, to draw them off for a while from the body of the Lord. The executioners next mounted the ladders to the crosses of the thieves. Two of them with their sharp clubs broke the bones of their arms above and below the elbows, while a third did the same above the knees and ankles. Gesmas roared frightfully, consequently the executioner finished him by three blows of the club on the breast. Dismas moaned feebly, and expired under the torture. He was the first mortal to look again upon his Redeemer. [310]

[JOHN 19:31–32] 31 Since it was the day of Preparation, in order to prevent the bodies from remaining on the cross on the sabbath (for that sabbath was a high day), the Jews asked Pilate that their legs might be broken, and that they might be taken away. 32 So the soldiers came and broke the legs of the first, and of the other who had been crucified with him.

THE cruel operation to which John alludes was sometimes inflicted as part of the punishment of crucifixion, but it was more often resorted to only as a means of hastening death when it seemed likely to be too long delayed. In order to avoid the necessity of protracted watching beside the instrument of torture, the executioners sometimes substituted increased agony for length of suffering. By means of a club the bones of the legs of the condemned were broken.

In the present instance, the Jews had very urgent reasons for acting as they did, for according to the Hebrew law it would be a desecration of the sacred soil of the Holy Land if the body of a criminal who had been executed were allowed to remain on the cross during the night. Moreover, it was the eve of the Jewish sabbath and of a sabbath of peculiar sanctity. Now the day was already far spent; everything must be finished before sunset. The two thieves were, therefore, dispatched to begin with. The first, who had railed at and insulted Jesus, yielded up his soul with yells of rage while the penitent one died in ecstasy without one moment of shrinking or of fear. Looking on at these last manifestations of cruelty the friends of Jesus shudder. They tremble for the sacred form of the Savior from which life has just departed. Will that body, which has already been so terribly maltreated, be subjected to this further indignity? No, no; that Jesus is really dead is to be proved in a very different manner, a more touching, may we not say in a providential manner? In every detail, in fact, the execution of the malefactors differed from that of Jesus Christ. The former were not nailed to the cross but bound to it with cords so that they died without any shedding of their blood. Jesus, on the contrary, was, throughout the whole of his martyrdom, a bleeding victim. Whereas the thieves were beaten to death like dangerous wild beasts, the Savior Christ poured out his blood to wash away the sins of the human race.

The Strike of the Lance [K17]

THE executioners appeared still to have some doubts as to the death of the Lord, and his friends, after witnessing the terrible scene just described, were more anxious than ever for them to withdraw. Cassius, the subaltern officer, afterward known as Longinus, a somewhat hasty, impetuous man of twenty-five, whose airs of importance and officiousness joined to his weak, squinting eyes often exposed him to the ridicule of his inferiors, was suddenly seized by wonderful ardor. The barbarity, the base fury of the executioners, the anguish of the blessed Virgin, and the grace accorded him in that sudden and supernatural impulse of zeal, all combined to make of him the fulfiller of a prophecy. His lance, which was shortened by having one section run into another, he drew out to its full length, stuck the point upon it, turned his horse's head, and drove him boldly up to the narrow space on top of the eminence upon which the cross was planted. There was scarcely room for the animal to turn, and I saw Cassius reining him up in front of the chasm made by the cleft rock. He halted between Jesus's cross and that of the good thief, on the right of our Savior's body, grasped the lance with both hands, and drove it upward with such violence into the hollow, distended right side of the sacred body, through the entrails and the heart, that its point opened a little wound in the left breast. [311]

[JOHN 19:33–37] 33 But when they came to Jesus and saw that he was already dead, they did not break his legs. 34 But one of the soldiers pierced his side with a spear, and at once there came out blood and water. 35 He who saw it has borne witness—his testimony is true, and he knows that he tells the truth—that you also may believe. 36 For these things took place that the scripture might be fulfilled, "Not a bone of him shall be broken." 37 And again another scripture says, "They shall look on him whom they have pierced."

AFTER having broken the legs of the thieves, the soldiers approached the Savior. To their great astonishment they found that he was already dead, so that the brutal operation of the crurifragium was quite unnecessary, for, as we have already said, its aim was merely to hasten death. The soldiers did not, therefore, dream of inflicting this indignity upon the body of the divine Master, and the apostle John sees in their refraining to do so a fulfilment of the scriptures. He probably alludes to the passages in Exodus and Numbers referring to the Paschal lamb, which was a type of the Messiah. Those offering sacrifices were strictly enjoined to respect the bones of the victims, and the greatest precautions were taken to avoid breaking them, lest the Almighty should be insulted by the mutilation of a sacrifice offered up in His honor. The Talmud tells us of severe penalties inflicted on those who transgressed this law, including the bastinado.

In order, however, to make quite sure of the death of Jesus, the centurion pierced his side with a spear and "forthwith" says the sacred text, "came there out blood and water." Though John insists on this fact he does not appear to consider it anything extraordinary. The Fathers of the Church see in this incident of the sacred drama the image of many very touching mysteries. "Even as Eve," they say, "was taken from the rib of Adam, so did the rib of Christ give birth to the second Eve who is the Church." As a matter of fact, the life of the Church is, so to speak, bound up with two fundamental rites which make of it one homogeneous whole. These two rites are Baptism, or the Sacrament of Regeneration, and the Eucharist, or the Sacrament of the Body and Blood of Christ. Now, water and blood are the fundamental elements of these two rites, and this is why, say the Fathers of the Church, they both flowed from the side of Jesus when he hung upon the cross.

The Confession of Longinus [K18]

⊕

WHEN with all his force he drew the blessed lance from the wide wound it had made in the right side of Jesus, a copious stream of blood and water rushed forth and flowed over his upraised face, bedewing him with grace and salvation. He sprang quickly from his horse, fell upon his knees, struck his breast, and before all present proclaimed aloud his belief in Jesus. The blessed Virgin, John, and the holy women, whose eyes were riveted upon Jesus, witnessed with terror the sudden action, accompanied the thrust of the lance with a cry of woe, and rushed up to the cross. Mary, as if the thrust had transfixed her own heart, felt the sharp point piercing her through and through. She sank into the arms of her friends, while Cassius, still on his knees, was loudly confessing the Lord and joyfully praising God. He was enlightened; he now saw plainly and distinctly. The eyes of his body, like those of his soul, were healed and opened.

All were seized with a sentiment of the deepest reverence at sight of the Redeemer's blood which, mixed with water, fell in a foamy stream into a hollow in the rock at the foot of the cross. Mary, Cassius, the holy women, and John scooped it up in the drinking cups they had with them, poured it into flasks, and dried the hollow with linen cloths. Cassius was entirely changed, deeply touched and humbled. He had received perfect sight. The soldiers present, touched also by the miracle they had witnessed, fell on their knees, striking their breast and confessing Jesus, from the wide opening of whose right side blood and water were copiously streaming. It fell upon the clean stone, and lay there foaming and bubbling. The friends of Jesus gathered it up with loving care, Mary and Magdalene mingling with it their tears. [311]

THE question has been raised, which side of the divine Master was pierced by the spear? It would at first sight appear natural that it should have been the left side, first, because of the position of the heart or rather because the heart is inclined toward the left, and secondly, because the left side was more easily reached by a blow delivered from the right. We are, in fact justified in supposing that the centurion held his spear in the right hand. In spite of all this, however, an opinion has long been pretty generally entertained that the wound was made on the right side. The Apocryphal Gospels of the Infancy of Christ and of Nicodemus, as well as the Ethiopian translation, also sanction this idea, and their view is perhaps not altogether without foundation in fact. Certain early painters also adopted it. One fact which may have led those authors to adopt this opinion is the testimony of Saint Bonaventure that Saint Francis of Assisi, when he received the stigmata, was pierced in the hands and feet and in the right, not the left side. . . . As we have already remarked, many legends are related about the centurion Longinus. One of these legends tells that he was blind, but that the stream of water and of blood which flowed from the heart of Jesus cured him alike of the blindness of the eyes, of his body, and of his soul. We have, however, seen from the account given by the evangelist that the conversion of Longinus resulted from totally different causes.

Jesus Alone on the Cross [K19]

⊕

ALL the above took place around the cross of Jesus soon after four o'clock, while Joseph of Arimathea and Nicodemus were making the purchase necessary for the burial of Christ. When the friends of Jesus on Golgotha were informed by Joseph of Arimathea's servants, who were come from cleaning and arranging the sepulcher, that their master had Pilate's permission to take down the sacred body and lay it in his own new tomb, John and the holy women returned at once to the city, to the quarter on Mount Zion. [311]

THE day which has been so crowded with events is drawing to a close; the spectators have left Golgotha and the two thieves have already been taken away. This was quickly accomplished, for all that was needed was to undo the ropes which kept the bodies in place, to fling those bodies into some hole near by and then to cover them over with stones, of which there were plenty about. In the case of Jesus a special request had been made and the orders of Pilate were being awaited. It was Joseph of Arimathea, according to Mark "an honorable counselor," that is to say a member of the great council or Sanhedrin, and a secret disciple of Christ, who had gone to crave the body of the Master. During this pause John and Mary Salome went into the town to collect all that was needed for the performance of the last melancholy offices for the sacred remains and for burying them in accordance with the usual rites. Already, finding the place deserted, and attracted by the smell of blood, the dogs, which swarm in Eastern towns, are prowling about Golgotha. They run to and fro sniffing for the bodies of the thieves, while in the air above hover eagles and vultures, wheeling slowly round, ready in their turn to pounce upon the quarry.

The Mother of Jesus, who still stands, and Mary Magdalene, who has fainted away at the foot of the cross, can neither of them leave. Even if they could believe him to be dead they could not tear themselves from the spot, but feel as if they must remain there forever. Absolute silence reigns around Golgotha; a thousand reasons keeping the crowds away from it and even preventing isolated passers-by from approaching. To begin with, the Sabbath is close at hand; it commences at sunset, after which all Jews will be occupied and absorbed with the ceremonies of the Passover. Moreover, dead bodies are looked upon as impure, and everyone would avoid being near them on the eve of so solemn a feast. Lastly, and above all, the extraordinary events which occurred on Golgotha but a few hours previously have led to the spot being dreaded, and all the spectators have fled from it; a few belated travelers at the most glide rapidly along the walls of rough stone, their furtive steps seeming rather to intensify than to disturb the loneliness of the scene.

Truly gloomy is the appearance of Golgotha! Two empty crosses stand out against the sky, while the third still bears the body of the divine victim, rigid in the immobility of death. At his feet are two silent women and all around him is the desert. The darkness has gradually dispersed and the weather is brightening somewhat, though it still looks threatening. A pale sun lights up the Mount of Olives, at the foot of which is the town, now in all the ferment of excitement usual at the time of the great feasts. The air is laden with a penetrating perfume, it is the scent of the incense, of which large quantities are being burnt in the temple. At regular intervals the sound of the trumpet rings out, now in short, now in long drawn-out blasts, summoning the worshippers to the evening ceremonies and regulating the order in which successive groups are allowed to enter the temple. Mary and the Magdalene remain motionless, utterly absorbed in their grief. What have they left to do but to wait? In any case, however, they could not leave the Lord. When Jesus was deserted by all others, these two women were ever true to him.

The Descent from the Cross [K20]

JOSEPH of Arimathea took leave of Pilate and went to meet Nicodemus, who was awaiting him at the house of a well-disposed woman. Nicodemus had purchased here a lot of aromatic plants and herbs for the embalming. Joseph of Arimathea bought a winding sheet of cotton, very fine and beautiful. His servants collected ladders, hammers, strong iron nails, water bottles, vessels, sponges, and all that was necessary for the work before them. It was still cloudy and foggy when they reached Golgotha, where they found their servants and the holy women, the latter sitting in front of the cross and in tears. As soon as the centurion Abenadar arrived, they began sadly and reverently that most holy labor of love, the taking down from the cross and preparing for burial of the sacred body of their Master, their Lord, their Redeemer. The most holy Virgin and Magdalene were seated upon the right side of the little mound between the cross of Dismas and that of Jesus. The other women were busied arranging the spices and linens, the water, the sponges, and the vessels. All were extremely touched. Their movements were marked by an air of solemn sadness and gravity.

Nicodemus and Joseph placed the ladders behind the cross and mounted, carrying with them a very long strip of linen, to which three broad straps were fastened. They bound the body of Jesus under the arms and knees to the trunk of the cross, and the arms they fastened in the same way at the wrists. Then, by striking upon strong pegs fixed against the points of the nails at the back of the cross, they forced out the nails from Jesus's hands. The lower part of the body, which in death had sunk down on the knees, rested now in a sitting posture upon a linen band that was bound up around the hands on the arms of the cross. While Joseph was striking out the left nail and allowing the left arm to sink down gently on the body, Nicodemus was binding the right arm in the same way to the cross, also the thorn-crowned head, which had fallen upon the right shoulder. The right nail was then forced out, and the arm allowed to sink into the band that supported the body. Abenadar the centurion had meanwhile, though with great effort, been driving out the enormous nail from the feet. Cassius reverently picked up the nails as they fell out, and laid them down together by the blessed Virgin. Next, removing the ladders to the front of the cross and close to the sacred body, they loosened the upper band from the trunk of the cross, and hung it on one of the hooks of the ladder. They did the same to the two other bands, which they hung on two of the lower hooks. Thus with the gently lowered bands, the sacred body sank by degrees to where the centurion Abenadar, mounted on portable steps, was waiting to receive it. He clasped the limbs below the knees in his arms and descended slowly, while Nicodemus and Joseph, holding the upper part in their arms, gently and cautiously, as if carrying a beloved and very severely wounded friend, came down the ladders step by step. In this way did that most sacred, that most terribly maltreated body of the Redeemer reach the ground. [315]

[JOHN 19:38] 38 After this Joseph of Arimathea, who was a disciple of Jesus, but secretly, for fear of the Jews, asked Pilate that he might take away the body of Jesus, and Pilate gave him leave. So he came and took away his body.

GOLGOTHA is hushed in silence now, and instead of the tumult of a short time ago nothing is heard but stifled sobs. The necessary orders for removing the beloved body from the cross as rapidly as possible are whispered from one to the other. Nicodemus and Joseph of Arimathea noiselessly make all the necessary arrangements for the delicate operation. This is how it was probably managed. To begin with, a long band of some material was placed across the chest and under the arms of Jesus, which band, passing over the crossbeam on either side of the title, and kept in place from behind by those who stood on the ladders, served to uphold the body for a moment or two when the cords were removed. The nails were then taken out of the hands; the arms were gently drawn down against the livid body, still bearing on it the marks of the blows, the injuries sustained in the various falls, the scourgings and the bonds. Then, the body, being still kept in place against the cross by the band, the nail was removed from the feet, and the centurion reverently received in swathing cloths the legs of the Savior. By gradually loosening the band of stuff upholding and wrapping round the sacred form it is now possible to let that form slowly glide into the arms of Mary, John, and Magdalene, who stand waiting to receive it. Their hands are swathed in linen brought from the town; it is only with the deepest reverence that they venture to touch the sacred remains; their sobs have ceased and a solemn silence reigns on Golgotha.

The Holy Virgin Receives the Body of Jesus [K21]

WHEN the blows of the hammer by which the nails were driven out resounded, Mary and Magdalene, as well as all that had been present at the crucifixion, were pierced with fresh grief, for the sound reminded them of that most cruel nailing of Jesus to the cross. They shuddered, as if expecting again to hear his piercing cries, and grieved anew over his death proclaimed by the silence of those blessed lips. As soon as the sacred body was taken down, the men wrapped it in linen from the knees to the waist and laid it on a sheet in his mother's arms which, in anguish of heart and ardent longing, were stretched out to receive it. The men then laid the sacred body on a sheet spread upon the mother's lap. The venerable head of Jesus rested upon her slightly raised knee, and his body lay outstretched upon the sheet. She pressed her lips to his bloodstained cheeks, while Magdalene knelt with her face bowed upon his feet.

The holy women helped in various ways, presenting when necessary vessels of water, sponges, towels, ointments, and spices. When not so engaged, they remained at a little distance attentively watching what was going on. Among them were Mary Cleophas, Salome, and Veronica, but Magdalene was always busied around the sacred body. Mary Heli, the blessed Virgin's elder sister, who was already an aged matron, was sitting apart on the earthwall of the circle, silently looking on. John lent constant assistance to the blessed Virgin. He went to and fro between the women and the men, now helping the former in their task of love, and afterward assisting the latter in every way to prepare all things for the burial.

The blessed Virgin's courage and fortitude, in the midst of her inexpressible anguish, were unshaken. With great care she opened the crown of thorns in the back and, with the assistance of others, removed it from Jesus's head. When the blessed Virgin had anointed all the wounds, she bound up the sacred head in linen, but the covering for the face, attached to that of the head, she did not as yet draw down. She embraced the sacred body of her Son, and weeping bitter tears, allowed her face to rest upon his. Magdalene's reverence for Jesus did not permit her to approach her face to his. She pressed it to his feet only. [315]

THE following is our view of the scene which now took place. Beyond the platform of Golgotha, on the same side as the garden of Joseph of Arimathea and not far from the sepulcher in which Jesus was to be buried, was a spot well fitted for the performance of the first of the touching rites which the Virgin was eager to perform for the sacred body of her divine Son. She was seated on some natural steps in the rock and the body of Jesus was laid near her, in such a manner that it could rest against her knees with the head upon her breast, so that she could lavish all her tenderness on it. Some warm water was provided close at hand, and with its aid the matted hair is freed from blood, the wounds are washed, and the crown of thorns, which is glued to the head with dried gore, is removed. The apostles and disciples, who have been looking on from afar ready to flee, venture to approach now that their enemies have left Golgotha. The holy women are also present, doing their best to aid the mother of the Savior. The crown of thorns when removed is put carefully aside.

The Body of Jesus Carried to the Anointing Stone [K22]

⊕

JOSEPH and Nicodemus had already been standing awhile at some distance waiting when John drew near the blessed Virgin with the request that she would permit them to take the body of Jesus, that they might proceed in their preparations for the burial, as the sabbath was near. Once more Mary closely embraced Jesus, and in touching words took leave of him. The men raised the most sacred body in the sheet upon which it was resting in the lap of his mother, and carried it down to the place where the burial preparations were to be made. They carried the body of Jesus a little distance down from Golgotha's summit to a cave on the side of the mount in which there was a beautiful flat rock. It was here that the men had prepared the place for embalming. I saw first a linen cloth, open-worked something like a net. Perhaps it was pierced like a net in order to allow the water used in washing to flow through it. [317]

[JOHN 19:39] 39 Nicodemus also, who had at first come to him by night, came bringing a mixture of myrrh and aloes, about a hundred pounds' weight.

THE head, face, hands, and arms, with the upper part of the sacred body, have been washed with lukewarm water, dried and anointed with spices by the Mother of Jesus. The mourners then prepare to descend to the foot of Golgotha, where, near the entrance to the so-called cave of Melchizedek, was a piece of rock flat enough to receive the corpse. There the disciples will complete the work begun by Mary, washing the feet, the legs, and the lower part of the body. They will then anoint with spiced unguents the wounds, the bruises, and the gaping holes made by the nails.

Now that the body of Jesus rests in the shroud, upheld by his friends, it seems instinct with a calm and majestic grandeur. The hair and beard are carefully arranged; the limbs seem to be stretched out in natural repose, and the features are restored to something of the beauty which rendered the Savior so attractive in life. The procession is soon formed; the sacred burden is carried by Nicodemus, Joseph of Arimathea, John, and the centurion. The Virgin follows, supported by her nearest relations, while Mary Magdalene, who is scarcely able to walk, follows her; the group of holy women succeeding the chief mourners, chanting psalms broken every now and then by their lamentations, which they no longer make any attempt to disguise.

The crown of thorns, with the sponges soaked with the precious blood and the vessels containing the water which has been used to wash the sacred corpse, are set apart, protected by a veil thrown over them. As for the nails which had fastened Jesus to the instrument of his death, they were left with the cross and its title. It would have been against the law to remove any of these things, for they were the property of the Roman authorities. It is to these scruples that we must, as it appears to me, attribute what would otherwise appear the inexplicable negligence of allowing the cross and the nails to be buried beneath the rubbish which accumulated during the long centuries succeeding the death of Christ.

The Holy Virgin Kisses the Face of Jesus on the Anointing Stone [K23]

JOHN once more conducted the blessed Virgin and the other holy women to the sacred remains of Jesus. Mary knelt down by Jesus's head, took a fine linen scarf that hung around her neck under her mantle and which she had received from Claudia Procula, Pilate's wife, and laid it under the head of her Son. Then she and the other holy women filled in the spaces between the shoulders and the head, around the whole neck and up as far as the cheeks with herbs, some of those fine threadlike plants, and the costly powder mentioned before, all of which the blessed Virgin bound up carefully in the fine linen scarf. Magdalene poured the entire contents of a little flask of precious balm into the wound of Jesus's side, while the holy women placed aromatic herbs in the hands and all around and under the feet. Then the men covered the pit of the stomach and filled up the armpits and all other parts of the body with sweet spices, crossed the stiffened arms over the bosom, and closely wrapped the whole in the large white sheet as far as the breast, just as a child is swathed. Then, having fastened under one of the armpits the end of a broad linen band, they wound it round the arms, the hands, the head, and down again around the whole of the sacred body until it presented the appearance of a mummy. Lastly, they laid the Lord's body on the large sheet, twelve feet long, that Joseph of Arimathea had bought, and wrapped it closely around it. The sacred body was laid on it crosswise. Then one corner was drawn up from the feet to the breast, the opposite one was folded down over the head and shoulders, and the sides were doubled round the whole person. [318]

[JOHN 19:40] 40 They took the body of Jesus, and bound it in linen cloths with the spices, as is the burial custom of the Jews.

THE disciples have completed their pious task; the body has been washed, embalmed, and, as was the custom among the Jews, linen bands have been wound round it before it was placed in its shroud. Finally, a second shroud would be placed over the beloved face, hiding it from the tender gaze of the mourners. The heavy clouds which had obscured the sky during the day are dispersed and the evening is fine. The women are now all grouped together, their faces veiled and their ample draperies entirely shrouding their figures, giving them the solemn, reserved appearance suitable to a funeral ceremony. The resinous torches are lighted now, to show the way to the tomb of Joseph of Arimathea, which is quite close by. The procession is ready to begin its progress thither.

Jesus Carried to the Tomb [K24]

THE men now laid the sacred body on the leathern litter and ran two poles along the sides. I thought right away of the Ark of the Covenant. Nicodemus and Joseph carried the front ends on their shoulders; Abenadar and John, the others. There followed the blessed Virgin, her elder sister Mary Heli, Magdalene, and Mary Cleophas. Then the group of women that had been seated at some distance: Veronica, Johanna Chusa, Mary Mark; Salome, the wife of Zebedee; Mary Salome, Salome of Jerusalem, Susanna, and Anna, a niece of Joseph. She was the daughter of one of his brothers, and had been reared in Jerusalem. Cassius and his soldiers closed the procession. The other women, namely, Maroni of Nain, Dinah the Samaritan, and Mara the Suphanite were at the time with Martha and Lazarus in Bethany. Two soldiers with twisted torches walked on ahead, for light was needed in the grotto of the sepulcher. I saw the procession halt at the entrance of the garden. It was opened by removing some of the poles, which were afterward used as levers for rolling away the stone from the door of the grotto. [318]

[JOHN 19:41] 41 Now in the place where he was crucified there was a garden, and in the garden a new tomb where no one had ever been laid.

THE new sepulcher given by Joseph of Arimathea is close at hand, not a stone's throw off the flat piece of rock where the washing and embalming of Jesus have taken place. Behind this spot, however, the ground suddenly rises, while the wall enclosing the garden makes it impossible to go straight to the tomb. The procession is therefore compelled to make a slight detour to avoid places so steep that the sacred burden would be shaken in a manner not at all consistent with the reverence due to it. The ground was not, in fact, then as level as it became later. The sun is setting; haste must be made, for the sabbath will very soon begin and the whole ceremony ought to be completed before that. This will explain how it was that there was something left to be done on the Sunday morning, and why the holy women will return to anoint yet again the body of the Lord.

The sky is clear; all the serenity of an evening in spring is once more restored. There is no wind, the smoke of the torches lighting up the tomb ascends straightly, the women shrouded in their mourning garments follow singing psalms, the sweet sound of their voices being heard afar off through the still air. The body of the Master is borne upon a kind of litter carried on their shoulders by John, Joseph of Arimathea, the centurion, and Nicodemus. Then comes Mary, accompanied by the holy women. On leaving the stone of anointing, the procession turns in the direction of the town, then, skirting along the spot where the crosses are lying, reaches the garden, passes beneath a few olive and fig trees, the shadows of which gradually deepen and lengthen, finally arriving, after having made an almost complete circuit of Golgotha, at the entrance to the sepulcher, which is reached by going down a few steps.

The Two Marys Watch the Tomb [K25]

⊕

THE holy women sat down upon a seat opposite the entrance of the grotto. [319]

[MARK 15:47] 47 Mary Magdalene and Mary the mother of Joses saw where he was laid.

THE precious body has been laid in the tomb; the last farewell has been silently taken. The mourners have filed past the corpse resting in the cubiculum, or little chamber, and have then slowly retired backward as we all regretfully leave a place we love. The stone, the wedges removed, has rolled into its groove, it has been firmly fixed once more and the sepulcher is closed. It is still, however, possible to enter the first chamber, for the outer aperture remains open. Everyone is gone now except two women who remain to watch the sacred spot from a distance. They intend to go back to it at the earliest possible moment to render yet more last services to the divine Master. At present, they must not dream of doing anything, for the sabbath has begun; they must content themselves with reviewing every detail of the interment, so that they may know what to do the next morning. This is what Mark implies when he says: "Mary Magdalene and Mary the mother of Joses beheld where he was laid." Then they take up their post on a rock opposite the entrance and wait. Time passes, but they are still there, they have too much food for meditation to be impatient. The night is closing in on them; still they do not move from their place, but with eager gaze they seem to strive to pierce through the stone closing the tomb, to the form of him they love.

Jesus in the Sepulcher [K26]

⊕

THE grotto, which was perfectly new, had been cleaned out and fumigated by Nicodemus's servants. It was very neat inside and was ornamented by a beautifully carved coping. The funereal couch was broader at the head than at the foot. It was cut out in the form of a body swathed in its bands and winding sheet, and slightly elevated at the head and foot. The four men carried the Lord's body down into it, set it down, strewed the stone couch with sweet spices, spread over it a linen cloth, and deposited the sacred remains upon it. The cloth hung down over the couch. Then, having with tears and embraces given expression to their love for Jesus, they left the cave. The blessed Virgin now went in, and I saw her sitting on the head of the tomb, which was about two feet from the ground. She was bending low over the corpse of her child and weeping. When she left the cave, Magdalene hurried in with flowers and branches, which she had gathered in the garden and which she now scattered over the sacred body. She wrung her hands, and with tears and sighs embraced the feet of Jesus. When the men outside gave warning that it was time to close the doors, she went back to where the women were sitting.

The men raised the cloth that was hanging over the side of the tomb, folded it around the sacred body, and then threw the brown cover over the whole. Lastly, they closed the brown doors, probably of copper or bronze, which had a perpendicular bar on the outside crossed by a transverse one. It looked like a cross. The great stone, intended for securing the doors and which was still lying outside the cave, was in shape almost like a chest or tomb, and was large enough for a man to lie at full length upon it. It was very heavy. By means of the poles brought from the garden entrance, the men rolled it into place before the closed doors of the tomb. The outside entrance was secured by a light door of wickerwork. All that took place in the grotto was by torchlight, for it was dark in there. [319]

[JOHN 19:42] 42 So because of the Jewish day of Preparation, as the tomb was close at hand, they laid Jesus there. [MARK 15:46] 46 And he bought a linen shroud, and taking him down, wrapped him in the linen shroud, and laid him in a tomb which had been hewn out of the rock; and he rolled a stone against the door of the tomb.

THE tomb hewn in the living rock is reached through a second rock-cut chamber. The body of Jesus is placed in a kind of trough. The opening giving access to the sepulcher is low, and those who enter it have to stoop. It is closed on the outside by a rounded stone not unlike a mill-stone running in a groove. This stone, heavy and difficult to move as it was, would engross the thoughts of the holy women when they came to visit the sepulcher on the morning of the Resurrection. Levers were generally used for moving stones of this kind, and once in place they were kept firmly in their grooves by wedges.

The Watch over the Tomb [K27]

PILATE wanted to have nothing more to do with the affair, so he said to them: "You have a guard. Go, guard it as you know." He, however, appointed Cassius to keep watch and give him an account of all that he observed. Thereupon I saw twelve men leaving the city before sunrise. They were accompanied by soldiers not dressed in the Roman uniform. They were temple soldiers, and looked to me like halbadiers. They took with them lanterns on long poles, in order to be able to distinguish things clearly in the dark, and also to have light in the gloomy sepulcher. When, on their arrival, they assured themselves that the sacred body was safe, they fastened a string across the doors of the tomb proper and another from that to the stone lying before them. Then they sealed the two together with a seal in the form of a half-moon. The twelve men returned afterward to the city, and the guard took up a position opposite the outer door of the sepulcher. Five or six took turns in watching, while some others presented themselves occasionally with provisions from the city.

Cassius never left his post. He remained most of the time in the sepulcher itself, sitting or standing before the entrance to the tomb, and in such a position that he could see that side at which rested the feet of the Lord. He had received great interior graces and had been admitted to the clear understanding of many mysteries. As such a condition, being almost all the time in a state of wonderful interior enlightenment, was something so new to him, he was, as it were, transported out of himself, wholly regardless of external things. He here became entirely changed, a new man. He spent the day in penance, thanksgiving, and adoration. [320]

[MATTHEW 27:62–66] 62 Next day, that is, after the day of Preparation, the chief priests and the Pharisees gathered before Pilate 63 and said, "Sir, we remember how that impostor said, while he was still alive, 'After three days I will rise again.' 64 Therefore order the sepulcher to be made secure until the third day, lest his disciples go and steal him away, and tell the people, 'He has risen from the dead,' and the last fraud will be worse than the first." 65 Pilate said to them, "You have a guard of soldiers; go, make it as secure as you can." 66 So they went and made the sepulcher secure by sealing the stone and setting a guard.

AFTER *their interview with Pilate, the members of the Sanhedrin, having obtained his authority, make their own arrangements for securing the tomb. It is now Saturday evening; the guard arrives and takes up its position; the lanterns are lit and a scribe comes to seal the round stone carefully. The Jews consider this a necessary precaution, to guard against the watchmen themselves, who might have been bribed by the friends of Jesus. The wax seals impressed, the man leans against the stone and becomes drowsy. The night is calm; the guards lie down upon the ground and watch in silence. Nothing is heard but the continuous barking of the dogs who prowl about in noisy bands all night.*

RESURRECTION · ASCENSION · DESCENT OF THE HOLY SPIRIT

The Eve of the Holy Resurrection

At the close of the sabbath, John, Peter, and James the Greater visited the holy women, to mourn with them and to console them. On their departure, the holy women enveloped themselves again in their mourning mantles, and retired to pray in the recesses strewn with ashes.

I saw an angel appear to the blessed Virgin. He announced to her that the Lord was near, and bade her to go out to the little gate belonging to Nicodemus. At these words, Mary's heart was filled with joy. Without saying a word to the holy women, wrapped in her mantle, she hastened to the gate in the city wall through which she had come on her return from the garden of the tomb.

It may have been *almost nine o'clock* when, in a solitary place near the gate, I saw the blessed Virgin suddenly halt in her hurried walk. She gazed as if ravished with joyous longing up at the top of the wall. Floating down toward her in the midst of a great multitude of the souls of the ancient patriarchs, I saw the most holy soul of Jesus, resplendent with light and without trace of wound. Turning to the patriarchs and pointing to the blessed Virgin, he uttered the words: "Mary, my mother!" and appeared to embrace her. Then he vanished. The blessed Virgin sank on her knees and kissed the ground upon which he had stood. She left the impress of her knees and feet upon the stone. Inexpressibly consoled, she hurried back to the women, whom she found busied preparing ointment and spices on a table. She did not tell them what had happened, but she consoled and strengthened them in faith.

The table at which the holy women were standing had an undersupport with crossed feet, something like a dresser, and it was covered with a cloth that hung down to the floor. I saw lying on it bunches of all kinds of herbs mixed and put in order, little flasks of ointment and nard water, and several flowers growing in pots, among which I remember one, a striped iris, or lily. The women packed them all in linen cloths. During Mary's absence, Magdalene, Mary Cleophas, Johanna Chusa, and Mary Salome went to the city to buy all these things. They wanted to go early next morning to scatter them over the body of Jesus in its winding sheet and pour upon it the perfumed water. I saw a part of it brought by the disciples from the dealer and left at the house without their going in to speak to the women.

*April 4, AD 33
Saturday, 9 PM*

Joseph of Arimathea Miraculously Set at Large

AFTER that I had a glimpse of Joseph of Arimathea praying in his prison cell. Suddenly the cell shone with light, and Joseph heard his name pronounced. I saw the roof raised just where the cornice joined it to the wall, and a radiant figure letting down a strip of linen that reminded me of one of those in which the body of Jesus had been wrapped. The figure commanded Joseph to climb up by holding on to it. Then I saw Joseph grasp the linen with both hands and, supporting his feet on the projecting stones of the wall, climb to the opening, a distance of about twelve feet. The roof immediately resumed its position when Joseph reached it, and the apparition disappeared. I do not know whether it was the Lord himself or an angel that released him.

I saw him running unnoticed a short distance along the city wall to the neighborhood of the Cenacle, which was situated near the south wall of Zion. He climbed down and knocked at the door. The disciples were assembled with closed doors. They were very sorrowful over Joseph's disappearance, for they credited the report that he had been thrown into a sewer. When they opened the door and he entered, their joy was as great as that which they experienced later on when Peter, freed from his prison, appeared before them. Joseph told them all about the apparition he had had. They were greatly rejoiced and consoled by his account; they gave him food and thanked God. *He left Jerusalem that night* and fled to Arimathea, his native place, where he remained until he received news that he might return to Jerusalem without fear of danger.

After the close of the sabbath, I saw Caiaphas and some other high priests in the house of Nicodemus, to whom, with an air of assumed benevolence, they were putting many questions. I do not now remember what subject they were discussing, but Nicodemus remained true and firm in his defense of the Lord, and so they parted.

The Night of Resurrection

ALL was quiet and silent around the holy sepulcher. About seven guards were in front and around it, some sitting, others standing. The whole day long Cassius maintained his stand inside the sepulcher at the entrance of the tomb proper, leaving it scarcely for a few moments. He was still absorbed in recollection. He was in expectation of something that he knew was going to happen, for extraordinary grace and light had been vouchsafed to him. *It was night*; the lanterns before the tomb shed a dazzling light. I saw the sacred body wrapped in its winding sheet just as it had been laid on the stone couch. It was surrounded by a brilliant light and, since the burial, two angels had in rapt adoration guarded the sacred remains, one at the head, the other at the foot. They looked like priests. Their whole attitude, their arms crossed on their breast, reminded me of the cherubim on the Ark of the Covenant, excepting that they had no wings. The whole tomb, and especially the resting place of the Lord, reminded me in a striking manner of the Ark of the Covenant at different periods of its history. The light and the presence of the angels may have been in some degree visible to Cassius, and it may have been on that account that he stood gazing so fixedly at the closed doors of the tomb, like one adoring the most blessed sacrament.

April 4–5, AD 33
Saturday, 11 PM–Sunday 12:30 AM

And now I saw the blessed soul of Jesus floating with the released spirits of the ancient patriarchs through the rock into the tomb, and showing them all the marks of ill-treatment upon his martyred body. The linen bands and winding sheet seemed to have been removed, for I saw the sacred body full of wounds; and it seemed as if, in some mysterious way, the indwelling divinity displayed before the souls the blessed body in the whole extent of its cruel laceration and martyrdom. It appeared to me perfectly transparent, its inmost parts disclosed to the eye. Its wounds, its sufferings, its pains could be seen even to their very depths. The souls gazed in mute reverence; they appeared to be sobbing and weeping with compassion.

My next vision was so mysterious that I cannot relate the whole of it in an intelligible manner. It was as if the soul of Jesus, though without restoring the sacred body to life by a perfect union with it, was transported in and with the body from the tomb. The two adoring angels raised the tortured body, not in an upright position, but just as it lay in the tomb, and floated with it up to heaven. The rock trembled as they passed through. Then it seemed to me that Jesus, between countless choirs of adoring angels ranged on either hand, presented his wounded body before the throne of his heavenly Father. Jesus's body seemed to have been resuscitated in a manner similar to that in which those of many of the prophets had been assumed by their souls after the death of Jesus and taken into the temple. They were not really alive, nor did they have again to die, for they were laid down by their souls without any forcible separation from

each other. I saw that the souls of the ancient patriarchs did not accompany the Lord's body to heaven.

I remarked a trembling in the rock of the sepulcher. Four of the guards had gone to the city to get something; the three others fell to the ground unconscious. They ascribed the shock to an earthquake, but knew nothing of the cause. Cassius, however, was very much agitated and frightened, for he had a clear view of what had happened without fully understanding it. He kept to his post, and with great devotion awaited what would next take place. Meanwhile the absent soldiers returned.

When the spices were prepared and packed in linen cloths ready to be taken to the tomb, the holy women again retired to their recesses and lay down on their couches to rest, because *they wanted to start before daylight* for Jesus's tomb. They had more than once expressed their anxiety as to the success of their design. They were full of dread lest the enemies of Jesus might waylay them when they went out. But the blessed Virgin consoled them. She bade them take some rest and then go courageously to the tomb, for no harm would befall them. And so they went to rest.

It was about eleven o'clock at night when the blessed Virgin, moved by love and ardent desire, could no longer remain in the house. She rose, wrapped herself in a gray mantle, and went out alone. I thought: Ah! How can they allow that blessed Mother, so full of sorrow and alarm, to go out alone under such circumstances. I saw her going sadly to the house of Caiaphas and then to Pilate's palace, which was a long way back into the city. And thus she traversed alone the whole way passed over by Jesus bearing his cross. She went through the deserted streets and paused at every spot upon which some special suffering or outrage had befallen the Lord. She looked like one seeking something lost. She frequently knelt down, felt around on the stones with her hand, and touched her lips to them, as if reverently touching and kissing something sacred, namely, the blood of Jesus. She beheld around her everything sanctified by contact with Jesus bright and shining, and her soul was entirely lost in love and adoration.

She went on until she approached Mount Calvary, when she stood quite still. It was as if the apparition of Jesus with his sacred, martyred body stepped before her. One angel preceded him, the two adoring angels of the tomb were at his side, and a multitude of released souls followed him. He seemed not to walk, but looked like a corpse floating along, environed with light. I heard a voice proceeding from him, which related to his mother what he had done in Limbo.

Now, he continued, he was about to come forth from the tomb alive, in a glorified body, and he bade her await him near Mount Calvary, on the stone upon which he had fallen. Then I saw the apparition going to the city, and the blessed Virgin kneeling and praying on the spot indicated by the Lord. *It may now have been past twelve o'clock*, for Mary had spent a considerable time in the Way of the Cross.

Then I saw the Lord's procession going over the whole of the same dolorous way. In a mysterious manner, the angels gathered up all the sacred substance, the flesh and the blood, that had been torn from Jesus during his Passion. I saw that the nailing to the cross, the raising of the same, the opening of the sacred side, the taking down from the cross, and the preparing of the holy body for burial, were shown to the souls in Jesus's train. The blessed Virgin also saw it all in spirit. She loved and adored.

Afterward it was as if the Lord's body rested again in the holy sepulcher. With it was all that had been torn from it during the Passion and replaced in an incomprehensible manner by the angels. I saw it as before, wrapped in the funereal bands and winding sheet, environed with dazzling splendor, the two adoring angels at the head and the foot of the tomb.

When the morning sky began to clear with a streak of white light, I saw Magdalene, Mary Cleophas, Johanna Chusa, and Salome, enveloped in mantles, leaving their abode near the Cenacle. They carried the spices packed in linen cloths, and one of them had a lighted lantern. They kept all hidden under their mantles. The spices consisted of fresh flowers for strewing over the sacred body, and also of expressed sap, essences, and oils for pouring over it. The holy women walked anxiously to the little gate belonging to Nicodemus.

The Resurrection of the Lord

THE BLESSED soul of Jesus in dazzling splendor, between two warrior angels and surrounded by a multitude of resplendent figures, came floating down through the rocky roof of the tomb upon the sacred body. It seemed to incline over it and melt, as it were, into one with it. I saw the sacred limbs moving beneath the swathing bands, and the dazzling, living body of the Lord with his soul and his divinity coming forth from the side of the winding sheet as if from the wounded side. The sight reminded me of Eve coming forth from Adam's side. The whole place was resplendent with light and glory.

And now I had another vision. I saw the apparition of a dragon with a human head coiling itself up out of the

April 5, AD 33
Sunday, Sunrise

abyss, as if right under the tomb upon which the Lord had been lying. It lashed its tail, and turned its head angrily toward the Lord. The risen Redeemer held in his hand a delicate white staff, on whose top floated a little standard. He placed one foot upon the dragon's head, and struck three blows of the staff upon its tail. At each stroke the monster seemed to contract, and at last sank into the earth, first the body, then the head, the human face still turned upward. I saw a similar serpent lurking around at the moment of Christ's conception. It reminded me of the serpent in Paradise and, I think, this vision bore reference to the Promise: "The seed of the woman shall crush the serpent's head." The whole vision appeared to me symbolical of victory over death, for as I watched the crushing of the serpent's head, the tomb of the Lord vanished from my sight.

Now I saw the Lord floating in glory up through the rock. [L1] The earth trembled, and an angel in warrior garb shot like lightning from heaven down to the tomb, rolled the stone to one side, and seated himself upon it. [L2] The trembling of the earth was so great that the lanterns swung from side to side, and the flames flashed around. The guards fell stunned to the ground and lay there stiff and contorted, as if dead. Cassius saw indeed the glory that environed the holy sepulcher, the rolling away of the stone by the angel, and his seating himself upon it, but he did not see the risen Savior himself. He recovered himself quickly, stepped to the stone couch, felt among the empty linens, and left the sepulcher, outside of which, full of eager desire, he tarried awhile to become the witness of a new and wonderful apparition. At the instant the angel shot down to the tomb and the earth quaked, I saw the risen Lord appearing to his blessed Mother on Mount Calvary. He was transcendently beautiful and glorious, his manner full of earnestness. His garment, which was like a white mantle thrown about his limbs, floated in the breeze behind him as he walked. It glistened blue and white, like smoke curling in the sunshine. His wounds were very large and sparkling; in those of his hands, one could easily insert a finger. The lips of the wounds formed the sides of an equilateral triangle which met, as it were, in the center of a circle, and from the palm of the hand shot rays of light toward the fingers.

The souls of the early patriarchs bowed low before the blessed Mother, to whom Jesus said something about seeing her again. He showed her his wounds, and when she fell on her knees to kiss his feet, he grasped her hand, raised her up, and disappeared.

When I was at some distance from the sepulcher I saw

fresh lights burning there, and I likewise beheld a large luminous spot in the sky immediately above Jerusalem.

The Holy Women at the Sepulcher

THE HOLY women, when the Lord arose from the dead, were near the little gate belonging to Nicodemus. They knew nothing of the prodigies that were taking place; they did not know even of the guard at the sepulcher, for they had remained shut up in their house the whole of the preceding day, the sabbath. They anxiously inquired of one another: "Who will roll away for us the stone from the doors?" Full of longing desire to show the last honors to the sacred body in the tomb, they had entirely lost sight of the stone. They wanted to pour nard water and precious balm over the sacred body and scatter their flowers and aromatic shrubs upon it; for to the spices of yesterday's embalming, which Nicodemus alone had procured, they had contributed nothing. They wished therefore to offer now to the body of their Lord and Master the most precious that could be obtained.

Salome had shared with Magdalene in defraying most of the cost. She was not the mother of John, but another Salome, a rich lady of Jerusalem, a relative of Joseph. At last the holy women concluded to set the spices on the stone before the tomb and to wait till some disciple would come who would open it for them. And so they went on toward the garden.

Outside the tomb the stone was rolled to the right, so that the doors, which were merely lying to, could now be easily opened. The linens in which the sacred body had been enveloped were on the tomb in the following order: the large winding sheet in which it had been wrapped lay undisturbed, only empty and fallen together, containing nothing but the aromatic herbs; the long bandage that had been wound around it was still lying twisted and at full length just as it had been drawn off, on the outer edge of the tomb; but the linen scarf with which Mary had enveloped Jesus's head lay to the right at the head of the tomb. It looked as if the head of Jesus was still in it, excepting that the covering for the face was raised.

When, as they approached, the holy women noticed the lanterns of the guard and the soldiers lying around, they became frightened, and went a short distance past the garden toward Golgotha. Magdalene, however, forgetful of danger, hurried into the garden. Salome followed her at some distance, and the other two waited outside.

Magdalene, seeing the guard, stepped back at first a few steps toward Salome, then both made their way together through the soldiers lying around and into the sepulcher. They found the stone rolled away, but the doors closed, probably by Cassius. Magdalene anxiously opened one of

them, peered in at the tomb, and saw the linens lying empty and apart. The whole place was resplendent with light, and an angel was sitting at the right of the tomb. [L3] Magdalene was exceedingly troubled. She hurried out of the garden of the sepulcher, off through the gate belonging to Nicodemus, and back to the apostles. Salome, too, who only now entered the sepulcher, ran at once after Magdalene, rushed in fright to the women waiting outside the garden, and told them of what had happened. Though amazed and rejoiced at what they heard from Salome, they could not resolve to enter the garden. It was not until Cassius told them in a few words what he had seen, and exhorted them to go see for themselves, that they took courage to enter. Cassius was hurrying into the city to acquaint Pilate of all that had taken place. He went through the gate of execution. When with beating heart the women entered the sepulcher and drew near the holy tomb, they beheld standing before them the two angels of the tomb in priestly robes, white and shining. The women pressed close to one another in terror and, covering their faces with their hands, bowed tremblingly almost to the ground. One of the angels addressed them. They must not fear, he said, nor must they look for the crucified here. He was alive, he had arisen, he was no longer among the dead. Then the angel pointed out to them the empty tomb, and ordered them to tell the disciples what they had seen and heard, and that Jesus would go before them into Galilee. They should, continued the angel, remember what the Lord had said to them in Galilee, namely, "The Son of Man will be delivered into the hands of sinners. He will be crucified and, on the third day, he will rise again." The holy women, shaking and trembling with fear, though still full of joy, tearfully gazed at the tomb and the linens, and departed, taking the road toward the gate of execution. They were still very much frightened. They did not hurry, but paused from time to time and looked around from the distance, to see whether they might not possibly behold the Lord, or whether Magdalene was returning.

Meanwhile Magdalene reached the Cenacle like one beside herself, and knocked violently at the door. Some of the disciples were still asleep on their couches around the walls, while several others had risen and were talking together. Peter and John opened the door. Magdalene, without entering, merely uttered the words: "They have taken the Lord from the tomb! We know not where" [L4]— and ran back in great haste to the garden of the sepulcher. Peter and John followed her, but John outstripped Peter. [L5]

Magdalene was quite wet with dew when she again reached the garden and ran to the tomb. Her mantle had slipped from her head down on her shoulders, and her long hair had fallen around loose. As she was alone, she was afraid to enter the sepulcher at once, so she waited out on the step at the entrance. She stooped down, trying to see through the low doors into the cave and even as far as the stone couch. Her long hair fell forward as she stooped, and she was trying to keep it back with her hands, when she saw the two angels in white priestly garments sitting at the head and the foot of the tomb, and heard the words: "Woman, why weepest thou?" She cried out in her grief: "They have taken my Lord away! I know not where they have laid him!" [L6] Saying this and seeing nothing but the linens, she turned weeping, like one seeking something, and as if she must find him. She had a dim presentiment that Jesus was near, and even the apparition of the angels could not turn her from her one idea. She did not appear conscious of the fact that it was an angel that spoke to her. She thought only of Jesus; her only thought was: "Jesus is not here! Where is Jesus?" I saw her running a few steps from the sepulcher and then returning like one half-distracted and in quest of something. Her long hair fell on her shoulders. Once she drew the whole mass on the right shoulder through both hands, then flung it back and gazed around.

About ten steps from the sepulcher and toward the east, where the garden rose in the direction of the city, she spied in the gray light of dawn, standing among the bushes behind a palm tree, a figure clothed in a long, white garment. Rushing toward it, she heard once more the words: "Woman, why weepest thou? Whom seekest thou?" [L7] She thought it was the gardener. I saw that he had a spade in his hand and on his head a flat hat, which had a piece of something like bark standing out in front, as a protection from the sun. It was just like that I had seen on the gardener in the parable which Jesus, shortly before his Passion, had related to the women in Bethany. The apparition was not resplendent. It looked like a person clad in long, white garments and seen at twilight. At the words: "Whom seekest thou?" Magdalene at once answered: "Sir, if thou hast taken him hence, show me where thou hast laid him! I will take him away!" And she again glanced around, as if to see whether he had not laid him someplace near. Then Jesus, in his well-known voice, said: "Mary!" Recognizing the voice, and forgetting the crucifixion, death, and burial now that he was alive, she turned quickly and, as once before, exclaimed: "Rabboni!" (Master!). She fell on her knees before him and stretched out her arms toward his feet. But Jesus raised his hand to keep her off, saying: "Do not touch me, for I am not yet ascended to my Father. But go to my brethren, and say to them: I ascend to my Father

and to your Father, to my God and to your God." [L8] At these words the Lord vanished. It was explained to me why Jesus said: "Do not touch me," but I have only an indistinct remembrance of it. I think he said it because Magdalene was so impetuous. She seemed possessed of the idea that Jesus was alive just as he was before, and that everything was as it used to be. Upon Jesus's words that he had not yet ascended to his Father, I was told that he had not yet, since his resurrection, presented himself to his heavenly Father, had not yet thanked him for his victory over death and for redemption. I understood by those words that the first fruits of joy belong to God. It was as if Jesus had said that Magdalene should recollect herself and thank God for the mystery of redemption just accomplished and his conquest over death. After the disappearance of the Lord, Magdalene rose up quickly and again, as if in a dream, ran to the tomb. She saw the two angels, she saw the empty linens, and hurried, now certain of the miracle, back to her companions.

April 5, AD 33
Sunday, Around Daybreak

It may have been about half-past three o'clock when Jesus appeared to Magdalene. Scarcely had she left the garden when John approached, followed by Peter. John stood outside the entrance of the cave and stooped down to look, through the outer doors of the sepulcher, at the half-opened doors of the tomb, where he saw the linens lying. Then came Peter. He stepped down into the sepulcher and went to the tomb, in the center of which he saw the winding sheet lying. It was rolled together from both sides toward the middle, and the spices were wrapped in it. The bandages were folded around it, as women are accustomed to roll together such linens when putting them away. The linen that had covered the sacred face was lying to the right next to the wall. It too was folded. John now followed Peter to the tomb, saw the same things, and believed in the resurrection. All that the Lord had said, all that was written in the scriptures, was now clear to them. They had had only an imperfect comprehension of it before. Peter took the linens with him under his mantle. Both again went back by the little gate belonging to Nicodemus, and John once more got ahead of Peter.

As long as the sacred body lay in the tomb, the two angels sat one at the head, the other at the foot, and when Magdalene and the two apostles came, they were still there. It seems to me that Peter did not see them. I heard John afterward saying to the disciples of Emmaus that, on looking into the tomb, he saw one angel. Perhaps it was through humility that he forbore to mention it in his Gospel, that he might not appear to have seen more than Peter.

Now, for the first time, I saw the guards arise from where they were lying on the ground. They took their lances, also the lanterns that were hanging on poles at the door of the entrance and shedding their light into the cave, and hurried in evident fear and trepidation to the gate of execution and into the city.

Meanwhile, Magdalene had reached the holy women and told them of the Lord's apparition. Then she too hurried on to the city through the neighboring gate of the execution, but the others went again to the garden, outside of which Jesus appeared to them in a white flowing garment [L.9] that concealed even his hands. He said: "All hail!" They trembled and fell at his feet. Jesus waved his hand in a certain direction while addressing to them some words, and vanished. The holy women then hastened through the Bethlehem gate on Zion, to tell the disciples in the Cenacle that they had seen the Lord and what he had said to them. But the disciples would not at first credit Magdalene's report, and, until the return of Peter and John, they looked upon the whole affair as the effect of women's imagination.

John and Peter, whom amazement at what they had seen had rendered silent and thoughtful, met on their way back James the Less and Thaddeus, who had set out after them for the tomb. They too were very much agitated, for the Lord had appeared to them near the Cenacle. Once I saw Peter, as they went along, suddenly start and tremble, as if he had just got a glimpse of the risen Savior. [L10]

The Guards' Statements

About an hour after the resurrection, Cassius went to Pilate, who was resting on his couch. Full of emotion, Cassius related all that had passed, the trembling of the rock, the descent of the angel, the rolling away of the stone, the empty winding sheet. Jesus, he said, was certainly the Messiah, certainly the Son of God. He was risen, he was no longer in the tomb. Pilate heard every detail with secret terror but, letting nothing appear, he said to Cassius: "Thou art a visionary! Thou didst act very unwisely by standing in the tomb of the Galilean. His gods have thereby acquired full power over thee, and it was they who conjured up all kinds of magic pictures before thee. I advise thee to say nothing of all this to the high priest, else it will be worse for thee." He pretended to believe that Jesus had been stolen away by the disciples, and that the guards had reported what they did in order to hide their own negligence; or because they were bribed, or even perhaps because they too had been bewitched. When Cassius left, Pilate again offered sacrifice to his gods.

Four of the soldiers returned from the tomb and went directly to Pilate with the same report. But he would listen to nothing more, and sent them to Caiaphas. The other guards went to a large court near the temple in which a number of aged Jews were gathered. These latter consulted together and came to the conclusion that they would, with money and threats, force the guards to report that the disciples had stolen the body of Jesus. But when the guards objected that their companions, who had informed Pilate of the whole affair, would contradict them, the Pharisees promised to make it all right with Pilate. Meanwhile the four guards who had been dismissed by Pilate arrived, but they adhered strictly to the account they had given to the governor. The report of Joseph of Arimathea's deliverance, in some unaccountable way, through the closed prison doors was already noised abroad and when the Pharisees, wishing to cast upon the soldiers the suspicion of having had an understanding with the disciples for the carrying off of Jesus's body, threatened them with severe punishment if they did not forthwith produce it, the men replied that they could no more do that than could the guard in Joseph of Arimathea's prison bring him back after he had disappeared. They defended themselves stoutly, and by no species of bribery could they be reduced to silence. Yes, they spoke even freely and openly of Friday's iniquitous judgment, and declared that it was on that account the Passover ceremonies had been interrupted. The four soldiers were seized and imprisoned. Jesus's enemies spread the report that his body had been stolen by the disciples; and the Pharisees, Sadducees, and Herodians caused the lie to be everywhere propagated, to be published in every synagogue in the whole world, accompanying it with slanderous abuse of Jesus. Their lies profited them little, for after Jesus's resurrection, many souls of holy deceased Jews appeared here and there to those of their descendants still susceptible of grace and holy impressions, and frightened their hearts to conversion. To many of the disciples also who, shaken in faith and disheartened, were dispersed throughout the country, similar apparitions appeared to console and strengthen them in faith.

The rising of the dead bodies from their tombs after the death of Jesus had no similarity whatever with the Lord's resurrection. Jesus arose in his renewed, glorified body, walked for some days alive upon the earth, and, in that same body, ascended into heaven in the sight of his friends.

April 5, AD 33
Sunday, An Hour Past Daybreak

But those other bodies were only corpses given to the souls merely as so many coverings. They were again laid down by them to await with us all the resurrection of the last day. Lazarus was raised from the dead, but he really lived and afterward died for the second time.

I saw the Jews beginning to purify, to wash and scour the temple. They strewed aromatic herbs, also ashes from the bones of the dead, and offered expiatory sacrifices. They cleared away the rubbish, covered the marks of the earthquake with boards and tapestry, and finished the Passover solemnities interrupted on the day of the feast.

With threats of punishment and excommunication, they tried to suppress all remarks and murmurs. They explained the disturbance of the feast and the damage done the temple as effects of the earthquake and the presence of the unclean at the sacrifices. They brought forward something from a vision of Ezekiel upon the risen dead, but I do not now remember how they applied it. Thus they quieted the people, for many had taken part in the crime. But it was only the great crowd of the obstinate and the incorrigible; all the better disposed were converted. They kept silence until Pentecost, when they proclaimed aloud their faith, later also in their native places through the teaching of the apostles. The high priests consequently began to lose courage. As early as the time of Stephen's ministry as deacon, Ophel and the eastern quarter of Zion could no longer contain the multitude of believers, so that they had to extend their huts and tents beyond the city, across the valley of Kidron to Bethany.

Annas was like one possessed. He was obliged to be confined, and he never again appeared in public. Caiaphas became like a madman devoured by secret rage. Simon of Cyrene went to the apostles after the sabbath, asking to be received among the baptized followers of Jesus.

The First Love Feast (*Agape*) after the Resurrection

IN the open entrance hall outside that of the holy Last Supper, Nicodemus prepared a repast for the apostles, the holy women, and the disciples. Thomas was not present at it. He kept himself in absolute retirement. All that took place at this feast was in strict accordance with Jesus's directions. During the holy Last Supper, he had given Peter and John, who were sitting by him and whom he ordained priests, detailed instructions relative to the blessed sacrament, with the command to impart the same to the other apostles, along with some points of his early teachings.

I saw first Peter and then John communicating to the eight other apostles, who were standing around them in a circle, what the Lord had entrusted to them, and teaching them the way in which he wished this sacrament to be dispensed and the disciples instructed. All that Peter taught was repeated in the selfsame manner by John. The apostles had put on their festal garments. Peter and John had, besides, a stole crossed on their breast and fastened with a clasp. The eight apostles wore a stole over one shoulder and across the breast and back. It fastened under the arm with a clasp crosswise. Peter and John had been ordained priests by Jesus; the others looked still like deacons.

After that instruction, the holy women, nine in number, entered the hall. Peter addressed them in some words of instruction. I saw John at the door receiving into the house of the master of the feast seventeen (as I counted) of the most trusty disciples, those that had been longest with the Lord. Zacchaeus, Nathaniel, Matthew, Barsabbas, and others were there. John served them while they were washing their feet and putting on festal garments, long white robes and girdles. Matthew was sent back to Bethany after Peter's discourse, in order there to reproduce, at a similar repast given in the house of Lazarus, the instructions just heard and the ceremonies witnessed. There were many disciples present at this feast.

And now a table was prepared in the entrance hall. It was so long that the seats of some of the disciples extended beyond the hall and into the courtyard, planted with trees, that surrounded the Cenacle. Three avenues were left open to the tables, in order to approach them with the servings of food. The holy women now sat together at one end of the same table with the men. They too wore long white garments. They were veiled, but without their faces being concealed. They sat cross-legged on little stools that had a kind of upright at the backs. Peter and John sat opposite each other at the center of the table. They closed the men's row, and then began the women's. The couches used at this feast were not like those at the Last Supper. They were low cushions. They looked as if they were woven, and were scarcely long enough to receive the upper part of the body, for they hardly reached below the knees. Each had before him a cushion raised upon two higher feet, which were fastened into cross-uprights. It stood in an oblique direction. All reclined near the table, the feet of one at his neighbor's back. At Simon's house and at the Last Supper, the guests reclined on stools of a different kind, the feet turned entirely out.

The meal was conducted with ceremony. The guests

prayed standing and ate lying, while Peter and John taught. At the end of the meal, a flat, ribbed loaf was placed before Peter, which he divided into small pieces as marked by the ribs. These he distributed right and left on two plates. A large cup was next sent round, and out of it each one drank. Although Peter blessed the bread, yet it was not a sacrament, only an agape, a love feast. Peter said that they should all desire to be one as was the bread that they were eating and the wine they were drinking. After that they sang psalms, standing.

When the tables were moved aside, the holy women retired to an apartment in the form of a half-circle at the end of the hall. The disciples ranged on either side, while the apostles walked up and down teaching and imparting to these ripe disciples all they could concerning the blessed sacrament. This was like the first catechetical instruction after Jesus's death. I saw also that they walked around among one another extending hands joyously declaring that they would have all things in common, would resign all things for one another, and would live perfectly united. A feeling of deep emotion stole over them. I saw them flooded with light and, as it were, dissolving into one another. All seemed to resolve into a pyramid of light in which the blessed Virgin appeared to be not only the apex, but the radiant center of all. All graces flowed in streams from Mary down upon the apostles, and from them back again through her to the Lord. This vision was symbolical of their union and the reciprocal relations existing among them.

Matthew, in the court of Lazarus's house, taught a great many more of the disciples who were not so well instructed as the others. They had the same kind of a meal and went through similar ceremonies.

Communion of the Holy Apostles

Early in the morning, Peter and John went with Andrew into the hall of the Last Supper and vested in their priestly robes, while the other apostles entered the antehall. Pushing aside the folds of woven tapestry, the three apostles entered the Holy of Holies, which was curtained in so as to form a little chamber. The ceiling, which was not so high as that of the hall, could be opened by a hanging cord ornamented with tassels, to admit light from the windows in the roof of the hall. The holy communion table stood therein. The chalice with the remains of the wine that Jesus had consecrated and the plate with what was left of the consecrated bread were standing in the compartments formed

like a tabernacle in a niche in the wall. A lamp was hanging, one branch of it lighted, before the blessed sacrament. They lighted the lamp of sacrifice that was suspended in the center of the hall, carried the communion table forward into the hall, placed the blessed sacrament on it in its case, and extinguished the lamp in the Holy of Holies. The other apostles, Thomas among them, took their places around the table. Of the bread consecrated by Jesus, the blessed sacrament of his body, there was still a great deal on the little plate, which stood on top of the chalice, the whole concealed under a bell-shaped cover surmounted by a knob. A white veil was thrown over it. Peter drew out the leaf from the base, spread the cover upon it, and placed on it the plate with the blessed sacrament. Andrew and John were standing behind him in prayer. Peter and John, bowing reverently, received the blessed sacrament. Then Peter sent the plate around, and each one communicated himself. Into the chalice, in which there was not so much of the wine consecrated by Jesus, they poured some wine and water, and drank of it. After that they sang psalms and prayed, covered the chalice, and carried it, along with the table, back to its place. This was the first divine service that I saw celebrated.

Thomas went after that to some little place near Samaria with a disciple from that part of the country.

The Disciples Going to Emmaus • *Jesus Appears to the Apostles in the Hall of the Last Supper*

LUKE had been among the disciples only a short time, but he had, before joining them, received John's baptism. He was present at the love feast and the instruction upon the blessed sacrament delivered by Matthew in the evening at Lazarus's, in Bethany. After the instruction he went, troubled and doubting, to Jerusalem where he spent the night in John Mark's house.

There he met several other disciples, among them Cleophas, a grandson of the paternal uncle of Mary Cleophas. He had been at the instructions and the love feast given in the house of the Last Supper. The disciples were talking about Jesus's resurrection and expressing their doubts. Luke and Cleophas, especially, were wavering in faith. As, moreover, the commands of the high priests were again made known, that no one should harbor the disciples of Jesus or supply them with food, both resolved to go together to Emmaus. They left the assembly. On leaving John Mark's house, one turned to the right and went around out of the city in a northerly direction, and the other took a route on the opposite side, as if not wishing to be seen together. One went straight out of the city, the other made his way between the walls and out by the gate, beyond which they again met upon a hill. They carried each a staff, and a bundle at his side. Luke had a leathern pocket. I saw him frequently stepping aside from the road and gathering herbs.

Luke had not seen the Lord during those last days, and had not been present at his instructions at Lazarus's. He had been more in the disciples' inn at Bethany and with the disciples in Machaerus. He had not long been a declared disciple, though he had always gone around with the rest and was very desirous of knowing what was going on.

I felt that both these disciples were anxious and doubting, and that they wanted to talk over all they had heard. They were especially put out at the Lord's being so ignominiously crucified! They could not understand how the Redeemer and Messiah could have been so shamefully ill-treated.

About the middle of their journey, Jesus drew near to them from a side path. As soon as they saw him, they went more slowly, as if wanting to let the stranger go on ahead, as if fearing to be overheard. But Jesus likewise slackened his pace, and stepped out on the road only after they were somewhat in advance. I saw him walking behind them for a little while, then drawing near and asking of what they were talking. [L11]

Where the road branched off outside of Emmaus (a pretty, clean little place) Jesus appeared as if he wanted to take that which ran southward to Bethlehem. But the two disciples constrained him to go with them into a house that stood in the second row of the city. There were no women in it, and it appeared to me to be a public house, for it looked as if a feast had lately been held in it. Some signs of it were still to be seen. The room was quadrangular and very neat. The table was covered, and reclining cushions lay around it, of the same kind as those used at the love feast on Easter day. A man put on it a honeycomb in a woven basketlike vessel, a large, four-cornered cake, and a small, thin, almost transparent Passover loaf. This last was set before the Lord as being the guest. The man that put the cake on the table appeared to be good, and he wore an apron, as if he were a cook or a steward. He was not present at the solemn breaking of the bread. The cake was marked by lines, the spaces between them being about two fingers wide. A knife was lying on the table. It was white, as if made of stone or bone, not straight, but bent

April 6, AD 33
Monday, Mid-Afternoon

crooked, and only as large as one of our large blades. Before eating the bread, they notched along the lines with the sharp edge of the knife, which edge was only at the point. For this reason they had to hold it near the point. The morsel previously notched they then broke off.

Jesus reclined at the table with the two disciples and ate with them of the cake and honey. Then taking the small cake, the ribbed one, he broke off a piece that he afterward divided into three with the short, white bone knife. These he laid on the little plate, and blessed. Then he stood up, elevated the plate on high with both hands, raised his eyes, and prayed. The two disciples stood opposite him, both intensely moved, and as it were transported out of themselves. When Jesus broke the little pieces, they opened their mouth and stretched forward toward him. He reached his hand across the table and laid the particle in their mouth. I saw that as he raised his hand with the third morsel to his own mouth, he disappeared. [L12] I cannot say that he really received it. The morsels shone with light after he had blessed them. I saw the two disciples standing a little while as if stupefied, and then casting themselves with tears of emotion into each other's arms.

This vision was especially touching on account of the Lord's mild and loving manner, the calm joy of the two disciples even before they knew him, and their rapture as soon as they recognized him and after he had disappeared. Cleophas and Luke hurried back at once to Jerusalem.

On the evening of the same day, many of the disciples and all the apostles excepting Thomas assembled with Nicodemus and Joseph of Arimathea in the hall of the Last Supper, the doors being closed. They stood ranged in a triple circle under the lamp that hung from the center of the ceiling, and prayed. They seemed to be engaged in some after-celebration of mourning or thanksgiving, for the Passover solemnities ended today in Jerusalem. All wore long white garments. Peter, John, and James the Less were vested in robes that distinguished them from the rest, and they held rolls of writing in their hands. Around their white, flowing garment, which was somewhat longer behind than before, they wore a girdle more than a hand in breadth. From it depended to below the knees scalloped strips, black like the girdle, and covered with large white letters. The girdle was knotted in the back, the ends crossing and reaching as low down as the strips in front. The sleeves were very wide, and one served as a pocket in which the prayer rolls could be stuck. Above the elbow of the left arm hung a broad maniple tripped with tassels of the same color and embroidered in the same way as the girdle. Peter wore a stole around his neck. It was broader from the shoulders down than it was around the neck, and was crossed and fastened on the breast with a little blank shield in the form of a heart and ornamented with stones. The two other apostles wore their stoles crossed under the arm, and had shorter strips to their girdles. When in prayer, all laid their hands crosswise on their breast. The apostles occupied the inner circle under the lamp; the two others were formed by the disciples. Peter, between John and James, stood with his back turned to the closed entrance of the house of the Last Supper; two only were behind him, and the circle was not closed in front of him, but open toward the Holy of Holies.

The blessed Virgin was, during the whole celebration, with Mary Cleophas and Magdalene in the hall outside, which opened into the supper room. Peter preached at intervals during the prayers.

I was surprised to see that although Jesus had appeared to Peter, John, and James, yet the greater number of the apostles and disciples would not fully believe in his resurrection. They still felt uneasy, as if his apparition was not a real and corporeal one, only a vision, a phantom, similar to those the prophets had had.

All had ranged again for prayer after Peter's instruction when Luke and Cleophas, hurrying back from Emmaus, knocked at the closed doors of the courtyard and received admittance. The joyful news they related somewhat interrupted the prayer. But scarcely was it again continued when I saw all present radiant with joyful emotion, and glancing in the same direction. Jesus was come in through the closed doors. He was robed in a long white garment simply girded. They did not appear to be really conscious of his approach, until he passed through the circles and stood in their midst under the lamp. Then they became very much amazed and agitated. He showed them his hands and feet and, opening his garment, disclosed the wound in his side. [L13] He spoke to them and, seeing that they were very much terrified, he asked for something to eat. I saw rays of light proceeding from his mouth. The apostles and disciples were as if completely ravished.

And now I saw Peter going behind a screen, or hanging tapestry, into a recess of the hall which one might fail to remark, since the screen was like the entire wainscoting. In the center of this recess, on the paschal hearth, stood the blessed sacrament. There was a side compartment into which they had pushed the table, which was one foot high, after they had eaten reclining around it under the lamp.

On this table stood a deep oval dish covered with a little white cloth, which Peter took to the Lord. In the dish were a piece of fish and some honey. Jesus gave thanks and blessed the food, ate and gave a portion of it to some, but not to all. To his Holy Mother also and the other women, who were standing in the doorway of the outer hall, he likewise distributed some.

After that I saw him teaching and imparting strength. The circles around him were still triple, the ten apostles forming the inmost. Thomas was not there. It appeared wonderful to me that part of Jesus's words and instructions was heard by the ten apostles only, though I ought not to say *heard*, for I did not see Jesus moving his lips. He was resplendent. Light streamed over them from his hands, his feet, his side, his mouth, as he breathed upon them. It flowed in upon them. They became interiorly recollected, and felt themselves endued with power to forgive sins, to baptize and heal and impose hands; and I saw that, if they drank any poisonous thing, it would be without receiving harm from it. But here I saw no talking with the mouth, no hearing with the ears. I knew not how it was, but I felt that Jesus did not impart these gifts with words, that he spoke not in words, and that all did not hear what he said; but that he infused these gifts substantially, with a substance as it were, with a flashing of light in upon their soul. Still, I do not know whether the apostles felt that they had received them in this way, or whether they thought that they had simply heard the words uttered naturally. I felt, however, that it was only the innermost circle, the apostles, that took or received these gifts. To me it was like an interior speech, but without a whisper, without the softest word.

Jesus explained to the apostles several points of holy scripture relative to himself and the blessed sacrament, and ordered the latter to be venerated at the close of the sabbath solemnities. He spoke of the sacred mystery of the Ark of the Covenant; of the bones and relics of ancestors and their veneration, thus to obtain their intercession; of Abraham, and of the bones of Adam which he had had in his possession and which he had laid on the altar when offering sacrifice. Another point relating to Melchizedek's sacrifice, which I then saw, I have forgotten, although it was very remarkable. Jesus further said that the colored coat which Jacob gave to Joseph was an emblem of his own bloody sweat on the Mount of Olives. At these words, I saw that coat of many colors. It was white with broad red stripes. It had three black cords on the breast, with a yellow ornament in the middle. It was full around the body so

April 6, AD 33
Monday Evening

that things could be put into it as into a kind of pocket, and girded at the waist. It was narrow below and had slits at the side to afford more room for walking. It reached to the ankles, was longer behind than before, and on the breast, was open down to the girdle. Joseph's ordinary dress reached only to the knee.

Jesus likewise told the disciples that Adam's bones, which had been preserved in the Ark of the Covenant, Jacob gave to Joseph along with the many-colored coat. I saw then that Jacob gave them to Joseph without the latter's knowing what they were. Jacob's love prompted him to bestow them upon Joseph as a means of protection, as a treasure, because he knew that his brothers did not love him. Joseph carried the bones hanging on his breast in a little pouch formed of two leathern tablets, not square, but rounded on top. When his brothers sold him, they took from him only the colored coat and the undergarment, leaving him a bandage round his loins and a scapular on his breast. It was under the latter that the little pouch hung. On going into Egypt, Jacob questioned Joseph about that treasure and revealed to him that it was Adam's bones. Again I saw the bones under Mount Calvary. They were white as snow and still very hard. Some of Joseph's own bones were preserved in the Ark of the Covenant.

Jesus spoke too of the mystery contained in the Ark of the Covenant. He said that that mystery was now his body and blood, which he gave to them forever in the Sacrament. He spoke of his own Passion and of some wonderful things relating to David of which they were ignorant and which he explained. Lastly, he bade them go in a couple of days to the region of Sichar, and there proclaim his resurrection. After that he vanished. I saw the apostles and disciples going around among one another, perfectly intoxicated with joy. They opened the doors, went in and out, and assembled again under the lamp, to sing canticles of praise and thanksgiving.

The Apostles Preaching the Resurrection

ON that same night a part of the apostles, at Jesus's bidding, betook themselves to Bethany, while some of them went around Jerusalem, for example, to Veronica. The older disciples remained in Bethany to teach the younger and weaker in the faith, which they did partly at the house of Lazarus and partly in the synagogue. Nicodemus and Joseph of Arimathea were staying at Lazarus's. The holy women were in a neighboring building surrounded by the same moat and courtyard that enclosed Lazarus's house. It had an entrance on the street, and was formerly occupied by Magdalene and Martha.

The apostles went with a troop of disciples, among them Luke, in the direction of Sichar. Peter said joyfully as they were setting out: "We shall go to the sea and catch fish," by which words he meant souls. They separated and went different ways, teaching at the inns and in the public places of the Passion and Resurrection of Jesus. This was a preparation for the conversions of Pentecost.

They met together again at the inn outside Thanat-Shiloh. Thomas also, with two disciples, joined them as they were gathered at a meal prepared for them by Silvan's father, who had care of the inn. The apostles told Thomas of the apparition of the risen Savior in their midst. But he raised his hands to silence them, and said that he would not believe it until he had touched his wounds. He did the same before the disciples when they declared to him that they had seen the Lord. Thomas had kept a little aloof from the followers of Jesus, and was thereby somewhat weakened in faith.

Peter taught till late at night in the school of Thanat-Shiloh. He spoke out quite freely of how the Jews had dealt with Jesus. He related many things of his last predictions and teachings, of his unspeakable love, of his prayer on the Mount of Olives, and of Judas's treachery and wretched end. The people were very much amazed and troubled at all they heard, for they loved Judas, who in Jesus's absence, had assisted many by his readiness to serve them, and had even wrought miracles. Peter did not spare himself. He recounted his flight and denial with bitter tears. His hearers wept with him. Then with still more vehement expressions of sorrow, he told of how cruelly the Jews had treated Jesus, of his rising again on the third day, of his appearing first to the women, then to some of the others, and lastly to all in general, and he called upon all present that had seen him to witness to his words. Upwards of a hundred hands were raised in answer to his call. Thomas, however, remained silent and responded by no sign. He could not bring himself to believe. Peter then called upon the people to leave all things, to join the new community, and to follow Jesus. He invited the less courageous to go to Jerusalem, where the faithful would share all they had with them. There was, he said, no reason to fear the Jews, for they were now themselves afraid. All were very much impressed by Peter's words, and many were converted. They wanted the apostles to remain longer with them, but Peter said that they must go back to Jerusalem.

The apostles cured many sick persons in Thanat-Shiloh, among whom were some lunatics and some possessed. They went about these cures just as Jesus had done, that is, they breathed upon the sick, they imposed hands while leaning over them. Some of these invalids Jesus had passed without curing on the occasion of his last visit to the place. The inhabitants of Thanat-Shiloh were very friendly toward the apostles. The disciples performed no cures, but they served the others, carrying, lifting, and leading the sick. Luke, who was a physician, now became quite a nurse.

I saw the Mother of God in Bethany. She was quiet and grave, more deeply absorbed in feelings of holy awe than in natural sorrow. Mary Cleophas was remarkably amiable and, of all the women, most like Mary. I often saw her leaning over her gently, consoling her in the most touching way.

Magdalene, in her sorrow and love, was above all fear. She was perfectly heroic and without a thought of danger. She took no rest, but often left the house, hurried through the streets with streaming hair, and wherever she found listeners, whether in their homes or in public places, she accused them as the murderers of the Lord, vehemently recounting all they had done to the Savior, and announcing to them his resurrection. If she found no one to listen to her, she wandered through the gardens and told it to the flowers, the trees, and the fountains. Oftentimes a crowd gathered around her, some offering her compassion, others insulting her on account of her past life. She was little esteemed by the crowd, for she had once given great scandal. I saw that her present violent conduct scandalized some of the Jews, and about five of them wanted to seize her, but she passed straight through them and went on as before. She had lost sight of the whole world, she sighed only after Jesus.

During the dispersion of the disciples and the Passion of the Lord, Martha had a heavy duty to fulfill and she still discharged it. Though torn with grief, she had to see to everything, to lend a helping hand everywhere. She had to feed the dispersed and wandering, attend to their wants, provide nourishment for all. Her assistant in all this, as well as in the cooking, was Johanna Chusa, a widow whose husband had been a servant of Herod.

Simon of Cyrene was now in Bethany with the disciples, among whom he found his two sons. He was a pious man from Cyrene who was accustomed to sojourn in Jerusalem during the Passover time, working for different families that knew him, doing up gardens and cutting hedges. He took his meals sometimes in this house, sometimes in

*April 10, AD 33
Friday Evening*

that. He was perfectly silent and upright. His sons were already some time among strangers and with the disciples without his knowing it, as occasionally happens to the children of the poor.

In those days, the emissaries of the high priests went throughout Jerusalem, visiting all the houses whose owners kept up communication with Jesus and the disciples, discharging them from whatever public employments they might happen to hold, and arresting any of Jesus's followers found there. Nicodemus and Joseph of Arimathea had, since Christ's burial, nothing more to do with the Jews. Joseph of Arimathea was something like an elder of a congregation. He always stood among the Jews like a man who, by his unobtrusive merit and multiplied good works modestly performed, had won the esteem of even the wicked. What very much rejoiced me was to see how Veronica's husband conceded to her when she told him that she would rather separate from him than from the crucified Jesus. I saw that he too was discharged from his public office. But I was informed that he bore it more for love of his wife than for love of Jesus. The Jews, moreover, caused the ways and paths to the Holy Sepulcher on Mount Calvary to be obstructed by ditches and hedges, because they had become a resort for many, and diverse moving incidents and miracles took place in them.

Pilate's interior disquietude drove him from Jerusalem. Herod, a couple of days previously, had gone to Machaerus, but finding no rest there, he proceeded to Madian. Here, where they had once refused to receive the Lord, they now opened the gates to the murderer.

I saw Jesus appearing in many places during these days, and lastly in Galilee, in a valley across the Jordan in which was a large school. Many people were standing together, speaking about him and expressing their doubts upon the report of his resurrection. He appeared among them, and vanished again after some words. I saw him appearing in this way in different localities.

The apostles very quickly returned from the region of Sichar. They sent a messenger on ahead to Bethany, to announce their return and to direct several of the disciples to go to Jerusalem for the sabbath. Others were commanded to celebrate it in Bethany, for they already had a certain law and order. The apostles only passed through the different places on the road without stopping. Thaddeus, James the Less, and Eliud went in their traveling dress, and ahead of the rest, to see the blessed Virgin and Mary Cleophas at John Mark's. As they had not seen the newcomers for a considerable time, the holy women were very much rejoiced. I saw that James was carrying on his arm a priestly vestment, a mantle, which the holy women in Bethany had made for Peter, and which he was taking to the house of the Last Supper.

It was so late when the apostles assembled in the house of the Last Supper that they could not partake of the meal prepared for them. *They had to begin the sabbath solemnities.* They at once put on their robes of ceremony, preceded of course by the customary foot washing. The lamps were lighted, and I already remarked some departure from the Jewish sabbatical ceremonies. First, the curtains were opened in front of the Holy of Holies, and the seat upon which Jesus had reclined at table at the institution of the Holy Eucharist was placed before it. They spread a cover over it, and laid upon it their prayer rolls. Peter knelt before it, John and James a little in the rear, the rest of the apostles behind them, and then came the disciples. When they knelt they bowed their heads to the ground, burying their faces in their hands. The cover was removed from the chalice, but the white linen cloth was still left hanging over it. Only those disciples were present who were already initiated into the mystery of the blessed sacrament, just as those chiefly had been taken on the journey to Sichar who had seen the Lord after his resurrection that they might be able to attest the fact.

Peter, with John and James at his side, delivered a meditation, or prayer, in which the holy Institution of the Lord and also his Passion were considered, and an interior sacrifice of prayer was offered. After that, standing under the lamp, they began the usual ceremonies of the sabbath. When all was over, they took a repast in the outer hall. In the supper hall itself I saw no more eating going on after the institution of the Holy Eucharist, excepting perhaps the taking of bread and wine.

On the occasion of his apparition through the closed doors, Jesus had taught the apostles the addition to the sabbath service that relates to the blessed sacrament.

The blessed Virgin was taken to Jerusalem by Mary Mark; and Veronica, who now went round with her openly, accompanied them, along with Johanna Chusa.

The blessed Virgin liked to be in Jerusalem, for she could there go alone in the twilight and darkness over the Way of Jesus's Passion, pray and meditate on the places upon which he had suffered or had fallen. And as she could not reach them all, on account of the Jews' having hedged some of them in and filled others up, she made the Holy Way at home, also, or in the open air, for she had all the

distances and the numbers connected with it deeply engraven in her soul, and thus she constantly revived, in her compassionate contemplations, the whole of that sorrowful journey of her Son.

It is a certainty that after the death of her Son, the blessed Virgin was first to begin the devotion of the Way of the Cross and the practice of meditating upon the bitter Passion, a practice she ever after continued.

The Second Love Feast (Agape) • Thomas Puts his Hand into the Marks of Jesus's Wounds

After the close of the sabbath, the apostles having laid aside their robes of ceremony, I saw a great meal spread in the outer hall. It was a love feast, such as had taken place on the preceding Sunday. Thomas must have celebrated the sabbath somewhere in the neighborhood, for I did not see him come in till after the meal, when they had again returned to the Cenacle. It was still early in the evening; the lamps were not yet lighted. Several of the apostles and disciples were in the hall, and I saw others entering. They robed themselves again in long white garments, and prepared for prayer as on the preceding occasion. Peter, John, and James again put on the vestments that distinguished them as priests.

While these preparations were being made, I saw Thomas entering the supper room. He passed through the apostles who were already robed, and put on his own long white garment. As he went along, I saw the apostles accosting him. Some caught him by the sleeve, others gesticulated with the right hand as they spoke, as if emphatically protesting against him. But he behaved like one in a hurry to vest and as if he could not credit the account given him of the wonderful things which had happened in that place. While all this was going on, a man entered the hall. He appeared to be a servant. He wore an apron and had in one hand a little lighted lamp, in the other a rod terminating in a hook. With the latter he drew down the lamp that was suspended from the center of the ceiling, lighted it, and again pushed it up. Then he left the hall! And now I saw the blessed Virgin, Magdalene, and another woman come into the house. The blessed Virgin and Magdalene entered the hall, Peter and John going to meet them. The third woman remained in the antechamber. The entrance hall was opened into the supper room, also some of the side halls. The exterior doors leading into the courtyard, as well as those of the court itself, were shut. A great many disciples were gathered in the side halls.

As soon as Mary and Magdalene entered, the doors were closed and all ranged for prayer. The holy women remained reverently standing on either side of the door, their arms crossed upon their breast. The apostles kneeling before the Holy of Holies, prayed again as before; then standing under the lamp, they sang psalms, in choirs. Peter stood before the lamp, his face toward the Holy of Holies, John and James the Less at his side. Right and left of the lamp were the other apostles. The side toward the

supper room and stepped between Peter and John who, like all the other apostles, fell back on either side.

Jesus did not enter walking properly so called, that is, in the usual way of mortals, and yet it was not a floating along, or hovering, as I have seen spirits doing. It reminded me, as I saw them all falling back, of a priest in his alb passing through a crowded congregation. Everything in the hall appeared to become suddenly large and bright. Jesus was environed with light. The apostles had fallen

Tiberias

Holy of Holies was left free. Peter stood between the two, his back to the door, so that the two holy women were standing behind him at some distance.

After some time there was a pause in the assembly, an intermission of prayer, or as if prayer was at an end, and they began to speak of going to the Sea of Tiberias and of how they would disperse. But soon they assumed an expression of rapt attention, called up by the approach of the Lord. At the same moment, I saw Jesus in the courtyard. He was resplendent with light, clothed in white garments and a white girdle. He directed his steps to the door of the outer hall, which opened of itself before him and closed behind him. The disciples in the outer hall saw the door opening of itself, and fell back on both sides to make room. But Jesus walked quickly through the hall into the

back from the radiant circle, otherwise they would not have been able to see him.

Jesus's first words were: "Peace be to you!" Then he spoke with Peter and John, and rebuked them for something. They had departed a little from his directions, in order to follow their own ideas about something, and consequently they had not met with success. It related to some of the cures they had sought to effect on their return from Sichar and Thanat-Shiloh. They had not followed Jesus's directions to the letter, and therefore had not been entirely successful. They had done something according to their own ideas. Jesus told them that if it happened again, they should act otherwise. Jesus now stepped under the lamp, and the apostles closed around him. Thomas, very much frightened at the sight of the Lord, timidly drew back. But

Jesus, grasping his right hand in his own right hand, took the forefinger and laid the tip of it in the wound of his left hand; then taking the left hand in his own left, he placed the forefinger in the wound of his right hand; lastly, taking again Thomas's right hand in his own right, he put it, without uncovering his breast, under his garment, and laid the fore and middle fingers in the wound of his right side. [L14] He spoke some words as he did this. With the exclamation: "My Lord, and my God!" Thomas sank down like one unconscious, Jesus still holding his hand. The nearest of the apostles supported him, and Jesus raised him up by the hand. That sinking down and rising up had some peculiar signification.

When Jesus grasped Thomas's hand, I saw that his wounds were not like bloody marks, but like little radiant suns. The other disciples were very greatly touched by this scene. They leaned forward, without, however, crowding, to see what the Lord was allowing Thomas to feel. I saw the blessed Virgin during the whole time of Jesus's stay, perfectly motionless, as if absorbed in calm, deep interior recollection. Magdalene appeared more agitated, yet manifesting far less emotion than did the disciples.

Jesus did not disappear immediately after Thomas's declaration of faith. He still continued to speak to the apostles, and asked for something to eat. I saw a little oval dish brought to him again from the partitioned recess in which the table stood. It was not precisely like that presented to him the first time. There was on it something that looked like a fish, of which he ate, then blessed and distributed what was left to those around him, beginning with Thomas.

Jesus then told them why he stood in the midst of them, although they had abandoned him, and why he did not place himself nearer to those that had remained faithful to him. He told them also that he had commissioned Peter to confirm his brethren, and explained why he had given him that charge. Then turning to them all, he told them why he wished to give them Peter for a leader, although he had so recently denied him. He must, he said, be the shepherd of the flock, and he enlarged upon Peter's zeal.

John brought on his arm from the Holy of Holies the large, colored, embroidered mantle that James had received from Mary and on which, in those last days, the holy women had worked at Bethany. Besides that, he brought also a hollow, slender staff, high and bent at the top like a shepherd's crook. It was shining and looked like a long pipe. The mantle was white with broad red stripes; and on it were embroidered, in colors, wheat, grapes, a lamb, and other symbols. It was wide, and long enough to reach to the feet. It was fastened over the breast with a little four-cornered metal shield, and bordered down the front with red stripes crossed by shorter ones on which were letters. It had a collar and a kind of hood, of a sky-blue color, which could be drawn up over the neck and head.

Peter next knelt down before Jesus, who gave him to eat a round morsel, like a little cake. I do not remember seeing any plate, nor do I know where Jesus got the morsel, but I do know that it shone with light. I felt that Peter received with it some special power, and I saw also strength and vigor poured into his soul when Jesus breathed upon him. This action of Jesus was not a simple, ordinary breathing. It was words, a power, something substantial that Peter received, but no merely spoken words. Jesus put his mouth to Peter's mouth, then to his ears, and poured that strength into each of the three. It was not the Holy Spirit himself, but something that the Holy Spirit was to quicken and vivify in Peter at Pentecost. Jesus laid his hands on him, gave him a special kind of strength, and invested him with chief power over the others. Then he placed upon him the mantle that John, who was standing next to him, was holding on his arm, and put the staff into his hand. While performing this action, Jesus said that the mantle would preserve in him all the strength and virtue that he had just imparted to him, and that he should wear it whenever he had to make use of the power with which he had been endued.

Peter addressed the assembly in his new dignity. He had become as it were a new being, a man full of vigor and energy. His hearers were greatly moved; they listened with tears. He consoled them, alluded to many things that Jesus had before told them, and which were now being fulfilled. He told them, as I still remember, that Jesus, during his Passion of eighteen hours, had borne insult and outrage from the whole world. In that discourse mention was made of how much was wanting to the completion of Jesus's thirty-four years. While Peter was speaking, Jesus vanished. No alarm, no exclamations of surprise broke in upon the attention with which Peter's words were received. He appeared to be endowed with strength entirely new. The discourse ended, they sang a psalm of thanksgiving. Jesus addressed neither his blessed Mother nor Magdalene.

Jesus Appears to the Holy Apostles at the Sea of Galilee

BEFORE going to the sea, the holy apostles went over the Way of the Cross to Mount Calvary, and thence to Bethany, from which place they took with them some disciples. They went by different routes and in several companies to the Sea of Galilee. Peter went with John, James the Greater, Thaddeus, Nathaniel, John Mark, and Silas, seven in all, to Tiberias, leaving Samaria to the left. All chose routes remote from cities. They went to a fishery outside Tiberias, which Peter had held on lease, but which was now rented by another man, a widower with two sons. They took a repast with this man, and I heard Peter saying that he had not fished here for three years.

They went aboard two ships, one somewhat larger and better than the other. They gave to Peter the choice of the former, into which he mounted with Nathaniel, Thomas, and one of the fisherman's servants. In the second ship were John, James, John Mark, and Silas. Peter would not suffer another to row. He wanted to do it himself. Although so distinguished by Jesus, he was exceedingly humble and modest, especially before Nathaniel, who was polished and educated.

They sailed about the whole night with torches, casting the nets here and there between the two ships, but always drawing them in empty. At intervals they prayed and sang psalms. *When day was beginning to dawn*, the ships approached the opposite side of the mouth of the Jordan, on the eastern shore of the sea. The apostles were worn out and wanted to cast anchor. They had laid aside their garments while fishing, retaining only a linen bandage and a little mantle. When about resuming their clothing preparatory to taking a little rest, they saw a figure standing behind the reeds on the shore. [L15] It was Jesus. He cried out: "Children, have you any meat?" They answered: "No!" Then he cried out again, telling them to cast the net to the west of Peter's ship. They did it, and John had to sail round to the other side of the ship. And now the net was so heavily filled that John recognized Jesus, and called to Peter across the silent deep: "It is the Lord!" At these words Peter instantly girded his coat about him, leaped into the water, and waded through the reeds to the shore where Jesus was standing. [L16] But John pushed on in a boat, very light and narrow, that was fastened to his ship.

Two of this kind were hooked together. They pushed one before the other, and crossed over it to land. It held only one man, and was needed only for shallow water near the land.

While the apostles were on the sea fishing, I saw the Savior floating out of the valley of Jehosaphat and surrounded by many souls of the ancient patriarchs whom he had freed from Limbo, also by others that had been banished to different places, caves, swamps, and deserts. During the whole period of these forty days, I saw Jesus, when not among the disciples, with the holy souls. They were principally from Adam and Eve down to Noah, Abraham, and other ancient leaders of the people. He went over all places

April 14–15, AD 33
Tues. Night–Wed. Morning

remarkable in his life, showing them all things, and instructing them upon what he had done and suffered for them, whereby they became indescribably quickened and through gratitude purified. He taught them, in a certain measure at this time, the mysteries of the New Testament, by which they were released from their fetters. I saw him with them in Nazareth, in the crib cave and Bethlehem, and in every place in which anything remarkable had happened to him. One could distinguish, by a certain weakness or vigor in the appearance of the souls, whether they animated men or women when on earth. I saw them in long, narrow garments that fell around them in shining folds, and floated behind in a long train. Their hair did not look like ordinary hair, but like rays of light, each of which signified something. The beards of the men were composed of similar rays. Though not distinguished by any external sign, yet I recognized the kings, and especially the priests that from the time of Moses had anything to do with the Ark of the Covenant. In the journeys of the Savior I always saw them floating around him, so that here too the spirit of order reigned in everything. The movements of these apparitions were exceedingly graceful and dignified. They seemed to float along, not exactly in an upright position, but inclining gently forward. They did not touch the earth like bodies that have weight, but appeared to hover just above the ground.

I saw the Lord arrive at the sea in company with these souls while the apostles were still fishing. Back of a little mound on the shore there was a hollow in which was a covered fireplace, for the use of the shepherds, perhaps. I did not see Jesus kindling a fire, catching a fish, or getting one in any other way. Fire and fish and everything necessary appeared at once in presence of the souls as soon as ever it entered into the Lord's mind that a fish should here be prepared for eating. How it happened, I cannot say.

The spirits of the patriarchs had a share in this fish and in its preparation. It bore some signification relative to the Church Suffering, to the souls undergoing purification. They were in this meal bound to the Church Militant by visible ties. In the eating of this fish, Jesus gave the apostles an idea of the union existing between the Church Suffering and the Church Militant. Jonah in the fish was typical of Jesus's stay in the lower world. Outside the hut was a beam that served for a table.

I saw all this before Jesus crossed the mound and went down to the sea. Peter did not swim, he waded through the water. The bottom could be seen, although the water was tolerably deep. Peter was already standing by Jesus when John came up. Those on the ship now began to cry to them to help draw in the net. Jesus told Peter to go bring in the fish. They drew the net to land, and Peter emptied it on the shore. In it were one hundred and fifty-three different kinds of fishes.[L17] This number signified that of the new believers who were to be gained at Thebez. There were on the ships several people in the employ of the fishermen of Tiberias, and they took charge of the ships and the fish, while the apostles and disciples went with Jesus to the hut whither he invited them to come and

awe stole over them and gave rise to solemn silence. Jesus was wrapped in a mantle, his wounds not visible.

After the meal, I saw Jesus and the apostles rise from table. They walked up and down the shore, and at last stood still while Jesus solemnly addressed Peter: "Simon, son of John, lovest thou me more than these?" Peter timidly answered. "Yea, Lord, thou knowest that I love thee!" Jesus said to him: "Feed my lambs!" And at the same instant I saw a vision of the church and the Chief Pastor. I saw him teaching and guiding the first Christians, and I

Sea of Galilee from Heights of Safed

eat. When they entered, the spirits of the patriarchs had vanished. The apostles were very much surprised to see the fire and a fish, not of their own catching, also bread and honeycakes. The apostles and disciples reclined by the beam while Jesus played the host.[L18] He handed to each on a little roll a portion of the fish from the pan. I did not see that the fish became less. He gave to them also of the honeycakes and then reclined with them at table and ate. All this took place very quietly and solemnly.

Thomas was the third of those that had on the ship a perception of Jesus's presence. But they were all timid and frightened, for Jesus was more spirit-like than before, and the whole meal and the hour had in them something full of mystery. No one dared ask a question. A feeling of holy

saw the baptizing and cleansing of the new Christians, who appeared like so many tender lambs.

After a pause, Jesus again said to Peter: "Simon, son of John, lovest thou me?" (They were walking all the time, Jesus occasionally turning and pausing while they regarded him with attention). Peter very timidly and humbly, for he was thinking of his denial, again answered: "Yea, Lord, thou knowest that I love thee!" Jesus again addressed him solemnly: "Feed my sheep!" Again I had a vision of the rising church and her persecutions. I saw the Chief Bishop gathering together the numerous scattered Christians, protecting them, providing them with shepherds, and governing them.

After another pause and still walking, Jesus said once

more: "Simon, son of John, lovest thou me?" I saw that Peter grew troubled at the thought that Jesus asked him so often, as if he doubted his love. It reminded him of his thrice-repeated denial, and he answered: "Lord, thou knowest all things, thou knowest that I love thee!" I saw that John was thinking: "Oh, what love must Jesus have, and what ought a shepherd to have, since he thrice questions Peter, to whom he confides his flock, concerning his love!" Jesus again said: "Feed my sheep! [L19] Amen, amen, I say to thee: when thou wast younger, thou didst gird thyself, and didst walk where thou wouldst. But when thou shalt be old, thou shalt stretch forth thy hands, and another shall gird thee, and lead thee whither thou wouldst not. Follow me!"

Jesus turned again to go on. John walked with him, for Jesus was saying something to him alone, but what it was I could not hear. I saw that Peter, noticing this, asked the Lord while pointing to John: "Lord, what will become of this man?" Jesus, to rebuke his curiosity, answered: "If I will have him to remain till I come, what is it to thee? Follow thou me!" And Jesus turning again, they went forward.

When Jesus said for the third time: "Feed my sheep!" and that Peter would in his old age be bound and led away, I had a vision of the spreading church. I saw Peter in Rome bound and crucified, also the martyrdom of the saints. Peter too had a vision of his own martyrdom and of John's future sufferings. While Jesus was predicting his death to Peter, the latter glanced at John and very naturally thought: "Shall not this man whom Jesus loves so dearly be crucified like him?" Putting the question to Jesus, he was answered with a rebuke. I had at this moment a vision of John's death in Ephesus. I saw him stretch himself out in his grave, address some words to his disciples, and die. After his death I saw his body no longer on earth, but in a place as resplendent as the sun off toward the southeast, and it seemed as if John here received something from above that he transmitted to the earth. I became aware also that some understand these words of Jesus falsely and think they mean: "I will that he *so* remain," or "If I will that he *so* remain." But they mean: "If I will that he *remains*." They therefore that heard these words thought that John would not die. But he did die. I had on this occasion, as I have said, a vision of his death and his subsequent sojourn.

The apostles and disciples went on a little farther with Jesus, who was instructing them upon their future conduct. He then vanished before them eastward of the sea toward Gerasa and they returned to Tiberias, though not by a route that would lead them past the place in which Jesus had given them to eat.

Of the fish that the apostles caught, none were used at that meal. When Jesus said that they should bring them ashore, Peter threw them in rows at Jesus's feet, that they might be numbered. By this it was acknowledged that they had caught the fish not by themselves and for themselves, but by his miraculous power and for him. When the fish were deposited on the shore, Jesus said to the apostles: "Come and eat!" and conducted them over the little hill, or mound, where the sea could no longer be seen, to the mud hut over the furnace. Jesus did not at once place himself at table, but went to the pan and brought to each a portion of fish on a piece of bread. He blessed the portions and they shone with light. The honeycakes were not in the pan. They were already prepared, and lay in a pile one above the other. Jesus distributed them, and when all were served, he too ate with them. There was only one fish in the pan, but it was larger than any they had caught. There was some mystery connected with this meal. The presence of the souls of the patriarchs and others, their participation in the preparation of the meal, and the subsequent call of Peter, gave me to understand that in this spiritual meal the Church Suffering, the holy souls, should be committed to Peter's care, should be incorporated with the Church Militant, and the Church Triumphant, in short, that they should occupy a third place in the church as a whole. I cannot explain how this was to be done, but I had in vision this intimate conviction. It was in reference to this also that Jesus closed with the prophecy of Peter's death and John's future.

Jesus next went with the souls of the ancient patriarchs to the country in which he had driven the demons into the swine. There he released some other souls that had been confined in dreary and desolate regions, for there were many possessed in these parts, and innocent people had here been murdered whose souls, according to God's decrees, were here condemned to sojourn.

Jesus went with the souls to Paradise also, which I distinctly saw as beautiful as ever. He explained to them all that their first parents had lost by their fall, and what a happiness it was for them that he could free them from its effects. I saw that the souls sighed indeed after redemption, though ignorant of the way in which it was to be effected, just as men on earth had only vague notions on the same point. Jesus walked with them and instructed them in a manner suited to their peculiar condition, as he had done in his communications with men upon earth. I again understood that man was created to fill up the places of the angelic choirs that had fallen from heaven. If the Fall had not taken place, men would have multiplied only until that number was reached, and then creation would have come to an end. But by the Fall, a dispersing, an arbitrary scattering, a transplanting arose mixed up with impurity and darkness; therefore is the punishment of death a necessary consequence, a real benefit, a real kindness to man. As to what is said of the end of the world, this much is certain: it will not end until all the wheat is separated from the chaff and those choirs of the fallen angels filled up with it.

I saw Jesus with the souls on great battlefields, explaining to them how they had been led to salvation. As he was speaking, I saw visions of the battles and everything connected with them, just as if they were going on under my eyes. I never saw anyone terrified in these ghostlike encounters. It was like a pleasant breeze blowing over the country, and joy abounded in all creatures. Jesus went with the ancient patriarchs to those regions also into which the apostles were first to carry the Gospel, and blessed them with his presence. In this way, he visited the whole world.

When Peter, with the three apostles and the three disciples, *returned that afternoon* to the fisherman Aminadab, who for the last two years had had possession of Peter's fishery, they took a meal with him. Peter related the miracle that they had witnessed, the apparition of the Lord, the meal, and the abundant draught of fish, and gave an instruction on leaving all things and following the Lord. The old fisherman, on seeing the ship approaching laden with fish and hearing from his sons who accompanied it an account of the same miracle, resolved at once to abandon all his worldly goods. The fish were distributed among the poor, the fishery was handed over to another, and he went that night with his two sons, Isaac and Josaphat, to join the disciples. Their route lay for some distance along the west side of the sea, and then turned off inland. The fisherman's intention was not perfectly pure. He thought that by leaving all he had he would get something in return.

Toward dawn the next morning, the apostles reached a synagogue of considerable size. It stood in an open field, surrounded by inns, and formed the central point of three villages. A great many disciples were here assembled, to whom Peter related the miracle of the draught of fishes and the meal, and repeated the words of Jesus. He taught in the school, taking for his subject the miraculous draught and the following of the Lord. There was a large gathering of people here, among them many sick, also some possessed. Peter was the only one that healed on this occasion, and he did it in the name of Jesus; the other apostles and disciples served and taught. All the good and those best disposed toward Jesus's doctrine were here gathered from the whole country around. Peter spoke also of the Lord's Passion and Resurrection, told how the apostles had seen him, and invited his hearers to follow him.

The people were carried away by Peter's words, for his whole deportment had undergone an entire change since the last two apparitions. He was full of inspiration, full of gentleness. He so touched the hearts of these people that all wanted to follow him right away, and he had to command many of them to go back to their homes.

Jesus Appears to the Five Hundred

FROM that last place, which was some hours south of Tiberias, Peter went with the other apostles, the disciples, and many of the people westward to an elevated region which had on the north an extraordinarily fertile valley. Even in the depth of winter, it was covered with beautiful, tall grass, for there was a brook running through it; but in hot weather it was parched. Sometimes the whole valley was inundated by the rains that flowed down the mountains in streams. Up on this plateau they came to a hill, around which lay houses with gardens behind them extending up its sides. The hill was not much higher than the houses themselves. Five pathways planted with hedges and trees ran up the hill, whose summit afforded ample space for about a hundred people to walk about freely. From it the view extended far around the country and over the Galilean sea. It was a very beautiful prospect. At no great distance arose the mountain of the multiplication of the loaves, and it was in this region that Jesus delivered his Sermon on the Mount. The well of Capernaum was at the base of this elevated plateau. The rest of the apostles, many of the disciples, and all the holy women were here, besides the Mother of God and Veronica. Peter's wife and daughter, the wives of Andrew and Matthew were come down from Bethsaida, along with many others. The apostles and disciples knew that they were all to meet here. They scattered around, some under sheds, some in the open air. Peter related to the apostles and the women the miraculous draught of fishes, and then went with them up the mountain, upon which the people had already been ranged by some of the disciples.

There was on it a hollow place in whose center stood a teacher's pillar overgrown with moss. One could mount into it as into a pulpit. The hollow in which the pillar stood was furnished with steps in tiers, so that the numerous audience could see over one another. Peter placed five apostles on the five several pathways that led up the mountain, and they taught the people, because all could not hear him, on account of the crowd. He himself stood on the pillar in the center, the apostles, disciples, and many of the people around him, and spoke of the Passion,

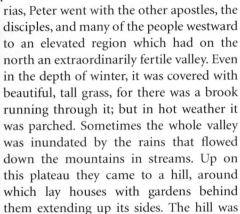

*April 15–16, AD 33
Wed. Afternoon–Thurs. Morning*

the Resurrection, the apparitions of the Lord, and the obligation of following him.

And now I saw Jesus approaching by the same route that Peter had come. He went up the mountain. The holy women, who were standing on one of the paths, prostrated before him, and he spoke to them as he passed. As, resplendent with light, he stepped in through the crowd, many shuddered and became alarmed. These did not remain faithful. Then Jesus went to the pillar on which Peter was standing. Peter resigned his place and took up a position opposite Jesus, who now addressed the multitude. He spoke of abandoning one's relatives, of following him, and of the persecution that they would have to endure. About two hundred of his hearers withdrew when they heard him talking of such things. All these were gone away, said Jesus. He had spoken to them mildly in order not to scandalize the weak. He uttered some very grave words upon the sufferings and persecution of those that would follow him upon earth, and he alluded to their eternal reward. He addressed these remarks to the apostles and disciples, as he had once before done in his last instruction in the temple. He told them that they should at first remain in Jerusalem. When he should have sent them the Spirit, they should baptize in the name of the Father, and of the Son, and of the Holy Spirit, and should at once establish a community. Then he told them how they should disperse, form distant communities, meet together once more, again separate for far-off countries, and receive at last the baptism of blood.

While Jesus was speaking, the spirits of the ancient patriarchs encircled the whole assembly, though invisibly. Jesus vanished. His disappearance was like a light suddenly extinguished in their midst. Many fell prostrate on their face. Peter again taught and prayed. This was Jesus's principal apparition in Galilee, where he taught and gave proof to all of his resurrection. The other apparitions were more secret.

Peter, Thaddeus, Andrew, and James the Less, I saw after that in another place, where they healed many sick whom lately in the region of Sichar they could not cure. Their fault was that, wishing to imitate the great dignity and reserve of Jesus in his demeanor, they did something extraordinary, they assumed an air of importance. They did not give humbly what they had received, but they gave it as coming from themselves, therefore success was not theirs. But now I saw them (and the sight touched me greatly) humbling themselves, kneeling down by the sick, and begging their pardon for failing to assist them. The

sick were all cured. There were people even from Kedar among them. The cured went with the apostles to Bethany for the sabbath.

Love Feast (Agape) in Bethany and in the House of the Last Supper • The Destruction of the Holy Places by the Jews

I SAW the apostles in Bethany, whither they were followed by about three hundred of the faithful, among them fifty women. They had given over their goods to the community. The blessed Virgin also had come from Jerusalem to Bethany, and was stopping in Martha and Magdalene's house. There was a great Love Feast of bread-breaking and passing round of the cup held in the open hall of Lazarus's court.

Peter afterward gave an instruction before a great multitude. There were some spies among the listeners. When Peter announced that they should leave all and join the community, and that he would give them what they needed, the spies laughed derisively. He had nothing himself, they said. He was only a poor fisherman, a vagrant, who could hardly support his wife at home. Peter still continued to teach, more on the command of Jesus than from any interior, quickening sentiment which the apostles received only with the Holy Spirit. He now spoke in the assemblies, excepting when the crowd was very great, for then he ordered some of the others to teach on various points. Since his reception of the mantle from Jesus and the meal of fish (which indeed was not a natural fish), at which he had received special power, he had become quite another being. All recognized him as the head, the mouth, the hand of the community. At Jesus's prediction on the seashore respecting Peter's death and John's future, at the command, "Feed my lambs!" I felt that Peter, in his successors, was forever to provide for the guiding and feeding of the flocks, while John should stand ever at the source of the water that was to refresh and irrigate the meadow and quicken the sheep. It seemed to me that Peter's influence belonged more to time, more to the exterior condition, and therefore was it divided among his successors; but that John's was more interior, that it consisted more in inspiration, in the sending abroad of inspired messengers. Peter was more like the rock, the edifice; John more like a wind, a cloud, a thunderstorm, a son of thunder, a voice sender. Peter was more like the frame, the cords, and the tone of a harp; John was the sighing of the breeze through its strings. I am unable to express in more significant words what I inwardly perceived.

April 16, AD 33
Thursday Afternoon–Evening

About fifty soldiers, the same that seized the Lord on the Mount of Olives, came from Jerusalem to Bethany. They were guards belonging to the temple and the high priests. Some deputies also of the Sanhedrin made their appearance at the council house in Bethany, and summoned the apostles before them. Peter, John, and Thomas presented themselves and replied boldly and openly to the charge that they convened assemblies and occasioned disturbance among the people. Soldiers were placed at Lazarus's. The deputies from Jerusalem interrogated the apostles publicly before the council house. The magistrates of Bethany opposed them, saying that if they knew anything against those men, they ought to take them into custody, but that they must not disturb the peace of the place by the presence of soldiers. Peter, in order to avoid giving offense, dismissed one hundred and twenty-three of the assembled faithful. Those from the greatest distance were directed to remain at the dwellings in the neighborhood, for they already had all things in common. The fifty women also withdrew and lived together in separate abodes. Peter gave orders for all to return to Bethany before the day of Christ's ascension.

The apostles, on leaving Bethany, went to the house of the Last Supper near Jerusalem, where they prayed under the lamp before the Holy of Holies. There were about seven disciples with them. They could no longer reach the house of the Last Supper through the city, for the road on that side had been partly destroyed by the Jews. They had to go to the left of the temple, and strike into the road taken by Peter and John on Maundy Thursday. There were numerous inns for the accommodation of strangers on this road, and the people living around these parts were not of pure Jewish origin. The Jews had expelled from their society and from public offices all that declared themselves for Jesus and that fraternized with the disciples. The places upon which Jesus fell during his sorrowful journey to Golgotha, or at which something noteworthy had happened, they cut through with ditches. The ways leading to the sections chiefly inhabited or frequented by the followers of Jesus, they walled up. It appeared to me very strange to see a person caught in such a street as in a blind alley, and have to turn round and come out again. Sometimes the friends of Jesus again opened the ways to Golgotha by night. All places around Jerusalem especially consecrated by the presence or the sufferings of Jesus, and on that account held in particular veneration by his followers, were maliciously laid waste by the Jews. The charming sites upon which Jesus had taught and tarried were rendered impassable and

closed in with hedges. In some places they actually dug pitfalls into which the pious pilgrim might fall, but I saw some of those vicious Jews plunging into them themselves. Mount Calvary was rendered unapproachable by hedges and beams. Its summit was dug up and the earth scattered like manure over the paths, also over the five grassy, heart-shaped plots that were formed by the pathways running up to the place of crucifixion. When they had taken away the mound that encircled the place of crucifixion, there remained a white stone. In it was a four-cornered hole about four feet deep, in which the cross had been planted. I saw the workmen toiling with crowbars, trying to upturn that stone, but the more they tried, the deeper it sank, so they buried it at last under some rubbish. The Holy Sepulcher alone was left unmolested, for that was Nicodemus's property. Christ's head, while in the tomb, lay toward the east. If a person on leaving the cave went around toward the south, he would have the sun directly above him, and the west on his right.

April 17, AD 33
Friday Evening

I was interiorly instructed that all demolishers of representations of the Holy Way of the Cross, of crucifixes, chapels or churches, of ancient devotions, of holy exercises and practices, and in general of all objects that draw us into closer relation with the history of Redemption, whether in building, picture, and writing, or by custom, festival, and prayer, will be judged with the enemies of Jesus's bloody footsteps and as belonging to them.

The Majesty and Dignity of the Blessed Virgin

On the evening of the following day, I saw the apostles and twenty of the disciples in the hall at prayer under the lamp. The blessed Virgin, all the holy women, Lazarus, Nicodemus, Joseph of Arimathea, and Obed were present. The prayer over, John addressed the apostles, and Peter, the disciples. They spoke in words full of mystery of their relations to the mother of the Lord and what she should be to them. During this instruction of the two apostles, which they based on a communication received from Jesus, I saw the blessed Virgin hovering over the assembly in a shining, outspread mantle whose folds embraced them all, and on her head descended a crown from the most holy Trinity through the open heavens above her. I no longer saw her kneeling outside the hall in prayer, and I had the conviction that Mary was the legitimate head of them all, the temple that enclosed them all. I think this vision was symbolical of what God designed to take place for the church at this moment through the exposition of the apostles upon Mary's dignity.

Toward nine o'clock, I saw a meal set in the outer hall. The guests wore festal robes and Mary her wedding garment. When at prayer, however, she wore a white mantle and veil. She sat between Peter and John at the table of the apostles, who were seated, their back to the court, the door of the hall in view. The other women and disciples were seated right and left at separate tables. Nicodemus and Joseph served. Peter carved the lamb, just as Jesus had done the paschal lamb. At the end of the meal, there was a breaking of bread and a passing around of blessed (not consecrated) bread and wine.

After that I saw the blessed Virgin with the apostles in the supper room. She was standing between Peter and John under the lamp. The Holy of Holies was open, and they were praying on their knees before it.

When midnight had sounded, the blessed Virgin, kneeling, received the blessed sacrament from Peter. He carried the bread that had been consecrated and broken by Jesus on the little plate belonging to the chalice. At that instant I saw Jesus appear to her, though not visible to the others. Mary was penetrated with light and splendor. She was still in prayer. I saw that the holy apostles were very reverent in their manner toward her. Mary next went to the little dwelling on the right of the entrance into the court of the Cenacle, in which she now had her apartment. Here standing she recited the Magnificat, the Canticle of the three youths in the fiery furnace, and the 130th Psalm. *The day was beginning to dawn* when I saw Jesus entering through the closed doors. He spoke long to her, telling her that she was to help the apostles, and explaining what she was to be to them. He gave her power over the whole church, endued her with his strength, his protecting influence, and it was as if his light flowed in upon her, as if he penetrated her through and through. I cannot express it. A covered way of mats across the court to the house of the Last Supper was made for the blessed Virgin, so that she could go from her little room to the Holy of Holies and the choir of the apostles and disciples. John also resided in the little dwelling. When Jesus appeared to Mary in her cell, I saw her head encircled by a crown of stars as it had been at her communion.

It was revealed to me also that as often as the blessed Virgin communicated, the form of the bread remained in her unchanged from one communion to another, so that she always adored in her breast the sacramental presence of the God-Man. During a period of persecution, after the stoning of St. Stephen, the apostles for a time refrained from consecrating. But even then the church was not without the blessed sacrament, for it was preserved in the

living tabernacle of Mary's most holy heart. I also learned at the same time that this was a grace entirely special, and that it could be imparted to the blessed Virgin alone.

Increase of the Community

THE NUMBER of the faithful continued to increase. Many came to join them, especially from the Galilean Sea, with asses laden with baggage. It kept some busy procuring them quarters. They generally stopped first at the disciples' inn outside Bethany, where the disciples dwelt in turn to receive the strangers, and give them advice and directions. The newcomers were sent by them to Lazarus, who owned many houses and dwellings. Many of them lived at Jerusalem also, in the quarter of Mount Zion. Only a few poor Jews were scattered around here. There were numerous old walls of extraordinary thickness, and vacant lots on which I saw asses grazing. Strangers who had come for the feast pitched their tents around this quarter. Besides the house of the Last Supper, there was another on Mount Zion, a very large, dilapidated old building (the Citadel of David), and numbers of the faithful found shelter under its surroundings. They dwelt in huts, or in lodgings adjoining them. I saw that people dwelt below in the massive walls, while on their top were erected tents of coarse tapestry.

The Chaldeans from Sikdor, whom Jesus had directed to the centurion of Capernaum, and who had from there returned to their homes, were now come back again in great numbers with their beasts of burden and baggage. Their beasts and packs were standing in the inner court of the large, dilapidated building. The Jews did not molest them; only the road to the temple mount and to the quarter of the city belonging to it was entirely walled up on the side of Mount Zion near the pool of Bethesda where the Christians were stopping. The community was thereby completely separated, cut off from the Jews.

I saw the newcomers resigning, for the good of the community, quantities of stuffs of fine and coarse, white and yellowish wool, carpets, canvas for tents, all in great rolls. Nicodemus and Joseph managed everything. Garments for religious service and baptism were made out of some, and some was given to the needy, all of whom were cared for.

There was, at the pool of Bethesda, an old synagogue formerly used only by strangers come for the feast. It stood at some elevation above the pool. The apostles now appropriated it to their own use. In it the newcomers assembled to be instructed by some of the apostles. But all these strangers were not at once admitted to the community, much less to the house of the Last Supper. I saw neither the apostles nor the disciples, nor these newly arrived again frequenting the temple. True, the apostles, having received the Holy Spirit, went there after Pentecost, but it was only that they might preach to the assembled multitude. Their temple was the house of the Last Supper that sheltered the blessed sacrament. The mother of all was the blessed Virgin. The apostles consulted with her, and she was for them like an apostle herself.

Peter's wife and daughter, Mark's wife, and other women had now come from Bethsaida to Bethany, where they dwelt under tents. They had no communication whatever with the men. They came into the presence of the apostles only for instruction, and they employed themselves in weaving and twisting long strips of stuff and coarse covers for tents, many of them working at the same time upon one piece. The blessed Virgin also, along with Martha and Magdalene, worked at embroidery,

April 19–May 11, AD 33

sometimes reclining, sometimes walking about, work in hand. I saw the blessed Virgin embroidering in delicate colors figures something like an apostle, or the Lord himself, on a yellow, brown, or sky-blue ground. The figures were not so enveloped in mantles as formerly. Once they embroidered a representation of the most holy Trinity. It was like God the Father handing the cross to the Son, who looked like a high priest. From both proceeded the Holy Spirit, though not in the form of a dove, for instead of wings there were arms. The figures were arranged more in a triangular form than one below the other. I have seen in the earliest churches of that period vestments that Mary had embroidered.

The apostles themselves lent a hand in preparing the dwellings of the newcomers. They carried to them wood and matting and wicker partitions, and worked hard. The poor were provided with clothing, and even their food was prepared for them, for Lazarus had contributed toward the foundation of a general fund.

The holy women, among whom was the wife of Zacchaeus, busied themselves in helping the newly arrived women. No one had anything of his own. He that brought something with him gave it up, and he that had nothing, received something. The house of Simon the Leper was crowded with disciples. Simon himself no longer dwelt in it, for he had resigned it to the community, and he now lived among the brethren. On the flat roof of the house there was formed, by means of movable wicker partitions, a kind of hall in which was placed an orator's chair. It was

reached from outside by steps in the wall. They built everywhere, they put up tents and sheds, they made use of every corner of walls and old buildings. There were also many vacant dwellings both here and in Jerusalem, for numbers of Jews went away after the crucifixion.

The newly converted and the baptized became so numerous after Pentecost that the apostles had to negotiate with the Jewish magistrates for procuring suitable dwelling-places for the newcomers. They sent Nicodemus, Joseph of Arimathea, Nathaniel, and others well known among the Jews, to the magistrates who were assembled, about twenty in number, in a hall over the gate of the women's porch. Three places outside the city and distant from the usual routes were assigned the converts: one to the west of Bethany, between it and Bethphage, where some huts and sheds were already put up; and two others south of Bethany, distant also from the highroads. In exchange for these, the disciples were to vacate the inn on the road outside Bethany, nor should they live permanently or put up at the inn beyond Jerusalem and on the road to Bethlehem, where Mary had stopped before her purification in the temple. I saw the magistrates indicating from the temple the regions named, the deputies carrying back the news to the community, some parties of the faithful going thither, and Peter and John pointing out to them sites for building. Supplies of all kinds were transported on asses, and water in great leathern bottles, to the place between Bethany and Bethphage, where there was no water. But when the Christians began to dig a well, water at once gushed forth. I saw Simon of Bethany, who had had a household of his own and understood domestic economy, under an awning near the pool of Bethesda, and he appeared to be noting down on a roll of parchment the goods and chattels of the people, who had brought with them sheep, goats, doves, and great birds with red beaks and legs. All were distributed to those in need of them, also covers and woollen stuffs for clothing. Admirable order was observed in this distribution. The women received their portion through the hands of women; the men, from men. There were people from the most widely scattered regions, who did not understand one another's language, but who with the greatest love handed over their property for distribution. The apostles alone understood all. Magdalene and Martha gave up their houses at Bethany to the new converts, and Lazarus delivered over all that he owned to the community. Nicodemus and Joseph of Arimathea did the same. They assumed the charge of providing for the community and distributing the alms. But when they were ordained priests, Peter appointed deacons in their place.

The Days Immediately Preceding the Ascension

JESUS communicated with the apostles quite naturally *in those last days*. He ate and prayed with them, walked with them in many directions, and repeated all that he had before told them. He appeared also to Simon of Cyrene as he was working in a garden between Bethphage and Jerusalem. Jesus, resplendent with light, approached him as if floating in the air. Simon fell on his knees and kissed the ground at Jesus's feet, who signed to him with his hand to keep silence, and then vanished. Some others that were working nearby likewise saw Jesus, and they too fell on their knees like Simon. When Jesus was walking with the apostles around Jerusalem, some of the Jews perceived the apparition, and were terrified. They ran to hide themselves, or to shut themselves up in their houses. Even the apostles and disciples accompanied him with a certain degree of timidity, for there was in him something too spiritual for them. Jesus appeared also in other places, Bethlehem and Nazareth for instance, to those especially with whom he and his blessed Mother had formerly had contact. He scattered blessings everywhere, and they that saw him believed and joined the apostles and disciples.

On the last day but one before the Ascension, I saw Jesus with five of the apostles approaching Bethany from the east, whither the blessed Virgin also, with other holy women, was coming from Jerusalem. Many of the faithful were gathered around Lazarus's house. They knew that Jesus was soon to leave them, and they wanted to see him once more and bid him goodbye. When Jesus had entered the house, these people were admitted into the spacious courtyard and the gates closed. Jesus took with the apostles and disciples some refreshments standing, and to the latter, who were weeping bitterly, he said: "Why do ye weep, dear brethren? Behold this woman! She is not weeping!" and he pointed to his blessed Mother, who was standing with the holy women at the entrance of the hall. A long table was set in the court for the numerous strangers. Jesus went out to them, blessed little rolls, and distributed them, after which he gave them a sign to retire. And now his blessed Mother humbly approached, to present to him a petition. But Jesus, checking her with a gesture of his hand, told her that he could not grant it. Mary thanked most humbly, and withdrew.

Jesus took a singularly touching leave of Lazarus. He gave him a shining morsel, blessed him, and extended to him his hand. Lazarus, who generally remained hidden in his own house, did not accompany Jesus when he left for Jerusalem with the apostles and disciples. They took the Palm Sunday route, though with many turnings into side ways. They went in four companies, allowing considerable distance to intervene between them. The eleven went on with Jesus; the holy women followed last. I saw Jesus shining with light, a conspicuous figure in their midst. The marks of his wounds were not always visible to me, but when I did see them, they were brilliant as the sun. All were anxious and greatly depressed. Some were in tears; others were talking to one another, saying: "He has often before vanished from us," for they did not want to think that he would really leave them. Peter and John alone appeared more calm, as if they understood the Lord better, for Jesus often spoke to them interiorly and explained to them many things. He often disappeared and then suddenly reappeared in their midst, as if desirous of preparing them for his final departure.

The way ran past charming little gardens where Jews were busy weaving and clipping the hedges, on which lovely bushes covered with flowers were growing in the form of pyramids. The laborers often covered their faces with their hands, fell to the earth, or fled among the shrubbery, I know not whether from fright and terror or from deep emotion. I do not know whether they saw the Lord, or whether they could not see him. Once I heard Jesus saying to the disciples: "After all these places shall have been converted to the faith by your preaching, and after others shall have driven the faithful away and laid all things waste—then shall come a sad time. Ye do not as yet comprehend me, but when ye will for the last time celebrate with me the Last Supper, then ye will understand me better."

Nicodemus and Joseph of Arimathea had prepared a meal, which was served in the entrance hall of the house of the Last Supper. The hall opened on all sides, and a passage ran from the left through the courtyard, which was planted with trees, to the little house with the kitchen hearth built near the surrounding wall. The covered walks on the right were opened into the courtyard, and here were set the tables for the disciples. They consisted of long planks only. The table for Jesus and the eleven was prepared in the entrance hall. On it stood little mugs and a large dish ornamented with delicate foliage, in which lay a fish along with some small rolls. On the disciples' table were fruits and three-cornered dishes containing honeycombs. Flat bone knives were placed around. Near every dish lay three slices of bread, for there was one dish for every three of the guests.

The sun had set and it was beginning to grow dark when Jesus drew near with the apostles. The blessed Virgin, Nicodemus, and Joseph of Arimathea received him at the gate. He went with his blessed Mother into her little abode, while the apostles proceeded to the entrance hall. When the disciples and holy women arrived somewhat later, Jesus joined the eleven in the hall. The table, only one long side of which they occupied, was higher than those in general use. The apostles reclined on cross-seats, but Jesus stood. At his side reclined John, who was more cheerful than the others. He was just like a child in disposition, now quickly troubled, and again full of consolation and joy. The lamp over the table was lighted. Nicodemus and Joseph served. I saw the blessed Virgin standing at the entrance of the Supper Room. Jesus blessed the fish, the bread, and the herbs, and passed them around with words of earnest instruction. I saw his words like rays of light issuing from his mouth and entering that of the apostles, into some quickly, into others slowly, according to their greater or less desire, their greater or less hunger after the teaching of Jesus. At the end of the meal, Jesus blessed the cup, drank from it, and then passed it around. This, however, was not a consecration.

The love feast over, all assembled outside the hall under the trees. Jesus addressed to them a long instruction, and ended by giving them his blessing. To his blessed Mother, who was standing in front of the holy women, he extended his hand. All were very much affected, and I felt that Magdalene ardently longed to embrace Jesus's feet. But she restrained her desire, for his demeanor was so grave that he inspired holy fear. When he left them, they wept very much. It was not, however, an exterior weeping; it was like the weeping of the soul. I did not see the blessed Virgin shedding tears. I never saw her actually weeping excepting when she lost Jesus, a boy of twelve, on her return journey from the Passover festival, and again when she stood under the cross after his death. *The assembly broke up before midnight.*

Jesus's Ascension into Heaven

On the night before his wonderful ascension, I saw Jesus in the inner hall of the house of the Last Supper with the blessed Virgin and the eleven. The disciples and the holy women were praying in the side halls. In the supper room the communion table was standing under the lighted lamp, and on it the Passover bread and chalice. The apos-

tles were in their robes of ceremony. The blessed Virgin was opposite Jesus who, as on Maundy Thursday, was consecrating bread and wine.

I saw the blessed sacrament entering the mouths of the apostles in the form of a luminous body, and Jesus's words at the consecration of the wine flowing into the chalice like a stream of red light.

During the last days, Magdalene, Martha, and Mary Cleophas received the blessed sacrament.

Toward morning, matins were solemnly recited as usual under the lamp. Jesus again imparted to Peter jurisdiction over the others, again laid upon him the mantle of which I have spoken, and repeated what he had said on the mountain by the Sea of Tiberias. He gave some instructions also on baptism and the blessing of water. During matins and the instructions I saw seventeen of the most confidential disciples standing in the hall behind the blessed Virgin.

Before leaving the house, Jesus presented the blessed Virgin to the apostles and disciples as their Mother, their Mediatrix, and their Advocate, and she bestowed upon Peter and all the rest her blessing, which they received bowing very low. At that instant I beheld Mary raised upon a throne, a sky-blue mantle around her, a crown upon her head. This was symbolical of her dignity as Queen of Mercy.

At dawn of day Jesus left the house of the Last Supper with the eleven. The blessed Virgin followed them closely; the disciples, at some little distance. They passed through the streets of Jerusalem where all was quiet, the inhabitants still buried in sleep. At each moment the Lord became more earnest, more rapid in speech and action. On the preceding evening he appeared to me much more sympathetic in his words to his followers. I recognized the route that they took as that of the Palm Sunday procession. I saw that Jesus went with them over all the paths trodden by him during his Passion, in order to inspire them by his teachings and admonitions with a lively appreciation of the fulfillment of the Promise. In every place in which some scene of his Passion had been enacted, he paused a moment to instruct them upon the accomplishment of the words of the prophets, upon the Promises, and to explain the symbolical relation of the place to the same. On those sites which the Jews had laid waste, over which they had thrown heaps of stones, through which they had opened ditches, or which they had rendered impassable in other ways in order to prevent their being venerated, Jesus ordered the disciples in his train to go on ahead and clear away all obstructions, which they quickly did. Then, bowing low as he passed, they allowed him to take the lead again while they followed. Just before the gate that led out to Mount Calvary, they turned aside from the road to a delightful spot shaded by trees. It was one of several places of prayer that lay around Jerusalem. Jesus paused to teach and comfort the little flock. *Meanwhile, day dawned brightly*; their hearts grew lighter, and they even began to think that Jesus would still remain with them.

New crowds of believers arrived, but I saw no women among them. Jesus again took the road that led to Mount Calvary and the Holy Sepulcher. But he did not follow it up to those points; he turned off and went around the city to the Mount of Olives. Some of the places on these roads consecrated to prayer and sanctified by Jesus's teaching, and which had been laid waste or hedged in by the Jews, were now restored by the disciples. The tools for their work they found in the gardens on their way. I remember round shovels that looked like our bake-oven shovels.

May 14, AD 33
Thursday, Morning–Noon

Jesus paused awhile with the crowd in an exceedingly cool and lovely spot covered with beautiful long grass. I was surprised to see that it was nowhere trodden down. The multitude that here surrounded Jesus was so great that I could no longer count them. Jesus spoke to them a very long time, like one who is about closing his discourse and coming to a conclusion. His hearers divined that the hour of parting was near, and yet they had no idea that the time still intervening was to be so short. The sun was already high, was already far above the horizon. I know not whether I express it rightly, for in that country it seems to me the sun is not so high as it is here. It always appears to me as if it were nearer to one. I do not see it as here, rising like a small globe. It shines there with far more brilliancy. Its rays are, on the whole, not so fine. They often look like a broad pathway of light. Jesus and his followers tarried here fully an hour. By this time the people in Jerusalem were all on the alert, amazed at the crowds of people they descried around the Mount of Olives. Out of the city, too, crowds were pouring in bands. They consisted of all that had gone out to meet Jesus on Palm Sunday. The narrow roads were soon thronged, though around Jesus and his own, the space was left free.

The Lord went only to Gethsemane, and from the Garden of Olives up to the summit of the mount. He did not set foot upon the path on which he had been arrested. The crowd followed as in a procession, ascending by the different paths that encircled the mount. Many even pressed through the fences and garden hedges. Jesus at each instant

shone more brightly and his motions became more rapid. The disciples hastened after him, but it was impossible to overtake him. When he reached the top of the mountain, he was resplendent as a beam of white sunlight. A shining circle, glancing in all the colors of the rainbow, fell from heaven around him. The pressing crowd stood in a wide circle outside, as if blending with it. Jesus himself shone still more brightly than the glory about him. He laid the left hand on his breast and, raising the right, turned slowly around, blessing the whole world. The crowd stood motionless. I saw all receive the benediction. Jesus did not impart it with the flat, open hand, like the rabbis, but like the Christian bishops. With great joy I felt his blessing of the whole world.

And now the rays of light from above united with the glory emanating from Jesus, and I saw him disappearing, dissolving as it were in the light from heaven, vanishing as he rose. [L.20] I lost sight of his head first. It appeared as if one sun was lost in another, as if one flame entered another, as if a spark floated into a flame. It was as if one were gazing into the *full midday* splendors of the sun, though this light was whiter and clearer. Full day compared with this would be dark. First, I lost sight of Jesus's head, then his whole person, and lastly his feet, radiant with light, disappeared in the celestial glory. I saw innumerable souls from all sides going into that light and vanishing on high with the Lord. I cannot say that I saw him becoming apparently smaller and smaller like something flying up in the air, for he disappeared as it were in a cloud of light.

Out of that cloud something like dew, like a shower of light, fell upon all below, and when they could no longer endure the splendor, they were seized with amazement and terror. The apostles and disciples, who were nearest to Jesus, were blinded by the dazzling glare. They were forced to lower their eyes, while many cast themselves prostrate on their faces. The blessed Virgin was standing close behind them and gazing calmly straight ahead.

After some moments, when the splendor began to diminish, the whole assembly in deep silence—their souls swayed by varying emotions—gazed fixedly up at the brightness, which continued visible for a long time. I saw two figures appear in this light. They looked small at first, but seemed to grow larger and larger as they descended. They were clothed in long white garments, and each held a staff in one hand. They looked like prophets. [L.21] They addressed the multitude, their voices like trumpets resounding loud and clear. It seemed to me that they could surely be heard in Jerusalem. They made no motion, stood perfectly still, and said: "Ye men of Galilee, why stand ye looking up to heaven? This Jesus who is taken up from you into heaven shall so come as you have seen him going into heaven." After these words the figures vanished. The brightness remained for a while longer and then disappeared like daylight retiring before the darkness of night. The disciples were quite out of themselves, for they now comprehended what had happened to them. The Lord had left them and gone to his heavenly Father! Many, stunned by grief and amazement, fell to the earth. When the glare had entirely died away, they arose again, and the others gathered around them. They formed groups, the blessed Virgin stepped forward, and so they stood for some time longer recovering themselves, talking together, and gazing upward. At last, the apostles and disciples went back to the house of the Last Supper, and the blessed Virgin followed. Some were weeping like children that refuse to be comforted, others were lost in thought. The blessed Virgin, Peter, and John were very calm and full of consolation. I saw, however, some among the different groups who remained unmoved, unbelieving, and full of doubts. They withdrew from the rest.

May 15–23, AD 33

On the top of the Mount of Olives, from which Jesus ascended, there was a level rock. On it he stood addressing the multitude before he blessed them and the cloud of light received him. His footsteps remained impressed on the stone, and on another the mark of one hand of the blessed Virgin. It was past noon before the crowd entirely dispersed.

The apostles and disciples now felt themselves alone. They were at first restless and like people forsaken. But by the soothing presence of the blessed Virgin they were comforted, and putting entire confidence in Jesus's words that she would be to them a mediatrix, a mother, and an advocate, they regained peace of soul.

A certain fear stole over the Jews in Jerusalem. I saw many closing doors and windows, others gathering together in groups. During the last days, they had experienced some peculiar feelings of alarm, which today were greatly intensified.

On the following days I saw the apostles always together and the blessed Virgin with them in the house of the Last Supper. At the last repast of Jesus, and ever after, I saw Mary when at prayer and the breaking of bread always opposite Peter, who now took the Lord's place in the prayer circle and at meals. I received at the time the impression that Mary now held a position of high importance among the apostles, and that she was placed over the church.

The apostles kept themselves very much aloof. I saw no one out of the great crowd of Jesus's followers going to them into the house of the Last Supper. They guarded more against persecution from the Jews and gave themselves up to more earnest and well-regulated prayer than did the disciples dispersed in bands throughout the other apartments of the same house. The latter went in and out more freely. I saw many of them also very devoutly traversing the way of the Lord by night.

At the election of Matthias to the apostolate, I saw Peter in the house of the Last Supper. He was clothed in his episcopal mantle and was standing in the center of the circle formed by the apostles. The disciples were gathered in the open side halls. Peter proposed Joseph Barsabbas and Matthias both of whom were standing off among the bands of disciples. There were some among these that wanted to be chosen in Judas's place. The two mentioned had never thought of such a thing, and had no desires on the subject. Next day the lots were cast, Barsabbas and Matthias being excluded from the assembly. When it was found that the lot had fallen on Matthias, someone went into the disciples' apartments and led him to the apostles.

The Holy Day of Pentecost

THE whole interior of the Last Supper room was, on the eve of the feast, ornamented with green bushes in whose branches were placed vases of flowers. Garlands of green were looped from side to side. The screens that cut off the side halls and the vestibule were removed; only the gate of the outer court was closed. Peter in his episcopal robe stood at a table covered with red and white under the lamp in front of the curtained Holy of Holies. On the table lay rolls of writing. Opposite him in the doorway leading from the entrance hall stood the blessed Virgin, her face veiled, and behind her in the entrance hall stood the holy women. The apostles stood in two rows turned toward Peter along either side of the hall, and from the side halls the disciples ranged behind the apostles took part in the hymns and prayers. When Peter broke and distributed the bread that he had previously blessed, first to the blessed Virgin, then to the apostles and disciples who stepped forward to receive it, they kissed his hand, the blessed Virgin included. Besides the holy women, there were in the house of the Last Supper and its dependencies one hundred and twenty of Jesus's followers.

After midnight there arose a wonderful movement in all nature. It communicated itself to all present as they stood in deep recollection, their arms crossed on their breast, near the pillars of the supper room and in the side halls, silently praying. Stillness pervaded the house, and silence reigned throughout the whole enclosure.

Toward morning I saw above the Mount of Olives a glittering white cloud of light coming down from heaven and drawing near to the house. In the distance it appeared to me like a round ball borne along on a soft, warm breeze. But coming nearer, it looked larger and floated over the city like a luminous mass of fog until it stood above Zion and the house of the Last Supper. It seemed to contract and to shine with constantly increasing brightness, until at last with a rushing, roaring noise as of wind, it sank like a thunder cloud floating low in the atmosphere. I saw many Jews, who espied the cloud, hurrying in terror to the temple. I myself experienced a childlike anxiety as to where I should hide if the stroke were to follow, for the whole thing was like a storm that had suddenly gathered, that instead of rising from the earth came down from heaven, that was light instead of dark, that instead of thundering came down with a rushing wind. I felt that rushing motion. It was like a warm breeze full of power to refresh and invigorate.

May 24, AD 33
Sunday Sunrise

The luminous cloud descended low over the house, and with the increasing sound, the light became brighter. I saw the house and its surroundings more clearly, while the apostles, the disciples, and the women became more and more silent, more deeply recollected. Afterward there shot from the rushing cloud streams of white light down upon the house and its surroundings. The streams intersected one another in sevenfold rays, and below each intersection resolved into fine threads of light and fiery drops. The point at which the seven streams intersected was surrounded by a rainbow light, in which floated a luminous figure with outstretched wings, or rays of light that looked like wings, attached to the shoulders. In that same instant the whole house and its surroundings were penetrated through and through with light. The five-branched lamp no longer shone. The assembled faithful were ravished in ecstasy. Each involuntarily threw back his head and raised his eyes eagerly on high, while into the mouth of every one there flowed a stream of light like a burning tongue of fire. It looked as if they were breathing, as if they were eagerly drinking in the fire, and as if their ardent desire flamed forth from their mouth to meet the entering flame. The sacred fire was poured forth also upon the disciples and the women present in the antechamber, and thus the resplendent cloud gradually dissolved as if in a rain of light. The flames descended on each in different colors and in different degrees of intensity. After that effusion of heavenly light, a joyous courage pervaded the assembly. All were full of emotion, and as if intoxicated with joy and confidence. They gathered around the blessed Virgin who was, I saw, the only one perfectly calm, the only one that retained a quiet, holy self-possession. The apostles embraced one another and, urged by joyous confidence, exclaimed: "What were we? What are we now?" The holy women too embraced. The disciples in the side halls were similarly affected, and the apostles hastened out to them. A new life full of joy, of confidence, and of courage had been infused into all. Their joy found vent in thanksgiving. They ranged for prayer, gave thanks and praised God with great emotion. The light meanwhile vanished. Peter delivered an instruction to the disciples, and sent several of them out to the inns of the Pentecost guests.

Between the house of the Last Supper and the pool of Bethesda there were several sheds and public lodging houses for the accommodation of guests come up for the feast. They were at this time very numerous, and they too received the grace of the Holy Spirit. An extraordinary movement pervaded all nature. Good people were roused interiorly, while the wicked became timid, uneasy, and still more stiff-necked. Most of these strangers had been encamped here since Passover, because the distance from their homes rendered a journey to and fro between that feast and Pentecost altogether impracticable. They were become, by all that they had seen and heard, quite intimate and kindly disposed toward the disciples, so that the latter, intoxicated with joy, announced to them the Promise of the Holy Spirit as fulfilled. Then too did they become conscious of a change within their own souls and, at the summons of the disciples, they gathered around the pool of Bethesda.

In the house of the Last Supper, Peter imposed hands on five of the apostles who were to help to teach and baptize at the pool of Bethesda. They were James the Less, Bartholomew, Matthew, Thomas, and Judas Thaddeus. The last-named had a vision during his ordination. It seemed to him that he was clasping to his breast the body of the Lord.

Before departing for the pool of Bethesda to consecrate the water and administer baptism, they received on their knees the benediction of the blessed Virgin. Before Jesus's ascension, this ceremony was performed standing. On the following days I saw this blessing given whenever the apostles left the house, and also on their return. The blessed Virgin wore on such occasions, and generally when she appeared among the apostles in her post of dignity, a large white mantle, a creamy white veil, and a scarf of sky-blue stuff that hung from her head down both sides to the ground. It was ornamented with embroidery, and was held firmly on the head by a white silken crown.

Baptism at the pool of Bethesda had been arranged by Jesus himself for this day's feast, and the disciples had, in consequence, made all kinds of preparations at the pool, as well as in the old synagogue that they had appropriated for their own use. The walls of the synagogue were hung with tapestry, and from the building down to the pool a covered tent-way was erected.

The apostles and disciples went in solemn procession, two by two, from the house of the Last Supper to the pool. Some of the disciples carried a leathern bottle of holy water and an asperges. The five apostles upon whom Peter had imposed hands separated, each taking one of the five entrances to the pool, and addressed the people with great enthusiasm. Peter stepped upon the teacher's chair that had been prepared for him in the third circle of the pool, counting from the outside one. This terrace was the broadest. The hearers filled all the terraces of the pool. When the apostles spoke, the multitude hearkened in amazement, for everyone listened to what sounded to him his own language. It was owing to this astonishment of the people that Peter lifted up his voice, as is recorded in the Acts of the apostles.

As many presented themselves for baptism, Peter, assisted by John and James the Less, solemnly blessed the water. The holy water, which they had brought in a leathern bottle from the house of the Last Supper, Peter sprinkled in fine streams far over the pool with an asperges. The preparations for baptism and the baptism itself occupied the whole day.

The neophytes approached Peter's chair in bands and by turns, the other apostles preaching and baptizing at the entrances. The blessed Virgin and the holy women were busy in the synagogue near the pool, distributing the white garments to the neophytes. The sleeves of these garments were bound over the hands with black bands, which were taken off after baptism and laid together in a pile. The neophytes leaned upon a railing. The water was scooped up in a basin and then with the hand poured three times over the head. It flowed again through a channel into the pool below. One basin held enough water for about ten couples. Every two baptized gave place to two neophytes upon whom they laid their hands as sponsors. Those baptized here today were they that had received John's baptism only.

The holy women too were baptized. The people added to the community today amounted to three thousand. That evening the apostles and disciples returned to the house of the Last Supper, where they took a repast and distributed blessed bread. Then came the evening prayer.

The Jews offered today in the temple little baskets containing two small loaves made of this year's grain. The baskets were deposited one upon another, until they formed high heaps, and they were afterward distributed to the poor. Once I saw that the high priest had in his hand a bunch of ears, thick like maize. Something like roots also was offered, and some kind of fruit unknown to me. The strangers under the sheds had asses laden with them, and the people made purchases of them. The bread was of their own baking. The apostles offered only the two loaves through Peter.

On the following days also, preaching and baptizing went on at the pool. Before the apostles and disciples went down for these duties, they received the blessing of the blessed Virgin.

The Church at the Pool of Bethesda

THE pool of Bethesda lay in a ravine of the valley that separated Mount Zion from the temple and the rest of that quarter of the city, and which declined eastward into the valley of Jehosaphat. It seemed to have been constructed in such a way as to cut off the view of the temple on the west, for on one side one could not see all around, as could be done on the others. The way to it was indeed broad enough, but the walls were partly overturned and the road was full of grass and sedge. Just at that point it ran down into a ravine that became greener in proportion to its depth. From the pool could be seen off to the southwest an angle of the Holy of Holies. The sheep pool lay to the north of the temple near the cattle market, and was entirely enclosed by a wall. From the house of the Last Supper, which stood on the eastern height of Mount Zion, the way led to the pool of Bethesda first to the east around the height of Zion, then wound in a half-circle to the north, then turned to the west, and lastly eastward again down into a curve. The whole of this quarter of Zion as far as the pool and across down into the valley of Jehosaphat, presented an appearance of desolation. In the dilapidated buildings were formed dwellings for the poor, on the slopes grew groves of juniper trees, and the hollows were covered with high grass and reeds. The Jews shunned this locality, so the new converts now began to settle in it.

The pool of Bethesda was oval in form and surrounded

by five terraces, like an amphitheater. Five flights of steps led down to the pool from these terraces to the little trough-like skiffs in which the sick who were seeking a cure were laid when waiting to be sprinkled by the bubbling waters. There was also in the pool a copper pump, which arose to nearly the height of a man above the surface of the water and was about as large around as a churn. A little wooden bridge with a railing led to it. I saw by the bridge a tube and piston, which were connected with the pump. When the piston was forced down, a valve was opened and a stream of water squirted out of the pump. By changes made in the opening, the stream could be increased or diminished and made to flow in different directions. The top of the pump could be closed also, and from side jets the streams could be made to spurt all around, like water from a watering pot. I often saw the sick in the skiffs rowing up to the pump to receive the streams over them. The entrance to the pool was usually closed. It was opened for the sick only. This pump was out of use, and on the Feast of Pentecost was not yet repaired, but a few days later I saw it restored. The terrace walls contained little vaulted halls in which were stone benches hollowed out in the form of a trough. They were for the accommodation of the sick. They could from all sides look down upon the pool, to see whether the waters were being stirred or not. The lowest terrace, the one nearest the pool, was provided with little parapets, or bars. The bottom of the pool was covered with shining white sand, through which three springs bubbled up and sometimes jetted above the surface of the water. The blood of the animals offered in sacrifice flowed through pipes under the altar in the temple down into the pool. With its surroundings and the old buildings in its vicinity, the pool covered a very large area. Before reaching it, one had to pass a wall through which there were only three openings. To the east of the pool, the valley made a steep descent, but westward, back of the pool, it was less deep and was spanned by a little bridge. The north side too was steep and overgrown, and on the northeast was a road conducting to the temple. But it was now gone to ruin and altogether impracticable. Little footpaths, however, led into the city, so that one did not have to go by the public gates. Jesus had often made use of these paths.

The whole pool had hitherto been out of use, for it as well as its surroundings had been allowed to fall to decay. Like many old sanctuaries of our own day, it was quite neglected. Only some poor people with lively faith still held it in veneration and visited it. After the healing of the

May 25–30, AD 33

paralytic by Jesus, the pool was again more frequented, though all the more hateful to the Pharisees. The outer walls were in some places quite in ruins, and many parts of the terraces were in a dilapidated condition. But now all was repaired. The fallen walls were partly replaced by movable screens, and from the pool to the synagogue was raised a covered tent-way.

The old synagogue, which was now erected into a church, was less hemmed in by buildings than the house of the Last Supper, whose court on one side adjoined a row of houses. I saw the apostles and disciples, after the Feast of Pentecost, working continually at the interior arrangements of the church. Peter, John, Andrew, and James the Less took turns in preaching at three different places around the pool and on the third terrace, upon which was Peter's chair of instruction. A great many of the faithful were always in attendance, and I often saw them prostrate on the ground in ardent prayer. Words cannot say what activity reigned throughout the whole community at all times. Weaving, plaiting, and every kind of work for the new church and for the poor were carried on.

The church was a large, long, quadrangular edifice with real windows high up in the walls. By means of steps in the wall, one could mount up on the outside to the flat roof, which was surrounded by a gallery. On it were three little cupolas that could be opened like draught holes. The inside, on the two lengths and one of the ends, was furnished with stone benches for the congregation, and the building was in all respects turned into a church. At one end was the altar, at such a distance from the wall that sufficient space was left behind for a sacristy, which was formed by wickerwork screens that reached from the altar to the side walls. These screens were covered in front with fine white stuff, on the other side with coarser. The altar was portable. It consisted of a long, four-cornered piece of wood covered, and resting on three steps. On either side, however, there was only a single step, which could be opened to allow carpets to be laid in, and the back of the altar likewise opened to receive the vestments. On it was a bell-shaped tabernacle with a fine white cover closed in front by two little metallic shields. There was a knob on top, by which it could be lifted. On either side of the tabernacle were branched lamps with burning wicks. The whole altar was enclosed by a white curtain with colored stripes, which was supported by a canopy. It hung down only a little below the top of the altar. The canopy itself formed a niche and depended by five straps from the hand of a figure embroidered by the holy women. It represented an old man in the robes of a high priest, a triangular halo around the head. It stood in a bowed posture, as if looking down through an opening in the cover, one hand outstretched as if giving a blessing, the other grasping the five straps of the canopy. The curtain was in one piece at the back, but in front it could be drawn to either side or closed with metal clasps.

From the raised altar down to the pulpit was a space set aside apart for the choir ceremonies of the apostles and disciples. After the holy Resurrection I saw them assembled every day in the Last Supper room for prayer in choir. The apostles stood along either side of the hall facing the Holy of Holies, while the disciples occupied the vestibule thrown open for the occasion. They sang and prayed in choirs. I saw Nicodemus, Joseph of Arimathea, and Obed present also. The blessed Virgin usually stood under the middle entrance of the vestibule, her face turned toward the Holy of Holies. She wore the long white mantle and was veiled. Jesus had himself arranged the choral service, and about the time of the eating of the fish at Tiberias, or perhaps during the meal itself, explained to the apostles the mysterious signification of this religious ceremony. He had repeated the same on the occasion of Thomas's touching his sacred wounds and giving testimony of his faith. Once also I saw that Jesus appeared to them while they were chanting in choir before daybreak. They daily assembled twice, in the evening till after dark, and before dawn in the morning. Below the pulpit the congregation was cut off from the choir by a grating, through many places of which the blessed sacrament could be reached to them. It was almost like the grating seen in cloisters. On either side of the pulpit there were small doors by which the apostles and disciples could enter the choir. The congregation was arranged in a certain order, the women separate from the men.

I saw the apostles and disciples going in procession with the blessed sacrament from the house of the Last Supper to the new church. Before setting out, Peter, standing in the entrance to the courtyard and surrounded by about twenty of the disciples, delivered a public discourse before many people. He spoke in fiery words. Many Jews ran to hear, and tried to interrupt him by advancing objections, but their efforts were fruitless. The discourse over, the procession wound down to the new church near the pool, Peter bearing in his hands the chalice containing the blessed sacrament. The chalice was covered with a white linen, something like a bag, which was suspended from his

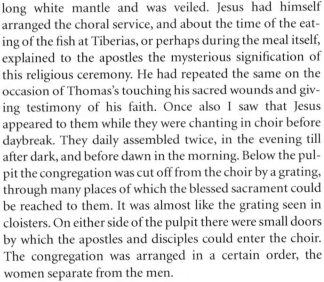

May 31, AD 33
Sunday, Daybreak

neck. The blessed Virgin walked after the apostles with the other women and the disciples. A part of the way was hung with screens of matting, and in the vicinity of the church the road was even covered in with awnings. The blessed sacrament was placed in the new tabernacle on the altar. The tray full of blessed bread had also been brought.

The floor of the church, like that of the house of the Last Supper in these latter days, was covered with colored carpets. The faithful entered barefoot.

The blessed sacrament was deposited in a vessel whose cover could be turned to one side. It lay in morsels on a plate that covered the bottom of the vessel and which could be raised by means of a handle, the more conveniently to get at them.

Peter Celebrates the First Holy Mass in the Last Supper Room

On the eighth day after Pentecost, I saw the apostles busily engaged the whole night in the house of the Last Supper, praying, etc. At *daybreak* they went with many of the disciples into the temple, to which the blessed Virgin and the holy women had preceded them. There appeared to be a feast going on, for in front of the entrance a triumphal arch had been erected upon which stood a figure holding a conqueror's sword. Beneath this arch Peter addressed a great crowd of people in powerful language. He told them openly that no punishment, neither scourging nor crucifixion, should deter them from publicly proclaiming Jesus Christ. He then entered the temple and preached from the teacher's chair that Jesus had so often occupied. Once I heard all the apostles and disciples interrupting Peter's discourse with a loud "Yes," as if in confirmation of his words. Afterward, when they were engaged in prayer, I saw a cloud of light hovering over the temple, and such rays streaming down upon them that the tiny flames of the lamps looked quite dim and red compared with them.

Toward eight o'clock that morning they left the temple. In the court of the pagans they formed in a long procession, two by two, first the apostles, after them the disciples, then the baptized and the newly converted. They proceeded across the cattle market to the sheep gate, out into the valley of Jehosaphat, and thence up Zion to the house of the Last Supper. The blessed Virgin and the other women had left the temple some time previously, in order to kneel alone before the blessed sacrament and pray. Magdalene prayed in the entrance hall sometimes standing, sometimes kneeling, or again prostrate on the ground, her arms outstretched. The other women had retired into their cells adjoining the church of Bethsaida. There they dwelt two together, occupying their time in washing and preparing the baptismal garments for the neophytes, and with the arrangement of such things for distribution.

When the procession reached the court of the Last Supper house, the new converts were ranged in order by the apostles outside the entrance hall. Peter and John went into the house and escorted the blessed Virgin to the door of the entrance hall. She was clothed in robes of ceremony. She wore the long white mantle with the embroidered facing down the sides, and over her veil the narrow scarf that hung down on either side and was kept in place by a wreath. Peter addressed the new converts and presented them to the blessed Virgin as to their common mother. He led them forward in bands of about twenty, one after another, and they received the benediction of the blessed Virgin.

After that I saw solemn service celebrated in the Last Supper room, into which the side halls and entrance hall were thrown open. In the sanctuary over the altar hung a festal wreath of green leaves and flowers. On either side of the chalice, that used at the Last Supper, were lighted lamps. The chalice was raised on a stand of some kind, and concealed under a little white cover. There was also on the altar a smaller chalice and some bread, both covered, and behind them a plate upon which stood two vessels, one for water, the other for wine. The plate was put aside; then the water vessel was placed at one end of the altar, the wine vessel at the other.

Peter, vested in his episcopal mantle, celebrated holy mass. John and James the Less served him. I saw all the ceremonies performed just as Jesus had performed them at the institution of the holy eucharist: the offertory, the pouring of wine into the chalice, the washing of the fingers, and the consecration. Wine and water were poured at different sides of the altar, on one end of which were lying the rolls of scripture. They were written in two columns and, by means of pegs placed higher or lower on the desk that supported them, they could be rolled or unrolled. When one leaf was read, it was thrown over the desk. There were many leaves lying one over another. After Peter had communicated, he handed his two assistants the sacrament, the bread and the chalice. Then John handed the sacrament first to the blessed Virgin, then to the apostles and the six disciples, who afterward received priestly ordination, and to many others. The communicants were kneeling, before them a narrow linen cloth, which two held on either side. I did not see the faithful partake of the chalice.

The six disciples who now received ordination were thereby advanced to a rank above the disciples, though below that of the apostles. Mary brought the vestments for them and laid them on the altar. The disciples ordained were Zacchaeus, Nathaniel, Joseph Barsabbas, Barnabas, John Mark, and Eliud, a son of the aged Simeon. They knelt, two by two, before Peter, who addressed them and read prayers from a little roll. John and James held lights in one hand and laid the other on their shoulders, while Peter imposed his on their head. Peter cut some hair from their head and placed it on the altar in the little plate; then he anointed their head and fingers from a box that John was holding. The vestments were next put on, the stole being crossed first under the arm and then in front over the breast. I saw that the ceremonies, though more solemn, were shorter than at the present day. At the close of the solemnity, Peter blessed the faithful with the large chalice of the Last Supper in which reposed the blessed sacrament.

Mary and the other women went after that to the church of the pool of Bethesda. The apostles, disciples, and the neophytes went thither also in procession with singing. Mary prayed there kneeling before the altar in the choir. Peter gave an instruction from the pulpit in reference to the order to be observed in the new community. No one, he said, was to have more than the others. All must share what they had and provide for the poor newcomers. His discourse, moreover, embodied thanks for the Savior's graces, and blessings upon the community.

Baptism was next administered, and several of the apostles were engaged in it. Two laid their hands upon the neophytes who, holding the railing of the little bridge that led to the pump, bowed their head to the stream issuing from it. Peter, who had put on his girdle over his white garment, turned the stream three times with his hand over the head of the neophyte, pronouncing the words at the same moment. I often saw a radiant cloud dissolving over the baptized, or a ray of light falling upon them. I saw that they were marvelously strengthened and, as it were, transfigured, transformed. It was most touching to see people from far-off countries leaving all that belonged to them, and coming hither to form one with the community of Jesus. At the edge of the pool burned a light on a pole, just such a one as those used by the guards at the Holy Sepulcher.

That evening in the entrance hall of the house of the Last Supper a meal was spread during which the blessed Virgin sat at table with the apostles, Joseph of Arimathea, Nicodemus, and Lazarus.

First General Communion of the New Converts • Choice of the Seven Deacons

ALL the baptized since Pentecost were instructed in the Bethsaida church upon the most blessed sacrament and prepared for its reception by six of the apostles robed in long white garments. They received it at the Holy Mass celebrated by Peter in the Bethsaida church, assisted by two of the apostles. Peter wore over his long, white robe and broad girdle with its flowing ends, a mantle that was taken out from the chest formed in the back of the altar. It was red and shining gold. It was like a large cape, deep in the back and pointed in front; and it fell so low over the shoulders that only the girdle could be seen at the side. It was fastened on the breast with three little shields. On the middle one just in front of the breast was the representation of a figure holding a loaf in one hand. The lowest shield, that nearest the points, or the ends of the mantle, bore on it a cross. On either shoulder was a figure formed of precious stones.

The altar was covered first with a red and over that a white transparent cloth, on which was laid another little white linen cloth like a corporal. On an oval plate lay a little pile of white bread sliced very thin and furrowed with lines for breaking. Beside it stood a white bowl with a foot like a low chalice, or ciborium, in which after being consecrated by Peter the bread broken into morsels was placed for distribution among the faithful. Besides all this, the chalice used at the Last Supper was standing full of wine on the altar. When, during holy mass, Peter uttered the words of consecration over the bread and wine, I saw the bread become luminous, while above the altar, as if issuing from a cloud, appeared a resplendent hand. It accompanied the movements of Peter's hand as he blessed the bread and wine, and did not disappear till all dispersed after receiving communion.

The apostles and disciples were the first to receive the blessed sacrament from Peter after his own communion. When the bowl, or ciborium, was emptied, Peter replenished it from the plate on the altar, and then proceeded with the distribution of the sacred species. The chalice also was handed by him to the apostles and to all the others. The communicants were so numerous that the church could not contain them, and many had to stand outside. The first to receive holy communion left the church in order to allow others to enter. The communicants did not kneel, but while receiving stood reverently bowed.

Before choosing the seven deacons, I saw the apostles gathered around Peter in the Last Supper room, where they assisted him in a solemn ceremony. They accompanied him to the Holy of Holies, where John laid upon him the mantle, another placed the mitre on his head, and another put the crosier into his hand. After all had received communion from Peter, robed in his sacred vestments and surrounded by the apostles, he addressed in the entrance hall a large crowd of disciples and new converts. He said among other things that it was not becoming for the Word of God to be neglected for the care of clothing and nourishment; consequently Lazarus, Nicodemus, and Joseph of Arimathea could not with propriety any longer oversee the temporal interests of the community as they had hitherto done, for they now had become priests. Then he added some words relative to the order observed in the distribution of alms, of household affairs, of widows and orphans. Stephen, a slender, handsome youth, stepped forward and offered himself for the services needed. Among others that did the same, I recognized Parmenas, who was one of the elder disciples. There were among them some Moors, still very young, who had not yet received the Holy Spirit. Peter laid his hands upon them and the stole crossed under their arm. While he did so a light was infused upon those that had not yet received the Holy Spirit. After that the treasures and goods of the community were delivered over to the seven deacons, and for their accommodation was assigned Joseph of Arimathea's house, which was not far from that of John Mark. John Mark helped them. The money was carried on asses, and consisted of bags filled with different kinds of coins. Some were like little stalks twisted into screws, others like stamped plate strung together on a little chain, and others again were in small, oval leaves. Most of the movables consisted of large packs of different stuffs, coverlets, clothing, also numbers of vessels and various kinds of furniture suitable for plain housekeeping.

On the day following the giving over of Joseph of Arimathea's house to the deacons, I saw the apostles dispersing into Judea.

Peter wrought more miracles than all the others. He drove out devils, raised the dead—yes, I even saw an angel going before him to the people and telling them that they should do penance and ask Peter for help.

I saw the healing of the lame man. It was about three hours after noon when Peter and John went up to the temple with several of the disciples. Mary and some of the holy women went too. A lame man had been brought on a litter and laid at the door of the temple. Peter and John, on their arrival, exchanged some words with him. Then I saw Peter standing under an awning in the open square on the south side of the temple, his back turned to that part of the edifice in which was the altar of sacrifice, and addressing the people in a fiery speech. During his instruction I saw the door of egress beset by soldiers and priests conferring together. And now I saw Peter and John, as they turned again toward the temple, accosted by the lame man and petitioned for alms. He was lying outside the door, a perfect cripple, leaning on the left elbow, while vainly striving to raise something with the crutch in his right hand. Peter said to him: "Look up!" and when the man obeyed, he continued: "I have no silver nor gold, but what I have, I give to thee! In the name of Jesus Christ of Nazareth, arise and walk!" Peter raised him by the right hand, while John grasped him under the shoulder. The man, full of joy and vigor, stood upon his feet, and I saw him leaping about cured, and running with shouts of triumph through the halls of the temple.

Twelve Jewish priests who were there seated on their chairs looked, with outstretched necks, in the direction of the tumult, and as the crowd around the cured man increased at every moment, they left their seats and withdrew. Peter and John went into the forecourt, and I saw the former mounting the teacher's chair from which Jesus had taught as a boy of twelve. The cured man was standing before him encompassed by a multitude of people, some from the city, others strangers from a distance. Peter preached long and in words full of inspiration. It was already dark when I saw him, along with John and the cured man, seized by the temple soldiers and thrown into a prison near the judgment hall in which he had denied the Lord. Next day all three were taken by the soldiers, and with much ill usage, up the same flight of steps upon which Jesus had stood, and there tried by Caiaphas and the other priests. Peter spoke with great warmth, after which they were set free.

The rest of the apostles had passed the night in the house of the Last Supper in continual prayer for the prisoners. When Peter and John returned and told them all that had taken place, their joy burst out into a loud act of thanksgiving, and the whole house shook, as if the Lord wanted to remind them thereby that he was still among them and had heard their prayer. Upon that, James the Less said that Jesus, when he appeared to him alone on the mountain in Galilee, had told him that after Peter and John, on going up to the temple, would be imprisoned and then set free, they should keep themselves somewhat retired for awhile.

On this news, I saw the apostles shutting up everything, and Peter, with the blessed sacrament suspended round his neck in a bag, going with the others to Bethany. They made the journey in three bands. The Mother of God and other women went also. While in Bethany, the apostles preached enthusiastically at the disciples' inn, at Simon's, and at Lazarus's. When they again returned to Jerusalem, they were more enthusiastic, more determined than ever. Peter, when teaching in the house of the Last Supper and in the church at the pool of Bethesda, declared that now was the time to discover who had preserved the Spirit sent by Jesus, now was the time to labor, to suffer persecution, and to give up all things. Whoever did not feel himself strong enough for this should depart. I saw that about a hundred of those that had most recently joined the community withdrew from the great crowd in the Bethsaida church.

When Peter, accompanied by John and seven other apostles, went again to teach in the temple, he found numbers of sick lying on litters under tents in the valley of Jehosaphat. Many others were lying around the temple in the court of the pagans and even up as far as the steps. I saw Peter performing most of the cures. The others did indeed effect some, but they helped Peter more than they cured. Peter cured those only that believed and were desirous of joining the community. In those places in which the sick lay in two rows opposite each other, I saw cured, Peter willing it, those upon whom his shadow fell, while he was busied with the opposite row.

THE LIFE OF MARY AFTER CHRIST'S ASCENSION

The Blessed Virgin Goes with John to the Neighborhood of Ephesus

ABOUT one year after the crucifixion of our Lord, Stephen was stoned, though no further persecution of the apostles took place at that time. The rising settlement of new converts around Jerusalem, however, was dissolved, the Christians dispersed, and some were murdered. *A few years later*, a new storm arose against them. Then it was that the blessed Virgin, who until that time had dwelt in the small house near the Cenacle and in Bethany, allowed herself to be conducted by John to the region of Ephesus, where the Christians had already made settlements. This happened a short time after the imprisonment of Lazarus and his sisters by the Jews and their setting out over the sea. John returned again to Jerusalem, where the other apostles still were. James the Greater was one of the first of the apostles who, after the division of the different countries had been made, left Jerusalem and started for Spain. I saw him on his departure in Bethlehem, where he concealed himself in the crib cave, and then with his companions secretly wandering through the country, for there were spies in search of them with orders to prevent their leaving Palestine. But James had friends in Joppa, and he succeeded in embarking. He sailed first to Ephesus in order to visit Mary, and thence to Spain. Shortly before his death, he visited Mary and John a second time in their home at Ephesus. Here Mary told him that his death would soon take place in Jerusalem. She encouraged and consoled him. James took

after trod the same. I saw James led out toward Mount Calvary. He continued his preaching all along the way, and thereby made many converts. When they bound his hands, he remarked: "Ye can bind my hands, but ye cannot bind the blessing, ye cannot bind my tongue!" A lame man was sitting by the roadside. He called to James, begging him to extend his hand and help him. James responded: "Come thou to me, and reach out thine hand to me!" The lame man arose, seized the fettered hands of the apostle,

Boat on the Shore near Joppa

leave of her and his brother John, and started for Jerusalem. It was at this period that he was brought into contact with Hermogenes and his pupil, both of whom he converted by his miracles. James was several times apprehended and taken before the synagogue. I saw that *shortly before Easter*, while he was preaching on a hill in an open square of Jerusalem, he was arrested. It must have been about this time, for I saw the customary encampments around the city. James was not imprisoned long. He was sentenced to death in the same place of trial as Jesus. The whole place, however, had undergone a change. Those sites upon which Jesus had trodden were no longer in existence, and I have always thought that none other ever

and was cured. I saw also the man that had denounced him. He was named Josias. His heart smote him. He hurried to the apostle and begged forgiveness. He declared himself for Christ and was likewise put to death. James asked him whether he desired baptism, and when Josias answered yes, he embraced and kissed him, saying: "Thou wilt be baptized in thy blood!" I saw a woman running with her blind child to James on the place of execution, and imploring its restoration to sight.

James was at first stationed near Josias on an elevated place, and the sentence proclaimed aloud. Then he was laid on a large stone, his hands bound to it, his eyes blindfolded, and his head struck off. This took place in the twelfth year after Jesus's death, or between 46 and 47 after the birth of Christ. I did not see James present at the death of the blessed Virgin in Ephesus. There was another in his place, a relative of the holy family, and one of the first among the seventy-two disciples. Mary died in the year 48 after the birth of Christ, thirteen years and two months after Christ's ascension. This was shown me in numbers, not in writing. First, I saw IV, and then VIII, which denoted the year 48; lastly, I saw XIII, and two full months.

The blessed Virgin's dwelling was not in Ephesus itself, but from three to four hours distant. It stood on a height upon which several Christians from Judea, among them some of the holy women related to her, had taken up their abode. Between this height and Ephesus glided, with many a crooked curve, a little river. The height sloped obliquely toward Ephesus. From the southeast one beheld the city as if lying just before him, at the foot of a mountain, but on nearer approach, he found the latter stretching still further away. From Ephesus, before which I saw great avenues with yellow fruit strewing the ground, narrow footpaths led up to this wild, overgrown height, upon which, to the circumference of about an hour, stretched a very solitary but fertile plain covered with smooth-trunked, wide-spreading trees, and containing clean rocky caves. These latter had, by means of light woodwork, been converted into hermitages by the early Christian settlers who had fled thither for refuge. These abodes, along with others that stood alone scattered here and there over the whole country, gave the region the appearance of a little village. From the top of this elevated plain, which was nearer to the sea than Ephesus, one could see both the city itself and the sea with its numerous islands. Not very far from the Christian settlement rose a castle whose occupant appeared to be a deposed king. John often visited him and finally converted him. At a later period, this place became a bishopric. Among the Christians settled here, I saw women, children, and some men. Not all of these people had contact with the blessed Virgin. Only some holy women came now and then for a visit, or to render her some assistance, for they saw to her needs. The locality was very retired and seldom visited by anyone, for no highway ran through it. The people of Ephesus did not trouble themselves about the little colony, and so they lived as if forgotten. The soil was fruitful, and the settlers owned some gardens and orchards. The only animals I saw in this place were wild goats.

Before John brought the blessed Virgin to this settlement, he had built for her a dwelling of stone very similar to her own at Nazareth. It stood among trees, and was divided into two apartments by the fireplace in the center. The fire was on the earth opposite the entrance, in a kind of furnace formed by the wall, which rose up on either side like steps to the roof of the house. In it was cut the flue, from which the smoke escaped through a tube that protruded above the flat roof.

The front room of the house was separated from the back by wicker screens placed on either side of the fireplace. Similar screens rested against the walls, right and left, the whole length of the house. They were used to form little apartments when needed, and could be easily put aside when the room was to be used as one. Mary's maid-servant used one of them as a sleeping apartment, and the others were occupied by the holy women of the settlement when they happened to come on a visit of some length.

To the right and left on either side of the fireplace, light doors opened through the wicker partition into the two back rooms, whose end walls were rounded and very pleasing to the eye, covered as they were with neatly wrought woodwork. The roof was rounded on the sides, and the beams above it were bound with wainscoting and twisted work, and ornamented with some simple imitation of foliage. In the most remote space of the rounded end Mary had her oratory, before which hung a curtain. Here in a niche in the wall was a kind of closet which, like a certain kind of tabernacle, could be made to open and close by revolving. In it was a crucifix about the length of one's arm. The arms were set into the trunk in an obliquely raised direction like that of Christ. This most simply carved crucifix was, I think, made by the blessed Virgin herself and John. It was constructed of three different kinds of wood: the whitish trunk was cypress wood, one arm of a brownish color was cedar, the other, which was yellowish, was made from wood of the palm tree. The top piece that supported the inscription was of polished yellow olive wood. The foot of the crucifix was set firmly in a stone like Christ's in the rock of Golgotha. At its foot lay a strip of parchment on which were inscribed some words of the Savior. The figure representing the Lord was formed simply of dark-colored lines cut into the cross. On either side of the crucifix stood a pot of flowers. I saw also lying near the cross a little linen, of which I had the intuitive knowledge that it was the one with which the blessed Virgin, after the taking down of the sacred body from the cross, had cleansed the wounds from blood; for as soon as I saw the little cloth, I had a vision of that exercise of her most sacred mother-love, in which she held the little linen in the same way as does the priest at the holy Mass when he is purifying the chalice. Mary had a similar crucifix, though only half as large, in the alcove in which she slept.

On the right of the oratory and against the rounded wall, was the alcove of the blessed Virgin. It was formed of two lightly woven screens of sapwood in its natural color. These stood at the head and the foot of the couch respectively; in front hung two curtains of tapestry that could be drawn and looped to either side. The couch was placed along the wall, which too was hung with tapestry. It was the length and breadth of a small bed, and consisted of a wooden frame about a foot and a half high. Over it a tester was stretched and fastened on the knobs of the four corners. The sides of the frame also were covered with tapestry, which hung down to the floor and was fringed with tassels. A round roll served as a pillow. The cover was of brownish checkered material. The ceiling of this little sleeping apartment was the loftiest in the house. It too was formed of wickerwork and, from the four corners to the center, ran up into a concave dome from which was suspended a branched lamp.

Here, on the last days before her death, I saw the blessed Virgin lying entirely enveloped in a white sleeping sheet; even her arms were wound up in it. The veil over her head was thrown up in crossfolds, but when conversing with men, she lowered it. Even her hands were uncovered only when she was alone. During those last days, I did not see her taking anything excepting the juice of a grapelike fruit with yellow berries, which the maid pressed out for her into a little cup.

By the wall to the left of the oratory and directly opposite the alcove, a recess was formed by means of wicker screens in which clothes and other things were kept. Besides some veils and girdles and the upper garment that Mary always wore when making the holy Way of the Cross, there hung in that recess two long robes, one white, the other sky-blue. The latter was a very delicate blue, and there was likewise a mantle of the same color. This was the robe in which Mary was married to Joseph. I saw too that Mary kept near her many of the garments of her divine Son, among them his woven tunic.

From that recess to the alcove extended a curtain by which the oratory could be concealed. When at work, Mary used to sit before this curtain and just between the recess and the alcove.

In this most silent and solitary little dwelling,† from which the abodes of the other settlers were distant about a quarter of an hour, lived the blessed Virgin alone with her maid, who procured for her the little that she needed for her support. There was no man in the house, and only at times was Mary visited by John or some other traveling apostle and disciple. Once I saw John entering the house. He was thin and looked older. He wore a long white garment girdled in folds, but which was now tucked up. He laid it aside on entering, and taking out another from under his mantle, put it on instead. There was an inscription in letters on this second one. He laid a maniple on his arm. The blessed Virgin was in a little private room from

which the maid conducted her to John. She was enveloped in a white robe and looked very weak. Her face was, as it were, transparent and white as snow. She appeared to be soaring upward on the wings of her ardent desires. Her whole life after her Son's ascension into heaven was stamped by an ever-increasing longing to be freed from earth. She retired with John to her oratory, pulled a band, or strap, upon which the tabernacle in the niche revolved and disclosed the crucifix of the length of one's arm standing between two vases of natural flowers. After Mary and John had prayed long on their knees before the crucifix, the latter arose and took from a metal box a roll of fine woollen stuff. Opening this, he took out a small piece of white bread, in shape four-cornered, that was carefully folded in white linen cloths. It was the most blessed sacrament, which with some words he gave to Mary. He presented to her no cup.

Mary's "Holy Way of the Cross" near Ephesus • She Visits Jerusalem

IN the neighborhood of her dwelling, the blessed Virgin had herself erected the stations of the Holy Way of the Cross. I saw her at first going alone and measuring off all the special points of the bitter Passion according to the number of steps which, after the death of her Son, she had so often counted. At the end of each definite number, she raised a memorial stone in remembrance of the special suffering there endured by her divine Son. I saw her with a sharp instrument, a stylus, recording what there had taken place and how many steps it was to it. If a tree happened to

† In 1891, after reading Anne Catherine Emmerich's description of Mary's home at Ephesus, two Lazarite priests from Smyrna set off to search for it. After five days' search in the mountainous area south of Ephesus they were guided by some local people to a ruined building located on the summit of an isolated hill. The site, and also the plan of the house, exactly fitted Anne Catherine's description. The priests learned that the place had been venerated down through the ages as Panaya Kapulu ("The House of the Holy Virgin"). Local villagers made annual pilgrimages there each year on August 15, the Festival of the Assumption of the Blessed Virgin Mary. Subsequent archeological investigations have confirmed the authenticity of Panaya Kapulu. The foundations of the original house date back to the first century. In the seventh century the building appears to have been enlarged and converted into a chapel in which Mary's Oratory became the main altar. At that time the entry was added and the fireplace wall removed. In 1898 the original hearthstones were discovered under the existing floor, still containing some ashes, petrified with age. In 1951 the Turkish government built a road up to the Holy Hill and the Society of Panaya, founded by the Archbishop of Smyrna, completely restored the ruins in accordance with the description in Anne Catherine's visions. In 1954 the Little Brothers of Jesus accepted the post of serving at Panaya Kapulu, now known as the Shrine of Our Lady of the Assumption.

be standing on that particular spot, she marked it as one of the stations, of which there were twelve. The way led to a grove, and there was the Holy Sepulcher represented by a cave in the side of a hill. After all the stations were definitively marked, the blessed Virgin made the Holy Way with her maid in silent meditation. When they reached a station, they sat down, meditated upon the mystery and its signification, and prayed. By degrees, the whole route was improved and more beautifully arranged. John gave orders for regular monuments to be set up. I saw also the cave representing the sepulcher being cleared out and made more suitable for prayer. The memorial stones lay in hollows of greater or less depth, which were covered with grass and flowers and surrounded by a hedge. They were of polished white marble. The thickness of the underlying surface could not be seen, on account of the grass. The faithful, when performing this devotion, carried a cross about a foot in length with a support which they placed in the little hollow on the upper surface of the stone while they were meditating, either kneeling or prostrate on their face. The path that ran in a hollow around the stone was wide enough for two persons to walk side by side. There were twelve such stones. When the devotion was ended, each was covered with a mat. The sides and base of all bore similar inscriptions in Hebrew characters, but the hollow places in which they rested differed, some being larger, others smaller. The first station, or that of the Mount of Olives, was in a little valley. There was a small cave in it, in which several could kneel together. The Mount Golgotha station was the only one not in a hollow. It was on a hill. For that of the Holy Sepulcher, one had to cross another hill on whose opposite side stood the memorial stone in a hollow. Thence one descended to the foot of the hill and into the tomb itself, in which later on Mary's remains rested. I think this tomb is still in existence under the surface of the earth, and that it will come to light someday.

Whenever I saw Mary making the Holy Way of the Cross, she wore an overgarment that fell in folds down the back as far as the feet. It was laid over the shoulders and was fastened under the collar by a button. It was girded round the waist, thus taking in the brownish underdress. It appeared to be a festal robe, for in accordance with ancient Jewish customs, a similar one had been worn also by Anne. Her hair was concealed under a yellowish cap, which was pointed on the forehead and gathered together in folds at the back of the head. A black veil of soft material hung down far below the waist. In this dress I saw her making the Way of the Cross. She had worn it at the crucifixion under the mantle of prayer, or mourning, which entirely enveloped her, and she wore it now only when performing this devotion. When at work in the house, she laid it aside.

The blessed Virgin was now very advanced in years, but she had in her appearance no other mark of age than that of a great longing, which at length effectuated her glorification. She was inexpressibly grave. I never saw her laugh. The older she grew, the whiter and more transparent became her face. She was thin, but I saw no wrinkle, no sign of decay in her. She was like a spirit. [L.22]

Once I saw the blessed Virgin and five other women making the Holy Way, along which she went first. She was perfectly white and transparent, indescribably touching to look upon. It seemed to me that she was now making the devotion for the last time. Among the holy women who were praying with her, there were several that had become acquainted with her in the first year of Jesus's teaching. One was a relative of the prophetess Anna, and another was the granddaughter of a maternal aunt of Elizabeth. I saw two of the women making the Way of the Cross by turns every morning and evening.

After Mary had lived three years in the settlement near Ephesus, she conceived a great desire to visit Jerusalem, so John and Peter escorted her thither. Several apostles were there assembled, of whom I remember Thomas. I think it was a council, and Mary assisted the apostles with her advice. On her arrival, I saw her in the evening twilight visiting, before she entered the city, the Mount of Olives, Mount Calvary, the Holy Sepulcher, and all the Holy Places around Jerusalem. The Mother of God was so sad, so moved by compassion, that she could scarcely walk. Peter and John supported her under the arms.

A year and a half before her death, she made one more journey from Ephesus to Jerusalem, and I saw her again visiting the Holy Places. She was unspeakably sorrowful, and she continually sighed: "O my Son! My Son!" When she came to the back gate of that palace where she had first seen Jesus passing with the cross and where he fell, she was so agitated by the painful remembrance that she too sank to the ground. Her companions thought her dying. They removed her to Zion, upon which the Cenacle was still standing, and in one of whose buildings she took up her abode. For several days she appeared to be so weak and so near death that her friends began to think of preparing her a tomb. She herself made choice of a cave on the Mount of Olives, and the apostles had a beautiful tomb built there by a Christian stonecutter. Many were of the opinion that she would really die; and so the report of her death spread abroad. But she recovered sufficient strength to journey back to Ephesus where, a year and a half later, she did indeed die. The tomb prepared for her on the Mount of Olives was ever after held in reverence, and at a later period a church was built over it. John Damascene, as I was told in vision, wrote from hearsay that the blessed

Virgin died in Jerusalem and was buried there. Her death, her assumption into heaven, and the site of her tomb, as I believe, God has allowed to be subjects of uncertain tradition that the pagan sentiments of the time might not penetrate Christianity, for the blessed Virgin might otherwise have been adored as a goddess.

The Apostles Arrive to be Present at the Blessed Virgin's Death

AS the blessed Virgin felt her end approaching, in accordance with the directions of her divine Son, she called the apostles to her by prayer. She was now in her sixty-third year. At the time of Christ's birth she was in her fifteenth. Before his ascension Jesus had made known to his most holy mother what she should say at the end of her earthly career to the apostles and some of the disciples who should be with her. He told her also that she should bless them, and that it would conduce very much to their welfare and eternal salvation. He entrusted to her also certain spiritual labors for the general good, which being accomplished, her longing after heaven was to be realized. Jesus had at the same time made known to Magdalene that she was to live concealed in the wilderness, and that Martha was to establish a community of women. He added that he himself would always be with them.

At the prayer of the blessed Virgin, the apostles received, through angels, an admonition to repair to her at Ephesus. In the various places in which they were, they had erected little churches here and there. Many of them were constructed merely of plaited rods, or branches, covered with clay, but all were of the same form as Mary's house, that is, three-cornered in the back. They were provided with altars for the celebration of holy mass. The journeys of the apostles, so distant, so exceedingly remote, were not made without divine assistance. Although they themselves were perhaps unconscious of it at the time, yet I do not doubt that they passed through many dangers in a supernatural manner. I often saw them walking unnoticed through the midst of a crowd. I have likewise seen that the miracles wrought by them among the various pagan nations were very numerous and of a different kind from those recorded of them in the holy scriptures. They labored everywhere according to the peculiar needs of the people. I saw that they carried about them the bones of the prophets or those of the first Christian martyrs, which relics they placed before them in time of prayer or when offering the holy sacrifice.

When called to Mary, Peter was in the region of Antioch with another apostle. Andrew, who had shortly before been in Jerusalem, but had there been persecuted, was not far from Peter. I saw them both on their way to Ephesus at places not very distant from each other. They passed the nights in those open inns that are met along the roads in hot countries. As Peter was lying one night near a wall, a resplendent youth approached him, took him by the hand, and bade him arise and hasten to Mary. On the way, the youth said, he would meet Andrew. Peter, who had grown stiff from age and fatigue, rose to a sitting posture and, clasping his hands round his knees to support himself, listened to the angel's words. Then he stood up, put on his mantle, girded himself, took his staff, and started on his journey. He soon came up with Andrew, who had been called by the same apparition. After traveling some distance they were met by Thaddeus, who also had received a similar warning. They journeyed together to Mary, with whom they found John.

Judas Thaddeus and Simon were in Persia when they received their summons. Thomas, who was in stature thick and short and had reddish-brown or auburn hair, was of all the apostles the farthest off. He arrived only after Mary's death. When the angel came to call him, he was praying in a hut built of reeds. With one very poor, simple servant, I saw him sailing alone in a little boat far over the waters. Then he journeyed across the country, turning aside from all the cities. A disciple now accompanied him. Thomas was in India when he received the warning. Before receiving it he had determined to go into Tartary, and he could not bring himself to change his plans. He always wanted to do so much, therefore it was that he was often behind time. So off he started northward almost across China, where Russia now is. Here he was called a second time. He obeyed the summons and hurried to Ephesus. The servant with him was a Tartar whom he had baptized. Thomas did not return to Tartary after Mary's death. He was pierced with a lance in India. I have seen that he set up a stone in this last-named country, upon which he knelt in prayer, and upon which the marks of his knees remained impressed. He told the people that when the sea would reach that stone, another would here preach Jesus Christ.

John had shortly before been in Jericho, for he often journeyed to Palestine. He usually abode in Ephesus, however, and the country around. Bartholomew was in Asia east of the Red Sea. He was handsome and very active, his complexion fair and his forehead high. He had large eyes, black curly hair, and a short, crisp beard, black and parted on the chin. He had already converted a king and all the royal family. Paul was not summoned. Those only were called that were related or acquainted with the holy family. Peter, Andrew, and John were the first to reach the blessed Virgin's house. She was already near death. She was lying calmly on her couch in her sleeping place. I saw the maidservant looking very sorrowful in this and that corner of the house, also outdoors, where she prayed prostrate with outstretched arms. I saw also two of Mary's sisters and five disciples coming together to the house. All looked tired and exhausted. They carried staves of various kinds, each according to his rank. They wore, under their hooded mantles of white wool, long albs of the same material fastened all the way down the front with little leather straps slit in the middle over little rolls like buttons. Both mantle and alb were girded high when traveling. Some had a pouch hanging from their girdle at the side. They embraced each other tenderly when they met. Many wept from mingled feelings of joy and sorrow at meeting on such an occasion. On entering the house, they laid aside their mantles, staves, pouches, and girdles; allowed their white robes to fall in broad folds down to their feet, and each put on a wide girdle inscribed with letters, which he had brought with him. Then with deep emotion they drew near Mary's couch to salute her, though she could now say only a few words. I did not see the travelers taking anything on their arrival, excepting some kind of beverage from a little flask, with which each one came provided. They did not sleep in the house, but outside under light awnings, which were put up on posts against the walls, and which were divided off and enclosed by movable screens and wickerwork.

I saw that the first to arrive prepared in the front apartment of the house a place suitable for prayer and offering the holy sacrifice. There was an altar covered with a red and over that a white cloth, and on it stood a crucifix, white like mother-of-pearl, and in shape like a Maltese cross. The cross could be opened. It contained five compartments, likewise cross-shaped. The middle one held the most blessed sacrament, while the others were intended respectively for chrism, oil, cotton, and salt. It was not quite a span, or nine inches, in length. Each of the apostles when traveling carried one like it on his breast. It was in this cross that Peter took to Mary the holy communion, during the reception of which the apostles stood bowing low, ranged in two rows from the altar down to her couch. The altar, before which was a stand with rolls of scripture hanging over it, was not in the center of the front apartment, where the fireplace stood, for that was still in use. It was placed near the wall on the right, and was put up and taken down every day.

When the apostles went all together into Mary's little sleeping chamber in order to take leave of her, they wore their long white albs and broad mantles. The screens that separated the front from the back of the house had been removed. The disciples and holy women remained standing in the front apartment. I saw that Mary sat upright, that the apostles knelt in turn at the side of her couch, and

that she prayed over each and blessed him with her hands laid upon him crosswise. She did the same to the disciples and to the women. One of the latter, who stood quite bent in two over Mary, received an embrace from her. When Peter stepped up to the couch, I saw that he had a roll of scriptures in his hand. Mary then addressed them in a body, and did all that Jesus had in Bethany directed her to do. I saw also that she told John what was to be done with her remains, and that he should see that her clothes were divided between her own maidservant and a maiden of the neighborhood who came sometimes to render her service. As she spoke, she pointed to the press, or partition, and I saw the maid going to it, opening and closing it.

Death, Burial, and Assumption of the Blessed Virgin

AND now the altar with its covers, one red, the other white, was placed in front of the crucifix of the blessed Virgin's own oratory. Peter here celebrated the Holy Mass with the same ceremonies as I had seen him first observe in the church at the pool of Bethesda. Tapers, not lamps, were burning on the altar. Mary was in a sitting posture on her couch during the whole celebration. Peter was vested in the large mantle and the pallium, whose colors glanced from white to red. These he wore over the white robe. The four apostles assisting him were also vested in festal mantles. After the communion, Peter gave the blessed sacrament to all present. During this Holy Mass, Philip arrived from Egypt. Weeping bitterly, he received the benediction of the blessed Virgin, and after the others the blessed sacrament.

Peter bore the blessed sacrament to Mary in the cross hanging on his breast, and John carried on a shallow dish the chalice containing the most sacred blood. This chalice was white, small as if for pouring, and of the same shape as that used at the Last Supper. Its stem was so short that it could be held with two fingers only. Thaddeus now brought forward a little incense basin. Peter first gave the blessed Virgin the last anointing, just as that sacrament is administered at the present day. Next he administered holy communion, which she received sitting up without support. Then she sank back again on her pillow, and after the apostles had offered a short prayer, she received the chalice from John, but not now in so upright a posture.

After communion, Mary spoke no more. Her countenance, blooming and smiling as in youth, was raised above. I no longer saw the roof of her chamber, and the lamp appeared to be suspended in the open air. A pathway of light arose from Mary up to the Heavenly Jerusalem, up to the throne of the most holy Trinity. On either side of this pathway I saw clouds of light out of which gazed angelic faces. Mary raised her arms to the Heavenly Jerusalem. Her body with all its wrappings was floating so high above the couch that I could see under it. A figure of light, also with upraised arms, appeared to issue from Mary. The two choirs of angels united under this figure and soared up with it, as if separating it from the body, which now sank back upon the couch, the hands crossed upon the breast. Many holy souls, among whom I recognized Joseph, Anne, Joachim, John the Baptist, Zechariah, and Elizabeth, came to meet her. But up she soared, followed by them, to her Son, whose wounds were flashing light far more brilliant than that which surrounded him. He received her and placed in her hand a scepter, pointing at the same time over the whole circumference of the earth. At last I saw—and the sight filled me with joy—a multitude of souls released from Purgatory and soaring up to heaven, and I received the surety that every year on the Feast of Mary's Assumption many of her devout clients are freed from Purgatory. The hour of Mary's death was made known to me as that of None, at which time also Jesus had died on the cross. Peter and John likewise must have seen the glory of Mary's blessed soul, for their faces were turned upward, but the other apostles were kneeling bowed to the ground. The body of the blessed Virgin lay radiant with light upon the couch, the eyes closed, the hands crossed upon the breast. All present knelt, adoring God.

At last the women covered the blessed remains with a sheet, put all the furniture of the house aside and covered it, even covering the fireplace. Then they veiled themselves and prayed together in a space in the front of the house, sometimes kneeling, sometimes sitting. The apostles too enveloped their head with the scarf they wore about their shoulders, and ranged in order for prayer. They took turns, two at a time, to kneel and pray at the head and feet of the blessed remains. I saw them exchanging places with one another four times in the day, and I likewise saw them making the Way of the Cross.

Andrew and Matthew were busy preparing the place of burial, which was the little grotto that Mary and John had arranged at the end of the Way of the Cross, to represent the Holy Sepulcher of Christ. It was not so large as Jesus's tomb, being scarcely as high as a man, and was surrounded by a little garden hedged in by stakes. A pathway ran obliquely down into it, and the stone couch, which was like a narrow altar, was hollowed on top to the shape of a body enveloped in its winding sheet, the head being a trifle higher than the foot. The station of Mount Calvary (the crucifixion) was on a hill nearby. No cross was erected on it, but there was one cut out on the stone. Andrew was

especially active in preparing the grotto, and setting up a door firmly in front of the tomb proper.

The blessed body was prepared by the women for burial. Among them I remember having seen a daughter of Veronica and John Mark's mother. They brought spices and pots of fresh herbs, in order to embalm it according to the Jewish custom. They closed the house, and worked by the light of lamps. They opened up the apartment back of the fireplace and removed the screens that enclosed the little alcove used by the blessed Virgin as a sleeping place, in order to have more room for their work of embalming. The wicker screens of the alcove were not again replaced, for immediately after the obsequies they, along with those of the clothes press, were put out of sight by the maidservant. Only the altar was allowed to remain standing before the crucifix in Mary's sleeping apartment. The whole house had now become like a little chapel in which the apostles prayed and celebrated the most holy and unbloody sacrifice. While the women were preparing the holy body for burial, the apostles prayed in choirs, sometimes in the front apartment, sometimes outside the house. The women went about their task most devoutly and reverently, just as had been done when preparing the most sacred body of Jesus for burial. The body of the blessed Virgin was lifted in the linen of the deathbed and laid in a long basket, which had a lid and which was filled with covers, so that when lying on them, it rose above the edge. The body was of a dry, indescribable whiteness as if shining with light, and of so little weight that, like a mere husk, it could be raised quite easily on the hands. The face was fresh and blooming. The women cut off some locks of hair to keep as relics. They laid bunches of herbs around the neck and throat, under the arms, and in the armpits.

Before the holy body was shrouded in its white garments and enveloped in the winding sheets, Peter celebrated the unbloody sacrifice on the altar of the oratory and gave holy communion to the other apostles. After that Peter and John approached the body in their mantles of ceremony. John carried a vessel of oil, with which Peter anointed, in the form of a cross and with accompanying prayers, the forehead, hands, and feet of the holy body, which was afterward entirely enveloped in linens by the women. They placed on the head a wreath of flowers, white, red, and sky-blue, as a symbol of Mary's virginity, and over the face a transparent veil, through which it could be seen encircled by the wreath. The feet also, which were bound up in aromatic herbs, could be traced through the linens that enveloped them. The arms and hands were bound crosswise on the breast. Thus prepared, the holy body was laid in a coffin of snow-white wood with a tightly fitting, arched cover, which was fastened down at the head, the foot, and in the middle, with gray straps. The coffin was then laid on a litter. Everything was done with the utmost solemnity, and all were penetrated with deep emotion. The sorrow of the mourners was more human and more openly expressed than at Jesus's burial, at which holy awe and reverence predominated.

When it was time to bear the coffin to the grotto, one half-hour distant, Peter and John raised it from the litter and carried it in their hands to the door of the house, outside of which it was again laid on the litter, which Peter and John then raised upon their shoulders. Six of the apostles thus carried it in turn. The coffin hung between the bearers as in a cradle, for the poles of the litter were run through leathern straps, or matting. Some of the apostles walked before the coffin praying, and after it came the women. Lamps, or lanterns on poles, were carried.

Before reaching the grotto, the litter was set down. Four of the apostles bore the coffin in, and placed it in the hollow of the tomb. All went, one by one, into the grotto, where they knelt in prayer before the holy body, honoring it and taking leave of it. Then the tomb was shut in by a wicker screen that extended from the front edge of the tomb to the top of the vaulted wall above. Before the entrance of the grotto they made a trench, which they planted so thickly with blooming flowers and bushes covered with berries that one could gain access to it only from the side, and that only by making his way through the underbrush.

On the night following the burial took place the bodily assumption of the blessed Virgin into heaven. I saw on this night several of the apostles and holy women in the little garden, praying and singing psalms before the grotto. I saw a broad pathway of light descend from heaven and rest upon the tomb. In it were circles of glory full of angels, in the midst of whom the resplendent soul of the blessed Virgin came floating down. Before her went her divine Son, the marks of his wounds flashing with light. In the innermost circle, that which surrounded the holy soul of Mary, the angels appeared like the faces of very young children; in the second circle, they were like those of children from six to eight years old; and in the outermost, like the faces of youths, I could clearly distinguish only the face, the rest of the figure consisting of perfectly transparent light. Encircling the head of the blessed

August 15, AD 44
9:30 PM

Virgin like a crown was a choir of blessed spirits. I know not what those present saw of all this. But I saw that some gazed up in amazement and adoration, while others cast themselves prostrate in fright upon the earth. These apparitions, becoming more and more distinct as they approached nearer, floated over the grotto, and another pathway of light issued from it and arose to the Heavenly Jerusalem. The blessed soul of Mary, floating before Jesus, penetrated through the rock and into the tomb, out of which she again arose radiant with light in her glorified body and, escorted by the entire multitude of celestial spirits, returned in triumph to the Heavenly Jerusalem.

Next day, when the apostles were engaged in choir service, Thomas made his appearance with two companions. One was a disciple named Jonathan Eleazar, and the other a servant from the most remote country of the three holy kings. Thomas was greatly grieved when he heard that the blessed Virgin was already buried. He wept with an abundance of tears quite astonishing to behold, for he could not forgive himself for coming so late. Weeping bitterly he threw himself, with Jonathan at his side, on the spot upon which the blessed soul of Mary had left her body, and afterward knelt long before the altar. The apostles, who had not interrupted their choir-chanting on account of his coming, now gathered around him, raised him up, embraced him, and set before him and his companions bread, honey, and some kind of beverage in little jugs. After that they accompanied him with lights to the tomb. Two disciples bent the shrubbery to one side. Thomas, Eleazar, and John went in and prayed before the coffin. Then John loosened the three straps that bound it, for it rose high enough above the trough-like couch to admit of being opened. They stood the lid of the coffin on one side and, to their intense astonishment, beheld only the empty winding sheets lying like a husk, or shell, and in perfect order. Only over the face was it drawn apart, and over the breast slightly opened. The swathing bands of the arms and hands lay separate, as if gently drawn off, but in perfect order. The apostles gazed in amazement, their hands raised. John cried out: "She is no longer here!" The others came in quickly, wept, prayed, looking upward with raised arms, and finally cast themselves on the ground, remembering the radiant cloud of the preceding night. Then rising, they took the winding sheet just as it was, all the grave linens, and the coffin to keep as relics, and returned to the house by the Holy Way, praying and singing psalms.

When they entered the house, John laid the folded linens on a little flap-table before the altar. Thomas and the others were in prayer, but Peter went a little apart, as if pondering some mystery. After that I saw him celebrating divine service at the altar before Mary's crucifix, and the apostles standing in order behind him, praying and singing. The women were standing in the doorways and by the walls of the fireplace.

The young servant that had come with Thomas looked quite unlike any of those present. He had small eyes, high cheekbones, forehead and nose remarkably flat, and his complexion was brownish. He was already baptized. He was perfectly innocent, and obeyed orders simply. He did all that he was told, remained standing or sitting wherever they told him to do so, turned his eyes in any direction indicated to see whatever was pointed out to him, and smiled upon everyone. When Thomas wept, he wept also. He always remained with Thomas, and I saw him dragging immense stones when Thomas was building a chapel.

I often saw the apostles and disciples standing together in circles and relating where they had been and giving their experience.

Before the apostles left Mary's house to journey again into distant parts, they rendered the grotto of the tomb wholly inaccessible by raising an embankment of earth before the entrance. At the rear, however, they made a low passage to the back wall of the tomb proper and an opening in the wall, by which one could look down upon it. This passage was known only to the holy women. Above the grotto they built a chapel of wood and wicker-work, and hung it with mats and tapestry. The little altar consisted of a stone slab; the step, too, was of stone. Behind the altar hung a strip of stuff on which was sewed or embroidered quite simply, in the colors of her festal robes, a picture of Mary. The little garden in front of the tomb, and especially the whole of Mary's Way of the Cross, was beautified by them. While engaged in this task of love, they prayed continually and chanted psalms. The apartment of the house in which Mary had had her oratory and sleeping alcove was converted into a little church. Mary's maid continued her abode in the front part of the house, and two of the disciples were left there by Peter for the benefit of the faithful dwelling in that section of the country.

The apostles, with tears and embraces, took leave of one another after they had once more celebrated solemn service in Mary's house. An apostle or disciple often returned at different times to pray there. I saw also that here and there, out of devotion and in reverence for the blessed Virgin, churches were built by the faithful in the same style as her house, and that her Way of the Cross and her tomb were for a long time devoutly visited by the Christians. I had a vision of those early times, just after Mary's assumption into heaven: A woman living near Ephesus, who entertained great love for Mary, visited her house. On her return she caused an altar like that she had seen there to be made, and covered it with a very costly cloth of tapestry. The woman was very poor, and had to defray the debt she thereby incurred by the sale of a piece of her property. Finding herself after some time in dire distress, she went, though very sorrowfully, to a married Christian and sold to her the beautiful altar cloth. But when the Feast of Mary's Assumption came round, I saw the poor woman very much troubled at no longer having the cloth with which to adorn her little altar. She went very humbly to the house of the purchaser, who meanwhile had given birth to twins, and begged her to lend her for the feast the cloth she had sold her, that she might adorn with it the altar of the blessed Virgin. But the present owner would not hear of lending it, and her husband repulsed the poor woman with the words: "Mary is dead and needs not the cloth; but my wife who bought it needs it." The poor woman went away sad, and complained to Mary of her want. Next night, I saw the blessed Virgin appear to the sleeping couple. She looked displeased and told them that, as a punishment of their hard and unchristian sentiments toward the poor devout woman, their children would die, and they themselves become poorer than the one whose request they had spurned. The couple awoke, and looked upon it at first as an empty dream. But on finding the twins dead, they recognized their offense with bitter lamentations. With many tears the husband and wife did penance. They received forgiveness from Mary, and the punishment in store for them was averted.

TISSOT ILLUSTRATIONS
[SECTION L]

The Passion and Death of Jesus Christ

⊕

The Resurrection · 430

The Angel Seated on the Stone of the Tomb · · · · 432

Mary Magdalene and the Women at the Tomb · · 434

Mary Magdalene Runs to the Cenacle · · · · · · · · 436

Peter and John Run to the Sepulcher · · · · · · · · · 438

Mary Magdalene Questions the Angels · · · · · · · · 440

Jesus Appears to Mary Magdalene · · · · · · · · · · · 442

Noli Me Tangere: Touch Me Not · · · · · · · · · · · · · 444

Jesus Appears to the Holy Women · · · · · · · · · · · 446

Apparition of the Risen Christ to Peter · · · · · · · · 448

The Pilgrims of Emmaus on the Road · · · · · · · · 450

He Vanished from Their Sight · · · · · · · · · · · · · · 452

The Appearance of Christ at the Cenacle · · · · · · 454

The Disbelief of Thomas · · · · · · · · · · · · · · · · · · 456

Christ Appears on the Shore of Lake Tiberias · · · 458

Peter Casts Himself into the Water · · · · · · · · · · · 460

The Second Miraculous Draught of Fishes · · · · · 462

Christ Shares a Meal with the Apostles · · · · · · · · 464

Feed My Lambs · 466

The Ascension Seen from Mount of Olives · · · · · 468

The Ascension Seen from Below · · · · · · · · · · · · · 470

The Holy Virgin in Old Age · · · · · · · · · · · · · · · · 472

The Resurrection [L1]

ALL was quiet and silent around the holy sepulcher. About seven guards were in front and around it, some sitting, others standing. The whole day long Cassius maintained his stand inside the sepulcher at the entrance of the tomb proper, leaving it scarcely for a few moments. He was still absorbed in recollection. He was in expectation of something that he knew was going to happen, for extraordinary grace and light had been vouchsafed to him. It was night; the lanterns before the tomb shed a dazzling light. I saw the sacred body wrapped in its winding sheet just as it had been laid on the stone couch. It was surrounded by a brilliant light and, since the burial, two angels had in rapt adoration guarded the sacred remains, one at the head, the other at the foot.

And now I saw the blessed soul of Jesus floating with the released spirits of the ancient patriarchs through the rock into the tomb, and showing them all the marks of ill-treatment upon his martyred body. The linen bands and winding sheet seemed to have been removed, for I saw the sacred body full of wounds; and it seemed as if, in some mysterious way, the indwelling divinity displayed before the souls the blessed body in the whole extent of its cruel laceration and martyrdom. I heard a voice proceeding from him, which related to his mother what he had done in Limbo. Now, he continued, he was about to come forth from the tomb alive, in a glorified body, and he bade her await him near Golgotha, on the stone upon which he had fallen. I then saw the risen Lord appearing to his blessed mother there. He was transcendently beautiful and glorious, his manner full of earnestness. His garment, which was like a white mantle thrown about his limbs, floated in the breeze behind him as he walked. It glistened blue and white, like smoke curling in the sunshine. His wounds were very large and sparkling. Later I saw the Lord floating in glory up through the rock. The earth trembled. The guards fell stunned to the ground and lay there stiff and contorted, as if dead. [388]

[MATTHEW 28:4–6] 4 And for fear of him the guards trembled and became like dead men. 5 But the angel said to the women, "Do not be afraid; for I know that you seek Jesus who was crucified. 6 He is not here; for he has risen, as he said. Come, see the place where he lay."

THE glorified Christ escapes from the tomb; silently he rises, his wounds shining luminously, his body, now triumphant over death, no longer subject to the laws to which it had previously submitted. In a moment he will disappear in space to reappear according to his promises. The sudden terror inspired by the earthquake, the blinding radiance which issues from the tomb, and the apparition of the angel seated within it plunge the guards into a kind of cataleptic state, and, as the sacred text tells us, "They became as dead men." The evangelist notes especially the effect produced on the soldiers by the sight of the angel: "for fear of him," he says, "the keepers did shake" as though a thunderbolt had fallen. They seemed to see the lightning flash and a terrible meteor flinging itself upon them to crush them to powder.

The Angel Seated on the Stone of the Tomb [L2]

⊕

NOW I saw the Lord floating in glory up through the rock. The earth trembled, and an angel in warrior garb shot like lightning from heaven down to the tomb, rolled the stone to one side, and seated himself upon it. At the instant the angel shot down to the tomb the earth quaked. [388]

[MATTHEW 28:2–3] 2 And behold, there was a great earthquake; for an angel of the Lord descended from heaven and came and rolled back the stone, and sat upon it. 3 His appearance was like lightning, and his raiment white as snow.

MATTHEW *attributes the earthquake which took place at the Resurrection to the descent of the angel of the Lord from heaven, and certain early commentators take this as a proof that the angel in question was Gabriel, the same messenger who had announced to Mary the coming birth of Jesus. Gabriel does, in fact, signify the power of God, and for that reason it would seem to be peculiarly appropriate that he should be associated with the Resurrection, that work of sovereign might. Moreover, add these doctors, it was fitting that the same angel should announce to the world the two births of the Son of Man: that to life on earth and that to life on high. There can be no doubt, they say, that many other celestial spirits were also present though invisible.*

Mary Magdalene and the Holy Women at the Tomb [L3]

⊕

THE holy women, when the Lord arose from the dead, were near the little gate belonging to Nicodemus. They knew nothing of the prodigies that were taking place; they did not know even of the guard at the sepulcher, for they had remained shut up in their house the whole of the preceding day, the sabbath. They anxiously inquired of one another: "Who will roll away for us the stone from the doors?" Full of longing desire to show the last honors to the sacred body in the tomb, they had entirely lost sight of the stone. At last the holy women concluded to set the spices on the stone before the tomb and to wait till some disciple would come who would open it for them. And so they went on toward the garden. When, as they approached, the holy women noticed the lanterns of the guard and the soldiers lying around, they became frightened, and went a short distance past the garden toward Golgotha. Magdalene, however, forgetful of danger, hurried into the garden. Salome followed her at some distance, and the other two waited outside. Magdalene, seeing the guard, stepped back at first a few steps toward Salome, then both made their way together through the soldiers lying around and into the sepulcher. They found the stone rolled away, but the doors closed, probably by Cassius. Magdalene anxiously opened one of them, peered in at the tomb, and saw the linens lying empty and apart. The whole place was resplendent with light, and an angel was sitting at the right of the tomb. [389]

[MARK 16:1–6] 1 And when the sabbath was past, Mary Magdalene, and Mary the mother of James, and Salome, bought spices, so that they might go and anoint him. 2 And very early on the first day of the week they went to the tomb when the sun had risen. 3 And they were saying to one another, "Who will roll away the stone for us from the door of the tomb?" 4 And looking up, they saw that the stone was rolled back;—it was very large. 5 And entering the tomb, they saw a young man sitting on the right side, dressed in a white robe; and they were amazed. 6 And he said to them, "Do not be amazed; you seek Jesus of Nazareth, who was crucified. He has risen, he is not here; see the place where they laid him."

IN the evening, when they see the guards arrive, the holy women withdraw and employ themselves in buying precious spices with which they intend to anoint yet again the sacred body of Jesus. They can get these spices now, for the sabbath ends at sunset, and from that moment the shops, which have been closed for the preceding twenty-four hours, are open again, so that all can buy the necessary provisions for that evening and the next morning. Their purchases completed, the holy women return together to the sepulcher. They are ignorant of the fact that seals have been set upon the stone, but they know that it is heavy and difficult to move, and they are considering whom they can ask to roll it back. Their embarrassment does not last long. When they return they find the guards prostrate, and in the midst of a bluish radiance they see a strange and supernatural figure seated at the entrance to the sepulcher. The tomb itself is open and filled with a surpassing glory of light. Jesus is no longer there. What can have become of him? They approach timidly, and then the angel, the first sight of whom has terrified them, announces the Resurrection.

Mary Magdalene Runs to the Cenacle [L4]

⊕

MEANWHILE Magdalene reached the Cenacle like one beside herself, and knocked violently at the door. Some of the disciples were still asleep on their couches around the walls, while several others had risen and were talking together. Peter and John opened the door. Magdalene, without entering, merely uttered the words: "They have taken the Lord from the tomb! We know not where"—and ran back in great haste to the garden of the sepulcher. [389]

[JOHN 20:1–2] 1 Now on the first day of the week Mary Magdalene came to the tomb early, while it was still dark, and saw that the stone had been taken away from the tomb. 2 So she ran, and went to Simon Peter and the other disciple, the one whom Jesus loved, and said to them, "They have taken the Lord out of the tomb, and we do not know where they have laid him."

AFTER *the entombment of Christ, the apostles lived together; their anxiety, shared by all the friends of Jesus, kept them assembled in one house. They waited in the guest-chamber, or rather they hid themselves there, dreading discovery and further persecution. This night, especially, they must have been agitated by vague presentiments, when they remembered certain mysterious words of the Master. Suddenly, on Sunday morning, that is to say, on the day following the sabbath, hasty knocks are heard at the door. Who can it be? What is happening? Are they to be arrested? Is the persecution of the disciples to be continued and must they flee again? Peter and John, who are more affectionately anxious and more eager about the Master than the others, are the first to open the door. It is Mary Magdalene who waits without; she rushes in like a hurricane, and, standing panting for breath on the threshold, she flings out the words without approaching nearer to the apostles: "They have taken away the Lord out of the sepulcher, and we know not where they have laid him." She is blinded by agitation. As long as Jesus was still there, living or dead, she could manage to control her grief and deceive herself, but now that he is gone, she becomes quite mad; she must find him at all costs, and she hurries back to the sepulcher, followed by most of her companions.*

Peter and John Run to the Sepulcher [L5]

⊕

MAGDALENE ran back in great haste to the garden of the sepulcher. Peter and John followed her, but John outstripped Peter. [389]

[JOHN 20:3–10] 3 Peter then came out with the other disciple, and they went toward the tomb. 4 They both ran, but the other disciple outran Peter and reached the tomb first; 5 and stooping to look in, he saw the linen cloths lying there, but he did not go in. 6 Then Simon Peter came, following him, and went into the tomb; he saw the linen cloths lying, 7 and the napkin, which had been on his head, not lying with the linen cloths but rolled up in a place by itself. 8 Then the other disciple, who reached the tomb first, also went in, and he saw and believed; 9 for as yet they did not know the scripture, that he must rise from the dead. 10 Then the disciples went back to their homes.

MARY Magdalene had no sooner left the guest-chamber before Peter and John hurry after her, running to the sepulcher as fast as they can. They had little more than half a mile to go to reach the tomb. In fact, Peter and John ran at their very utmost speed, for they were all eagerness to verify for themselves the agitated account of the holy women. John, younger and more active than his companion, out-runs him, but, out of respect for the chief of the apostles, he will wait for him before actually entering the sepulcher. The Church is, in fact, already founded and Peter has been solemnly named as the rock on which it was built; it is, therefore, fitting that he should be the first to authenticate the miracle. Peter then enters the tomb to find the cubiculum empty and to "see the linen clothes lie, and the napkin, that was about the head of the Lord, not lying with the linen clothes, but wrapped together in a place by itself." It is very certain, although the sacred text says nothing on the subject, that these precious shrouds were not left in the sepulcher; they were relics far too valuable to the community of which Peter was the chief. He must have taken them away, and the Church thus became the owner of the priceless treasures. The fact of the Resurrection being now beyond a doubt, the account of the holy women being confirmed by the sight of the empty sepulcher, the two apostles, convinced, as we are told by John, of the truth, "went away again unto their own home."

Mary Magdalene Questions the Angels in the Tomb [L6]

⊕

MAGDALENE was quite wet with dew when she again reached the garden and ran to the tomb. As she was alone, she was afraid to enter the sepulcher at once, so she waited out on the step at the entrance. She stooped down, trying to see through the low doors into the cave and even as far as the stone couch. She saw the two angels in white priestly garments sitting at the head and the foot of the tomb, and heard the words: "Woman, why weepest thou?" She cried out in her grief: "They have taken my Lord away! I know not where they have laid him!" Saying this and seeing nothing but the linens, she turned weeping, like one seeking something, and as if she must find him. She had a dim presentiment that Jesus was near, and even the apparition of the angels could not turn her from her one idea. She did not appear conscious of the fact that it was an angel that spoke to her. She thought only of Jesus; her only thought was: "Jesus is not here! Where is Jesus?" I saw her running a few steps from the sepulcher and then returning like one half-distracted and in quest of something. [390]

[JOHN 20:11–13] 11 But Mary stood weeping outside the tomb, and as she wept she stooped to look into the tomb; 12 and she saw two angels in white, sitting where the body of Jesus had lain, one at the head and one at the feet. 13 They said to her, "Woman, why are you weeping?" She said to them, "Because they have taken away my Lord, and I do not know where they have laid him."

IT is somewhat difficult to follow the order of events; but with a little care we can, with the aid of the various details given, form a very accurate picture of what took place. This is our own idea: Mary Magdalene, followed by the other two Marys, is the first to arrive, and she finds the actual tomb empty, though the angels are in the antechamber. She takes no notice of them, but while the other holy women are questioning them she rushes away to the guest-chamber to tell the apostles that the body of the Lord has disappeared. She makes no allusion to the angels; they are quite secondary considerations with her. However this may be, there is no doubt that the apostles hastened to the tomb, and when they returned, meeting the holy women by the way, they took them back with them with the exception of Mary Magdalene, who went alone to the tomb, still not knowing what to think and feeling sure of but one thing: that the Savior has disappeared.

There she is, then, alone in the garden weeping, and in the midst of her tears she approaches the tomb to look into it once more. She now sees two angels seated where the body of Jesus had lain, one at the head, the other at the feet. She feels no emotion at this sight; what she seeks is more to her than any angels, everything else gives way to her anxiety, and she addresses the heavenly messengers as she would any ordinary mortals. One of them says to her: "Woman, why weepest thou?" and she returns with strange persistence to her original thought: "They have taken away my Lord, and I know not where they have laid him."

Jesus Appears to Mary Magdalene [L7]

⊕

ABOUT ten steps from the sepulcher and toward the east, where the garden rose in the direction of the city, she spied in the gray light of dawn, standing among the bushes behind a tree, a figure clothed in a long, white garment. Rushing toward it, she heard once more the words: "Woman, why weepest thou? Whom seekest thou?" She thought it was the gardener. I saw that he had a spade in his hand and on his head a flat hat, which had a piece of something like bark standing out in front, as a protection from the sun. It was just like that I had seen on the gardener in the parable which Jesus, shortly before his Passion, had related to the women in Bethany. The apparition was not resplendent. It looked like a person clad in long, white garments and seen at twilight. At the words: "Whom seekest thou?" Magdalene at once answered: "Sir, if thou hast taken him hence, show me where thou hast laid him! I will take him away!" And she again glanced around, as if to see whether he had not laid him someplace near. [390]

[JOHN 20:14–15] 14 Saying this, she turned round and saw Jesus standing, but she did not know that it was Jesus. 15 Jesus said to her, "Woman, why are you weeping? Whom do you seek?" Supposing him to be the gardener, she said to him, "Sir, if you have carried him away, tell me where you have laid him, and I will take him away."

THE question has often been asked: how was it that Mary Magdalene did not recognize Jesus when he appeared to her near the tomb, but took him for the gardener? And many different explanations have been given. The evangelist does, in fact, say that after she heard the Savior call her "Mary" "she turned herself back" to answer. She had, therefore, in the first instance spoken without turning round, her eyes fixed obstinately on the sepulcher, and it is, therefore, not surprising, taking into account her confusion and the difficulty of believing in a resurrection, that she did not at the first moment recognize the divine Master. The way in which she refers to that Master is remarkable; she merely uses the pronoun "him," as if the whole world must be cognizant of her loss. "Sir," she says, "if thou have borne him hence, tell me where thou hast laid him, and I will take him away." There is something grand in those last words! Mary Magdalene does not consider her weakness, everything seems possible to her if she can but recover him she loves. She only demands one thing: "Tell me where thou hast laid him, and I will take him away." This boldness is sublime, and is one of the characteristic touches which give the gospels their incomparable impress of truthfulness. That of John especially, as we have more than once remarked, is almost always marked by exceptional powers of observation, combined with the charm of the most perfect simplicity.

Noli Me Tangere: Touch Me Not [L8]

⊕

THEN Jesus, in his well-known voice, said: "Mary!" Recognizing the voice, and forgetting the crucifixion, death, and burial now that he was alive, she turned quickly and, as once before, exclaimed: "Rabboni!" (Master!). She fell on her knees before him and stretched out her arms toward his feet. But Jesus raised his hand to keep her off, saying: "Do not touch me, for I am not yet ascended to my Father. But go to my brethren, and say to them: I ascend to my Father and to your Father, to my God and to your God." At these words the Lord vanished. After the disappearance of the Lord, Magdalene rose up quickly and again, as if in a dream, ran to the tomb. She saw the two angels, she saw the empty linens, and hurried, now certain of the miracle, back to her companions. It may have been about half-past three o'clock when Jesus appeared to Magdalene. [390]

[JOHN 20:16–18] 16 Jesus said to her, "Mary." She turned and said to him in Hebrew, "Rabboni!" (which means Teacher). 17 Jesus said to her, "Do not hold me, for I have not yet ascended to the Father; but go to my brethren and say to them, I am ascending to my Father and your Father, to my God and your God." 18 Mary Magdalene went and said to the disciples, "I have seen the Lord"; and she told them that he had said these things to her.

IT is from the familiar sound of her own name that Mary Magdalene recognizes the risen Savior. "Mary!" it is the name none but intimate friends use, and it is impossible not to respond to it. She is moved to the very depths of her soul by that one word, and she eagerly replies: "Master!" In an instant all her grief is gone; mad with joy she flings herself down, thinking to resume her old place at the feet of Jesus and to embrace them as she had done on Golgotha. But the time is gone by for such familiarity; Jesus has taken up again a life which he can no longer share with his disciples, he can now only permit them to indulge in distant homage. He therefore gently repels her who would fain touch him and sends her, the "apostle of the apostles" as she is called in the Catholic liturgy, to take to the brethren the news of his approaching Ascension.

Jesus Appears to the Holy Women [L9]

⊕

MEANWHILE, Magdalene had reached the holy women and told them of the Lord's apparition. Then she too hurried on to the city through the neighboring gate of the execution, but the others went again to the garden, outside of which Jesus appeared to them in a white flowing garment that concealed even his hands. He said: "All hail!" They trembled and fell at his feet. Jesus waved his hand in a certain direction while addressing to them some words, and vanished. The holy women then hastened through the Bethlehem gate on Zion, to tell the disciples in the Cenacle that they had seen the Lord and what he had said to them. [391]

[MATTHEW 28:8–10] 8 So they departed quickly from the tomb with fear and great joy, and ran to tell his disciples. 9 And behold, Jesus met them and said, "Hail!" And they came up and took hold of his feet and worshiped him. 10 Then Jesus said to them, "Do not be afraid; go and tell my brethren to go to Galilee, and there they will see me."

Apparition of the Risen Christ to Peter [L10]

SCARCELY had she left the garden when John approached, followed by Peter. John stood outside the entrance of the cave and stooped down to look, through the outer doors of the sepulcher, at the half-opened doors of the tomb, where he saw the linens lying. Then came Peter. He stepped down into the sepulcher and went to the tomb, in the center of which he saw the winding sheet lying. It was rolled together from both sides toward the middle, and the spices were wrapped in it. The bandages were folded around it, as women are accustomed to roll together such linens when putting them away. The linen that had covered the sacred face was lying to the right next to the wall. It too was folded. John now followed Peter to the tomb, saw the same things, and believed in the resurrection. All that the Lord had said, all that was written in the scriptures, was now clear to them. They had had only an imperfect comprehension of it before. Peter took the linens with him under his mantle. Both again went back by the little gate belonging to Nicodemus, and John once more got ahead of Peter. John and Peter, whom amazement at what they had seen had rendered silent and thoughtful, met on their way back James the Less and Thaddeus, who had set out after them for the tomb. They too were very much agitated, for the Lord had appeared to them near the Cenacle. Once I saw Peter, as they went along, suddenly start and tremble, as if he had just got a glimpse of the risen Savior. [391]

[LUKE 24:34] 34 Who said, "The Lord has risen indeed, and has appeared to Simon!" [LUKE 24:32] 32 They said to each other, "Did not our hearts burn within us while he talked to us on the road, while he opened to us the scriptures?" [JOHN 20:6–7] 6 Then Simon Peter came, following him, and went into the tomb; he saw the linen cloths lying, 7 and the napkin, which had been on his head, not lying with the linen cloths but rolled up in a place by itself.

WHEN Peter and John had seen for themselves that the body of Jesus was no longer in the tomb, they must have separated, each going his own way, for there is nothing about John in the account of the Lord having appeared to Peter, given by Luke, who is the only one of the evangelists to relate the incident, though his account was confirmed later by Paul in the First Epistle to the Corinthians, where he says: "He was seen of Cephas, then of the twelve." In our engraving, Peter is represented on his way back to the Cenacle, when suddenly Jesus appears to him, his body radiating light. He shows his now glorious wounds to his wondering disciple, reminds him by a gesture of his triple denial, which he will later make him retract by a triple protestation of love. From this moment, however, it is very evident that Peter is forgiven, and his confusion is that of surprised affection rather than of fear. He has wept so much, since the time of his fall!

The character of Peter, as it comes out in the gospels, presents curious contrasts. He is at once generous, eager, devoted, easily alarmed, and timid. He wants to call down fire from heaven on the towns which reject his Master, yet he himself denies him three times. He draws his sword in the garden and dashes blindly into the midst of the soldiers, cutting off the ear of one of them, but directly afterward he runs away with the other disciples. At the house of Caiaphas, whither he hastens, not without courage, after John, he cannot face the questions of a mere servant, but a look from Jesus is enough to recall him to himself, and later he will know how to die. When Jesus was about to wash his feet in the Cenacle, he protested: "Thou shalt never wash my feet," but when the Lord replied: "If I wash them not thou hast no part with me," he rushed at once from one extreme to the other, crying: "Not my feet only but also my hands and my head." Such was Peter, with his sympathetic and deeply interesting temperament, but he had great need of the Holy Spirit to become a pillar of the Church and the rock on which that Church was to be built.

The Pilgrims of Emmaus on the Road [L11]

LUKE had been among the disciples only a short time, but he had, before joining them, received John's baptism. He was present at the love feast and the instruction upon the blessed sacrament delivered by Matthew in the evening at Lazarus's, in Bethany. After the instruction he went, troubled and doubting, to Jerusalem where he spent the night in John Mark's house. There he met several other disciples, among them Cleophas, a grandson of Mary Cleophas's paternal uncle. He had been at the instructions and the love feast given in the house of the Last Supper. The disciples were talking about Jesus's resurrection and expressing their doubts. Luke and Cleophas, especially, were wavering in faith. As, moreover, the commands of the high priests were again made known, that no one should harbor the disciples of Jesus or supply them with food, both resolved to go together to Emmaus. They left the assembly. On leaving John Mark's house, one turned to the right and went around out of the city in a northerly direction, and the other took a route on the opposite side, as if not wishing to be seen together. One went straight out of the city, the other made his way between the walls and out by the gate, beyond which they again met upon a hill. They carried each a staff, and a bundle at his side.

Luke had a leathern pocket. I saw him frequently stepping aside from the road and gathering herbs. Luke had not seen the Lord during those last days, and had not been present at his instructions at Lazarus's. He had been more in the disciples' inn at Bethany and with the disciples in Machaerus. He had not long been a declared disciple, though he had always gone around with the rest and was very desirous of knowing what was going on. I felt that both these disciples were anxious and doubting, and that they wanted to talk over all they had heard. They were especially put out at the Lord's being so ignominiously crucified! They could not understand how the Redeemer and Messiah could have been so shamefully ill-treated.

About the middle of their journey, Jesus drew near to them from a side path. As soon as they saw him, they went more slowly, as if wanting to let the stranger go on ahead, as if fearing to be overheard. But Jesus likewise slackened his pace, and stepped out on the road only after they were somewhat in advance. I saw him walking behind them for a little while, then drawing near and asking of what they were talking. Where the road branched off outside of Emmaus Jesus appeared as if he wanted to take that which ran southward to Bethlehem. [394]

[LUKE 24:13–27] 13 That very day two of them were going to a village named Emmaus, about seven miles from Jerusalem, 14 and talking with each other about all these things that had happened. 15 While they were talking and discussing together, Jesus himself drew near and went with them. 16 But their eyes were kept from recognizing him. 17 And he said to them, "What is this conversation which you are holding with each other as you walk?" And they stood still, looking sad. 18 Then one of them, named Cleophas, answered him, "Are you the only visitor to Jerusalem who does not know the things that have happened there in these days?" 19 And he said to them, "What things?" And they said to him, "Concerning Jesus of Nazareth, who was a prophet mighty in deed and word before God and all the people, 20 and how our chief priests and rulers delivered him up to be condemned to death, and crucified him. 21 But we had hoped that he was the one to redeem Israel. Yes, and besides all this, it is now the third day since this happened. 22 Moreover, some women of our company amazed us. They were at the tomb early in the morning 23 and did not find his body; and they came back saying that they had even seen a vision of angels, who said that he was alive. 24 Some of those who were with us went to the tomb, and found it just as the women had said; but him they did not see." 25 And he said to them, "O foolish men, and slow of heart to believe all that the prophets have spoken! 26 Was it not necessary that the Christ should suffer these things and enter into his glory?" 27 And beginning with Moses and all the prophets, he interpreted to them in all the scriptures the things concerning himself.

JESUS remained longer with the disciples on the road to Emmaus than on any other occasion after his resurrection. As a rule, he showed himself but for a few instants, said a few words, scarcely allowing anyone to touch him, but this time he walked with the two apostles for an hour. They laid their hands on his shoulders, they listened to his voice and were touched by his words, yet he seemed to them so much like any other man that they invited him to supper. He accepted, went in with them and "sat down to meat." How was it that, seeing him in so tangible a form before them, they did not recognize him? "Their eyes were holden," says the sacred text. On other occasions it was as he appeared that he made himself known, now it was as "he vanished out of their sight" that he revealed himself. This sudden disappearance opened their eyes more fully even than the breaking of the bread which first led to their recognition of the divine Master.

He Vanished from Their Sight [L12]

BUT the two disciples constrained him to go with them into a house that stood in the second row of the city. There were no women in it, and it appeared to me to be a public house, for it looked as if a feast had lately been held in it. The table was covered, and reclining cushions lay around it. A man put on it a honeycomb in a woven basketlike vessel, a large, four-cornered cake, and a small, thin, almost transparent Passover loaf. Jesus reclined at the table with the two disciples and ate with them of the cake and honey. Then taking the small cake, the ribbed one, he broke off a piece that he afterward divided into three with a short, white bone knife. These he laid on the little plate, and blessed. Then he stood up, elevated the plate on high with both hands, raised his eyes, and prayed.

The two disciples stood opposite him, both intensely moved, and as it were transported out of themselves. When Jesus broke the little pieces, they opened their mouth and stretched forward toward him. He reached his hand across the table and laid the particle in their mouth. I saw that as he raised his hand with the third morsel to his own mouth, he disappeared. I cannot say that he really received it. The morsels shone with light after he had blessed them. I saw the two disciples standing a little while as if stupefied, and then casting themselves with tears of emotion into each other's arms. This vision was especially touching on account of the Lord's mild and loving manner, the calm joy of the two disciples even before they knew him, and their rapture as soon as they recognized him and after he had disappeared. Cleophas and Luke hurried back at once to Jerusalem. [394]

[LUKE 24:28–30] 28 So they drew near to the village to which they were going. He appeared to be going further, 29 but they constrained him, saying, "Stay with us, for it is toward evening and the day is now far spent." So he went in to stay with them. 30 When he was at table with them, he took the bread and blessed, and broke it, and gave it to them. [LUKE 24:31] 31 And their eyes were opened and they recognized him; and he vanished out of their sight.

The Appearance of Christ at the Cenacle [L13]

ON the evening of the same day, many of the disciples and all the apostles excepting Thomas assembled with Nicodemus and Joseph of Arimathea in the hall of the Last Supper, the doors being closed. All wore long white garments. Peter, John, and James the Less were vested in robes that distinguished them from the rest. Peter wore a stole around his neck. The apostles occupied the inner circle under the lamp; two other circles were formed by the disciples. Peter, between John and James, had his back turned to the closed entrance of the house of the Last Supper, and the circle was not closed in front of him, but open toward the Holy of Holies. I was surprised to see that although Jesus had appeared to Peter, John, and James, yet the greater number of the apostles and disciples would not fully believe in his resurrection. They still felt uneasy, as if his apparition was not a real and corporeal one, only a vision, a phantom, similar to those the prophets had had.

All had ranged again for prayer after Peter's instruction when Luke and Cleophas, hurrying back from Emmaus, knocked at the closed doors of the courtyard and received admittance. The joyful news they related somewhat interrupted the prayer. But scarcely was it again continued when I saw all present radiant with joyful emotion, and glancing in the same direction. Jesus was come in through the closed doors. He was robed in a long white garment simply girded. They did not appear to be really conscious of his approach, until he passed through the circles and stood in their midst under the lamp. Then they became very much amazed and agitated. He showed them his hands and feet and, opening his garment, disclosed the wound in his side. He spoke to them and, seeing that they were very much terrified, he asked for something to eat. After this I saw him teaching and imparting strength. The circles around him were still triple, the ten apostles forming the inmost. Thomas was not there. [395]

[JOHN 20:19–20] 19 On the evening of that day, the first day of the week, the doors being shut where the disciples were, for fear of the Jews, Jesus came and stood among them and said to them, "Peace be with you." 20 When he had said this, he showed them his hands and his side. Then the disciples were glad when they saw the Lord.

YET another very striking apparition of Jesus is recorded, which took place shortly after he vanished away at Emmaus on the evening succeeding the sabbath. The doors were closed, yet he passed through them without effort, thanks to the new conditions of his life since his resurrection, and suddenly stood in their midst. It was indeed he, and to prove it he showed them his hands and his pierced side, the disciples recognizing him joyfully. Whereas he had previously appeared to but one or at the most two or three at a time, he now manifested himself to the infant Church. Luke, with his usual tact, understood this well, and that is why he gives to his narrative something of the seal of a medical statement: "Behold my hands and my feet, that it is I myself: handle me, and see; for a spirit hath not flesh and bones, as ye see me have." And when he had thus spoken, he showed them his hands and his feet. And while they yet believed not for joy, and wondered, he said unto them, Have ye here any meat? And they gave him a piece of a broiled fish, and of a honey comb. And he took it, and did eat before them."

The Disbelief of Thomas [L14]

AFTER that he vanished. On that same night a part of the apostles, at Jesus's bidding, betook themselves to Bethany, while the rest set out for Jerusalem. The apostles went with a troop of disciples, among them Luke, in the direction of Sichar. They met together again at the inn outside Thanat-Shiloh. Thomas also, with two disciples, joined them as they were gathered at a meal prepared for them by Silvan's father, who had care of the inn. The apostles told Thomas of the apparition of the risen Savior in their midst. But he raised his hands to silence them, and said that he would not believe it until he had touched his wounds. Peter taught till late at night in the school of Thanat-Shiloh. He told of how cruelly the Jews had treated Jesus, of his rising again on the third day, of his appearing first to the women, then to some of the others, and lastly to all in general, and he called upon all present that had seen him to witness to his words. Thomas, however, remained silent and responded by no sign. He could not bring himself to believe.

After the close of the sabbath, I saw a great meal spread in the outer hall. While these preparations were being made, I saw Thomas entering the supper room. He passed through the apostles. As he went along, I saw the apostles accosting him. After some time there was a pause in the assembly, and they began to speak of going to the Sea of Tiberias and of how they would disperse. But soon they assumed an expression of rapt attention, called up by the approach of the Lord. At the same moment, I saw Jesus in the courtyard. He was resplendent with light, clothed in white garments and a white girdle. The disciples in the outer hall saw the door opening of itself, and fell back on both sides to make room. But Jesus walked quickly through the hall into the supper room and stepped between Peter and John who, like all the other apostles, fell back on either side. Jesus was environed with light.

The apostles had fallen back from the radiant circle, otherwise they would not have been able to see him. Jesus's first words were: "Peace be to you!" He now stepped under the lamp, and the apostles closed around him. Thomas, very much frightened at the sight of the Lord, timidly drew back. But Jesus, grasping his right hand in his own right hand, took the forefinger and laid the tip of it in the wound of his left hand; then taking the left hand in his own left, he placed the forefinger in the wound of his right hand; lastly, taking again Thomas's right hand in his own right, he put it, without uncovering his breast, under his garment, and laid the fore and middle fingers in the wound of his right side. He spoke some words as he did this. With the exclamation: "My Lord, and my God!" Thomas sank down like one unconscious, Jesus still holding his hand. The nearest of the apostles supported him, and Jesus raised him up by the hand. That sinking down and rising up had some peculiar signification. [400]

[JOHN 20:24–29] 24 Now Thomas, one of the twelve, called the Twin, was not with them when Jesus came. 25 So the other disciples told him, "We have seen the Lord." But he said to them, "Unless I see in his hands the print of the nails, and place my finger in the mark of the nails, and place my hand in his side, I will not believe." 26 Eight days later, his disciples were again in the house, and Thomas was with them. The doors were shut, but Jesus came and stood among them, and said, "Peace be with you." 27 Then he said to Thomas, "Put your finger here, and see my hands; and put out your hand, and place it in my side; do not be faithless, but believing." 28 Thomas answered him, "My Lord and my God!" 29 Jesus said to him, "Have you believed because you have seen me? Blessed are those who have not seen and yet believe."

Christ Appears on the Shore of Lake Tiberias [L15]

THEY went aboard two ships, one somewhat larger and better than the other. They gave to Peter the choice of the former, into which he mounted with Nathaniel, Thomas, and one of the fisherman's servants. In the second ship were John, James, John Mark, and Silas. Peter would not suffer another to row. He wanted to do it himself. Although so distinguished by Jesus, he was exceedingly humble and modest, especially before Nathaniel, who was polished and educated.

They sailed about the whole night with torches, casting the nets here and there between the two ships, but always drawing them in empty. At intervals they prayed and sang psalms. When day was beginning to dawn, the ships approached the opposite side of the mouth of the Jordan, on the eastern shore of the sea. The apostles were worn out and wanted to cast anchor. They had laid aside their garments while fishing, retaining only a linen bandage and a little mantle. When about resuming their clothing preparatory to taking a little rest, they saw a figure standing behind the reeds on the shore. It was Jesus. He cried out: "Children, have you any fish?" They answered: "No!" Then he cried out again, telling them to cast the net to the west of Peter's ship. They did it, and John had to sail round to the other side of the ship. And now the net was so heavily filled that John recognized Jesus. [401]

[JOHN 21 4–6] 4 Just as day was breaking, Jesus stood on the beach; yet the disciples did not know that it was Jesus. 5 Jesus said to them, "Children, have you any fish?" They answered him, "No." 6 He said to them, "Cast the net on the right side of the boat, and you will find some." So they cast it, and now they were not able to haul it in, for the quantity of fish.

IN this incident Jesus once more demonstrates to his disciples in an unmistakable manner the reality of his resurrection, and employs two methods, each supplementary to the other. In the first place, he repeats a miracle, that of the great draught of fishes, which will at once insure his recognition. But, as he could have worked that miracle by virtue of his divine power without his actual palpable presence, he invited his disciples to eat of the fish and partook of their meal himself as he had done in the Cenacle. The whole scene bears a remarkable impress of poetry and of truth. This man in white robes standing alone upon the shore in the calm of the early morning and hailing a boat in the offing is enough to attract attention, but how much more impressive is his appearance when it is remembered that he is the very man whom those in the boat bore to the tomb a few days before.

The word pulmentarium *used in the Vulgate will be noticed. It indicates the food the fishermen of that day were in the habit of eating, and consisted of a kind of boiled pulse or a mixture of beans and various vegetables, sometimes also of figs, nuts, and grapes all cooked together and flavored according to taste. With bread it was the staple of every meal.*

Peter Alerted by John to the Presence of Christ Casts Himself into the Water [L16]

⊕

JOHN recognized Jesus, and called to Peter across the silent deep: "It is the Lord!" At these words Peter instantly girded his coat about him, leaped into the water, and waded through the reeds to the shore where Jesus was standing. But John pushed on in a boat, very light and narrow, that was fastened to his ship. Two of this kind were hooked together. I saw all this before Jesus crossed the mound and went down to the sea. Peter did not swim, he waded through the water. The bottom could be seen, although the water was tolerably deep. Peter was already standing by Jesus when John came up. [401]

[JOHN 21:4–8] 4 Just as day was breaking, Jesus stood on the beach; yet the disciples did not know that it was Jesus. 5 Jesus said to them, "Children, have you any fish?" They answered him, "No." 6 He said to them, "Cast the net on the right side of the boat, and you will find some." So they cast it, and now they were not able to haul it in, for the quantity of fish. 7 That disciple whom Jesus loved said to Peter, "It is the Lord!" When Simon Peter heard that it was the Lord, he put on his clothes, for he was stripped for work, and sprang into the sea. 8 But the other disciples came in the boat, dragging the net full of fish, for they were not far from the land, but about a hundred yards off.

FISHERMEN when at work, especially in the shallow waters inshore, often wore nothing more than a little linen girt about their loins and reaching half way down their thighs, as prescribed by Jewish law. To this, however, they added a net slung over their backs and wound round their bodies, which served as a bag for holding fish. Their nets were, as already stated, of the kind known as sweep-nets. In the winter the upper part of the body was covered, but the climate was so mild that the limbs could be left bare and untrammeled in the spring. At the time of year of which we are speaking it was already warm on the lake. When Peter heard John say: "It is the Lord," he put his gibbeh on again out of respect to the Master and cast himself into the sea. The water was, no doubt, only up to his thighs, for where the seine-net could be used, the lake cannot have been deep, and the beach was not encumbered with rocks as in the north. A hundred steps would bring Peter to the land, while his companions also approached to join him who had hailed them. The account of John is full of typical details betraying an eye-witness, and, when this is borne in mind, the passage quoted above is pregnant with import. The character of the two apostles, Peter and John, is clearly brought out. John is the first to see the Lord, Peter takes the first decisive step. John looks on and meditates, Peter acts and rushes forward. Throughout the remainder of their lives the same peculiarities distinguished them, one is full of the zeal and activity of the missionary, the other of thoughtful contemplation.

The Second Miraculous Draught of Fishes [L17]

⊕

THOSE on the ship now began to cry to them to help draw in the net. Jesus told Peter to go bring in the fish. They drew the net to land, and Peter emptied it on the shore. In it were one hundred and fifty-three different kinds of fishes. This number signified that of the new believers who were to be gained at Thebez. [402]

[JOHN 21:10–11] 10 Jesus said to them, "Bring some of the fish that you have just caught." 11 So Simon Peter went aboard and hauled the net ashore, full of large fish, a hundred and fifty-three of them; and although there were so many, the net was not torn.

IT was with the seine-net that the disciples fished. One end of a long narrow net was made fast on land and the boat was then steered out into the offing, gradually paying out the net, the greater portion of which with its weights sank to the bottom, while the upper edge, provided with corks, floated freely on the surface of the water. When the net had been thus stretched out in a straight line toward the offing, the boat described a wide circle round it, taking the other end back to the land. All the fish in the path of the net were taken and were towed in by the fishermen wading in the water.

Having reached the shore with their load, the disciples found themselves face to face with Jesus, who, addressing them in the old familiar way, invited them to eat with him. In their astonishment they know not what to say. They recognize him. It is indeed he, and yet they remember having laid him in the tomb. Full of emotion, they hold their peace and "none durst ask him, Who art thou? knowing that it was the Lord." It is indeed a grand scene, and it alone would be enough to prove the authenticity of the gospel account and the reality of the resurrection. May we not see in this meal, which is evidently symbolical, an emblem of the spiritual and material aid upon which the disciples could rely in the new era which was about to begin? Even as the miraculous draught of fishes was, as we have seen, a symbol of the marvelous work which would be accomplished by the divine assistance? Others see in the lake an emblem of the field of work and in the firm land one of the eternal reward, so often symbolized in the scriptures by a feast of which the elect will partake, and over which God Himself will preside.

Christ Shares a Meal with the Apostles [L18]

I SAW the Lord arrive at the sea while the apostles were still fishing. Back of a little mound on the shore there was a hollow in which was a covered fireplace, for the use of the shepherds, perhaps. I did not see Jesus kindling a fire, catching a fish, or getting one in any other way. Fire and fish and everything necessary appeared at once in presence of the souls as soon as ever it entered into the Lord's mind that a fish should here be prepared for eating. How it happened, I cannot say. The apostles were very much surprised to see the fire and a fish, not of their own catching, also bread and honeycakes. The apostles and disciples reclined while Jesus played the host. He handed to each on a little roll a portion of the fish from the pan. I did not see that the fish became less. He gave to them also of the honeycakes and then reclined with them at table and ate. All this took place very quietly and solemnly. [402]

[JOHN 21:9, 12–13] 9 When they got out on land, they saw a charcoal fire there, with fish lying on it, and bread... 12 Jesus said to them, "Come and have breakfast." Now none of the disciples dared ask him, "Who are you?" They knew it was the Lord. 13 Jesus came and took the bread and gave it to them, and so with the fish.

Feed My Lambs [L19]

AFTER the meal, I saw Jesus and the apostles rise from table. They walked up and down the shore, and at last stood still while Jesus solemnly addressed Peter: "Simon, son of John, lovest thou me more than these?" Peter timidly answered. "Yea, Lord, thou knowest that I love thee!" Jesus said to him: "Feed my lambs!" And at the same instant I saw a vision of the church and the Chief Pastor. I saw him teaching and guiding the first Christians, and I saw the baptizing and cleansing of the new Christians, who appeared like so many tender lambs. After a pause, Jesus again said to Peter: "Simon, son of John, lovest thou me?" (They were walking all the time, Jesus occasionally turning and pausing while they regarded him with attention). Peter very timidly and humbly, for he was thinking of his denial, again answered: "Yea, Lord, thou knowest that I love thee!" Jesus again addressed him solemnly: "Feed my sheep!" Again I had a vision of the rising church and her persecutions. I saw the Chief Bishop gathering together the numerous scattered Christians, protecting them, providing them with shepherds, and governing them. After another pause and still walking, Jesus said once more: "Simon, son of John, lovest thou me?" I saw that Peter grew troubled at the thought that Jesus asked him so often, as if he doubted his love. It reminded him of his thrice-repeated denial, and he answered: "Lord, thou knowest all things, thou knowest that I love thee!" I saw that John was thinking: "Oh, what love must Jesus have, and what ought a shepherd to have, since he thrice questions Peter, to whom he confides his flock, concerning his love!" Jesus again said: "Feed my sheep! Amen, amen, I say to thee: when thou wast younger, thou didst gird thyself, and didst walk where thou wouldst. But when thou shalt be old, thou shalt stretch forth thy hands, and another shall gird thee, and lead thee whither thou wouldst not. Follow me!" [403]

[JOHN 21:15–19] 15 When they had finished breakfast, Jesus said to Simon Peter, "Simon, son of John, do you love me more than these?" He said to him, "Yes, Lord; you know that I love you." He said to him, "Feed my lambs." 16 A second time he said to him, "Simon, son of John, do you love me?" He said to him, "Yes, Lord; you know that I love you." He said to him, "Tend my sheep." 17 He said to him the third time, "Simon, son of John, do you love me?" Peter was grieved because he said to him the third time, "Do you love me?" And he said to him, "Lord, you know everything; you know that I love you." Jesus said to him, "Feed my sheep. 18 Truly, truly, I say to you, when you were young, you girded yourself and walked where you would; but when you are old, you will stretch out your hands, and another will gird you and carry you where you do not wish to go." 19 (This he said to show by what death he was to glorify God.) And after this he said to him, "Follow me."

AFTER the repast, Jesus rose and moved away, the apostles following him with Peter at their head. Jesus then led the latter apart and asked the searching question: "Simon, lovest thou me more than these?" He wished to remind him of his former protestation: "Though all these should be offended because of thee, yet will I not be offended." But he was also anxious to give him a chance of expressing his repentance and receiving forgiveness. Peter, with the humility which came from the remembrance of his fall, replied "Yea, Lord; thou knowest that I love thee." He does not say "more than these," and he does not dare use the word love in its highest and spiritual sense as Jesus himself had used it; he uses a term signifying rather to cherish or to be personally attached to, than to love. Receiving this answer, Jesus confides to him the care of his sheep. But it was not enough: a second, a third time Jesus asks the same question, substituting the last time the word signifying to cherish for that meaning to love, as if he would assure himself even of that minimum of affection which is all that Peter in his humility claims. Then "Peter was grieved." He was moved to the very depth of his soul, and, daring no longer to trust his own heart, of which he remembers the weakness all too bitterly, he appeals to Christ, who knows everything, and it is only on meeting his gaze, which is the unmistakable guarantee of his love, that he ventures to say: "Lord, thou knowest that I love thee." And Jesus said to him yet again: "Feed my sheep," thus making him the shepherd of souls.

The Ascension as Seen from the Mount of Olives [L20]

⊕

THE Lord went only to Gethsemane, and from the Garden of Olives up to the summit of the mount. He did not set foot upon the path on which he had been arrested. The crowd followed as in a procession, ascending by the different paths that encircled the mount. Jesus at each instant shone more brightly and his motions became more rapid. The disciples hastened after him, but it was impossible to overtake him. When he reached the top of the mountain, he was resplendent as a beam of white sunlight. A shining circle, glancing in all the colors of the rainbow, fell from heaven around him. The pressing crowd stood in a wide circle outside, as if blending with it. Jesus himself shone still more brightly than the glory about him. He laid the left hand on his breast and, raising the right, turned slowly around, blessing the whole world. The crowd stood motionless. I saw all receive the benediction. With great joy I felt his blessing of the whole world.

And now the rays of light from above united with the glory emanating from Jesus, and I saw him disappearing, dissolving as it were in the light from heaven, vanishing as he rose. It appeared as if one sun was lost in another, as if one flame entered another, as if a spark floated into a flame. It was as if one were gazing into the full midday splendors of the sun, though this light was whiter and clearer. Full day compared with this would be dark. I saw innumerable souls from all sides going into that light and vanishing on high with the Lord. I cannot say that I saw him becoming apparently smaller and smaller like something flying up in the air, for he disappeared as it were in a cloud of light. Out of that cloud something like dew, like a shower of light, fell upon all below, and when they could no longer endure the splendor, they were seized with amazement and terror. The apostles and disciples, who were nearest to Jesus, were blinded by the dazzling glare. They were forced to lower their eyes, while many cast themselves prostrate on their faces. The blessed Virgin was standing close behind them and gazing calmly straight ahead. [411]

[ACTS 1:9] 9 And when he had said this, as they were looking on, he was lifted up, and a cloud took him out of their sight.

THE *resurrection of Jesus is to a certain extent incomplete so long as his glorious ascension is still unaccomplished. He has resumed his body, he has still to take his own place again, and that he is about to do. After he had given his last instructions to his disciples, Luke tells us that "he led them out as far as Bethany, and he lifted up his hands and blessed them. And it came to pass while he blessed them he was parted from them and carried up to heaven." The same disciple, in the Acts of the Apostles, adds a few characteristic details about the luminous cloud and the angels which appeared. It is evident that the cloud did not resemble a chariot destined to bear the glorified body of Jesus to heaven, but was simply a veil hiding from the disciples what became of that body, endowed as it now was with special powers. It may perhaps have undergone a kind of dematerialization, fading away in the light, to take form again where he was to reign eternally. Or perhaps he may have been merely transported to heaven in the twinkling of an eye, by virtue of his divinity. However that may have been, he suddenly faded from sight, and where he had been, a cloud stretched like a veil, hiding the mysteries of God. The apotheosis is complete. Jesus is gone to sit down at the right hand of his Father, from whence he shall some day come, according to his promise, to judge the world.*

The Ascension as Seen from Below [L21]

⊕

AFTER some moments, when the splendor began to diminish, the whole assembly in deep silence—their souls swayed by varying emotions—gazed fixedly up at the brightness, which continued visible for a long time. I saw two figures appear in this light. They looked small at first, but seemed to grow larger and larger as they descended. They were clothed in long white garments. They looked like prophets. They addressed the multitude, their voices like trumpets resounding loud and clear. It seemed to me that they could surely be heard in Jerusalem. They made no motion, stood perfectly still, and said: "Ye men of Galilee, why stand ye looking up to heaven? This Jesus who is taken up from you into heaven shall so come as you have seen him going into heaven." After these words the figures vanished. The brightness remained for a while longer and then disappeared like daylight retiring before the darkness of night. The disciples were quite out of themselves, for they now comprehended what had happened to them. The Lord had left them and gone to his heavenly Father! Many, stunned by grief and amazement, fell to the earth. When the glare had entirely died away, they arose again, and the others gathered around them. They formed groups, the blessed Virgin stepped forward, and so they stood for some time longer recovering themselves, talking together, and gazing upward. At last, the apostles and disciples went back to the house of the Last Supper, and the blessed Virgin followed. Some were weeping like children that refuse to be comforted, others were lost in thought. The blessed Virgin, Peter, and John were very calm and full of consolation. [411]

[ACTS 1:9–12] 9 And when he had said this, as they were looking on, he was lifted up, and a cloud took him out of their sight. 10 And while they were gazing into heaven as he went, behold, two men stood by them in white robes, 11 and said, "Men of Galilee, why do you stand looking into heaven? This Jesus, who was taken up from you into heaven, will come in the same way as you saw him go into heaven." 12 Then they returned to Jerusalem from the mount called Olivet, which is near Jerusalem, a sabbath day's journey away.

THE ascension is not merely the personal glorification of Jesus, it is also an event of the last importance to the human race. It is the completion of the creation, interrupted by the fall of the first man. The design of God in creating man was to make of him the conscious and free agent of his own salvation, the sharer in the divine bliss and glory. Man by his sin had hindered the realization of this plan, but he could not frustrate it. By the resurrection of Christ we see man set free from death and restored to his first hopes of eternal life, but his salvation is not yet completed. By the ascension God permits man, redeemed through Christ, to share with him in the divine glory, and thus realize in him the original idea of the creation. Only thus can that idea achieve completion. Not yet, however, is the end of all things. The ascension not only completes the work of our redemption through Christ, it lays the foundations of its realization in every one of us who is of Christ. In this consists its importance for the church.

There remain now but two promises to be fulfilled; the sending of the Holy Spirit, which shall continuously supply the church on earth with the grace of the risen Savior, and that last prophecy uttered in the judgment hall of Caiaphas: "Hereafter shall ye see the Son of Man sitting on the right hand of power and coming in the clouds of heaven," a coming which will summon the elect to share the ascension of the Master and to become partakers of his glory, even as Jesus prayed in the sublime petition offered up on the eve of his death. "Father, I will that they also whom thou hast given me, be with me where I am; that they may behold my glory which thou hast given me; for thou lovedst me before the foundation of the world."

It is not for us to dwell now on this last subject, these final chords of the divine symphony. We have been relating the life on earth of Jesus; that life ends for us in the apotheosis of the ascension. The cloud which "received Christ from sight" is like the curtain which falls at the close of a drama. We will not attempt to raise it, but let us each and all withdraw to "ponder," as the Virgin did, these things in our hearts.

The Holy Virgin in Old Age [L22]

⊕

THE blessed Virgin was now very advanced in years, but she had in her appearance no other mark of age than that of a great longing, which at length effectuated her glorification. She was inexpressibly grave. I never saw her laugh. The older she grew, the whiter and more transparent became her face. She was thin, but I saw no wrinkle, no sign of decay in her. She was like a spirit. . . . After Mary had lived three years in the settlement near Ephesus, she conceived a great desire to visit Jerusalem, so John and Peter escorted her thither. Several apostles were there assembled, of whom I remember Thomas. I think it was a council, and Mary assisted the apostles with her advice. On her arrival, I saw her in the evening twilight visiting, before she entered the city, the Mount of Olives, Mount Golgotha, the Holy Sepulcher, and all the Holy Places around Jerusalem. The Mother of God was so sad, so moved by compassion, that she could scarcely walk. Peter and John supported her under the arms.

A year and a half before her death, she made one more journey from Ephesus to Jerusalem, and I saw her again visiting the Holy Places. She was unspeakably sorrowful, and she continually sighed: "O my Son! My Son!" When she came to the back gate of that palace where she had first seen Jesus passing with the cross and where he fell, she was so agitated by the painful remembrance that she too sank to the ground. Her companions thought her dying. They removed her to Zion, upon which the Cenacle was still standing, and in one of whose buildings she took up her abode. For several days she appeared to be so weak and so near death that her friends began to think of preparing her a tomb. She herself made choice of a cave on the Mount of Olives, and the apostles had a beautiful tomb built there by a Christian stonecutter. Many were of the opinion that she would really die; and so the report of her death spread abroad. But she recovered sufficient strength to journey back to Ephesus where, a year and a half later, she did indeed die. The tomb prepared for her on the Mount of Olives was ever after held in reverence, and at a later period a church was built over it. John Damascene, as I was told in vision, wrote from hearsay that the blessed Virgin died in Jerusalem and was buried there. Her death, her assumption into heaven, and the site of her tomb, as I believe, God allowed to be subjects of uncertain tradition that the pagan sentiments of the time might not penetrate Christianity, for the blessed Virgin might otherwise have been adored as a goddess. [423]

*A Station of Mary's Own Way of the Cross in Ephesus,
drawn by Cl. Brentano, after Anne Catherine*

APPENDICES

Appendix I
Chronology of the Life of Jesus 477

Appendix II
The Hebrew Calendar 493

Appendix III
*Reconstruction of the Hebrew Calendar for
the Time of Jesus's Ministry Based on
Anne Catherine Emmerich's
Calendar Indications* 495

Appendix IV
A Summary of the Chronicle 500

Appendix V
*Commemoration of the Events
in the Life of Jesus* 508

Ancient Stairwell in Jerusalem

APPENDIX I

Chronology of the Life of Jesus Christ

MANY have been impressed and deeply affected by Anne Catherine Emmerich's account of the life of Jesus,[†] yet until now it has been generally viewed merely as useful for the edification of the soul. However, as we shall see, Anne Catherine's account is not only edifying and uplifting but also, on the whole, *true*. We say "on the whole," because it would be nearly impossible to check every detail. What can be said is that, at least with respect to *space* (the geography and topography of Palestine) and *time* (the historical dating of the Christ events), Anne Catherine's account of the life of Jesus is very accurate indeed, and from this it follows that considerable confidence may be placed in her visions as a whole.

We are currently not long past the 2,000[th] anniversary of the birth of Jesus, and the question arises whether modern astronomical-chronological research can help determine this date, and others in the life of Jesus, with a high degree of certainty. We believe that, on the basis of these visions, such dates can in fact be established, as will be set forth in what follows. And as stated earlier, it has proven possible, furthermore—with the help of Anne Catherine's descriptions (supplemented by the gospels)—to reconstruct a day-by-day chronicle of Jesus's life for much of his ministry. The authenticity of Anne Catherine's chronicle can, moreover, be independently verified by applying astronomical chronology to her calendar indications. The results of such astronomical-chronological research show that Anne Catherine's descriptions of the life of Jesus during his ministry are consistent throughout with respect to the calendar, thus providing an internal control on the chronological validity of her descriptions of the rest of the life of Jesus.

Historical Overview

By the very nature of its subject matter, this chronological study is concerned with dates. The motivation to carry out the research leading to the dating of events in the life of Jesus was not simply to determine these dates, but rather, having determined them, to *apply* them. An immediate application was the computation of planetary positions on various dates with a view to unveiling the mystery of the star of the Magi and other mysteries. One way of exploring

the veracity of Anne Catherine's visions is to compute planetary positions against the background of the signs of the zodiac for major events in the life of Jesus, and to see whether a harmony prevailed between these configurations of the heavenly bodies above and the events and miracles of the earthly life of Jesus below, paying special attention to those places where in her visions Anne Catherine makes specific reference to astronomical events. However, in order to compute these planetary configurations, the relevant dates had first to be established. Once discovered, these dates—or rather, their connection with certain time intervals in Jesus's life—reveal a profound wisdom that sheds new light upon the very nature of his life, as will emerge in what follows.

One could argue, of course, that Christianity has managed quite well until now without knowing the exact dates of Jesus's life, and that such details are in any case irrelevant to the central mysteries of salvation and redemption. Without claiming in any way that such knowledge is necessary, or even important, for the salvation of the human being or for redemption, the point of this study is that these dates, once known, can be worked with and understood in such a way that a deeper relationship to Jesus is made possible; indeed, they open the door to a new perspective on Jesus Christ.

Paradoxical though it may seem, it is precisely knowledge of the concrete details of Jesus's life that enables us to comprehend him in a new way. These details enable us to explore the heavenly correspondences that existed during Jesus's life on Earth. At the same time, they open a new dimension of Christianity, one attuned to Christ as a cosmic reality, and it is upon this reality that this study aspires to shed some light.

With the closing of two millennia of Christianity, it would seem the time has come for humanity to approach the mystery of the Christ anew. Here we may recall his words concerning "the sign of the Son of Man in heaven" (Matt. 24:30), which imply a universal dimension of Christianity and call for humanity to look to the signs in the heavens and to begin to decipher them, as did the Magi of old. To lay a firm foundation for such an understanding of Christianity, however, we must first establish secure dates for the life of Jesus. To begin, then, let us consider his date of birth, for this is the obvious starting point for our whole inquiry.

---

† See *Abbreviations and Endorsements* for some testimonials.

The Date of Birth

The birth of Jesus is traditionally celebrated by the Church on December 25. Prior to AD 354, however, the chosen date was January 6. Both of these dates, as shown below, are based on correspondences—that is, they are symbolical and not necessarily based on historical fact. Our first inquiry, then, will examine the underlying significance of these traditional dates.

Let us first consider January 6, which is, incidentally, the date of the nativity still celebrated in the Armenian Church. This date was chosen in the course of the third century AD as the day on which to commemorate the birth of Jesus. Who made this choice and why?

To answer these questions, we must imagine the climate of early Christianity in Egypt—for it was above all in Alexandria, the city founded by Alexander the Great in 332 BC, that the Church flourished most vigorously at that time. Here the ancient mystery-wisdom tradition of Egypt and the newly-emerging Christian religion met and clashed. Among the Church Fathers who lived and worked in Alexandria were Clement of Alexandria (ca. AD 150–215) and Origen (ca. AD 185–254).

These and other early Church Fathers were faced with a multitude of religious cults that derived from various ancient mystery traditions. As "apologists," they undertook the task of representing Christianity, which, they argued, differed from all pagan cults in its claim to *historicity*. Whereas the traditional mystery cults were directed primarily to polytheistic worship, Christianity emphasized the worship of the One—the Son of God, who had lived on Earth as a human being. Christianity is in fact centered on the being of Christ, the Second Person of the Godhead, who passed through *birth* and *death*. This distinguishes Christianity from all other religions, cults, and beliefs: Christianity has its basis in *the historical fact* of the life, death, and resurrection of Christ Jesus.

Although Christianity rests squarely on this historical event, and is unique among religious traditions in this regard, the dates of Jesus's birth and death were not transmitted—at least no record of them has yet been discovered. The only two calendrical details recorded in the Gospel of St. John set the crucifixion on the day of preparation for the Passover, which is said to have fallen on a Friday, that is, the day before the sabbath, that year (the sabbath begins on Friday evening).

Nor is much help with dating to be expected from Jewish or Roman historians. To those in power at that time in Jerusalem (Pontius Pilate, Herod Antipas, and the priests and Pharisees comprising the Sanhedrin), Jesus was only a carpenter's son from Nazareth who—because he had taught and healed throughout the land and had agitated the people, drawing a following largely from ordinary folk—had died a common criminal's death upon a cross.

No official source bothered to record anything more concerning Jesus of Nazareth. The startling paradox, then, is that the historical fact upon which Christianity rests—and it is precisely this historicity that sets Christianity apart—is nowhere documented, with the exception of the witness borne later by the four gospels. Yet none of these mentions any explicit dates, even though they do contain a few calendrical indications. The early Church Fathers were thus faced with solemnizing an historical fact for which they had no exact date. They wished, quite naturally, to celebrate the birth and death of the Messiah each year, but in the absence of any transmitted dates, how could they proceed?

In the case of the *death* and *resurrection*, the solution was straightforward. Since the resurrection took place on the Sunday following the feast of the Passover, the annual commemoration of this event was specified to take place on the Sunday after the spring Full Moon, for the latter always coincided more or less with the onset of the Passover festival. In fact, in the year AD 33 the spring Full Moon (the first Full Moon after the vernal equinox) fell on Friday, April 3, the day of the crucifixion.[†] By fixing Easter Sunday as the Sunday after the first spring Full Moon, the "archetype" established in the year AD 33 recurs each year, although usually only approximately, since the spring Full Moon falls (on average) on a Friday only once every seven years.

But what of the commemoration of the *birth* of Christ Jesus? The Alexandrian Church Fathers in the third century chose January 6, and this date spread then throughout the Church. Their choice was influenced by the mystery cults prevailing in Egypt at that time. For instance, St. Epiphanius of Salamis (ca. AD 315–403) wrote concerning the festival in Alexandria dedicated to the goddess Koré, which was celebrated each year on the night of January 5/6: "On this night Koré—the Virgin—gave birth to Aion" (*Panarion* 51, 22, 10). This festival was essentially a solar cult, for Aion was identified with Helios, the Sun, believed by the Egyptians to be born (or reborn) on January 5/6. But why was this date chosen for the birth of Jesus?

---

† It should be noted that only in the twentieth century did it become possible, through astronomical chronology applied especially to Anne Catherine's visions, to establish the true historical date of the crucifixion (see below, *The Date of the Crucifixion*). Prior to this, the above-mentioned rule had been applied to determine the date of Easter Sunday without any definite knowledge, generally speaking, of the original date (April 5, AD 33, as we shall see) on which the resurrection in fact took place according to the research here presented.

Evidently the sages then living in Egypt believed that, in the Julian calendar (introduced by Julius Caesar in 46 BC), the winter solstice occurred on January 5/6. This was for them the date transmitted by tradition as the longest night of the year. In actual fact the longest night of the year at the time of Jesus was December 22/23, but this was apparently not generally known to the people of Alexandria, who adhered to the traditional date. It is difficult to believe, however, that the reason for the two-week discrepancy between the traditional date and the actual date for the celebration of the winter solstice was entirely due to ignorance of the astronomical facts. Perhaps it was due to an error that arose with the introduction of the Julian calendar in place of the traditional Egyptian calendar. However that may be, the early Christians did take note of the solar phenomenon of the winter solstice, and we must remember that there was a natural correspondence for them between Christ and the Sun. Anastasios Sinaita of the Eastern Church wrote, for example:

> Helios (the Sun) has the first place in the sky and leads the heavenly dance. So is Christ, who is the spiritual Sun, placed above all the heavenly hierarchies and powers, for He is the leader, the door to the Father. (*Hexaemeron* 5)

To early Christians the identification of Christ with the spirit of the Sun was self-evident. For them, Christ was the Sun of righteousness, and the physical Sun was his outward symbol. Such analogic thinking was also prevalent in Egypt at that time and has been called the *hermetic* mode of thought, after the Egyptian sage Hermes. The presiding axiom of this mode of thinking is summarized in the so-called Emerald Table: "That which is above is like unto that which is below, and that which is below is like unto that which is above." Early Christians living in Egypt and influenced by this hermetic mode of thought conceived of the physical Sun as an outer manifestation, or symbol, of the spiritual Sun (Christ). Just as the physical Sun was thought to be born (or reborn) each year on January 6, so did the Church Fathers of Alexandria apparently believe the birth of Christ to have fallen on this day.

The Church Fathers in the *West* arrived at the date of December 25 for the nativity by the same reasoning, for it was believed in Rome that the winter solstice—again, the longest night of the year—fell on December 24/25. Although more accurate than the traditional date of January 5/6 celebrated in Egypt, the longest night of the year at the time of Christ was in fact, as we have said, December 22/23. Nevertheless, the Roman followers of Mithras held their festival dedicated to the Invincible Sun on December 25. On this day each year they celebrated the triumph of the Sun over the powers of darkness, which they held to be

at their height on the night of December 24/25, the longest night of the year according to their belief.

Just as the Sun (Helios) was thought to be born (or reborn) on December 25 of each year, after which its light and warmth would begin to increase, so the Roman Christians—since they had no historical testimony regarding the actual day of Jesus's birth—considered that it too must have taken place on this day. The parallel is clear: the birthday of the physical Sun, Helios, ought to fall on the same day as that of its archetype, the spiritual Sun—Christ. Thus, by AD 354, December 25, previously the festival of the Invincible Sun, was being celebrated as the day of the nativity:

> But they name this day (December 25) also "the birthday of the Invincible Sun." Truly, who is as invincible as Our Lord, who cast down and triumphed over death? And if they call this day "the birthday of the Sun" then He is the Sun of righteousness, of whom the prophet Malachi said: "to the God-fearing His name will arise as the Sun of righteousness, and salvation is beneath His wings." (From a homily by St. John Chrysostom; cf. A. Wilmart; "La collection des 38 homelies latines de St. Jean Chrysostome," *Journal of Theological Studies*, vol. 19, 1918, pp. 305–327.)

We see then that the traditional dates assigned to the nativity were derived by way of *analogy*. In both cases the nativity was determined to coincide with the longest night of the year, *symbolizing* the birth of the Christ Sun. The actual moment of birth was (and still is) celebrated at midnight: December 24/ 25 in the West; January 5/6 in the East. If the underlying symbolism is understood, December 25 is still an appropriate date to celebrate the birth (or rebirth) of the spiritual Sun (Christ), for December 25 comes just three days after the winter solstice, which at the present time falls on December 21/22.

When in the fourth century Roman Christians adopted December 25 (in preference to January 6) as the date of the nativity, they nevertheless still continued to celebrate January 6, regarding it then as the date of the *baptism in the Jordan* rather than of the birth of Jesus. Moreover, since the three kings were believed to have visited the newborn child shortly after his birth, January 6 came to be celebrated also as the date of the Adoration of the Magi. The term *epiphany*, meaning "appearance," was associated with January 6, for it was believed that on this day, the star appeared over the place of Jesus's birth and that on this same day thirty years later the dove appeared above him at the baptism.

The tradition of celebrating January 6 as the date of the baptism in the Jordan appears to derive from the gnostic Basilides, who taught in Alexandria in the second century AD. Clement of Alexandria mentions a gnostic sect, followers of Basilides, that celebrated the baptism on this day (*Stromata* I, 146, 1, 2). It was certainly again by way of analogy with the mystery cult of Koré in Alexandria that the gnostics adopted January 6 as the date of the baptism: for them, *the baptism of Jesus* was actually the *birth of Jesus Christ*. This was their interpretation of the words the Father pronounced at that moment: "Thou art my Son whom this day I have begotten" (Luke 3:22).

The gnostics maintained therefore that the *real* birth of Christ occurred at the baptism and that the date of January 6 corresponded to the baptism—the descent of Christ onto Earth—rather than to the physical birth of *Jesus*. They believed that, at the baptism, the *divine* being of Christ united with the *human* being of Jesus and was "born" at that moment. And so, they celebrated this "birth"—i.e., the baptism—each year on that day.

This practice spread subsequently to Rome, and January 6 is still celebrated by the Church as the date of the baptism. As we shall see later, the historical baptism actually occurred in autumn, not in the middle of winter. But first we turn our attention to the determination of the true birth date of Jesus.

The visions of Anne Catherine as recorded by Clemens Brentano include detailed descriptions of the nativity itself, as well as precise geographical indications of its location in a cave at the south end of a hill to the east of Bethlehem. The Constantine-Basilica, which St Helena had built above the cave of the nativity, still stands on this very spot today. Anne Catherine communicated the following about the timing of the birth:

> The Blessed Virgin spent the sabbath in the Cave of the Nativity in prayer and meditation.... In the *afternoon of the sabbath*, when it is the Jewish custom to go for a walk, Joseph took the Blessed Virgin through the valley behind the cave to the tomb of Maraha, Abraham's nurse.... Mary had told Joseph that *tonight at midnight* would be the hour of the child's birth, for then the nine months since the Annunciation would have been completed.... [That night] I saw the radiance around the Blessed Virgin growing ever greater.... Meanwhile the Blessed Virgin, borne up in ecstasy, was now gazing downwards, adoring her God, whose Mother she had become and who lay on the Earth before her in the form of a helpless newborn child. I saw our Redeemer as a tiny child, shining with a light that overpowered all the surrounding radiance, and lying on the carpet at the Blessed Virgin's knees. (*LBVM*, 191–193 [emphasis added])

According to this description, the birth took place around midnight on the day after the sabbath. Since the Jewish sabbath falls on Saturday, and the Jewish day begins at sunset, the sabbath day extends from sunset Friday to sunset Saturday. The birth took place, therefore, around the midnight between Saturday and Sunday. This is the first detail to take note of.

Anne Catherine's visions indicate also that the birth took place during the Jewish month of Kislev. This is evident from her description of events following the birth. She states that the child was circumcised at dawn the day after the sabbath following the birth, that is, Sunday morning, one week after the birth (cf. Luke 2:21). Regarding the next sabbath, and the beginning of the Feast of the Dedication of the Temple, she says:

> This feast really begins on the 25th day of the month of Kislev, but as this fell on the evening of Friday . . . in the year of Jesus's birth, that is to say on the eve of the sabbath, it was postponed to the evening of Saturday . . . or the 26th day of Kislev. It lasted eight days. [Thus the sixth day after the circumcision was the 25th day of Kislev, so that the circumcision happened on the nineteenth day of Kislev and the birth of Jesus on the twelfth day of Kislev.] (*LBVM*, 240–241)

Readers already familiar with the writings that describe Anne Catherine's visions will realize that references to the calendar dates on which she *had* the relevant visions have been omitted. It is only the *Jewish* calendar dates and festivals communicated by Anne Catherine that are relevant, not the modern calendar dates on which she experienced the visions. At the time of Jesus, the Jewish calendar, not the Julian calendar employed by the Romans, was in use in Palestine. Hence it is clearly the Jewish calendar that is of primary importance in all chronological matters pertaining to the life of Jesus.

Thus the date of the crucifixion mentioned in the Gospel of St. John refers to the Jewish calendar: namely, the day of preparation for the Passover, the 14th day of the month of Nisan. In AD 33 this was the same as April 3 in the Julian calendar. However, the date "April 3" would have been meaningless for the majority of Jews living in Palestine at that time. For them, this day was "Nisan 14." Similarly, the date Kislev 25 was known throughout Palestine as the start of the Feast of the Dedication. Indeed, it is the communication of this date in relation to the sabbath that provides a key to the dating of the birth of Jesus. Assuming that Anne Catherine's indication is correct, the birth took place thirteen days before this feast, on Kislev 12, around midnight Saturday/Sunday.

For astronomical chronology, then, the problem is to determine when, historically, for those years in which the birth of Jesus might have taken place, Kislev 25 coincided in fact with the sabbath (Friday/Saturday); or, which leads to the same result, when Kislev 12 coincided with Saturday/Sunday.

Knowledge of the Jewish calendar is obviously necessary

to answer this question. Here it suffices to point out that the occurrence of the New Moon more or less coincided with the start of a new month in the calendar of ancient Israel. A New Moon festival was celebrated on the evening of the first day of the new month, and the months were reckoned as "hollow" or "full," depending on whether they comprised 29 or 30 days (these usually alternated). In this way, the months corresponded closely with the phases of the Moon, for on average 29½ days (actually 29.53 days) elapse from one New Moon to the next.

At some time in the history of Israel, a set of rules for specifying the Jewish calendar was devised, primarily to reconcile the inevitable discrepancies between solar and lunar reckoning. In principle, the first (Nisan), third (Sivan), fifth (Ab), seventh (Tishri) and eleventh (Shebat) months were consistently full, each containing 30 days, while the second (Iyyar), fourth (Tammuz), sixth (Elul), and tenth (Tebeth) months were consistently hollow, each containing 29 days. The remaining months—the eighth (Heshvan or Marcheshvan), the ninth (Kislev), and the twelfth (Adar)—could be either full or hollow. As we shall see when we look into Anne Catherine's calendar indications, these rules seem to have been applied in general—but not rigorously—by the time of Jesus.[†]

This method of counting alternate months of the year as either full or hollow did not guarantee that the months would remain precisely in step with the phases of the Moon. However, it was possible to regulate the sequence of months to coincide with the phases of the Moon—especially in the eighth and ninth months, Heshvan and Kislev, which could be either full or hollow. Therefore we can understand that, by the eighth or ninth month (Heshvan or Kislev), the occurrence of the New Moon could sometimes fall *after* the start of the new month. The month of Kislev in which Jesus was born actually started 1⅓ days *before* the astronomical New Moon. But how is it possible to establish this?

To do so, we need to know in what year the birth of Jesus fell. For this, the following statement by Anne Catherine provides the necessary clue: "Christ reached the age of thirty-three years and three times six weeks. I say three times six, because that figure was in that moment shown to me three times one after the other" (*LBVM* p. 145).

Assuming that the crucifixion took place on Friday, April 3, AD 33 (see below), the birth must have occurred in the year 2 BC, which is also the year favored by some early Christian writers, among them Epiphanius.

To be precise, the birth took place, according to Anne Catherine, on Kislev 12 in 2 BC, and it follows from this

that Christ Jesus attained the age of thirty-three on Kislev 12 in AD 32.[‡] Since the astronomical New Moon at the start of the month of Kislev in AD 32 took place on November 21 at 9:15 PM Jerusalem time, the first day of the month of Kislev could possibly have started at sunset the following day, November 22, in which case Kislev 1 that year would equate with November 22/23. This means that Kislev 12, eleven days later, may well have coincided with December 2/3 in the year AD 32, exactly four calendar months prior to the crucifixion on April 3 of the following year. Even if Kislev 12 did not coincide precisely with December 2/3, AD 32, it must have been within a day or two of this date.

Counting from Tuesday, December 2, AD 32, to Friday April 3, AD 33, gives seventeen full weeks plus a fraction (Tuesday to Friday), corresponding closely with the indication that "Jesus reached the age of thirty-three years and three times six weeks." In other words, thirty-three years elapsed between Kislev 12, 2 BC, and Kislev 12, AD 32; and a further eighteen weeks elapsed before the crucifixion.

Having provisionally established 2 BC as the birth year, the task remains to determine the Julian calendar date of Kislev 12 in that year.

The New Moon at the start of the month of Kislev in 2 BC occurred at 1:20 AM Jerusalem time on November 27. Very often the first day of the Jewish month began at sunset on the same calendar date following the occurrence of the astronomical New Moon. In this case, Kislev 1 would equate with November 27/28, and Kislev 12 with December 8/9. However, since December 8 in 2 BC was a Monday, it does not fulfill the first condition referred to above, namely, that in the birth year of Jesus, Kislev 12 coincided with Saturday/Sunday. To fulfill this condition in 2 BC, Kislev 12 must correspond to Saturday/Sunday, December 6/7.

Thus, in the light of Anne Catherine's indications, the birth of Jesus took place around midnight December 6/7 2 BC (see Table 1).

TABLE 1: THE BIRTH OF JESUS

The New Moon denoting the start of the month of Kislev took place at 1:20 AM Jerusalem time on November 27, 2 BC. However, Kislev 1 had already started at sunset on November 25, 1⅓ days prior to this. (* denotes sabbath)

[†] See *Appendices II–IV.*

[‡] Note that in the historical method of dating there is no year 0, and the count goes straight from 1 BC to AD 1. Someone born in 2 BC would have attained the age of 1 in 1 BC, the age of 2 in AD 1, and the age of 3 in AD 2, etc., and the age of 33 in AD 32.

Kislev 1	Tue/Wed	25/26 Nov	New Moon Festival
Kislev 2	Wed/Thu	26/27 Nov	
Kislev 3	Thu/Fri	27/28 Nov	
*Kislev 4	Fri/Sat	28/29 Nov	
Kislev 5	Sat/Sun	29/30 Nov	
Kislev 6	Sun/Mon	30/1 Dec	
Kislev 7	Mon/Tue	1/2 Dec	
Kislev 8	Tue/Wed	2/3 Dec	
Kislev 9	Wed/Thu	3/4 Dec	
Kislev 10	Thu/Fri	4/5 Dec	
*Kislev 11	Fri/Sat	5/6 Dec	
Kislev 12	Sat/Sun	6/7 Dec	Birth of Jesus
Kislev 13	Sun/Mon	7/8 Dec	
Kislev 14	Mon/Tue	8/9 Dec	
Kislev 15	Tue/Wed	9/10 Dec	
Kislev 16	Wed/Thu	10/11 Dec	
Kislev 17	Thu/Fri	11/12 Dec	
*Kislev 18	Fri/Sat	12/13 Dec	
Kislev 19	Sat/Sun	13/14 Dec	Circumcision
Kislev 20	Sun/Mon	14/15 Dec	
Kislev 21	Mon/Tue	15/16 Dec	
Kislev 22	Tue/Wed	16/17 Dec	
Kislev 23	Wed/Thu	17/18 Dec	
Kislev 24 Thu/Fri		18/19 Dec	Feast of the Dedication of the Temple started
*Kislev 25 Fri/Sat		19/20 Dec	
Kislev 26 Sat/Sun		20/21 Dec	

The sequence of days in the month of Kislev, 2 BC, is listed in Table 1, where the day count shows that Kislev 1 fell on November 25/26. The preceding month of Heshvan, having completed 29 (or more likely 30) days, the New Moon festival of Kislev could have been celebrated on the evening of Tuesday, November 25 in 2 BC. Assuming that dusk, which denoted the start of the new day, occurred around 5:20 PM Jerusalem time on November 25, the New Moon then fell 32 hours later, at 1:20 AM Jerusalem time on November 27. Thus Kislev 1 started 32 hours (= 1⅓ days) prior to the astronomical New Moon. By counting 30 days in that month of Kislev, making it a "full" month, the start of the next month (Tebeth) would have been brought back closer into step with the Moon's phases.

Using Anne Catherine's indications, we can establish, then, that the birth of Jesus took place around midnight between Saturday and Sunday, December 6/7, in 2 BC.†

This result differs by one year and eighteen days from the most famous dating of Jesus's birth, that made by Dionysius Exiguus in AD 525. Dionysius concluded that the birth took place on December 24/25, 1 BC, that is, just one week prior to January 1, AD 1, the date that Dionysius chose as the beginning of the Christian era. Considering that Dionysius had little upon which to base his study, apart from a few remarks by the early Church Fathers, the date he arrived at for the birth of Jesus is remarkably close to the actual historical date of December 6/7, 2 BC, which it has been only recently possible to determine.

Some readers may object that December 6/7, 2 BC, is untenable as the birth date of Jesus, since Herod the Great is generally held to have died in 4 BC. This assumption is the primary reason most modern biblical chronologists place the birth of Jesus before 4 BC. Without tackling the problem of dating the death of Herod at this point, it will have to suffice to refer to the work of the theologian Florian Riess (*Das Geburtsjahr Christi*, Freiburg, 1880), supported more recently by Ormond Edwards (*The Time of Christ*, Floris Books, Edinburgh, 1986), both of whom conclude that Herod died no more than three months after the lunar eclipse on January 10 in 1 BC. Ormond Edwards bases his conclusion on evidence presented by coins minted close to the beginning of Herod's reign, combined with a new consideration of the Jewish historian Josephus's count of the years of his reign.

The Date of the Baptism

The first two verses of the second chapter of the Gospel of St. Luke state:

1. "In those days a decree went out from Caesar Augustus that all the world should be enrolled."
2. "This was the first enrollment, when Quirinius was governor of Syria."

This reference to Quirinius was examined thoroughly by Emil Schürer in his book, *The History of the Jewish People in the Age of Christ Jesus*. According to Schürer, Quirinius was very likely governor of Syria in 3–2 BC, and definitely so in AD 6–7. Our date for the birth—December 6/7, 2 BC—fits well, then, with this chronological indication given in the Gospel of St. Luke.

Two further important chronological indications are given in the third chapter of the Gospel of St. Luke:

---

† Elsewhere Anne Catherine said: "The actual date of Jesus's birth, as I always see it, is four weeks earlier than its celebration by the Church" (*LBVM*, 165). This remark holds true if the original date of birth celebrated by the Church is taken (i.e., January 6), for the historical date was December 6 (or rather the night of December 6/7).

1–3. "In the fifteenth year of the reign of Tiberius Caesar, Pontius Pilate being governor of Judea, and Herod being tetrarch of Galilee . . . the word of God came to John the son of Zechariah in the wilderness; and he went into all the region about the Jordan, preaching a baptism of repentance for the forgiveness of sins."

21–22. "Now when all the people were baptized, and when Jesus also had been baptized and was praying, the heaven was opened. . . . Jesus, when he began his ministry, was about thirty years of age."

Let us combine these references with Anne Catherine's indications and see whether we can close in on the date of the baptism in the Jordan. Here Luke's statement regarding "the fifteenth year of the reign of Tiberius" is of central importance. According to J. K. Fotheringham, who applied astronomical chronology to establish the date of the crucifixion as April 3, AD 33:

> Technical chronology proves just as decisively that the fifteenth year of Tiberius was the year AD 28–29. . . . The only question is whether the fifteenth year of Tiberius began in Nisan (spring) of AD 28 or in the autumn of that year. (*TC*, 146)

Subsequently Ormond Edwards was able to establish from evidence provided by the dating of a coin that the fifteenth year of Tiberius in fact extended from the autumn of AD 28 to the autumn of AD 29. The specification of the fifteenth year of Tiberius thus tallies precisely with Anne Catherine's indication that "the word of God" came to John during the month of Nisan. As we shall see, the Nisan concerned was in the year AD 29. In other words, John began his baptizing activity after the month of Nisan (spring) of AD 29.

The Gospel of St. Luke states that, at the baptism, Jesus "was about thirty years of age." According to our calculations, Jesus turned thirty on Kislev 12, AD 29. If Luke's "about thirty years" is interpreted in a strict sense, the baptism must have taken place toward the end of the year 29 (since Kislev 12 corresponded approximately to December 5/6 that year). With the help of Anne Catherine's indications, however, it is possible to arrive at an exact date.

As in the case of her description of the *birth* of Jesus, where the date Kislev 12 in the Jewish calendar was found by counting back from the beginning of the Feast of the Dedication (Kislev 25), so can the date of the *baptism* be determined by counting back from the beginning of the Feast of Tabernacles (Tishri 15) in the autumn of AD 29.

In her day-by-day account of the travels of Jesus in the period after the baptism, Anne Catherine mentions three sabbaths before the beginning of the Feast of Tabernacles, when Jesus approached the town of Dibon on the east side of the Jordan (northeast of the place of baptism). Again it

is the sabbath—the seventh day—that provides the key to the specification of the weekdays, for Anne Catherine beheld the start of the Feast of Tabernacles as on the third day after the sabbath, that is, Tuesday (starting Monday evening), since the sabbath is Saturday (starting Friday evening). This means, according to her account, that Tishri 15 fell on Monday/Tuesday in the year of the baptism.

In AD 29, the New Moon at the start of the month of Tishri occurred at 5:00 PM Jerusalem time on Monday, September 26. At sunset on this date, the first day of Tishri must have begun; and then, fourteen days later, at sunset on Monday, October 10, the fifteenth day of Tishri would have begun. Since Tishri is the seventh month of the year, it is reckoned as a "full" month (30 days) and the preceding month (Elul) as "hollow" (29 days). Counting back three sabbaths (Saturdays) from Monday, October 10, we arrive at Saturday, September 24, in the year 29 AD, which means that the sabbath would have started at sunset on Friday, September 23. This sabbath was the twenty-seventh day of the month of Elul (Elul 27, see Table 2).

TABLE 2: THE BAPTISM OF JESUS

The New Moon denoting the start of the month of Tishri took place at 5:00 PM Jerusalem time on September 26, AD 29. The first day of the month of Tishri (Tishri 1) started at sunset on this day. (*denotes sabbath)

Elul 26	Thu/Fri	22/23 Sept	Baptism
*Elul 27	Fri/Sat	23/24 Sept	
Elul 28	Sat/Sun	24/25 Sept	
Elul 29	Sun/Mon	25/26 Sept	
Tishri 1	Mon/Tue	26/27 Sept	New Moon Festival
Tishri 2	Tue/Wed	27/28 Sept	
Tishri 3	Wed/Thu	28/29 Sept	
Tishri 4	Thu/Fri	29/30 Sept	
*Tishri 5	Fri/Sat	30/1 Oct	
Tishri 6	Sat/Sun	1/2 Oct	
Tishri 7	Sun/Mon	2/3 Oct	
Tishri 8	Mon/Tue	3/4 Oct	
Tishri 9	Tue/Wed	4/5 Oct	
Tishri 10	Wed/Thu	5/6 Oct	
Tishri 11	Thu/Fri	6/7 Oct	
*Tishri 12	Fri/Sat	7/8 Oct	
Tishri 13	Sat/Sun	8/9 Oct	
Tishri 14	Sun/Mon	9/10 Oct	
Tishri 15	Mon/Tue	10/11 Oct	Start of the Feast of Tabernacles

We turn now to Anne Catherine's description of the events surrounding the baptism:

Jesus, walking more quickly than Lazarus, reached John's place of baptism two hours before him.... A crowd more numerous than usual was assembled to whom John was with great animation preaching of the nearness of the Messiah and of penance, proclaiming at the same time that the moment was approaching for him to retire from his office of teacher. Jesus was standing in the throng of listeners. John felt his presence. He saw him also, and that fired him with zeal and filled his heart with joy. But he did not on that account interrupt his discourse, and when he had finished he began to baptize. He had already baptized very many and it was drawing on ten o'clock, when Jesus in his turn came down among the aspirants to the pool of baptism. John bowed low before him, saying "I ought to be baptized by thee, and comest thou to me?" Jesus answered: "Suffer it to be so now, for so it becometh us to fulfill all justice that thou baptize me and I by thee be baptized." He said also: "Thou shalt receive the baptism of the Holy Spirit and of blood." [After the baptism] Jesus journeyed that same day with his followers the distance of a couple of hours towards Jerusalem to a little, obscure place whose name sounded like Bethel.... Jesus celebrated the sabbath in this place (pp. 231–233).

From the above description, it is evident that Jesus was baptized on the morning of the day preceding the sabbath, i.e., at 10:00 AM on Friday morning. Since this was the first of three sabbaths that elapsed in the period from the baptism to the start of the Feast of Tabernacles, it must have been the sabbath of Friday/Saturday, September 23/24.

The baptism therefore took place at 10:00 AM, on Friday, September 23, AD 29—or Elul 26 in the Jewish calendar (see Table 2).

From Elul 26 to Kislev 12 is two and one-half months, which means that Jesus was two and one-half months short of his thirtieth birthday when he was baptized. This fits the chronological indication, given by St. Luke, that Jesus was about thirty years of age; and it concurs with the supposition of many early Christian authors that the baptism took place in the autumn.

Having established this much, let us now consider the date of the crucifixion.

The Date of the Crucifixion

St. Matthew states in his gospel (27:51) that the hour of Jesus's death was 3:00 PM, whereas St. John in his gospel indicates the day of preparation for the Passover, on Friday—prior to the commencement of the sabbath (19:14, 31). Taken together, it is apparent that the crucifixion occurred at 3:00 PM on Friday, Nisan 14. We know also that it took place when Pontius Pilate was procurator of Judea, so the date would be between AD 26 to 36, according to the Jewish historian Josephus (*Antiquities* 18:35, 89).[†]

We can determine which years Nisan 14 fell on a Friday —since Nisan 14 must occur on a Full Moon—the only years it could have been were AD 27, 30, 33, and 36.[‡] St. Luke tells us that John the Baptist's ministry began in Tiberius' fifteenth year (3:1–2). As this equates with AD 28–29, the crucifixion could not have occurred in AD 27. Similarly, AD 36 is not plausible if the remark that Jesus "when he began his ministry was about thirty years of age" is taken seriously (Luke 3:23), for there is no indication in the gospels that Jesus's ministry lasted six years.[††] This leaves only AD 30 and AD 33.

The ministry of John the Baptist, however, began in AD 28–29, thus the crucifixion could not have taken place in the year AD 30, which would mean that his ministry lasted little more than one year—from the baptism until the Passover in AD 29, and then one year to the Passover in AD 30. But since three Passovers are explicitly mentioned by St. John, AD 30 is also unacceptable (2:13, 6:4, 11:55). This leaves the year AD 33 as the only possible year for the crucifixion. Astronomically, Nisan 14 in the year AD 33 equated with Friday, April 3.

This date, determined by J.K. Fotheringham,[‡‡] is the only possible date of the crucifixion according to astronomical chronology, as based on the indications in the gospels, and it accords exactly with the account of the life of Jesus given by Anne Catherine. She also stated that at the crucifixion the Moon was full (*BL*, 172). This was the case on April 3, AD 33. The exact moment of the Full Moon was 7:45 PM (Jerusalem time), just 4¾ hours after the death on the cross.

Having established the date of the baptism—and therewith the start of the ministry—to be Friday September 23, AD 29, and the date of the crucifixion as April 3, AD 33, we are now in a position to reconstruct Jesus's ministry on the basis of Anne Catherine's daily communications. But before we undertake this, we must look in detail at the question of the duration of the ministry.

† Ormond Edwards, *The Time of Christ* (Edinburgh: Floris Books, 1986), p.147; cf. also Harold W. Hoehner, "Chronological Aspects of the Life of Christ," *Bibliotheca Sacra* 131 (1974), p. 335.

‡ J.K. Fotheringham, "Evidence of Astronomy and Technical Chronology for the Date of the Crucifixion," *Journal of Theological Studies* 35 (1934), pp. 146–162.

†† Hoehner, op. cit., p. 335.

‡‡ Fotheringham, ibid.

The Duration of Jesus's Ministry

Throughout the history of Christianity, many theories have been put forward concerning the length of Jesus's ministry. The estimates most frequently referred to are:

(1) a *one-year* ministry, advocated by Clement of Alexandria and Origen (second/third centuries), since only one Passover is mentioned in the synoptic gospels (Mark 14:1);
(2) a *two-year* ministry, supported by Epiphanius (fourth century), since the Gospel of St John mentions three Passovers;
(3) a *three-year* ministry, propounded by Eusebius (third/fourth centuries), who thought that in addition to the three Passovers mentioned in the Gospel of St John (2:13; 6:4; 11:55), there was an extra year of Jesus's ministry between the Passovers mentioned in 2:13 and 6:4.

In each of these three estimates, the actual duration is usually reckoned as somewhat longer than the exact period in years. Thus, if the traditional date of the baptism (January 6) is taken as the date of baptism, then the Passover follows about three months later, since the Passover coincides more or less with Easter. This means that the duration of the ministry would have been reckoned to be one and one-quarter, two and one-quarter, or three and one-quarter years.

In light of Anne Catherine's indications, as we have shown, the baptism occurred on the morning of Friday, September 23, AD 29, when Jesus was approaching thirty years of age. Moreover, as shown above, the crucifixion took place on the afternoon of Friday, April 3, AD 33, when he was thirty-three years and eighteen weeks old.

From these dates it is possible to establish that the duration of Jesus's ministry was approximately three and one-half years. This length of time is indicated indirectly also in a passage of the Gospel of St. Luke that immediately follows the account of the baptism and the temptation in the wilderness. After the temptation, Luke reports that Jesus went up to Galilee,

and came to Nazareth, where he had been brought up; and he went to the synagogue, as his custom was, on the sabbath day. And he stood up to read; and there was given to him the book of the prophet Isaiah. He opened the book and found the place where it was written: "The Spirit of the Lord is upon me, because he has anointed me to preach good news to the poor. He has sent me . . . to proclaim the acceptable year of the Lord." And he closed the book, and gave it back to the attendant, and sat down; and the eyes of all in the synagogue were fixed on him. And he began to say to them, "Today this scripture has been fulfilled in your hearing." . . . And he said, "Truly, I say to you no prophet is acceptable in his own country. But in truth I tell you, there were many

widows in Israel in the days of Elijah, when the heaven was shut up for three years and six months." (Luke 4:16–25)

This chronological indication of three and one-half years in the Gospel of St. Luke can be interpreted as an indirect reference to the duration of Jesus's ministry.

We also read in the Letter of James: "Elijah was a man of like nature with ourselves and he prayed fervently that it might not rain, and for three years and six months it did not rain on the Earth" (James 5:17).

Christ, however, came as the "wellspring of the water of eternal life" (John 4:14), which gushed forth during the three and one-half years of his ministry, thus "balancing out" the three and one-half years of Elijah.

The drought in the days of Elijah, "when the heaven was shut up for three years and six months," was compensated during the ministry of Jesus, who said to the Samaritan woman at Jacob's well: "Every one who drinks of this water will thirst again, but whoever drinks of the water that I shall give him will never thirst; the water that I shall give him will become in him a spring of water welling up to eternal life" (John 4:13–14).

An interval of about three and one-half years is also referred to in the Book of Daniel (12:11), where a period of desolation lasting 1,290 days is mentioned. Again, in the Book of Revelation, an interval of three and one-half years is mentioned several times:

(1) "[T]hey will trample over the holy city for forty-two months" (11:2);
(2) "And I will grant my two witnesses power to prophesy for 1,260 days" (11:3);
(3) "And the woman fled into the wilderness, where she has a place prepared by God, in which to be nourished for 1,260 days" (12:6);
(4) "And the beast . . . was allowed to exercise authority for forty-two months" (13:5).

Since three and one-half years amounts to 1,278 days, the period of 1,260 days is slightly less, and that of 1,290 days slightly more, than three and one-half years, whereas forty-two months is exactly three and one-half years. The time-periods given in Apocalypse texts (1) and (2) are more or less identical. Here the principle of "balancing out" is indicated, which can be thought of in terms of cosmic scales of justice. If the Antichrist is "allowed to exercise authority for forty-two months," this is because Christ's influence held sway on Earth for the three and one-half years, between the baptism in the Jordan and the resurrection.

A further indication of the working of the cosmic scales of justice is that, according to (1), the anti-Christian powers despoil that which is holy for three and one-half years, and according to (2), the two witnesses of God are able to prophesy for three and one-half years. Furthermore, the "forty-two months" of the Antichrist concurs with the "period of desolation" of 1,290 days spoken of by the prophet Daniel.

On a cosmic scale, the three and one-half "years of grace" of Jesus Christ's ministry balance out the three and one-half years during which the Antichrist will be allowed to exercise his authority on Earth. It is quite extraordinary also that, when the number of days is counted from the baptism (Friday, September 23, AD 29) to the resurrection, (Sunday, April 5, AD 33), the same 1,290 days reappears.

The Gap in Anne Catherine Emmerich's Account of the Ministry

As mentioned earlier, Anne Catherine began to communicate her day-by-day account of the ministry of Jesus to Clemens Brentano on July 29, 1820. Counting the days from then till her death on February 9, 1824, yields 1,290 days, the same period of approximately three and one-half years again! Theoretically, therefore, it would have been possible for her to relate the *entire* 1,290 days of the ministry of Jesus, from the baptism up to the resurrection, assuming that she was attuned to Jesus's life day by day in her own life, which, as will emerge in the following, was indeed the case.

In fact, however, owing to a six-month period in 1823 during which Clemens Brentano was away, and owing to shorter periods of illness during which she was unable to relate anything, the period of 1,290 days was reduced to less than three years of reported visions. This must be taken into account in reconstructing Jesus's ministry from her communications, for it implies that there must be a gap in her account. But where does this gap lie? And why did it escape the notice of Clemens Brentano and others who have occupied themselves with Anne Catherine's visions?

To answer these questions, it will be helpful to provide an overview of these visions. From the start of her daily communications concerning the ministry, which began on July 29, 1820, six main periods can be distinguished:

(a) *July 29, 1820–March 29, 1821*: The last eight months of the ministry, leading up to the crucifixion.
(b) *March 30, 1821–June 1, 1821*: The crucifixion, the resurrection, and subsequent events.
(c) *June 2, 1821–April 28, 1823*: The four months prior to the baptism; then from the baptism to the sending out of the apostles.
(d) *April 29, 1823–October 21, 1823*: No communication (due to Clemens Brentano's absence).
(e) *October 22, 1823–January 8, 1824*: Reconstruction of the first eleven weeks of period (d), from the sending out of the apostles onward.

(f) *January 9, 1824– February 9, 1824*: Day-by-day communications concerning the ministry resumed, then discontinued (due to ill health).

These six periods do not take into account brief interruptions in the visions owing to illness or other causes, nor are all the boundaries between the periods exact.

When Clemens Brentano returned after his six-month absence, period (d), he found, much to his disappointment, that during this time Anne Catherine had continued to receive a day-by-day revelation of Jesus's ministry throughout the period. On Tuesday, October 21, 1823, he read to her his last notes, which had ended on April 28, at the point where, in the mountains northwest of Garisma, Jesus was teaching the disciples in preparation for their apostolic missions. When Brentano finished reading these notes, Anne Catherine said that she saw everything again with her spiritual vision and promised that she would continue the revelation as best she could from the point at which it had been broken off.

Thus she resumed on Wednesday, October 22, with the vision that belonged to Wednesday, April 30, communicating all she had then beheld after the dispersion of the apostles. She proceeded in this way, reconstructing a period of almost eleven weeks, until Thursday, January 8, 1824, after which she stopped communicating the "lost" day-by-day ministry any further, thus leaving a gap in the record.

Brentano believed that the revelation up to July 13, 1823 completed the cycle that Anne Catherine had begun on July 29, 1820. From this date onward, until March 29, 1821, she had revealed, day by day, the last eight months of the ministry up to the crucifixion. He was convinced that the revelation of the entire ministry had been given him at this point, excepting fifteen missing days (July 14 to July 28). The fact is, however, that 313 days were missing, not fifteen days, which can be shown by reference to Anne Catherine's own communications.

With the publication in Germany, beginning in 1980, of Clemens Brentano's original notes, new insight into the duration of Jesus's ministry was made possible.[†] A three-volume edition of *The Life of Our Lord and Savior Jesus Christ* (based on Clemens Brentano's notes) had been published after Brentano's death by Rev. Carl Schmöger. The fact that Rev. Schmöger changed an important detail

---

† *BL* (1980), *LJ* i (1983), and *LJ* ii (1985), three volumes of Brentano's original Emmerich notes, were *edited* for publication in the historical-critical edition of the complete works of Clemens Brentano (Frankfurt Goethe-Haus Edition). *LJ* iii and other Emmerich-related volumes planned for the historical-critical edition of the complete works of Clemens Brentano have remained unpublished until the present day (2015). Fortunately, the Belgian Emmerich specialist

in the course of his editing only came to light with the publication of the original notes. This detail was communicated by Anne Catherine on Tuesday, September 11, 1821, and relates to the period preceding the baptism in the Jordan. Her account of the baptism itself followed seventeen days later, on Friday, September 28, 1821.

According to our earlier investigations, the historical date of the baptism was Friday, September 23, AD 29, which corresponds to Elul 26 in the Jewish calendar. By subtracting seventeen days from the date that Anne Catherine communicated the detail in question, September 11, 1821, we arrive at Tuesday, September 6, AD 29, which corresponds to Elul 9 that year.

On Elul 9, Anne Catherine saw Jesus and five disciples travel after dark (the night of Monday/Tuesday) from Kisloth—near Mount Tabor—to Nazareth. Instead of entering Nazareth, however, they stayed with a small community of Essenes living close by. Jesus was put up in the house of an old Essene named Eliud. During the course of the day (Tuesday) his mother, Mary, came to the house of Eliud and talked with Jesus. The English translation of Rev. Schmöger's edition reads:

> Jesus conversed much with his mother on this day, for she came to him two or three times. He told her that he would go up to Jerusalem *three* times for the Passover, but that the last time would be one of great affliction for her. (*LJC* i, 366 [emphasis added]; correction on p. 322, Book I.)

According to the original notes, however, Jesus told Mary that he would travel to Jerusalem *four* times for the Passover (*LJ* i, 90–91). Historically, these four journeys took place during the month of Nisan in the spring of the years AD 30, 31, 32, and 33. At the fourth Passover, on the day of preparation (Nisan 14, AD 33), the crucifixion took place. If this indication concerning four Passovers had been taken seriously, and not been changed to three, the true duration of the ministry (three and one-half years) would have been discovered long ago.[†] But why was it changed to three?

Anne Catherine's report that Jesus said he would go to Jerusalem *four* times for the Passover was changed because Clemens Brentano, and later Rev. Schmöger, believed that her two and one-half year day-by-day revelation gave a complete account of the ministry, apart from a short fifteen-day gap. For this reason Clemens Brentano wrote in a footnote: "She made a slip of the tongue; it should be three times" (*LJ* i, 90); and Rev. Schmöger changed the text accordingly from *four* to *three*. However, when various statements made by Anne Catherine are taken in conjunction with certain indications given in the Gospel of St. John, it becomes evident that the gap was in fact about ten months (313 days) in length, that the ministry therefore lasted three and one-half years, and that there were four Passovers rather than three.

In the tenth chapter of the Gospel of St. John, prior to the raising of Lazarus, it is written that Jesus was in Jerusalem for the Feast of the Dedication: "It was the Feast of the Dedication at Jerusalem; it was winter, and Jesus was walking in the temple, in the portico of Solomon" (John 10:22–23).

Now, the Feast of the Dedication of the Temple, as referred to earlier, began on Kislev 25, falling in December or late November. But in Anne Catherine's day-by-day descriptions of the travels of Jesus, she nowhere describes him as visiting Jerusalem at this time of the year. The following observations regarding the four Feasts of the Dedication can be made on the basis of her descriptions:

First Feast of the Dedication. The evening of the day after the sabbath, Sunday evening, December 18, AD 29, was the start of Kislev 25 in the Jewish calendar. On that evening Jesus celebrated the beginning of the Feast of the Dedication in the synagogue at Thebez in Samaria (present-day Tubas, about nine miles northeast of Jacob's well). He was on his way to Galilee for the wedding at Cana. (see Book I, pp. 387ff)

Second Feast of the Dedication. On the evening of the start of the sabbath, Friday evening, December 8, AD 30, Kislev 25 began. On that evening Jesus taught in the synagogue at Capernaum, on the north side of the Sea of Galilee (Lake Tiberias). During the following period (lasting over two

---

Jozef De Raedemaeker began in 1998 the monumental work of transcribing (from the old German style used by Brentano)—and then subsequently publishing—Brentano's original, *unedited* Emmerich notes: *Anne Catherine Emmerick, Visions from Brentano's Diaries: First Edition of the Original Texts* (Mechelen, Belgium: Privately printed by Jozef De Raedemaeker, 2003–2007). This private edition is now superseded by Jozef De Raedemaeker's publication—again privately—in 2009 of a CD of the complete notes that Clemens Brentano made as Anne Catherine Emmerich described her visions. This privately produced CD comprises all of Brentano's Emmerich-related notes, on the basis of which all the editions of publications of Anne Catherine Emmerich's works have hitherto been compiled.

[†] Further corroboration that the ministry lasted three and one-half years is given in Anne Catherine's account of the words spoken by Jesus on October 6, AD 29, two weeks after the baptism. "They then spoke of John's great zeal, and remarked upon the handsome and strong appearance of Jesus. Jesus answered that in three and one-half years' time they would see nothing more of strength and beauty in his appearance; his body would become so disfigured as to be unrecognizable." *This reference, shortly after the baptism, to the disfiguring of his body through the crucifixion,* clearly indicates a period of three and one-half years for the ministry.

weeks), he visited various towns to the northwest of the Sea of Galilee. (see Book II, p. 175)

Third Feast of the Dedication. Missing from Anne Catherine's account.

Fourth Feast of the Dedication. In November and December, AD 32, Jesus was crossing the Arabian desert after visiting Chaldea, prior to returning to Palestine in January, AD 33, for the three months leading up to the crucifixion. (see Book II, pp. 517 ff.)

It is evident from the above that the reference in the Gospel of St. John to Jesus's presence in Jerusalem at the Feast of the Dedication can only refer to AD 31. As if he were somehow aware of this, Fr. Helmut Fahsel, in his description of Anne Catherine's account of the Tuesday prior to Passion week (historically Tuesday, March 24, AD 33), wrote the following:

Early that morning he taught the disciples (in Bethany) in the house where they were staying (belonging to Lazarus). During the day he spoke in the Temple (in Jerusalem), without the presence of the Pharisees. The disciples, stimulated by what he had taught them, asked him concerning the meaning of "Thy Kingdom come." Jesus spoke at length about this, and also that he and the Father are one (John 10:30), and that he would go to the Father (John 16:16)—all of which he had already touched upon once before in Jerusalem at the Feast of the Dedication. (*WJW*, 377)

This must refer to Jesus's presence in Jerusalem at the Feast of the Dedication in AD 31. In that year, Kislev 25 started on the evening of November 28. With the help of St. John's gospel, then, a detail belonging to the "missing year" is filled in, allowing us to deduce that Jesus was in Jerusalem for the Feast of the Dedication at the end of November/start of December in the year AD 31.

The only further relevant information provided in the Gospel of St. John is that Jesus "went away again [after the Feast of the Dedication] across the Jordan to the place where John at first baptized, and there he remained. And many came to him; and they said, 'John did no sign, but everything that John said about this man was true.' And many believed in him there." (John 10:40–42)

Chapter 11 begins with the account of Lazarus's illness, death, and resuscitation from the dead by Jesus. Now, according to Anne Catherine's account of the last period of Jesus's ministry, the raising of Lazarus occurred at the end of the month of Tammuz in AD 32 (see Appendix III, where the date of the raising of Lazarus is identified as July 26, AD 32, which corresponds to Tammuz 28). This implies that there is a gap of almost eight months in the Gospel of St. John, separating Chapter 10 and Chapter 11:

from the Feast of the Dedication, which ended on December 5, AD 31, to the raising of Lazarus on July 26, AD 32. All that we are told by St. John about Jesus's activity during this period is that "he went across the Jordan to the place where John first baptized." (John 10:40)

Most of this eight-month period falls in the "missing period." In fact, the missing period starts in the summer of AD 31 and extends to a point several weeks before the raising of Lazarus. *But, apart from Jesus's visit to Jerusalem for the Feast of the Dedication in AD 31, can we establish that any other event took place during this missing period?*

Here again the Gospel of St. John can support us. Comparing this gospel with Anne Catherine's description, we can see that the two accounts agree chronologically. It emerges that the other three gospels are not arranged strictly chronologically, and that the order of certain events they present is occasionally displaced. *The Gospel of St. John, in contrast, is chronologically accurate; and the sequence of events it presents conforms to the historical account given by Anne Catherine. More than any other gospel, that of St. John should be able, then, to help us fill in details of the missing period of the ministry.*

We have shown above that the presence of Jesus in Jerusalem at the Feast of the Dedication, as described in the Gospel of St. John, belongs to the missing year. Although Anne Catherine nowhere recounts this event directly in her day-by-day account of the ministry, she nevertheless refers to it (as a forthcoming event) toward the end of the period prior to the missing ten months:

When he and the disciples started for Bethsaida, they directed their steps to the south of the Jordan bridge. On their way they came, this side of Bethsaida, to an inn where his mother, the widow of Nain, Lea, and two other women were waiting to take leave of him, because he was now going to teach on the other side of the Jordan. Mary was very much afflicted. She had a private interview with Jesus, in which she shed abundant tears and begged him not to go to Jerusalem for the Feast of the Dedication of the Temple. . . . He told her that he must fulfill the mission for which his Father had sent him. . . . (see Book II, p. 407)

This reference to Jesus's intention to travel to Jerusalem for the Feast of the Dedication could have made it clear to Clemens Brentano, and also to Rev. Carl Schmöger, that her revelation of the ministry was incomplete. Taken together with her indications concerning four Passovers, they could have deduced that a period amounting to *somewhat less than one year* was missing from her account of the ministry. Unfortunately, neither took the necessary step.

But let us return to the Gospel of St. John in order to determine what else of the missing period may be revealed there.

To orient ourselves, let us turn to Chapter 6. There it is mentioned that "the Passover, the feast of the Jews, was at hand" (John 6:4). Following this, St. John describes the feeding of the five thousand, the walking on the water, and the sermon in the synagogue at Capernaum where Jesus referred to himself as the bread of life. All of this accords with Anne Catherine's account.

According to the chronicle of the ministry established on the basis of her visions,[†] the feeding of the five thousand took place on the afternoon of Monday, January 29, AD 31, on a mountain close to the town of Bethsaida-Julius. That same night—Monday/Tuesday—the walking on the water occurred. And, after visiting some places around the Sea of Galilee, Jesus then arrived in Capernaum on the last day of January and began his teaching concerning the bread of life. On the evening of the sabbath, Friday evening, February 2, AD 31, he continued this teaching in the synagogue at Capernaum (John 6:52–59). On the next day, Saturday, February 3, AD 31, he taught again in the synagogue, and there arose a great dispute with some of his disciples who sided with the Pharisees (John 6:60–66). Jesus then withdrew from the synagogue and met with his close disciples that evening on a hill at the north end of the town. It was here that he spoke the words recorded at the close of Chapter 6: "Did I not choose you, the twelve, and one of you is a devil?" (John 6:70) Chapter 7 then begins:

> After this Jesus went about in Galilee; he would not go about in Judea, because the Jews sought to kill him. Now the Jews' Feast of Tabernacles was at hand.... After his brothers had gone up [to Jerusalem] to the feast, then he also went up, not publicly but in private (John 7:1–2, 10).

As the Feast of Tabernacles was celebrated in the autumn, beginning on Tishri 15, there is a gap of 7½ months between Chapter 6 and Chapter 7 of St. John's Gospel. The period extending from the evening of Saturday, February 3, AD 31, to the evening of Wednesday, September 19 (Tishri 15), AD 31, is unaccounted for, but it was during this period of 7½ months that the Passover referred to in Chapter 6 ("the Passover, the feast of the Jews, was at hand," John 6:4) must have taken place. Anne Catherine in fact described Jesus's presence in Jerusalem for this Passover festival, as well as his subsequent journey back to Galilee, where the transfiguration on Mount Tabor took place on the night April 3/4, AD 31, exactly two years before the crucifixion, on April 3, AD 33.

Following the transfiguration, Anne Catherine contin-

[†] See the following section, *Dates of Some of the Major Events in the Ministry of Jesus*.

ued her day-by-day description of the ministry through April, May, June, and part of July, reaching the point where Jesus visited the ruined citadel of Datheman close by the so-called "David's Way" (Book II, p. 469).

At this point, Sunday, July 8, AD 31, her narrative broke off, and here the missing period begins, extending to the point where she renewed her daily account of the ministry several weeks before the raising of Lazarus. As the raising of Lazarus occurred on July 26, AD 32, the missing period must have lasted until the summer of AD 32—more precisely, until May 16. The events related in Chapters 7, 8, 9, and 10 of St. John's gospel fall within this missing period (July 9, AD 31 to May 16, AD 32).

Summarizing these chapters briefly from a chronological point of view:

Chapter 7 describes Jesus in Galilee and then recounts his presence in Jerusalem at the Feast of Tabernacles, relating historically to the week Wednesday, September 19 to Wednesday, September 26, AD 31 (Tishri 15–22); the last day of the feast, referred to in John 7:37 as "the great day," might have been Tishri 23 (sometimes called "the day of joy").

Chapter 8 describes Jesus teaching in the temple at Jerusalem.

Chapter 9 relates the healing of the man born blind.

Chapter 10 describes Jesus's presence in Jerusalem at the Feast of the Dedication, historically the week of Wednesday, November 28 to Wednesday, December 5, AD 31 (Kislev 25–Tebeth 2), and indicates that, after this, Jesus went "across the Jordan to the place where John at first baptized." (John 10:40)

Of the missing period (summer AD 31 to summer AD 32), which Chapters 7 through 10 of St. John's Gospel refer to, Anne Catherine's day-by-day account mentions only the forthcoming Feast of the Dedication in the late autumn of AD 31. Here the only precise chronological references—either from Anne Catherine or St. John's Gospel—are those concerning the Feast of Tabernacles and the Feast of the Dedication. Thus the missing ten-month period of Jesus's ministry is really more or less completely lost to us due to various circumstances that hindered Anne Catherine from giving the full revelation before she died.

Dates of Some of the Major Events in the Ministry of Jesus

Having established the date of the birth of Jesus, the date of the baptism in the Jordan, the length of the ministry, and the dates of the missing period (ten months) in Anne Catherine's account, we now find it possible to construct a daily chron-

icle of Jesus's ministry, following the life of Jesus day by day from the baptism (Friday, September 23, AD 29) to the crucifixion (Friday, April 3, AD 33), with the exception of the missing ten-month period extending from July 9, AD 31 to May 16, AD 32.

Indeed, excepting such events as the healing of the man born blind, which took place during these missing ten months, we can now date most of the events in the ministry of Christ Jesus—as described by Anne Catherine—with a high degree of accuracy.

The dates of some of the major events thus established are as follows:

TABLE 3
DATES OF SOME OF THE MAJOR EVENTS

Birth of Jesus	Midnight	Dec 6/7	2 BC
Baptism in the Jordan	10:00 AM	Sept 23	AD 29
Start of the Forty Days in the Wilderness	Dusk	Oct 21	AD 29
End of the Forty Days in the Wilderness	Sunset	Nov 30	AD 29
Wedding at Cana (Jn. 2:1–12)	Morning	Dec 28	AD 29
Healing of Nobleman's Son (Jn. 4:43–54)	1:00 PM	Aug 3	AD 30
Raising of the Youth of Nain (Lk. 7:11–17)	9:00 AM	Nov 13	AD 30
Raising of Jairus' daughter (Mk. 5:35–43)	Evening	Dec 1	AD 30
Beheading of John the Baptist	Evening	Jan 3	AD 31
Healing of the Paralyzed Man (Jn. 5:1–14)	Evening	Jan 19	AD 31
Feeding of the Five Thousand (Jn. 6:16–21)	4–6:00 PM	Jan 29	AD 31
Walking on the Water (Jn. 6:16–21)	Night	Jan 29/30	AD 31
Transfiguration (Mk. 17:1–8)	Midnight	April 3/4	AD 31
Raising of Lazarus (Jn. 11:1–44)	Morning	July 26	AD 32
Triumphant Entry into Jerusalem (Mk. 21:1–11)	Morning	March 19	AD 33
Crucifixion	3:00 PM	April 3	AD 33
Resurrection	Sunrise	April 5	AD 33
Ascension	Noon	May 14	AD 33
Whitsun (Pentecost)	Dawn	May 24	AD 33

At first sight, it may seem that the findings presented in this inquiry are of a speculative nature. This impression may easily arise due to its rather rapid and concise manner of presentation. To describe the findings adequately would necessitate writing a volume much longer than the present one, as the findings required both a long process of preliminary research and the establishment of new hermeneutic principles. Only at the end of this process did the accuracy of these conclusions seem sufficiently confirmed to present here. Readers wishing to achieve this degree of certainty for themselves must carefully weigh the results presented, mindful that a wealth of description had to be omitted. Nevertheless, these findings, if carefully and conscientiously evaluated, will reveal their strong probative value.

The Probative Value of the Visions

We have shown how it is possible to ascertain the dates of the birth and baptism of Jesus on the basis of the Jewish calendar dates of these events communicated by Anne Catherine. The question arises: How trustworthy are her visions? Why should any degree of confidence be placed in her communications?

An answer to this question is provided by the fact that, if all of Anne Catherine's statements concerning the Jewish calendar are considered in connection with the particular days of the week on which the events she describes took place, a remarkable agreement with the reconstructed Jewish calendar for the period AD 29–33 becomes apparent (a detailed analysis of this is given in Appendix III).

From this analysis we can see clearly that Anne Catherine could not possibly have contrived these dates. In Table 2, for example, concerning the Feast of Tabernacles—which always begins on the evening of Tishri 15 in the Jewish calendar—it is apparent that the start of Tishri 15 fell on a Monday evening, exactly as Anne Catherine described.

In this case, the likelihood of her accuracy with regard to the weekday of this Jewish date was only one in seven, so this one statement alone cannot be taken as unusually significant—it could simply have been a fortunate coincidence. However, to be accurate thirteen times consecutively (see Appendix III) is a different matter altogether, for the probability in this case is one in 96,889,010,407 or nearly one in 100 billion!

The only possible conclusion to be drawn is that she was speaking the truth, especially bearing in mind that she was a simple, uneducated woman who knew nothing of the intricacies of the Jewish lunar calendar, which modern astronomical computational methods are now able to compute back two thousand years with a high degree of accuracy. From the standpoint of probability theory, then, it is clear that, at least with respect to dates, she was speaking the truth (leaving aside the intriguing question of how this was possible).

Apart from dates, however, there are other points to be considered. One is that her account of the life of Jesus agrees by and large with the testimony of the four gospels, the primary historical source, of course, for facts of Jesus's life.

Anyone familiar with the account in the gospels will recognize it, greatly expanded and in much more detailed form, in Anne Catherine's descriptions, thus supporting the authenticity of her visions. Her descriptions of Jewish customs at the time of Jesus are recognized by experts as being, on the whole, remarkably precise.

> Archeologists were frequently amazed at the accuracy and exactitude with which Emmerich described the household fittings and utensils and customs of the people of Israel. (*WJW*, 11)

And in the Foreword to his book *Die Reiche der heiligé drei Könige* ("The Kingdoms of the Three Kings"), Anton Urbas writes:

> Since Anne Catherine Emmerich names the places visited by the Savior on his journeys and describes them in such precise detail, I took recourse to travel guides and atlases of Palestine so as to check the accuracy of her indications. The more comparisons I made, the more I came to the conclusion that Anne Catherine Emmerich had greater knowledge of the Holy Land and knew more concerning Jewish customs than all the geographers and archeologists in the whole world. (quoted in *WJW*, 11)

This brings us to the next point: *the geography and topography* of the Holy Land as described in Anne Catherine's account of Jesus's daily travels. These descriptions are very precise, as often as not giving the geographical direction in which Jesus traveled and the length of time he took to journey from one place to the next. Fr. Helmut Fahsel gathered all these descriptions together and found that they were mutually consistent and agreed precisely with the actual topography of Palestine. On the basis of Anne Catherine's indications, Fr. Fahsel was able to construct the detailed maps of Palestine for the time of Jesus included in this volume. These maps were first published in his monumental *Der Wandel Jesu in der Welt*. They present clear, consistent solutions to archeological riddles to which only vague, uncertain proposals have been given up until now.

For example, among archeologists there is no agreement on the location of Bethsaida, the hometown of the disciples Peter, Andrew, and Philip. Some modern archeologists identify Bethsaida with Bethsaida-Julias, the ruins of which have been located on the hill et-Tell, just east of the Jordan and some two and a half miles north of where the Jordan flows into the Sea of Galilee. Anne Catherine, however,

clearly situated Bethsaida-Julias at the site of et-Tell, but sees Bethsaida as a little fishing village on the north shore of the Sea of Galilee, about two and a half miles southeast of Capernaum (*WJW*, 459). In light of this description, the ruins of Bethsaida would now lie beneath the waters of the lake, since the ruins of Capernaum have been located on the present northern lake shore of the Sea of Galilee. She even explained that a shift in the geography of the lake shore arose on account of an earthquake (*WJW*, 466).

Many other examples could be given regarding the solution, or possible solution, of archeological riddles on the basis of Anne Catherine's visions. (The discovery of the site of Mary's house near Ephesus, referred to in the Introduction, is a most striking example.) Her indications concerning the locations of various miracles are especially significant. Fr. Fahsel's detailed research makes it possible to accurately locate most of these places.

One example is the Mount of Beatitudes, where the sermon on the mount (Matt. 5:1–7:28) and the feeding of the five thousand (John 6:1–15) took place. Despite the explicit reference in John's gospel that before the feeding of the five thousand "Jesus went to the other side of the Sea of Galilee" (John 6:1) and in the Gospel of Mark that after the miraculous feeding Jesus and the disciples crossed back across the lake and "came to land at Galilee" (Mark 6:53), most archeologists now locate the Mount of Beatitudes close to Galilee on the northwest side of the Sea of Galilee. Each year hundreds of thousands of tourists visit the Church of the Beatitudes (built upon the hillcrest of Eremos at the supposed site of the sermon on the mount) and the Church of the Loaves and Fishes at Tabgha at the foot of Eremos (the supposed location of the miracle of the feeding of the five thousand) in the belief that these were the actual historical sites. However, Anne Catherine's account of the geographical location of the Mount of Beatitudes—in agreement with the Gospels of Mark and John—points to a site on the other side of the Sea of Galilee. Her description is so detailed that Fr. Fahsel was able to identify the site of the hill quite precisely on the northeast side of the lake, overlooking the Sea of Galilee.

Considering these points as a whole, there is good reason to place considerable confidence in Anne Catherine's visions. This does not mean that everything she described is wholly accurate. She was human, not infallible. The same can be said of Clemens Brentano, who wrote down her visions as she described them. It is quite possible that mistakes in his transcription of her account occurred and that, for one reason or another, errors crept into the text. Nevertheless, as far as the dates communicated by Anne Catherine are concerned, the probability of error is, as shown in *Appendix II*, extraordinarily low, and this seems justification enough for accepting her calendar indications as a reliable basis for dating the life of Jesus Christ.

The Names of Places

The place names provided in this text were given by Anne Catherine herself. Her geographical descriptions were sufficiently detailed to enable these places—most of which are now completely unknown—to be located fairly accurately. In *Der Wandel Jesu in der Welt,* Fr. Helmut Fahsel, as has been mentioned, drew up a series of detailed maps of Palestine. He related each map to a specific period covered in Jesus's ministry and entered onto it the places named by Anne Catherine that Jesus visited during the period in question. All these maps have been reproduced in the present text. As a help in comparing with present-day maps of Palestine, the modern names (usually Arabic) of mountains, plains, and valleys have been entered on Fr. Fahsel's maps. The dotted lines indicate the approximate route taken by Jesus on his travels during the period in question. The small half-circle denotes the beginning and the arrowhead the end of each particular journey. The next map then continues the route taken during the next period of time.

APPENDIX II

The Hebrew Calendar

DURING the time of the Babylonian captivity (sixth century BC), certain elements of Babylonian culture were assimilated by the Jewish people, one of which was the Babylonian lunar calendar.

The months of both the Babylonian and the Hebrew calendars are determined by the Moon's cycle, and thus average about 29½ days (the exact period from one New Moon to the next is 29.531 days). If a year contained exactly twelve lunar months, its length would be about 12 x 29½ = 354 days, some eleven days shorter than the solar year of 365 days.

In order that the lunar calendar not fall out of step with the seasons of the solar year, the loss of these eleven days is compensated for by adding one extra lunar month approximately every three years. An intercalary year—a leap year—contains *thirteen* lunar months, and the Babylonians discovered that a nearly perfect concordance with the solar year could be established by distributing seven leap years within a cycle of nineteen lunar years. This principle also underlies the Jewish calendar, in which the 3rd, 6th, 8th, 11th, 14th, 17th, and 19th years of each 19-year cycle are leap years.

The names of the months of the Hebrew calendar are:

Nisan, Iyyar, Sivan, Tammuz, Ab, Elul, Tishri, Marcheshvan (Heshvan), Kislev, Tebeth, Shebat, and Adar. In a leap year there are two months of Adar: Adar I and Adar II.

Normally the months comprise alternately 30 and 29 days, designated as *full months* and *hollow months* respectively. This yields the following (ideal) pattern:

Nisan (30), Iyyar (29), Sivan (30), Tammuz (29), Ab (30), Elul (29), Tishri (30), Heshvan (29), Kislev (30), Tebeth (29), Shebat (30), Adar (29).

This pattern would be adequate if the lunar month contained exactly 29½ days; but, since the exact number is 29.531 days, there are deviations from this ideal.

Thus, in a leap year, Adar I always has 30 days and Adar II 29 days. Moreover, Heshvan often becomes a full month of 30 days, while Kislev may in certain years become a hollow month of 29 days. Owing to the complex rules of this system, there is no easily recognizable pattern for the occurrence of Kislev and Heshvan as full or hollow months. But on average about 55% of Heshvan months are hollow and about 75% of Kislev months are full. The three possibilities in any given year are:

(1) Heshvan and Kislev both hollow (about 25% of the time)
(2) Heshvan hollow and Kislev full (about 30% of the time)
(3) Heshvan and Kislev both full (about 45% of the time)

This means that in the course of twenty years, on average, possibility (1) occurs five times, possibility (2) six times, and possibility (3) nine times. In the specification of the Hebrew calendar, the determination of whether possibility (1), (2), or (3) applies in any given year is completely independent of the 19-year cycle. It has nothing to do with whether the year in question is a common year or a leap year.

It was not until the fourth century AD that the patriarch Hillel II made public the system of calculating the Jewish calendar. Prior to this step, the determination of the calendar had been a closely guarded secret of the Sanhedrin, the supreme court in Jerusalem, and it is not known exactly when this system was first applied by them.

From the calendar indications communicated by Anne Catherine, however, it proved possible—with the help of astronomical calculations—to reconstruct the Jewish calendar for much of the period of Jesus's ministry. This reconstruction is presented in Appendix III, and shows that the Hebrew calendar at the time of Christ followed the pattern of full and hollow months described above, but with one exception: in the year AD 30, the month of Iyyar was full instead of hollow. Thus, it would seem that by the time of Jesus the set of rules used by the Sanhedrin for determining the calendar had become more or less fixed, but not absolutely rigid.

Prior to the application of these rules, the beginnings of each month were sanctified and announced by the Sanhedrin after at least two witnesses had testified that they had seen the lunar crescent of the New Moon.

Since each month had to contain 29 or 30 days, the search for the new lunar crescent started at dusk on the evening after the 29th day. If it was sighted and ratified by the Sanhedrin, the start of the new month was announced that evening throughout Israel by the kindling of night fires, sending out messengers, and hanging flags on the roofs of synagogues.

The sanctification of the New Moon was celebrated in a festival lasting one day if the preceding month was hollow; otherwise the thirtieth day of the old month was counted (and was celebrated as the first day of a two-day New Moon festival), and the new month would begin on the following evening, in which case the New Moon festival lasted two days, since it included the thirtieth day of the old month and the first day of the new one. (It should be remembered that the day in the Jewish calendar begins at dusk and extends to dusk the following evening). This ratification procedure ensured that the lunar months did in fact keep in step with the actual phases of the Moon.

When this observational system was replaced by a set of rules, it was essential that the rules ensure that months remain in step with the Moon's phases. This function was served by the *Molad* calculation (the determination of the conjunction of the Sun and Moon), and the *Moladoth* (the elapsed time from one Molad to the next). The Moladoth is calculated at 29 days, 12 hours, and 793 parts of an hour.

It is also assumed that the very first Molad—the conjunction of the Sun and Moon at the time of the creation of the world on Tishri 1 of the year 1 of the Jewish world era—took place two days, 5 hours, and 204 parts of an hour after 6 PM (Jerusalem time) on the start of Tishri 1. By repeatedly adding multiples of the Moladoth to this original Molad, each new Molad could be determined.

The first day of each month in the Jewish calendar begins close to the Molad—that is, close to the astronomical conjunction of the Sun and Moon. The exact rules concerning the relationship between the computed Molad and the start of day 1 of the month are complex; however, the basic intention of these rules was to adjust the start of day 1 (in relation to the Molad) so that it coincided with the day that would have been sanctified by the Sanhedrin, based on direct observation of the New Moon.

In other words, the rules shifted the start of day 1 after the Molad in such a way as to approximate the time interval from the Molad to the evening on which the New Moon became visible in Jerusalem after the conjunction. In practice this means that the (civil) calendar date on which day 1 of a given month starts is generally either the same as, or one or two days later than, the calendar date on which the astronomical conjunction between the Sun and Moon takes place.

Prior to the application of these rules for the Hebrew calendar, a special committee of the Sanhedrin had the task of determining leap years, in which a thirteenth month (Adar II) was inserted before Nisan to ensure that the Passover (starting Nisan 15) would take place in spring. Originally, various signs were taken as indicators that spring had actually arrived—whether the barley was ripe, the fruit on the trees had grown properly, the winter rains had stopped, or the young pigeons were fledged. If these signs were fulfilled, there was no need for the intercalation of an extra month. In this way the Hebrew calendar was adjusted to keep in step with the passage of the actual seasons.

When the calendar rules were applied, the intention was to ensure its continued synchronization with the seasons. Since the vernal equinox—when the Sun begins its passage northward from the celestial equator—is the primary decisive astronomical factor for the onset of spring, the rules underlying the application of the 19-year cycle should specify that the Molad (conjunction of Sun and Moon) preceding day 1 of the month of Nisan should fall as close as possible to the vernal equinox. This is the theoretical basis of the Hebrew calendar.

To make the 19-year cycle fit in practice, this theory, though generally correct, may occasionally not work. As Appendix III shows, the conjunction of the Sun and Moon preceding day 1 of the month of Nisan fell on March 22 in AD 30, March 12 in AD 31, March 30 in AD 32, and March 19 in AD 33. These dates nonetheless all fall relatively close to the date of the vernal equinox, March 22–23, during the time of Jesus.

APPENDIX III

Reconstruction of the Hebrew Calendar for the Time
of Jesus's Ministry Based on Anne Catherine Emmerich's Calendar Indications

FROM the description of the Jewish calendar in Appendix II, it should be evident that the occurrence of the Molad (conjunction of Sun and Moon), which always falls close to the start of day 1 of a new month, is decisive for the specification of the calendar.

And so a first step in reconstructing the Hebrew calendar is to compute the civil calendar date of the conjunction of the Sun and Moon in Jerusalem time each month, as listed in column 2 of the table below. The table lists a reconstruction of the months of the Hebrew calendar for the four years from June AD 29 to May AD 33, the time covering the 3½ year period of Jesus's ministry.

In the first column the name of each month is given, with an indication whether it was *a full* 30–day, or a *hollow* 29–day month. The pattern of full and hollow months conforms exactly with the description of the calendar in Appendix II, with the single exception that the month of Iyyar in AD 30 contained 30 days instead of 29 days.

The second column lists the time (in Jerusalem) and the date (civil calendar) of the conjunction of Sun and Moon as computed astronomically.

The third column gives the length of time (in days and hours) that elapsed from the conjunction to the start of day 1 of the corresponding lunar month. Here, for the sake of simplicity, day 1 is assumed to start at 6:00 PM Jerusalem time, on the given calendar date, though it actually starts at dusk. In the rare event that the astronomically computed conjunction of the Sun and Moon occurred *after* 6 PM on the given date, the time interval is prefixed with a minus (–) sign. Note that the civil calendar used in the Roman empire at the time of Christ was the Julian calendar, which is similar to, but not identical with, the modern Gregorian calendar now in use throughout the world.

The fourth column gives the civil calendar date on which day 1 of the lunar month commenced, starting at dusk.

Many of the dates in this column were determined from Anne Catherine's calendar indications, as described in the preceding text; the remaining dates were simply reconstructed on the basis of the usual pattern of full and hollow months.

RECONSTRUCTION OF THE JEWISH CALENDAR
from June AD 29 to May AD 33

MONTH	CONJUNCTION OF SUN AND MOON Time (Jerusalem time) and Date		TIME INTERVAL Days and Hours	START OF DAY 1 at dusk on:	
Sivan (30)	02:20, 1 June	AD 29	-0d. 8h.	31 May	AD 29
Tammuz (29)	13:31, 30 June	AD 29	0d. 4h.	30 June	AD 29
Ab (30)	23:10, 29 July	AD 29	-0d. 5h.	29 July	AD 29
Elul (29)	08:01, 28 August	AD 29	0d. 10h.	28 August	AD 29
Tishri (30)	16:58, 26 September	AD 29	0d. lh.	26 September	AD 29
Heshvan (29)	02:51, 26 October	AD 29	0d. 15h.	26 October	AD 29
Kislev (30)	14:07, 24 November	AD 29	0d. 4h.	24 November	AD 29
Tebeth (29)	02:46, 24 December	AD 29	0d. 15h.	24 December	AD 29
Shebat (30)	16:33, 22 January	AD 30	0d. lh.	22 January	AD 30
Adar (29)	07:15, 21 February	AD 30	0d. lh.	21 February	AD 30
Nisan (30)	22:41, 22 March	AD 30	-0d. 5h.	22 March	AD 30
Iyyar (30)	14:31, 21 April	AD 30	0d. 3h.	21 April	AD 30
Sivan (30)	06:06, 21 May	AD 30	0d. 12h.	21 May	AD 30
Tammuz (29)	20:40, 19 June	AD 30	0d. 2h.	20 June	AD 30
Ab (30)	09:43, 19 July	AD 30	0d. 8h.	19 July	AD 30

RECONSTRUCTION OF THE JEWISH CALENDAR
from June AD 29 to May AD 33

Tishri (30)	08:07, 16 September	AD 30	0d. 10h.	16 September	AD 30
Heshvan (30)	18:45, 15 October	AD 30	0d. 23h.	16 October	AD 30
Kislev (30)	05:36, 14 November	AD 30	ld. 12h.	15 November	AD 30
Tebeth (29)	16:39, 13 December	AD 30	ld. lh.	15 December	AD 30
Shebat (30)	03:47, 12 January	AD 31	ld. 14h.	13 January	AD 31
Adar (29)	15:09, 10 February	AD 31	2d. 3h.	12 February	AD 31
Nisan (30)	03:13, 12 March	AD 31	ld. 15h.	13 March	AD 31
Iyyar (29)	16:27, 10 April	AD 31	2d. lh.	12 April	AD 31
Sivan (30)	06:51, 10 May	AD 31	ld. 11h.	11 May	AD 31
Tammuz (29)	22:00, 8 June	AD 31	ld. 20h.	10 June	AD 31
Ab (30)	13:13, 8 July	AD 31	ld. 5h.	9 July	AD 31
Elul (29)	04:02, 7 August	AD 31	ld. 14h.	8 August	AD 31
Tishri (30)	18:13, 5 September	AD 31	ld.0h.	6 September	AD 31
Heshvan (29)	07:46, 5 October	AD 31	ld. 10h.	6 October	AD 31
Kislev (30)	20:32, 3 November	AD 31	0d. 21h.	4 November	AD 31
Tebeth (29)	08:22, 3 December	AD 31	1d. 10h.	4 December	AD 31
Shebat (30)	19:08, 1 January	AD 32	0d. 23h.	2 January	AD 32
Adar I (30)	05:07, 31 January	AD 32	ld. 13h.	1 February	AD 32
Adar II (29)	14:49, 29 February	AD 32	2d. 3h.	2 March	AD 32
Nisan (30)	00:54, 30 March	AD 32	ld. 17h.	31 March	AD 32
Iyyar (29)	11:54, 28 April	AD 32	2d. 6h.	30 April	AD 32
Sivan (30)	00:10, 28 May	AD 32	ld. 18h.	29 May	AD 32
Tammuz (29)	13:51, 26 June	AD 32	2d. 4h.	28 June	AD 32
Ab (30)	04:59, 26 July	AD 32	ld. 13h.	27 July	AD 32
Elul (29)	21:18, 24 August	AD 32	1d. 21h.	26 August	AD 32
Tishri (30)	14:08, 23 September	AD 32	ld. 4h.	24 September	AD 32
Heshvan (29)	06:27, 23 October	AD 32	ld. 12h.	24 October	AD 32
Kislev (30)	21:14, 21 November	AD 32	0d. 21h.	22 November	AD 32
Tebeth (29)	10:03, 21 December	AD 32	ld. 8h.	22 December	AD 32
Shebat (30)	21:04, 19 January	AD 33	0d. 21h.	20 January	AD 33
Adar (29)	06:43, 18 February	AD 33	ld. 11h.	19 February	AD 33
Nisan (30)	15:32, 19 March	AD 33	ld. 2h.	20 March	AD 33
Iyyar (29)	00:03, 18 April	AD 33	ld. 18h.	19 April	AD 33
Sivan (30)	08:53, 17 May	AD 33	ld. 9h.	18 May	AD 33
Crucifixion	Nisan 14	3 PM Friday	April 3		AD 33
Resurrection	Nisan 16	dawn Sunday	April 5		AD 33
Ascension	Iyyar 25	noon Thursday	May 14		AD 33
Whitsun (Pentecost)	Sivan 6	dawn Sunday	May 24		AD 33

Remarks Concerning the Reconstruction of the Table of Months of the Hebrew Calendar from June AD 29 to May AD 33

The reconstructed table of months of the Hebrew calendar may be divided into four periods:

(1) Sivan AD 29–Elul AD 29
(2) Tishri AD 29–Tammuz AD 31
(3) Ab AD 31–Ab AD 32
(4) Elul AD 32–Sivan AD 33

The first period covered by Anne Catherine's daily communications comprises the four months leading up to the baptism in the Jordan. It starts with the travels of Jesus after his move from Nazareth to Capernaum, and ends with his baptism on Elul 26. During this period the regular occurrence of the sabbath is referred to by Anne Catherine, but she does not mention any festivals that can be linked to the Hebrew calendar. Her indications concerning the sabbath enable the days of the week to be determined, but with no explicit point of reference within the Hebrew calendar.

The dating of her daily communications for this period is therefore by extrapolation backward from period (2), for which Anne Catherine *does* give explicit calendar indications. This extrapolation is effected simply by counting the seven-day sabbath rhythm backward during the summer of AD 29. Similarly, the reconstruction of the Hebrew calendar for this period was made by extrapolating back from period (2), and is securely defined on the basis of statements made by Anne Catherine.

Period (2) covers Anne Catherine's daily communications from the baptism to the start of the "missing period," where her communications were ended by her death. During this period she not only communicated the seven-day rhythm running through Jesus's ministry, but also referred repeatedly to various Hebrew festivals.

These references, together with the sabbath rhythm, make it possible to reconstruct the calendar with great certainty. Almost all the calendar references given by Anne Catherine during this period are mutually supporting, so there can be little doubt concerning their authenticity. It would be virtually impossible to concoct such a set of consistent and mutually supporting calendar references and communicate them over a period of almost twenty-two months—Anne Catherine being a simple woman of humble peasant origin with no knowledge of the intricacies of the Hebrew calendar.

Period (3) contains the "missing period" consisting of the 313 days absent in Anne Catherine's daily communi-

cations concerning Jesus's ministry. Since there are no communications to go on, the Hebrew calendar is in this case reconstructed by simply filling in the missing months between periods (2) and (4) through extrapolation forward from period (2) and backward from period (4).

Period (4) includes the time leading up to and immediately following the crucifixion, including Whitsun. This was the first period revealed by Anne Catherine when she began her daily communications, which were much shorter than her later communications belonging to periods (1) and (2). One possible reason for this is that, since Clemens Brentano initially had difficulty understanding her dialect, some things may not have been written down.

Unfortunately, the brevity of the communications during the period leading up to the crucifixion offer no indications concerning festivals in the Hebrew calendar. The sole exception is the time of the crucifixion itself, which was described (in agreement with the Gospel of Saint John) as taking place on the day of preparation for the Passover—Nisan 14 in the Hebrew calendar.

Anne Catherine indicates that the crucifixion of Jesus began at approximately 12:15 PM Jerusalem time and lasted until shortly after 3:00 PM (*BL*, 320, 346). Not long after the beginning of the crucifixion, she relates that trumpets sounded from the temple to announce the slaying of Passover lambs. This occurred at about 12:30 PM rather than the usual time of 3:00 PM because in AD 33 the day of preparation was on Friday, and the slaying had to be completed before the start of the sabbath that evening (*LJC* iii, 281). The Gospel of Saint John also states that the day of preparation was on Friday.

Now, we previously established that the date of the crucifixion was in fact Friday, April 3, AD 33.[†] And so, on the basis of the weekly sabbath rhythm throughout the period of communications leading to the crucifixion, the dates of events during this period were determined by following the sabbath rhythm back from the date of the crucifixion, with some modifications (see Appendix IV). Similarly, the months of the Hebrew calendar were extrapolated back from Nisan 14 on the day of the crucifixion, and the months of Iyyar and Sivan following after Nisan were added on. Thus, the ascension took place at midday on Thursday, Iyyar 25 and Whitsun at dawn on Sunday, Sivan 6, the Feast of Weeks.

---

† See Appendix I, *Chronology of the Life of Jesus Christ.*

Discussion of Anne Catherine Emmerich's Calendar Indications

It is evident that the calendar indications of Anne Catherine during Period (2) are of key significance for dating Jesus's ministry, as well as providing authenticity for her communications.

Taking a closer look, we see that the very first calendar indication she gave concerns the start of the Feast of Tabernacles on Monday evening after the baptism (*LJ* i, 186). Since the Feast starts on Tishri 15, and since three sabbaths had occurred following the baptism, it is easy to determine that the baptism occurred at 10:00 AM on Friday, Elul 26, or September 23, AD 29 (see Table 2, p. 483). Therefore Tishri 1 began on the evening of Monday, September 26, AD 29 (as listed in column 5, line 5 of our reconstructed table of months, p. 495).

The next calendar indication relates to the start of the Feast of Dedication, which coincides with Kislev 25 in the Hebrew calendar. According to Anne Catherine, Kislev 25 in that year began on a Sunday evening (*LJ* i, 248). Historically this must have been Sunday, December 18, AD 29, from which it follows that Kislev 1 started on the evening of Thursday, November 24, AD 29 (see column 4 of the Table, in this and all similar references below).

Shortly after this, when Christ Jesus was in Cana for the wedding, she identified the start of the third day in Cana as Tebeth 4 (*LJ* i, 265). This began Tuesday evening, and on the following morning the wedding took place—the morning of Wednesday, December 28, AD 29. Thus Tebeth 1 commenced on the evening of Saturday, December 24, AD 29 (see column 4 of the Table). This is confirmed by the reference to the evening of the sabbath (Friday) as the beginning of Tebeth 7 (*LJ* i, 281).

The New Moon festival celebrating the start of the month of Shebat fell on a Monday—beginning Sunday evening (*LJ* i, 300). She describes the flags for the New Moon festival hanging from long flagstaffs on the roof of the synagogue, and large knots tied at intervals on the staves, the number of knots signifying the month just begun—in this case eleven knots for Shebat, the eleventh month. This was the evening of January 22, AD 30.

In the next month, Adar, the calendar indication given by Anne Catherine refers to the start of the Feast of Purim, beginning on Adar 14, a Monday evening, or March 6, AD 30 (*LJ* i, 336). This means that Adar 1 commenced on the evening of Tuesday, February 21, AD 30.

There is another calendar indication for the onset of the New Moon festival at the beginning of the month of Nisan, on a Wednesday evening, March 22, AD 30 (*LJ* i, 348).

There are no calendar communications, in the months of Iyyar and Sivan, until Tammuz 17, where Anne Catherine speaks of the day of fasting (Tammuz 17) commemorating the broken tablets of the Law on Mt. Sinai (*LJ* i, 401). The beginning of Tammuz 17 was on a Thursday evening, July 6, AD 30; Tammuz 1 therefore started on Tuesday evening, June 20, AD 30.

The New Moon festival of the month of Ab began on a Wednesday evening, on July 19, AD 30 (*LJ* i, 443). This is confirmed by the reference to the start of Ab 18 on Saturday evening after the sabbath (*LJ* ii, 38).

Anne Catherine speaks of the onset of the New Moon festival of the month of Elul, on the start of the sabbath (*LJ* ii, 84), August 18, AD 30. This is confirmed by the reference to the morning of Elul 24 on a Monday morning (*LJ* ii, 191). The reference (*LJ* ii, 199) to Tishri 1 on Sunday, followed by the reference (*LJ* ii, 204) to the day of Tishri 2 on Monday, indicates the start of the month of Tishri on Saturday evening, which equated historically with Saturday, September 16, AD 30. Similarly, she speaks of the start of the month of Marcheshvan on Monday evening (*LJ* ii, 283). This means that Heshvan 1 began on the evening of Monday, October 16, AD 30.

The next calendar reference is to the onset of the New Moon festival on Wednesday evening (*LJ* ii, 401), signifying that Kislev 1 commenced on the evening of Wednesday, November 15, AD 30.

Up to this point, all of Anne Catherine's calendar indications are mutually supporting and consistent with one another and with the seven-day cycle of weekdays and with the Hebrew calendar for the period under consideration. But with the next reference, concerning the beginning of the Feast of Dedication, we encounter a one-day discrepancy:

> However, today was Friday, Kislev 24 and because this evening the sabbath coincided with Kislev 25, the Feast of Dedication, the festival began already yesterday evening with the start of Kislev 24. (*LJ* ii, 486)

To be consistent with all her foregoing calendar indications, it is easily shown that Kislev 24 must have started on Friday evening and not, as the above statement implies, on Thursday evening. *This is the first contradiction that emerges from Anne Catherine's statements concerning the calendar.* It is clearly a matter of miscommunication, for the very next calendar indication definitely implies that Kislev 24 started on Friday evening. This reference (*LJ* 503) mentions the coincidence of the New Moon festival with the sabbath (i.e., Tebeth 1 started on the evening of Friday, December 15 AD 30). Thus Kislev 24, exactly one week prior to Tebeth 1, also commenced on Friday evening.

At present (2015), only the first two volumes (*LJ* ii) of the original notes by Clemens Brentano of Anne Catherine's account of Jesus's ministry have been published. Thus the calendar indications cited henceforth derive from the original edition of Anne Catherine Emmerich's *Das Leben unseres Herrn und Heilands Jesu Christi* (*LHHJC*).[†]

The next calendar indication concerns the New Moon festival, which is said to have started on Friday evening (*LHHJC* ii, 294). Here again there is a discrepancy of one day, for, to be consistent with the foregoing calendar statements, the first day of the month of Shebat must have started on Saturday evening, January 13, AD 31. However, it should be noted that as Anne Catherine generally communicated her visions either on the day she had them, or the day after, it is quite possible that a one-day discrepancy could occur occasionally in her narrative.

The next calendar indication states that the New Moon festival was celebrated "yesterday and today," referring to a Monday (*LHHJC* ii, 367), which can be taken to mean that Shebat 30 started on Sunday evening and Adar 1 on Monday evening. If this interpretation is correct, Adar 1 commenced on the evening of Monday, February 12, AD 31, in conformity with the preceding calendar dates. This is followed by a reference (*LHHJC* ii, 381) to the Purim festival starting on Monday (i.e., historically Monday, February 26, AD 31). Since the Purim festival starts on Adar 14, this implies that Adar 14 equated with Monday evening, whereas in fact Adar 15 started on Monday evening. (The Purim festival lasts for two days, Adar 14–15). Again there is a discrepancy of one day in Anne Catherine's communications with regard to the actual historical occurrence of the days of the Jewish calendar.

Then comes the calendar indication for the Passover meal, for which Jesus and his disciples gathered at Lazarus's castle. This feast, which is always on the evening of Nisan 15, was on Tuesday evening (*LHHJC* ii, 415), equating with Tuesday, March 27, AD 31. This means that Nisan 1 began on the evening of Tuesday, March 13, AD 31, which agrees with our findings, thus confirming the authenticity of this calendar indication for the Passover.

The last calendar indication in period (2) concerns the start of the Feast of Weeks on Wednesday evening (*LHHJC* iii, 83). The Feast of Weeks occurs on Sivan 6–7. Since Sivan 6 started on Wednesday evening, May 16, AD 31, it follows that Sivan 1 commenced on the evening of Friday, May 11, AD 31—again in agreement with our findings.

In summary, it emerges from the above that of the twenty calendar indications given by Anne Catherine in

period (2), only three do not fit exactly with the established pattern. In these three cases, however, there is only a one-day variation from the otherwise consistent calendar pattern. As mentioned already, this one-day difference may well be due to the fact that Anne Catherine communicated her visions either on the same day on which she had them or on the day after. Overall, the calendar indications are in fact virtually completely consistent, that is, mutually supporting and in accord with the actual months of the Hebrew calendar for the period of Anne Catherine's description of the ministry of Christ Jesus—on the whole, historically accurate indeed. If any reader remains skeptical here, it is worthwhile to consider the odds of the foregoing calendar indications being arbitrary.

Summarizing the foregoing: the first thirteen calendar indications are correct, and of the last seven indications three display a one-day discrepancy. What is the probability of making a correct indication of the weekday for a given date? The answer is obviously 1 in 7. To give the correct weekday twice in a row is $1/7 \times 1/7$, that is, 1 in 49. Similarly, to be able to say the correct day of the week for given historical dates three times in a row is $1/7 \times 1/7 \times 1/7$, or 1 in 343. And the probability of indicating the correct weekday thirteen times in a row is 1 in 96,889,010,407, or almost 1 in 100 billion. Further, the probability of giving the sequence she did, in which seventeen of the twenty weekdays are correct, is one in 373,996,603,229,683. Technically the odds should be reduced by a factor of seven, since one of her weekday indications was pivotal in the correlation with the actual historical weekdays, but even reducing by a factor of seven, the odds are still enormous, the first figure being one in 13,841,287,201 (1 in 14 billion) and the second, one in 53,428,086,175,669 (1 in 53 trillion). The only possible conclusion is that Anne Catherine's calendar indications are true (albeit sometimes with a one-day discrepancy).[‡]

[†] As mentioned in the Introduction, in 2009 Jozef De Raedemaeker published in 38 volumes his edition of Brentano's complete notes of the visions of Anne Catherine. These notes hold great promise for future calendrical research of the sort presented here.

[‡] The probability that the dates were random was subsequently revised by Robert Powell, in collaboration with two other mathematicians, to one in *four hundred and thirty five billion*. (The reliability and trustworthiness of Anne Catherine's account is more fully discussed in Powell's *Chronicle of the Living Christ* (Great Barrington, MA: Anthroposophic Press, 1996.) In other words, it can be stated with virtually 100 per cent certainty—as the application of probability theory to Anne Catherine's calendar indications verifies—that the dates determined from her visions are the authentic, actual dates of the events she describes.

APPENDIX IV

A Summary of the Chronicle

IN the following summary of Anne Catherine's chronicle of the ministry, it will emerge that the last part of the reconstruction of the calendar discussed in Appendix III can be viewed in another way. In that Appendix we specified four periods extending over four years, starting with Jesus's first major journey, which took place during the first half of the month of Sivan in AD 29:

Period 1: Sivan AD 29–Elul AD 29 (up to the baptism)
Period 2: Tishri AD 29–Tammuz AD 29 (up to the start of the missing period)
Period 3: Ab AD 31–Ab AD 32 (the missing period)
Period 4: Elul AD 32–Sivan AD 33 (up to Whitsun/Pentecost)

In the analysis of Anne Catherine's calendar indications undertaken in Appendix III, it was shown that she gave a number of calendar indications for Period (2) which are consistent and mutually supporting. These indications, taken together with her regular reference to the seven-day (sabbath) rhythm running throughout the chronicle, enabled us to determine this part of the chronicle with great exactitude; e.g., it can be said with a high degree of certainty that the feeding of the five thousand took place on the afternoon of Monday, January 29, AD 31, the transfiguration on Mount Tabor on the night of April 3/4, AD 31, etc. Since Period (1) and Period (2) were communicated together—that is, consecutively, with the seven-day (sabbath) rhythm running throughout—it is not unreasonable to extend the sabbath rhythm backward in time from the securely-defined Period (2) to Period (1). In this way, for example, the date of the baptism on the morning of Elul 26, equating with Friday, September 23, AD 29, is obtained (see Table 2 in the first part of this book). Comparing the derived historical dates for the events in Periods (1) and (2) with the calendar dates upon which Anne Catherine communicated these events, a pattern emerges:

EVENT	HISTORICAL DATE	CALENDAR DATE (ACE)
Baptism	September 23	September 28
Feeding of 5000	January 29	February 3
Transfiguration	April 3/4	April 8/9

It is evident that a simple five-day difference exists between the calendar date on which Anne Catherine made her communication and the historical date in the Julian calendar. This five-day difference holds throughout Periods (1) and (2). But it should be recalled here that during the last part of Period (2) Anne Catherine was obliged to re-narrate the course of the ministry after Clemens Brentano had been away for almost six months. The last eleven weeks of Period (2) were communicated in this way. For example, what she related on the morning of Sunday, December 7, 1823, referred to what she had seen the day before, and was a repetition of what she had seen originally on Saturday, June 14, 1823, during Clemens Brentano's absence. In this period of almost eleven weeks leading up to Anne Catherine's death, Brentano always dated the text with the earlier (original) date, thus maintaining continuity of dates throughout Period (2).

Is the account of the chronicle in these last eleven weeks of Period (2), as re-narrated almost six months later, as reliable as the account for the preceding part of the chronicle? This question has often been raised because it was during this time that Anne Catherine spoke of a journey Jesus undertook to Cyprus that lasted five weeks: from Wednesday, April 25, to Thursday, May 31, AD 31. Since there is no record of such a journey in the four gospels, doubt has naturally been cast upon this account.

Of crucial importance for determining the reliability of Anne Catherine's account of this period is her communication concerning the celebration of the Feast of Weeks, which took place when, according to her visions, Jesus was on the island of Cyprus.

As with all her communications, the sabbath rhythm forms the backbone of the chronicle because it specifies the weekdays. For the eleven weeks under consideration at the end of Period (2), the sabbath rhythm continues on smoothly from the preceding period.

On the morning of Thursday, November 13, 1823, Anne Catherine narrated her vision of the Feast of Weeks, which Brentano dated as representing a "repetition" of what she had experienced on Wednesday, May 21, 1823. Subtracting five days to obtain the historical date gives Wednesday, May 16, AD 31. Anne Catherine's description for this day included the preparations for the Feast of Weeks, which is celebrated on Sivan 6 and Sivan 7 in the Hebrew calendar, fifty days after Passover (Nisan 15).

She saw Jesus at the town of Mallep, in the middle of the north side of Cyprus. There was a Jewish colony living there. Preparations were being made for the start of the Feast of Weeks that evening, which Jesus attended in the synagogue in Mallep. This would indicate that Sivan 6 started at dusk on the evening of Wednesday, May 16, AD 31; and indeed, it is evident from the table of the reconstructed Hebrew calendar in Appendix III that Sivan 6, AD 31 did start on a Wednesday evening. This strongly confirms that, despite the time-lag of almost six months in the reporting of her visions, Anne Catherine's account for the last eleven weeks of Period (2) is as reliable as her earlier revelations.

We now come to Period (3), the "missing period"—that part of the ministry unreported by Anne Catherine due to her untimely death. It was during this "missing period" that the events described in Chapters 7, 8, 9, and 10 of St. John's Gospel took place, including the healing in Jerusalem of the man born blind.

According to the description in Chapter 9 of the Gospel of St. John, this healing took place on the sabbath, i.e. either on a Friday evening, or on a Saturday morning or afternoon before sunset. As discussed previously, the calendar indications given in Chapter 7 (Feast of Tabernacles) and Chapter 10 (Feast of Dedication) of St. John's Gospel permit us to establish that this healing took place after Friday, September 28, and before Thursday, November 29, AD 31.

The earliest possibility would have been Saturday, September 29, AD 31; but this would entail compressing into the space of one day (before sunset) all that is described in Chapter 8 as well as the healing of the blind man in Chapter 9. Alternatively, the following dates (Friday/Saturday) are possible for this healing in AD 31: October 5/6, October 12/13, October 19/20, October 26/27, November 2/3, November 9/10, November 16/17, and November 23/24.

Since Jesus was in Jerusalem at some time both before and after the healing, the first sabbath (October 5/6) and the last sabbath (November 23/24) seem more likely possibilities, as it is unlikely that he remained in Jerusalem the whole time, because of the persecution directed against him there. Further research will be necessary to penetrate more accurately into the details of the "missing period," but this example gives some indication of the method employed.

Let us now turn our attention to Period (4): the eight months leading up to the crucifixion and the following two months until Whitsun. It is only the eight months leading up to the crucifixion that will occupy us, since these belong to the ministry, and Anne Catherine communicated the sabbath rhythm running more or less continuously throughout this period. Having determined the date of the crucifixion as Friday, April 3, AD 33, it is a simple matter to historically date Anne Catherine's account of Period (4) by retracing the sabbath rhythm retrospec-

tively. In this way, the raising of Lazarus, described in Chapter 11 of St. John's Gospel, is found to have occurred on the morning of Saturday, October 11, AD 32. (However, as we shall shortly see, this was not the correct date.)

As for Periods (1) and (2), where there is a correspondence between the historical dates and the actual calendar dates on which Anne Catherine made her communications—the historical dates being obtained simply by subtracting five days from the calendar dates—for Period (4), does this correspondence also seem to hold true? This is evident in the case of the following two examples:

EVENT	HISTORICAL DATE	CALENDAR DATE (ACE)
Raising of Lazarus	Oct. 11, AD 32	October 7
Crucifixion	April 3, AD 33	March 30

The correlation shows that the historical date is given by adding four days to the calendar date on which Anne Catherine communicated the event in question. It will emerge that, whereas this correspondence holds good for the latter part of Period (4) leading up to the crucifixion, it becomes questionable for the early part of Period (4) to which belongs the raising of Lazarus.

If it is accepted that this simple correspondence (adding 4 days) applies to the whole of Period (4), it must be concluded that the date of the raising of Lazarus was October 11, AD 32, as just mentioned. In order to consider this date more closely, however, it is necessary to look at all of Period (4) leading up to the crucifixion. Let us do so on the assumption that October 11, AD 32, is the correct date—that is, let us assume that the correspondence applies to the whole of Period (4) just as the other correspondence (subtracting 5 days) applies to the whole of Periods (1) and (2).

After he raised Lazarus, Jesus had to flee because the news caused a great uproar in Jerusalem that it led to the Pharisees' determination to have him put to death. Anne Catherine described how he left Bethany and went with the apostles back to Galilee, traveling up the east side of the Jordan to the town of Chorazin, northeast of the Sea of Galilee. On October 12, 1820, she saw Jesus with his apostles and disciples in Chorazin. Adding four days, this would yield the historical date October 16, AD 32—five days after the raising of Lazarus.

Here in Chorazin she heard Jesus describe to the apostles and disciples that he would now part company with them and go on a journey. He told them to which towns they should go and teach, and which towns they should avoid. According to Anne Catherine, he also said that he would be away for about three months, and that they should then meet him at Jacob's well near Shechem.

In the Jewish calendar the historical date October 16, AD 32, equates with Tishri 23; adding three months gives Tebeth 23, which equates with the historical date January 14, AD 33. Now, on January 9, 1821, Anne Catherine was in an ecstatic condition and suddenly cried out joyfully:

O! He has arrived there! How joyfully they go up to welcome him! He is at Jacob's Well. They are weeping for joy. They are washing his feet, and the feet of the disciples. There are about twelve here from this region, young shepherds who accompanied him to Kedar; also Peter, Andrew, John, James, Philip, and one other! They were expecting him here. (*LHHJC* iii, 348)

Adding four days gives as the historical date of Jesus's arrival at Jacob's Well, January 13, AD 33, equating with Tebeth 22. This corresponds exactly to the statement concerning a three-month period of absence owing to a journey, and seems to confirm the simple rule of four days taken as our basic assumption for Period (4).

This assumption becomes questionable, however, if Anne Catherine's account of the journey is taken seriously; it is evident that it would have been impossible to accomplish the journey in three months. In order to investigate this, let us look in detail at her description of the journey, determining dates simply by adding four days to the calendar dates on which she described its various stages. (Note: since this journey is not described in Fr. Helmut Fahsel's *Der Wandel Jesu in der Welt*, the original 1860 edition of *Das Leben unseres Herrn und Heilands Jesu Christi nach den Gesichten der gottseligen Anna Katharina Emmerich aufgeschrieben von Clemens Brentano* has been consulted [abbreviated *LHHJC*].)

Preliminary Remarks

According to the correspondence described above, it was in Chorazin on Thursday, October 16, AD 32, that Anne Catherine beheld a preview of the journey made by Jesus. After describing him visiting many towns (mostly unnamed), she said:

I also perceived that Jesus would go to Egypt and visit Heliopolis, where he had lived as a child. . . . He will return from the other side, via Hebron. . . . Jesus stated he would be away about three months. They would then definitely find him again at Jacob's Well near Shechem. (*LHHJC* iii, 251)

Further applying the correspondence of adding four days, we arrive at the following table of events belonging to the journey made by Jesus.

Dates obtained by applying the rule of adding four days; description of the main stages of Jesus's journey:

AD 32

Thursday, October 16

Jesus, in Chorazin, told the disciples he was going on a journey.

Saturday, October 18

This evening Jesus went to Bethsaida with Andrew, Peter and Philip. They traveled by moonlight.

Monday, October 20

Jesus and the three apostles traveled the whole day and part of the night through East Galilee to the land of the Amorites (Basan).

Tuesday, October 21

In Basan three youths and a group of disciples met up with Jesus. Jesus said "that he and the three youths would travel alone through Chaldea and the land of Ur, where Abraham had been born, and would go through Arabia to Egypt. The disciples should spread out and teach here and there within the boundaries [of Palestine]; he would also teach wherever he went. Once again he specified that they would meet at Jacob's Well after three months." (*LHHJC* iii, 254)

Wednesday, October 22

At daybreak Jesus parted company with the apostles and disciples. They were much downcast. Jesus wanted to take only the three youths with him, who were sixteen to eighteen years old.

Friday, October 24

Jesus and the three youths arrived in Kedar, not far from the easternmost boundary of Israel, where they celebrated the sabbath in the synagogue.

Thursday, November 25

After teaching for one month in and around Kedar, Jesus and the three youths left Kedar and set off east across the desert.

Friday, December 12

Jesus arrived at the tent-city of the three kings, where they had settled after returning to Chaldea from Bethlehem. Only two of the kings (Mensor and Theokeno) were still alive, the third (Sair) had died some years previously. Jesus was met by Mensor; Theokeno was bedridden.

Tuesday, December 16

Jesus left the two kings and journeyed further east, accompanied by the three youths.

Thursday, December 18

They arrived in the town of Atom, Chaldea.

Sunday, December 21

Jesus left Atom and traveled southeast, arriving at Sikdor that evening.

Monday, December 22

Jesus and the three youths, having been joined by a fourth youth, left Sikdor and, traveling past Babylon on the Euphrates, went east to Mozian on the Tigris, arriving on the evening of Tuesday, December 23.

Wednesday, December 24

Jesus and his companions left Mozian and traveled south toward Ur, the birthplace of Abraham.

Friday, December 26

Toward evening they arrived in Ur, the journey time from Mozian to Ur being about thirty hours.

Sunday, December 28

This morning Jesus and the four youths left Ur and traveled west.

Wednesday, December 31

In the evening Jesus and the four youths arrived at a town in Egypt.

AD 33

Thursday, January 1

They left this town and traveled toward Heliopolis.

Friday, January 2

Around 4 PM they arrived in Heliopolis, where Jesus had been as a child.

Sunday, January 4

In the morning they left Heliopolis and went east toward Palestine.

Thursday, January 8

In the evening they arrived in Beersheba in Israel, and journeyed further the next morning toward Hebron.

Friday, January 9

Toward evening they arrived at Bethain near Hebron, where they celebrated the sabbath in the synagogue. They left Bethain after the close of the sabbath on the evening of January 10, and traveled north toward Shechem.

Tuesday January 13

Having traveled by night to avoid being seen, Jesus and the youths arrived by dawn at Jacob's Well.

A glance at the main stages of the journey to Chaldea and Egypt from Palestine and back, as described by Anne Catherine, shows that the first part of the journey, from Kedar to Ur, could conceivably have been accomplished in the time stated, but that the journey from Ur to Egypt would have been impossible in the time allowed. According to the account, Jesus left Ur on the morning of Sunday, December 28, and arrived at a town in Egypt on the evening of Wednesday, December 31, AD 32, *three days later*. Since the entire journey from Palestine to Ur, with stopovers at various places, took one month (from Kedar, November 25 to Ur, December 26), the far longer journey

from Ur to Egypt could not possibly have been accomplished in so short a time-span.

It may be helpful to consider the approximate distances involved:

JOURNEY	DISTANCE	TIME ALLOWED IN ACE
Kedar to Ur	over 600 miles	31½ days
Crucifixion	over 900 miles	5½ days

As we contemplate this riddle, consider the following words of Anne Catherine, in which she describes the transition in her visions from Chaldea to Egypt: "Since yesterday evening I did not see Jesus and the youths stop anywhere. They traveled continuously, to begin with in the open, sandy desert, then traversing gently climbing hills, then in a land with more green. . . ." (*LHHJC* iii, 341)

It seems that the day-by-day account of the long journey through the Arabian desert is simply compressed into one night in her vision. The impression of a break at this point in the continuity of Anne Catherine's narrative is strengthened by the fact that up to this point the sabbath is explicitly mentioned every seven days, whereas at Jesus's arrival in Heliopolis (according to her account on a Friday, shortly before the start of the sabbath), the sabbath is not mentioned. All that is said is that on that evening "the Lord was led into the synagogue by a very old man. . . . I saw Jesus teach and pray." And on the next day, "Jesus taught again in the synagogue." (*LHHJC* iii, 345) In fact, this probably was the sabbath, since Jesus was in the synagogue that evening and the following morning, but it is not explicitly stated, whereas prior to this, throughout the journey to Ur in Chaldea, the sabbath is explicitly referred to every seven days.

A closer scrutiny of the text, however, reveals a solution, but it means discounting the statement that Anne Catherine attributed to Jesus: that he would be away "about three months" (*LHHJC* iii, 251), and that the apostles should meet him at Jacob's Well near Shechem after three months. (*LHHJC* iii, 254) The above-tabulated chronicle of Jesus's journey fits this specification of three months exactly. Nevertheless, the three months do *not* conform to another indication made by Anne Catherine, one that we have hitherto ignored on account of its uncertainty. This is the statement she made on Monday or Tuesday, November 6 or 7, 1820, referring to Jesus's stay in the town of Sichar-Kedar not far from the easternmost boundary of Israel:

There began one of the first festivals which God commanded the Israelites to celebrate; I believe it was the New Moon festival. It was held that evening in the synagogue. (*LHHJC* iii, 273)

On the assumption that the rule of adding four days to Anne Catherine's calendar dates holds here also, Monday or Tuesday, November 6 or 7, would equate historically with Monday or Tuesday, November 10 or 11, AD 32. However, referring to the table of the reconstructed Hebrew calendar in Appendix III, it can be seen that these dates equate with Heshvan 18 or 19 in the Jewish calendar—nowhere near day 1 of the month! This statement concerning the New Moon festival (celebrated in the evening, at the commencement of day 1 at the start of a new Jewish month) does not fit then with the rule of adding four days.

But what if we take this problematic calendar indication seriously? If true, it would mean that Jesus was in Sichar-Kedar on a Monday or Tuesday on the evening of which day 1 of the new month in the Jewish calendar started. Let us therefore look through the table of the reconstructed Hebrew calendar in Appendix III to see if there was any Jewish month that started on a Monday or Tuesday in AD 32. We find two possibilities:

Nisan 1, AD 32 started on the evening of Monday, March 31; Elul 1, AD 32 started on the evening of Tuesday, August 26.

The first case can be ruled out, since we may assume that Jesus must have been in Jerusalem for the Passover festival that started on Nisan 15 (April 15, AD 32). The second case is plausible, however, so let us assume that it is true, and, in light of this assumption, take a fresh look at Period (4).

As a starting point, we can reconsider the raising of Lazarus, which Anne Catherine described as taking place on a Saturday morning, thirty-one days prior to the above-mentioned New Moon festival. Under our new assumption, the historical date of the raising of Lazarus would be thirty-one days prior to Tuesday, August 26—that is, Saturday, July 26, AD 32. Under our old assumption (rule of adding four days) it took place on Saturday, October 11, AD 32, since the calendar date on which Anne Catherine spoke of the raising of Lazarus was Saturday, October 7.

The old assumption was based on the rule: add four days. The new assumption yields the rule: subtract two months and twelve days (−73 days). The total difference between the historical dates arrived at is therefore two months and sixteen days (−77 days). This period of two months and sixteen days is gained for the journey to Chaldea and Egypt if it is assumed that Anne Catherine's vision of the journey through the Arabian desert was compressed into one night. In other words, 2½ months can be added to the journey time, so that the statement concerning a three-month absence can now be modified to 5½ months. We need not go into the question whether 2½

months was the actual journey time across the Arabian desert to Egypt, but it is certainly clear that the journey from Ur to Heliopolis and back to Beersheba in Palestine becomes more plausible if two months and twenty-seven days are allowed rather than a mere eleven days.

There are two further minor points in Anne Catherine's description of the journey that support this new assumption. Referring to our summary of the main stages of the journey listed above, for the date Saturday, October 18, AD 32, we read: "This evening Jesus went to Bethsaida with Andrew, Peter, and Philip. They traveled by moonlight."

Now, the thin waning crescent of the Moon rose on the eastern horizon only 31 hours before sunrise on the morning of Sunday, October 19, AD 32, so it was hardly possible to travel by moonlight that night. Under the new assumption, we have to go back two months and sixteen days from Saturday, October 18 to Saturday, August 2, AD 32. On that night the waxing Moon reached first quarter and so would have been high in the heavens at sunset, illuminating the journey that evening.

For Tuesday, November 25, AD 32 (in our summary), we read: "Jesus and the three youths left Kedar and set off eastward across the desert." Anne Catherine also describes their arrival that evening at a heathen tent village, where a festival of star worship was being celebrated: "They cried out especially loudly as the Moon and other stars rose across the horizon." (*LHHJC* iii, 288)

Since the waxing crescent of the New Moon was already visible above the horizon at sunset on the evening of Tuesday, November 25, AD 32, the foregoing statement does not really make sense. Under the new assumption, however, subtracting two months and sixteen days from November 25, we arrive at Tuesday, September 9, AD 32. On this evening the almost Full Moon rose across the eastern horizon some four hours after sunset.

There is yet another reason for believing that the new assumption is true. It concerns the raising of Lazarus, which, under this assumption, took place on Saturday morning, July 26, AD 32. Now, reading both Anne Catherine's account and that in the eleventh chapter of the Gospel of St. John, one cannot help but get the impression that Jesus deliberately waited a few days before raising Lazarus from the dead. But there is a complication. If the new assumption *is* accepted as true, Anne Catherine's report that Jesus said he would be away about three months does not hold good. In fact, however, there is a simple explanation for this statement about a three month absence; but in order to follow it we must take another look at Anne Catherine's entire revelation of the ministry, this time on the basis of the new assumption. Under these circumstances, a period of two months and sixteen days must be subtracted from all the dates prior to December 31, AD 32 in the above table listing the dates of Jesus's journey from Israel to Ur. Also, the four periods covered by her revelation need to be slightly amended as follows:

(1) Sivan AD 29–Elul AD 29 (up to the baptism)
(2) Tishri AD 29–Tammuz AD 31 (up to the start of the missing year)
(3) Ab AD 31–Iyyar AD 32 (the missing period)
(4a) Iyyar AD 32–Tebeth AD 32/33 (period including the raising of Lazarus and the journey to Chaldea and Egypt)
(4b) Tebeth AD 32/33–Sivan AD 33 (from the return to Israel, to Pentecost /Whitsun, including the crucifixion)

Here the missing period, period (3), is reduced by 2½ months; and period (4) is correspondingly lengthened by 2½ months, which have been added to the journey time. Note that period (4) is now divided into two: (4a) and (4b). The relationship between the calendar dates of Anne Catherine's communications and the historical dates, under the new assumption, is:

periods (1) and (2) subtract 5 days
period (4a) subtract 73 days (2 months and 12 days)
period (4b) add 4 days

But how is it that the calendar dates of period (4a) of Anne Catherine's revelation of the ministry differ so much from the historical dates, whereas the calendar dates of most of her revelation harmonize so closely with the historical dates?

First, it should be noted that period (4a) was the very first period of the ministry communicated by Anne Catherine, starting in July 1820. But as early as September 1818 Clemens Brentano had been taking notes of much that Anne Catherine narrated from her visions. This period from September 1818 to July 1820 was plagued with difficulties that worked to prevent the free communication by Anne Catherine of her visions. (It must be remembered that she had visions from the Old and New Testaments almost continuously throughout her life.) It was only Brentano's patience and perseverance throughout all these difficulties that cleared the way and established the possibility of daily communications.

During this time the visions communicated by Anne Catherine seem to have been drawn fairly randomly from the life of Jesus. For example, on February 27, 1820, she had a vision of the transfiguration on Mount Tabor (*LHHJC* iii, 197–198), the historical date of which was the night of April 3/4, AD 31. Here the calendar date of her communication of this event is widely separated from the

historical date. Then the regular daily communications of the ministry started suddenly on July 29, 1820, signifying the start of period (4a). It is not surprising, therefore, that the beginning of period (4a), which under the new assumption equates with the historical date May 17, AD 32, should also be widely separated in time from the calendar date of Anne Catherine's communications.

It was only during the course of the regular daily communications that a process of harmonization could take place, in which the calendar dates and the historical dates fell into step with one another, to become separated by a matter of only days. For this harmonization to take place, at some point a jump in the communications had to occur. All the evidence indicates that this was some time during the journey from Ur back to Palestine (via Heliopolis). This "adjustment" entailed the loss of eleven weeks (77 days). Since 77 is a multiple of seven, the sabbath rhythm could continue, as if in regular sequence; but the entire day-by-day account of the long journey through the Arabian desert was left out, having been compressed into a single day and night. Under this hypothesis the calendar indication (New Moon Festival) and details of astronomical phenomena referred to above are accounted for.

As Anne Catherine often said, a higher intelligence was at work guiding her communications. Under the new hypothesis, it seems as though the omission of 77 days was a calculated jump, planned in advance. And the statement concerning a three-month absence from Palestine does not refer to the actual journey time but to the calendar date on which Anne Catherine was to resume her description of the ministry after Jesus's return to Palestine.

What Anne Catherine saw was that in three months Jesus would be back in Palestine at Jacob's Well near Shechem; *but this refers to the timing of her visions.* Since 2½ months were omitted, the *actual* period of Jesus's absence was 5½ months. However, as far as her *visions* were concerned, it was three months, which would seem to explain her reference to a three-month absence. This tentative conclusion will have to suffice until it is possible for further research in relation to the entirety of Emmerich's visions.

There still remain several questions concerning Jesus's journey to Chaldea and Egypt. For example, considering the great distance involved, would this journey have been physically possible? Anne Catherine repeatedly remarked, in her visions of Jesus's travels, her astonishment at the speed with which he walked. Although the distance from Palestine to Ur to Heliopolis and back to Palestine is great, it is not beyond the bounds of possibility that someone capable of walking swiftly for long distances could have accomplished the journey in 4½ months. (4½ months, since of the 5½ months, one month was spent at the beginning of the journey in and around Kedar, not far from the easternmost boundary in Palestine.)

Nevertheless, other questions remain unanswered regarding the provisions needed by Jesus and his young traveling companions on their trek across the desert, a journey presumably made mainly by night because of the great heat. Why is there no mention of this journey in the four gospels or any other sources? And what could the purpose of this journey have been? Anne Catherine reported the following explanation given her by the intelligence (*angelos*) guiding her communications:

> I also received instruction as to why this journey of Jesus remained so concealed. I recall that Jesus said to his apostles and disciples that he wanted to withdraw somewhat in order to be forgotten. They themselves knew nothing of this journey. The Lord took only simple youths with him, who would not be outraged at the pagans and would not pay attention to everything. I believe also that he strictly forbade them to speak about it, whereupon one of the youths responded naively: "Although you forbade the man born blind, after he received his sight, to say anything about it, he did so nevertheless, and he was not punished." Whereupon Jesus replied: "That took place to the glory of God, but this (journey) would give rise to much outrage." I understood that the Jews and even his apostles would have been outraged to a certain extent if they had learned that he had visited the pagans. (*LHHJC* iii, 330–331)

All that is said in the Gospel of St. John, after the raising of Lazarus, is:

> Jesus therefore no longer went about openly among the Jews, but went from there to the country near the wilderness, to a town called Ephraim; and there he stayed with the disciples. Now the Passover of the Jews was at hand.... (John 11:54–55)

The impression here is that Jesus retreated for a time to a place near the desert, which is obviously the impression that the apostles and disciples had. But that he was away for 5½ months, during which time he visited Chaldea and Egypt, is not in any way indicated in the text of St. John's Gospel or in any other gospel account. And after returning to Palestine early in January AD 33, three more months elapsed before the Passover festival, at which the crucifixion and resurrection took place.

On the journey, according to Anne Catherine, Jesus gave instruction to the pagans and made it clear that he had come not only for the Jews but for them also. For the people of Israel, who were the pagans? The people of Egypt and Chaldea were the closest and most important ones. The father of Israel, Abraham, had been born in Ur in Chaldea, and the Jewish people had lived in Chaldea at the time of the Babylonian captivity. Chaldea was therefore of great significance to the people of Israel. Similarly, from the time of the patriarch Jacob, whose son Joseph had been sold as a slave and carried off to Egypt, the Jewish nation had lived in Egypt, until the exodus led by Moses. Jesus himself as a child had been obliged to flee Israel with his parents, because of Herod the Great, and the holy family had then lived for a time at Heliopolis in Egypt. So Egypt also represented an important station on the path of the people of Israel.

The journey made by Jesus to Chaldea and Egypt retraced the path of the people of Israel, a path retraced immediately prior to the last three months of the life of the Messiah in Israel, leading up to the Mystery of Golgotha. This journey by the Son of God was therefore a brief recapitulation of the steps made by God's chosen people just before the sacrifice on Golgotha, which represented the culmination of the history of Israel.

Another reason for this journey by Jesus was to visit the three kings who had paid him homage as a child. After the three kings had left Bethlehem, they went south of the Dead Sea and returned east, toward Babylon, across the desert. But before reaching Babylon they stopped at a place in pleasant surroundings and settled there, living in tents. Just as they had been warned in a dream not to return to Herod, so too they received instruction to settle at this place and wait for the King of the Jews to visit them there. However, when Jesus came, only two of the three kings were still alive: Mensor (Melchior) and Theokeno (Casper); the third king, Sair (Balthasar) had died nine years before. Mensor and Theokeno, by now very old, were overjoyed when Jesus told them that he was the child they had visited so many years ago.

Jesus told them that he had come for the pagans as well as for the Jews, that he had come for all who believed in him. The two kings then said that it was now time for them to leave their land; after having waited so long, they wanted to accompany Jesus on his return to Judea. Jesus replied that his kingdom is not of this world. Moreover, he said that they would only take offense and be shaken in their belief if they were to see how he would be despised and mistreated by the Jews.

He spoke of his mission, now approaching its end, and that it was a secret withheld from the Jews that he was there with them. The Jews would have already murdered him if he had not slipped away. But he had wanted to come and see the kings, because of their faith, hope, and love, before being delivered up and put to death.

He said that three years after his return to the Heavenly Father, he would send his disciples to them. And indeed, three years later, the apostles Thomas and Judas Thaddeus came to the two remaining kings and baptized them, as well as others living there. According to the account by Anne Catherine, Mensor was baptized *Leandor* and Theokeno was christened *Leo* (*LHHJC* iii, 305–306, 318, 576–577).

Anne Catherine's account of Jesus's journey to the three (or rather, two) kings, and thence to Ur and Heliopolis before returning to Palestine, adds a new dimension to our understanding of the life of the Messiah. The three kings had been the first to recognize and acknowledge his coming, a fact that implies he came not just as the Savior of the people of Israel, but of all who believe in him. And this is confirmed explicitly by Jesus's journey outside of Palestine, undertaken toward the end of his ministry, immediately prior to the three months leading up to his death.

Much of Jesus's last three months was spent in Jerusalem and Bethany, during which time the confrontation with the Pharisees built to a climax.

At the start of the month of Adar, on the evening of Thursday, February 19, AD 33, six weeks prior to the Last Supper, Jesus went to Jerusalem, where he remained —either in Bethany or Jerusalem—until the crucifixion. Four weeks later, toward the end of the month of Adar, on the 28th (Thursday, March 19, AD 33), Jesus made his triumphant entry into Jerusalem. This event actually occurred two weeks prior to the Last Supper. (Traditionally it is celebrated on Palm Sunday, in the belief that it took place just four days prior to the celebration of the Last Supper on Maundy Thursday.) On the day of his triumphant entry into Jerusalem, there was a total eclipse of the Sun.

Jesus had taught at the temple in Jerusalem during much of this last six-week period, but intensified his teaching activity after making his triumphant entry into the city on a donkey. During these last two weeks he taught in two different ways, depending on the nature of his auditors. When the scribes and Pharisees were present, he attacked them for their hypocrisy and lack of humility, as, for example, in the words of Chapter 23 of the Gospel of Saint Matthew, that he spoke in the temple on Tuesday, March 24, AD 33. When speaking to his apostles and disciples alone, however, he gave instruction concerning the future, as in the words of Chapter 24 of the Gospel of Saint Matthew, that he spoke on the Mount of Olives on Thursday, March 26, AD 33.

Sometimes he was able to teach the apostles and disciples in the temple without being disturbed by the presence of the scribes and Pharisees, as on the last occasion that he taught there (Tuesday, March 31, AD 33), when he spoke of the truth and fulfillment of his teachings. He went on to say that now he must fulfill what he had taught: It is not enough simply to believe; one must also fulfill one's belief. No one, not even the Pharisees, could accuse him of having taught anything false. Now, however, he wanted to fulfill the truth he had taught, and must ascend to the Father. Before departing, though, he wanted to bestow upon them all that he had. He had neither money nor possessions, but wanted to give them his might and his powers, to found a union with them to the end of time—a still more inward union than the present one. He wanted also to unite all of them together as members of one body (*LHHJC* iii, 415).

Then, on the evening of the Last Supper, he instituted the holy sacrament, saying: "Now a new era and a new sacrifice is beginning, which will last until the end of the world" (*BL*, 8384). With the Last Supper the ministry of Christ Jesus came to a close, and his Passion began, lasting until the following afternoon and culminating in the death on the cross at 3:00 PM on Friday, April 3, AD 33.

APPENDIX V

Commemoration of Events in the Life of Jesus

THE FOLLOWING discussion concerns modern, contemporary dates in relation to some of the historical dates in the life of Jesus. With the help of these dates it is possible to relive events in the life of Jesus in a meditative way day-by-day in connection with the *cosmic memory* of these events. By cosmic memory is meant the date when the Sun at the particular event under consideration returns to the same position in the zodiac as its location at that event during Jesus's life—referred to in the following as the *cosmic commemoration* of the event.

For example, taking the baptism in the Jordan (historical date: Friday, September 23, AD 29), we find that the cosmic commemoration of this event equates with October 18/19 at the present time.[†] The reason for this shift from the historical date of September 23 to October 18/19 at the present time has to do with the astronomical phenomenon known as the "precession of the equinoxes." As another example we may take the cosmic commemoration of the changing of water into wine at the wedding at Cana (historical date: Wednesday, December 28, AD 29), which occurs on January 22/23 at the present time. The *Sun Chronicle* that follows gives the modern dates of cosmic commemoration for 115 of the most significant events in the life of Jesus.

For the sake of more readily enabling a commemorative "living into" the chronicle of Jesus's life day-by-day, the commemoration of events may be undertaken also *on the same weekday* as that on which they occurred. For example, as the baptism in the Jordan took place at about 10 o'clock on the morning of Friday, September 23, AD 29, a meditative contemplation of this event would be appropriate on the *Friday closest to* October 18/19 in any given year. Similarly, as the wedding at Cana occurred on the morning of Wednesday, December 28, AD 29, the miracle of the changing of water into wine can be commemorated on the *Wednesday closest to* January 22/23 in any given year. Why is it important to observe the weekdays on which events in Jesus's life took place?

It is a fact that Anne Catherine's visions of the day-by-day unfolding of Jesus Christ's ministry were attuned to the historical weekdays. Other stigmatists have reported the same phenomenon of the significance of the weekdays in relation to the life of Jesus—stating, for example, that

for them the event of his crucifixion is a reality of mystical experience every Friday.

In the case of Anne Catherine, every Friday evening she beheld the commencement of the sabbath, the original meaning of which is *seventh day*. That is, since for her the sabbath day—as the seventh day—was the last day of the week, every Friday evening signified the start of the sabbath and every Saturday evening denoted the commencement of the first day of the week.[‡] Thus the weekdays were imbued with meaning for Anne Catherine on account of her attunement to the life of Jesus, and this was relevant—at least in some cases—to her experiences of the historical events on particular weekdays.

Let us take as an example the miracle of the healing of the paralyzed man at the pool of Bethesda in Jerusalem. This took place historically on Friday, January 19, AD 31. Anne Catherine describes how, on the afternoon of this day, Jesus and the disciples went to the pool of Bethesda and healed many, including a number who were blind. It was while departing the pool of Bethesda that Jesus healed the paralyzed man who had lain there for 38 years.

According to Anne Catherine's description, at the time of the healing the sabbath had just commenced. In other words, the sun had already set on this Friday of the healing of the paralyzed man. It was the fact of the healing of the paralyzed man having occurred on the *sabbath* that led to the persecution of Jesus: "And this was why the Jews persecuted Jesus, because he did this on the sabbath" (John 5:16). From this example it is possible to grasp something of the significance of the weekdays in the life of Jesus, and hence to appreciate their importance for a meditative reliving of the day-by-day unfolding of his ministry. In the case of this example then, it would be appropriate to contemplate the healing of the paralyzed man on the *Friday closest to* February 14 in any given year—in order to attune to the *weekday as well as to the date of cosmic commemoration* (February 14) of this event.

In general, then, a meditative "living into" the chronicle of Jesus Christ's ministry is enhanced by taking the weekdays into account in addition to the dates of cosmic commemoration.

[†] Note that the modern dates can vary by a day or so depending upon the occurrence of leap years, etc.

[‡] For the Semitic peoples of antiquity the "day" began at dusk and lasted until shortly after sunset the following day.

Sun Chronicle of Events in the Life of Jesus Christ

The Sun's sidereal Longitude	Event in the Life of Jesus Christ † indicates events where only the date is known (no time indication); * indicates events where there is a time indication, but it is only very approximate	Historical Date	Present Date of Sun's Arrival at Same Longitude
♈			
0° Aries 23	*The Cursing of the Fig Tree	Fri 3/20/33	Apr 14/15
0° Aries 33	†Theophany (Second)	Fri 3/20/33	Apr 15
4° Aries 24	"Woe Upon the Pharisees"	Tue 3/24/33	Apr 18/19
5° Aries 52	The Enmity of the Pharisees	Mon 3/26/31	Apr 20/21
6° Aries 21	Teaching of the Second Coming (First)	Thur 3/26/33	Apr 20/21
7°Aries 41	†Theophany (First)	Wed 3/28/31	Apr 22/23
9° Aries 57	Healing of the Woman Born Crippled	Fri 3/30/31	Apr 24/25
10° Aries 5	The Visitation	Sun 3/30/2 BC	Apr 24/25
10° Aries 14	Teaching of the Second Coming (Second)	Mon 3/30/33	Apr 25
12° Aries 22	The Last Anointing	Wed 4/1/33	Apr 27
13° Aries 20	The Last Supper	Thur 4/2/33	Apr 28
13° Aries 26	The Night of Gethsemane, Jesus Sweats Blood	Thur 4/2/33	Apr 28
13° Aries 28	The Betrayal by Judas	Thur 4/2/33	Apr 28/29
13° Aries 36	The Trial by Caiaphas	Fri 4/3/33	Apr 28/29
13°Aries 41	Peter's Denial	Fri 4/3/33	Apr 28/29
13° Aries 44	The Trial by Pontius Pilate	Fri 4/3/33	Apr 28/29
13° Aries 51	The Scourging	Fri 4/3/33	Apr 28/29
13° Aries 52	The Crowning with Thorns	Fri 4/3/33	Apr 28/29
13° Aries 54	The Sentence of Death	Fri 4/3/33	Apr 28/29
13° Aries 58	The Carrying of the Cross	Fri 4/3/33	Apr 28/29
13° Aries 59	The Nailing to the Cross	Fri 4/3/33	Apr 28/29
13° Aries 59	The Transfiguration	Wed 4/4/31	Apr 28/29
14° Aries 0	Christ Raised Upon the Cross	Fri 4/3/33	Apr 28/29
14° Aries 6	The Crucifixion	Fri 4/3/33	Apr 28/29

14° Aries 36	†Twelve-year-old Jesus in the Temple	Sun 4/3/12	Apr 29/30
14° Aries 57	†The Descent into Hell	Sat 4/4/33	Apr 29/30
15° Aries 39	The Resurrection	Sun 4/5/33	Apr 30–May 1
16° Aries 29	The Cleansing of the Temple	Thur 4/6/30	May 1/2
17° Aries 0	The Appearance on the Road to Emmaus	Mon 4/6/33	May 1/2
19° Aries 4	† The Night Conversation with Nicodemus	Sun 4/9/30	May 4
22° Aries 4	†The Appearance to the Eleven	Sat 4/11/33	May 7
23° Aries 32	The Healing of Man with Dropsy	Fri 4/13/31	May 8/9
25° Aries 19	†The Appearance to the Seven	Wed 4/15/33	May 10/11
26° Aries 50	†The Appearance to the Five Hundred	Thur 4/16/33	May 12
28° Aries 56	❖Retrieval of John the Baptist's Head from Machaerus	Thur 4/19/31	May 14/15
♉			
2° Taurus 46	Mary Receives Communion	Thur 4/23/33	May 18
19° Taurus 5	Healing of Three Blind Boys	Thur 5/10/31	June 4/5
23° Taurus 19	The Ascension	Thur 5/14/33	June 8/9
26° Taurus 26	†Blessing of the Children	Sat 5/17/32	June 11/12
♊			
2° Gemini 35	Pentecost	Sun 5/24/33	Jun 18/19
8° Gemini 49	†The Call of Zacchaeus	Fri 5/30/32	June 24/25
11° Gemini 21	Peter Cures a Lame Man	Tue 6/2/33	June 27/28
12° Gemini 37	The Birth of John the Baptist	Wed 6/4/2 BC	June 29
19° Gemini 17	†The Healing of Two Blind Men	Tue 6/10/32	July 5/6
21° Gemini 11	†The Healing of Ten Lepers	Thur 6/12/32	July 7/8
♋			
1° Cancer 7	The Teaching of Baptism by Fire	Sat 6/23/31	July 18/19
22° Cancer 43	The Death of Lazarus	Tue 7/15/32	Aug 9/10
♌			
2° Leo 37	"I Am the Resurrection and the Life"	Fri 7/25/32	Aug 20
2° Leo 50	Conversation with Samaritan Woman at Jacob's Well	Wed 7/26/30	Aug 20/21
3° Leo 4	†The Raising of Lazarus	Sat 7/26/32	Aug 20/21
10° Leo 36	The Healing of the Nobleman's Son	Thur 8/3/30	Aug 28/29

19° Leo 37	Pharisees Try to Cast Jesus from the Brow of a Hill	Sat 8/12/30	Sept 6/7
22° Leo 46	The Death of Mary	Sat 8/15/44	Sept 9/10
23° Leo 17	The Assumption of Mary	Sun 8/16/44	Sept 10/11
26° Leo 15	The Healing of Peter's Mother-in-Law	Sat 8/19/30	Sept 13/14
♍			
9° Virgo 28	The Raising of Nazor	Mon 9/1/32	Sept 27
11° Virgo 57	The Healing of Mara the Suphanite	Mon 9/4/30	Sept 29/30
16° Virgo 3	The Birth of Mary	Fri 9/7/21 BC	Oct 3/4
17° Virgo 3	The Conception of John the Baptist	Mon 9/9/3 BC	Oct 4/5
23° Virgo 27	Transfiguration Before Eliud the Essene	c. Midnight Fri/Sat 9/15/16/29	Oct 11/12
♎			
0° Libra 40	The Raising of a Pagan Child	Sat 9/23/30	Oct 18/19
0° Libra 50	The Baptism of Jesus	Fri 9/23/29	Oct 18/19
6° Libra 3	The Healing of Theokeno	Sun 9/28/32	Oct 23/24
13° Libra 40	The Healing of the Blind Youth Manahem	Fri 10/6/30	Oct 31/Nov 1
14° Libra 48	John the Baptist's "Behold the Lamb of God"	Fri 10/7/29	Nov 1/2
29° Libra 21	The Start of the Forty Days in the Wilderness	Fri 10/21/29	Nov 16/17
♏			
1° Scorpio 22	The Arrival of Attarus	Sun 10/23/29	Nov 18/19
1° Scorpio 50	The Calling of Judas	Tue 10/24/30	Nov 18/19
6° Scorpio 49	The Calling of Thomas	Sun 10/29/30	Nov 23/24
15° Scorpio 1	†The Healing of the Son of Achias	Mon 11/6/30	Dec 1/2
17° Scorpio 19	The First Conversion of Mary Magdalene	Wed 11/8/30	Dec 4
19° Scorpio 0	The Healing of the Centurion's Servant	Fri 11/10/30	Dec 5/6
22° Scorpio 1	The Raising of the Youth of Nain	Mon 11/13/30	Dec 8/9
24° Scorpio 11	*John the Baptist's "Heal the Blind"	Wed 11/15/30	Dec 10/11
27° Scorpio 22	† The First Raising of the Daughter of Jairus	Sat 11/18/30	Dec 13/14
28° Scorpio 26	The Calling of Matthew	Sun 11/19/30	Dec 14/15
♐			
0° Sag 44	†Jesus Stills the Storm	Tue 11/21/30	Dec 17

2° Sag 20	The Healing of the Man Born Blind	Fri 11/23/31	Dec 18/19
4° Sag 23	†The Healing of Mary Cleophas	Sat 11/25/30	Dec 20/21
5° Sag 45	The Miraculous Draught of Fishes	Sun 11/26/30	Dec 22
6° Sag 51	†The First Temptation	Sun 11/27/29	Dec 23
7° Sag 53	†The Second Temptation	Mon 11/28/29	Dec 24/25
8° Sag 54	†The Third Temptation	Tue 11/29/29	Dec 25/26
9° Sag 58	The End of the Forty Days in the Wilderness	Wed 11/30/29	Dec 26/27
10° Sag 41	The Calling of Andrew	Thur 12/1/29	Dec 26/27
10° Sag 46	The Second Raising of the Daughter of Jairus	Fri 12/1/30	Dec 27
13° Sag 49	Jesus Bestows his Power upon the Twelve	Mon 12/4/30	Dec 30
15° Sag 37	†The Healing of the Demons in Gergaza	Wed 12/6/30	Jan 1
16° Sag 4	The Birth of Jesus	Sat 12/6/2 BC	Jan 1
17° Sag 9	The First Walking on the Water	Fri 12/8/30	Jan 2/3
17° Sag 35	The Conception of Mary	Thur 12/8/22 BC	Jan 3
17° Sag 59	Mary Goes to the Temple	Mon 12/8/19 BC	Jan 3
19° Sag 49	The Commissioning of the Twelve	Sun 12/10/30	Jan 5
23° Sag 40	The Circumcision of Jesus	Sun 12/14/2 BC	Jan 9
29° Sag 8	The Calling of Peter	Mon 12/19/29	Jan 14
	♑		
4° Cap 29	†The Calling of Philip	Sat 12/24/29	Jan 19/20
6° Cap 0	†The Second Conversion of Mary Magdalene	Tue 12/26/30	Jan 21
6° Cap 15	The Adoration of the Magi	Sun 12/26/6 BC	Jan 21
8° Cap 18	The Turning of Water into Wine	Wed 12/28/29	Jan 23
11° Cap 21	The Raising of a Man at Cana	Sat 12/31/29	Jan 26
14° Cap 39	†The Death of John the Baptist	Thur 1/4/31	Jan 29/30
20° Cap 13	*The Revelation of John the Baptist's Death	Tue 1/9/31	Feb 4
26° Cap 3	The Presentation of Jesus in the Temple	Thur 1/15/1 BC	Feb 10
	♒		
0° Aqu 35	The Healing of the Paralyzed Man	Fri 1/19/31	Feb 14
7° Aqu 38	The Healing of the Man with a Withered Hand	Fri 1/26/31	Feb 21
10° Aqu 37	The Feeding of the Five Thousand	Mon 1/29/31	Feb 24

10° Aqu 54	†The Second Walking on the Water	Tue 1/30/31	Feb 24/25
14° Aqu 47	The Teaching of the Bread of Life	Fri 2/2/31	Feb 28
19° Aqu 41	The Raising of the Daughter of an Essene	Tue 2/7/30	March 4/5
24° Aqu 34	†The Healing of the Syrophonecian Woman	Mon 2/12/31	Mar 9/10
⊬			
13° Pisces 41	The Flight to Egypt	Thur 3/2/5 BC	Mar 28/29
16° Pisces 13	The Conception of Jesus	Thur 3/6/2 BC	Mar 31/Apr 1
25° Pisces 16	The Feeding of the Four Thousand	Thur 3/15/31	Apr 9/10
28° Pisces 41	Peter Receives the Keys to the Kingdom	Mon 3/19/31	Apr 13
29° Pisces 24	†The Triumphant Entry into Jerusalem	Thur 3/19/33	Apr 13/14

Aaron (disciple), son of Jesse, I: 63–64; II: 97, 99

Aaron, brother of Moses), I: 102, 120, 149–50, 153, 177, 303, 318, 358; II: 50, 57, 371, 498

Abdias, I: 56–57

Abel, I: 121–22, 125, 352, 483; II: 36, 365; III: 119

Abenadar, I: 61, 67–68, 82; III: 224, 302–4, 310, 314–15, 318, 320

Abgar of Edessa, King, I: 48, 57, 84, 458–59; II: 17

Abigail, II: 53–55, 494

Abiram, II: 405

Abisai, I: 326

Abner, I: 326

Abraham, I: 56, 84, 114, 118–21, 125, 128–30, 132, 134–42, 144, 147, 149, 151, 160–61, 166, 184–86, 194–95, 205, 212, 297, 310, 312, 314–15, 335, 339, 347, 352, 354, 360, 362, 396–97, 493, 520, 522, 524; II: 15, 28, 34, 36–38, 72, 76, 78, 80–82, 90–91, 136, 144, 208, 210–11, 213, 304, 334–36, 346, 365, 371, 375, 380, 409, 465, 481–82, 484, 498–99, 502, 504, 513–16, 520; III: 18, 74, 195, 304, 322–23, 359, 395, 401, 480, 502–3, 506

Absalom, I: 435; II: 207, 314; III: 39, 119, 139

Achaz, King, II: 4

Achias (Roman officer), I: 61; II: 103–5, 137, 149, 151, 223

Achzib, II: 185

Acicus, II: 509

Adam, I: 23, 113–22, 125, 129, 140–41, 145, 158, 161, 166, 183, 218, 302, 314–15, 483; II: 5, 36, 74, 76, 365, 376; III: 6, 84, 87–88, 92, 115, 221, 275, 277, 323, 325, 331, 351, 365, 388, 395–96, 401

Adonis, I: 318

Aegeas (judge) I: 43

Afthages, I: 47

Agabus, II: 15

Ahab, King, II: 59, 377

Alertz, Clemens August, I: 13

Alexander Jannaeus, I: 398

Alexander the Great, II: 105; III: 478

Alexander, son of Simon of Cyrene, III: 213, 267, 279, 478

Aman, I: 413; II: 316

Amandor, son of Veronica (Seraphia), I: 62, 64, 84, 91, 303, 305; II: 162, 303

Amandor. See Nathaniel of Cana

Ambrose, St., III: 277

Aminadab, I: 62, 64, 355; II: 57; III: 404

Ananias, I: 153, 163

Andrew the Apostle, I: 29, 38–39, 41–42, 45–46, 52–53, 55, 62–64, 102–3, 232, 298, 300, 305, 316, 321–23, 336–37, 339, 342–45, 371, 373–80, 382, 390, 394,

396–99, 403, 405–6, 408, 412, 419, 459, 463, 471–73, 484, 486, 491, 494, 496–97, 515; II: 1, 3, 5, 7–8, 17–19, 23, 30–33, 41, 45, 55, 65, 70, 84, 105, 137, 149–52, 155–58, 163, 169, 185, 187, 195, 243, 298, 300, 306, 321–22, 324, 333, 344, 399, 474, 481–82, 522–26, 528, 530; III: 3, 10, 76, 80, 129, 261, 393, 404–5, 415, 424, 426, 491, 502

wife of, I: 41; II: 523–24, 528

Angels, I: 18–19, 71–72, 77, 81, 113–14, 117–22, 132, 134–36, 139–43, 161–63, 165–67, 169, 175, 178, 182, 195–96, 199, 201, 215–16, 222, 229–31, 235, 261, 329, 333, 344–45, 347, 351–52, 354–55, 358, 360, 366–70, 384, 447, 463, 483, 499, 502, 510; II: 62, 340, 376, 390, 465, 486, 507; III: 15, 80–81, 84–87, 92–93, 97, 106, 111, 116, 145, 199, 203, 210, 217–18, 221, 305, 307, 323–24, 387–90, 404, 424, 426–27, 441, 469

Angels at the Nativity. See Angels

Anna, mother of Samuel, I: 151, 161, 167

Anna, eldest daughter of Cleophas, I: 64; II: 92, 105–6, 189, 191, 197, 208

Anna, a niece of St. Joseph, I: 69; III: 318

Anna Cleophas, I: 67, 89, 91

Anna (prophetess), I: 58, 88, 92, 176–77, 197, 216–17, 219, 226, 231, 235, 294, 313, 316, 326–29, 332, 348, 422; III: 196, 322, 423

Annadias, I: 65; II: 523

Annas, I: 111, 336; III: 82, 93–96, 99, 101–2, 106–7, 109, 117, 119, 163, 192, 195, 198, 207, 209, 301, 307, 392

Anne (St. Anne, Mother Anne), I: 73, 77–78, 83, 90, 120, 135, 138, 151–52, 153–58, 160–72, 174–83, 185, 187–89, 197, 199, 201, 211, 214–15, 217–20, 229, 234–35, 298, 303, 305–6, 313–15, 348, 364–65, 378, 384, 393, 397, 412, 496; II: 8–9, 94–95, 100, 145, 148, 166, 184, 194, 204, 206, 352, 479, 526, 528; III: 110, 192, 203, 214, 323, 423, 426

Antichrist, I: 26, 323; III: 485–86

Antigonus, I: 520; II: 103

Antipater, I: 517; II: 201

Aphras, I: 155

Apis, I: 133, 163

Apollinaris, I: 40

Aquinas, St. Thomas, I: 37, 420, 505, 513

Aram (disciple), I: 62, 65, 356, 363–64, 374, 376–77, 390, 477; II: 87; III: 204

Arastaria (disciple), I: 62, 64, 83, 91, 156, 305–6, 311

Archos (Essene prophet), I: 154–55, 308

Aretas, I: 478–79

Aristobolus, I: 65; II: 8, 13–14, 23

Arnim, Achim von, I: 1

Arphaxad, I: 129

Asenath, I: 127, 133, 145–49, 224

Asher, tribe, I: 148; II: 184–85, 313, 319

Asphas (Aspax), unicorn god, II: 513

Astarte, I: 317–18, 518

Athalia, I: 93, 87–88; II: 137, 139–40

Augustus, Emperor, I: 58, 193, 197, 257; III: 482

Azarias, son of Ananias, I: 163

Azarias, nephew of Mensor, II: 509–13

Azor, I: 65; II: 351, 353, 360, 362

Bactrians, I: 129

Balaam, I: 205; II: 50, 60, 409, 465, 467

Balak, II: 50, 467

Balthasar (Balthazar), I: 204; II: 59; III: 506

Barabbas, III: 200–201, 203

Barnabas, I: 29–30, 65; II: 14, 351, 353–54, 360, 362, 366–73, 376, 384–85, 390, 399; III: 417

Barsabbas, Joseph, I: 45, 54–55, 58, 64, 78, 90, 235, 298, 314, 336, 512, 515; II: 8, 39, 41, 51, 60, 82, 93, 149, 154, 177, 211, 213, 306, 313–14, 327, 332–33, 407; III: 113, 392, 412, 417

Bartholomew (Naphtali), I: 29, 46–47, 49, 53, 56, 62–64, 294, 380, 459–60; II: 83–86, 90, 92, 137, 147, 151, 306, 314, 316, 403–4, 470, 472; III: 2–3, 76, 80, 113, 413, 424

Beloved Disciple. See also John, son of Zebedee, III: 161, 221, 295

Belus, I: 130, 462; II: 393–94

Benedict, St., I: 218

Benjamin, I: 145, 259

Benjamin (tribe), I: 214, 355, 362, 376, 403; II: 51, 64, 74, 214; III: 181

Benjamin of Edon, II: 486

Berger, Ludwig, I: 13

Bernardini, Archbishop, I: 3

Beshalach, II: 218

Bismark, Otto von, I: 13

Boaz, I: 259, 319; II: 91

Bonaventure, St., III: 367

Bonoi Ben Gorion, I: 457

Boos, Martin, I: 26

Brentano, Christian, I: 10

Brentano, Clemens, I: 1–2, 10–14, 17, 24, 26, 29–30, 69; III: 75, 480, 486–88, 491, 497–500, 505

Bridget, St., I: 165

"Brothers of the Lord", I: 62, 64, 77, 90

Caesar Augustus. See Augustus, Emperor

Caesar, I: 100, 111; II: 82, 239; III: 11, 55, 206–7, 479

Caiaphas, I: 51, 103, 111; II: 62; III: 10, 27, 78, 82, 93–96, 99, 101–3, 105–17, 119,

161, 163, 165, 179, 183, 192, 195, 198, 207, 209, 212, 214, 217, 235, 259, 265, 306–7, 313, 320–21, 386–87, 391–92, 419, 449, 471

Cain, I: 121–22, 125, 483; II: 36, 365; III: 117, 119

Caisar of Atom, I: 65; II: 511–13

Caius, son of Salathiel, II: 491

Caleb, son of Jairus, I: 362

Caleb, son of Jesse, I: 63–64; II: 97, 99

Canaanites, I: 431; II: 34, 36, 287

Candace, Queen, II: 212

Caspar, I: 204

Cassius, I: 61; II: 224, 304, 310–11, 314–15, 317–20, 323, 386–89, 391. *See also* Longinus

Catherine of Alexandria, St., II: 367, 395; III: 94

Causur, King of, I: 204

Celidonius (Sidonius), I: 59

Cephas, I: 38, 42, 379; II: 137; III: 115, 449

Chaldeans, I: 65, 204; II: 513; III: 4–5, 407

Chariot, Essene, I: 355, 362, 402

Child of Promise,
　Blessed Virgin Mary, I: 176
　Christ. *See* Christ, as Child of Promise
　Isaac, I: 141
　Mary Heli, II: 77, 90
　Mary Cleophas, I: 90
　Seth, I: 121, 352

Children of Israel, I: 120, 136, 138, 145, 151, 338–40, 345, 357, 364–65, 376, 397, 419, 435, 469, 475, 492–93; II: 3, 12, 36, 41, 48, 52, 57, 125, 186, 312, 365, 371, 387, 518; III: 18

Chilion, I: 88; II: 43–44

Christ, *passim*
　as *Bread of Life*, I: 108, 512; II: 165, 303–5, 318, 323, 364; III: 19, 89, 109, 489
　as *Child of Promise*, I: 198, 263
　as *Eternal Word*, III: 111, 221, 300
　as *Incarnate Word*, I: 388
　as *King of the Jews*, I: 207, 209, 265, 348, 418; II: 26–27, 48, 493, 497, 501–2, 504–5, 507, 509, 511; III: 194, 196–98, 200, 205, 208, 221, 224, 227, 231, 239, 257, 281, 310, 506
　as *Lamb of God*, I: 334, 356, 373, 420–21, 435, 449, 480, 501; II: 29, 214, 340; III: 103, 206, 209, 221
　as *Messiah*, I: 34, 37, 41, 49, 58, 60, 62, 83, 97, 99–100, 102, 106, 108, 139–40, 151, 154, 157, 163, 176–77, 179–80, 184–85, 188, 206, 208, 216, 227, 231, 294–95, 297–98, 300–303, 311–14, 316–18, 323, 325–28, 334, 336, 338, 340, 342–45, 348, 351, 362–63, 369, 373, 378, 380, 382–83, 388, 394, 396, 411, 429, 437, 448, 459, 462, 488–89, 491–93, 496, 513; II: 3, 5, 11–12, 17, 22, 26–27, 30, 37–41, 43, 50, 56, 58, 64, 67, 85, 107, 145, 163, 177, 179–80, 207, 214, 323–24, 326,

352, 358–59, 361, 372, 384, 394–98, 400–401, 403, 406, 409, 465, 467, 492, 494, 500–501, 504; III: 11, 57, 111, 117–18, 120, 169, 171, 185, 194, 200, 214, 277, 308, 365, 391, 394, 478, 484, 506–7
　as *New Adam*, III: 87, 221
　as *Paschal Lamb*, I: 419–21; II: 214, 218, 329, 331, 340; III: 75, 103, 105, 116, 193, 195, 206, 209, 221, 223, 321, 365
　as *Redeemer*, I: 19, 119–20, 141, 160–61, 170, 183, 279, 334, 448; II: 9, 37, 40–41, 48, 57, 214, 218, 222, 329, 343, 376, 479, 495, 499; III: 6, 84, 87–90, 92, 116, 194–96, 203, 208–10, 212, 219–20, 224, 277, 299–300, 304, 310–11, 314–15, 322–24, 345, 351, 388, 391, 480
　as *Savior*, I: 16, 24, 138, 149, 151, 156, 163, 165, 176, 184, 189, 193, 197, 205–6, 210, 229–31, 261, 302, 328–29, 334, 340, 343, 367, 384, 415, 418, 420, 429, 437, 443, 501; II: 20, 22, 27, 29, 57, 87, 91–92, 150, 160, 208, 214, 277, 340, 465, 49, 487, 499, 517; III: 15, 80, 84–85, 91–92, 94, 96, 103, 106, 114, 118, 123, 135, 141, 143, 145, 165, 179, 183, 192, 194, 196, 198, 200–202, 205, 208, 216, 218–19, 221, 229, 231, 235, 237, 259, 273, 277, 287, 299, 304, 311, 323–24, 331, 337, 349, 351, 359, 363, 365, 371, 373, 375, 388, 391, 396–97, 401, 417, 421, 441, 443, 445, 471, 491, 507
　as *Son of David*, I: 393; II: 84, 166, 174, 179, 189, 191, 259, 275, 309, 473, 455; III: 11, 37, 112, 194
　Temptations of,
　　in Gethsemane, III: 82–88, 141, 143
　　in Wilderness, I: 367–71, 441, 443, 445, 447; III: 196, 485

Christians, I: 2, 40–41, 44–45, 48, 50, 55, 57, 59–60, 75, 85, 87, 118, 235, 297, 308, 310, 333, 515; II: 14, 139, 263, 319, 359, 369, 396, 468, 474; III: 65, 88, 97, 100, 215, 222, 267, 312, 318, 322, 329, 402, 407–8, 419, 421, 428, 479

Christmas, I: 17, 22, 196, 204, 218, 507, 517

Chrysostom, St. John, III: 479

Church Fathers, III: 478–79, 482

Clare, St., III: 311

Claudia Procula, III: 192, 195–96, 200, 203, 206, 208–9, 229, 317, 361

Clement of Alexandria, III: 478–79, 485

Cleophas, Alpheus, I: 45, 53–55, 90–91, 219, 235, 314, 336; II: 137, 154, 269

Cleophas, Anna, I: 64, 67, 89, 91, 105–6, 189, 191, 197, 208

Cleophas, brother of Joseph, I: 85, 89, 91

Cleophas, husband of Mary Heli, I: 57, 62, 64, 77, 90, 165, 167, 219; III: 71, 75, 281

Cleophas, James, II: 210

Cleophas, Mary, I: 45, 53–56, 58, 64, 67–72, 77–79, 85–86, 88, 90–92, 166–67,

170, 174, 188–89, 218–19, 235, 292, 297–98, 303, 305, 315, 316, 326, 328–30, 336, 382, 402–3, 411, 419, 424, 491; II: 8, 39, 137, 154, 157–58, 160, 163, 167, 194, 287, 322, 403, 407, 468, 475; III: 20, 75, 81, 86, 100, 199, 203, 218, 224, 300, 302–3, 310, 316, 318, 386, 388, 393, 395, 397, 410

Cleophas of Emmaus, I: 232; II: 39; III: 312, 393–95

Cleophas, Susanna. *See* Susanna of Jerusalem

Cleophas, Little. *See* Nathanael

Cocharia, I: 62, 64, 83, 91, 156, 305–6, 311

Cornelius the Centurion, I: 60; II: 136, 141, 151–52, 154–55, 158, 175, 198, 223, 306, 343, 346, 398, 408; III: 4

Costa, father of St. Catherine, II: 367

Ctesiphon, I: 45, 129; II: 179–80; III: 203, 224, 303

Cuppes (Serena), pagan priestess, II: 506–7, 509–10, 513

Cyrenius (governor of Syria), I: 257

Cyrinus of Cyprus, I: 63, 67; II: 74, 100–02, 151, 350, 352–54, 356, 358, 361–62, 384
　sons of, II: 350, 353, 356, 358, 384

Cyrinus of Dabrath, II: 149, 362

Cyrinus of Egypt (playmate of Jesus), II: 193

Cyrus (Sirius, Syrus), father of Manahem of Coreae), II: 73

Dagon (an idol), I: 55

Daniel, I: 152; II: 27, 74, 515; III: 486

Datula, I: 28

David, King, I: 102, 141, 156, 178, 192, 222, 283, 317, 354, 399, 407, 429, 435, 520; II: 41, 62, 75, 78, 90–91, 97, 168, 176, 205, 207–8, 314, 406, 465, 492, 498, 504; III: 3, 39, 72, 119, 194, 325, 359, 396

Deborah (prophetess), I: 151; II: 97, 218–19

Degas, Edgar, I: 2

Demetrius, son of Salathiel, II: 491

Deodatus, I: 65, 229; II: 519

De Raedemaeker, Jozef, I: 1, 29; III: 487, 499

Derketo (goddess/idol), I: 127–28, 130–32; II: 365

Deutsch, Fr. Brenard F., I: 2

Devil, I: 15–16, 18, 22, 50, 82, 100, 102, 108, 110, 123, 125–26, 132, 134, 148, 167, 197, 296, 300, 358–59, 364, 370, 380, 390, 393, 441, 443, 445, 497, 500, 510–11; II: 8, 13, 21, 43, 57, 78, 80, 87, 94, 110, 137–38, 150, 159, 166, 168–71, 173–74, 176, 189, 199, 202, 223, 297, 309, 318, 321–22, 341, 343, 479, 512, 526, 529–30; III: 4, 10, 22, 69, 90, 97, 102, 107, 109, 205, 307. *See also* Satan *and* Lucifer

Dinah the Samaritan Woman, I: 63, 67–68, 73–74, 81, 85, 87–90, 92, 486–92, 505, 513; II: 65, 80–81, 88, 105–6, 110, 140, 150, 152, 167, 175, 189, 197, 283, 348, 352; III: 318, 320–21

Dinah, daughter of Jacob, I: 144–45
Dinotus (Pharisee), I: 60; II: 31–33
Dionysius the Areopagite, I: 224; III: 351
Dionysius the Carthusian, I: 509
Dismas (the good thief), III: 222–24, 300, 305, 310, 314
Djemschid, I: 123, 126–28; II: 374–76
Dothanites, II: 92

Ebionite Christians, II: 263
Ebionites, I: 437
Edwards, Ormond, III: 482–84
Egyptians, I: 130, 133, 137, 145–49, 225, 227, 339; II: 46–47, 77, 381–82; III: 478
Ela, I: 91
Eleazar, II: 409
Elia, grandson of Matthan, brother of Joseph), I: 95; II: 99
Eliachim, I: 71, 75
Eliezer, I: 357
Elijah (prophet), I: 34, 109, 121, 123, 132, 154, 162–63, 165, 180, 300–303, 332, 337–38, 340, 365, 370, 401, 411, 435, 462, 475, 493, 496, 500–502, 517, 519, 523; II: 12–14, 56–60, 63, 99, 102, 146, 304, 312–13, 326, 340, 342, 352, 359, 363, 365, 377, 393; III: 485
Elijah, brother of Joseph, I: 64; II: 99
Elimelech of Bethlehem, I: 89; II: 44
Elisha, I: 118, 338, 365, 379, 401, 407, 464, 493, 515, 517; II: 12, 33, 63, 75, 82, 90, 93, 343, 359
Eliud (Siricius), I: 65; II: 482, 487–88, 495, 510, 522–23, 526; III: 7, 20, 31, 397, 417
Eliud, Essene of Nazareth, I: 60, 78, 83, 90, 94, 155–58, 214–15, 220, 309, 312–22, 325, 367, 413–14, 500, 515; II: 11; III: 487
Jesus transfigured before, I: 321–22, 500; III: 509
Eliud (husband of Ismeria, father of Anne), I: 75, 90, 155–156
Eliud, 2nd husband of Anne, I: 214–215, 220
Eliud, 2nd husband of Maroni, daughter of Sobe, father of Martialis, I: 83, 94, 156; II: 100
Eliud, son of the aged Simeon, III: 4
Elizabeth, cousin of Mary, I: 75, 77, 83, 155, 161, 165, 167, 177–78, 183–88, 197, 201, 205, 222, 226, 230–31, 251, 279, 296, 300, 310, 315, 429; II: 91, 205, 207–8, 210–11, 213, 393–94; III: 4, 323, 423, 426
Elizabeth, wife of Aaron, II: 57
Emerentia, I: 151, 155
Emily. *See* Ratimiris
Emmerich, Anne Catherine, I: 1–15, 17–18, 20–22, 24–26, 29–30, 40, 42, 48, 58, 60, 67–72, 77–78, 82–84, 86, 88–89, 111, 292, 298, 303, 325, 343, 352, 366, 390, 409, 516, 518–19, 522–23; II: 37, 50, 306, 404, 467, 475, 484, 495, 500, 517–18, 522; III: 6, 70, 75, 80, 82, 157, 269, 303, 311, 313, 316, 319, 351, 422, 477–78, 480–

93, 495, 497–508
Emorun (Moruni), I: 154–55
Enoch, I: 118, 122–23, 126–27, 135, 148; II: 63, 304
Enoi, I: 341
Enue (widow with flow of blood), sister-in-law of Lea, I: 93, 509; II: 164–165, 167, 257, 267, 319–20, 343, 364, 397
her uncle, II: 320
Enue, sister of Elizabeth and daughter of Emerentia and Aphras, I: 94, 155, 165, 167–168
Enue, daughter of Stolanus and Emorrun, I: 95,
Epaphras, III: 215
Ephraim, I: 148
Ephraim (tribe), II: 81; III: 147
Eremenzear (Hermas), I: 65; II: 482, 484, 502, 510–12, 514, 522–23, 526; III: 6–8, 20
Esau, I: 142–44, 362–63; II: 34, 45, 68, 100–101, 150, 308
Esdras, II: 180
Esra, II: 54
Essenes, I: 45–46, 48, 60, 62, 64–65, 78, 84, 90, 188, 198–200, 215, 226, 231–32, 305–8, 312–15, 318–20, 322–23, 340, 355, 362, 367–68, 370, 376, 387, 401–2, 412–14, 418, 473, 496, 500, 512, 515, 523; II: 11–13, 16–18, 39, 53, 73–74, 77, 180, 184, 193–95, 206–7, 211, 213–15, 330, 352, 358, 360–62, 467; III: 110, 193, 214, 308, 487
in Family of the Blessed Virgin Mary, I: 152–58, 164–65
Esther, I: 412–14; II: 316
Esther (Egyptian idol), I: 318. *See also* Astarte)
Eusebius, III: 147, 485
Eustachius, I: 62, 64, 84, 91, 300, 305, 367, 390
Eve, I: 114–21, 138, 141, 158, 161, 166, 302, 327, 352, 483; II: 5, 36, 365, 376; III: 6, 15–16, 84, 87, 92, 316, 323, 325, 365, 388, 401
Ezekiel, I: 302; II: 73–74, 194, 346, 350, 357, 359, 392

Fabian, Pope, III: 80
Fahsel, Fr. Helmut, I: 4–5, 109; III: 488, 491–92, 502
Fey, Clara, I: 13, 17; II: 145, 400
Five Hundred, the, II: 388, 401; III: 305, 404–5
Fotheringham, J.K., III: 483–84
Frances of Rome, St., I: 22
Francis of Assisi, St., I: 7; III: 367

Gabriel (Archangel), I: 136, 139, 183, 279, 329; III: 305, 323, 433
Gad, I: 147; II: 83, 480
Galileans, I: 192, 287, 339; II: 206, 326–27, 329–30, 335, 338, 345–46, 349, 385; III: 67, 110
Garescha. *See* Stolanus
Gentiles, I: 300, 355, 360, 421; II: 17, 20,

22, 30, 34, 40, 48, 55, 70, 82–83, 101, 104, 157–58, 163, 168, 172, 223, 306, 311, 325, 352, 354, 363, 370, 396, 504
Gergeseans, II: 170–74, 176, 318, 347, 350, 362, 404; III: 84
Gesmas (the bad thief), III: 222, 224, 310
Gideon, II: 51–52, 170
Gileadites of Jabes, II: 96–97
Gnostics, I: 437, 480
God the Father, I: 24, 39, 72, 74, 82, 90, 98, 103, 105, 141, 157, 183, 201, 232, 234, 292, 311, 322, 329–30, 344, 347, 349, 352–55, 363–68, 373–77, 388–89, 392, 396, 420–21, 423, 467, 473, 475, 479–80, 482, 488, 491–93, 497, 499–500, 502–3, 514; II: 1, 5–6, 15–16, 22, 26–29, 31–33, 40, 67, 88–89, 94–95, 101, 104, 107–8, 142–43, 152, 159, 172, 177, 179, 181–82, 194, 202–4, 218, 224, 289, 303, 305, 307, 312, 317, 326, 331–35, 340, 344, 349, 357, 361–64, 374, 376–77, 383, 403–4, 406–7, 486–87, 490–92, 494, 497, 499, 507–8, 513, 520, 528; III: 3, 6, 12–13, 15, 18, 25, 77–78, 81–82, 85–89, 92, 97, 106–7, 111–12, 116, 145, 183, 195, 203, 210, 224, 261, 287, 301–3, 305, 322, 339, 341, 343, 387, 390, 405, 408, 412, 465, 471, 480, 488, 506–7
Godolias, II: 56
Goliath, I: 222, 283, 354, 429
Gossner, Johannes Evangelista, I: 26
Gouyet, Abbé Julien, I: 2

Ham, I: 125–26, 129, 133; II: 37; III: 219
Hanna, I: 16
Hay, servant of Job, I: 138
Heber, I: 129, 136; II: 76
Helena, St. (Empress), I: 181, 341, 365; III: 227, 235, 241, 249, 275, 313, 480
Heli, father of Mary Heli andVirgin Mary. *See* Joachim
Heli of Hebron, I: 94; II: 330, 332; III: 71–73, 123
Heli (high priest), II: 96
Helia, I: 160
Heliachim (Joachim), son of Cleophas), I: 62, 64, 77; II: 158, 177, 194
Hensel, Luise, I: 13
Hensel, Wilhelm, I: 13
Hermas. *See* Eremenzear
Hermes (Egyptian sage), III: 479
Hermogenes, I: 44; III: 420
Herod Agrippa I, King, I: 45
Herod Antipas, I: 34, 36, 42, 100, 107, 298, 394, 458, 496; II: 26, 31, 336; III: 82, 231, 478
Herod the Great, I: 106, 517–18; III: 63, 231, 482, 506
Herod the Elder, I: 480; III: 192–94
Herod of Pera and Galilee, II: 53
Herodians, I: 36, 103, 106–10, 521; II: 15, 25–31, 34, 40, 101, 107, 144, 146–47, 149, 167, 199, 201, 221–22, 224, 302, 329–30, 338, 348, 385; III: 4, 96, 102, 194, 391

Herodias, I: 110, 339, 394; II: 198–200, 214–15, 283; III: 198

Hillel, I: 457; III: 493

Hiram, King, I: 462

Holofernes, I: 306, 345, 413; II: 25, 81

Holy Family, I: 56, 60, 63–64, 79, 85, 90–91, 137, 153, 163–64, 177, 184, 189, 198–99, 211–16, 218–20, 222–30, 232–35, 239, 273, 275, 279, 281, 283, 287, 294, 298, 313, 316, 319, 322–23, 327, 334, 345, 347, 352–54, 356, 380, 385, 389, 397, 414, 431, 483, 517, 520, 533; II: 39, 150, 204, 206–7, 209–10, 215, 518–20; III: 73, 214, 222, 308, 421, 424, 506

Holy Innocents (Bethlemite babes), II: 492; III: 84, 196, 226

Holy Spirit, I: 21, 29–30, 33, 37, 39, 59, 119, 141, 151, 170, 175, 180, 183, 185, 189, 195, 199, 230, 241, 247, 249, 253, 255, 271, 302, 308, 310, 332–34, 341, 343–45, 347, 357–58, 360, 362, 364–65, 371, 373–74, 392, 394, 396, 441, 445, 489, 516; II: 16, 72, 159, 179, 208, 218, 326, 343–44, 359, 403, 435, 463, 471, 478–79; III: 3, 17–18, 65, 81, 87, 100, 106 195, 305, 316, 322, 400, 405, 408, 413, 418, 449, 471, 484. *See also* Spirit, the.

Holy Trinity, I: 77, 119, 160–62, 165–66, 183, 198, 217–18, 329, 502; II: 48, 340, 498; III: 84, 406, 408, 425

Hom, I: 124–28, 388

Idol of Baal, II: 59

Ignatius of Antioch, II: 343, 457; III: 151

Ignatius, II: 401

Isaac (Patriarch), I: 120, 125, 142–44, 147, 185, 314, 354, 362, 522; II: 34, 36, 56, 100–101, 136, 208, 227, 409; III: 210, 322, 404

Isaiah, I: 153, 179, 185; II: 3–4, 11, 20–21, 29–33, 40, 50, 54, 59, 67, 72, 76, 168, 186, 224, 526; III: 171, 485

Ishmael, II: 481, 490, 495

Isis, I: 56, 133, 146

Ismeria (Essene) I: 78, 90, 155–56

Israel of Cana, I: 298

Israelites, I: 133, 135, 138, 148–52, 155–56, 163, 176, 216, 340–41, 345, 357, 365, 399, 418, 422, 429, 494; II: 38, 48, 50–52, 57–58, 63, 76–77, 97, 136, 216, 224, 338, 352, 381–82, 394, 401, 406, 465; III: 323, 503

Issachar of Dothan, I: 48, 61, 99; II: 89–94, 99, 197, 359; III: 147

Issachar (tribe), II: 99, 359; III: 147

Jacob (patriarch), I: 119, 134, 138, 141–48, 213, 302, 323, 325, 335, 352, 360, 262, 378, 401, 488, 493, 518, 522; II: 34, 38, 44–46, 68, 80–81, 83, 94, 100–101, 136, 208, 308, 352, 481, 524; III: 13, 208, 304, 322, 395–96, 506

Jacob, father of St. Joseph, I: 178

Jacob, House of, I: 183

Jacob, son of Sebadje, I: 64

Jacob, son of Matthan, I: 156

Jairus of Capernaum, I: 43, 60, 512; II: 26, 136, 150–52, 163–165, 168, 175, 223, 225, 232–33, 287, 319, 397, 400, 408; III: 5, 490, 509, 512

Jairus the Essene (of Phasael), I: 60, 362–63, 401–2, 512; II: 40, 76–77

Jairus, son of Mary Heli and Obed, I: 78, 90, 95

Jairus, younger brother of Obed, II: 530

James the Greater (James of Zebedee), I: 30, 38, 41–45, 63–64, 69, 78–79, 83, 91, 102–3, 155, 165, 232, 298, 300, 322, 379–80, 392, 402–3, 459, 484, 486, 491, 497, 500–501, 512–13, 515; II: 3–4, 17–18, 23, 29–30, 33, 44–45, 65, 105–6, 137, 141, 149, 151, 155–57, 165, 168–169, 195, 208, 306, 308, 321, 326, 339, 401, 409, 468, 472–74, 477, 522, 529; III: 1, 3, 5, 76, 78, 80, 83, 89, 91, 139, 141, 318, 320, 386, 395, 398, 400–401, 419–20, 502

James the Less, I: 29, 41–42, 45, 48, 54–58, 63–64, 67, 69, 90–91, 235, 253, 298, 305, 314, 322, 336, 339, 379, 387, 403, 408, 460, 463, 473, 484; II: 17–18, 55, 65, 92–93, 137, 154, 177, 183, 298, 306, 313, 321, 353, 360, 362, 376, 390, 398–99, 524–26, 528, 530; III: 2–3, 7, 17, 74, 76–77, 96, 129, 151, 212, 281, 320, 391, 394, 397–400, 405, 413–15, 417, 419

James, son of Cleophas and disciple of John the Baptist, I: 62, 90; II: 137, 158, 194, 207, 210, 213

Jane of Valois, St., I: 6

Japhet, son of Sebadje, I: 64, 232

Japhet, son of Noah, I: 124–26, 129; II: 37; III: 303

Jebusites, race of, II: 56

Jehoram, King, II: 63

Jehovah, I: 353, 396, 437, 471; II: 77; III: 197

Jephthah, II: 44–48, 51, 85, 467
daughter of, II: 44–48, 53, 467

Jephthah, son of Achias, I: 61; II: 104–5, 137, 151

Jeremiah, I: 152–53, 314, 493, 517; II: 53, 63, 74, 155, 204, 209–10, 321, 326, 370, 376; III: 181, 306

Jerome, St., II: 263, 283; III: 147, 183, 235

Jesse of Dabrath, I: 61; II: 97, 99–100, 102

Jesse (Old Testament), I: 155, 166, 179

Jethro, I: 147, 149; II: 50, 53, 57, 63–64, 224, 368, 375

Jezebel, I: 58, 294, 301; II: 59, 377

Joab, I: 326

Joachim, father of Mary Heli and Virgin Mary, I: 73, 77–78, 83, 90–91, 95, 119–20, 151, 155–58, 160–72, 174–77, 179–80, 188, 192, 214, 232, 245, 313–15, 323, 384; II: 94–95, 184, 204, 352, 479; III: 214, 323, 426

Joachim, King, II: 155

Johanna Chusa, I: 65, 67–72, 81, 86–87, 92, 215, 303, 313, 326, 328–29, 377–78,

402, 416, 431, 475, 482, 485, 497; II: 70, 88, 105, 189, 197, 204, 207, 211, 214, 216, 349, 395, 530; III: 100, 103, 214–15, 217–18, 318, 386, 388, 397–98

Job, I: 56, 128, 130–33, 136–39, 144, 205; II: 37–38, 74, 76, 81–82, 509–10; III: 171

John the Baptist, I: 30, 33–37, 41–42, 45, 48, 52, 55, 59, 62–65, 77, 83, 86, 89–91, 102, 108–10, 132, 136, 143, 155, 162, 177, 187–88, 191, 197, 201, 214, 220, 226, 229–32, 235, 259, 279, 283, 292, 296–98, 300–303, 305–8, 310–11, 313, 316–17, 319, 321–23, 325–27, 330–49, 352–53, 356–60, 362–65, 367, 371, 373–77, 379–80, 390, 392, 394, 396–97, 399, 401, 416, 418, 420, 422, 424, 429, 433, 435, 458–60, 462–63, 471, 473, 477–80, 482, 484, 491–92, 502, 515, 517, 520–21, 523; II: 4, 14, 16–17, 20, 22, 24, 26–29, 31–32, 37, 39–41, 43, 45, 48, 55, 62–63, 65, 68, 70, 73–74, 83, 92–93, 102, 105, 107, 137, 143–48, 150, 152, 154, 158–61, 167, 175, 177, 180, 183, 191, 194, 196–200, 203, 205–15, 217, 219, 222–23, 239, 304–5, 314, 334, 342, 349, 358–59, 385, 394, 401, 409, 443, 465, 479, 481, 524; III: 2, 11, 51, 84, 99–100, 214, 223, 306, 310, 323, 359, 414, 484

John, son of Zebedee, I: 23, 41–45, 61–64, 67, 69, 72, 76–79, 83, 90, 103, 165, 182, 321–23, 337, 379–80, 388, 392, 402–3, 408, 459, 462, 484, 491, 500–501, 512–13, 515; II: 3–4, 17–18, 23, 30, 45, 55, 65, 70, 105, 137, 149, 151, 155–57, 165, 169, 176–77, 184, 196–97, 201–2, 204–8, 217, 298, 306, 308, 316, 321, 323, 326, 339, 343, 350, 403, 409, 443, 468, 470–71, 474, 477, 480, 484, 512, 522–25; III: 1, 3–5, 7, 13, 17, 20–21, 49, 71–83, 85, 89, 91, 93, 98, 102, 108–11, 113–15, 119–20, 123, 127, 129, 131, 135, 141, 151, 161, 163, 177, 195–200, 204, 208, 212–13, 217–18, 220, 224, 235, 253, 265, 300–307, 310–11, 314, 316–19, 321–23, 331, 333, 337, 339, 341, 363, 365, 369, 371, 389–95, 398–403, 405–10, 414–15, 417–27, 437, 439, 443, 449, 461

John Mark, I: 29, 59, 65, 86, 92, 313, 326–27, 331, 343–44, 384, 414, 416, 419; II: 380, 524, 528, 530; III: 1, 5, 10, 14, 16, 20, 74, 100, 393, 397, 400–401, 426

John of Gischala, II: 102–3

Jonadab, I: 62, 64, 200, 294, 296, 377; II: 193–94; III: 219, 317

Jonah (prophet of Shiloh), I: 492–93; II: 191, 267, 306, 323–24

Jonah (Jonas), father of Peter, I: 38–39, 42, 54, 62, 314 II: 326

Jonas, father of Simeon [Justus], I: 64, 78, 90–91; II: 160

"Jonah in the fish", III: 401

Jonas of Salamis, I: 65; II: 356, 358, 360–62, 366
and his father. *See above*

Jonathan, half-brother of Peter, I: 62,

64, 385, 392, 403, 408, 419, 484; II: 59
Jonathan, son of Saul, II: 75, 465
Jonathan Eleazar, III: 427
Josephus, Flavius, III: 63, 329, 482, 484
Joses, son of Matthan, I: 156
Joses, nephew of Bartholomew, I: 137, 151
Joshua, I: 220, 259, 340–41, 357, 376, 475, 521; II: 74, 400, 427
Joseph, husband of Mary, I: 58–59, 62–63, 69, 73, 77, 89, 97, 99, 102, 133, 156, 164, 177–96, 198–201, 205, 208–15, 217–20, 222–29, 232–34, 243, 245, 253, 259, 273, 275, 285, 287, 294, 303, 314–16, 346–47, 352, 355, 358, 387, 398, 401; II: 81, 91, 207, 219, 395, 398, 505, 519; III: 110, 192, 219, 322, 426
  death of, I: 73, 98, 235–36, 333, 371; II: 194
Joseph Barsabbas, I: 45, 54–55, 58, 64, 78, 90, 235, 298, 314, 336, 512, 515; II: 8, 39, 41, 51, 60, 82, 93, 149, 154, 177, 213, 306, 313–14, 327, 332–33, 407; III: 113, 412, 417
Joseph of Arimathea, I: 30, 45, 59, 61–62, 65, 67–68, 84, 86, 91, 336–37, 343–44, 356–57, 363–64, 373–77, 386, 397, 416, 418–19, 424, 477, 482; II: 65, 87–88, 163, 183, 204–5, 207–8, 210–11, 217–18, 397, 409, 530; III: 1, 19, 71–72, 81, 86, 102–3, 108, 110, 114, 117, 204, 212, 214, 222, 275, 277, 279, 297, 307, 310–13, 318, 320–21, 329, 331, 369, 371, 373, 375, 377, 379, 386, 391, 394, 396–97, 406, 408–10, 416–18
Joseph, son of Jacob, I: 121, 127, 138, 145–50, 166, 224, 325, 378, 411; II: 30, 33, 46, 57, 83, 92, 159, 191, 193, 210, 215, 382, 506
Josias, III: 420
Judas Iscariot, I: 30, 48–52, 56–58, 60, 62–64, 75, 77, 85, 90, 103, 108, 294, 337, 362, 367, 483–84, 513, 521; II: 82–90, 92–94, 137, 140, 149, 158, 169, 172, 177, 305, 351–53, 394, 403, 528, 530; III: 3, 5–6, 10, 13–15, 19–22, 49, 74–76, 79–81, 86, 93–97, 100, 102, 105, 109, 115, 117–19, 127, 129, 133, 141, 147, 151, 187, 198, 324, 396, 412
Judas Maccabeus, I: 354–55; II: 201
Judas Thaddeus, I: 29, 41–42, 45–46, 48, 54–58, 63, 69, 78, 84, 90–91, 235, 314, 322, 336, 339, 403, 460, 484, 504; II: 21, 84, 87, 93, 154, 300, 306, 313, 327, 351, 393, 398–99, 489, 491, 512–13, 528–30; III: 3, 76, 127, 129, 391, 397, 400, 405, 413, 424, 507
Judas, son of Sebadje, 232
Judas of Gamala/Judas the Golanite, II: 326–27, 329–30, 336, 338, 346, 385
Judges,
  Scripture, II: 44, 51, 81, 406, 409, 467; III: 316
  Position, I: 336, 493; II: 40, 50, 81, 406; III: 107–8, 110, 163, 165, 177, 191, 206,

323
Judith, I: 306, 345, 413; II: 25
Jupiter (god), I: 97; II: 495

Karaites sect, II: 63–64
Keturah, II: 90–91, 502, 512
Kolaya, I: 62, 64, 84, 91, 300, 305, 311, 316; II: 8
Korah, II: 163, 405
Koré (goddess), III: 478, 480

Laban, I: 139, 143; II: 34, 68, 150, 409
Lais of Nain, I: 93; II: 87–88, 137, 139–40
Lazarus, I: 30, 49, 58–60, 62, 75, 79–81, 84–86, 88, 92, 103, 235, 294–95, 300, 316–18, 326–31, 342–46, 357–58, 363–64, 370–71, 377–80, 385–87, 394, 397–98, 402–3, 406, 414–16, 418–19, 421–22, 475, 477–78, 480, 482–85, 491–92, 505, 513, 515; II: 14, 39, 65, 73, 78, 83–85, 87–88, 94, 177, 180, 184, 187–90, 197, 204–8, 212, 214, 219, 222, 303, 308–9, 326–27, 329–30, 332–33, 348–49, 375, 380, 397–99, 409, 443, 473, 524–25, 528–30; III: 1–6, 8, 11–12, 21–22, 74, 85, 100, 102, 113, 192, 215, 312, 320–21, 359, 406–9, 417–19
  raising of, II: 475–80, 484, 523; III: 15, 19, 27, 197, 392, 487–89, 501
Lazarus (of the parable), II: 316, 331, 333–35, 341; III: 90
Lea (widow), I: 62, 64, 91, 305, 311, 313, 328–30; II: 407
Lea, sister-in-law of Enue, I: 93; II: 165, 167, 343, 397
Leah, wife of Jacob, II: 34
Leander, I: 204. *See also* Mensor
Lentulus, I: 197, 475, 477
Leo, I: 204; III: 507. *See also* Theokeno
Leopold zu Stolberg, Count Friedrich, I: 13
Levi, father of Matthat, I: 156
Levi, friend of Holy Family, I: 73, 97, 235, 292, 298, 316
Levi. *See* Matthew
Levites, I: , I: 141, 156, 174–75, 233–34, 341, 344, 406, 420, 522; II: 34, 38, 45–53, 56–58, 62, 68, 70, 99, 179–84, 207, 210–11, 218, 309, 321, 351, 393–94, 396–97, 409, 529; III: 63, 357
Limberg, Fr., I: 12
Livias, I: 478; II: 105
Longinus (Cassius), I: 61, 115; III: 224, 304–5, 310–11, 314–15, 317–20, 323, 367, 386–89, 391. *See also* Cassius (Longinus
Lot, I: 88, 139–40, 312, 360; II: 15, 28
Louis XI, King, I: 6
Louis St., III: 239, 257
Lucifer, I: 113, 229; III: 324. *See also* Devil *and* Satan
Ludgarde, St., I: 14, 17
Luke, I: 509; III: 71, 263, 277, 312, 341, 349, 393–97, 449, 469, 484–85
Lysia, sister of Thomas, I: 48

Maacha, II: 314
Maccabees, I: 153, 201
  Feast of the Maccabees, I: 201, 415
  War of the Maccabees, II: 82, 201, 467
Mary Magdalene (Magdalene), I: 39, 48, 50–51, 58–60, 67–74, 79–86, 90–92, 161, 230, 294–95, 306, 316, 318, 328–31, 339, 363–64, 371, 393, 398, 414, 431, 478, 483–84, 490, 513; II: 44, 88, 90, 135, 140–41, 149, 175, 193, 195, 197, 204–5, 215–16, 218, 222, 329, 332, 348, 364, 395, 397, 443, 445, 468, 473, 477–78, 523–25, 528–29; III: 4, 9–11, 15, 19–22, 49, 74, 81, 84–86, 91–94, 100, 112, 114–15, 119–20, 171, 195–96, 199–200, 203–4, 217–20, 224, 265, 277, 281, 293, 299–300, 302–3, 305, 310–11, 314–19, 331, 335, 341, 369, 371, 375, 381, 386, 388–91, 395–400, 408, 410, 416, 424, 437, 441, 443
  First Conversion, I: 401–3; II: 105–10
  Second Conversion, II: 188–91, 204
Magi, I: 48, 57–58, 65, 97, 129, 132, 137, 139, 143, 177, 190, 197, 202–6, 265, 338, 348, 351, 355, 418, 458, 463, 472, 496, 518; II: 17, 48, 50, 57, 152, 210, 212, 465, 482, 484, 499–500, 517, 530; III: 318, 477, 479, 502, 506–7
Mahlon, I: 89; II: 43
Malachi (prophet), I: 152, 500–502; II: 64, 74–75, 97, 99–102, 107, 159, 180, 184, 304–5, 340, 352, 372, 376, 380, 465; III: 72, 107, 479
Malchus, III: 97, 100, 114, 155, 157, 177
Manahem of Coreae (Essene), I: 62; II: 72–74, 87–88, 93–94; II: 163, 177, 342, 380, 408; III: 113, 509
Manahem (prophet), I: 158, 364,
Manasseh, I: 62, 64, 148, 318, 355; II: 3, 81
Manasseh (tribe), II: 49, 51, 82
Manet, Edouard, I: 2
Mara the Suphanite, I: 74, 88–89, 92, 513; II: 42, 44, 65, 70, 105, 108, 175, 191, 197, 203, 314, 348, 395; III: 318, 320
Maraha, great-aunt of Jesus, I: 62, 64, 78, 90, 156, 165, 195, 305–6, 311, 411
Maraha, nurse of Abraham, I: 138, 339, 352, 360; III: 480
Marcella, maidservant of Martha, I: 59–60, 79; II: 468
Marcion, I: 40
Mark (Evangelist), I: 59, 64, 69; II: 123, 247, 491; III: 161, 267, 285, 361, 369, 381, 408
Maroni (widow of Nain), I: 38, 40, 44, 67–68, 83, 88–89, 91, 156, 497, 512, 522; II: 16, 100, 136–37, 141, 143–44, 152, 158, 163, 189, 197, 348, 396; III: 318, 320–21
Martha, I: 58–60, 67–68, 79–82, 84–92, 294, 316–17, 326–30, 362, 370, 377–78, 385, 388–89, 402–3, 414, 416, 424, 482–83, 497; II: 39, 44, 70, 88, 92, 105–6, 110, 140, 152, 167, 175, 188–91, 197, 204, 215–16, 218, 348, 395, 443, 468, 473, 477–79, 523, 528–29; III: 4, 11, 86, 100, 102, 113,

192, 217–18, 224, 318, 320–21, 396–97, 405, 408, 410, 424

Martialis (youth of Nain), I: 38, 40, 44, 83, 91, 512; II: 100, 137, 142–43, 157, 162, 395

Mary (Virgin), I: 16–17, 23, 30, 42, 45, 69, 83–84, 90, 93, 97, 102, 119–20, 133, 135, 137–38, 147, 151, 155–72, 174–95, 197–201, 205, 209–20, 222–29, 232–35, 243, 245, 251, 259, 275, 279, 285, 287, 292, 294, 297, 303, 306–7, 312–17, 322–23, 325–31, 334, 346–47, 351, 354, 358, 362, 367, 371, 378, 382–90, 393, 398, 401, 408–9, 411–12, 414–15, 419, 421, 477–78, 48, 491–92, 497, 520, 522; II: 4, 6, 18, 30–31, 50, 74, 80–81, 88, 91–92, 94, 100, 106, 110, 136–37, 141, 163, 167–68, 189–91, 204–11, 219, 223–24, 306, 348 395, 398, 400, 407, 505, 509, 518, 520, 523–24, 528–30; III: 1, 4, 10, 13–14, 19, 49, 71, 74, 82, 86, 94, 97, 102, 115, 120, 195–96, 200–201, 203–4, 208, 212, 214, 217–18, 224, 265, 281, 293, 300, 311, 315–17, 320–22, 333, 337, 369, 371, 375 379, 386, 388, 393, 397, 399–400, 406–10, 412, 417–18, 420–28, 433, 487

Annunciation of, I: 182–83, 201; III: 196, 480

as Ark of the Covenant, I: 160, 170, 175–76, 186, 314, 328

as Blessed Mother, I: 16, 349, 354; II: 514; III: 3, 74, 93 102, 195, 208–9, 212–13, 219, 300–301, 315, 387–88, 400, 409–10

as Blessed Virgin, I: 3, 23, 43, 50, 53 64, 67, 71, 75–78, 88, 90–91, 93, 139, 162–63, 165, 167, 178–79, 181–85, 187–91, 194–96, 198–200, 206, 210–12, 215–16, 218–19, 222–25, 227–29, 232, 303, 305–6, 310, 313–15, 25, 327–28, 330, 333, 346–48, 354, 358, 370, 387–88, 412, 491; II: 39, 80–81, 83, 89, 105, 110, 140, 160, 189, 207–8, 214, 329, 398, 475, 477, 487, 495, 519, 523, 528, 530; III: 6–7, 20–21, 71, 73–76, 79–81, 92–93, 99–100, 112, 114–15, 120, 195, 199, 203–4, 207, 212, 214, 217–20, 224, 235, 265, 267, 277, 281, 287, 300, 303, 309–12, 314–23, 386–88, 393, 395, 397–98, 400, 405–14, 416–17, 419–28, 480

as Mary of Nazareth, I: 38, 42, 45, 53, 57, 62, 77–78, 90, 523

as Mediatrix, I: 388; II: 195, 410, 412

as Mother of God, I: 16, 24, 78, 182, 186, 197–98, 205, 210, 214, 216, 232, 303, 310, 386; II: 213, 365, 514, 524; III: 21, 195, 203, 214, 397, 404, 419, 423

as Queen of Mercy, III: 410

as Virgin Mary, I: 2–3, 38–45, 47–48, 53, 58–59, 67–68, 71, 73–77, 79, 82, 85–86, 88, 90–92, 165, 279, 305–6, 329, 382; II: 163, 403, 517, 523–24; III: 71, 106

Birth of, I: 165–67

Espousal of, I: 178–82

Immaculate Conception of, I: 117, 157–64, 175, 328, 352, 517

Naming and Presentation of, I: 167–76

Purification of, I: 188, 201, 211, 215–17, 233, 255, 287

Visitation of, I: 177, 183–87; II: 207

Mary Cleophas, I: 45, 53–56, 58, 64, 67–72, 77–79, 85–86, 88, 90–92, 166–67, 170, 174, 188–89, 218–19, 235, 297–98, 303, 305, 313, 316, 326, 328–30, 336, 382, 402–3, 411, 419, 424, 491; II: 8, 39, 137, 154, 157–58, 160, 163, 167, 194, 287, 332, 407, 475; III: 20, 75, 81, 86, 100, 199, 203, 218, 224, 300, 302–3, 310, 316, 318, 386, 388, 393, 395, 397, 410

Mary Heli, I: 57–58, 62, 64, 67–68, 77–78, 90, 165–68, 170, 174, 218–20; II: 39, 137, 177, 194, 206–7, 211, 332, 475; III: 71, 75, 199, 203, 218, 316, 318–19

Mary of Hebron, I: 86, 92

Mary of Nain, I: 83, 91

Mary Mark, I: 40, 59, 65, 67–68, 70, 83, 86, 92, 326–27, 330, 384, 416, 419, 421, 424, 463, 482; II: 100, 197, 480; III: 1, 7, 74–75, 86, 92–93, 100, 102–3, 218, 318–19, 398

Mary, mother of Joses, I: 67, 69; III: 381

Mary of Cana, I: 298

Mary of Egypt, I: 335; II: 58

Mary Salome, I: 38, 42, 67–70, 72, 78–79, 90, 155, 298, 326, 328–30; II: 215, 329, 468, 477; III: 86, 100, 265, 277, 318, 369, 386

Mary Zebedeus, II: 477

Mathathias, II: 520

Matthan, I: 156

Matthat, father of Heli, I: 156

Matthew, I: 29, 46, 54–56, 78, 90–91, 300, 310, 314, 336, 393, 513, 515; II: 152, 154–58, 160–62, 165, 167, 185, 187, 189, 195, 239, 297, 303, 306, 322, 324, 401, 408–9, 468, 479–81; III: 3, 10, 76, 129, 177, 285, 341, 359, 392–93, 404, 413, 426

Matthias, I: 3, 57–58, 64, 77, 85, 90–91, 380; II: 48, 86, 137; III: 412

Maximin, I: 59

Melchior, I: 204; III: 506

Melchizedek, I: 84, 118, 125, 128, 130, 134–36, 139–41, 149, 152, 212, 318, 335, 341, 360, 363, 396–97; II: 37–38, 74–75, 374–76, 380, 409, 481, 495, 504, 508; III: 74, 80, 277, 351, 375, 395

Mendelssohn, Fanny, I: 13

Mensor (Leander), I: 136, 197, 202, 204, 207–11, 335; II: 482, 500–505, 507–13; III: 4, 502, 506–7

Merari, race of, I: 406

Mercuria (pagan priestess), II: 362, 364, 367, 369, 390, 393, 396, 407

Messiah

Micah, II: 465

Michael (Archangel), I: 136, 369

Michol, daughter of Ozias, I: 61; II: 75, 201–3

Midianites, II: 51–52, 57, 81, 170

Mira of Heliopolis, I: 65

Mithras (Mytor, Mitras), II: 513; III: 479

Mizraim, I: 130, 133

Mnason, I: 65; II: 351, 353, 379, 386–88, 390, 399, 405, 407

Moloch, II: 59–61, 63; III: 181

Money-changers, I: 105; III: 43

Moruni. See Emorun

Moses, I: 49, 118–20, 131–34, 138, 141, 148–53, 155, 161, 166, 168, 170, 178–79, 185, 195, 197, 226, 259, 275, 303, 314–15, 318–19, 347, 357, 376, 383, 393, 397, 409, 445, 462, 467, 493, 500–502; II: 3, 12, 14, 21, 47, 50, 53, 57–59, 64, 139, 144, 194, 224, 303–4, 334, 340, 346, 359, 367, 371, 375, 381–82, 387, 401; III: 74–75, 261, 323, 401, 506

Moses, father of Mnason, II: 386

Mosoch, I: 124, 126

Müller, Wilhelm, I: 13

Naaman, II: 12–13, 63, 336

Nahum (prophet), I: 518–19; II: 180

Naomi, aunt of Lazarus, I: 58, 175–76, 197, 217, 271, 315, 318,

Naomi of Bethlehem, wife of Elimelech, mother of Ruth, I: 89, 302; II: 43

Naomi of Dabrath, II: 99–100

Nathan, brother of Solomon, I: 95, 156

Nathaniel Chased, I: 46–47, 53, 56, 62–64, 91, 294, 371, 373, 378, 380, 383–85, 387, 402–3, 406, 408, 419, 427, 460, 463, 471–73, 484, 496–97, 512; II: 1, 21, 30, 32–33, 91, 105, 163, 177, 184, 327, 351, 393, 404, 529; III: 71, 74–75, 96, 100, 113, 392, 400–401, 408, 417

Nathaniel (Little Cleophas), I: 64, 89, 91–92, 94, 117, 235

Nathaniel of Capernaum (Amandor), bridegroom of Cana, I: 43, 62–64, 91, 298, 378–80, 386, 388, 402–3, 408, 419, 451, 463, 477, 484, 494; II: 2, 21, 59–60, 89–90, 177, 306, 398, 403; III: 4

Nazarites, I: 308, 310; II: 73, 309; III: 55

Nazor, II: 493–95

Nebuchadnezzar, King, I: 265; II: 82, 515

Nehemiah, II: 180, 218; III: 95

Neumann, Theresa, I: 5

Nicanor, I: 271

Nicodemus, I: 30, 59, 61, 63, 67–68, 71–72, 84, 87, 91, 326–28, 331, 343–44, 397, 416, 419, 424, 457, 482, 513; II: 102, 205, 207–8, 218, 308–9, 479–80, 524, 530; III: 1, 7, 12–13, 19–20, 22, 71–73, 78, 81, 86, 102–3, 108, 110, 114, 117, 214–15, 222, 307, 310–15, 317–20, 322, 367, 371, 375, 386, 388–90, 392, 394, 396–97, 406–10, 416–18

Nimrod, I: 130–31

Noah, I: 118, 120–21, 123–29, 139–40, 148, 151, 161, 312, 314; II: 37, 72, 76, 365,

375; III: 18, 74, 219, 275, 277, 359, 401

Obed, I: 59–60, 62, 65, 78, 326–27, 332, 337, 343–44, 357, 380, 384–86, 398, 406, 414, 416, 418–20, 422, 477, 482, 484, 496; II: 80–82, 137, 530; III: 73, 204, 506, 416
Oberdorfer, Marie, I: 26
Onan, II: 352
Origen, III: 478, 485
Orpah, I: 88–89; II: 43–44
Osiris (god), I: 133, 146
Overberg, Bernard, I: 12–13
Ozias, I: 61; II: 201–3

Pagan Philosophers, I: 57, 65, 128; II: 362–66, 374–78, 385, 398–99
Palsied man, II: 164
Pan (god), I: 518; III: 309, 351
Paralyzed man (38 yrs.), II: 216–18, 330; III: 113, 155
Parmenas, I: 62, 64, 78, 91, 187, 296–98, 303, 342; II: 9, 13–14, 23, 33, 194; III: 418
Paul, I: 29–30, 61, 308, 520; II: 14, 102–4, 117, 137, 140, 201, 369, 484, 491; III: 3, 208, 235, 267, 277, 424, 449
Paula, St., I: 194
Peter the Apostle, I: 23, 29–30, 38–45, 48, 53–56, 58, 62–64, 72–73, 76, 78–79, 83, 90–91, 102–3, 108, 153, 182, 197, 235, 271, 300, 305, 310, 313, 316, 322–23, 333, 336–37, 339, 371, 373–74, 378–80, 382, 392–93, 402–3, 408–9, 411–12, 419, 422, 459–60, 462–63, 465, 472–73, 484, 490, 500–501, 503–4, 512–13, 515, 518–19; II: 3–8, 17–21, 23, 59, 84, 105, 141–42, 149–52, 154–56, 167–69, 173–77, 180, 183, 195–97, 201–7, 243, 293, 298, 301, 306, 308, 321, 324, 326–27, 339–44, 350, 401, 403–6, 409, 443, 468, 471, 474, 481–82, 522–24, 526, 528; III: 1–5, 7, 10, 12–13, 18–19, 21, 71–83, 89, 93, 96–97, 102, 108–10, 112–15, 123, 127, 129, 131, 139, 141, 143, 151, 155, 161, 171, 177, 179, 265, 307, 309, 320, 386, 389–96, 398–410, 412–19, 423–28, 437, 439, 449, 461, 467, 491, 502, 504
Peter's mother-in-law, I: 39, 348; II: 4, 7, 18, 23, 160, 399
Petronella, I: 38
Pharaoh, I: 133–34, 139, 145, 147–49, 226–27, 275; II: 57, 381–82
Pharisees, I: 42, 44, 47–48, 50–51, 55, 58–59, 63, 86, 89, 97–110, 134, 164, 177, 192, 235, 294, 306, 410–13, 315, 318–19, 323, 328, 331, 336, 338, 345–46, 362–63, 367, 369–70, 375–76, 394, 398, 403, 405, 413, 416, 418–22, 424, 429, 433, 459, 462, 464, 473, 475, 478, 482–83, 485, 492–96, 511, 523; II: 1–5, 9, 11–22, 26–27, 30–31, 33–34, 37–40, 42–44, 59, 64, 72–74, 76–78, 80, 82, 84, 86–88, 90–96, 99–101, 103, 106–9, 136–37, 139, 141, 143–44, 146, 148–52, 154–55, 157–59, 163–64, 166–67, 174–76, 179–87, 189–91, 193–

95, 200, 202–4, 209–10, 214, 216–19, 221–24, 297, 302–5, 307, 314, 316, 319–25, 330–36, 338, 340, 342–43, 345–49, 359, 364, 384–88, 394–97, 400–401, 403, 405–9, 468, 471–74, 480, 523–24; III: 1–6, 11–20, 22, 27, 37, 51, 55, 61, 74, 82, 86, 93–99, 101–2, 107, 109–10, 119–20, 147, 157, 192, 197–200, 202, 206–7, 209–18, 220–21, 224, 279, 295, 300–302, 304–9, 311, 314, 391, 415, 478, 488–89, 501, 507
Philip, I: 45, 52–53, 56, 62–64, 298, 305, 336, 339, 373, 379–80, 382–83, 484, 491; II: 18, 59, 84, 87, 177, 212, 298, 300, 306, 321, 481–82, 522; III: 3, 9–10, 45, 76, 96, 129, 425, 491, 502, 504
Philip (tetrarch), I: 375, 379, 518; II: 44, 53–54, 318
Philistines, I: 407, 429; II: 36, 53, 96–97, 101; III: 199
Phinehas, II: 50
Pilgrim, I: 10, 12–15, 18–19, 23–26; II: 369. *See* Brentano, Clemens
Pius IX, Pope, I: 13
Polymius, King, I: 47
Pontius Pilate, I: 100, 109–11, 177, 225–26; II: 200–201, 211–12, 216, 219, 326–27, 329–30, 335–36, 338–39, 356, 361, 384–85; III: 55, 82, 93, 105–6, 115, 117–20, 157, 191–212, 216–17, 221–22, 224, 227, 229, 231, 233, 241, 243, 245, 247, 251, 253, 281, 289, 300–302, 304, 307–12, 314, 317, 320, 341, 361, 369, 385, 387, 389, 391, 397, 478, 484
Potiphar, I: 145–48, 224
Powell, Robert, I: 2; II: 467; III: 499

Queen of Heaven (pagan goddess Derketo), II: 365
Quirinius, governor of Syria, III: 482

Rachel, I: 139, 143–44, 178, 259; II: 34, 361
Raphael (Archangel), I: 67; III: 305, 323, 357, 433
Ratimiris (Emily), II: 512–13
Rebecca, I: 138, 142–44; II: 34, 36–37, 409
Rechabites, I: 522; II: 53–54, 56, 58, 369, 371–72, 309
Reuben, son of Jacob, I: 145, 148
Reuben (priest), I: 158
Reuben (innkeeper), I: 353
Rhoda, I: 83; II: 100
Riess, Florian, III: 482
Roman Commandant of Salamis, II: 360–61, 364, 367, 369, 390–91, 395
Romans, I: 100, 107, 192, 300, 345, 408; II: 25, 55, 82, 101–2, 338; III: 96, 115, 198, 201, 206, 209, 218, 221, 237, 285, 339, 480
Rufus, son of Simon of Cyrene, III: 213, 267, 279
Ruth, I: 61, 259, 302, 319, 384; II: 43–44, 91, 486

Sabbas, I: 45, 54, 64, 78, 235, 298, 314, 336
Sabia, I: 93; II: 87–88, 137, 139–40
Sadducees, I: 51, 105–7, 109, 192, 197, 208, 297, 306, 338, 376, 429, 493–94, 520, 523; II: 27, 29–30, 37–38, 40, 59, 64, 76, 91, 93, 99–103, 107, 137, 181–82, 184, 200, 209, 216, 221–22, 302, 324, 335, 348, 408–9; III: 11, 37, 94, 96, 102, 109, 224, 391
Sadoch (Zadok), son of Cleophas, I: 63–4, 77, 90, 95; II: 137, 158, 177, 207, 210
Sadoch (Pharisee), II: 103
Sair, I: 197, 202, 204, 208, 210, 213; II: 500–501, 504–5; III: 502, 506
Salathiel, II: 4, 491–95
Salome, daughter of Jairus, I: 60, 339, 512; II: 150, 163–64, 166–68
Salome of Jerusalem, I: 67, 69–70, 72, 85; II: 215, 329; III: 86, 92–93, 100, 103, 217, 218, 224, 302–3, 310, 316, 318, 388–89
Salome, step-daughter of Herod, I: 36, 339; II: 198–200; III: 231
Samanenses, I: 125, 130, 135–36
Samaritan Jews, I: 88, 99, 336, 362, 378, 414, 463, 466, 468, 487–88, 490–92, 494, 496; II: 5, 18, 22, 80–81, 84, 196, 336
Samson, II: 394, 407; III: 199, 316
Samuel (Book of), II: 405, 465
Samuel (disciple), II: 195
Samuel (prophet/judge), I: 151, 222, 354–355, 493, 522; II: 97, 406
Sarah, maid of Magdalene, I: 59–60
Sarah, wife of Abraham, I: 139, 141–42, 166, 339; II: 90, 208
Sarah, wife of Tobias, I: 163
Sarziri (Stolanus), I: 154–55
Satan, I: 18, 22, 47, 51–52, 113, 117, 119, 126, 130–31, 138, 229, 324, 344, 351, 366–70, 443, 510–11; II: 2–3, 16, 36, 88, 94, 108, 137, 170, 175, 306, 327, 335–36, 344–45, 398, 404, 506–7, 511, 514; III: 13, 81, 84–85, 87–89, 94–95, 97, 103, 105–6, 111, 115, 118–20, 196. *See also* Devil *and* Lucifer
Saturnin, I: 45, 62–63, 65, 102, 232, 342–45, 347, 349, 352–53, 356–57, 360, 373–77, 379–80, 390, 394, 396, 398–99, 416, 418, 422, 459–60, 462–63, 465, 472–73, 477, 482–84, 486, 491, 493, 496, 504, 513, 515; II: 7–8, 13–14, 23, 33, 51, 82, 84, 93, 150–52, 155–56, 158, 161–63, 165, 169, 177, 195, 211–12, 300, 313, 319, 351, 394; 482, 529; III: 113
Saul, I: 308, 407, 493, 517; II: 75, 95–97, 176, 349, 406
Schubert, Franz, I: 13
Schmöger, Rev., III: 486–88
Schürer, Emil, III: 482
Sebadja of Nazareth, I: 64
Segola, I: 149; II: 57, 377
Seraphia. *See* Veronica

Selam (Sela) of Kedar, I: 65; II: 526, 530

Semiramis, I: 123, 125, 128–36, 148; II: 365, 409; III: 74

Serena. *See* Cuppes

Sephora, wife of Moses, I: 149; II: 50

Seth, I: 121, 125, 134, 138, 148, 352; II: 76, 331

Seventy-Two Disciples, I: 59, 88, 206, 366, 370, 490; II: 180, 297–98; III: 421

Sheba, Queen of, II: 218, 221, 331

Shechemites, I: 144, 358, 487, 491; II: 5, 80–81

Shem, I: 122, 125–26, 129–30, 139; II: 37; III: 219, 277

Sidonius (Celidonius), man born blind, I: 59

Silas (young disciple), I: 43, 57, 65; II: 73, 482, 486, 491, 510, 522–23, 526; III: 6–8, 20, 74, 400–401

Silent Mary, I: 59, 80, 90, 92, 316, 328–30, 363–64, 370, 515; II: 204, 216 death of, I: 364, 420–24

Silvanus of Nazareth, I: 64; II: 528, 530

Simeon (aged priest), I: 58–59, 65, 83, 86, 91–92, 167, 197, 216–19, 231, 235, 285, 294, 297, 328–30, 348, 377, 416; III: 1, 71, 73, 196, 214, 217, 306–7, 322

Simeon of Gath-Hepher, I: 60; II: 193

Simeon the Samaritan, I: 60, 463–65; II: 393–94

Simon of Bethany. *See* Simon the Pharisee

Simon of Cyrene, I: 416; III: 82, 213, 215–16, 267, 273, 279, 312, 392, 397

Simon of Iscariot, I: 49; II: 89, 93

Simon the Leper. *See* Simon the Pharisee

Simon the Magician, III: 4, 231

Simon the Pharisee, I: 50, 59, 81, 330, 416, 418–19; II: 42, 76–77, 107–9, 123, 139, 218–19, 332, 529; III: 9–10, 13, 19–21, 408

Simon Zabulon. *See* Simon the Pharisee

Simon the Zealot, I: 40, 42, 45–46, 49, 54–58, 63–64, 69, 78, 90–91, 235, 314, 322, 336, 339, 403; II: 84, 86, 94, 154, 306, 327, 393, 528; III: 3, 76, 129, 424

Sinaita, Anastasios, III: 479

Sirach, I: 83–84, 91, 305; III: 103, 213–14, 269

Sisera, II: 51

Sisters of the Annunciation, I: 6

Sobe, I: 64, 78, 83, 90–91, 156, 165, 298, 378, 384

Soentgen (family), I: 6

Soentgen, Clara, I: 17

Solomon, I: 138, 156, 225, 317, 382, 462; II: 41, 77–79, 147, 189, 218, 221, 293, 352; III: 1, 72, 107, 112, 331

Solomon, father of Mary Salome), I: 78, 90, 155

Spirit, the (Spirit of the Lord, Spirit of God), I: 146, 149, 217, 251, 271, 334, 344, 356, 365, 369, 396, 437, 441, 445, 457, 499; II: 11, 73, 275, 380; III: 12–13, 115, 405, 419

Star Worshippers, I: 132, 163, 205; II: 494–99, 510, 518, 526; III: 196

Stephen, I: 21, 48, 64, 75; II: 139, 335, 407; III: 3, 100, 213, 392, 407, 418–19

Stewart, Lori, I: 2

Stolanus (Garescha, Sarziri), Essene grandfather of Anne, I: 154–55,

Susanna Alpheus, I: 78, 90–91; II: 175, 189, 197

Susanna of Jerusalem, I: 67, 69, 85, 91, 171, 326, 330, 346, 362, 416, 482; II: 167, 197, 207; III: 100, 103, 217, 318

Syrophoenician Woman, I: 93, 522; II: 308–12, 353

Tertullian, III: 351

Thaddeus, Judas. *See* Judas Thaddeus

Tharzissus, I: 65; II: 8, 13–14, 23, 33

Themeni, I: 62, 65, 356, 363–64, 374, 376–77, 390, 477; III: 204

Theokeno (Leo), I: 197–98, 202, 204, 207–8, 210, 213; II: 500–505, 507; III: 502, 506–7

Thomas, I: 39, 43, 46–48, 50, 56–58, 62–64, 204, 380, 392, 460, 500, 517; II: 90, 92–94, 96, 105, 137, 149, 151, 176–77, 180–81, 184–85, 195, 306, 313, 350, 393–94, 403–4, 484, 500, 506–7, 512–13, 516, 528, 530; III: 3, 10, 13, 76, 96, 129, 392–96, 398–402, 406, 413, 416, 423–24, 427–28, 507

Three Kings, the. *See* Magi

Tiberius Caesar, I: 429, 518; III: 55, 208, 318, 483–84

Tissot, J. James, I: 2, 4, 30, 449; III: 351

Titus, II: 486, 495; III: 39, 277

Tobias, I: 163–64, 166, 345, 393, 473; II: 307, 494–95

Trophimus, I: 65; II: 102

Tubal, I: 124, 126

Tubalcain, I: 122

Uis (Ois), servant of Job, I: 138

Urbas, Anton, III: 491

Veronica, I: 57, 64, 67–68, 81, 83–86, 88–89, 91–93, 174, 218, 303, 305, 313, 326–27, 330, 337, 362–63, 384–86, 388, 402, 416, 475, 482–83, 485, 497; II: 65, 70, 88, 105–6, 161–62, 183, 189, 197, 207, 211, 303, 395–96, 468, 479–80, 530; III: 7–8, 19–20, 73, 75, 78, 82, 93, 100, 103, 193, 204, 213–15, 217–18, 269, 271, 316, 318, 396–98, 404, 426

Virgo, III: 509–10

Von Droste-Vischering, Cl. A., I: 12

Von Gerlach, Ludwig, I: 13

Von Max, Gabriel, I: frontispiece

Wesener, Dr. Franz, I: 9–11

Witch of Endor, II: 96–101, 349

Widow of Nain. *See* Maroni

Wilmart, A., III: 479

Yahel, II: 51

Zacchaeus of Jericho, I: 61, 65; II: 468, 471–72, 484–85, 523, 529–31, 553; III: 3, 113, 392, 408, 417, 509

Zadoch (Essene), III: 193, 301, 308

Zarah (Zerah), I: 58, 294

Zebedee, I: 42–44, 55, 64, 67–68, 78, 89–90, 155, 165, 298, 300, 302, 392, 403, 412, 419; II: 6, 23, 92, 137, 155, 157, 161–62, 287; III: 3, 318

Zebulon (tribe), I: 152, 406; II: 99

Zechariah, father of John the Baptist), I: 60, 77, 83, 91, 140, 160–61, 166, 168, 170, 172, 174–75, 177–78, 184–88, 214, 218, 222, 230–31, 292, 296, 313, 315, 333, 419–20; II: 39, 62, 73, 91, 183–84, 205, 207, 209–11, 213–16, 380, 385, 394, 396, 399, 479; III: 51, 214, 306–7, 322–23, 426

Zedekiah, II: 82

Zilpah, II: 83

Zimri, II: 50

Zoroaster, I: 123, 128, 132

Zorobabel, centurion, I: 60, 110, 415, 524; II: 1–5, 7, 18, 21, 23, 74, 105, 136, 141, 149–52, 155, 158, 175, 198, 206, 211, 223, 306, 347, 398, 400, 408; III: 308

Zosimus, II: 58

INDEX OF PLACES AND SUBJECTS

(*p.* = present-day name)

Abel-Mehola, I: 136, 372, 379, 517; II: 33–40, 68, 77, 80, 219–20; Maps 8, 20

Abez, I: 528; II: 66, 94–98, 150, 223; Maps 21, 22

Abila (Abila Decapoleos), I: 149, 517; II: 35, 56–60, 377; Map 20

Abraham's Well, II: 80, 82

Abram, I: 517; II: 178, 182–87; Map 24

Abyssinia, I: 46–47

Achajachala (Acajaja), I: 203–4; Map: Journey of the Three Kings

Acre, III: 119–20, 191, 198, 200, 251

Adam, II: 41; III: 351

Adam's tomb, III: 325

Adama, I: 459, 461–62, 465–73, 475, 482, 517; II: 17, 105; Map 16

Adoration of the Magi, I: 209–11, 269, 348; II: 465; III: 479, 506–7, 512

Adummin (Adommim), I: 398–99, 517; Map 12

Advent, I: 22, 164

Africa, I: 133; II: 427; III: 267

Agape, III: 392–93, 398–99, 405

Agony in the Garden, III: 19

Ain et-Tin, II: 161

Aïn-Karim, I: 251, 279, 283, 429

Aïn siti Mariam, II: 293

Aïn sitti Mariam (El Rogel), I: 279

Aineil-Aramiyeh, valley, II: 293

Ainon (*p.* Ed-Damije), I: 34–35, 37, 88–89, 92, 135, 143–44, 189, 292, 298, 300–301, 334–38, 342, 354, 360–61, 373, 424, 459, 462–63, 477–80, 492, 517, 520; II: 2, 16, 28, 35, 38–39, 41–48, 50, 55, 65–71, 76, 88, 94, 314, 468; Maps 7, 20–21

Akbara, I: 518

Akko (Ptolemais), I: 517, 519, 522; II: 385, 391, 393

Akrabis (Accrabata, Acrabeta, *p.* Agraba), I: 391, 394–95, 517; II: 66, 70–73, 76, 80; Maps 10–11, 21

Alexandria, I: 271; III: 94, 478–80, 485; Maps 38, 40

Alexandrium, I: 517; II: 74–75, 525, 530; III: 1; Maps 38–39

Amathus, II: 60

Amead, I: 482

Amen, The, II: 218

Amichores-Libnath (Amead-Sichor, Sichor-Libnath, Sihor, Labanath), I: 60, 461–65, 473, 515, 517; II: 393; Map 16

Amma, Mount, I: 326

Ammonitis, II: 470

Amthar (Aram), II: 334, 341, 447, 453

Anathoth (*p.* Anata), I: 517; II: 193, 204, 465; Map 25

Angelic Gloria, I: 352

Anim, I: 220, 353

Anointing stone, III: 317–18, 375

Anointings (of Jesus) by,
Blessed Virgin, III: 317, 375
Magdalene, I: 51; II: 110, 188; III: 10, 15, 19–22, 49, 94, 112
Mara the Suphanite, II: 67
Syrophoenician Woman's daughter, II: 311
Enue's daughter, II: 319–20
Angels, III: 199

Ante-Lebanon Mountains, I: 301

Antioch, I: 40, 55; II: 457, 520; III: 74, 424

Antipatris, I: 61, 110, 517; II: 192, 200–204, 212; Map 25

Antonia Citadel/Tower, I: 172, 369, 443; II: 329–30, 338, 385; III: 39, 63, 191, 203, 251, 277, 306, 312

Apheke (*p.* Afula), I: 47, 83, 310, 392, 410, 414, 517; II: 90, 92, 96, 99; Map 14

Apochryphal Gospel of Nazarenes, II: 263

Apostles, Mount of the, II: 526–27; Map 39

Appolonia, I: 110; II: 212

Arabia, I: 41, 46, 58, 64, 131–32, 134, 136, 225, 294, 310, 335–36, 340, 357, 462, 469, 478–79, 491; II: 223, 318, 321, 375, 386, 482, 494, 520; III: 502

Aram (Amthar). *See* Amthar (Aram)

Arbela, I: 378–79, 408

Arga (*p.* Suf), I: 517; II: 35, 47, 49–52, 64

Argob, I: 517; II: 15, 17, 49, 53, 316, 318, 320–21, 402, 408; Maps 27, 32

Arimathea, I: 386

Ark, Noah's, I: 114, 121, 123–27, 140, 312, 314; II: 37, 72, 74

Ark, of the Covenant, I: 119–20, 125, 136, 141, 145, 147–54, 160–61, 166, 170, 175–76, 178, 185–86, 220, 227, 241, 314–15, 328, 339, 340–41, 344–45, 356, 358, 364–65, 377, 396–97, 401, 437, 488; II: 49–50, 52–53, 62, 71, 183, 208, 212, 218, 382, 492, 509; III: 72, 75, 318, 379, 387, 395–96, 401

Armenia, I: 46, 58

Armenian Church, III: 478

Aruma (Ruma), I: 134, 357–63, 400, 402–3, 517; II: 66, 74–78, 201, 233; Maps 7, 12, 21

Asach, II: 350

Ascalon, I: 132; II: 85

Ascension, I: 2, 14, 91, 218, 500; II: 486, 491, 512–13; III: 409–11, 445, 490

Aser, II: 81–83

Aser-Michmethath (*p.* Tayasir), I: 517; II: 66, 78, 80–81, 83–84, 192, 219; Maps 21, 25

Asia, I: 41, 46, 55, 318; II: 16; III: 309, 318, 424

Askar (Sichar), I: 87; III: 396–99, 405, 457, 503–4

Asphas, or Aspax, II: 513

Assyria, I: 345

Ataroth (*p.* Attara), I: 105, 492–95, 517; II: 83, 86, 90, 328, 335–38, 449; Maps 18, 28

Athens, I: 320; II: 14

Atom, I: 65; II: 509–14, 517; III: 502

Attarus, Mount, I: 361, 365, 517, 523; Map 7

Augsburg, I: 26

Auranitis, II: 466

Azanoth, I: 82, 517; II: 178, 188–91, 223, 392–97; Maps 24, 31

Azo (*p.* Ajlun), I: 517; II: 35, 49–52, 81

Baal-Hermon, II: 313

Babylon, I: 56–57, 130, 132, 134–35, 152, 204, 227, 273, 275; II: 3, 59, 73, 365, 514; III: 55, 503, 506

Babylonian Captivity, I: 152, 314, 336, 378, 522; II: 163, 386, 409; III: 493, 506

Bahurim, I: 417, 424, 517; II: 477; Maps 15, 36

Balsam Garden, I: 223–24, 229

Basan, II: 49, 51, 70, 219, 302, 370, 482; III: 502

Battlefield of Ezekiel's Vision, I: 299, 302; Map 2

Bavaria, I: 5, 26

Beatitudes, II: 163, 167, 175, 177, 181–85, 195–96, 222, 224, 253, 298, 300–304, 323, 370–71, 386–87, 407

First Beatitude ("Blessed are the poor in spirit…"), II: 162–63, 175, 195–96, 300, 305

Second Beatitude ("Blessed are the meek…"), II: 163, 181, 195–96, 300

Third Beatitude ("Blessed are those who mourn…"), II: 195–96, 300

Fourth Beatitude ("Blessed are those who hunger and thirst for righteousness…"), II: 168, 195–96, 300

Fifth Beatitude ("Blessed are the merciful…"), II: 220–22, 224, 300

Sixth Beatitude ("Blessed are the pure of heart…"), II: 167, 300

Seventh Beatitude ("Blessed are the peacemakers…"), II: 323

Eight Beatitude ("Blessed are those who are persecuted for righteousness' sake…"), II: 323, 370, 408

Beatitudes, Mount of, I: 392; II: 153, 299, 318, 321–23, 346; III: 491

Beeroth (*p.* el Bireh), I: 287

Beersheba, I: 65, 517; II: 483, 520–21; III: 503–4; Maps 37–38

Beheading of John the Baptist, I: 36, 75, 110, 232; II: 198–200, 211, 223, 285; III:

490

Beit-Saour, I: 259, 261
Belus river, I: 130, 462; II: 393–94
Birket el Sultan, II: 293
Birket Mamilla, II: 293
Berlin, I: 1, 12–13
Berotha, I: 461, 472–77, 504
Bersabea, I: 273
Bet She'an (Scythopolis), I: 379, 393, 480, 517–20; II: 33, 80, 97
Bethabara, I: 62, 365, 372–75, 379, 401, 435, 459, 473, 492, 518; II: 410, 468–74, 480, 528, 530; Maps 8, 33, 35, 40
Bethagla (*p.* Ain Hajla), I: 35, 338, 395, 397–99, 518; Map 11
Beth-Anoth (Bethanoth, ruins Bet Enun), I: 518
Bethain, II: 193, 208, 469, 475, 520–22; III: 503; Maps 25, 35, 38
Bethan, I: 518; II: 178, 180–81, 183; Map 24
Bethanat, I: 391–92, 403, 518; II: 176, 178–81; Maps 10, 24
Bethany (Eizariya), I: 50–51, 58–59, 68, 75–76, 80, 82, 85–86, 88–92, 103, 158, 172, 192, 235, 294–95, 316, 318, 325–28, 331, 338, 345, 362–63, 397, 412, 414–24, 431, 458, 477–78, 480–85, 490, 513, 515, 518; II: 27, 39, 42, 70, 73, 76–77, 87–88, 106, 110, 193, 203–4, 215, 219, 329–35, 369, 407, 435, 472–73, 475–78, 480, 523, 528–30, 563; III: 1–2, 4–12, 16–22, 27, 29, 39, 49, 63, 71, 74, 94, 100, 123, 171, 313, 318, 320–21, 379, 390, 392–94, 397–98, 400, 405–9, 419, 425, 443, 451, 457, 469, 488, 501, 507; Maps 1, 5, 15, 17, 25, 28, 36, 40
Beth-Arabah, I: 102, 334, 338, 347, 349, 356, 397, 518; Maps 5–7, 11
Betharbel, I: 378
Betharamphtha-Julias (Amatha), I: 518; II: 52–54, 61; Map 20
Bethel (Luz, *p.* Beitin), I: 345, 522
Bethel, I: 41, 62, 143, 323, 333, 343, 345, 377, 394, 518, 522; II: 74, 524–25; III: 484; Maps 5, 35
Bethesda, I: 136, 307, 314, 362, 396, 471; II: 113, 200–201, 206, 216–17, 285, 291, 330–33, 336, 407, 524; III: 5, 18, 95, 101, 109, 112–13, 155, 192, 212, 216, 251, 275, 331, 407–8, 413–17, 419, 425, 508
Beth-Horon, I: 56, 63, 171, 176, 217, 477, 483–85, 518; II: 74, 203–4, 212
Beth-Horon, Lower (*p.* Beit Ur et Tahta), I: 518; II: 204
Beth-Horon, Upper (*p.* Beit Ur el Fauqa), I: 63, 518; II: 204; Maps 17, 25
Bethjesimoth (Bethsimoth, *p.* ruins Suweima), I: 376, 518; II: 470; Maps 8, 35
Beth-Lechem (*p.* Bet Lehem), I: 518; II: 397; Map 31
Bethlehem, I: 17, 44, 57, 61, 65, 68, 72, 89, 97, 102, 122, 135, 172, 178–81, 188–215, 218–20, 225, 229, 231, 233, 235, 243,

255, 257, 259, 261, 263, 265, 267, 273, 277, 287, 302–3, 306, 319, 338, 345–52, 355–56, 358, 362, 364, 384, 397–98, 401, 414–15, 420, 485, 491–92, 502, 518–520; II: 43–44, 81, 91, 94, 197, 205–6, 209–10, 213, 293, 361, 395, 465, 502, 504–5, 507, 509, 511, 515, 530; III: 1, 7, 25, 214–16, 219, 273, 275, 311–14, 391, 394, 401, 408–9, 419, 447, 451, 480, 502, 506; Map: Journey of the Three Kings; Map 6
Bethphage, I: 86; II: 332, 529; III: 1, 6–8, 16, 39, 92, 99, 408–9
Bethsaida (Bezatha), I: 38, 41, 52, 63–64, 73, 78, 91, 135, 165, 232, 292, 295, 297–98, 305, 322, 333, 337, 378, 382, 390, 392–93, 403, 406, 409, 411, 427, 439, 473, 477, 479, 518; II: 4–8, 18–20, 23, 129, 133, 140, 152, 154, 157–58, 162–63, 170, 172–73, 189, 235, 237, 243, 297–98, 301, 303–4, 322, 324, 335, 344, 346, 399, 406–8, 417, 423, 433, 455, 480–81, 528; III: 45, 404, 408, 416, 418–19, 488, 491, 502, 504; Maps 3, 18–19, 23, 27, 29, 32, 36
Bethsaida-Julias (*p.* ruins, et-Tell), I: 63, 504, 518; II: 7, 17, 152, 154, 162–63, 168, 297, 301, 303, 318, 321–22, 325, 345–46, 407–8, 491; Maps 27, 29, 32
Bethsames, II: 53
Bethsop, I: 316, 518; Map 7
Bethsoron, II: 212
Bethulia, I: 46, 62, 107, 136, 292, 295, 305–7, 312, 390, 403, 405, 477, 480, 518; II: 23–27, 33, 102, 105, 110, 141, 183, 189, 191, 212, 223, 302, 314, 326–27, 341; Maps 1, 3, 10, 13, 19, 25, 27, 28
Beth-zur (Bethsur, *p.* Beit Sahur), I: 518; Map 25
Bezek, I: 515, 518; II: 33, 38–43, 221–22; Map 20
Black Forest, II: 375
Black Sea, I: 56, 122, 136
Blessing, the, I: 117, 119–20, 125, 141–45, 148–49, 151–52, 160–61, 163, 166, 314, 327, 347, 362, 488; II: 100; III: 74. *See also* Promise, the
Book of Esther, I: 413–14
Bosra (Beestra, *p.* Busra), I: 518–19, 521–24; II: 409; Map 34
Bread and wine, I: 24, 128, 136, 140–41, 146, 151, 318, 360, 384, 389; II: 37, 42, 107, 374, 376, 494–95, 504, 507–8, 512; III: 74, 80–81, 89, 131, 398, 407, 410, 418
Brook Kerith, I: 302; II: 56, 60
Brook Kidron, III: 16, 39, 83, 93, 95, 98–99, 104, 119, 147, 157, 189, 215, 346
Burning Bush, I: 166, 195

Cabul, I: 483, 515, 519; II: 319, 352; III: 308, 483
Caesarea, II: 201, 319–21, 325, 338
Caesarea-Phillipi (Paneas, Baniyas), I: 93, 509, 518–23; II: 164, 318–21, 323–25, 339, 343, 364, 408, 431, 439; Map 27

Cairo, I: 273, 275, 281, 520
Calling of the Apostles, I: 62–64; II: 147, 243
  of Andrew, I: 41, 63; II: 155–56
  of Bartholomew, I: 46, 460; II: 83–84
  of James the Greater, I: 44, 63; II: 155–56
  of James the Lesser, I: 45
  of John, I: 42, 63; II: 155–56
  of Judas Iscariot, II: 85–86
  of Jude Thaddeus, I: 56–57, 484
  of Matthew, I: 54; II: 153–54
  of Nathaniel Chased, I: 383
  of Philip, I: 379, 382
  of Simon Peter, I: 38–39, 63, 379; II: 155–56
  of Simon the Zealot, II: 83–84
  of Thomas, II: 92–93
Calvary, Mount. *See* Golgotha
Cana (*p.* Kafr Kanna), I: 38, 43, 45, 53, 56, 59, 61–64, 78, 91, 135, 181, 214, 232, 245, 297–98, 307, 371, 378–86, 389–90, 392, 394, 403, 409, 411, 421–22, 451, 453, 504, 518; II: 1–2, 21, 39–40, 93, 121, 158, 306, 314, 353, 403–4, 486; III: 498; Maps 2, 9, 18, 26, 31
Canaan, I: 93, 107, 125, 134, 138, 148, 470, 493; II: 30, 36, 40, 144, 427; III: 74
Capernaum (Kafr Nahum), I: 38, 44, 46, 50, 53, 60, 62–64, 73–74, 78–79, 90–91, 97, 99–103, 110, 182, 235, 292, 294–98, 300, 304, 310, 314, 316, 320, 322, 333, 343, 357, 371, 380–84, 390, 393, 402–3, 409, 411–12, 419, 427, 451, 455, 462–63, 473, 477–78, 480, 491, 494, 496–97, 508, 518–19; II: 2–8, 12–13, 15–23, 26, 40, 59, 88, 96, 102, 106, 136–37, 140, 148–51, 155, 158–59, 174, 183, 223, 303, 398–406, 408; III: 102, 491; Maps 1, 3, 9, 10, 13–14, 16–19, 22–23, 25–26, 29, 31–32, 35–36, 40
Carmel, Mount, I: 64, 153, 162, 164, 180, 302–3, 339, 367–68, 411, 519; II: 393, 557; Map 2
Casaloth, I: 83; II: 99
Caspian Sea, I: 197
Caucasus, I: 126, 128, 137, 205
Causur, I: 204–5
Cave of the Nativity, I: 44, 97, 122, 179, 194–95, 198–201, 209–15, 259, 338, 351–52, 393, 398, 401; III: 419, 480
Cenacle, I: 39–40, 51, 58, 70–72, 75, 86, 88–89, 294, 421–22; II: 217–19, 407; III: 3, 19, 71–73, 75–76, 78–83, 86, 93, 95, 102, 119, 125, 131, 133, 192, 215, 311, 319–22, 386, 388–89, 391–92, 398, 407, 419, 423, 437, 447, 449, 473
Cendevia, II: 393
Chabul (Cabul, Chabalon), I: 464, 483, 515, 519; II: 319, 352; III: 308; Map 16
Chaldar, II: 513
Chaldea, I: 103, 132, 138–39, 142, 163, 265; II: 482, 500, 516–17; III: 4, 488, 502–6
Chalice, I: 43, 77, 119, 125, 140–41, 145–

46, 149, 154, 161, 175, 178, 197, 202, 227, 370; II: 505, 512, 514; III: 71, 73–75, 78–81, 84–85, 89–90, 92–93, 97, 131, 133, 135, 153, 200, 209, 393, 398, 407, 410, 416–18, 421, 425
Chel, III: 37, 47, 51, 63
Chennai, I: 48
Chim, I: 320–21, 519; Map 4
China, I: 121; III: 424
Chisloth, I: 83, 310–11, 405–6; II: 191, 193, 339
Chisloth-Tabor (Chesulloth, Casaloth *p.* Iksal), I: 63, 104, 302, 313, 405–7, 519; Maps 2, 4, 13, 25
Chorazin, I: 519; II: 7, 155, 157, 161, 167–68, 170, 219, 298, 322–24; III: 309, 501–2
Chorazin, Little, I: 393, 519; II: 297, 303, 323
Chorazin, Great, I: 357, 360, 393, 519; II: 155, 157, 167, 480; Maps 7, 27, 36
Chronology, I: 2, 4, 133–34; II: 37, 77; III: 477–513
Chume. *See* Heliopolis
Church of the Copts, I: 275
Church of the Holy Sepulcher, III: 183, 283, 313
Church Militant, I: 501; III: 325, 401, 403
Church of Saint Anne, II: 291
Church of Santa Croce di Gerusalemme, III: 227
Church Suffering, III: 325, 401, 403
Church Triumphant, I: 164, 501; III: 81, 403
Cidessa, I: 333
Circumcision, The, I: 200–201
Coesfeld, I: 1
Column of Reproach, III: 235
Consoler, I: 37; II: 375–76, 380, 465, 513
Constantine-Basilica, III: 480
Constantinople, I: 84
Conversions,
 of adultress, II: 68
 of Claudia, wife of Pontius Pilate, III: 229
 of Clemens Brentano, I: 11, 24
 of Cornelius the Centurion, III: 4
 of Dinah the Samaritan, I: 85, 87–88, 92, 486–91
 of Longinus, I: 367
 of Mara the Suphanite, I: 89, 92, 513; II: 42–44, 204
 of "obstinate Jew," I: 467–68
 of Pagan Philosophers, I: 57; II: 375–76
 of Saul (Paul), II: 103, 491; III: 3
 of Sirach, I: 91
 See also Mary Magdalene, First Conversion, Second Conversion
Coreae, I: 65, 519, 524; II: 71–74, 87–88, 342, 465; Maps 21, 28
Corinthian Gate, I: 271
Court of the Gentiles, I: 421; III: 47, 51, 63

Court of Israel, I: 419, 423; III: 55
Court of the Treasure, III: 61
Court of the Women/Gazophylacium, I: 208, 271, 433; II: 549; III: 53, 55, 61
Creation, I: 113–18, 120, 327, 499, 501, 503, 506; II: 36, 40, 67, 140, 339, 376, 390, 497–98; III: 13, 305, 345, 403, 405, 471, 494
Crete, II: 500
Crib Cave. *See* Cave of the Nativity
Crown of Thorns, I: 6, 14–15, 366; III: 203, 205, 207, 209–11, 213, 217, 219, 239, 241, 251, 253, 257, 259, 267, 285, 287, 316, 373
Cross, St. Andrew's, I: 41
Crusades, II: 291
Cydessa (Cydassa, Cedesa), I: 519; II: 105, 187, 306; Map 26
Cyprus, I: 56–57, 61, 65, 128, 132, 515, 519, 521–23; II: 75, 84, 137, 350–54, 367–68, 388–91, 395–98; III: 500

Daberath (Dabaritta, *p.* Dabburiya), I: 519; Map 22
Dalmanutha, I: 519; II: 15, 170, 301–2, 324, 347, 408–9; Map 26
Damascus, I: 48, 64, 87–89, 92, 490, 497, 521; II: 65, 85, 239, 314, 321, 369
Damascus Gate, III: 104
Damna (Dimnah), I: 519; II: 105–6, 137, 189–91, 223, 397–98; Maps 24–25, 31
Dan (Lais, Lesem), I: 93, 147, 335, 365, 385, 519; II: 307–9, 427; Map 26
Datheman (Dathema, *p.* Ataman), I: 519; II: 467; III: 489; Map 33
David's Way, I: 519; II: 465–67; Map: Journey of the Three Kings; Map 34
Day of Judgment/the Judgment, I: 484, 492, 494; II: 21, 29, 107, 194, 267, 335, 344, 372, 382, 393, 400, 495, 522; III: 47, 116, 325,
Dead Sea, I: 36, 135–36, 205, 212, 222, 231, 259, 265, 296, 335, 341, 353, 396–97, 441, 445, 517–24; II: 86, 90, 209, 213, 220, 481; III: 331, 501, 506; Map 1
Debbaseth, I: 46, 460; II: 84, 147, 393
Deborah's Canticle, II: 97
Decapolis, II: 125, 156, 170, 173–74, 221, 316, 322, 344, 347, 350, 352, 409, 427, 433; III: 309, 360
Der Wandel Jesu in der Welt, I: 4; III: 491–92, 502
Deluge (Flood), I: 122–25, 132, 136–37, 312, 314; II: 37, 48, 375–76; III: 303
Dibon, II: 73; Maps 6–8
Dion (Dium, Dia), I: 519; II: 61–64; Map 20
Divine Law, I: 115; II: 376
Divine Prototype, I: 118
Djifneh, II: 565
Doch, II: 80; Maps 38, 40
Dothaim, I: 107, 296–97, 310, 411–12, 519; II: 25, 27–31, 187, 189, 197, 340–42, 455; Maps 1, 4, 14, 24, 29
Dothan, I: 48, 61, 99, 136, 336, 411, 519;

II: 89–94, 100, 193, 196–97, 220; Map 21
Doves, Valley of the, I: 136, 524; Map 22
Dragon(s), I: 595; II: 353, 506–07; III: 89, 218, 388
Dschebl, I: 519
Dschebl ed-Dedebe, II: 337; Map 29
Dschebl Dschamle, II: 337; Map 29
Dülmen, I: 1–2, 5, 10, 12, 409; II: 353; III: 100, 312

Earthquake, II: 347; III: 82, 305–9, 314, 351, 357, 392
Easter, I: 39, 45, 68–70, 72, 79, 85–86, 90, 92; II: 522; III: 4, 82, 394, 420, 478, 485
Ebez, I: 517
Edessa, I: 48, 57, 458; II: 17
Edom (Edon), I: 519; II: 38, 486, 488
Edrai (*p.* Der'a), I: 518–19; II: 409; Map 33
Edron valley, I: 311–13; Map 4
Egypt, I: 41, 53, 56–57, 65, 103, 120, 127, 130–35, 137–39, 145–49, 151, 153, 163, 166–67, 178, 185, 190, 193, 197, 205, 219–20, 224, 226–30, 275, 303, 310, 315–16, 318, 334–35, 338, 345, 348, 353–54, 376, 397, 414, 419, 491, 501; II: 16, 50, 57–58, 76, 80–81, 103, 186, 193–94, 207–10, 218, 340, 352–53, 377, 384, 481–82, 497, 508, 519–20, 539; III: 75, 84, 196, 201, 222, 396, 425, 478–79, 502
Eilabun, I: 517
El Bireh, I: 287
El Rogel, II: 293
Eleale (El'aleh, *p.* El'Al), I: 375, 519; Map 8
Eleutheropolis, II: 8, 406–7
Elijah, cave of, I: 154, 165, 303; II: 58
Elijah's pillar, I: 517
Elizabeth, Cave of, I: 296; Map 1
Elkasa (Elkese, Elkosh), II: 179–81, 183, 307; Maps 24, 26
Elkosh, I: 519
El Rogel (Aïn siti Mariam), II: 293
Emerald Table, II: 479
Emmaus, I: 64, 184, 232, 294, 379, 427; II: 39, 215, 312, 390, 393–95
Endor (Ain-dor, *p.* 'En Dor), I: 316–18, 494, 497, 519; II: 94–96, 180, 196, 336, 349; Map 4
Engedi (Engaddi), II: 396
Engannim, I: 220, 493–94, 496–97; II: 1–2, 141; Map 18
Ensemes (Ain-Semes), I: 353, 357, 519; II: 527; Maps 5, 39
Enzannim, I: 353
Ephesus, I: 2–3, 40–41, 43–45, 47, 53, 75–77, 182; II: 491; III: 2–4, 74, 403, 419–24, 428, 491
Ephra, II: 51
Ephraim (Ephron, *p.* Taiyiba), I: 148, 354, 520; II: 81, 565; III: 147, 506; Maps 38, 40
Ephraim, Cave of, I: 350; Map: Flight of

the Holy Family to Egypt; Map 6
Ephrata (Hebrew name of Bethlehem), I: 207, 259, 267; II: 465
Ephron, I: 155, 222, 323, 354–55, 520; II: 52–53, 64, 302, 327, 329, 370, 523, 530
Ephron, Desert of, I: 326, 328; II: 45, 94
Ephron, Mount, I: 222, 323, 353–54
Esdrelon, I: 316, 321, 393, 407, 411, 460; II: 51, 90, 95, 97, 141, 196–97, 336, 394, 557
Etam, III: 25
Eternal life, I: 85, 108, 115, 347, 457, 491; II: 28, 46, 115, 304–6, 331, 406, 423, 463, 495, 551; III: 107, 109, 193, 215, 299, 471, 485
Eternal salvation, I: 24; III: 424
Eternal Word. *See* Christ, as Eternal Word
Ethiopia, I: 55
Eucharist, I: 1, 84, 181; II: 289; III: 80–81, 135, 365, 398, 417
Euphrates, I: 65, 522, 535; II: 239, 513–15; III: 503
Exhortation to the Apostles, II: 176
Expiation of Christ, I: 189

Fall, The, I: 114–18, 151, 161, 183, 302, 314–15, 387; II: 5, 36, 48, 67, 74, 344, 365, 376, 498; III: 6, 84, 86, 403
Fall of the Angels, I: 103, 117
Feasts
  Feast of the Apparition of the Star, I: 504–9
  Feast of Atonement, I: 62; II: 322
  Feast of the Dedication of Solomon's Temple, II: 77
  Feast of the Dedication of the Temple (Feast of Lights), I: 378–79, 415; II: 77, 174, 179–81, 407; III: 480, 482–83, 487–89, 498, 501
  Feast of the Dedication of the Temple of Zorobabel, I: 415
  Feast of Ennorum, II: 221
  Feast of the Expulsion of the Sadducees, II: 209
  Feast of the New Moon, I: 397–98, 418, 478; II: 78, 147, 209, 309, 490
  Feast of Purim, I: 412–14; II: 313, 316; III: 498–99, 412–13
  Feast of Tabernacles, I: 158, 160, 357, 359–60, 375–76, 414; II: 34, 37, 52, 56, 59, 65, 67–70, 73–74, 76–77, 90, 96, 101, 220, 397, 467; III: 483–84, 489–90, 498, 501
  Feast of Weeks, II: 379–81; III: 497, 499–500
  Feeding of the 4,000, Mount of, II: 323; Map 27
  Feeding of the 5,000, Mount of, II: 298–300; III: 491
Fig tree, accursed, III: 9
Flamske, I: 1
Flight into Egypt, I: 219–23, 318, 348, 353–54; II: 80–81, 207–8, 519–20, 530; III: 196

Forty Days in the Wilderness, I: 62, 330, 346, 364–71, 441, 447, 517, 523; III: 490
Fountain of Mary, I: 137
France, I: 2, 60, 79–80, 427; III: 318

Gabaa, I: 485, 520
Gabara (*p.* ruins, Madin), I: 63, 81–82, 92, 318, 503, 520; II: 105–10, 136, 140–41, 188–89, 347–49, 362, 404, 407; Map 22
Gabatha, I: 190
Gabbatha (Gk. Lithostrotos), III: 192, 207–9, 241, 245, 247, 251, 253, 255, 259, 265, 301
Gadara (Gadar, *p.* Hamat Gader), I: 393, 512, 517, 520; II: 58–61, 64; Map 20
Galgala (near Gush Halav), I: 520; II: 180; Map 24
Galilee, I: 41, 45–46, 58–60, 62, 64, 90, 109–10, 235, 245, 257, 279, 292, 294–96, 300, 318, 326, 331, 336, 340, 371, 374, 401, 405, 427, 460, 478, 482, 515; II: 2, 17, 23, 27, 103, 157, 188, 205–8, 210–11, 267, 302, 487, 524; III: 194–95, 308, 397, 405, 419, 501–2; Maps 15–16
Gamala, II: 15–16, 167, 170, 326, 330, 336, 338
Ganges, II: 510
Garden of Gethsemane, I: 43, 51, 79, 103, 482; II: 435, 470; III: 93, 96, 98, 139, 141, 147, 151, 157, 181
Garden of Olives, II: 338; III: 83, 86, 93, 96, 98–99, 109, 114, 141, 157, 309, 411, 469
Garisima (Garis, Garsis), I: 64; II: 349–50; Map 29
Garisma, I: 520; III: 486
Garizim, Mount, I: 220, 323, 463, 486, 488, 492; II: 74, 78, 86, 219; III: 309
Gath-Hepher, I: 60, 135, 477, 520, 524; II: 191, 197; Maps 16, 25
Gaul, I: 168, 180; III: 381
Gaulanitis, I: 64
Gaulon, II: 315; Map 27
Gaza, I: 140, 222–23, 229, 273, 281, 303, 352, 354; II: 352, 380; III: 199; Map: Flight of the Holy Family to Egypt
Gazora, II: 400
Gebea (Gibea, Gibeath, *p.* Jenin), I: 520
Gehenna, III: 241
Genesis, I: 259, 411, 518, 522; II: 44, 56, 76, 82, 181
Gennabris (Ginnabris, Sennabris), I: 46, 53, 60, 62–64, 103, 107, 109, 378–83, 402–3, 462, 494, 520; II: 23, 27–33, 79, 155; Maps 9, 13, 19
Gerasa, I: 360, 362, 520; II: 16–17, 49, 154, 169–70, 344; III: 309, 403; Maps 7, 19, 20, 23
Gergesa, I: 296, 520; II: 157, 168–74, 298, III: 309; Map 23
Gerizim (Garizim), I: 1990, 486, 488; II: 30, 327
Gessur, I: 57, 61, 231, 520; II: 53, 313–14,

390, 396, 398–99; III: 2–3; Map 27
Giah, I: 326; Map 5
Gihon, spring, II: 200, 285, 293; III: 216, 313, 317
Gihon, valley, III: 25, 181, 215, 304, 349, 355
Gilboa, Mount, I: 407; II: 94–95, 223
Gilead, I: 61, 143, 520, 523; II: 14–16, 75, 86, 96, 409, 484; III: 2–3; Map 19
Gileaditis, II: 15, 35, 410; Map 33
Gilgal, I: 62, 220, 225, 356–61, 363, 374, 376, 459, 482, 520; Map 6
Ginea, I: 414, 492–94, 520; II: 90, 197, 204, 327, 333, 336, 475, 477, 530; Maps 14–15, 17–18, 36
Gischala (Gis-Halab), I: 61, 520; II: 102–5, 137, 141, 157, 206, 306; Map 22
Golan, I: 520; II: 318, 327, 339
Golden Gate, I: 151, 158, 160–62, 174–75, 315; II: 94; III: 312
Golgotha, I: 67–68, 71, 76, 85–86, 122; II: 371; III: 82, 209–13, 215–19, 235, 259, 261, 265, 267, 269, 273, 275, 277, 279, 281, 283, 285, 289, 295, 299, 301–5, 307–8, 310–14, 319–20, 325, 329, 331, 335, 337, 345, 347, 351, 369, 371, 373, 379, 389, 406, 421, 423, 445, 506
Gomorrha, I: 135, 312, 374, 396, 520; II: 37, 82, 107, 169, 191, 195
Good Friday, I: 21, 52, 84, 151; III: 82, 235, 325
Gophna (Jifna), I: 85, 91, 171, 180, 233, 245, 287, 323, 520; II: 204; Map 5
Goshen, Land of, I: 225, 227
Gospels, Apocryphal, I: 243, 253; III: 367
Grail, I: 84
Greece, I: 41, 55; II: 84, 158, 360, 427; III: 9–10
Gur, I: 322–23, 520; Map 4

Hadad-Rimmon (Adaremmon, Maximianopolis), I: 520; Maps 28–29
Haifa, I: 419, 521–22; II: 391–94; Map 31
Hail Mary, The, I: 165
Hammoth Dor, II: 310
Hanathon, I: 63, 390–92, 520, 523; II: 176, 407; Map 10
Hareth, Forest of, I: 520; II: 75
Hauran Mountains, I: 65, 522–23; II: 417
Hausen, I: 26
Hay (ha'Ai, *p.* ruins, Haiyan), I: 138, 394, 482, 520; Map 11
Hazezon-Thamar (Asesonthamar, earlier, En Gedi), I: 396–97, 520; Map 11
Heavenly Jerusalem, I: 23, 26, 77, 134, 161, 175, 322, 335, 345, 469; III: 324, 425, 427
Hebron, I: 45, 62, 135–36, 140, 172, 177, 183–84, 200, 220, 235, 294, 296–97, 339, 354, 419–20, 520, 522; II: 26, 39, 73–74, 90–91, 194, 197–98, 205–12, 215, 218, 223, 303, 330, 332, 349, 352, 361, 380,

399, 407, 474, 481; III: 71, 86, 100, 123, 216, 308, 502; Maps 1, 15, 25

Heliopolis (On, Chume), I: 57, 133, 145, 163, 197, 205, 224–27, 273, 275, 520–21; II: 481, 518–19; III: 502–7; Map: Flight of the Holy Family to Egypt; Map 37

Helios, III: 478–79

Hermon, Mount, I: 158, 317, 521; II: 33, 313

Herod's Castle, I: 86, 313, 318, 477; II: 212, 349

Herodium, I: 59, 318, 480

Hesebon (Heshbon), I: 36, 110, 477, 480; II: 211, 222, 301

Hexaemeron, III: 479

Hieromax (or Heiromax), river, I: 297, 521; II: 56; Map 1

Hinnom (caves/valley), III: 105, 113, 117, 119, 179, 181, 189, 304, 349, 355

Hippos (Hippene, *p.* Susitha), I: 393, 521; II: 169–70, 173; Map 10

Holy Communion, I: 21, 23, 76, 140; II: 62, 508; III: 393, 418, 425–26

Holy of Holies, I: 151, 160–61, 170, 176–79, 241, 243, 358, 419; II: 62, 68; III: 14–15, 72, 81, 103, 106, 112, 196, 202, 221, 229, 235, 295, 306, 315, 322, 393, 395, 398–400, 406–7, 412, 414, 416, 418, 455

Holy Sepulcher, I: 61, 68–72, 76, 79, 82, 85–86, 90, 92, 399; III: 183, 275, 283, 313, 320, 386, 388, 397, 406, 411, 417, 423, 426, 431, 473

Honey, I: 98, 142, 146–47, 187, 198, 209, 211, 222, 230–31, 283, 315, 327, 329, 354, 388, 398, 411, 460, 472, 479, 489, 504; II: 3, 13, 34, 42, 52, 62, 65, 89, 92, 95, 105, 163, 177, 206, 211, 221, 300, 311, 313, 349, 366, 370–72, 377, 385–86, 391, 398, 404, 465, 471–72, 481, 486, 488, 496, 504, 514–15, 525; III: 20–21, 394–95, 402–3, 409, 427, 455

Horeb, Mount, I: 153, 226; II: 50

House of David, I: 156, 179–80, 243, 358, 415; II: 44

House of Mary (Panaya Kapulu), I: 2–3, 86, 416, 424; II: 398; III: 1, 7, 74–75, 86, 92–93, 100, 102, 422

Hukok (*p.* Huqoq), I: 521; II: 177, 179; Map 24

Hunin, II: 299; Map 26

Huttenried, I: 26

Idumaea, III: 237

Immaculate Conception, I: 117, 157–64, 175, 328, 352, 517

India, I: 46, 48, 121, 128–20; II: 375; III: 424

Instruction, Mount of, I: 473, 520, 523; II: 98, 105–10, 153, 178, 337, 349, 401, 404, 407; Maps 10, 16, 22–24, 26, 29, 32

Iraq, II: 477; Map 36

Ischariot (Keriyot, Karioth), I: 521; III: 147; Map 21

Israel, I: 57, 136, 148, 166, 271, 281, 314,

329, 344–45, 355, 377, 421; II: 46–48, 51, 53, 63, 68, 83, 97, 101, 136, 143, 159, 161, 174, 313, 359; III: 481, 502–3, 505

Italy, III: 197, 210, 311

Jabbok River, I: 143–44, 522; II: 44–45, 49, 68

Jabesh (Jabes)-Gilead, I: 143; II: 49, 53, 96, 400

Jacob's well, I: 63, 67, 87–88, 92, 303, 486–91, 505, 521, 523; II: 115, 198, 481–82, 520–22; III: 485, 487, 501–3, 505; Maps 2, 17, 38

Jaffa (Japha), I: 42, 78, 90, 281, 517; II: 137

Jahza, I: 365

Jenin Route, I: 520; II: 557

Jericho, I: 35–36, 61–62, 85, 103, 137, 208, 263, 292, 313, 315, 323, 329, 331, 334, 337, 342, 355, 357, 362, 364–65, 367, 373, 390, 399, 441, 445, 457, 464, 482, 496, 515, 521; II: 5, 37, 39, 71, 342, 400, 408, 435, 463, 470–474, 480, 482, 484, 520, 522–26, 528, 553, 555; III: 3, 424; Maps 35, 38

Jerusalem, I: 29–30, 37, 40, 43, 45, 48, 50–51, 55–59, 65, 73, 75–76, 83–85, 91–92, 99–103, 111, 114, 136, 140, 153, 171–74, 177–78, 207, 226, 232–35, 259, 313, 315–16, 325, 327–28, 333, 336, 341–45, 348, 369, 374, 397, 416–20, 423, 443, 484–85, 493–94, 496, 521; II: 3–5, 20–21, 27, 32, 40, 71, 103, 107, 137, 139, 173, 176, 185, 194, 203, 306, 215–19, 229, 285, 326, 329–32, 346, 372, 388–89, 393, 395, 403, 407, 435, 477, 530; III: 3, 5–16, 33, 39, 71–75, 103–6, 109, 194, 251, 308, 312–13, 389, 397–98, 411, 419–21, 423–25, 487–89; Map: Journey of the Three Kings; Maps 1–2, 5, 7, 15, 25, 28, 36, 40

Jethro, I: 147

Jezreel (*p.* Yizre'e), I: 61, 81, 92, 308–10, 393, 402–3, 406–7, 480, 497, 521; II: 141, 293, 336; Maps 3–4, 10, 12–13

Jezreel, Plain of (*p.* Merdsch Ibn Amir), I: 500, 504; II: 92; Maps 4, 22

Jezreel, Valley of, II: 33

Jogbeha, I: 521; II: 61–65; Maps 20–21

Joppe (Joppa), I: 40, 44; II: 350, 354, 360, 385, 396, 398–99; III: 215, 222, 302, 312, 420

Jordan River, I: 4, 33–35, 46, 59, 62, 80, 103, 108, 121, 136, 153, 162, 190–91, 206, 232, 292, 296–98, 334, 337–47, 349, 353–54, 457, 359, 371–76, 390, 393–98, 429, 435, 441, 479; II: 14–16, 30–31, 39–41, 60, 63, 80, 101, 220, 302, 319, 324, 346, 362, 388, 465, 468, 480–82, 524–36; III: 3, 309, 401, 479, 483, 485, 489–91, 497, 508

Josaphat (Jehosaphat), Valley of, I: 122, 158, 172, 279; II: 216, 435, 481, 551; III: 18, 27, 39, 63, 65, 71, 74–75, 82–83, 92–93, 95, 99–100, 159, 192, 204, 401, 404, 414, 416, 419

Joseph's well, I: 411–12; II: 48

Jotopata (Jotapata), I: 102, 107, 521; II: 10, 23–27, 105, 220, 349; III: 102; Map 19

Journey of the Three Kings, I: 202–5, 496; II: 48, 409, 465

Judah, I: 33, 147, 208, 259, 323, 346, 397, 399, 493, 496; II: 50, 57, 81, 352, 386; III: 147, 181

Judea, I: 45, 55, 75, 99–100, 136, 163, 198, 206, 208, 222, 229, 267, 294, 334, 370, 374, 409, 411, 415, 478; II: 2, 5, 15, 18, 23, 27, 49, 53, 59, 65, 80, 90, 123, 137, 155, 168, 180, 193, 201, 247, 267, 352, 357, 371, 380, 383, 394, 481, 484, 497, 520, 525; III: 418, 484, 525; Map 17

Jutta, I: 36–37, 42, 75, 92, 177, 197, 201, 231, 292, 419–20, 521, 524; II: 205–16, 219, 474–75; Maps 15, 25

Kabul, I: 382

Kades-Nephthali, I: 504, 521; II: 307–8; Map 26

Kadumin, valley, II: 97

Kallirrhoe, I: 298

Kalounieh, I: 429

Kamon, I: 521; II: 44–45

Kaphar-Sheba, II: 201

Kapharot, I: 521; II: 349–50; Map 29

Kastoul, I: 429

Kedar, I: 57, 65, 231, 359, 521; II: 173, 484–90, 494–95, 517, 522, 526, 530; III: 20, 405, 502–4, 506; Map: Journey of the Three Kings; Map 37

Kedesh, I: 380, 382, 472–73; II: 309

Keriyot (Karioth, Ischariot). *See* Ischariot

Kibzaim, I: 376–79, 485, 521; Maps 8, 17

Kidron, I: 215, 265, 423, 463; III: 16–17, 39, 83, 93, 95, 98–99, 101–2, 119, 139, 147, 157, 181, 189

Kimki (Chimki), I: 101, 188–89, 255, 311–13, 521; Map 4

Kiriathaim, I: 521; II: 182–85; Map 24

Kishion (Kiseon, Kedes), I: 307, 521; Map 3

Kishon River, I: 316, 321; II: 97, 141, 144, 147, 197, 336, 391, 393, 395, 397

Kision. *See* Kishion

Kition, I: 521; II: 386, 389–90; Map 30

Konnersreuth, I: 5

Kore, I: 521; Maps 33–34

Kyrenia, I: 521; II: 377, 386–89; Map 30

Kythria, I: 65; II: 366–71, 373, 375–76, 384–86, 388, 390; Map 30

Lais, I: 519; II: 307, 320

Lake of Crocodiles, I: 451

Land of Goshen, I: 149, 225, 227

Lanifa (Cypriot village), I: 128; II: 375–76, 386

Lapethos, II: 377, 387

Last Supper, I: 29–30, 39, 43, 48, 50–51, 79, 84, 92, 119, 125, 140, 145, 161, 175, 197, 374, 386, 389, 419; II: 210, 214, 218, 330, 479–80, 508; III: 3, 17–18, 71, 73–

74, 78, 80, 93, 210, 392–95, 398, 406–10, 412–19, 425, 451, 455, 471, 507

Lazarus, castle of, I: 294, 416, 422, 424, 482; II: 218. 332; III: 499

Lazarus, country home of, II: 475, 477; Maps 14, 17, 28, 36

Lebanon, I: 292, 300–303, 469; II: 253, 417; III: 331; Map 2

Lebona, I: 179, 377, 521; II: 75, 219; Map 25

Lebonah (near *p.* Lubban Shaqiya), I: 521; II: 327; Map 28

Leccum, I: 521; II: 177, 345–46; Map 29

Legio, I: 220, 414

Leontes River, II: 351

Leper's Chamber, I: 433

Leppe, I: 521; II: 375, 377, 386; Map 30

Libnath (Libna, Lebna, Labana, Lobna), I: 60, 522; II: 211–12, 393; Map 25

Limbo, I: 21, 166, 368, 506; II: 107, 203, 222; III: 92, 221, 295, 303, 305, 308, 323–25, 343, 357, 359, 387, 401, 431

Loaves and Fishes, II: 277, 300, 323; III: 491

Lord's Prayer, I: 392, 501; II: 20, 224, 295, 298, 300–305, 307–8, 318, 339, 360, 366, 370–71, 373, 385–87, 407, 415, 423, 498, 528

Luz (*not* Bethel/Luz), I: 345–46, 522

Lydda, II: 215

Machaerus, I: 36–37, 86, 92, 109–10, 158, 399, 477–80, 517; II: 28–29, 39, 74, 83, 92–93, 145, 158, 175, 198–201, 205, 211–16, 219–20, 223, 285, 298, 349, 385, 470, 481; III: 100, 309–10, 394, 397, 451

Machmas, II: 204, 206, 208

Machpelah, Cave of, I: 522; II: 208, 520; Map 25

Madian (Manathea), I: 205, 364; II: 470; III: 397; Map: Journey of the Three Kings; Map 35

Madras, I: 48

Madrid, III: 183

Magdala (near *p.* 'En Gev), I: 58–59, 80–81, 192, 294–96, 300, 306, 318, 328, 427, 522; II: 168–71, 173, 301–2, 324, 417, 437; Map 23

Magdalum (*p.* Migdal), I: 393, 402–3, 490

Mahanaim, I: 522; II: 44–45, 143–44; Map 20

Malachi, Cave of, Map 22

Malta, II: 491

Mamre, Grove of, II: 78, 208, 222

Maraha, Cave of, I: 352

Mallep (*p.* Bellapaise), I: 522; II: 373–75, 377, 380, 382, 384–90, 396; III: 500–501; Map 30

Mar Saba, III: 101

Mar-Elias, Hill of, I: 259

Marriage, Mystery of, II: 487–94

Marseille, I: 44, 60, 79, 84

Matarea, I: 56, 65, 137, 197, 226–29, 275; Map: Flight of the Holy Family to

Egypt

Media, I: 204–5

Mediterranean Sea, I: 79, 273, 517, 522

Megiddo (Magiddo), I: 37, 100, 135, 323, 522; II: 143–51, 158, 186, 336; Map 22

Memphis, I: 226–27, 56, 133–35, 147, 149, 197

Men's Court, I: 443, 271; III: 53

Mensor's Island Castle, I: 204

Merom, Lake (*p.* Hula Reserve), I: 459, 462, 465, 517, 521–24; II: 105, 195, 325

Meroz, I: 50, 63, 93, 522; II: 83–90, 92, 137, 355; Map 21

Mesopotamia, I: 65, 103, 143, 148; II: 36, 367

Michmas, I: 323

Michmethath, I: 60, 135; II: 81–83, 86, 89

Midian, I: 147, 522; II: 81, 481

Misael (Masal), I: 462, 522; II: 393–94, 401; III: 316; Map 31

Milk Cave, I: 138, 193

Mizpah (Maspha, *p.* Nabi Samwil, Shemu'el), I: 340, 354–55, 362, 364, 522; II: 46–47, 51, 73, 465; Map 6

Moab, Mountains of, I: 265, 441, 445

Moabites, I: 88, 92, 360, 399, 467

Moreh's grove, I: 520; Map 15

Moriah, Mount, III: 33

Mount of the Apostolic Mission, II: 407

Mount of Beatitudes, II: 314, 318, 321–23, 346; III: 491; Maps 23, 26

Mount of Olives, I: 23, 76, 83, 86, 121–22, 154, 233–34, 287, 416, 482–84, 517; II: 39, 62, 305–6, 209, 215, 287, 317, 330–32, 339, 429, 535; III: 7–8, 10, 13–16, 19, 27, 31, 39, 63, 65, 71, 74, 81–93, 95–96, 98, 100, 102, 105, 114–15, 117, 119–20, 139, 141, 151, 159, 179, 189, 195, 200, 209, 277, 300–301, 369, 395–96, 406, 411–13, 423, 473, 507; Map 25

Mountain of the Prophets, I: 120, II: 63

Mount of Scandals, III: 119, 189

Mountain Sermons, I: 74–75, 91–92, 99; II: 362

Mozian, I: 522; II: 514–17; III: 503; Map 37

Münster, I: 8, 12–13; II: 30, 90

Museum, Brooklyn, I: 2

Naasson, I: 522; II: 183–84; Map 24

Nablus (Shechem), I: 87–88, 144, 190, 317, 325–26, 378, 486–87, 489–92, 494, 505, 517, 523; II: 5, 78, 83, 201, 482, 520, 522–23; III: 501–3, 505

Naddabar, I: 55

Nain (Naim, *p.* Nein), I: 38, 40, 44, 67, 83, 88–89, 91, 93, 100, 135, 156, 494, 497, 512, 522; II: 1, 16, 84, 87–88, 99–100, 121, 136–37, 139, 141–45, 147, 150, 152, 157–58, 160, 162–63, 166, 181, 193, 195, 223, 231, 336, 348, 384, 386, 389–91, 395–98, 407; III: 5, 318, 320, 379, 488; Maps 18, 22, 31

Naioth, I: 485

Nantes, I: 2

Naos Basilica, III: 45, 51

Naphtali, I: 46, 294, 427, 515, 522; II: 180, 184–85, 307; Map 26

Naples, I: 40

Nazara, I: 220, 414, 504, 522; Map: Flight of the Holy Family to Egypt; Map 14

Nazareth, I: 45–47, 60, 62, 73, 77–79, 97–98, 101, 105, 135, 139, 155, 157, 161, 165, 167–68, 171, 174, 180–90, 197, 199, 208, 215, 218–22, 229, 231–35, 257, 294–98, 302–21, 326, 333, 336, 338, 342, 346, 355, 357, 368, 383, 392–94, 403, 405, 411–14, 416, 419, 421, 427, 451, 493–94, 500, 503, 505, 511, 515, 522; II: 1–3, 5, 7–16, 18, 21, 26, 39–40, 91, 95, 106, 137, 141, 144–45, 147–48, 158, 160–61, 166–69, 193–96, 204, 223–24, 336, 385, 393–95, 475, 522, 526; III: 3, 12, 102, 147, 309, 401, 409, 421, 485, 487, 497; Map: Flight of the Holy Family to Egypt; Maps 1–4, 14, 19, 25, 40

Nazarite's Chamber, I: 43

Nebo (Nabo), I: 399, 401, 522; II: 468; Maps 12, 35

Nebo, Mount, I: 357, 399, 441, 445, 522

Nejel, I: 392

New Covenant, I: 152, 308, 314

New Moon Festival, I: 382, 407, 460, 477; II: 78, 144, 1181, 308; III: 481, 493–94, 498–99, 505

Nicaea, III: 309

Nicanor Gate, I: 271; II: 551

Nile River, I: 133, 147, 149, 224–27, 275, 518

Nineveh, I: 130, 132, 358; II: 267; III: 55

Nobah (near Lake Merom), I: 522; II: 316, 318, 324; Map 27

Nobah in Hauran (near Behem, Bosra), II: 409; Map 34

Old Cairo, I: 273, 275, 281

Old Testament, I: 5–6, 14, 118, 139, 261, 345, 352; II: 28; III: 53, 343

On. *See* Heliopolis

Ono (near Kasr el-Jehud), I: 35, 46, 62, 102, 301, 303, 334, 342, 379, 390, 394, 397–98, 401, 403, 458–59, 478, 522; II: 70, 212; Maps 11–12

Ophel, II: 291, 330, 369, 407; III: 73, 95–96, 99–102, 105, 107, 120, 123, 147, 159, 195, 312, 392

Ophel Gate, III: 107, 139

Ophra, I: 313, 316, 374–75, 398, 522; II: 73–75, 84; Maps 8, 21

Ornithopolis, I: 64, 93, 522; II: 84, 308–13, 319, 352–54, 396, 399; Maps 26, 29

Ozensara (*p.* Uzzen Se'ereh), I: 171, 522–23; II: 201, 203–4; Map 25

Paderborn, I: 13

Padiaios, river, II: 390

Palestine, I: 2, 33–34, 50, 44, 47, 57, 73,

102, 106, 122, 130, 132, 134–36, 139, 144, 153, 162, 167, 169, 182, 190, 194, 218, 225, 259, 292, 298, 302–3, 370–71, 469, 471, 473, 511; II: 17, 34, 56, 63, 67, 239, 277, 289, 353, 359, 361, 363–64, 367, 369, 384–85, 389–91, 396, 406, 409, 459, 465, 481–82, 484–85, 501, 557; III: 206, 305, 351, 420, 424, 477, 480, 488, 491–92, 502–7

Panaya Kapulu. *See* House of Mary

Paneas, I: 93, 382, 518; II: 157, 168, 173, 316, 408; III: 309

Parables, I: 104, 109, 318, 351, 375, 382; II: 4, 44, 46, 67, 78, 81, 88, 100, 104, 137–41, 144, 147–48, 156, 162–63, 177, 224, 364, 371, 486, 468, 470, 472, 482, 484, 487, 497, 507; III: 109, 112, 390
of animals, II: 55
of bees, II: 489
of building, I: 311
of the different soils, II: 52, 181
of the Father's mansions, II: 490
of the fig (fruitless) tree, I: 375, 505; II: 346, 472
of the fisherman, II: 393, 401
of the Good Samaritan, I: 398–99, 482, 496; II: 336, 385, 405, 475
of the Good Shepherd, I: 349; II: 30, 179–80, 201, 204, 344–45, 409, 465, 482, 484; III: 88
of the grain of wheat, II: 495
of the harvest, II: 103, 141, 367
of the hidden treasure, II: 157, 198
of the houses on sand and solid ground, II: 325
of the innkeeper, I: 347
of the king and servant, II: 222
of the king's garden, III: 6
of the king's son, I: 344; II: 5–6, 29, 377, 486, 488
of the kingdom of God, II: 161, 168, 196
of the laborers in the vineyard, I: 322, 463; II: 83, 316, 325, 401
of the Lord's Prayer, II: 385
of the lost coin (drachma), I: 483–84; II: 37, 198
of the lost sheep, I: 67; II: 44, 345
of the malefactors in Adummin, I: 399
of the marriage feast, I: 234
of the master of the feast, II: 31, 198, 346–47
of the mustard seed and faith, I: 311
of the obedient and disobedient sons, III: 2
of the persecuted prince, I: 348
of the Pharisee and Publican, II: 93
of plowing, sowing, and reaping, I: 349, 351, 484; II: 180, 201–2, 204, 465, 482, 484
of the prodigal son, II: 38, 52, 67, 220–22, 485, 490
of the rich man and Lazarus, II: 331, 333–34
of the sower, III: 141, 154, 179–80

of the talents, II: 21, 81, 84, 400
of the Three Kings, I: 463
of the unjust steward, I: 311, 317, 469–70, 482; II: 82, 470, 488
of the vine, I: 376; II: 488–89, 491
of the vineyard owner, I: 98, 317, 483–85, 492; II: 201–2, 377, 400
of the watchful servants, II: 405, 495
of the wedding at Cana, I: 387–89
of the wheat and tares, I: 475; II: 28, 141, 154, 400; III: 1
of the wise and foolish virgins, II: 82–83, 186, 403; III: 14

Paradise, I: 113–16, 120–21, 123, 158, 161, 166, 183, 218, 231, 302, 387, 483; II: 5, 36, 63–64, 220; III: 6, 82, 84, 221, 299–300, 324, 388, 403

Passover, I: 232, 234, 292, 313, 375, 382, 388–89, 484, 494; II: 293, 381; III: 82, 123, 135, 227, 357, 369, 410

Passovers during Ministry
First (AD 30), I: 62, 101, 393, 398, 409, 419–20, 422, 458; II: 27, 31, 75, 91, 93, 139, 155; III: 484
Second (AD 31), I: 63, 308; II: 173, 218, 309, 326–27, 329–33, 345, 350, 354, 356–57, 361–62, 379; III: 133, 500
Third (AD 32), I: 313; III: 487–88, 504
Fourth (AD 33), III: 9, 13–14, 18, 71–80, 86, 95–96, 102–3, 105, 110, 113, 119, 125, 129, 198–200, 216, 221, 227, 263, 322, 357, 391–92, 478, 480, 484, 497, 506

Patras, I: 65, 342, 504; II: 152, 158
Pella, I: 296, 388–99; II: 85; III: 3
Pelusium, I: 273, 281; Map: Flight of the Holy Family to Egypt

Pentecost, I: 30, 39, 59, 81, 85, 307, 467; II: 93, 137, 345, 372, 375, 379–81, 384–85, 395, 397, 524; III: 9–10, 39, 81, 108, 309, 392, 396, 400, 408, 413, 415–16, 418

Peraa (Perea), I: 523; Maps 1, 36
Persia, I: 56–57, 370, 439; II: 235, 239; III: 55, 424
Persian Gulf, I: 524
Peter's Fishery, I: 38, 42, 44–45, 54, 56, 58, 63, 379; II: 7, 23, 84, 141, 152, 161, 168; III: 404; Map 2
Peter's House, II: 6–7, 17–21, 23, 136, 150, 158, 160, 162, 164, 167, 173–76, 223, 297, 303, 342, 399–401; III: 309
Phasael, I: 60, 362–63, 402–3, 512, 523; II: 40, 76–78; Maps 7, 12
Phiala, Lake (*p.* Berekhat Ram), I: 521; II: 314, 316, 319, 321; Map 27
Philadelphia, I: 524
Phoenicia, I: 382; II: 223
Pilate's Palace, II: 329; III: 118, 120, 192, 196–99, 201–2, 205, 301, 307–8, 312, 387
Piscina Probatica, II: 293. *See also* Pool of Bethesda
Place of Baptism, First, I: 417, 424, 459, 517, 520, 523; Map 15
Place of Baptism, Second, I: 63, 372–73, 394, 417, 459, 523; Maps 8, 15

Place of Baptism, Third, I: 301, 334, 379, 390, 458–59, 522–24; Maps 5–6, 11–12, 15, 38
"Place of Grace", I: 466–68, 471, 520
polytheism, II: 357
Pool of Bethesda, I: 136, 307, 314, 362, 396, 471; II: 200–201, 206, 216–17, 291, 330–33, 336, 407, 524; III: 5, 18, 95, 101, 109, 112–13, 155, 192, 212, 216, 331, 407–8, 413–16, 419, 425, 508. *See also* Piscina Probatica
Pool of Hezekiah (amygdalum), II: 293; III: 25, 273
Porch of the Temple, I: 443
Praetorium, II: 385; III: 191–92, 199, 201, 205, 227, 229, 235, 241, 243, 249
Prophet Mountain (Mount of the Prophets), I: 120, 128
Promise, the, I: 106, 119, 121, 128, 140, 148, 151, 155–56, 161, 166, 176, 207, 232, 234, 327, 351, 353, 355, 358, 377, 411, 488–89; II: 3, 72, 74, 93, 95, 104, 107, 159, 186, 208, 352, 365–66, 370–71, 376, 403; III: 6, 300, 323, 388, 410, 413. *See also* Blessing, the
Promised Land, I: 148, 151, 265, 345, 353, 357, 397, 409, 435, 493–94; II: 3, 30, 40, 48, 352, 367, 383, 401, 465
Prophecy,
of destruction of Jerusalem, I: 177; III: 14, 63, 322
of Star of Bethlehem, I: 205
of Abraham, I: 138
of Simeon, I: 285; III: 196,
Protevangelium of St. James the Less, I: 259
Provence, I: 80
Ptolemais (Akko), I: 517; II: 385, 391, 393

Quarantinia, Mount (*p.* Quruntul), I: 363, 365, 369, 523; Maps 7–8

Rabbath-Ammon, I: 524
Raisings from the Dead, I: 109, 511–13, 516; II: 26, 334
in the plot of the Sadducees, I: 493–94
of the child at Gadara, I: 512; II: 59–60, 145
of the daughter of Jairus the Essene, I: 402–3, 512; II: 40, 77, 163
of Lazarus, I: 59–60, 80, 103, 318, 491, 505, 513; II: 327, 443, 475–79, 501, 504–6; III: 8, 11–12, 15, 19, 392, 487–89, 501, 504–6
of the man fallen from the tower (in Capernaum), I: 390
of Martialis, son of the widow of Nain, I: 38, 40, 44, 83, 512, 522; II: 100, 141–42, 150, 158, 195, 395; III: 5
of Nazor, II: 493–94
of Salome, daughter of Jairus the Synagogue Official, I: 43, 60, 512; II: 150–52, 164
Ramah (*p.* Ram), I: 277, 523; II: 333–35;

Map 28

Ramath-Gilead (Ramath-Mizpa, Hag Gilead, *p.* Salt), I: 523; Map 20

Rameses, I: 229

Ramoth Valley, II: 47, 49, 53, 70

Red Sea, I: 46, 132–33, 145, 149, 151, 338, 345; II: 48, 64, 218–19, 367, 381, 386; III: 424

Regaba, I: 523; II: 318, 321, 323–24; Map 27

Regaba, Fortress of, II: 315

Rehob, I: 523; II: 313; Maps 26–27

Rhodes, I: 275

Rimon, I: 523; II: 336, 339, 397; Map 31

Rod of Aaron, I: 150, 152, 154–55, 166, 314

Romantic Movement, I: 1

Rome, I: 22, 40, 44, 57, 84, 110–11, 172, 197, 475; II: 53, 168, 212, 219, 360, 362, 369, 491, 497; III: 183, 215, 227, 241, 249, 257, 271, 281, 309, 403, 479–80

Royal Porch, III: 27, 37, 45

Russia, III: 424

Safed, heights of, III: 402

Saint-Baume, I: 60, 79

Saïs, I: 133–34

Salamis, I: 57, 61, 65, 523; II: 354, 356, 358–64, 366–71, 373, 377, 380, 384–86, 388, 390, 395, 399; III: 478; Map 30

Salcha (Selcha, *p.* Salkhad in Hauran), I: 523; II: 409, 465; Map 34

Salem, I: 136, 140, 144, 162, 189, 292, 298, 333–35, 360, 363, 402, 478, 480, 523; II: 41–42, 75–76, 467–68; Map 21

Samaria (Sabastiya), I: 40, 44, 56, 65, 180, 189–90, 220, 251, 281, 292, 294, 298, 302–3, 323, 329–30, 349, 376–77, 402, 411, 414–15, 419, 424, 431, 439, 459–60, 463, 468, 480, 484–86, 488–92; II: 1–2, 5, 27, 30, 34, 41, 59, 63, 71, 80, 83, 86, 90, 93, 103, 106, 108, 175, 196–97, 219, 223, 235, 239, 342–43, 352, 472–73, 475, 482, 522, 524, 557; III: 3, 393, 400, 487; Maps 3, 17

Sanhedrin, I: 51, 83–84, 101–3, 107, 267, 303, 332, 336, 338–39, 354, 423; II: 18, 59, 103, 200, 209, 297; III: 67, 94, 108, 112, 118, 120, 157, 208, 214, 231, 245, 269, 307, 361, 369, 385, 406, 478, 493–94

Santiago de Compostela, I: 45

Saphet (Safad, Zefat), I: 47, 136, 523; II: 176–83, 325, 345; Map 24

Saragossa, I: 44–45

Sarepta (Sarephat, Zarphat, *p.* Sarafand), I: 300–302, 523; II: 12–13, 58, 312–13, 352–53, 377; Maps 2, 6

Sarona/Saron, I: 40, 97; II: 215

Saul's well, I: 517; II: 95–97

Scala Santa, III: 249

Scopus, Mount, III: 39, 277

Scythopolis (Bet She'an), I: 379, 393, 480; II: 33, 80, 97, 180

Sea of Galilee, I: 38–39, 43, 46–47, 54–

55, 59, 73, 80–81, 107, 109, 162, 192, 292, 295, 297, 300, 305, 307, 313, 318, 333, 356, 360, 363, 376, 390, 392–93, 409, 412–13, 424, 502–3, 515, 519; II: 5–6, 13, 17, 97, 108, 152, 155, 162, 170, 243, 298, 324, 334, 353–54, 403, 482, 525; III: 308–9, 400–403, 487–89, 491, 501

Sealed Fountain, II: 293; III: 25

Seleucia, I: 459, 462, 470–73, 482, 523; II: 195; Maps 16, 28

Sermon on the Mount, I: 63, 504; II: 87–88, 105, 162–64, 168, 289, 298, 304, 314, 323, 348, 375; III: 202, 404, 491

Sepphoris, Greater, I: 523; II: 8–9, 11; Maps 3, 14

Sepphoris, Little, I: 523; II: 8–9, 11, 26; Maps 3, 14, 19

Shathaf, I: 429

Shechem (Sichem, *p.* Nablus), I: 87–88, 144, 190, 317, 325–26, 378, 486–87, 489–92, 494, 505, 523; II: 5, 78, 83, 201, 482, 520, 522–23; III: 501–3, 505; Maps 17, 38

Sheep Gate, II: 291; III: 39, 112, 120, 192, 202, 211, 241, 251, 265, 312, 416

Sheep Pool, III: 43, 63, 192, 206, 211, 241, 414

Shiloh, I: 151, 376–78, 523; II: 51, 71–73, 361, 565; III: 102, 139; Maps 8, 21

Sichar, I: 87, 151, 349, 362, 486–87, 523; II: 78, 335, 481, 487, 490–91, 493; III: 20, 396–99, 405

Sichar-Kedar, II: 487–88; III: 503–4

Sidon (Zidon, *p.* Saida), I: 54–55, 193, 300–302, 310, 314, 336, 382, 403, 405, 451, 459, 483, 523–24; II: 75, 84, 154, 180, 308, 352–53, 360; Maps 2, 16

Sikdor, I: 65; II: 513–14, 517; III: 4–5, 502–3

Siloam, Pool of, I: 279, 293; II: 467; III: 181

Siloam, Tower of, I: 110; II: 203, 285; III: 100

Sinai, II: 518

Sinai, Mount, I: 141, 150, 152, 165, 314, 368, 467, 493; II: 50, 218, 224, 379–81, 518, 520; III: 94, 498

Sion (*not* Mount Zion), I: 261, 523; II: 394–95; Map 31

Soba, I: 429

Sodom, I: 135, 140, 142, 312, 360, 374, 396, 520; II: 37, 82, 107, 169, 191, 195

Sogane, I: 39, 64, 523; II: 325; Map 27

Solomon's Porch, II: 551; III: 43

Sondermühlen, I: 13

Songs of the Degrees, I: 291

Spain, I: 44–45; II: 137; III: 419–20

St. Maries-de-la-Mer, I: 60

Succoth, I: 36, 138, 144, 189, 357, 360, 424, 478, 517, 523; II: 41, 45, 65, 68, 70–71, 76; Maps 7, 21

Swamp of Cendevia, II: 393

Shunem (*p.* Sulam, Shumen), I: 406–8, 523; II: 92, 94, 96, 195–97; Maps 13–14, 25

Stigmata, I: 1, 9, 14–15, 17; III: 367

Stigmatization, I: 7–9

Suckling Cave, I: 194–96, 211–12, 352

Susa Gate, III: 27

Switzerland, III: 197, 210, 216, 281

Sychar, I: 48, 63, 303; II: 115; Map 8

Syria, I: 58, 125, 132, 190, 257, 294, 310, 462; II: 16, 125, 157, 219, 223, 356, 524, 557; III: 3, 482

Tabor, I: 83, 135, 408, 419; II: 147–48, 193, 195, 215, 302, 318, 336, 361–62, 395; Map 29

Tabor, Mount, I: 43, 63–64, 79, 135–36, 302–3, 307–8, 310, 357, 403, 405–6, 411, 437, 499–501, 515, 523; II: 1, 86, 95, 97–99, 101–2, 141, 147, 163, 180, 191, 193, 223, 339–42, 344, 397, 403; III: 487, 489, 500, 505; Maps 22, 25

Talmud, I: 271; II: 181; III: 53, 365

Tarascon, I: 80

Tarichea, I: 55, 295, 333, 379–80, 523; II: 13–17, 33, 169, 220, 301–2, 347; III: 309; Maps 9, 19, 26, 29

Tartary, III: 424

Taurus Mountains, III: 511–12

Tel-Aviv, I: 59

Ten Commandments, I: 493; II: 12, 20, 68, 72, 125, 164, 181

Tent City, I: 57; II: 495–96, 499–502, 504, 509–11, 513, 517; III: 502; Map: Journey of the Three Kings; Map 37

Terebinth Valley, I: 283, 429

Terebinthe Moreh, I: 221; Map: Flight of the Holy Family to Egypt

Thaanach (*p.* ruins, Ta'nakh), I: 179, 524; II: 393–96, 407; Map 31

Thanat-Shiloh (*p.* ruins, Ta'na), I: 524; II: 78–80, 197–98, 200, 335, 528; III: 396–97, 399; Maps 21, 25, 28, 40

Thantia (Thainata), I: 524; II: 465, 467; Map 34

Thebes, I: 133–34

Thebez (*p.* Tubas), I: 189, 294, 297, 308, 378–79, 491–92, 524; II: 76, 80, 83, 86; III: 402, 487; Map 8

Thebez, Mount, I: 294, 297

Thirza, I: 109, 414–15, 492, 524; II: 219–22, 338, 385; III: 85, 102, 197, 308

Thisbe, I: 472–73, 475

Throne of Grace, I: 150

Tiberias, I: 55, 179, 182, 294–95, 318, 323, 326, 378–79, 403, 439, 451; II: 23, 33, 84, 155–56, 170, 173, 195, 198, 206, 220, 235, 301–2, 336, 339, 347, 417, 423, 526; III: 231, 308, 399–404, 410, 416

Tigris, river, I: 129, 522; II: 513–15; III: 503

Tower of Babel, I: 125, 128–30; II: 37, 76, 375

Transfiguration (before the Apostles), I: 43–44, 79, 140, 357, 437, 499–501, 523; II: 189, 339–42; III: 489–90, 500, 505

Transfiguration (before the Essene Eliud), I: 322

Tree of Knowledge, I: 115–16, 118, 218

Tree of Life, I: 115; III: 221, 231
Tyre (Zor, *p.* ruins, Sour), I: 63, 382,
    405, 459–62, 465, 483, 515, 524; II: 75,
    84, 105, 180, 308, 310, 319, 351–53, 360,
    365, 390; III: 239; Map 16
Tyropeon valley, III: 39, 45, 191, 251

Ulama (*p.* Ullama), I: 408–9, 524; II: 33
Unicorn, I: 114; II: 513
Upper Galilee, I: 109, 478, 482; II: 17,
    19–20, 31, 140, 151, 195–96, 221, 297, 313,
    321, 339, 350; III: 309
Ur, I: 57, 138–39, 524; II: 37, 482, 513–17;
    III: 502–7; Map 37

Valley of the Shepherds, I: 196, 200,
    209, 215, 349, 352, 397, 502; II: 213, 482;
    Maps 6, 11
Venice, III: 183
Via Dolorosa, III: 235, 249, 265
Vulgate, I: 257; III: 459

Wad el-Kafren, I: 35

Wadi el-Kelt, I: 400; Map 12
Wadi Nimrin, I: 35
Wadi Sha'ara, I: 304; Map 3
Wady Urtas, III: 25
Walking on Water, I: 502–3; II: 172–73,
    298, 301, 419, 421; III: 489
    by St. Peter, II: 172–73, 301
        First Episode, 172–73
        Second Episode, II: 301
Way of Sorrows, I: 28
Way of the Cross, I: 17, 43, 76, 177; III:
    195, 212, 217, 310, 388, 398, 400, 406,
    422–23, 426, 428
Wedding at Cana, I: 38, 45, 53, 56, 59,
    63, 298, 377–79, 384–90; II: 1, 306, 403,
    487, 508
Wells of the Virgin (Aïn-sitti Mariam),
    I: 279
Widow's mite, III: 13–14, 61

Xystus Bridge, III: 37, 45

Zabulon (Zebulon) Valley, I: 45, 52, 62,

81, 155, 157, 165, 167, 307, 313, 322, 524;
    II: 9, 95, 105, 144, 147–48, 184–85, 224,
    314; Maps 3, 19, 31
Zarqa River, I: 292
Zarthan, I: 341; II: 41
Zedad, I: 473, 477, 524; Map 16
Zion, I: 150, 369; II: 20, 40, 59, 78; III:
    71, 73, 103, 105, 123, 139, 181, 183, 212,
    235, 251, 265, 312, 320, 322, 386, 391–92,
    413–14, 416, 423, 473
Zion, Mount, I: 58, 180, 231, 294, 317,
    326, 421–23, 523; II: 217–18, 479–80; III:
    17, 39, 45, 71, 99, 102, 105, 111, 119–20,
    192, 211, 215, 311–12, 407, 414
Zorobabel (estate), Maps 22, 31

28184946R00335